Agile Estimation Techniques and Innovative Approaches to Software Process Improvement

Ricardo Colomo–Palacios
Universidad Carlos III de Madrid, Spain

Jose Antonio Calvo–Manzano Villalón
Universidad Politécnica de Madrid, Spain

Antonio de Amescua Seco
Universidad Carlos III de Madrid, Spain

Tomás San Feliu Gilabert
Universidad Politécnica de Madrid, Spain

T0320585

A volume in the Advances in Systems Analysis, Software Engineering, and High Performance Computing (ASASEHPC) Book Series

Information Science REFERENCE
An Imprint of IGI Global

Managing Director:	Lindsay Johnston
Production Editor	Jennifer Yoder
Development Editor:	Allyson Gard
Acquisitions Editor:	Kayla Wolfe
Typesetter:	John Crodian
Cover Design:	Jason Mull

Published in the United States of America by
Information Science Reference (an imprint of IGI Global)
701 E. Chocolate Avenue
Hershey PA 17033
Tel: 717-533-8845
Fax: 717-533-8661
E-mail: cust@igi-global.com
Web site: http://www.igi-global.com

Library of Congress Cataloging-in-Publication Data

Agile estimation techniques and innovative approaches to software process improvement / Ricardo Colomo-Palacios, Jose Antonio Calvo-Manzano Villalon, Antonio de Amescua Seco and Tomas San Feliu Gilabert, editors.
    pages cm
  Includes bibliographical references and index.   ISBN 978-1-4666-5182-1 (hardcover) -- ISBN 978-1-4666-5183-8 (ebook) -- ISBN 978-1-4666-5185-2 (print & perpetual access) 1. Agile software development. 2. Computer software--Development. I. Colomo-Palacios, Ricardo, 1973- editor of compilation.
  QA76.76.D47A3823 2014

    005.1--dc23
    2013044979

This book is published in the IGI Global book series Advances in Systems Analysis, Software Engineering, and High Performance Computing (ASASEHPC) (ISSN: 2327-3453; eISSN: 2327-3461)

British Cataloguing in Publication Data
A Cataloguing in Publication record for this book is available from the British Library.

All work contributed to this book is new, previously-unpublished material. The views expressed in this book are those of the authors, but not necessarily of the publisher.

For electronic access to this publication, please contact: eresources@igi-global.com.

Advances in Systems Analysis, Software Engineering, and High Performance Computing (ASASEHPC) Book Series

Vijayan Sugumaran
Oakland University, USA

ISSN: 2327-3453
EISSN: 2327-3461

MISSION

The theory and practice of computing applications and distributed systems has emerged as one of the key areas of research driving innovations in business, engineering, and science. The fields of software engineering, systems analysis, and high performance computing offer a wide range of applications and solutions in solving computational problems for any modern organization.

The **Advances in Systems Analysis, Software Engineering, and High Performance Computing (ASASEHPC) Book Series** brings together research in the areas of distributed computing, systems and software engineering, high performance computing, and service science. This collection of publications is useful for academics, researchers, and practitioners seeking the latest practices and knowledge in this field.

COVERAGE

- Computer Graphics
- Computer Networking
- Computer System Analysis
- Distributed Cloud Computing
- Enterprise Information Systems
- Metadata and Semantic Web
- Parallel Architectures
- Performance Modeling
- Software Engineering
- Virtual Data Systems

IGI Global is currently accepting manuscripts for publication within this series. To submit a proposal for a volume in this series, please contact our Acquisition Editors at Acquisitions@igi-global.com or visit: http://www.igi-global.com/publish/.

Titles in this Series

For a list of additional titles in this series, please visit: www.igi-global.com

Agile Estimation Techniques and Innovative Approaches to Software Process Improvement
Ricardo Colomo-Palacios (Universidad Carlos III de Madrid, Spain) Jose Antonio Calvo-Manzano Villalón (Universidad Politécnica De Madrid, Spain) Antonio de Amescua Seco (Universidad Carlos III de Madrid, Spain) and Tomás San Feliu Gilabert (Universidad Politécnica De Madrid, Spain)
Information Science Reference • copyright 2014 • 312pp • H/C (ISBN: 9781466651821) • US $215.00 (our price)

Enabling the New Era of Cloud Computing Data Security, Transfer, and Management
Yushi Shen (Microsoft, USA) Yale Li (Microsoft, USA) Ling Wu (EMC, USA) Shaofeng Liu (Microsoft, USA) and Qian Wen (Endronic Corp, USA)
Information Science Reference • copyright 2014 • 336pp • H/C (ISBN: 9781466648012) • US $195.00 (our price)

Theory and Application of Multi-Formalism Modeling
Marco Gribaudo (Politecnico di Milano, Italy) and Mauro Iacono (Seconda Università degli Studi di Napoli, Italy)
Information Science Reference • copyright 2014 • 314pp • H/C (ISBN: 9781466646599) • US $195.00 (our price)

Pervasive Cloud Computing Technologies Future Outlooks and Interdisciplinary Perspectives
Lucio Grandinetti (University of Calabria, Italy) Ornella Pisacane (Polytechnic University of Marche, Italy) and Mehdi Sheikhalishahi (University of Calabria, Italy)
Information Science Reference • copyright 2014 • 292pp • H/C (ISBN: 9781466646834) • US $190.00 (our price)

Communication Infrastructures for Cloud Computing
Hussein T. Mouftah (University of Ottawa, Canada) and Burak Kantarci (University of Ottawa, Canada)
Information Science Reference • copyright 2014 • 583pp • H/C (ISBN: 9781466645226) • US $195.00 (our price)

Organizational, Legal, and Technological Dimensions of Information System Administration
Irene Maria Portela (Polytechnic Institute of Cávado and Ave, Portugal) and Fernando Almeida (Polytechnic Institute of Gaya, Portugal)
Information Science Reference • copyright 2014 • 321pp • H/C (ISBN: 9781466645264) • US $195.00 (our price)

Advances and Applications in Model-Driven Engineering
Vicente García Díaz (University of Oviedo, Spain) Juan Manuel Cueva Lovelle (University of Oviedo, Spain) B. Cristina Pelayo García-Bustelo (University of Oviedo, Spain) and Oscar Sanjuán Martinez (University of Carlos III, Spain)
Information Science Reference • copyright 2014 • 426pp • H/C (ISBN: 9781466644946) • US $195.00 (our price)

www.igi-global.com

701 E. Chocolate Ave., Hershey, PA 17033
Order online at www.igi-global.com or call 717-533-8845 x100
To place a standing order for titles released in this series, contact: cust@igi-global.com
Mon-Fri 8:00 am - 5:00 pm (est) or fax 24 hours a day 717-533-8661

Editorial Advisory Board

Ulises Juárez Martínez, *Instituto Tecnológico de Orizaba, Mexico*

Cuauhtémoc Lemus, *Research Centre in Mathematics (CIMAT, A.C.), Mexico*

Jorge Manjarrez Sánchez, *Research Center in Mathematics (CIMAT), Mexico*

Antonia Mas, *Universitat de les Illes Balears, Spain*

Fuensanta Medina-Dominguez, *Universidad Carlos III de Madrid, Spain*

Manuel Muñoz Archidona, *Universidad Carlos III de Madrid, Spain*

Jezreel Mejía, *Research Centre in Mathematics (CIMAT, A.C.), Mexico*

Antoni Lluis Mesquida, *Universitat de les Illes Balears, Spain*

Hugo A. Mitre, *Research Center in Mathematics (CIMAT), Mexico*

Arturo Mora-Soto, Universidad Carlos III de Madrid, Mexico

Fernando Moreira, *Universidade Portucalense Infante D. Henrique, Portugal*

Edrisi Muñoz, *Research Centre in Mathematics (CIMAT, A.C.), Mexico*

Mirna Muñoz, *Research Centre in Mathematics (CIMAT, A.C.), Mexico*

Victor Navarro Belmonte, *Research Center in Mathematics (CIMAT), Mexico*

Martha Omorodion, *Federal University of Technology, Nigeria*

Carmen Pages, *Universidad de Alcalá, Spain*

Adriana Peña Perez-Negron, *Universidad de Guadalajara, Mexico*

Manuel Pérez-Cota, *Universidade de Vigo, Spain*

Mery Pesantes, *Research Centre in Mathematics (CIMAT, A.C.), Mexico*

Raquel Poy, *Universidad de León, Spain*

Jorge Luis Risco Becerra, *University of São Paulo – Escola Politécnica, Brazil*

Alvaro Rocha, *LIACC Universidade do Porto, Portugal*

Josefina Rodríguez-Jacobo, *Centro de Investigación Científica y de Educación Superior de Ensenada (CICESE), Mexico*

Tomás San Feliu, Universidad Politécnica de Madrid, Spain

Sodel Vázquez Reyes, *Universidad Autónoma de Zacatecas, Mexico*

Perla Velasco-Elizondo, *Autonomous University of Zacatecas, Mexico*

Table of Contents

Section 1
Innovative Agile Development and Estimation Techniques

Chapter 1

Hugo A. Mitre, Research Center in Mathematics (CIMAT), Mexico
Leonardo Bermon-Angarita, National University of Colombia, Colombia

Chapter 2

Gloria Piedad Gasca-Hurtado, Universidad de Medellín, Colombia
Jaime Alberto Echeverri Arias, Universidad de Medellín, Colombia
María Clara Gómez, Universidad de Medellín, Colombia

Chapter 3

Jorge Manjarrez Sanchez, Research Center in Mathematics (CIMAT), Mexico
Victor Navarro Belmonte, Research Center in Mathematics (CIMAT), Mexico

Chapter 4

Tomás San Feliu Gilabert, Universidad Politécnica de Madrid, Spain
Magdalena Arcilla, Universidad Nacional de Educación a Distancia, Spain

Section 2
Software Process Improvement

Detailed Table of Contents

Section 1
Innovative Agile Development and Estimation Techniques

Chapter 1
Hugo A. Mitre, Research Center in Mathematics (CIMAT), Mexico
Leonardo Bermon-Angarita, National University of Colombia, Colombia

Currently, agile methods are replacing traditional process-based methods in the software industry. However, process-based software development still matters because of its degree of reusability in new projects. Some problems arise when Knowledge Management (KM) is not correctly aligned with processes, such as lack of productivity and process improvement. In this chapter, the authors present a case study of applying two proposals of process libraries in an agile software development division. The researchers and the software development division worked with a Kanban dashboard, eXtremme Programming (XP), and SCRUM practices, adapted to Process Assets Library (PAL) and to Process Practice Library (PPL) in three software projects in order to find experiences of tacit and explicit knowledge that have an impact on process improvement and productivity. Under results and discussion, the authors present the good and bad practices.

In this chapter, the authors present the automatization of a technique for identifying the risks that may affect software acquisition projects. The proposed technique can have an impact in two software acquisition areas: 1) acquisition software contract for: Fully Developed (FD) software, Modified-Off-The-Shelf (MOTS) software, and Commercial-Off-The-Shelf (COTS) software; and 2) information technology services contract, which can be a result of using the required technological tools for the operation of any organization. In both cases, it is indispensable to manage and address (track) the risks that may affect the success of any project type mentioned above.

Chapter 3

The main goal of a good software design is to achieve high modularity in order to promote reusability, maintainability, and reduce costs. Coupling and cohesion are two among the many measures that quantify the degree of modularity of a system. An ideal modular design is highly cohesive and lowly coupled. This chapter presents a review of some important metrics to numerically quantify coupling and cohesion and the assessment of some tools to automate their calculation in medium and large Java programs.

Chapter 4

This chapter reviews the estimation techniques in software development focused on small teams and provides useful estimation guidelines for software practitioners. The techniques selected are based on one principle: easy to learn, easy to apply. The authors have included both agile techniques and traditional techniques. Agile techniques are suitable for small teams. Nevertheless, traditional techniques, like PROBE, have proven to be useful. Finally, they discuss sustainable estimation infrastructure.

Chapter 5

Mobile app markets have experienced remarkable growth during the last year. The increasing number of apps available on the market and the revenue that developers and companies obtain is significant enough to seriously consider the way apps are developed. The ever-changing environment in which apps are developed makes agile methodology convenient to follow. Although agile methodologies allow the development team to quickly adjust the requisites to the new customer's needs, there is a lack of research on how they can be explicitly adapted to develop mobile apps. There are many Websites that explain how to code a mobile app, but there is not enough information about other stages in the development process. Adapting an agile methodology for mobile apps would provide development teams with a clear guide to successfully develop an app without missing any step in the development process. This chapter proposes an agile mobile app development process, including processes and activities to be followed as well as the roles involved in these activities. Marketing issues are also considered in the proposed development process as they are necessary to publicize the mobile app. This process has been applied for over two years in the development of the institutional apps at Carlos III University of Madrid.

Chapter 6

In Software Engineering, personality traits have helped to better understand the human factor. In this chapter, the authors give an overview of important personality traits theories that have influenced Software Engineering and have been widely adopted. The theories considered are Myers-Briggs Type Indicator, Big Five Personality Traits, and Belbin Roles. The influence of personality traits has provided remarkable benefits to Software Engineering, especially in the making of teams. For software project managers, it is useful to know what set of soft skills correlates to a specific team role so as to analyze how personality traits have contributed to high performance and cohesive software engineering teams. The study of software engineers' personality traits also helps to motivate team members. Creating teams that involve compatible individuals, each working on tasks that suit them, and having a motivated team improves team performance, productivity, and reduces project costs.

Section 2
Software Process Improvement

Chapter 7

Organizational process improvement offers a key opportunity for organizations to become more efficient. As a consequence, the software industry, among others, is more interested in software process improvement. However, one of the most common issues identified when an organization tries to implement a software process improvement initiative is the difficulty that they face in selecting the reference model and its adaptation to the current organization scenario. Moreover, selecting the wrong reference model according to the way the organization works becomes a trigger to increase resistance to change. This chapter presents a methodology that allows the use of a multi-model environment as a reference model so that the organization can select best practices that best fit the way it works to implement software process improvement. The results of the implementation of an improvement using the methodology proposed are also presented.

This chapter summarizes a set of relevant aspects that may have a strong influence on the effectiveness of software process improvement and, as a consequence, on the competitiveness of software companies. Also included are the results obtained from a survey carried out in large companies on their processing needs in order to be more competitive. The organizational structures seen in different projects highlight the relevance of suitable processes as well as a culture of individual and organizational commitment. With this focus in mind, this chapter provides detailed information about teams, their construction and performance so that they can be effective in developing and implementing the processes. Finally, the chapter provides information about successful change management as well as advice on qualification of the workforce and technological tendencies, which is of key importance to achieve the objectives of competitiveness and process improvement.

Chapter 9

In general, software process improvement entails significant benefits such as increased software product quality, decreased time and development cost, and decreased risks. To obtain these, organizations must apply knowledge management because the identification of new knowledge is considered key to success when improving software processes. Existing knowledge is, however, difficult to find, and when found, it is often difficult to reuse in practice. This is due to the fact that a considerable part of the knowledge that is useful for executing software processes is tacit and not all of it can be captured and made explicit. The purpose of this chapter is to present a framework for software process improvement based on the enrichment of organizational knowledge by means of the acquisition of tacit knowledge from individuals working in different teams and environments. The framework includes the specification of roles, processes, and tools, and is based on a process asset library and the introduction of configuration and change management mechanisms.

The complexity of decision making in software process development and the need for highly competitive organizations require new supporting tools to coordinate and optimize the information flow among decision levels. Decision levels are related to strategic planning, tactical process management, and operational activities development and control. This chapter presents the theory for developing a framework that integrates the different decision levels in software development companies in order to reach their business objectives. Furthermore, the proposed framework coordinates the information exchange among the different modeling paradigms/conventions currently used.

Recently, many micro and small-sized enterprises (MSEs) have implemented a model-based Software Process Improvement (SPI) initiative. An initiative like this is a knowledge-intensive activity that uses and creates knowledge related to multiple areas (SPI knowledge) that should be managed. However, MSEs do not usually manage their SPI knowledge, which results in its erosion and eventual loss. This chapter discusses the importance of Knowledge Management (KM) for those MSEs that are implementing an SPI initiative. It also presents the knowledge created or required to accomplish the implementation of this type of initiative. Finally, it discusses the characteristics that a software tool should have to effectively support this KM process.

Chapter 12

Software architecture is a very important software artifact, as it describes a system's high-level structure and provides the basis for its development. Software architecture development is not a trivial task; to this end, a number of methods have been proposed to try to systematize their related processes to ensure predictability, repeatability, and high quality. In this chapter, the authors review some of these methods, discuss some specific problems that they believe complicate their adoption, and present one practical experience where the problems are addressed successfully.

In the multimodel improvement context, Software Organizations need to incorporate into their processes different practices from several improvement technologies simultaneously (i.e. CMMI, PSP, ISO 15504, and others). Over the last few years, software process architectures have been considered a means to harmonize these technologies. However, it is unclear how to design a software process architecture supporting a multimodel environment. In this chapter, an overview of the method to design a software process architecture is presented, identifying basic concepts, views, phases, activities, and artifacts. In addition, important aspects in the creation of this method are explained. This method will assist process stakeholders in the design, documentation, and maintenance of their software process architecture.

This chapter describes the experience of a Spanish software company founded in 2000, which bet strongly on quality as the way to progress towards maturity. The authors discuss the continuous evolution the company experienced through the implementation of quality standards. The actions related to the deployment and improvement of both the management and production processes are detailed. The most significant results and lessons learned during the improvement path are presented. The experience gained from continuous improvement has facilitated the deployment of a knowledge reuse strategy that enables an effort and cost reduction when implementing a new quality standard.

Software process development in software engineering does not seem to offer a solid view of what they have in reality. Although many models have already been developed, recommended, or even used in the industry, these proposals have still not been able to come to terms with what is available. This chapter evaluates the benefits and limitations of some of the software development models while offering a comparative analysis and data on their real usage. In particular, an attempt has been made to evaluate the problems and strengths of a good variety of software process models and methodologies. Some conclusions and lines of future research are presented.

Chapter 16

Using a large sample of Spanish organizations, in this chapter, the authors empirically reveal the state of health of the Spanish software industry in terms of software process improvement, both in the monitoring of working methodologies and the usage of tools, and they provide the necessary information in order to understand the real skills and efforts to improve the quality of products and end-user services. Having found that a significant number of organizations do not have specific training programs or their own software quality department, it is an essential point of departure for professionals to increase awareness of the need to implement quality processes to improve the competitiveness of the company. The state of knowledge of the methodologies aimed at quality and existing national and international standards shows that these are barely known by professionals in Spanish companies, especially among SMEs and micro-enterprises. However, most Spanish small businesses and large enterprises think the CMMI model best suits their needs, both business and technical. This growing interest is the main reason behind the fact that Spain has almost 38% of the European CMMI certifications, including 22 new certifications since 2010, and is the fourth country in the world in terms of number of CMMI appraisals.

There is a vast amount of literature showing the effects of social networks in different organizational settings, such as innovation, knowledge transfer, leadership, and organizational culture. Recently, business process literature has recognized the impact of Social Network Analysis (SNA) in process improvement by observing the real collaborative relationships between employees, or the SNA impact in detecting communication structures in a large software team. However, little is known about how the teams' network structures may impact on the teams' productivity. This chapter analyzes different network properties that may have an impact on the teams' productivity and generates knowledge that may help to improve processes in the organizations.

Money is one of the most important things for enterprises today. Computer Centers represent a large part of the total costs of enterprises, irrespective of their size. This chapter describes some (real) ways to convince enterprises to use Cloud computing in order to save money and obtain better returns from their computer (hard and soft) resources.

Foreword

This book, *Agile Estimation Techniques and Innovative Approaches to Software Process Improvement*, appears at an opportune time, when the area of Software Process Improvement is going through transformational stages with significant innovative approaches. In this Foreword, we extract from a presentation made at Zacatech 1.0 and expand on it to incorporate new innovative initiatives in software process improvement presented at the SEPG Europe 2012. The text chronicles the evolution of the area prior to and after the creation of the Software Engineering Institute with the introduction and adoption of capability maturity models worldwide. It then refers to agile methodologies, which are now seeing increasing adoption in the improvement of the software development process. It culminates with recent initiatives at the SEI, which deal with new approaches to software engineering process improvement.

Software Process Improvement has been a recurrent theme in Software Engineering for many years, going back to the time when the need for the management of the software development process was identified as a major problem area, circa 1982, and later, in 1983, in the DoD Software Technology for Adaptable, Reliable Systems (STARS) strategy. Earlier, there were very few software engineering practices that produced consistent, well-documented, or well-understood results. Supporting software tools were often ad-hoc. Yet, successful software development programs and a growing body of literature were beginning to emerge. IBM had mature efforts that had proven effective. When, in 1984, the Software Engineering Institute (SEI) was founded, the theme was reemphasized. The SEI strategic plan—supported by DoD and defense contractors—was recognized as a fundamental activity. The SEI recruited Watts Humphrey from IBM and the Process Management Framework Project was created in 1986. In order to elicit a consensus on practices leading to improved software development, under the auspices of the Air Force Program Manager, the SEI conducted a study of "best practices," and workshops were held with leading software professionals in the defense industry, commercial industry, and academia. It was at this time that a number of Software Process Improvement Networks, SPINs, were created in the software engineering community worldwide. The outcome of the workshops was the enumeration of 18 practices to use as models for the work of organizations, and a subsequent SEI Maturity Questionnaire identified 18 key process areas and a 5-level model of organizational maturity based on the implementation of the process areas. More precise definitions of the practices and the model resulted in seminal contributions of the SEI, to wit: *Software Capability Maturity Model* in 1991; *Capability Maturity Model for Software, Version 1.1*. The following technical reports and/or books attracted considerable attention in the software community: *Managing the Software Process*; *Software Engineering Process Group Guide*; *An Analysis of SEI Software Process Assessment Results: 1987-1991*.

In response to a request of the Air Force for establishing ways for the Acquisition Offices to assess the maturity of their contractors, the SEI then developed the Software Capability Evaluation (SCE).

Training and documentation supported its use by the DOD acquisition community. The SCE method was widely used in software-intensive systems acquisitions by the organizations serving the DOD. This provided an incentive for the use of the SEI's CMM to achieve improvements in management and technical practices. The evolution of this work is a de-facto standard for evaluating and improving process management in software and systems engineering. After the first CMM for use in software development, the SEI proceeded to create a powerful framework for processes in multiple disciplines, which eventually led to the development of maturity models for other areas: People CMM, for managing human assets; Systems Engineering CMM; and eventually in the cyber security area, the CERT Resilience Management Model, released in 2010.

A landmark in the evolution of maturity models was the Capability Maturity Model Integration (CMMI), developed to improve the usability of maturity models by integrating many different models into one framework. Currently, CMMI models are available in three areas: product and service development (CMMI for Development); service establishment, management, and delivery (CMMI for Services); and product and service acquisition (CMMI for Acquisition). The software engineering, management and measurement processes defined by CMMI have seen widespread adoption with implementations in 74 countries on 6 continents. The CMMI has reached a level of maturity itself, which precludes further research supported by the DOD. Consequently, while recognizing its importance and future developments, it has now been transferred from the SEI to the CMMI Institute, a separate entity of Carnegie Mellon University.

Recognizing the great impact that the methodology and principles of the Capability Maturity Model had in the software engineering process improvement, they were extended to the people who actually do the work—the practicing engineers. The Personal Software Process (PSP) was built on the principle that every engineer who works on a software system must do quality work to produce a quality system. The development of the PSP began with the application of CMM principles to writing small software programs. Further refinement led to a disciplined personal framework. This allows engineers to establish and commit to effective engineering and management practices for their software projects.

Recognizing that effective engineers must be able to work on teams, the Team Software Process (TSP) was developed to help development teams establish a mature and disciplined engineering practice toward producing secure, reliable software in less time and at lower costs. The TSP has been applied in small and large organizations in a variety of domains with well-documented results: productivity improvements of 25% or more, testing costs and schedule reductions of up to 80%, and cost savings of 25-50% per software product release.

Agile software development (http://en.wikipedia.org/wiki/Agile_software_development) refers to a group of software development methods based on iterative and incremental development, where requirements and solutions evolve through the collaboration between self-organizing, cross-functional teams. It promotes adaptive planning, evolutionary development and delivery, and a time-boxed iterative approach, and encourages rapid and flexible response to change. It is a conceptual framework that promotes foreseen interactions throughout the development cycle. The Agile Manifesto introduced the term in 2001 (http://agilemanifesto.org/).

So-called *lightweight agile* software development methods evolved in the mid-1990s as a reaction against *heavyweight waterfall* methods, which were characterized by their critics as a heavily regulated, regimented, micromanaged, waterfall model of software development. Proponents of lightweight agile methods contend that they are a return to development practices from early in the history of software development.

Early implementations of agile methods include Rational Unified Process (1994), Scrum (1995), Crystal clear, Extreme Programming (1996), Adaptive Software Development, Feature Driven Development, and Dynamic Systems Development Method (DSDM) (1995). These are now typically referred to as agile methodologies, after the Agile Manifesto.

Looking to the future, the SEI has established the following initiatives (SEI Blog, 2012): Innovating Software for Competitive Advantage, Securing the Cyber Infrastructure, Accelerating Assured Software Delivery for the Mission, Advancing Quantitative Methods for Engineering Software. These initiatives reflect the increasing role that agile methods are playing in the research and development funded by the SEI.

In Innovating Software for Competitive Advantage, the area focuses on creating innovations to revolutionize the development of secure systems-of-systems. Examples of projects are incremental and Iterative architecture for agile software, architecture patterns to secure key quality attributes in systems-of-systems, and optimizing resources for mobile platforms at the edge.

In Securing the Cyber Infrastructure, the area focuses on enabling with well-informed confidence the use of ICT technologies to guaranty a secure connected world. Examples of projects are static analysis checker for C/C++ coding patterns and patterns for architecting enterprise IT systems to improve resilience against insider threats.

In Accelerating Assured Software Delivery for the Mission, the area focuses on guarantying a predictable return in the mission of the acquisition, operation, and maintenance of resilient software. A challenge here would be to produce for the DOD an empirical base to establish opportunities, conditions, and thresholds for the use of agile methods. Examples of Projects are patterns for joint acquisition programs and contingency models to evaluate the applicability of the agility in resilient software systems in critical missions.

In Advancing Quantitative Methods for Engineering Software, the area focuses on the sustainability, affordability, and availability of software-reliant systems through data-driven models, measurement, and management methods. This area has some challenges, like improving costs at the beginning of the life cycle in the acquisition and being able to construct incrementally agile methods in software development. Examples of Projects are methods and tools for estimating probabilistically software costs and models and methods of engineering, management, and measurements practices.

Angel G. Jordan
Carnegie Mellon University, USA

Angel G. Jordan *is University Professor of Electrical and Computer Engineering and Robotics, Emeritus and Provost Emeritus, at Carnegie Mellon University. He obtained the degree Licenciado en Ciencias Físicas in the Universidad de Zaragoza in 1952. From 1952-1956, he worked as an electronic engineer in the Spanish Naval Ordnance Laboratory in Madrid. Dr. Jordan came to Carnegie Mellon University in 1956 as an instructor in electrical engineering and as a graduate student and obtained his M.S. and Ph.D. in electrical and computer engineering in 1959. He was an assistant professor from 1959-62, associate professor from 1962-66, and attained the rank of professor of electrical and computer engineering in 1966. He was the Head of the Department of Electrical and Computer Engineering from 1969-79, the Whitaker Professor of Electrical Engineering from 1972-80, the Dean of Carnegie Institute of Technology (the engineering college) from 1979-83, and Provost of Carnegie Mellon from 1983-1991. His research interest over the years has been in semiconductors, including integrated circuits and smart sensors for robotics applications and software engineering. In all these areas, he has made significant contributions to engineering, science, and technology resulting in many publications in refereed journals, monographs, conference papers and* *presentations, and reports. Dr. Jordan is active in national and international science and technology research and education issues, does extensive consulting work, serves on various boards in the U.S. and abroad, and holds memberships in prestigious engineering and science associations, such as the National Academy of Engineering in the US and the Real Academia de Ingeniería in Spain. He is a Fellow of the IEEE and the AAAS. He was the founder of the Software Engineering Institute, where he has been twice Acting Director, and co-founder of the Robotics Institute. He is Doctor Honoris Causa of the Universidad Politécnica de Madrid, the Universidad Pública de Navarra, and the Universidad Carlos III.*

REFERENCES

SEI Blog. (2012). Retrieved from http://www.blog.sei.cmu.edu/

Preface

In recent years, Software Process Improvement (SPI) has emerged as the dominant approach for delivering improvements to the software product in software development organizations (Shih & Huang, 2010). SPI initiatives have been around for many years with the growing globalization of software development is making them increasingly important (Niazi, Babar, & Verner, 2010).

SPI is a systematic approach to increase the efficiency and effectiveness of a software development organization and to enhance software products (Unterkalmsteiner, et al., 2012). In other words, software process improvement methods help to continuously refine and adjust the software process to improve its performance (Petersen & Wohlin, 2010). According to Müller, Mathiassen, and Balshøj (2010), it dates back to the founding of the Software Engineering Institute at Carnegie Mellon University in 1984 and the publishing of Watts Humphrey's book *Managing the Software Process*. Since then, many of the software development organizations think about existing models and standards, such as ISO 9000 series of standards, ISO 15504, the Capability Maturity Model (CMM), and the Capability Maturity Model Integrated (CMMI) from the Software Engineering Institute (SEI) (Sun & Liu, 2010). SPI attempts to change how software professionals think and act in their everyday organizational activities. SPI involves understanding existing processes and changing these processes to improve product quality and reduce cost and development time (Shih & Huang, 2010).

As a result of its importance, there are many works devoted to investigate SPI initiatives and aspects including its implications with teams dynamics (O'Connor & Basri, 2012; Yilmaz & O'Connor, 2011), knowledge management (Jahn & Nielsen, 2011; Montoni & Cavalcanti da Rocha, 2011; Vlaanderen, Brinkkemper, & van de Weerd, 2012), people issues and approaches (Calvo-Manzano, et al., 2012; Korsaa, et al., 2012; Matturro & Saavedra, 2012; Ply, Moore, Williams, & Thatcher, 2012), implementation strategies (Niazi, Wilson, & Zowghi, 2005), certification (Messnarz, Bachmann, Ekert, & Riel, 2010; Nevalainen & Schweigert, 2010), cultural problems (Elliott, Dawson, & Edwards, 2009; Muller, Kraemmergaard, & Mathiassen, 2009; Niazi, 2009; Passos, Dias-Neto, & da Silva Barreto, 2012), process adaptations to small and medium companies (Clarke & O'Connor, 2012; Espinosa-Curiel, Rodríguez-Jacobo, & Fernández-Zepeda, 2011; Garcia, Pacheco, & Calvo-Manzano, 2010; Habra, Alexandre, Desharnais, Laporte, & Renault, 2008; O'Connor, 2012; Sulayman, Urquhart, Mendes, & Seidel, 2012), measuring effectiveness (Iversen & Ngwenyama, 2006; van Solingen, 2004, 2009), integrations with lean methods (Petersen & Wohlin, 2010), agile approaches (Akbar, Hassan, & Abdullah, 2011; Ringstad, Dingsøyr, & Moe, 2011), or the study of its success factors (Dyba, 2000; Munk-Madsen & Nielsen, 2011; Niazi, 2009, 2011), citing just the most relevant and recent cases.

Process improvement related to outsourcing has grown rapidly, and two new topics, contract engineering and risk management, have risen. However, the number of reported cases of failure is increasing. The failure is caused by many factors, including: inadequate project management, poor requirements definition, inadequate supplier selection, deficiencies in technology selection, and the lack of change management controls. The majority of project failures could be avoided if the acquirer learns how to prepare or evaluate properly the contracts. Risk management is also critical to the success of acquisition projects. Managing risk is essential to project activities every day to achieve the projects' objectives and hence its success.

Another management topic that is always included in process improvement is the estimation process. There are aspects of the process that are peculiar to software estimating. Some of the unique aspects of software estimating are driven by the nature of software as a product. Other problems are created by the nature of the estimating methodologies. One of the first key points in any estimate is to understand and define the system to be estimated. Software process improvement is an opportunity for put in place new estimation techniques tailored to new approaches.

Organizations have recognized that the control of their software processes affect the success of their projects. A new research line based on process improvement in very small enterprises has arisen in order to facilitate competitive capabilities for this environment. Team Software Process (TSP) and Scrum are frameworks that allow organizations focus on real business value. They guide teams in managing schedule and quality.

As a result of its influence, SPI has become the primary approach for improving software quality and reliability, employee and customer satisfaction, and return on investment (Mathiassen, Ngwenyama, & Aaen, 2005). However, even when many organizations are motivated to implement software process initiatives, not all of them know how best to do so. This situation increases the need to develop methodologies that allow implementing process improvements focused on the needs of organizations and in a pace supported by them. Nevertheless, in order to be useful, these methodologies need to evolve. In this book, the use of knowledge management, and most recently, ontologies, social networks, and cloud computing (new ways for implementing improvements) are presented.

The scope of software process improvement goes far, including a wide range of possibilities such as putting in place new estimation techniques tailored to new approaches, combining agile methodologies with defined process in order to get better results. Finally, and not less importantly, process improvement could be implemented in outsourcing environments having better contracts or having a better risk identification. These topics are also developed in the book. In what follows, the organization of the book and the sections that it contains are shown.

ORGANIZATION

The book is structured into two sections with the following major themes:

Section 1: Innovative Agile Development and Estimation Techniques
Section 2: Software Process Improvement

The next paragraphs provide a short introduction to each chapter.

Section 1

Section 1, "Innovative Agile Development and Estimation Techniques," includes a set of six chapters. This section is devoted to presenting techniques ranging from a proposal of process libraries for agile environments and a study of risk management techniques, including a review of estimation in small teams and how to apply agile process to develop mobile apps. The section ends by exploring the impact on development of the personalities of team members.

Chapter 1 presents a case study of applying two proposals of process libraries in an agile software division. Based on a study of the practices of a set of three projects, Hugo A. Mitre and Leonardo Bernon-Angarita identify the good and bad practices.

Chapter 2 is titled "Technique for Risk Identification of Software Acquisition and Information Technologies." In this chapter, Gloria P. Gasca-Hurtado, Jaime A. Echeverrri, and Maria Clara Gómez present an approach for applying risk identification in any acquisition project.

Chapter 3, "Assessing Modularity in Java Programs," by Jorge Manjarrez and Víctor Navarro, presents a review of important metrics to quantify coupling and cohesion, and the assessment of tools to automate their recollecting in medium and large Java programs.

Chapter 4, "Estimating Methods for Small Teams," by Tomás San Feliu Gilabert and Magdalena Arcilla, reviews the estimation techniques focused on small teams. The techniques are based on one principle: easy to learn, easy to apply.

Chapter 5, "Adapting Agile Practices to Mobile Apps Development," by Alberto Heredia, Javier García-Guzman, Roberto Esteban-Santiago, and Antonio Amescua, proposes an agile mobile app development process. Marketing issues are also considered in the proposed process, as they are necessary to advertise the mobile app.

Chapter 6, "The Influence of Personality Traits on Software Engineering and its Applications," by Adrián Casado-Rivas and Manuel Muñoz-Archidona, reviews the personality traits theories that have been widely adopted. The study of personality traits helps to motivate team members.

Section 2

The main objective of this section is to provide an overview of the field of the Software Process Improvement by collecting various research works form different domains. Chapters 8 and 9 provide background information on software process improvement. Chapters 10, 11, and 12 give information on applying the knowledge management to process improvement. Chapters 13 and 14 provide guidance on defining software architecture processes. Chapters 15 and 16 present case studies of successful improvement experiences and analyze their benefits. Chapter 17 focuses on studies related to how organizing teams and their training needs. Finally, chapter 18 provides guidance on contracting outsourcing and cloud services.

The information in this book is designed to provide a comprehensive foundation of the strategies and techniques to improve teams, departments and organizations.

Chapter 7 by Mirna Muñoz and Jezzreel Mejia presents a methodology that allows the use of a multi-model environment as a reference model. An organization can select best practices that best fit in the way the organization works to implement process improvement.

Chapter 8 is titled "Some Key Topics to be Considered in Software Process Improvement." In this chapter, Gonzalo Cuevas, Jose A. Calvo-Manzano, and Iván García present a set of relevant aspects that may have a strong influence on the effectiveness of software process improvements. This chapter provides information about successful change management as well as advice on qualification of the workforce and technological tendencies.

In chapter 9, Alberto Heredia, Javier García-Guzmán, Fuensanta Media-Domínguez, and Arturo Mora-Soto present a study titled "Managing Tacit Knowledge to Improve Software Processes." The aim of this chapter is to present a framework for process improvement based on the enrichment of organizational knowledge by means of the acquisition of tacit knowledge.

Chapter 10 is titled "Towards Knowledge Management to Support Decision Making for Software Process Development," by Edrisi Muñoz and Elizabeth Capón-García. It presents a proposal of framework to integrate the different decision levels in software development companies in order to reach their business objectives.

Chapter 11 is titled "Software Process Improvement in Small Organizations: A Knowledge-Management Perspective." In this chapter, Ismael Espinosa-Curiel, Jose A. Fernández-Zepeda, Ulises Gutiérrez-Osorio, and Josefina Rodríguez-Jacobo discuss the importance of Knowledge Management for micro and small-sized enterprises that are implementing a software process improvement initiative. The authors present the knowledge created or required to accomplish the implementation of this type of initiative. A proposal of requirements for a support knowledge management tool is presented.

Chapter 12, "On Software Architecture Processes and their Use in Practice," by Perla Velasco-Elizondo and Humberto Cervantes, reviews methods for software architecture development and their adoption issues. A positive experience where the adoption issues were addressed successfully is presented.

Chapter 13 is titled "A Method to Design a Software Process Architecture in a Multimodel Environment: An Overview" and is authored by Mery Pesantes, Jorge L. Risco-Becerra, and Cuauhtémoc Lemus. The work presents an overview of the method to design software process architecture. This method will assist process stakeholders in the design, documentation, and maintenance of the software process architecture.

In chapter 14, Antonia Mas and Antonio L. Mesquida present a study titled "A Successful Case of Software Process Improvement Programme Implementation." The work describes the experience of a Spanish company founded in 2000, which bet strongly on quality as the way to progress towards maturity. The authors discuss the continuous evolution of the company experiences through the implementation of quality standards. The experience obtained from continuous improvement has helped to deploy a knowledge reuse strategy.

In chapter 15, Sanjay Misra, Martha Omorodion, Luis Fernández-Sanz, and Carmen Pages present a study titled "A Brief Overview of Software Process Models: Benefits, Limitations, and Application in Practice." The aim of this work is to evaluate the benefits and limitations of some of the software development models while offering a comparative analysis and data on their usage.

Chapter 16 is titled "Learning to Innovate: Methodologies, Tools, and Skills for Software Process Improvement in Spain" and authored by Félix A. Barrio and Raquel Poy. In this chapter, the authors attempt to empirically reveal the health of Spanish organizations in terms of software process improvement. The analysis found that a significant number of organizations do not have specific training programs or a software quality department.

Chapter 17 is titled "Social Network Analysis for Processes Improvement in Teams." In this chapter, Alejandra García-Hernández examines different social network properties that may have an impact on the team's productivity. A second goal is to generate knowledge that may help to improve processes in the organization.

The final chapter in the book, chapter 18, is titled "Cloud Computing Decisions in Real Enterprises" by Manuel Pérez-Cota, Ramiro Gonçalves, and Fernando Moreira. The authors describe the different computational models and their impact on business. It presents a proposal of a framework to integrate the different decision levels in software development companies in order to reach their business objectives. This work examines the critical elements of cloud computing and establishes potential risk items. Finally, it identifies different users' needs and different cloud computing services.

CONCLUSION

This book presents original works and interesting case studies arising from research with the Agile estimation techniques and Innovative Approaches to Software Process Improvement. The goal of this book has been to put together in one place the papers presented in the First International Conference on Software Process Improvement 2012. This book aims to promote the ideas and technologies that promote the use of the new techniques to improve the process at all stages of software development and IT services. The book is organized into two sections to cover Agile techniques and Software Process Improvement. The chapters offer ideas on adapting agile techniques, selecting best practices in multi-model environments, introducing knowledge management initiatives, and introducing innovation in software improvement.

Ricardo Colomo-Palacios
Universidad Carlos III de Madrid, Spain

Jose Antonio Caolvo-Manzano Villalón
Universidad Politécnica de Madrid, Spain

Antonio de Amescua Seco
Universidad Carlos III de Madrid, Spain

Tomás San Feliu Gilabert
Universidad Politécnica de Madrid, Spain

REFERENCES

Akbar, R., Hassan, M. F., & Abdullah, A. (2011). A review of prominent work on agile processes software process improvement and process tailoring practices. In J. M. Zain, W. M. bt Wan Mohd, & E. El-Qawasmeh (Eds.), Software engineering and computer systems (Vol. 181, pp. 571–585). Berlin: Springer.

Calvo-Manzano, J. A., Cuevas, G., Gómez, G., Mejia, J., Muñoz, M., & San Feliu, T. (2012). Methodology for process improvement through basic components and focusing on the resistance to change. *Journal of Software: Evolution and Process*, 24(5), 511–523. doi: doi:10.1002/smr.505

Clarke, P., & O'Connor, R. V. (2012). The influence of SPI on business success in software SMEs: An empirical study. *Journal of Systems and Software*, 85(10), 2356–2367. doi:10.1016/j.jss.2012.05.024

Dyba, T. (2000). An instrument for measuring the key factors of success in software process improvement. *Empirical Software Engineering, 5*(4), 357–390. doi:10.1023/A:1009800404137

Elliott, M., Dawson, R., & Edwards, J. (2009). An evolutionary cultural-change approach to successful software process improvement. *Software Quality Journal, 17*(2), 189–202. doi:10.1007/s11219-008-9070-7

Espinosa-Curiel, I. E., Rodríguez-Jacobo, J., & Fernández-Zepeda, J. A. (2011). A framework for evaluation and control of the factors that influence the software process improvement in small organizations. *Journal of Software Maintenance and Evolution: Research and Practice.* doi:10.1002/smr.569

Garcia, I., Pacheco, C., & Calvo-Manzano, J. (2010). Using a web-based tool to define and implement software process improvement initiatives in a small industrial setting. *IET Software, 4*(4), 237–251. doi:10.1049/iet-sen.2009.0045

Habra, N., Alexandre, S., Desharnais, J.-M., Laporte, C. Y., & Renault, A. (2008). Initiating software process improvement in very small enterprises: Experience with a light assessment tool. *Information and Software Technology, 50*(7–8), 763–771. doi:10.1016/j.infsof.2007.08.004

Iversen, J., & Ngwenyama, O. (2006). Problems in measuring effectiveness in software process improvement: A longitudinal study of organizational change at Danske data. *International Journal of Information Management, 26*(1), 30–43. doi:10.1016/j.ijinfomgt.2005.10.006

Jahn, K., & Nielsen, P. A. (2011). A vertical approach to knowledge management. *International Journal of Human Capital and Information Technology Professionals, 2*(2), 26–36. doi:10.4018/jhcitp.2011040103

Korsaa, M., Johansen, J., Schweigert, T., Vohwinkel, D., Messnarz, R., Nevalainen, R., & Biro, M. (2012). The people aspects in modern process improvement management approaches. *Journal of Software: Evolution and Process.* doi:10.1002/smr.570

Mathiassen, L., Ngwenyama, O. K., & Aaen, I. (2005). Managing change in software process improvement. *IEEE Software, 22*(6), 84–91. doi:10.1109/MS.2005.159

Matturro, G., & Saavedra, J. (2012). Considering people CMM for managing factors that affect software process improvement. *IEEE Latin America Transactions, 10*(2), 1603–1615. doi:10.1109/TLA.2012.6187605

Messnarz, R., Bachmann, O., Ekert, D., & Riel, A. (2010). SPICE level 3 - Experience with using e-learning to coach the use of standard system design best practices in projects. In A. Riel, R. O'Connor, S. Tichkiewitch, & R. Messnarz (Eds.), *Systems, software and services process improvement* (Vol. 99, pp. 213–221). Berlin: Springer. doi:10.1007/978-3-642-15666-3_19

Montoni, M. A., & Cavalcanti da Rocha, A. R. (2011). Using grounded theory to acquire knowledge about critical success factors for conducting software process improvement implementation initiatives. *International Journal of Knowledge Management, 7*(3), 43–60. doi:10.4018/jkm.2011070104

Muller, S. D., Kraemmergaard, P., & Mathiassen, L. (2009). Managing cultural variation in software process improvement: A comparison of methods for subculture assessment. *IEEE Transactions on Engineering Management, 56*(4), 584–599. doi:10.1109/TEM.2009.2013829

Müller, S. D., Mathiassen, L., & Balshøj, H. H. (2010). Software process improvement as organizational change: A metaphorical analysis of the literature. *Journal of Systems and Software*, *83*(11), 2128–2146. doi:10.1016/j.jss.2010.06.017

Munk-Madsen, A., & Nielsen, P. A. (2011). Success factors and motivators in SPI. *International Journal of Human Capital and Information Technology Professionals*, *2*(4), 49–60. doi:10.4018/jhcitp.2011100105

Nevalainen, R., & Schweigert, T. (2010). A European scheme for software process improvement manager training and certification. *Journal of Software Maintenance and Evolution: Research and Practice*, *22*(4), 269–277. doi: doi:10.1002/spip.438

Niazi, M. (2009). Software process improvement implementation: Avoiding critical barriers. *CROSS-TALK: The Journal of Defense Software Engineering*, *22*(1), 24–27.

Niazi, M. (2011). An exploratory study of software process improvement implementation risks. *Journal of Software Maintenance and Evolution: Research and Practice*. doi:10.1002/smr.543

Niazi, M., Babar, M. A., & Verner, J. M. (2010). Software process improvement barriers: A cross-cultural comparison. *Information and Software Technology*, *52*(11), 1204–1216. doi:10.1016/j.infsof.2010.06.005

Niazi, M., Wilson, D., & Zowghi, D. (2005). A framework for assisting the design of effective software process improvement implementation strategies. *Journal of Systems and Software*, *78*(2), 204–222. doi:10.1016/j.jss.2004.09.001

O'Connor, R., & Basri, S. (2012). The effect of team dynamics on software development process improvement. *International Journal of Human Capital and Information Technology Professionals*, *3*(3), 13–26. doi:10.4018/jhcitp.2012070102

O'Connor, R. V. (2012). Evaluating management sentiment towards ISO/IEC 29110 in very small software development companies. In A. Mas, A. Mesquida, T. Rout, R. V. O'Connor, & A. Dorling (Eds.), *Software process improvement and capability determination* (Vol. 290, pp. 277–281). Berlin: Springer. doi:10.1007/978-3-642-30439-2_31

Passos, O. M., Dias-Neto, A. C., & da Silva Barreto, R. (2012). Organizational culture and success in SPI initiatives. *IEEE Software*, *29*(3), 97–99. doi:10.1109/MS.2012.52

Petersen, K., & Wohlin, C. (2010). Software process improvement through the lean measurement (SPI-LEAM) method. *Journal of Systems and Software*, *83*(7), 1275–1287. doi:10.1016/j.jss.2010.02.005

Ply, J. K., Moore, J., Williams, C. K., & Thatcher, J. (2012). IS employee attitudes and perceptions at varying levels of software process maturity. *MIS Quarterly-Management Information Systems*, *36*(2), 601.

Ringstad, M. A., Dingsøyr, T., & Moe, N. B. (2011). Agile process improvement: Diagnosis and planning to improve teamwork. In R. V. O'Connor, J. Pries-Heje, & R. Messnarz (Eds.), *Systems, software and service process improvement, communications in computer and information science* (pp. 167–178). Berlin: Springer. doi:10.1007/978-3-642-22206-1_15

Shih, C.-C., & Huang, S.-J. (2010). Exploring the relationship between organizational culture and software process improvement deployment. *Information & Management*, *47*(5–6), 271–281. doi:10.1016/j.im.2010.06.001

Sulayman, M., Urquhart, C., Mendes, E., & Seidel, S. (2012). Software process improvement success factors for small and medium web companies: A qualitative study. *Information and Software Technology*, *54*(5), 479–500. doi:10.1016/j.infsof.2011.12.007

Sun, Y., & Liu, X. (2010). Business-oriented software process improvement based on CMMI using QFD. *Information and Software Technology*, *52*(1), 79–91. doi:10.1016/j.infsof.2009.08.003

Unterkalmsteiner, M., Gorschek, T., Islam, A. K. M. M., Cheng, C. K.,,Permadi, R. B., & Feldt, R. (2012). Evaluation and measurement of software process improvement: A systematic literature review. *IEEE Transactions on Software Engineering*, *38*(2), 398–424. doi:10.1109/TSE.2011.26

van Solingen, R. (2004). Measuring the ROI of software process improvement. *IEEE Software*, *21*(3), 32–38. doi:10.1109/MS.2004.1293070

van Solingen, R. (2009). A follow-up reflection on software process improvement ROI. *IEEE Software*, *26*(5), 77–79. doi:10.1109/MS.2009.120

Vlaanderen, K., Brinkkemper, S., & van de Weerd, I. (2012). On the design of a knowledge management system for incremental process improvement for software product management. *International Journal of Information System Modeling and Design*, *3*(4), 46–66. doi:10.4018/jismd.2012100103

Yilmaz, M., & O'Connor, R. V. (2011). A software process engineering approach to improving software team productivity using socioeconomic mechanism design. *SIGSOFT Softw. Eng. Notes*, *36*(5), 1–5. doi:10.1145/2020976.2020998

ADDITIONAL READING

Dogru, A. H., & Biçer, V. (2011). *Modern software engineering concepts and practices: Advanced approaches*. Hershey, PA: IGI Global.

Fauzi, S. S., Nasir, M. N., Ramli, N., & Sahibuddin, S. (2012). *Software process improvement and management: Approaches and tools for practical development*. Hershey, PA: IGI Global.

Liu, X., & Li, Y. (2012). *Advanced design approaches to emerging software systems: Principles, methodologies and tools*. Hershey, PA: IGI Global.

Ramachandran, M. (2011). *Knowledge engineering for software development life cycles: Support technologies and applications*. Hershey, PA: IGI Global. doi:10.4018/978-1-60960-509-4

Rech, J., & Bunse, C. (2012). *Emerging technologies for the evolution and maintenance of software models*. Hershey, PA: IGI Global.

Zahran, S. (1998). *Software process improvement*. Reading, MA: Addison-Wesley.

Acknowledgment

The editors would like to acknowledge the help of all the people involved in this project and, more specifically, the authors and reviewers that took part in the review process. Without their support, this book would not have become a reality.

Firstly, the editors would like to thank each one of the authors for their contributions. Our sincere gratitude goes to the chapter authors who contributed their time and expertise to this book.

Secondly, the editors wish to acknowledge the valuable contributions of the reviewers regarding the improvement of quality, coherence, and content presentation of chapters. Most of the authors also served as referees; we highly appreciate their double task. Our special thanks to David Forest for his valuable comments.

A special thanks to Dr. Ángel Jordán for writing the Foreword.

Our special thanks also go to the publishing team at IGI Global for considering the edited book proposal academically and publishing it for the intended readership. If not for them, this effort would have no meaning at all. In particular, we would like to thank Erin O'Dea, Jan Travers, Allyson Gard, and Monica Speca for their endless support and cooperation.

Dr. Colomo-Palacios would like to thank his (lovely and beautiful) wife, Cristina, a constant source of inspiration, encouragement, and endless love, and Rodrigo, the charming kid.

Dr. Calvo-Manzano would like to thank his loving family: Magdalena and all his children, Ana, Manuel, and María.

Dr. Amescua wants to thank two wonderful sisters, Mercedes and Carmen Campos, and Enrique González-Ruano, his father and reference model, whom he has always trusted and who has supported his teaching and research activity in the public university.

Dr. San Feliu Gilabert wants to thank his family. They encouraged him to pursue the dream to be a professor.

Ricardo Colomo-Palacios
Universidad Carlos III de Madrid, Spain

Jose Antonio Caolvo-Manzano Villalón
Universidad Politécnica De Madrid, Spain

Antonio de Amescua Seco
Universidad Carlos III de Madrid, Spain

Tomás San Feliu Gilabert
Universidad Politécnica De Madrid, Spain

Section 1
Innovative Agile Development and Estimation Techniques

Chapter 1
Process and Productivity Improvement in Agile Software Development with Process Libraries:
Case Study

Hugo A. Mitre
Research Center in Mathematics (CIMAT), Mexico

Leonardo Bermon-Angarita
National University of Colombia, Colombia

ABSTRACT

Currently, agile methods are replacing traditional process-based methods in the software industry. However, process-based software development still matters because of its degree of reusability in new projects. Some problems arise when Knowledge Management (KM) is not correctly aligned with processes, such as lack of productivity and process improvement. In this chapter, the authors present a case study of applying two proposals of process libraries in an agile software development division. The researchers and the software development division worked with a Kanban dashboard, eXtremme Programming (XP), and SCRUM practices, adapted to Process Assets Library (PAL) and to Process Practice Library (PPL) in three software projects in order to find experiences of tacit and explicit knowledge that have an impact on process improvement and productivity. Under results and discussion, the authors present the good and bad practices.

DOI: 10.4018/978-1-4666-5182-1.ch001

1. INTRODUCTION

During these last years, agile methods are becoming more important and rapidly replacing traditional methods for software development companies (Laanti, Salo, & Abrahamsson, 2011). But this does not mean the demise of software development based on processes. The time and effort to create a project process description is significantly reduced when a reusable process is instantiated instead of building the process from scratch (Hollenbach & Frakes, 1996).

One concern for creating a process description is that software developers do not usually follow the process to search and create knowledge required to develop and improve their activities (Jean-Claude & Oquendo, 2004). There are two types of knowledge leading the software development process: knowledge acquired through experience (known as tacit knowledge), and the technical knowledge stored in documents (known as explicit knowledge). Nonaka (1994) describes explicit knowledge as stored in textbooks, software products and documents, and implicit (tacit) knowledge as stored in the minds of people in the form of memory, skills, experience, education, imagination and creativity. One way to organize knowledge is to use and manage repositories of process assets known as a Process Asset Library (PAL). A PAL captures, understands and uses processes to improve productivity (Jalote, 2002).

Since the information on agile software development is easy to obtain, one can say that explicit knowledge is less worrisome than tacit. Also, there are benefits from applying practices derived from experiences - tacit knowledge - to agile methods, such as the improvement of customer collaboration, fixing problems while work is in progress and learning with pair programming (Dybå, Dingsøyr, & Moe, 2004). Other important practices of agile methods are stand-up meetings (Levy & Hazzan, 2009) and iteration retrospective. However, there is no evidence of productivity and process improvement of knowledge management having an impact on agile methods in a real case study. Our research goal is to:

Find experiences of how the use of tacit and explicit knowledge has an impact on productivity in agile software development and process improvement.

In this article, we provide evidence of process improvement and productivity from agile software development teams. For the case study, we used two process libraries: PAL was applied to two small projects and the PPL (Process Practice Library) to a small project in a software company. PPL was adapted and improved in the agile software process and the technical needs of the software company.

This article is organized as follows: section two presents the PAL and PPL proposals; section three describes the case study; section four analyzes and discusses the results; and the last section presents the conclusions.

2. PROCESS LIBRARIES

Before this proposal, there were two process-oriented libraries: the first was a Web-based library oriented towards small software companies to provide organized and searchable repository of process assets and to cover the needs of process guidance for the Capability Maturity Model (CMMI) (Calvo-Manzano, Cuevas, & San Feliu, 2008). The second was a wiki-based library (Wiki 2.0 offering dynamic content) oriented towards small and medium software companies with the aim of searching, creating and modifying the tacit and explicit knowledge of process assets, called PAL (García, Amescua, Sánchez, & Bermón, 2011). A process asset can help to understand, capture, and use the process. Moreover, the assets generated in previous projects can be stored in the wiki at the end of the projects and reused in future projects. Reuse of these assets can save developers time and effort because the assets encapsulate the explicit and tacit knowledge of the organization. The optimal proposal used in the software industry is PAL.

PAL was correctly validated with students, but the software industry is different. This is why we decided to use it in two small projects of a software division in Mexico in order to improve productivity and introduce an agile method to the software division. After gaining experience from the two projects, the Process Practices Library (PPL) proposal was created according to the needs and culture of the software development team, and then tested in a small software project.

2.1 PAL

The Process Assets Library (PAL) is a repository of process assets that seeks to facilitate the use and learning of an agile software process with wiki technology. Wiki enables software teams to write documents collaboratively in a repository.

As seen in Figure 1, the structure of PAL is presented in a UML (Unified Modeling Language) class diagram. This model is described in general terms as follows:

PAL is used in a software *organization* with *n projects* operated by the *process team*, *develop-*

ment team and *PAL administrator*. The process team creates, evaluates, edits, and enhances the knowledge; the development team uses the knowledge stored in the wiki repository; and the PAL administrators manage users and contents. Each project can have process assets instances containing *structured knowledge* (explicit), such as the work product, examples, technical procedure; and *non-structured knowledge* (tacit), such as lessons learned and discussions. The *process elements* are agile software development processes and tailoring guidelines.

This proposal also has a guide to follow core, support and advanced functions. The *Core functions* are the knowledge management activities for acquisition, organization, utilization, preservation, distribution and reuse of knowledge. The *support functions* are defined for change control, user management and measurement of the wiki. The advanced functions address project and deployment processes in the software organization.

2.2 Proposal of PPL

The Process Practices Library (PPL) is an adapted Wiki repository of practices for agile software development. Our decision to change assets for practices was based on experience in the use of

Figure 1. UML meta-model for the PAL structure

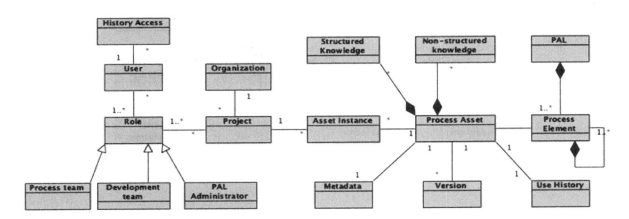

complex and dispersed information of the process assets. The technical information from process assets was uncontrollable because of the technologies of software development projects. These experiences are detailed in section four.

PPL integrates the tacit and explicit knowledge in agile software development practices represented in a pattern (template of practice) and aligned to the agile software development process.

As seen in Figure 2, the structure of PAL is presented in a UML class diagram. A *project* is operated by two roles: the *development team* (e.g. junior developer, senior developer, project leader and technical leader) and the *knowledge administrator* (this person performs the core and support functions). A *project* can have *n processes*, and in turn each *process* is composed of *n practices*. Each *practice* is composed of an *entry and exit criteria*, and *explicit knowledge* and can aggregate *n tacit knowledge*. The practice can be seen in a template as follows:

- **Definition of practice:** Describes the purpose of the practice after completing the template instructions.
  - **Practice pertains to process:** This is a textual field that provides the process of this practice.
  - **Practice pertains to activity:** This textual field represents the activity of the Business Process Modeling Notation (BPMN) Process aligned with this practice. The Object Management Group (OMG) has developed a BPMN standard to "provide a notation that is readily understandable by all business users, from the business analysts that create the initial drafts of the processes to the technical developers responsible for implementing the technology that will perform those processes, and finally, to the business people who will manage and monitor those processes." BPMN can be seen at http://

Figure 2. UML meta-model for the PPL structure

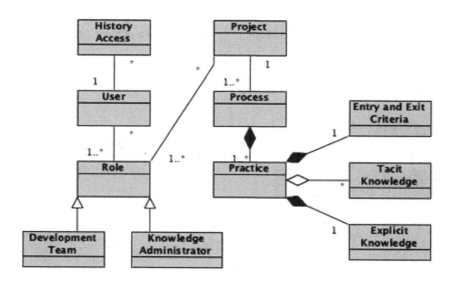

www.cimat.mx/~hmitre/process.png. In short, each practice template is aligned with each activity of the agile software development process.

- **Roles:**
  - ○ **Role co-ordinator:** This role is responsible for conducting this practice.
  - ○ **Collaborator:** Collaborators are involved in the implementation of this practice, but they are not responsible for the output products.
  - ○ **Reviewers:** These are the roles that verify that the practice has been successfully completed.
- **Practice:**
  - ○ **Entry products:** Work products necessary to start this practice
  - ○ **Entry criteria:** These are the criteria for the incoming information to initiate this practice.
  - ○ **Practice:** This describes the execution order of the practice in simple steps.
  - ○ **Output products:** These are the resulting work products on completion of this practice.
- **Learning:**
  - ○ **Presentations:** These are slides describing how to follow this practice in detail.
  - ○ **References:** They are the books, articles and magazines that can be useful for continuing this practice.
  - ○ **Discussion:** These are suggestions and discussions of the role of the co-ordinator and/or the collaborator and/or the reviewer.

3. DESCRIPTION OF THE CASE STUDY

3.1 Research Method

Our research was identified as action research (Runeson & Höst, 2008); hence, our research goals were defined and focused on improvement and productivity. Moreover, our implementation process was based on the suggested spiral case study process (Andersson & Runeson, 2007). The spiral process represents the actors who perform their corresponding activity, such as: setting scope and goals, data collection, data analysis and results, and corrective actions taken. Our collaboration scheme for data collection and filtering can be seen in Figure 3. Researchers can interchange ideas, suggestions and instructions with the technical leader and, in turn, the technical leader with the development team and the QA leader for project coaching, and with the customer to meet their expectations of user stories. Finally, researchers and the technical leader can save the project data in a Wiki repository.

3.2 Context

This study was performed in the telecommunications company Compulogic, specifically in its software division in Zacatecas, Mexico.

The company uses Thin Client technology so that deploying work stations for developers is easy. This has helped the company's daily operations to avoid many maintenance headaches. Thin Clients are seen as components of a broader computer infrastructure, where many clients share their computations with the same server. As such, thin client infrastructures can be viewed as providing some

Figure 3. Collaboration scheme for data collection

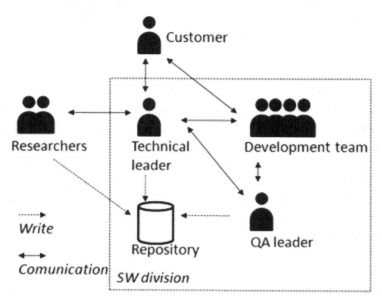

computing service via several user-interfaces. This is desirable in contexts where individual fat clients have much more functionality or power than the infrastructure either requires or uses.

Our first agile software development based on Kanban, Extreme Programming (XP) and SCRUM can be seen in Table 1.

Three projects were developed for this study: the Quality Schools Programs Project (QSP), the Construction Supervision Project (SCS) and the Collaborations of Small and Medium Enterprises (CSMEs). The context of projects are presented as follows:

- **Context of the Quality Schools Programs Project (QSP):**
  - **Customer Profile:** Quality Schools Program (QSP) is a government program that tries to improve basic education in Mexico. It has several lines of action but the most important is that it provides financing to make improvements in schools.
  - **Basic work process:** The basic mechanism is a school finds some form of donation from parents or other benefactors and the federal government matches their donations. Each state has control of their own schools and decides some specific rules to distribute the money amongst the schools in the state. In this project, the state involved was Zacatecas. Since the federal government matches every donation, they also need to have control of these expenses. And having this control for 466 schools in the state system is difficult. Moreover, in order to serve all the schools, there are only five accountants and one state coordinator to sign every check the schools get.
  - **Users:** Direct users: 5 accountants and 1 state coordinator. Indirect users: 1 governor, 466 school principals and 466 Parent Teacher Association presidents.
  - **Software Tools:** PHP programming with Yii Framework were used. Yii is an open source, object-oriented,

Table 1. Initial agile software development process presented in a Kanban dashboard

Kanban Column (Sub-Process)	Description
Backlog	Where all the user stories that are known to the system are added.
Selected	User stories that are selected to work on this iteration. Once a user story leaves this column it should also have been decomposed in several user stories if needed.
Development	The actual coding of the user story and its unit tests. They are done in Pair Programming.
Unit Testing	The Extreme Programming sense tests should be carried out before the actual code but some flexibility is allowed here. This column simply tries to make sure that developers "test everything that could possibly break" (Jeffries, Anderson, & Hendrickson, 2000).
Big Story Integration	In this process those user stories that were decomposed in sub-stories during the Selected phase are re-integrated.
Acceptance Testing	One of the members of the Quality Assurance team helps the pair write the acceptance tests for this user story.
Integration	In this column all the stories for the iteration are kept together to present them to the customer. Also at this stage, all the unit tests are run together. In the QPS project all tests were run by hand. In the SCS and CSMEs projects these tests are run automatically by the Continuous Integration Server.
Ready to Deploy	Storage of finished user stories that have not been pushed to production.
Deployment	Code is delivered to the customer or pushed to the production server.

component-based Model-View-Controller (MVC) PHP Web application framework.

○ **System Goal:** QSP Zacatecas approached Compulogic to develop a system that would allow them to more closely control the expenses for all the schools, make the job of the accountants easier and the state co-ordinator could send the money to schools in an automated way.

○ **Personnel:** 7 junior developers with less than one years' experience in software development, 2 senior developers with an average of 5 years' professional experience, 1 project leader with 20 years' experience in administrative roles and 1 technical leader with 10 years' experience in software development.

● **Context of School Construction Supervision Project (SCS):**

○ **Customer Profile:** Zacatecas Institute for School Construction is a state office in charge of building and maintaining public schools. They are responsible for building from one classroom to a whole university campus.

○ **Basic work process:** A project is developed and then opened to public tender. Once a contractor wins the tender, they do the actual construction; but the institute is responsible for supervising the project.

○ **System Goal:** The basic use case is a supervisor going to the construction site, taking pictures of the progress and notes on the overall progress of the work. Then a report is written and pictures of the construction are uploaded. The director and governor follow the progress of the different constructions through a dashboard.

○ **Users:** Direct users: 12 construction supervisors, 1 head of construction and 1 state coordinator. Indirect users: 1 governor, 400 schools per year.

○ **Software Tools:** The basic coding tools (PHP language, Yii framework) were used. But in this project, the team emphasized Continuous Integration. Other tools included, apart from the previous tools mentioned:

- CruiseControl General Continuous Integration, a tool and an extensible framework for creating a custom continuous build process.
- PhpUnderControl add-on application to CruiseControl for the PHP language. It is an application for the continuous integration tool, CruiseControl, which integrates some of the best PHP development tools. Therefore, phpUnderControl comes with a command line tool that performs all the modifications to an existing CruiseControl installation.
  - **Personnel:** 7 junior developers with less than one year's experience in software development, 2 senior developers with an average of 5 years' professional experience, 1 project leader with 20 years' experience in administrative roles and 1 technical leader with 10 years' experience in software development.
- **Collaborations of Small and Medium Enterprises (CSMEs):**
  - **Customer profile:** Small or medium enterprises looking to be part of a supply chain in a collaborative way.
  - **Basic work process:** Site of collaboration between companies, governments, educational institutions and the population. It is a social network that allows interaction between them in order to achieve cohesion between business projects, free-lancers and governments supported by educational institutions. It also allows the strengthening of supply chains, find-

ing suppliers, creating chains, project sharing, knowledge transfer, identifying specific needs and the adoption of business models for the benefit of members.

- **System goal:** Offer, improve, renovate, and develop projects, a variety of resources, tools and services that users have in a reciprocal process of teaching and learning.
- **Development time:** One week per iteration with 16 iterations planned.
- **Users:** Small or medium enterprise.
- **Software tools:** PHP language, Yii framework, CruiseControl and PhpUnderControl.
- **Personnel:** 4 junior developers with less than one years' experience in software development, 1 senior developer with an average of 5 years' professional experience and 1 technical leader with 10 years' experience in software development.

3.3 Plan

Our *research goal* is to find experiences of how the use of tacit and explicit knowledge has an impact on productivity on agile software development and process improvement.

Before the projects, the eXtremme Programming (XP) and SCRUM agile methods with a Process Asset Library (PAL) were used as the main training resource. XP is a software development methodology that is intended to improve software quality and responsiveness to changing customer requirements. It advocates frequent "releases" in short development cycles (timeboxing), which is intended to improve productivity and introduce checkpoints where new customer requirements can be adopted. SCRUM is an iterative and incremental agile software development framework for managing software projects and product or application development. Its focus is on a flexible, holistic product development strategy where a development team works as a unit to reach a common goal. Our initial approach for software development was PAL (Process Assets Library) (García et al., 2011). That is why PAL was used as a training tool. Our *training* schedule was 4 hours per day for 6 weeks.

The projects were performed consecutively in the following order:

- **QSP:** Two weeks per iteration with four iterations planned.
- **SCS:** Two weeks per iteration with five iterations planned.
- **CSMEs:** One week per iteration with 16 iterations planned.

The measures designed to be collected for each project are categorized as follows:

- **Measures that indicate tacit knowledge implementation:**
  - **Number of stand-up meetings:** The entire team holds a daily stand-up meeting, which usually takes place in the morning for 10 to 15 minutes. In these meetings, each team member presents the status of his or her development tasks in small sentences and what he or she plans to accomplish during the day, both with respect to the development tasks and personnel role. When needed, one sentence can be added by each team member during his or her turn with respect to anticipated problems.
  - **Number of customer meetings:** The target is to get an on-going feedback from the customers (face to face) and to move on according to their needs. Such an on-going interaction avoids the need to speculate about the customers' needs, which may lead to incorrect working assumptions. This

practice implies that in agile software development all team members have access to the customer during the entire development process.
  - **Number of retrospectives:** At the end of each project iteration, a meeting called retrospective is carried out with the entire team. Retrospective meetings give the team a chance to tap into discoveries about what works or does not work in their environment. Moreover, during these meetings, for each iteration project some measures are saved in the Wiki repository, for example Perfect Engineering Hours (PEH) and PEHs per day.
  - **Number of processes improved or added:** Technical leader's improvement of the agile software development process.
- **Measures of productivity of software development teams. The purpose of the following steps is to measure project development productivity:**
  - **Perfect Engineering Hours (PEH):** This is a subjective measurement of the complexity of a user story. It is roughly defined as if developers worked in a perfect state with no distractions and totally focused on how many hours it would take to finish this task (Cohn, 2005).
  - **Burn down charts:** This chart represents productivity in time by iteration. The outstanding work (or backlog) is often on the vertical axis, with time along the horizontal. That is, it is a run chart of outstanding work. It is useful for predicting when all of the work will be completed. It is often used in agile software development methodologies such as Scrum. However, burn down charts can be applied to any project containing

measurable progress over time. For this kind of burn down chart, we use the PEH as the Y-Axis and the iterations as the X-Axis. Moreover, we depict the planned (initial estimation), re-planned (new estimation in each iteration) and actual lines (real work performed at the end of iteration).

4. ANALYSIS OF RESULTS AND DISCUSSION

4.1 Results

Below are the results of projects with a breakdown of iterations and the results at the end of each project. The results are categorized into project productivity and tacit knowledge factors.

- **Productivity of the software development team of (include: the) QSP Project:**
  - ○ **Iteration 1:** As seen in Figure 4, during this first iteration, there was a great deal of discovery on how the Yii framework worked and how to update the process assets. However, the software development team did not take into account the learning curve

to plan the re-planned line. For this reason, the estimation of this iteration wasn't accurate causing an undesired impact on productivity.

- ○ **Iteration 2:** During this iteration, we set up a testing-only team for the unit testing sub-process. Also, we set up Work-In-Process (WIP) limits in the Kanban dashboard, at the top of the Kanban columns in order to control the maximum workload of the software development team. WIP limits imply that a pull system is implemented in parts or all of the workflow. The pull system will act as one of the main stimuli for continuous, incremental and evolutionary changes to the system. Our mistake was to mix hard User Stories with easy. Hence, we were too far from the re-planned line.
- ○ **Iteration 3:** We started to use regression testing creating process assets that were difficult to control, and with the lack of code review to avoid the rework. So, our productivity was not close to the re-planned line.
- ○ **Iteration 4:** Since we saw that no iteration had improved, we decided to

Figure 4. Burn Down Chart of the QSP project

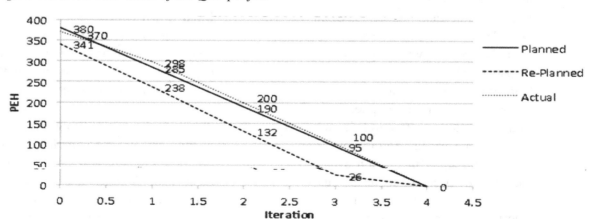

plan aggressively but, in the end, it went slower than re-planned but near the planned finishing on time.

- **Tacit knowledge factors:**
  - **Number of stand-up meetings:** 40.
  - **Number of customer meetings:** 5.
  - **Number of retrospectives:** 4.
  - **Number of processes improved or added:** Retrospectives helped us to add the code review in the next process.

- **Productivity of the software development team of the SCS Project:**
  - **Iteration 1:** As seen in Figure 5, the first iteration was slow due to the learning curve of process assets management in PAL. Moreover, we added a column to Kanban to include the Code Review to avoid rework.
  - **Iteration 2:** During this iteration we made a prototype of a difficult algorithm on a spreadsheet so that it was easier to codify. But, for developers (include: it) was complicated to update Wiki assets, so assets were distributed in the technologies used to develop the software and not in the Wiki. Consequently, we were still far from the re-planned PEH.
  - **Iteration 3:** Here we assigned a new developer to the project. This was a mistake as two were needed right from the beginning. PAL provides much information. Training a new developer on how to manage the new process assets was too complex. Even with the training of the new hire, the results show that PAL was the iteration closest to the planned and re-planned line.
  - **Iteration 4:** We wasted a full day on a feature that was not really needed. That affected the whole system and this created problems and bugs throughout the codebase.
  - **Iteration 5:** We left the easiest stories for last. We now think that these stories were overestimated because several members of the team then had experience on how to develop these kinds of stories, which led to a big increase in productivity.

- **Tacit knowledge factors:**
  - **Number of stand-up meetings:** 47.
  - **Number of customer meetings:** 6.

Figure 5. Burn Down Chart of the SCS project

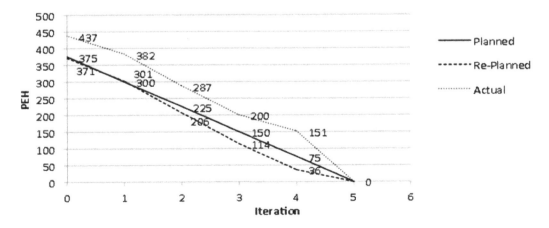

- Number of retrospectives: 6.
  - Number of processes improved or added: Retrospectives and customer meetings help us to identify the need for a usability review for the next process.

- **Productivity of the software development team of the CSMEs Project:**
  - **Iteration 1-9:** As seen in Figure 6, the productivity of the software development team was not a problem. With the practices oriented towards an agile development process of PPL, the developers managed its process assets into their corresponding technology, specifically with CruiseControl and PhpUnderControl. However, after the third iteration, the unit test practice was used once again. Finally, the experience and the lack of management in assets within the Wiki led to disuse of PPL.

- **Tacit knowledge factors:**
  - **Number of stand-up meetings:** 28.
  - **Number of customer meetings:** 5.
  - **Number of retrospectives:** 9.
  - **Number of processes improved or added:** None.

4.2 Discussion

4.2.1 Tacit and Explicit Knowledge that Have an Impact on Productivity

The tacit knowledge of PAL and PPL required in their templates was never updated. The culture of the development team and collaborators interfered in their responsibility to maintain the knowledge of their assets or practices. In sum, this culture is do it quickly and well but undocumented.

Despite the learning curve in the first two projects, the developers mentioned that the practices of the agile software development, such as the pair programming and the stand-up meetings helped to improve software development productivity. For stand-up meetings, it is a confirmation previously presented by the authors (Levy & Hazzan, 2009). Pair programming was also very supportive, but we suggest putting the asset maintenance in charge of someone who is not programming at that moment.

Concerning the explicit knowledge, during the CSMEs Project, the productivity was clearly improved due to the fact that the developers rapidly assimilated the explicit knowledge of PPL and learned to preserve their assets in their corresponding software development technology. But, concerning tacit knowledge, the same difficulty that happened using PAL happened to PPL; they were unable to maintain the experience generated to the assets or practices.

Figure 6. Burn Down Chart of the CSMEs project

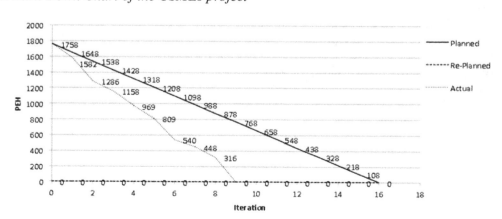

4.2.2 Tacit and Explicit Knowledge that Have an Impact on Process Improvement

In the first two projects, we realized that customer collaboration and the retrospectives are valuable practices to improve the agile process.

- Retrospectives and customer meetings helped us to identify the need for a usability review. During the SCS Project, customers made several corrections to the software product about usability, and for this reason, an improvement of the software development process was identified during retrospective meetings.
- Retrospectives and Burn Down Charts helped us to add the code review. After finishing the QSP Project and after the conclusions of retrospectives with the results of Burn Down Charts, the senior developer and technical leader added the code review sub-process to avoid the rework.

With the discovery of these two sub-processes we made a significant improvement to the PPL proposal. The code review and usability review sub-processes were added in the new process (BPMN) and aligned with the PPL practices.

4.2.3 Other Discussion

Concerning the alignment of Knowledge Management (KM) and development processes, the first version of the Kanban dashboard used the process expressed in PAL, and from each iteration thereafter, the dashboard evolved with other practices. As shown earlier, PAL was useful as a training method, but not for the productivity of software teams. And PPL was designed to align KM with the agile process, but failed in maintaining management.

Regarding the classic problems Anderson (2010) says that when he presented agile methods

to different teams, some of them said that it was not practical. As time passed, he learned that when people said "It isn't practical" what they really meant was "It doesn't apply in my context." The software division basically made several classic mistakes:

1. We tried to "push harder" trying to make it practical (i.e. to develop more PEHs than the iterations speed would allow).
2. We tried to avoid a major rework, making a better software product, but we ended up wasting a day's work for the entire team.
3. We did not have a decomposition process during the first two projects. However, during third one, we defined a well-known practice template to have as part of the BPMN process.

We think this offers a valuable lesson in team building: It is good to let the team make mistakes as long as they go through a reflection process that allows the team to learn and correct those mistakes and finally create a new proposal. What we want to convey is an incremental improvement of the processes.

5. CONCLUSION

In this article, three projects were analyzed to discover the experiences of applying PAL and PPL in a real case study. We found good and bad experiences that had an impact on productivity and process improvement. The best practices identified are:

- The stand-up meetings and pair programming helped to improve software development productivity.
- Retrospectives, customer meetings and burn down charts helped to improve the software development process.
- Practice-based development helped improve productivity significantly.

And the bad practices that reduced productivity and process improvement are:

- Adding a developer during project execution.
- Introducing process assets without software development technology integration.
- Discard the learning curve for iteration planning.

Finally, sacrificing the idea of process assets led to more productivity, and it also led to lack of knowledge management. For future work, we suggest preserving process assets, but integrating them into the software development technology synchronized with the library. In this way, it is possible to keep the agile manifest and preserve the process asset terminology.

ACKNOWLEDGMENT

This case study was supported by the Mexican National Council on Science and Technology (CONACYT, Consejo Nacional de Ciencia y Tecnología) through the project *Innovation Network Planning, Execution, Control and Continuous Improvement Process Oriented Software Development of Regional Market Based on Agile Methods* (Red de Innovación para la Planeación, Ejecución, Control y Mejora Continua de Procesos Orientados al Desarrollo de Software en el Mercado Regional Basado en Métodos Ágiles).

REFERENCES

Anderson, D. J. (2010). Kanban. In *Successful evolutionary change for your technology business*. Blue Hole Press.

Andersson, C., & Runeson, P. (2007). A spiral process model for case studies on software quality monitoring—Method and metrics. *Software Process Improvement and Practice*, *12*(2), 125–140. doi:10.1002/spip.311

Calvo-Manzano, J. A., Cuevas, G., & San Feliu, T. (2008). A process asset library to support software process improvement in small settings. In *Proceedings of EuroSPI 2008, CCIS 16* (pp. 25–35). Berlin: Springer-Verlag.

Cohn, M. (2005). *Agile estimating and planning*. Englewood Cliffs, NJ: Prentice Hall.

Dybå, T., Dingsøyr, T., & Moe, N. B. (2004). *Process improvement in practice: A handbook for IT companies*. Boston: Kluwer Academic.

García, J., Amescua, A., Sánchez, M.-I., & Bermón, L. (2011). Design guidelines for software processes knowledge repository development. *Information and Software Technology*, *53*(8), 834–850. doi:10.1016/j.infsof.2011.03.002

Hollenbach, C., & Frakes, W. (1996). Software process reuse in an industrial setting. In *Proceedings of the 4th International Conference on Software Reuse* (ICSR '96) (pp. 22–30). IEEE.

Jalote, P. (2002). *Software project management in practice*. Reading, MA: Addison-Wesley Professional.

Jean-Claude, D., & Oquendo, F. (2004). Key issues and new challenges in software process technology. *Novatica. European Journal for the Informatics Professional*, *5*(5), 15–20.

Jeffries, R., Anderson, A., & Hendrickson, C. (2000). *Extreme programming installed*. Reading, MA: Addison-Wesley Professional.

Laanti, M., Salo, O., & Abrahamsson, P. (2011). Agile methods rapidly replacing traditional methods at Nokia: A survey of opinions on agile transformation. *Information and Software Technology*, *53*(3), 276–290. doi:10.1016/j.infsof.2010.11.010

Levy, M., & Hazzan, O. (2009). Knowledge management in practice: The case of agile software development. In *Proceedings of Cooperative and Human Aspects on Software Engineering* (pp. 60–65). IEEE.

Nonaka, I. (1994). A dynamic theory of organizational knowledge creation. *Organization Science*, *5*(1), 14–37. doi:10.1287/orsc.5.1.14

Runeson, P., & Höst, M. (2008). Guidelines for conducting and reporting case study research in software engineering. *Empirical Software Engineering*, *14*(2), 131–164. doi:10.1007/s10664-008-9102-8

KEY TERMS AND DEFINITIONS

Agility in Software Development: Means to strip away as much of the heaviness, commonly associated with the traditional software-development methodologies, as possible to promote quick response to changing environments, changes in user requirements, accelerated project deadlines and the like (Erickson, Lyytinen, & Siau, 2005).

Knowledge: Is an important concept of this article. But it is common to confuse the concepts of knowledge and information. Information is a flow of messages, while knowledge is created and organized by the every flow of information, anchored on the commitment and beliefs of its holder (Nonaka, 1994). In the same way there are two types of knowledge: *Tacit knowledge* is stored in the minds of people in the form of memory, skills, experience, education, imagination and creativity. And the *explicit knowledge* is stored in textbooks, software products and documents (Nonaka, 1994).

Process Asset: Is defined as "any or all process related assets, from any or all of the organizations involved in the project that can be used to influence the project's success" (Indelicato, 2008). These include plans, procedures, historical information, schedules, risk data and earned value data.

The Process Practice: Term was taken from CMMI (Capability Maturity Model Integration). This term in CMMI is defined as "an activity that is considered important in achieving the associated specific goal. The specific practices describe the activities expected to result in achievement of the specific goals of a process area" (CMMI Product Team, 2002). In our case, the alignment of the practices was assigned to the agile development process and has the purpose to achieve the requirements of a project.

Chapter 2
Technique for Risk Identification of Software Acquisition and Information Technologies

Gloria Piedad Gasca-Hurtado
Universidad de Medellín, Colombia

Jaime Alberto Echeverri Arias
Universidad de Medellín, Colombia

María Clara Gómez
Universidad de Medellín, Colombia

ABSTRACT

In this chapter, the authors present the automatization of a technique for identifying the risks that may affect software acquisition projects. The proposed technique can have an impact in two software acquisition areas: 1) acquisition software contract for: Fully Developed (FD) software, Modified-Off-The-Shelf (MOTS) software, and Commercial-Off-The-Shelf (COTS) software; and 2) information technology services contract, which can be a result of using the required technological tools for the operation of any organization. In both cases, it is indispensable to manage and address (track) the risks that may affect the success of any project type mentioned above.

1. INTRODUCTION

Different fields of science study the implementation of risk management. However, a large percentage of projects in the software industry are never finished or underperform before the expected time (Gibbs, 1994), (Ropponen & Lyytinen, 1997).

DOI: 10.4018/978-1-4666-5182-1.ch002

These facts make it necessary to study project risk management.

Currently, organizations do not incur high costs to produce software that solves individual needs. On the other hand, it is increasingly common to adapt applications to meet unique requirements that are integrated with the existing ones. Also, all types of organizations are increasingly dependent on software to execute their daily tasks. On the other hand, software is becoming more complex and the software industry has had to incorporate new technologies to keep up with a competitive market. Simultaneously, this allows to distribute data and functionality through high-speed networks and increasingly specialized devices (Jones, 1995).

The use of modern techniques and safety protocols is essential in the acquisition of Information Technologies Products and Services (IT-PS), but even with these, the software presents a high number of security failures. Additionally, the development methodologies adopted exceed budget limits and schedules established. Incorporating human beings in these activities results in failures, either through lack of safety perception, lack of skills at different stages or ignorance of a rule, among other factors. If the human component is not dealt with properly, then projects are vulnerable to large losses (Johnson, 2006).

There is a widespread belief within the software industry that an integrated software security is needed, from the earliest stages of system development, in order to ensure privacy, integrity, availability and authenticity of the products so that final products could be delivered on time and within budget.

2. RISK MANAGEMENT FROM THE ACQUISITION ORGANIZATION'S POINT OF VIEW

Currently, organizations have increased their capacity of IT-PS acquisition, and few continue to develop software in-house. This phenomenon occurs for various reasons, such as:

1. Increased demand for IT-PS in organizations
2. High costs of maintaining development teams with technical skills than can support Information Technology (IT) demand.

3. Increasing number of competitive organizations with high technical capabilities for developing Information Technology (IT).

Therefore, organizations nowadays adopt IT-PS acquisition as a business strategy to improve operational efficiency. This is accomplished using the suppliers' capabilities to offer quality solutions quickly, at a lower cost and with the most appropriate technology (Software Engineering Institute, 2010).

2.1 Types of IT-PS Acquisition Projects

The different types of acquisition projects can be classified under various criteria. For example: (i) depending on the type of development team (inside or outside the organization) (Nelson, 1996); (ii) depending on the type of product being acquired (IEEE, 1998); (iii) depending on the function of the existing relation between the development team and the end user (Baker & Fisher, 2007); (iv) depending on the type of work to be performed by the external organization ("Extreme Chaos," 2001).

A classification of different types of acquisition projects that include software acquisition projects patterns is summarized as follows (Vega Zepeda, Gasca-Hurtado, Calvo-Manzano, 2012):

1. **Acquisition of fully developed software, developed using traditional methodologies:** Acquiring a fully developed software allows the customer to control and participate in the software development cycle. When using a traditional methodology, control can be exercised by reviewing the artifacts generated during the process of software construction.

2. **Acquisition of fully developed software, developed using agile methodologies:** If software development is done using agile methodologies, it requires greater involve-

ment and commitment by the customer (This is one of the principles of agile methodologies). Control must be executed in a manner that does not detract the agility of the process by incorporating many extra tasks or excessive documentation.

3. **Acquisition of completed commercial-off-the-shelf-software (COTS):** A *COTS* is a product that can be acquired from a commercial seller, where the customer cannot specify particular requirements. Instead, customers must search among alternative components for the one that best suits their needs. Management and control in these types of projects are aimed at managing the selection of the most appropriate component.

4. **Acquisition of some COTS components that will be assembled for a development performed by an inside team:** In this pattern the most complex aspect is the selection of the right components to meet part of the requirements of developing a system. If these components are going to be assembled by an inside team, the customer can have absolute control over the activities of the development team.

5. **Acquisition of some COTS components that will be assembled for a development performed by an outside team:** The customer must control the right selection of the components. This is a complex activity if the selection is made outside his or her organization. Additionally, it is necessary to control the suppliers' software development processes.

6. **Acquisition of different COTS components that will be assembled by an inside team:** In this case, the selection of components is developed internally and that makes it possible to control the selection process. Since, there is no development, but only assembly of components, the activities to manage are different.

7. **Acquisition of different COTS components that will be assembled by an outside team:** The customer must ensure that the outside team select the right components to be assembled. As there is no development, the control activities are different.

8. **Acquisition of a modified-off-the-shelf-software (MOTS) that will be adapted by an inside team**: This pattern has some similarities to customized software development. It differs in the fact that development does not start from scratch; it is based on the acquired component. While there are some similar management activities between both patterns, it is important to ensure that the most appropriate component that allows to improve the software product construction is selected. Control is easier because the work and selection are internal activities.

9. **Acquisition of a modified-off-the-shelf-software (MOTS) that will be adapted by an outside team:** In this case it is necessary to ensure that the outside team select the most appropriate component. The customer must also control the supplier's adaptation process.

Independent of the type of acquisition that the organization decides on, the acquisition project of IT-PS must be managed carefully. Some of the critical factors that contribute to the failure of these projects are: (1) poor project management, (2) inability to articulate customer needs, (3) poor requirements definition, (4) inadequate suppliers selection and contracting, (5) lack of procedures for selection of development technology and (6) lack of changes control.

It is true that the responsibility for the failure or success of the project is shared between supplier and customer. However, both parties aim for success rather than failure. Both are interested in avoiding failure. This can be achieved if the customer is prepared properly for contracting and supporting her IT-PS suppliers management (Software Engineering Institute, 2010).

Part of the preparation to avoid the failure of acquisition projects consists of first considering the critical factors previously mentioned, i.e. the deficiencies in the management process of acquisition projects. In project acquisition management, the customer must be fully involved in the project. The latter prevents loss of control (of the project), and ensures that the project meets h: the defined schedule, the deadlines and also that the chosen technology is feasible.

The fact that the customer is actively involved in the project requires her to develop other responsibilities that demand more than the simple integration testing, operational transition and meeting needs of the delivered IT-PS, issues that normally appear at the end of the project.

Involving the customer in the acquisition process and during the IT-PS development requires support mechanisms. These mechanisms have been designed for many years; some of them are related to the standards and models, focused on collecting the various recommendations that can be taken into account by the clients when they participate in an IT-PS acquisition environment.

The next section presents a review of the different recognized standards and models in the IT-PS acquisition environment.

3. SOFTWARE ACQUISITION STANDARDS

There are different efforts that seek to define mechanisms to manage and establish appropriate processes for the projects involved in an IT-PS acquisition environment.

Next, some selected models and standards are presented. For this selection the following criteria were defined:

- Make reference to the software purchase (acquisition),
- Have major use in the industry, and
- Have information available.

From these criteria, the following standards and models have been selected: 1) ISO/IEC 12207 standard, 2) IEEE 1062 standard, 3) CMMI-ACQ model, 4) eSCM-CL model.

In the following section, a brief description of each one of the standards and models mentioned is presented.

3.1 ISO/IEC 12207 Standard - Information Technology/ Software Life Cycle Processes

ISO/IEC 12207 Standard - Information Technology/Software Life Cycle Processes is related to the definition of software life cycle process, its interface with other processes and the high-level relationships that govern these interactions.

The usefulness of this standard and the reception of the industry, specifically the software industry, led to an update of its approach in 2008 (International Organization for Standardization, 2008).

This standard is applicable to IT-PS acquisition because structures and acquisition processes aim to facilitate the communication among customers, suppliers and other actors involved in the process. This standard proposes a life cycle that includes the definition, control and improvement of the software processes.

In addition it can be used as support in supplier contracting activities, monitoring and acceptance of the IT-PS, because it provides guidance for the development of IT-PS acquisition contracts.

3.2 IEEE 1062
Standard - Recommended Practice
for Software Acquisition

IEEE 1062 Standard - Recommended Practice for Software Acquisition is a framework with the same relevance of models such as: SW-CMM (Software Engineering Institute, 2002), SA-CMM (Cooper & Fisher, 2002), ISO 9000 (Asociación Española de Normalización y Certificación AE-NOR, 1996), ISO/IEC 15504 (Organization for Standardization/International Electrotechnical Commission, 2004).

It describes a practice that can be used for the acquisition of any IT-PS and for any type of computational platform, regardless of its size and complexity. It is focused on the MOTS (modified-off-the-shelf-software) or FD (partially to fully outsourced FD) products acquisition (Institute of Electrical and Electronics Engineers, 1998). This feature highlights the IEEE 1062 standard within the range of standards and models for IT-PS acquisition.

Part of its structure is focused on standardizing the software acquisition phases and establishing quality characteristics required for acquisition planning. Additionally, it promotes best practices to assess the ability of the supplier to meet the needs of the acquiring organization.

Related to software, this standard aims to promote best practices to evaluate and modify the software that the supplier is offering to the organization.

3.3 CMMI-ACQ Model

The CMMI-ACQ Model provides guidance for applying CMMI best practices in an organization that acquires IT-PS. These best practices are focused on initiating and managing IT-PS acquisition to satisfy the needs of customers and end users. This model involves the suppliers in order to offer useful and appropriate artifacts in the context of the acquisition process.

CMMI-ACQ Model is based on CMMI Model Foundation or CMF (i.e., model components common to all CMMI models and constellations), the CMMI Acquisition Module (Bernard, Gallagher, Bate, & Wilson, 2005) and the CMM-SA Software Acquisition Model (Cooper & Fisher, 2002).

This model provides a wide set of best practices for IT-PS acquisition since it recognizes the relevance of the customer at the same level as the developer. This is one reason why the customer must participate actively in processes such as: product integration, requirements development and technical solution. Also, the supplier must interact in the project management to improve the IT-PS to be acquired.

3.4 ESourcing Capability Model
for Client Organizations

The eSourcing Capability Model for Client Organizations (eSCM-CL) provides a set of best practices for acquiring organizations that allow to evaluate and improve their ability to promote effective relationships with suppliers and better manage projects that are in an acquisition environment (ITSqc Carnegie Mellon, 2006). This model establishes tasks for the acquiring organization such as: the development of acquisition strategy (sourcing), the acquisition planning and the supplier selection. It recommends strategies to establish the appropriate agreement with the IT-PS supplier, the management of a successful offer of IT-services and the supervision of the contracts to completion.

3.5 Summary and Comparison
of Standards and Models

Table 1 presents a summary of the standards and models described in the previous section. This summary allows to make a comparison from the point of view of the features that are of interest for this study.

First, we analyzed the standard approach to the proposal (A) as wells as its goal. In addition, its dimensions and weaknesses (DW) related to IT-PS acquisition environment were established.

Also, we determined the most relevant features for this work in order to establish comparison criteria among the standards and models analyzed and summarized in Table 1. After the comparison, the results were tabulated in a template designed to characterize each standard in terms of features related to risk management in the area of IT-PS acquisition (see Table 2).

These results allowed to identify certain important aspects for this work. Initially, the importance of the CMMI-ACQ model is highlighted. Table 2 shows a complete traceability of this model according to the characteristics of analysis and key aspects to the success of the IT-PS ac-

Table 1. Summary of standards and models

N*	A*	Goal	DW*
ISO/IEC 12207 Standard	Software Acquisition	Acquire a product or service that meets client needs.	Identification of the IT-PS acquisition as a core process of Information Technologies and definition of the tasks to follow the acquisition. *It lacks a complete definition and description of the acquisition best practices and better specification of its approach.*
IEEE 1062 Standard	Software Acquisition	Standardize the software acquisition process of the organizations; keep in mind aspects such as the quality and the assessment of the supplier capacity.	It is a software acquisition process framework. Its structure defines nine key steps for the acquisition process. *It lacks definitions and description of software engineering best practices that support the acquisition process.*
CMMI – ACQ Model	Software Acquisition	Establish a few practices focused on the necessary activities for supplier contracting, the beginning of the acquisition project and the contract award decision, as well as the software acquisition management, the measurement system and the acceptance criteria of the supplier artifacts, among others.	It describes all the practices of the process areas oriented and aligned with the activities of the customer. *It lacks guides, tools and methodologies that enable acquiring organizations to know how to implement the practices of the process areas that comprise it.*

N: Name; A: Approach; DW: Dimensions and Weaknesses

Table 2. Tabulation of results

Standard or Model / Features	ISO 12207	IEEE 1062	CMMI-ACQ	eSCM-CL
Process definition for IT-PS acquisition	✓	✓	✓	✓
Best practices definition for IT-PS acquisition projects			✓	✓
Acquisition environment oriented	✓	✓	✓	✓
Recommendations for organizations that acquire IT-PS	✓	✓	✓	✓
Risk management in IT-PS acquisition environments			✓	
Risk management practices focused on IT-PS acquisition environments			✓	

quisition project. In relation to risk management, this model includes a risk management process in its structure as a key process in the IT-PS acquisition projects management.

A (thorough review of the proposal made by the CMMI-ACQ model for the risk management process, allows to highlight the recommendations for software acquiring organizations in relation to the techniques required to achieve effective management of their risks.

These techniques are so useful that the Software Engineering Institute (SEI) has developed a risk taxonomy for risk identification based on questions (Carr, Konda, Monarch, Ulrich, & Walker, 1993). This technique is oriented to software development and is focused on providing ways to identify risks from the point of view of developers or software development teams.

The proposal presented in this work is based on the taxonomy established by the SEI (Carr et al., 1993). However, this proposal focuses on customer processes.

Later on in this chapter, a useful technique for identifying, analyzing and managing risks related to an IT-PS acquisition environment is proposed.

4. PROPOSAL OF A RISK MANAGEMENT TECHNIQUE

It has been mentioned that deficiencies in project management have a negative impact and as a result there are serious problems that affect its success. Risk management is a process that contributes to project management. Therefore, the use of project management best practices, such as the identification, analysis and risk management, helps to solve the failing causes of IT-PS acquisition projects.

The implementation of the identification, analysis and risk management must be supported by techniques that facilitate and make such implementation operational (Software Engineering Institute, 2010).

The proposal establishes a technique for identifying risks in a quick and simple manner. This approach reflects the SEI proposal, adapted to identify environmental risks of IT-PS acquisition and from the point of view of the acquiring organization. It also takes into account others taxonomies structures, such as Safety taxonomy of Requirements (Firesmith, 2005) and a unified reference of accidental failures of critical software (López, 2005).

Based on a method for the construction of a taxonomy, called Taxonomy Construction Method-TCM (Gasca-Hurtado, 2010), a taxonomy focused on the classification of risks associated with IT-PS acquisition projects has been designed.

This taxonomy takes into account the following aspects:

- Typical or common risks for which a project may fail. These risks have been identified from an analysis of relevant projects in IT-PS acquisition environments (United States Government Accountability Office, 2009a), (United States Government Accountability Office, 2009d), (United States Government Accountability Office, 2009e), (United States Government Accountability Office, 2009c), (United States Government Accountability Office, 2009b).
- The ISO/IEC 12207 standard takes into account the integration of the IT-PS acquisition process and software development.
- Good practices recommended by the IEEE 1062 standard to establish processes and the recommended order to be followed for the implementation of a proposed IT-PS acquisition.

Recommendations and practices in risk management in the CMMI-ACQ (RSKM) for structuring implementation of risk management techniques, such as risk identification from taxonomies.

4.1 Structure of the Taxonomy

Establishing the structure of the taxonomy was an activity carried out through:

- Interviews with experts in the risk area.
- Entrepreneurs and software developers working with clients, and
- Documentary analysis (this activity includes the study of standards, models and other taxonomies).

Furthermore, the information was gathered through a systematic review method (Calvo-Manzano, Cuevas, Gasca-Hurtado, & San Feliu, 2009). The structure of the taxonomy is divided into three categories as shown in Figure 1.

From the information obtained during the application of the Taxonomy Construction Method (TCM), the risk taxonomy structure during the software acquisition process is outlined. Figure 2 shows a list of components according to the structure of the method validated through TCM.

4.2 Structure of the Questionnaire

The purpose of the questionnaire was to build up a risk identification tool for IT-PS acquisition projects through a set of questions.

The questions were designed and ordered from the taxonomy structure (see Figure 2). This design responds to the need for identifying risks from questions. The classification of the questions corresponds to a structure that guides the life cycle

Figure 1. Structure of the taxonomy

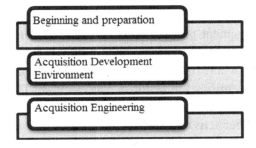

Figure 2. Structure of taxonomy

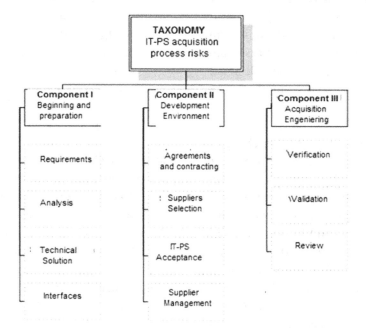

of a proposed IT-PS acquisition (Singh, 1995). This classification allows to expose not only the risks explicitly described in the instrument of questions designed, but also those that the project risk management team could identify.

The questionnaire is the basis of the risk identification technique. Its main objective is to improve the pace at which the risk management process is carried out, with full coverage of the acquisition process. Furthermore, this technique maintains continuity of the project and organization, and uses risk management results in similar projects.

Risk identification is the first phase of the risk management process. This phase is considered the most important one since it allows to focus on the whole risk management process. A correct risk identification result in success in an IT-PS acquisition project.

Other activities such as risk mitigation can be carried out through the use of techniques and tools developed for other sectors, due to their capacity to adapt to an IT-PS acquisition project.

Two types of questions were designed: a) multiple choice questions with a single answer, and b) multiple-choice questions with multiple answers. Examples of these two types of questions are shown in Figures 3 and 4.

4.3 Implementation Procedure

This questionnaire allows to consolidate the taxonomy as a risk identification technique with features like:

- Defining each risk identified from the taxonomy.
- Selecting the step or phase of an IT-PS acquisition project requiring the implementation of the risk management process.
- Analyzing the risks through a qualitative assessment.
- Prioritizing the identified risks for permitting the establishment of mitigation actions and risk control.

Figure 3. Single-answer questions

<u>Establishment of the request package</u>
[Are the requirements and evaluation criteria and do they allow to seek proposals from potential suppliers?]

33. Has the request package been defined taking into account all the basic elements?

Supplier Specification
Process, product and service level
Guide for prospective suppliers about how to answer the request
Description and evaluation criteria of proposals
Documentation related to requirements (Project plan)
.Request process schedule
Procedure to ask questions and contact details

Figure 4. Multiple-answer questions

34. ¿ Have you defined the project scope in the specifications of the supplier?

(Yes) (34.a) ¿Does the specifications of the supplier established according to project scope?

(Yes) (35.b) ¿The project scope has been defined taking into account all the elements?

- WBS (Work Breakdown Structure)
- Task dictionary

To implement the technique, a procedure has been defined, which include the steps to identify risks in IT-PS acquisition projects. It also includes the definition of activities, as well as a description of every input and output for each activity. The roles of participants have been established and should be taken into account when performing risk identification.

This guide is composed of four activities: preparation and commitment, training and analysis, risk identification, consolidation and communication, as shown in Figure 5.

4.4 Risk Management Technique Automation

This technique aims to assess the risks associated with a proposed acquisition of software from a holistic vision. Therefore, questions are used to define and assess the risks identified. When a risk is identified it can be divided into components, and a chosen design pattern should be applied because it allows to handle the complexity that can emerge from this approach in a recursive manner (see Figure 6).

A comparison with similar projects was executed, and taking into account the structure of the prototype, it was designed in Microsoft Excel. This implementation may take into account aspects such as usability and speed of implementation.

The selected architecture is object oriented to facilitate reuse and proposes a layered development to address the development of the prototype in a better way.

Figure 7 shows a prototype interface that is under construction.

Figure 5. Guide for the implementation of the technique

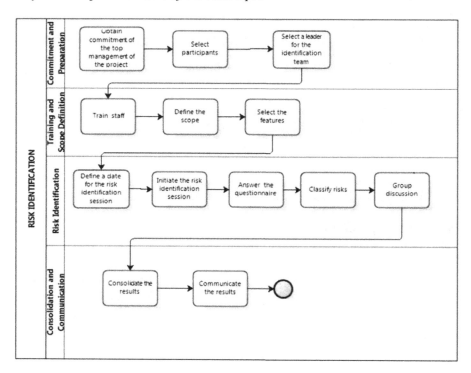

Figure 6. Architectural design patterns

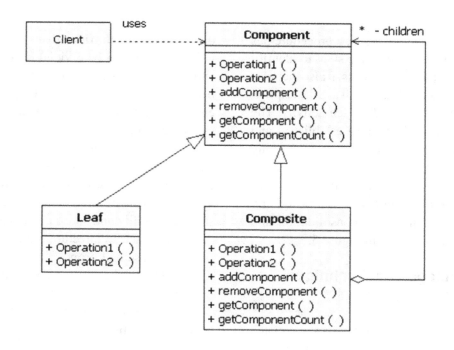

Figure 7. GUI prototype

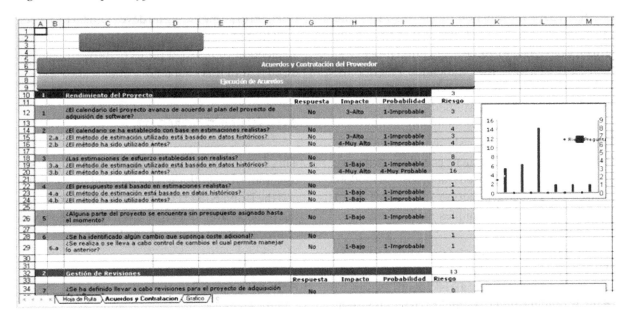

5. CONCLUSION

Organizations' strategies to improve quality, reduce costs and get information technology solutions and software at the right time are improving over time. This tendency has increased the number of organizations that decide to outsource software and acquire Information Technologies Products and Services (IT-PS) and, at the same time, in-house software development has decreased drastically.

This phenomenon occurs for different reasons, such as: a) Increasing demand SP-IT in organizations, b) high maintenance costs for development teams with technical capabilities that can handle the demands of information technology, and c) the increasing number of competitive organizations with high technical capabilities for developing Information Technology (IT).

As more organizations start IT-PS acquisition projects, their needs become greater. Some of these needs are addressed by standards and models that offer useful guidelines for such projects, contracts diversity and IT-PS acquisition projects types such

as: acquisition of customized products, development with traditional methodologies, developed with agile methodologies, acquisition of a complete COTS product, acquisition of some COTS components that will be assembled by an internal team, acquisition of some COTS components that will be assembled by an external team, acquisition MOTS components to be adapted by an internal team and acquisition of MOTS components to be adapted by an external team, among other types of projects that can be set both in organizations and in terms of research.

However, projects should be carefully managed regardless of the type of contract. Otherwise, the consequences of poor project management, inability to articulate the customer's needs, poor definition of requirements, inadequate recruitment and selection of suppliers, lack of procedures for selecting the technology for development and lack of control over changing requirements become factors of project failure.

A key aspect in successful IT-PS acquisition processes is risk management. Within risk management, a key phase to properly manage risks is identification. In this sense, some standards such as ISO/IEC 12207 Information Technology/Software Life Cycle Processes and others that have been properly designed to guide acquisition processes, such as IEEE 1062 Recommended Practice for Software Acquisition, the CMMI-ACQ and the eSCM-CL models were studied.

This study focuses on analyzing approaches and dimensions about risk management. The analysis concludes that there is a clear necessity for supporting the proposed standards and models focused on IT-PS acquisition (as CMMI-ACQ y eSCM-CL) with techniques such as the ones proposed in this chapter.

The risk management process is a key factor in IT-PS acquisition projects that can be developed by three general activities: a) risk identification, b) analysis of identified risks and c) risk mitigation. It requires the use of techniques in each phase that allow organizations to expedite the process of identification and mitigating of risk.

The proposed technique identifies risks from a risk taxonomy based on a series of questions pre-configured by the team responsible for managing the risks of an IT-PS acquisition project.

We have built a structure that classifies risks of IT-PS acquisition projects via three categories: i) beginning and preparation, ii) development environment and iii) acquisition engineering. The numbered categories are part of the taxonomy structure, its relationships and components (elements and attributes). Thus, the taxonomy that classifies risks and supports the identification phase of these projects is completed.

Based on the established taxonomy, a technique to identify risks emerges. It is based on questions which are constructed to determine and develop a questionnaire with two types of questions a) single-answer questions and b) multiple-answer questions. This technique is automated through the development of a prototype of an application to implement the technique in a real environment. This prototype is designed in Microsoft Excel and it is projected to be designed for a Website in its final version. The defined architecture is object-oriented to allow reuse and development by layers.

The validation will take place by means of a selection of typified projects through patterns discussed in this chapter.

ACKNOWLEDGMENT

This work is funded by the Vicerrectoría de Investigación, from both the Universidad de Medellín and the Universidad Politécnica de Madrid, under the project title: "Identificación de Riesgos para el Proceso de Outsourcing de Software."

REFERENCES

Asociación Española de Normalización y Certificación AENOR. (1996). *ISO 9000*. Asociación Española de Normalización y Certificación.

Baker, E., & Fisher, M. (2007). *Basic principles and concepts for achieving quality*. Software Engineering Institute.

Bernard, T., Gallagher, B., Bate, R. A., & Wilson, H. (2005). *CMMI acquisition module, version 1.1 software engineering institute* (Technical Report CMU/SEI-2005-TR-011). Pittsburgh, PA: Carnegie Mellon.

Calvo-Manzano Villalón, J. A., Agustín, G. C., Hurtado, G. G., & San Feliu Gilabert, T. (2009). State of the art for risk management in software acquisition. *ACM SIGSOFT Software Engineering Notes, 34*(4), 1–10. doi:10.1145/1543405.1543426

Carr, M. J., Konda, S. L., Monarch, I., Ulrich, F. C. A., & Walker, C. F. (1993). *Taxonomy-based risk identification*. Software Engineering Institute.

Cooper, J. A., & Fisher, M. (2002). *Software acquisition capability maturity model version 1.03 (CMU/SEI-2002-TR-010)*. Pittsburgh, PA: Software Engineering Institute Carnegie Mellon.

Extreme Chaos. (2001). The Standish Group.

Firesmith, D. (2005). *A taxonomy of security-related requirements*. Software Engineering Institute.

Gasca-Hurtado, G. P. (2010). *Metodología para la gestión de riesgos de adquisición de software en pequeños entornos MEGRIAD. (Tesis para optar al grado de Doctor)*. Madrid, Spain: Universidad Politécnica de Madrid.

Gibbs, W. W. (1994). Software's chronic crisis. *Scientific American*, *271*(3), 86–95. doi:10.1038/scientificamerican0994-86

IEEE. (1998). *IEEE recommended practice for software acquisition*. Institute of Electrical and Electronics Engineers.

Institute of Electrical and Electronics Engineers. (1998). *IEEE Std 1062: 1998 recommended practice for software acquisition software engineering standards committee of the IEEE computer society*. IEEE.

International Organization for Standardization. (2008). *Systems and software engineering —Software life cycle processes (ISO/IEC 12207)*. Author.

ITSqc Carnegie Mellon. (2006). eSCM-CL v1.1, part 1. Pittsburgh, PA: Carnegie Mellon.

Johnson, J. (2006). *My life is failure: 100 Things you should know to be a successful project leader*. West Yarmouth, MA: Standish Group International.

Jones, C. (1995). Risks of software system failure or disaster. *American Programmer*, *8*(3), 2–9.

López, P. (2005). *Taxonomía unificada de referencia de fallos accidentales de software crítico*. (PhD Dissertation). Universiad Politécncia de Madrid, Madrid, Spain.

Nelson, P., Richmond, W., & Sidmann, A. (1996). Two dimensions of software acquisition. *Communications of the ACM*, *39*(7), 29–35. doi:10.1145/233977.233986

Organization for Standardization/International Electrotechnical Commission. (2004). *International standard ISO/IEC 15504 software process improvement and capability determination*. Author.

Ropponen, J., & Lyytinen, K. (1997). Can software risk management improve system development: An exploratory study. *European Journal of Information Systems*, *6*(1), 41–50. doi:10.1057/palgrave.ejis.3000253

Singh, R. (1995). *International standard ISO/IEC 12207 software life cycle processes*. Federa Aviation Administration.

Software Engineering Institute. (2002). *Capabitlity maturity model integration - CMMI-SE/SW, V1.1*. Author.

Software Engineering Institute. (2010). *CMMI for acquisition, version 1.3*. Author.

United States Government Accountability Office. (2009a). *Challenges in aligning space system components (Vol. GAO 10-55)*. Washington, DC: Author.

United States Government Accountability Office. (2009b). *DOD faces substantial challenges in developing new space systems*. Washington, DC: Author.

United States Government Accountability Office. (2009c). *Issues to be considered for army's modernization of combat systems*. Washington, DC: Author.

United States Government Accountability Office. (2009d). *Many analyses of alternatives have not provided a robust assessment of weapon system options (Vol. GAO 09-665)*. Washington, DC: Author.

United States Government Accountability Office. (2009e). *Opportunities exist to achieve greater commonality and efficiencies among unmanned aircraft systems*. Washington, DC: Author.

Vega Zepeda, V., Gasca-Hurtado, G. P., & Calvo-Manzano, J. A. (2012). *Identifying patterns of software acquisition projects through the application of the MECT method*. Paper presented at the Information Systems and Technologies (CISTI). Madrid, Spain.

KEY TERMS AND DEFINITIONS

Acquisition: According to the CMMI-ACQ Model of the Software Engineering Institute, acquisition is the process of obtaining products or services through.

IT Service Management: According to Margaret Rouse TI Service Management is a process-based practice intended to align the delivery of information technology (IT) services with needs of the enterprise, emphasizing benefits to customers. ITSM involves a paradigm shift from managing IT as stacks of individual components to focusing on the delivery of end-to-end services using best practice process models.

ITIL: According to Margaret Rouse, Information Technology Infrastructure Library (ITIL) is a globally recognized collection of best practices for information technology (IT) service management.

Risk Management: In the acquisition context and taking in to account the CMMI-ACQ model, the risk management is an organized, analytic process used to identify what might cause harm or loss (identify risks); to assess and quantify the identified risks; and to develop and, if needed, implement an appropriate approach to prevent or handle causes of risk that could result in significant harm or loss.

Security Management: Security management is one of the five key functional areas of network management as defined by the International Standardization Organization. Security Management provides the means by which the security services, mechanisms and security related information are managed.

Service Strategy: The objective of ITIL Service Strategy is to decide on a strategy to serve customers. Starting from an assessment of customer needs and the market place, the Service Strategy process determines which services the IT organization is to offer and what capabilities need to be developed. Its ultimate goal is to make the IT organization think and act in a strategic manner.

Supplier Agreement: According to the CMMI-ACQ Model of the Software Engineering Institute, supplier agreement is a documented agreement between the acquirer and supplier. Supplier agreements are also known as contracts, licenses, and memoranda of agreement.

Taxonomy: According to Margaret Rose Taxonomy is the science of classification according to a pre-determined system, with the resulting catalog used to provide a conceptual framework for discussion, analysis, or information retrieval. In theory, the development of a good taxonomy takes into account the importance of separating elements of a group (taxon) into subgroups (taxa) that are mutually exclusive, unambiguous, and taken together, include all possibilities. In practice, a good taxonomy should be simple, easy to remember, and easy to use.

Chapter 3
Assessing Modularity in Java Programs

Jorge Manjarrez Sanchez
Research Center in Mathematics (CIMAT), Mexico

Victor Navarro Belmonte
Research Center in Mathematics (CIMAT), Mexico

ABSTRACT

The main goal of a good software design is to achieve high modularity in order to promote reusability, maintainability, and reduce costs. Coupling and cohesion are two among the many measures that quantify the degree of modularity of a system. An ideal modular design is highly cohesive and lowly coupled. This chapter presents a review of some important metrics to numerically quantify coupling and cohesion and the assessment of some tools to automate their calculation in medium and large Java programs.

1. INTRODUCTION

The objective of the software business is to create good software developed in time, within budget and that comply with requirements. In order to achieve this, the software should be easy to understand, maintain, test, evolve and manage. This motivates to elicit a modular design: the whole is divided in small independent modules of functionality; hence reducing the system's complexity and each module could be developed and

managed independently by collaborating teams, perhaps geographically distributed. Moreover, these modules can be reused in new systems, reducing development time and costs, or can be replaced by more efficient ones without introducing bugs, changing operations or lines of code, at least ideally. However, such an ideal state does not exist and system parts are tied because of their interactions.

The importance of good quality software for the business is indicated in the Measurement and Analysis process of CMMI Level 2. It states among the measurement objectives (The CMMi easy button, 2012) that it:

DOI: 10.4018/978-1-4666-5182-1.ch003

- Reduces time to delivery.
- Reduces total lifecycle cost.
- Delivers specified functionality completely.
- Improves prior levels of quality.
- Improves prior customer satisfaction ratings.
- Maintains and improves the acquirer/supplier relationships.

Reusability and all the other desirable properties of good software can be attained with modules due to their well-defined boundaries, which are established by a lean interface that specifies a set of responsibilities and capabilities. Having a lean interface means the module has a small number of duties and hence increases its flexibility. One of the first persons to point out this idea was Parnas (1972) with his information-hidden principle that established the basis for encapsulation, one of the fundamental concepts in object-oriented programming and other paradigms, such as Aspect Oriented Programming (Tarr, 1999).

Unfortunately, just saying a system is good is not enough; one must state objectively the degree of goodness and in terms of what. A system is good if it has a good level of modularity measured in terms of coupling and cohesion, and to express it numerically one must compute some metrics of a software system with some known tools and compare them with their manually obtained baseline. A system is said to be good if it has low coupling between components and high cohesion inside a component.

The metrics for coupling and cohesion can be calculated manually by an engineer who understands the corresponding formulas and definitions in the literature on this subject, but the size of the system matters. A small system can be manually analyzed but a system bigger than a hundred classes makes this task hard, error prone and not achievable in a reasonable time. To ease the calculation of coupling and cohesion metrics for big projects, some tools have been developed. However, these tools do not always

provide accurate results; even for a human being it is hard enough to apply the concepts implied by a metric. Many modularization principles are implemented by language constructs created after the proposal of the metrics and thus they do not have a precise corresponding variable to denote them; or sometimes the metrics are conceived for a different programming language. Hence, this is an active research subject.

In this chapter, we first review some fundamental concepts to evaluate modularity by means of coupling and cohesion. Then we review some fundamental metrics and, based on these metrics, we perform an empirical evaluation to assess the quality of a system manually and by using some automated tools. This study will also allow the reader to understand the difficulty even for these tools to correctly evaluate the parameters involved in quantifying coupling and cohesion.

2. BASIC CONCEPTS

A recurring problem in software systems is that, as it increases in size and functionality, it becomes harder to code, test and maintain. Even changing a small part can be a hard task in time and cost due to the system's complexity. To avoid this problem and keep the system simple, we must design a system with two concepts in mind: coupling and cohesion.

2.1 Coupling

Software coupling indicates the number of relationships between system components. This relationship can be by association or containments. The more dependencies a component has, the more susceptible it is to change because changes in the other components it has relationships with can trigger changes in its inputs and outputs. Also, if many components depend on one component, it acquires too many responsibilities and so it is very sensitive to modification because it can cause an external functionality to break.

A system with high coupling between its parts also increases costs and is difficult to test, maintain and understand. Coupling is also an indicator of software failure propensity.

Coupling can be used to make the component stable. Understanding stability allows the programmer to follow the Stable Abstractions Principle; this will be discussed in the next section.

2.2 The Stable Abstractions Principle (SAP)

The Stable Abstractions Principle (Martin, 2007) states that a component should be as abstract as stable. This means a component must be in one of the following ideal states:

- Be totally stable and abstract to avoid the concrete code limits extensibility of the design.
- Be totally unstable and concrete and hence its own stability allows to change more easily the concrete code.

The components of a system must comply with one of these two ideal categories to attain a balance between stability and level of abstraction. In section 3, we present practical examples to quantify them numerically.

2.3 Cohesion

There are two cohesion levels: class and library.

2.3.1 Class Level Cohesion

It refers to how the elements of a class are correctly grouped together; this means the functionality it implements is related and the class has only one responsibility as in the *single responsibility principle* (Martin, 2002).

The Single Responsibility Principle says that to have robust classes that are easy to understand and modify, it is necessary that they have a single duty. This principle defines the responsibility of a class as a reason for change. If one can think of several reasons to change a class then the class has many responsibilities.

A class with more than one responsibility can have undesirable effects on the system. One of these is that classes are harder to understand because so many responsibilities obfuscate their internal working. Another problem is that these kinds of classes have a greater tendency to introduce bugs during maintenance or modification. The mixing of responsibilities conveys the risk of collateral affectations in changing one of them.

2.3.2 Library Level Cohesion

It is important that in our design each class be a cohesive unit, but it is equally important that the distribution of the classes in libraries be also cohesive to guarantee that our libraries can be reused and distributed with a level of confidence without causing problems in new systems.

To verify this, the application of the following three principles when structuring a system into libraries (Martin, 2007) is proposed.

2.4 The Reuse/Release Equivalence Principle

A group of classes, which are expected to be useful for another application, could be a class library. It is not worth making a library with just one class or one that requires the support of many others to make something useful. In the same way we must consider including only classes that are useful for the target domain of application in order the keep them slim and clean.

2.5 The Common Reuse Principle

This principle states that if we use one class of a library all the others must also be reused. This can be interpreted that a library must contain only related classes. Incorporation of unrelated classes within a library can be a sign of introducing dependencies that are not valuable for the reuse in mind and will complicate the management of the library.

2.6 The Common Closure Principle

The classes in a library must be closed to the same genre of changes. A change that affects a library affects all the classes within it, but not other libraries. This is equivalent to the Single Responsibility Principle applied to libraries that basically tries to improve a library's maintainability and the user system by keeping changes in only one library and thus reducing the time of validation, re-compiling and installation.

Having a highly cohesive design can induce a low coupling and conversely having a low coupled design may induce a high cohesion. These are desirable properties and, in order to quantify their degree within a system, they must be measured objectively and quantitatively.

3. METRICS

Some metrics have been created to evaluate the level of coupling and cohesion of a system. Some of the most relevant are cited in the next section.

3.1 Coupling Metrics

- **Efferent coupling at class level (Cec):** Is the number of classes directly referenced by a class. A class with a Cec greater than 50 must be revised because it probably has more than one responsibility and is a candidate for refactoring (JArchitect, 2012).

- **Afferent coupling at class level (Cac):** Is the number of classes referencing directly a class (JArchitect, 2012).
- **Efferent coupling at library level (Ce):** Is the number of external classes referenced by the classes within the library. This metric can be interpreted as a measure of dependency. A high level of efferent coupling indicates a high degree of dependency and thus tendency to involuntary change, and the fragility of the component used when the external dependencies change (Martin, 2007).
- **Afferent coupling at library level (Ca):** Is the number of external classes referencing directly the classes of this library. This metric can be interpreted as a level of responsibility; a high afferent coupling indicates high responsibility and is thus hard to change (Martin, 2007).

Evidently, a combination of high responsibility and high instability implies elements prone to become a bottleneck during development and maintenance.

3.2 Derived Metrics of Coupling

Instability (I): Represents the resistance of a library to change. It is calculated with efferent coupling over the total coupling of the library (Reißing, 2001). Its value can be established as a relation between the level of dependency and the level of responsibility.

$$I = Ce / \left(Ce + Ca \right)$$

Its range of values goes from 0, where a library is considered stable, to 1 where the library is considered totally unstable.

Level of Abstraction (A): Represents how abstract a component is. It is obtained by dividing the number of abstract classes by the total number of classes (Martin, 2007).

$$A = TCA \, / \, TC$$

Where:

TCA = total number of abstract classes (including interfaces)

TC = total number of classes

The range of values of this metric is [0,1], where 0 means the component has no abstract classes and 1 that it is totally abstract.

Principal sequence: With a calculated value for the stability (I) and level of abstraction metrics (A) a relationship between them can be established. It is considered that there are two types of ideal components: those which are at a maximum level of abstraction and stability, and those which are maximally concrete and unstable (Martin, 2002). This, according to the *Stable Abstraction Principle* (Martin, 2000), is hard to achieve, so it is established that the components ideally should be as concrete as abstract. When these two characteristics are on the same level it can be said that the component is on the principal sequence as it is equally concrete as it is abstract.

As explained in (Martin, 2007), the ideal would be for all the components to be balanced in their abstraction and stability level, and far from the undesirable states where components present several problems. When a component has level 0 of abstractness and level 0 of instability; in other words, it is concrete and stable, but then it is hard to extend and change. If a component has level 1 of abstractness and instability level 1, it is at the maximum level of instability and abstractness. This means it has no method definition within it, zero functionality implemented and because it is also at the maximum level of instability, it is not reliable for others to reference it. This case should be considered for refactoring.

Distance from the principal sequence (D): To have a numerical value which indicates how far or near a component is from the principal sequence, the value D is computed as follows:

$$D = \left(A + I + 1 \right) / \sqrt{2}$$

The range of values for $D \in \left[0, 0.707\right]$, where 0 means the component is directly over the principal sequence and 0,707 means the value is far from it.

Normalized distance from the principal sequence (D'): it is normalized because its range of values is [0,1], where 0 means the component is on the principal sequence and 1, the component is the furthest away possible. We will use this metric in the case study section. It is computed by:

$$D' = A + I - 1$$

3.3 Cohesion Metrics

Lack of Cohesion of Methods (LCOM): this metric tries to capture the cohesion of the methods of a class. It considers the pairs of similar methods (those that share one or more instance variables) and pairs of dissimilar methods (those that do not share instance variables). This metric is calculated by (Chidamber, 1994; Hitz, 1995)

$$if\,NPS > NPNS\;LCOM = NPNS - NPS$$
$$if\,NPS \leq NPNS\;LCOM = 0$$

Where:

NPNS = number of dissimilar pairs
NPS = number of similar pairs

This formula focuses on the similarity of methods as a Boolean value (true or false), thus it is not convenient as it does not indicate the intensity of the relationship.

Lack of Cohesion of Methods Henderson Sellers (LCOMHS): This metric tries to capture the cohesion of the methods of a class. It considers the similarity of the methods as the number of instance variables accessed in common. It is calculated by (Sellers, 1996):

$$LCOMHS = \left(\frac{Sum\left(MF\right)}{F} - M \right) / \left(1 - M\right)$$

Where:

M is the number of methods in a class
F is the number of instance variables
MF is the summation of all MF values for all the instance variables in the class.

This formula was conceived to improve the deficiencies of *LCOM*, and measures the degree of the relationship gradually. The range of values is [0,1], where 0 means total or perfect cohesion while 1 represents a class without cohesion and each method accesses its own instance variables (Chidamber, 1994) and indicates that the class has more than one responsibility and should be refactorized.

Relational cohesion (H): measures the internal cohesion of libraries, how many dependencies the classes have within them.

$$H = \left(R + 1\right) / N$$

Where:

R is the number of relationships between the classes in the library
N is the number of classes in the library

In this formula the mutual dependencies are counted twice, once for each direction (Martin, 2007). A desirable value for *H* is $1.5 < H < 4$ because a higher value can indicate coupling problems and may require some classes to be merged in more cohesive units [JA].

More detailed information on the topic of this section can be found in (Martin, 2007).

4. CASE STUDY

In this section, we empirically assess the reliability of some automated tools to measure the already presented metrics of coupling and cohesion in Java source code. First, we present the tools used, and then we describe the target system and the evaluation methodology.

A summary of the tools and their capabilities is shown in Table 1.

Based on their capabilities, the most important tools are:

- JArchitect 3.1 (10 metrics) and the corresponding CQL Query Edit
- CodePro Analytix 1.3.8 (5 metrics)

The other tools have few metrics or are outdated, although the more important feature for us is their precision in the results. However, we have considered them in our empirical study.

A final consideration is that JArchitect provides an interface CQL Query Edit, which uses a SQL query language to evaluate the metrics. In the corresponding evaluation, we have provided the used query to compute the metric.

Experimental Settings: The Java project used to measure coupling and cohesion is a Web interface to control and access financial resources; it was organized originally into two libraries:

- **Core:** Contains database access layer and business logic, and 32 classes.
- **Web:** Contains everything about user interaction through the Web, and 70 classes.

This project was slightly modified to include new libraries with code specifically designed to probe and challenge some metrics. These libraries are:

Table 1. A summary of some automated tools to calculate metrics in Java programs and their capabilities

Metric	JArchitect JavaDepend	JDepend	Eclipse Metrics	CodePro Analytix	Metrics reloaded
Cec	●				●
Ce	●	●		●	●
Cac	●				●
Ca	●	●		●	●
I	●			●	
A	●			●	
D'	●			●	
LCOM	●		●		
LCOMHS	●				
H	●				

- **The CohesiveProject:** A project done to have a high relational cohesion.
- **RelationalCohesionProject:** A project done to have a medium relational cohesion.
- **NonCohesiveProject:** A project done to have a low relational cohesion.
- **ClassProject:** A project that contains classes with different levels of afferent coupling, efferent coupling and lack of method cohesion. This project is used to evaluate these class metrics including lack of method cohesion of Henderson Sellers.

Methodology: First, we calculated manually every metric. This result is taken as a baseline to assess the quality of the tools, so it is used to calculate the percentage of error with the formula:

$$\%Error = \frac{tool - manually}{manually}\,x100$$

If the absolute value of the difference in the numerator is not used, the negative sign will indicate that the tool provides an under estimation of the metric compared with the manual result. From this comparison we can establish if the tool is accurate enough. In case of any difference in the results, we try to provide an explanation.

4.1 Afferent Coupling at Class Level

The query to compute this metric for JArchitect is

```
SELECT TYPES WHERE TypeCa >=0.
```

The results are presented in Table 2. In most cases there is no coincidence between results. One reason is that JArchitect counts the references in a different way; only those that are used by a method execution of the referenced class. Indeed, a simple variable declaration of the referenced type should count as a reference. Although there are cases in which it is not possible to figure out a reason for the wrong count, it is possible that the bytecode analysis influences the results. We can conclude that from the code of Clase1 where there is only one reference to this class.

Table 2. Results for afferent coupling at class level metric

Analyzed Class	Baseline	JArchitect	%Error
Clase1	1	3	200.00
Clase2	2	1	-50.00
Clase3	2	1	-50.00
Clase4	3	1	-66.67
Clase5	3	2	-33.33
Clase6	0	0	0.00
Clase7	0	0	0.00
Clase8	2	1	-50.00
Clase9	2	2	0.00
Clase10	5	3	-40.00
Clase11	6	5	-16.67
Clase12	5	4	-20.00
Clase13	5	3	-40.00
Clase14	5	3	-40.00
Clase15	5	3	-40.00
Clase16	4	2	-50.00
Clase17	4	2	-50.00
Clase18	4	2	-50.00
Clase19	4	2	-50.00
Clase20	4	2	-50.00

4.2 Efferent Coupling at Class Level

The query to compute this metric for JArchitect is

```
SELECT TYPES WHERE Ce >=0.
```

Again as in the last metric, for JArchitect having a class reference of a class is not enough but it must invoke at least one of its methods, which does not happen in many situations and hence the difference in the results. It is also important to note that Clase8 and Clase9 are enumerations which do not make reference to any class other than Object, but as they are declared with a reserved Java keyword they can be seen as a special case.

There is another particular case that makes this tool fail: it does not count the references in the Java annotations, hence the mismatch in Clase3,

which contains annotations. Even if annotations may be considered as less important as they do not contain executable code, and due to their nature, they are less susceptible to change.

4.3 Afferent Coupling at Library Level

The query to compute this metric for JArchitect is

```
SELECT TYPES WHERE JarCa >=0.
```

Here we use the Core library. The mismatch seems to arise from a double counting of the classes that have a reference. Hence, we validated this with a new query, SELECT TYPES FROM PROJECTS "web" WHERE IsUsing "core," that searches the references of the Web Library to the Core library (see Figure 1).

The result of this query shows a list of classes with duplicate elements, in addition to TransferCompletePage that in fact does not make a reference to Core. This indicates a possible bug that doubles the counting of the references under certain conditions. However, in CodePro Analytix, there is no problem with the results.

4.4 Efferent Coupling at Library Level

The query to compute this metric for JArchitect is

```
SELECT PROJECTS WHERE JarCe >=0.
```

In this test, none of the tools produced the correct result; each tool seems to have a particular origin for this.

- **JArchitect:** This is near the baseline. Its imprecision arises from not counting references to enum types. Maybe it is not as bad as the enum types even if they are classes, do not have complex functionality within and are not susceptible to changes.

Figure 1. Afferent coupling at library level with JArchitect

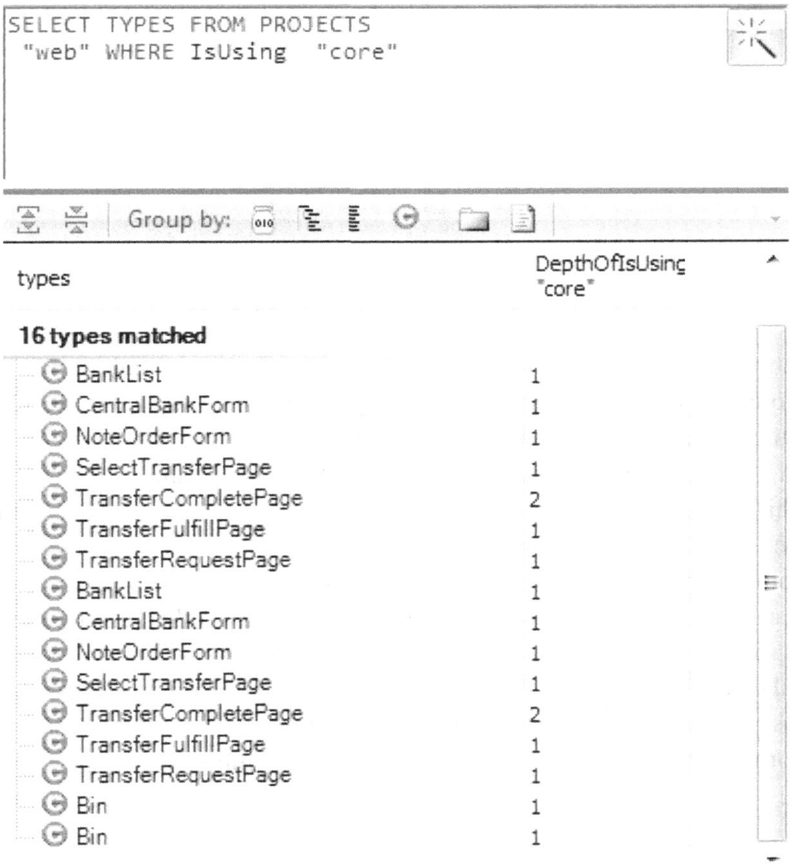

• **CodePro Analytix:** In this case the differences with the baseline are large because this metric computes all the classes that have a reference to external libraries. This is not correct because it should count instead the number of external classes referenced within the library.

The result provided is worthless because it has the same value when referencing 100 external classes as when referencing just one. Additionally, finding a class without external references is almost impossible because a class with zero external references probably does nothing as it references at least the basic Java types!

It is important to note that it seems to have the required elements to provide the correct result as the tab "Externally referenced types" shows a listing that contains external references that must be added to have the total efferent coupling (Figure 2). This indicates that the tools could provide the correct results.

4.5 Instability

This metric relies on Ce and Ca, but the two tools used gave a different result from the one that was obtained manually. For this reason, we are just going to verify whether these values are used correctly to compute instability. Table 3 shows the values of instability calculated manually for

Figure 2. External types referenced in Codepro Analytix

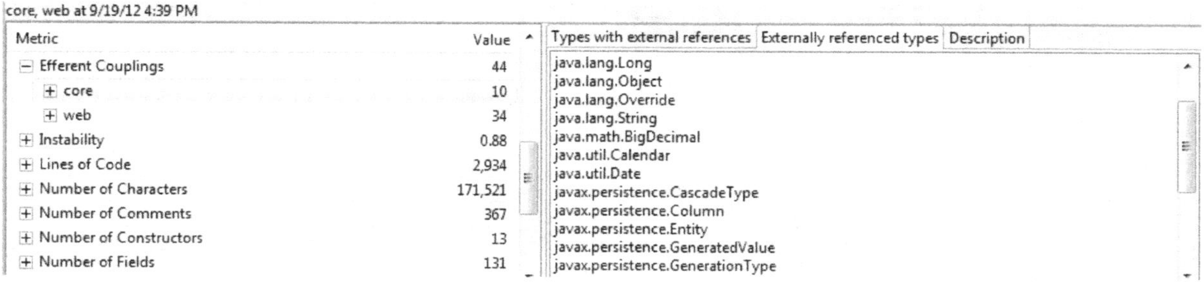

core, web at 9/19/12 4:39 PM			
Metric	Value ▲	Types with external references | Externally referenced types | Description	
⊟ Efferent Couplings	44	java.lang.Long	▲
⊞ core	10	java.lang.Object	
⊞ web	34	java.lang.Override	
⊞ Instability	0.88	java.lang.String	
⊞ Lines of Code	2,934	java.math.BigDecimal	≡
⊞ Number of Characters	171,521	java.util.Calendar	
⊞ Number of Comments	367	java.util.Date	
⊞ Number of Constructors	13	javax.persistence.CascadeType	
⊞ Number of Fields	131	javax.persistence.Column	
		javax.persistence.Entity	
		javax.persistence.GeneratedValue	
		javax.persistence.GenerationType	▼

both case study libraries, using the previously obtained afferent coupling and efferent coupling.

Next, we take the values obtained with JArchitect for Ce and Ca and compute instability manually. We call this semi-manual and it is shown in the second column in Table 3. Then we execute JArchitect over both libraries; this is the third column, and we can see they are the same. So, even if the values for Ce and Ca do not match those of the manual calculation, the instability is consistent with those obtained only with the tool.

The query to compute this metric for JArchitect is

```
SELECT PROJECTS WHERE Instability
>=0.
```

The result can be seen in Table 4.

Table 3. Instability values obtained manually

Library	Manual Calculation
Core	0.867
Web	1

Table 4. Instability values obtained with JArchitect

Library	Semi-Manual	JArchitect
Core	0.754	0.754
Web	1	1

For Codepro Analytix we used a similar approach. First, we took the Ce and Ca values, computed instability manually and then executed the tool to obtain the value for instability, and again, they matched. The values are shown in Table 5.

For this metric both tools obtained a correct value of instability, taking their own Ce and Ca values. But as we have previously seen, they differ from those obtained manually. For this reason we show, in Table 6, a comparison of the manual values compared to the tool values. The minus sign indicates an under estimation.

4.6 Level of Abstraction

The query to compute this metric for JArchitect is

```
SELECT PROJECTS WHERE Abstractness
>=0.
```

This evaluation matches the values of the tools with the manual calculation. The results are given in Table 7. This metric is easy to compute and does not represent a challenge.

Table 5. Instability values obtained with Codepro Analytix

Library	Semi-Manual	Codepro Analytix
Core	0.81	0.81
Web	1	1

Table 6. Comparison of instability values

Library	Manually	JArchitect	%Error	Codepro Analytix	%Error
Core	0.867	0.754	-13.03	0.81	-6.57
Web	1	1	0	1	0

Table 7. Comparison of Level of abstraction results

Library	Manually	JArchitect	%Error	Codepro Analytix	%Error
Core	0.375	0.375	0%	0.375	0%
Web	0	0	0%	0	0%

4.7 Normalized Distance from the Principal Sequence (*D'*)

Again, this metric relies on the previous value of instability, which in turn relies on the efferent and afferent coupling values. Both tools gave a different result compared with the one obtained manually. So, here it is verified manually that they obtain consistent results for the normalized distance from the principal sequence metric. First, the baseline for this metric is computed. INCOMPLETE SENTENCE In Table 8, we show manually calculated values of D' for the libraries using the instability and level of abstraction manual values.

And then for JArchitect (see Table 9): The query to compute this metric for JArchitect is

```
SELECT PROJECTS WHERE NormDistFrom-
MainSeq >=0.
```

For Codepro Analytix, see Table 10 and Figure 3.

From Tables 10 and 11, we observe that both tools obtained the same value as those obtained semi-manually. They applied correctly the formula for metric D', but the difference in the underlying metrics results is a mismatch with the manual baseline; this difference is shown in Table 11. The minus sign indicates an under estimation.

4.8 Lack of Cohesion of Methods (LCOM)

The query to compute this metric for JArchitect is

```
SELECT TYPES WHERE LCOM >=0.
```

Table 8. Manual calculation of normalized distance from the principal sequence

Library	Manual Calculation
Core	0.242
Web	0

Table 9. Normalized distance from the principal sequence with JArchitect

Library	Manual Calculation	JArchitect
Core	0.129	0.129
Web	0	0

Table 10. Normalized distance from the principal sequence with Codepro Analytix

Library	Manual Calculation	Codepro Analytix
Core	0.18	0.18
Web	0	0

Figure 3. Normalized distance from the principal sequence with Codepro Analytix

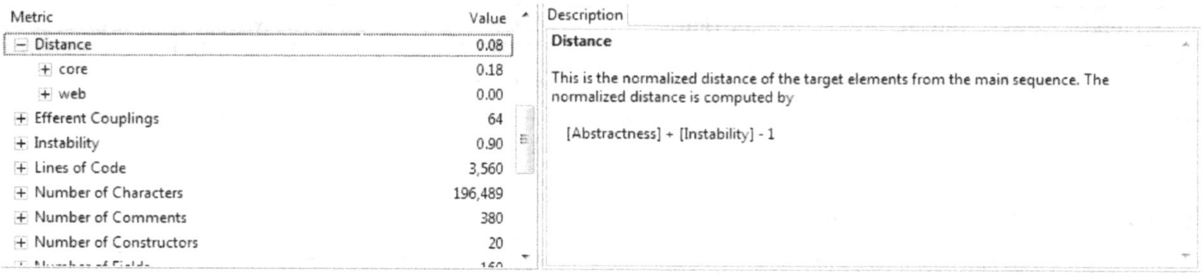

Metric	Value
− Distance	0.08
+ core	0.18
+ web	0.00
+ Efferent Couplings	64
+ Instability	0.90
+ Lines of Code	3,560
+ Number of Characters	196,489
+ Number of Comments	380
+ Number of Constructors	20

Description

Distance

This is the normalized distance of the target elements from the main sequence. The normalized distance is computed by

[Abstractness] + [Instability] - 1

Table 11. Comparison of normalized distance from the principal sequence results

Library	Manual Calculation	JArchitect	%Error	Codepro Analytix	%Error
Core	0.242	0.129	-46.6	0.18	-25.61
Web	0	0	0	0	0

But JArchitect does not use the formula given by Chidamber and Kemerer; instead it uses [JA]:

$$LCOM = 1 - \left(sum\left(MF\right) / M * F\right)$$

Where:

M is the number of methods in a class
F is the number of instance variables in the class
MF is the number of methods in a class that uses a given instance variable
Sum(MF) is the summation of all MF values for all instance variables in the class and

$LCOM \in [0,1]$ (see Table12)

4.9 Lack of Cohesion of Methods Henderson Sellers (LCOMHS)

The manual calculation of this metric is compared with that of JArchitect and Eclipse Metrics continued. The query to compute this metric for JArchitect is

Table 12. Comparison of LCOM results

Analyzed Class	Manual Calculation	JArchitect
Clase1	4	0.4
Clase2	4	0.4
Clase3	0	0
Clase4	10	0.78889
Clase5	10	1
Clase6	1	0.66667
Clase7	10	0.97778
Clase8	0	0
Clase9	0	0
Clase10	6	0.8
Clase11	8	0.5
Clase12	1	0.333
Clase13	0	0
Clase14	0	0
Clase15	8	0.5
Clase16	0	0
Clase17	13	0.71429
Clase18	36	0.95
Clase19	1	0.5
Clase20	10	0.83333

```
SELECT TYPES WHERE LCOMHS >=0.
```

The results are shown in Table 13.

From this table it is observed that neither JArchitect nor Eclipse Metrics gives the expected values. JArchitect differs in less %Error and one can suppose that it may take into account inherited methods. We contacted the developers of JArchitect and they supplied a corrected version. On the other hand, Eclipse metrics gives higher %Errors and seems abandoned.

4.10 Relational Cohesion

To evaluate this metric, only JArchitec was used. The query used to compute this metric is

```
SELECT PROJECTS WHERE Relational Co-
hesion >=0.
```

We also modified the source code to have three levels of cohesion and tested their detection by the tool. For this metric all the results of the tools match their manual value (Table 14).

4.11 Summary of Results

In Table 15 we offer a comparison of the results obtained for a metric between the tools and manually, in terms of the quadratic mean of the %Error for all cases where it was evaluated.

Finally, we want to make some comments about the tools.

Table 13. Comparison of results for LCOMHS metric

Analyzed Class	Manual Calculation	JArchitect	%Error	Eclipse Metrics	%Error
Clase1	0.667	0.5	-25.00%	0	-100.00%
Clase2	0.667	0.5	-25.00%	0	-100.00%
Clase3	0.000	0	0.00%	0	0.00%
Clase4	1.183	0.94667	-20.00%	0	-100.00%
Clase5	1.250	1.2	-4.00%	0	-100.00%
Clase6	2.000	1	-50.00%	0	-100.00%
Clase7	1.217	1.1733	-3.56%	1.867	53.45%
Clase8	0.000	0	0.00%	0	0.00%
Clase9	0.000	0	0.00%	0	0.00%
Clase10	1.333	1	-25.00%	0	-100.00%
Clase11	0.750	0.6	-20.00%	0	-100.00%
Clase12	1.000	0.5	-50.00%	1	0.00%
Clase13	0.000	0	0.00%	0	0.00%
Clase14	0.000	0	0.00%	0	0.00%
Clase15	0.750	0.6	-20.00%	0	-100.00%
Clase16	0.000	0	0.00%	0	0.00%
Clase17	1.000	0.83333	-16.67%	1	0.00%
Clase18	1.063	1.0556	-0.65%	0	-100.00%
Clase19	1.500	0.75	-50.00%	1.5	0.00%
Clase20	1.250	1	-20.00%	0	-100.00%

- **JArchitect:** This is a tool that computes all the metrics of relevance to this study, but three out of eleven have a mismatch with the baseline. This is a large fraction of incorrect values and the reason for this seems to come from the fact that in addition to source code analysis, it also analyzes the compiled files. The compiling process can introduce data that are not always clear at first glance. This appears to be its weakness, but the developers are willing to improve it.

- **Codepro Analytix:** This tool calculates five out of eleven relevant metrics for this study, but only two have a match. The three mismatches appear to be easy to correct within the same tool. However, this project has been on standby since September 2012. Its transition to open source can be helpful.

- **Eclipse Metrics Continued:** This tool calculates one out of eleven relevant metrics for this study and it is the only one to have a mismatch with the baseline. Being an open source project makes it somewhat easier to fix and improve.

Table 14. Results for relational cohesion

Project Analyzed	Manual Calculation	JArchitect	%Error
CohesiveProject	3.25	3.25	0%
RelativelyCohesiveProject	2.25	2.25	0%
NoCohesiveProyect	0.25	0.25	0%

Table 15. Comparison of the results for all metrics in terms of quadratic mean

Metric	JArchitect	Codepro Analytix	Eclipse Metrics C.
Afferent coupling at class level (Cac)	mismatch 60.26%.		
Efferent coupling at class level (Cec)	mismatch 69.15%.		
Afferent coupling at library level (Ca)	mismatch 70.71%.	Correct	
Afferent coupling at library level (Ca)	Correct	mismatch 59.13%.	
Instability (I)	Correct formula but wrong data used led to a mismatch of 9.21%.	Correct formula but wrong data used led to a mismatch of 4.64%.	
Level of Abstraction (A)	Correct	Correct	
Normalized distance from the principal sequence (D')	Correct formula but wrong data use lead to a mismatch of 32.75%.	Correct formula but wrong data use lead to a mismatch of 18.10%.	
Lack of Cohesion of Methods (LCOM)	mismatch 71.02%.		
Lack of Cohesion of Methods Henderson Sellers (LCOMHS)	mismatch 23.75%.		mismatch 71.71%.
Relational cohesion (H)	Correct		

4.11.1 Some Lessons

The errors of these tools can be categorized into two groups:

- **Error in counting code elements:** This is the most common error and can be seen as an inaccurate or incomplete code analysis, very hard to fix, and may involve mistaken concepts in the counting or flawed counting techniques.
- **Error in metric formula application:** It is the less common error, but it can ruin all previous analytical processes and counting in the last step.

If it is envisioned to build a new tool or improve an existing one, it will be necessary to consider the aforementioned errors and provide methods to avoid them. Proposed points to be considered are:

- Define what a relation between classes is and how to count it.
- Verify that the implementation that is carried out maintains the result within the range of accepted values.
- If bytecode is analyzed, find the way to differentiate between source code defined and compile time generated ones.

5. CONCLUSION

We have seen in practice the difficulty in assessing numerically the quality of a system in terms of coupling and cohesion. Even for small or medium sized problems their quantification challenges a programmer or automated tools. Language constructs, compile time transformations among others, affect the precision of their results. In spite of that, automated tools are needed for large projects because it is a hard task to do manually.

Modularity can be achieved at different levels of abstraction, and the reader must consider evaluating other aspects of the software to assess the quality of modularity.

5.1 Future

Include more tools to automate the calculation of metrics. Measure modularity by hand and with automated tools, in programs designed by aspects and with OSGi.

REFERENCES

Chidamber, S. R., & Kemerer, C. F. (1994). A metrics suite for object oriented design. *IEEE Transactions on Software Engineering*, *20*(6), 476–493. doi:10.1109/32.295895

Hitz, M., & Montazeri, B. (1995). Measuring coupling and cohesion in object-oriented systems. In *Proceedings of the International Symposium on Applied Corporate Computing* (Vol. 50, pp. 75-76). Academic Press.

JArchitect. (2012). *Java metrics*. Retrieved December 2013 from http://www.javadepend.com/Metrics.aspx

Martin, R. C. (2000). *Design principles and design patterns*. Object Mentor.

Martin, R. C. (2002). The single responsibility principle. In *The principles, patterns, and practices of agile software development* (pp. 149–154). Upper Saddle River, NJ: Prentice Hall.

Martin, R. C., & Martin, M. (2007). *Agile principles, patterns, and practices in C*. Upper Saddle River, NJ: Prentice-Hall PTR.

Parnas, D. L. (1972). On the criteria to be used in decomposing systems into modules. *Communications of the ACM*, *15*(12), 1053–1058. doi:10.1145/361598.361623

Reißing, R. (2001). Towards a model for object-oriented design measurement. In *Proceedings of 5th International ECOOP Workshop on Quantitative Approaches in Object-Oriented Software Engineering* (pp. 71-84). ECOOP.

Sellers, B. H. (1996). *Object-oriented metrics: Measures of complexity*. Upper Saddle River, NJ: Prentice-Hall, Inc.

Tarr, P., Ossher, H., Harrison, W., & Sutton, S. M., Jr. (1999). N degrees of separation: Multi-dimensional separation of concerns. In *Proceedings of the 21st International Conference on Software Engineering* (pp. 107-119). ACM.

The CMMi Easy Button. (2012). *CMMI level 2 - MA*. Retrieved 10th December 2013, from http://www.software-quality-assurance.org/cmmi-measurement-and-analysis.html

KEY TERMS AND DEFINITIONS

Cohesion: Is a metric to evaluate the degree of self-containment and isolation concerning the responsibilities of a module. Single responsibility is ideal to promote reusability and enhance software modularity.

Coupling: Is an indicator of the dependencies and responsibilities between modules in a software system. The less is better, because it frees a module to change without much affecting the system functionality.

Software Metric: A quantitative or qualitative measure to evaluate an aspect of a program at code level or design level.

Software Modularity: A method to simplify software design and programming by dividing the whole into small and independent parts (modules) of functionality. This modularity improves coding, testing, maintainability and reuse.

Chapter 4
Estimating Methods for Small Teams

Tomás San Feliu Gilabert
Universidad Politécnica de Madrid, Spain

Magdalena Arcilla
Universidad Nacional de Educación a Distancia, Spain

ABSTRACT

This chapter reviews the estimation techniques in software development focused on small teams and provides useful estimation guidelines for software practitioners. The techniques selected are based on one principle: easy to learn, easy to apply. The authors have included both agile techniques and traditional techniques. Agile techniques are suitable for small teams. Nevertheless, traditional techniques, like PROBE, have proven to be useful. Finally, they discuss sustainable estimation infrastructure.

1. INTRODUCTION

The main objective of this chapter is to present software estimation techniques that are easy to apply. Experts have been writing about software estimation for more than four decades (Shepperd, 2012). They have developed numerous techniques for software estimates. However, the knowledge does not make a person an expert estimator. There are numerous problems that arise during the estimation process (Jørgensen, 2004). Small teams need to use simple but effective techniques. The problem is to combine these simple techniques with low deviation.

Software estimation research is focused on improving techniques in order to reduce estimation deviation (Jorgensen, 2009). Software projects are influenced by numerous factors that are embodied in complex algorithms. Software practitioners do not have the time to learn the intensive mathematical support required to understand estimation models. In software engineering, as in similar disciplines, perhaps the most stable result is that simple models typically perform just as well as the more sophisticated models.

DOI: 10.4018/978-1-4666-5182-1.ch004

This paper emphasizes techniques, procedures and simple formulas that are directly used by software practitioners.

1.1 Estimation Challenges

Effort estimation for software development depends on limited understanding of requirements, often complicated, but uncertainty is derived from requirements changes and lifecycle progress. Although idiosyncrasies in projects drive effort estimations, differences in organizational capabilities further affect the validity and reliability of these estimations.

Traditionally, estimation is a critical activity in developing project economics to determine if a project is a sound investment (Sommerville, 2004). But, in Agile environments, estimation is a way to create a shared understating of the requirements, and a shared understanding of the solution (Cottmeyer, 2011). When teams have problems estimating, it is almost never an estimation problem, but rather a shared understanding problem. Some of the most common problems relate are on the product side as insufficient understanding of business problems, insufficient requirements decomposition and insufficient business involvement. Other understanding problems come from technical debt, quality, or even just teams that are unfamiliar with the technologies. All of these problems result in making estimations without a clear understanding of what needs to be done. In order to achieve better estimates, it is necessary to generate a shared understanding.

One way is to develop an estimation process focused on four key attributes (SQCC, 2011):

- **Credibility:** The estimation technique must be visible and provide assurance that the best possible prediction has been made.
- **Confidence:** Estimates provided at particular points in the life cycle have a proven probability of being correct and a proven variability.

- **Control:** Actual results can be compared against selected estimates as part of the measurement process. Problems and potential problems can be identified and addressed before they have an impact on commitments.
- **Continuity:** A well-defined estimation technique and well-documented results allow personnel to understand fully the basis of the previous estimates and to identify areas which have changed since the original estimates were produced.

Normally, these factors rely on collective knowledge. However, the quality of organizational databases of lessons learned varies greatly. Although the databases generally contain volumes of technical data, they are unmanageable because of the sheer quantity of data. Another caution for using data from previous projects is that the context for the historical number is not fully understood.

Another aspect of estimation is understanding the risks that could affect a project. Teams have a limited pool of projects to assess the reasonableness of estimates and overly narrow perspectives of what risks could emerge.

A human aspect is the lack of specialized skills for performing estimation (Jorgensen, 2007). There is very little estimation talent in the industry. Much of the new talent entering the software industry is focused on technology development.

And finally, there is a deadline driven culture, where the estimation results are often used to manage only the scope, ignoring commitment and shared understanding.

1.2 Estimation Principles

There are some basic principles from traditional methodologies:

- Estimation is a process that needs a good knowledge of product and process.
- If a process is well defined, the estimation task is easier.

Traditional methods (Schwaber, 2009) for estimates start by handling a large amount of information. Estimates are made by comparing the planned product with previous products. By breaking new products into smaller parts and comparing each part with data on similar parts of previous products, it is possible to establish the size of the new product. This strategy works well for estimating stable products. However, software as a new product development has the following characteristics:

- It is rarely possible to create unchanging and detailed specifications early.
- Near the beginning, it is not possible to have reliable estimations. Adaptive steps driven by feedback cycles are required.

As mentioned by Martin Fowler (Beck, 2001): "Plans are only as good as the estimates that the plans are based on, and estimates always come second to actuals. The real world has this horrible habit of destroying plans." From Agile approaches we have some helpful principles that are a start to estimating new products:

- The customer has the right to an overall plan, to see progress and to be informed of schedule changes, whereas the developer has the right to make and update his/her own estimates and to accept responsibility instead of having responsibility assigned to him.
- Forecasting tomorrow's weather is much more difficult than saying what the weather was like yesterday.
- Don't try to be too sophisticated; estimates will never be anything other than approximate, however hard you try.

And Scrum methodology (Schwaber, 2009) has the following Agile principles for estimation:

- If estimating is difficult, the agile approach increases the feedback:
  - Shorten the time from estimating to feedback about accuracy of estimate.
  - Increase the frequency of estimating.
  - Sketch out options and get feedback from the customer before doing detailed estimating.
- If the future is unclear, then you must not estimate too far into the future. This is a way to eliminate waste.
- If the requirements and assumptions are not really clear, the team should develop multiple estimates ("Options Thinking"):
  - Communicate the constraints / assumptions of the estimates rather than just the numbers. Base estimation on facts, rather than on speculation. Use actual data obtained from what happened in the past.
  - Discuss the constraints / assumptions with the customer and the customer can give feedback to better align the team's understanding with the business drivers.
- Validate estimates by comparing them with other estimates / experience, use simple rules, triangulation and intuitive decision-making.
- The agile approach relies on self-organization of the team, continuous learning and emergence of estimates (besides requirements and design). In order to gain an understanding of the amount of effort to develop the product or system, Agile methods recommend:
  - Making a greater effort to reach this estimate for higher priority than lower priority items, since the lower priority items may change prior to being developed.
  - Not to spend too much time on estimating. The goal of the estimates is to gain a general understanding of the cost of the system or product. This is used to determine whether it is economical to develop it. Be aware of diminishing returns.

An additional recommendation from (Schwaber, 2009) is: "use the people who will be staffing the project teams to make the estimates. If they aren't known yet, people of equal skills and project domain knowledge should make the estimates. Do not have experts or outsiders make the estimates. Their estimates are irrelevant to those who will actually be doing the work."

The Product Owner role works with the business departments and the development organization to develop estimates (to analyze, design, develop, document, and test the functionality, i.e. whole lifecycle), usually in person days.

2. AVAILABLE TECHNIQUES

In an Agile environment, the estimation process is continuous. Schwaber (2009) tells us: "Estimating is an iterative process. Estimates change as more information emerges. If you can't get a believable estimate for a top priority backlog item, lower its priority (to delay working on that item until you know more about it). Alternatively, keep them high priority but reclassify them as an issue. The work to turn this issue into a required functionality might take ten days, so estimate the issue at ten days."

2.1 Methods Focused on Agile Estimates

Among all different estimation methods, there are specific methods that are more applicable to agile projects, mainly because Delphi Wideband, Planning Poker and User Stories do not require detailed specifications.

2.1.1 Method 1: Delphi Wideband Approach

Delphi wideband and planning poker techniques are very similar. Wideband Dephi (Boehm, 2000) is a structured group estimation technique. The basic Delphi technique calls for several experts to create independent estimates and then hold a group meeting to get the experts to converge on, or at least agree to on, a single estimate. However, an assertive individual can dominate the group. Boehm and his colleagues formulated an alternative method called Wideband Delphi technique. Table 1 describes this Wideband Delphi technique.

Most of the steps can be performed either in person or electronically via e-mail or chat software. Performing the steps electronically can help preserve anonymity. One function of the coordinator is to prevent people with strong personalities from having influence on estimates.

Wideband Delphi is useful if you are estimating work in a new business area, working on a new technology, or working with unfamiliar software.

2.1.2 Method 2: Planning Poker

Planning poker is an iterative approach to estimating (Cohn, 2004), (Moloken, 2004), (Mahnič, 2012). Planning poker is also called Scrum poker. It is a variation of the Wideband Delphi technique. The idea behind planning poker is very simple. Individual stories are presented for estimation.

Table 1. Wideband Delphi description

Step	Description
1	The Coordinator presents each expert with a specification and estimation form.
2	The Coordinator calls a group meeting in which the experts discuss estimation issues related to the project at hand. If the group agrees on a single estimate without much discussion, the coordinator assigns someone to play devil's advocate.
3	Estimators give their individual estimates to the coordinator anonymously.
4	The Coordinator prepares and distributes a summary of the estimates on an iteration form and presents this form to the estimators.
5	The Coordinator calls a group meeting to discuss variations in their estimates.
6	Estimators vote anonymously on whether they want to accept the average estimate. If any of the estimators votes "no," they return to step 2.
7	The final estimates could be a single estimate like the basic Delphi technique or a range created through Delphi discussion.

After a period of discussion, each participant chooses a numbered card that represents his or her estimate.

In planning poker, each team member has index cards with numbers printed on them. The most popular sequence of number involves doubling each card (0, ½, 1, 2, 4, 8, etc.) or the Fibonacci sequence (1, 2, 3, 5, 8, 13, etc.). The Fibonacci sequence is generally more popular. Table 2 summarizes the steps.

Planning Poker works because:

- Those who do the work, estimate it.
- Estimators are required to justify estimates.

The estimate is the result of a live discussion. The group submitted less optimistic estimates than the individuals. The results show that the group-based estimates are closer to the effort expended on the actual project than the individual expert estimates. The ability of the group to identify a greater number of the activities required is a possible explanation for this increase in accuracy.

2.1.3 Method 3: User Stories

A user story describes functionality that will be valuable to either a user or purchaser of a system or software. A user story is a very high-level definition of a requirement, containing enough information so that the developer can produce an estimate of effort to implement it. User stories are composed of three aspects:

- A written description of the story used for planning and as a reminder ("Card").
- Conversations about the story that serve to flesh out the details of the story ("Conversation").
- Tests that convey and document details and that can be used to determine when a story is complete ("Confirmation").

Table 2. Planning poker description

Step	Description
1	One team member (preferably the customer or product owner) kicks off a discussion on a feature, and the whole team asks questions and normalizes on the scope and breadth of the feature.
2	At the end of the discussion, a vote is taken. Each team member privately selects a card representing his or her estimate.
3	When all the team members are ready with their estimate, they all hold up an index card with their estimate on it. It's important for everyone to do so at the same time so that they are not influenced by their peers.
4	If everyone holds up cards with the same number, the estimate is official, and it is recorded. If there is no consensus, you investigate why and a new round of estimation is made.

While the Card may contain the text of the story, the details are worked out in the Conversation and recorded in the Confirmation.

The size of the story is given in "story points" (an abstract unit). The team defines how a story point translates to effort. Typically one story point is equal to one ideal day of work. The total amount of story points that a team can deliver during one iteration is called "team velocity." Developers are responsible for estimating the effort required to implement the things that they will work on, including stories. The implication is that because you can only do so much work in one iteration, the size of the work items (including stories) will be affected when those work items are addressed. Although it may be feared that developers do not have the requisite estimating skills, and this is often true at first, the fact is that it does not take long for people to get pretty good at estimating when they know that they are going to have to live up to those estimates. The entire team, using the experience of all members, similarly to the "Wideband Delphi" approach, develops the estimate for the entire story.

If you have adopted the pair programming practice, then a user story must be implemented by two people in a single iteration/sprint. Therefore, if you're working in one-week iterations each user story must describe less than one week's worth of work. Large user stories would need to be broken up into smaller stories to meet this criterion. Table 3 describes the summarized steps.

It is important that user stories can be coded and tested between half a day and two weeks by one or two programmers.

User stories encourage deferring detail – it allows (us) to spend little or no time thinking about a new feature until we are sure that the feature is needed. Stories discourage us from pretending we can know and write everything down in advance. Because user stories shift emphasis toward talking and away from writing, important decisions are not captured in documents (that are unlikely to be read anyway). Instead, important aspects about stories are captured in automated acceptance tests and run frequently.

Table 3. User stories description

Step	Description
1	Developers gather information using techniques like user interviews, questionnaires, or workshops and write a collection of user stories.
2	The customer selects a story from the collection and reads it to the developers. The developers ask as many questions as they need and the customer answers them.
3	When there are no more questions, each developer writes an estimate on a card, without showing the estimate to the others. When everyone has finished writing an estimate, the developers turn over their cards.
4	If estimates differ, the high and low estimators explain their estimates. At this point the team discuss it. The customer clarifies issues as they come up.
5	After the group has discussed the story, the developers again write their estimates on cards. When everyone has finished writing a revised estimate, the developers turn over their cards. If there is no consensus, you investigate why. A new round of estimation is made. If estimates converge then it can be used for the story.
6	The customer selects a new story from the collection and returns to step 2. At the end, the team counts the number of story points.

The estimates are verified with previous estimates. Periodically, you can re-estimate a story, which gives you a chance to incorporate additional information.

At the end of each iteration the team count the number of story points they completed and add up the ideal time in all the stories to determine the team's velocity. Each developer measures his or her velocity by tracking his or her accomplishments in every iteration. The developer can only sign up for the same number of day's worth of tasks the next time (Care should be taken not to use this data against the developer).

User stories work because those who do the work estimate it.

2.2 Traditional Methods

There are many standards and well-known traditional methods. Traditional methods are usable directly in agile environments, but they need well-defined requirements. Using traditional methods like Function Points, Use Case Points or PROBE in an agile environment could be useful. The estimates need to be updated at every iteration if any function is added, changed or removed.

2.2.1 Method 4: Function Points

The International Function Points Group (IFPUG) defines functions points as "measuring software size by quantifying the functionality provided to the user based solely on logical design and functional specifications." Function Points were defined by Allan J. Albrech in 1979 and were designed to meet three goals:

- Gauge delivered functionality in terms users can understand.
- Be independent of technique, technology, and programming language.
- Give a reliable indication of software size during early design.

There is a convention in the industry that a project with 3 to 500 function points is considered a small project; projects between 500 and 1000 function points, medium projects; and projects greater than 1000 function points, big projects.

A function point count is used to "estimate the functional size of a project before the development phase. If you have a list of the functionalities, using the estimated count method, it will be possible to know the functional size of the project with an error margin of 15%."

From the function point count or estimation, the effort and cost of the project by roles and disciplines are derived.

From a final count at the end of a project, the functional size to determine how much money to charge the client is measured. Many projects are based on function points. Companies pay by function points instead of by hours. It is good because the client will pay by size of the functionality, not by the hours or lines of code used to develop it.

2.2.1.1 Function Point Types

There are two types of functionality – Data Functions to count size of the data part of the project (e.g. schema files) and Transactional Functions to count size of the transactional functions of the project (e.g., WSDL files). Data functions are data structures like tables, schema files, text files, and any type of data perceived by the user as a repository for business information. There are two types of data functions – Internal Logical Files (ILF) to count data functions from the project scope and External Interface Files (EIF) to count data functions from outside scope but used by any transactional function of the project scope. To determine the total number of function points of a data function, we use/d a complexity table as follows (see Table 4):

ILF and EIF are composed of record element types (RET) and data element types (DET). A RET is a data subgroup and a DET is a data element only, a field. In a Person file for example,

Table 4. Complexity weights

Function Type	Complexity-Weight		
	Low	Average	High
Internal Logical Files	7	10	15
External Interface Files	5	7	10
External Inputs	3	4	6
External Outputs	4	5	7
External Inquiries	3	4	6

we can have a subgroup called Address to group the Zip Code, Street, City, State and Country fields. Any elementary field in the File (ILF or EIF) will be a DET, like Person name (for example). The complexity level for ILF and EIF types is computed using Table 5.

Transactions functions are functions responsible to do the user functionalities and meet business requirements. For example, transaction functions are the operations of the SOA services.

There are three types of transaction functions: External Input (EI), External Output (EO) and External Inquiry (EQ). External Inputs (EI) are functionalities used to insert or update business information in one or more data functions. An input is considered to be unique if it has different data or format, or if it requires different processing. There is a complexity table available to count EI (see Table 6). External Outputs (EO) are func-

Table 5. Complexity levels

For Internal Logical Files and External Interface Files			
		Data Elements	
Record Elements	1-19	20-50	51+
1	Low	Low	Avg.
2-5	Low	Avg.	High
6+	Avg.	High	High

53

Table 6. Complexity levels

For External Input			
		Data Elements	
File Types	1-4	5-15	16+
0 or 1	Low	Low	Avg.
2-3	Low	Avg.	High
4+	Avg.	High	High
For External Output and External Inquiries			
		Data Elements	
File Types	1-5	6-19	20+
1	Low	Low	Avg.
2-3	Low	Avg.	High
4+	Avg.	High	High

tionalities used to return derived or calculated business information to the user (or consumer of the service). In a return of a group of data, if any DET (field) is a result of a calculation or math operation, the transaction will be an EO. If two or more fields are inserted, merged, processed before returning the result to the user, the transaction will be an EO too. An output is considered to be unique if it has different data or format, or if it requires different processing. There is a complexity table available to count EO (see Table 6).

External Inquiries (EQ) are functionalities used to return the information requested by the user without calculations, transformations or internal processing. The data is returned as is to the user's data repository. A query is a set of selection criteria that are used to extract information from an existing database. Like External Input and External Output, there is a complexity table available to count EQ. Table 7 describes the summarized steps.

Function Points work to facilitate dialogue between the user and the developer. Many types of data sources can be used throughout development. Moreover, the count is unaffected by language or tools used to develop the software.

2.2.2 Method 5: Estimating Use Case Points

The model presented here is essentially the same as published by Geri Schnaider and Jason Winters in their book, *Applying Use Cases* (Schnaider, 2001). The Use Case Points (UCP) method provides the ability to estimate the man-hours of a software project required from its use cases. Based

Table 7. Function point counting process

Step	Description
1	The estimator defines the application boundary and describes the system in general terms.
2	The estimator counts the instances of each function type.
3	The estimator determines the complexity of each instance using lookup tables.
4	The estimator uses another lookup table to assign a numeric value to each object based on its function type and complexity.
5	The estimator multiplies the count by the corresponding weight for each type and complexity level.
6	The estimator sums the results and gives the total number of unadjusted function points.
7	The estimator adjusts this total to account for system characteristics.

on work by Gustav Kramer, the UCP analyzes the use case actors, scenarios and various technical and environmental factors and summarizes them into an equation.

The UCP equation is composed of three variables:

1.   Unadjusted Use Case Points (UUCP).
2.   The Technical Complexity factor (TCF).
3.   The Environment Complexity Factor (ECF).

The process starts by considering the actors. For each actor, it determines whether the actor is simple, average or complex. A simple actor represents another system with a defined Application Programming Interface (API). An average actor is either another system that interacts through a protocol such as TCP/IP or a person interacting through a text-based interface. A complex actor is a person interacting through a graphical user interface (GUI).

The number of simple, average and complex actors must be counted. Table 8 contains the weight factor for each actor type. The quantity of each type of actor is multiplied by the weight factor and the total is summed up.

It should be apparent that the weighted values used to modify the quantity of actors (in this section, as in subsequent sections) are valid only if the impact they have on the result is backed up by feedback from historical data. In the case of actors, the feedback from historical data is used to adjust the definition of simple, average or complex.

For each Use Case, determining whether it is simple, average or complex is based on the number of transactions in a Use Case, including secondary scenarios. For this purpose, a transaction is defined as an atomic set of activities that is performed entirely or not at all. A simple Use Case has up to 3 transactions, an average Use Case has 4 to 7 transactions, and a complex Use Case has more than 7 transactions.

If analysis classes have been defined for the system, and also those used to implement a particular Use Case, this information is used in place of transactions to determine the Use Case complexity (Note: Used Use Cases or extended existing Use Cases do not need to be considered).

The number of simple, average and complex Use Cases is counted. Table 9 contains the weight factor for each Use Case Type. Multiply the quantity of each type of Use Case by the weight factor and sum up the total. The total for actors is added to the total for Use Cases to determine the Unadjusted Use Case Points (UUCP).

Weighting technical factors is an exercise to calculate a Use Case Point modifier, which will modify the UUCP by the weight of the technical factors. Start by calculating the technical complexity of the project. This is called the technical complexity factor (TCF). To calculate the TCF, go through the following table and rate each factor from 0 to 5. A rating of 0 means the factor is irrelevant for this project, and 5 means it is essential (Table 10).

For each factor, multiply its rating by its weight from the table. Add the resultant values together

Table 8. Weighting actors for complexity

Actor Type	Description	Weight Factor
Simple	Defined API.	1
Average	Interactive or protocol-driven interface.	2
Complex	Graphical user interface.	3

Table 9. Weighting use cases for complexity

Use Case Type	Description	Weight Factor
Simple	Up to 3 transactions	5
Average	4 to 7 transactions	10
Complex	More than 7 transactions	15

Table 10. Weighting technical factors

Technical Factor	Factor Description	Weight Factor
T1	Must have a distributed solution	2
T2	Must respond to specific performance objectives	1
T3	Must meet end-user efficiency desires	1
T4	Complex internal processing	1
T5	Code must be reusable	1
T6	Must be easy to install	.5
T7	Must be easy to use	.5
T8	Must be portable	2
T9	Must be easy to change	1
T10	Must allow concurrent users	1
T11	Includes special security features	1
T12	Must provide direct access for third-parties	1
T13	Requires special user training facilities	1

Table 11. Weighting experience factors

Experience Factor	Factor Description	Weight Factor
E1	Familiar with FPT software process	1
E2	Application experience	0.5
E3	Paradigm experience (OO)	1
E4	Lead analyst capability	0.5
E5	Motivation	0
E6	Stable Requirements	2
E7	Part-time workers	-1
E8	Difficulty of programming language	-3

to get the total Technical Factor. The Technical Factor does not directly modify the UUCP. To calculate Technical Complexity Factor (TCF), multiply Technical Factor by 0.01 and then add 0.6.

Calculate the size of the software (Use Case) project by multiplying UUCP times TCF.

Note on Reusable Components: Reusable software components should not be included in this estimate. Identify the UUCP associated with the reusable components and adjust the size of the software accordingly.

The experience level of each team member can have a great effect on the accuracy of an estimate. This is called the Experience Factor (EF) (see Table 11).

To calculate EF, go through the preceding table and rate each factor from 0 to 5. For factors E1-E4, 0 means no experience in the subject, 3 means average, and 5 means expert. For E5, 0 means no motivation on the project, 3 means average, and 5 means high motivation. For E6, 0

means unchanging requirements, 3 means average amount of change expected, and 5 means extremely unstable requirements. For E7, 0 means no part-time technical staff, 3 means, on average, half of the team is part-time, and 5 means all of the team are part-time. For E8, 0 means an easy–to-use programming language is planned, 3 means the language is of average difficulty, and 5 means very difficult language is planned for the project.

For each factor, multiply its rating by its weight from the table. Add the resultant values together to get the total Experience Factor. The Experience Factor is adjusted by multiplying by 0.03 and adding 1.4. To calculate final Use Case Points (UCP), multiply the size of the software by the experience factor.

The Use Case Points are very similar to Function Points.

2.2.3 Method 6: PROBE Method

The Proxy method is characterized by a systematic use of historical data. PROBE stands for PROxy Based Estimating and it uses proxies or objects as the basis for estimating the likely size of a product (Humphrey, 05). With PROBE, engineers first determine the objects required to build the product described by the conceptual design. Then they determine the likely type and number of methods

Table 12. C++ Class size in LOC per item

Category	Very Small	Small	Medium	Large	Very Large
Calculation	2.34	5.13	11.25	24.66	54.04
Data	2.60	4.79	8.84	16.31	30.09
I/O	9.01	12.06	16.15	21.62	28.93
Logic	7.55	10.98	15.98	23.25	33.83
Set-up	3.88	5.04	6.56	8.53	11.09
Text	3.75	8.00	17.07	36.41	77.66

for each object. They refer to historical data on the sizes of similar objects they have previously developed and use linear regression to determine the likely overall size of the finished product. The example object size data in Table 12 shows the five size ranges the Personal Software Process (PSP) uses for C++ class.

Since object size is a function of programming style, the PROBE method shows engineers how to use the data on the programs they have personally developed to generate size ranges for their personal use. Once they have estimated the sizes of the objects, they use linear regression to estimate the total amount of code they plan to develop. To use linear regression, engineers must have historical data on estimated versus actual program size for at least three prior programs. Table 13 describes the PROBE method.

Step 1: Generate the conceptual design. For the size estimate you must start with a conceptual design. The requirements deal with what the user wants or needs. To make a good plan, you need an estimate for what you intend to build. The conceptual design is your first cut at the product's design. This design establishes the expected product objects and their functions. This is a preliminary design; it is not a full design. You produce it only to make a size estimate.

Step 2: Determine object type and size. The next step in the PROBE method is to determine what objects are called for by the conceptual

Table 13. PROBE description

Step	Description
1	Generate conceptual design.
2	Determine object type and size.
3	Determine category and size.
4	Determine LOC from historical data.
5	Estimate size of reused parts and base additions.
6	Adjust estimated size with linear regression.

design. Then, using historical data on object size, you can estimate total object size. After you have divided the product into parts, you check to see if you have historical data on them. If a part does not match any element in your database, you re-examine it to see if you have refined it to a proper level. If a part does not fit a category, you will most likely find it to be a composite of several basic parts. You should then refine it into those parts.

If an object is at the right level and does not belong to any of the existing categories, then you estimate its size as a new category.

Step 3: Determine category and size. For every object you must determine its category and judge how its size compares with those in the database in its category. There are five different relative sizes: very small, small, medium, large and very large.

Step 4: Determine LOC from historical data. A table of actual size range for category contains a summary of historical data. The PROBE divides historical data into categories that represent different kinds of work. For example, developing text-handling parts is different from implementing algorithm computation. The next step is to divide the size data into very small, small, medium, large, and very large size ranges. For each category, the average size belongs to the medium relative size. Using this table you can match the relative size and category to obtain the probable LOC size per method. Then, you can compute the estimated LOC of an object multiplying by the number of methods.

Step 5: Estimate size of reuse parts and base additions. If you can find available parts that provide the functions required by the conceptual design, you may be able to reuse them. The total estimated size is the sum of estimated LOC of objects.

Step 6: Adjust estimated size with linear regression. A way to calculate total adjusted program size using personal characteristics is to look at your historical behavior. For example, if you apply the linear regression to your historical data and the result is a slope of 1.25, then your historical data are showing that the finished program is 25 percent bigger than the total estimated size of the objects it contains. Once you have an estimate of the total size of the objects, you add 25 percent to get the estimate for the program. Usually, the estimated and projected sizes are strongly related and the linear regression method is used to represent this relationship.

The PROBE method works (Grutter, 2002) because:

- The developers do the work and/or estimate the work using their parameters.

- The developers collect their data and use them.
- It allows accurate time, size and defects estimates.

3. SUSTAINABLE ESTIMATION INFRASTRUCTURE

Size estimation is the summation of individual elements using established methods and valid data, based on what is known today. In this context a critical function is to have the available valid data. The quality of organizational databases varies greatly. Although the databases generally contain volumes of technical data, they are unmanageable because of the sheer quantity of data. Another caution for using data from previous projects is that the context for the historical projects is not well documented. Relevant historical data should be used from similar systems to project estimates of new systems.

In this context we can identify three possible states about estimation infrastructure:

- An initial state is characterized by not having any operating data. Data exists but can be scattered or data may not be comparable. Historical data are sometimes invalid, unreliable or unrepresentative. One possible strategy is to rely on data and/or models brought from the industry.
- A more advanced state is when the organization collects data by introducing action mechanisms in the projects or recreating data from previous projects. The organization relies on a standard process that emphasizes the quality of data.
- A high maturity state. The organization has accurate historical data and this historical data provide valuable information for strengthening the credibility of estimates.

It is important to highlight that all estimation methods are based on comparing the characteristics of the product to be developed with previous data. Previous data can be lessons learnt and previous experiences that can be coded or non-coded, i.e. based only on previous experience without having estimator documentary support.

To have a sustainable infrastructure it is necessary to codify previous experience through data collection and processing for future estimates and model calibration. According to the state, different strategies are available, but the most important is to generate a historical dataset.

Initially, the focus must be to collect data. Collecting historical data and dedicating the time needed to do this continuously is a challenge for organizations. Many types of data, technical, schedule, and cost, need to be collected. This data can be collected in a variety of ways, such as from/form databases of past projects, interviews and focus groups. In order to face this challenge, the organization should start with a very small set of data. Examples of commonly used measures (McConnell, 2006) include the following:

- **Size:** Lines of code or something else you can count after the software has been released.
- **Effort:** The person-days or person-months.
- **Time:** Probably, calendar-days, or calendar-months.
- **Defects:** This is important data about software quality.

After the estimate is complete, the data need to be well documented, protected, and stored for future use in retrievable databases. These data sets will provide enough data to calibrate organizational estimation models. It will allow you to compute derived measures such as lines of code per person-month. If you do not start this small data set, you can end up with data that are defined inconsistently across projects, which makes the data meaningless.

Historical data and project data are both useful and can support the creation of accurate estimates. With historical data, you use an assumption that the next project will go the same way as the last few projects did. Productivity is an organizational attribute that cannot easily be varied from project to project. Estimates always involve some sort of calibration, either implicitly or explicitly.

This concept showed up in the Extreme Programming as "Yesterday weather." The weather today won't always be the same as it was yesterday, but it is more like yesterday's weather than like anything else (Beck & Fowler, 2001).

3.1 Calibrating Techniques

Calibration is used to convert counts to estimates. The estimates can be calibrated using any of the three kinds of data (McConnell, 2006):

- Industry data, which refer to data from other organizations that develop the same basic kind of software.
- Historical data, which refer to data from the organization that will conduct the project being estimated.
- Project data, which refer to data generated earlier in the same project, being estimated.

A simple technique to calibrate data is triangulation. Triangulation is defined in the Agile literature as the process of establishing the size of a user story to two other stories for the purpose of increasing the reliability of the estimate (Cohn, 2006). The triangulation technique is based on yesterday's weather rule. This rule says: "You'll do as much today (in the next iteration) as you actually got done yesterday (in the last iteration)."

The first estimate (at the beginning of the project, when there is no yesterday) is the hardest and least accurate. Fortunately, you only have to do it once. After the first few estimates have been made, verify them by relating them to each other. Triangulation confirms estimates by comparing the story to multiple other stories.

- A two-point story should be half the effort of a four-point story.
- A three-point story should be roughly larger than a two-point story, but yet smaller than a four-point story.

Although not exact, triangulation is an effective means for a team to verify that they are not gradually altering the meaning of a story point. It builds on intuitive decision-making.

This rule helps to prevent inconsistent data. Moreover, this technique allows to track all kinds of changes to the team, new technology and changes in products.

4. CONCLUSION

In a small team environment, with frequent changes that cannot be anticipated, estimation must be done in an incremental and adaptive way. Due to a lack of time and resources, the estimates can no longer be a sophisticated, big approach by highly skilled estimators at the beginning of the project.

The researchers suggest a number of estimation models and methods, but none is best suited for all projects and all software companies. Agile approaches to estimation look extremely simple, but they work quite well. Traditional techniques in this paper offer comparable or similar usability features.

No estimation technique has been shown to be superior in all cases (Basha, 2010). No one model is best for all situations and environment. But, historical data play a vital role in prediction. Use of a model with historical data can produce good results. In order to achieve this goal a good sustainable measurement infrastructure is necessary. All data collection activities must be documented as to source, time, units and context information. Com-

prehensive documentation during data collection greatly improves quality and reduces subsequent effort in developing the estimate.

If the organization does not have any historical data, it is possible to use industry data, which are adequate but not better. Data are the foundation of every estimate. How good the data are affects the estimate's overall credibility (Estimating, 2009). A key step in developing a sound estimate is to collect valid and useful data. A good monitoring policy is always required to make estimation a success. In order to know the level of accuracy it is necessary to compare actual data against estimates periodically (Jørgensen, 2012).

Finally, every technique and method requires a little bit of modification according to the local environment. Most development does not remain static; they tend to change in people, technology and context. Developing an estimate should not be a one-time event, but rather, a recurrent process. There are estimation techniques that allow adapting estimates to continuous changes.

ACKNOWLEDGMENT

This work is sponsored by everis Foundation and Universidad Politécnica de Madrid through the Software Process Improvement Research Chair for Spain and Latin American Region.

REFERENCES

Basha, S., & Ponnurangam, D. (2010). Analysis of empirical software effort estimation models. *International Journal of Computer Science and Information Security*, 7(3), 68–77.

Beck, K., & Fowler, M. (2001). *Planning extreme programming*. Reading, MA: Addison-Wesley Professional.

Boehm, B. W., Madachy, R., & Steece, B. (2000). *Software cost estimation with Cocomo II with Cdrom*. Upper Saddle River, NJ: Prentice Hall PTR.

Cohn, M. (2004). *User stories applied: For agile software development*. Reading, MA: Addison-Wesley Professional.

Cottmeyer, M. (2011). *The real reason we estimate*. Retrieved December 2013 from http://www.leadingagile.com/2011/09/the-real-reason-we-estimate/

Grütter, G., & Ferber, S. (2006). The personal software process in practice: Experience in two cases over five years. In Proceedings of Software Quality—ECSQ 2002, (pp. 165-174). ECSQ.

Humphrey, W. S. (2005). *Psp (sm), a self-improvement process for software engineers*. Reading, MA: Addison-Wesley Professional.

Jørgensen, M. (2004). A review of studies on expert estimation of software development effort. *Journal of Systems and Software*, 70(1), 37–60. doi:10.1016/S0164-1212(02)00156-5

Jorgensen, M., Boehm, B., & Rifkin, S. (2009). Software development effort estimation: Formal models or expert judgment? *IEEE Software*, 26(2), 14–19. doi:10.1109/MS.2009.47

Jorgensen, M., & Grimstad, S. (2012). Software development estimation biases: The role of interdependence. *IEEE Transactions on Software Engineering*, 38(3), 677–693. doi:10.1109/TSE.2011.40

Jorgensen, M., & Shepperd, M. (2007). A systematic review of software development cost estimation studies. *IEEE Transactions on Software Engineering*, 33(1), 33–53. doi:10.1109/TSE.2007.256943

Mahnič, V., & Hovelja, T. (2012). On using planning poker for estimating user stories. *Journal of Systems and Software*, 85(9), 2086–2095. doi:10.1016/j.jss.2012.04.005

McConnell, S. (2006). *Software estimation: Demystifying the black art*. Microsoft Press.

Moløkken-Østvold, K., & Jørgensen, M. (2004). Group processes in software effort estimation. *Empirical Software Engineering*, 9(4), 315–334. doi:10.1023/B:EMSE.0000039882.39206.5a

Schneider, G., & Winters, J. P. (2001). *Applying use cases: A practical guide*. Que Publishing.

Schwaber, K. (2004). *Agile project management with Scrum*. Microsoft Press.

Shepperd, M., & MacDonell, S. (2012). Evaluating prediction systems in software project estimation. *Information and Software Technology*, 54(8), 820–827. doi:10.1016/j.infsof.2011.12.008

Sommerville, I. (2004). *Software engineering*. International Computer Science Series.

SSQC. (2011). Software estimation bootcamp. In *Proceedings of the SEPG Conference 2011*. Portland, OR: SEPG.

KEY TERMS AND DEFINITIONS

Agile Software Development: Technopedia.com defines Agile Software Development as a lightweight framework that promotes iterative development that promotes iterative development across the lifecycle of the project, a close collaboration between the development team and business side, constant communication, and tightly-knit teams.

Estimate: Webster dictionary defines it as: 1. To form an opinion or judgment about. 2. To judge or determine generally but carefully (size, value, cost, etc.). According McConnell an estimate is a prediction of how long a project will take or how much it will cost. But estimation on software projects interplays with business targets, commitments and control. Targets are business needs or desirable objectives to achieve. A commitment is a promise to deliver defined functionality at certain time and a certain quality.

Function Point: A function point is method of measuring the functionality of a proposed software development from the point of view of user.

PROBE: PROxy-Base Estimation is a method based on use of proxy or object to produce accurate estimates. The proxy size measure should closely relate to effort equired to develop the product. The proxy content of a product should be automatically countable (Humphrey, 05).

User Stories: Extreme programming.org define a user story as things that the system needs to do for the customers written by the customers. They are in the format of about three sentences of text written in the customers terminology.

Chapter 5
Adapting Agile Practices to Mobile Apps Development

Alberto Heredia
Universidad Carlos III de Madrid, Spain

Javier Garcia-Guzman
Universidad Carlos III de Madrid, Spain

Roberto Esteban-Santiago
Universidad Carlos III de Madrid, Spain

Antonio Amescua
Universidad Carlos III de Madrid, Spain

ABSTRACT

Mobile app markets have experienced remarkable growth during the last year. The increasing number of apps available on the market and the revenue that developers and companies obtain is significant enough to seriously consider the way apps are developed. The ever-changing environment in which apps are developed makes agile methodology convenient to follow. Although agile methodologies allow the development team to quickly adjust the requisites to the new customer's needs, there is a lack of research on how they can be explicitly adapted to develop mobile apps. There are many Websites that explain how to code a mobile app, but there is not enough information about other stages in the development process. Adapting an agile methodology for mobile apps would provide development teams with a clear guide to successfully develop an app without missing any step in the development process. This chapter proposes an agile mobile app development process, including processes and activities to be followed as well as the roles involved in these activities. Marketing issues are also considered in the proposed development process as they are necessary to publicize the mobile app. This process has been applied for over two years in the development of the institutional apps at Carlos III University of Madrid.

DOI: 10.4018/978-1-4666-5182-1.ch005

1. INTRODUCTION

Currently, mobile app development is booming to satisfy the rapid growth in demand for apps, according to data from the Gartner research group (2012). Although there is a great deal of information about coding apps for mobile devices, there is very little information on how to complete the entire development process.

Agile methodologies are often adopted for mobile software development because of their characteristics. The development of an app should be relatively quick and straightforward. Small teams must deliver upgraded versions in short periods of time to meet customers' needs and expectations (Abrahamsson, 2007).

These agile methodologies, however, attempt to strive for universal solutions as opposed to situation appropriate solutions. As a consequence, they usually lack significant aspects that are specific to mobile apps, such as the co-joint management of a portfolio of apps to develop; mechanisms to involve end-users in the process of validating and upgrading the apps; or marketing-related practices to differentiate the app as a product, identify the target customers and consider other activities to publicize the app and follow up the marketing efforts.

To tackle all these problems, a development process based on agile methodologies was tailored specifically for mobile apps. We decided to use agile methodologies because they adapt quickly to changes, which is very important in the highly dynamic and competitive market of mobile apps. The inclusion of marketing activities in the proposed development process is considered innovative because agile methodologies do not usually include marketing phases in their processes.

This chapter aims at showing how agile methodologies are used in a mobile app development project. Different processes to be followed throughout the entire project are further described along with their corresponding activities and the appropriate roles for each one of these activities.

Thus, the apps produced following the process proposed in this chapter are likely to be better developed and have greater success in the mobile apps market.

2. BACKGROUND

Agile methodologies have been applied since the 90s for software development. Due to the growth of light applications oriented to mobile devices, agile is currently one of the most adopted methodologies for mobile software development (Shen, Yang, Rong, & Shao, 2012).

The characteristics of all agile methodologies are based on the Agile Manifesto (Agile Alliance, 2001) which emphasizes: individuals and interactions over processes and tools, working software over comprehensive documentation, customer collaboration over contract negotiation, and responding to change over following a plan.

There are also twelve principles behind the Agile Manifesto. The first one states that the highest priority is to satisfy the customer through early and continuous delivery of valuable software, as working software is considered the primary measure of progress. Another cornerstone of agile development is to welcome changing requirements because agile processes harness change for the customer's competitive advantage. Agile methodologies also encourage motivated individuals working in self-organizing teams composed of both business people and developers. The team should be able to maintain a constant pace indefinitely, paying continuous attention to technical excellence and good design, and reflecting on how to become more effective. To do so, good communication is key and agile methods consider face-to-face conversation as the most efficient and effective method of conveying information to and within a development team. Finally, agile principles state that the team should choose simpler solutions until more complexity is needed because simplicity allows to maximize the amount of resources not expended.

Recently, numerous agile methodologies have appeared, each with different characteristics (Dybå & Dingsøyr, 2008). However, all of them share the following attributes: incremental, cooperative, straightforward and adaptive (Abrahamsson, Warsta, Siponen, & Ronkainen, 2003). Incremental refers to small software releases, with rapid development cycles. Cooperative refers to a close customer and developer interaction. Straightforward implies that the method itself is easy to learn and to modify and that it is sufficiently documented.

These characteristics of agile methodologies make them suitable for mobile app development (Abrahamsson, 2007). The development of an app should be relatively quick and straightforward. Small teams must deliver upgraded versions in short periods of time to meet the customer's needs and expectations. And this must be done maintaining an appropriate product quality and reducing development costs.

Some of the most popular methodologies are eXtreme Programming (Beck, 1999), Scrum (Schwaber & Beedle, 2002) and Kanban (Anderson, 2010).

2.1 Extreme Programming

eXtreme Programming (XP) (Beck, 1999), created by Kent Beck, is an incremental and iterative software development method that stresses customer satisfaction through rapid creation of high-value software, skillful and sustainable software development techniques, and flexible response to change.

This method was probably one of the first agile methods. It emphasizes collaboration among users and software developers, the creation of running software in the very early stages of a project and skillful development practices. XP is based on four values:

- **Communication:** Communication among software developers and other stakeholders is promoted through pair programming, daily stand-up meeting, and the Planning Game. Communication is promoted through customer involvement in writing acceptance tests and the Planning Game.
- **Simplicity:** This applies not only to the design of software, but to other things such as requirements and project management tools. For example, XP encourages the use of simple paper index cards to write a brief description of feature and task requests if more formal artifacts can be avoided.
- **Feedback:** In the short term feedback is driven by the XP practice of test-first development with unit tests. It also comes from the practice of continuous integration; a broken build tells the story. When a customer writes a feature description, programmers immediately estimate it, so customers are aware of the effort. The practice of using a daily tracker provides the team and customers with feedback on progress for the iteration. On a wider scale, the customer-written acceptance tests provide feedback. Short iterations give the customer the chance to see an incrementally evolved partial system, and clarify or redirect the requirements.
- **Courage:** The courage to develop and make changes fast emerges from the support of the other values and practices and modern technologies.

The project lifecycle proposed by XP is composed of the following stages:

1. Like many projects, XP can start with exploration. Some software requirements may be written in terms of user stories to be satisfied by the software to develop. Moreover, rough estimations are provided for each user story.

2. In the Release Planning Game, customers and developers complete the user stories specification and rough estimates, and then decide what to do for the next release.

3. For the next iteration, in the Iteration Planning Game, customers pick stories to implement. They choose stories based on current status and their latest priorities for the next release. Developers then break the stories into many short, estimated tasks. Finally, a review of the total estimated task-level effort may lead to readjustment of the chosen stories. Overtime is seriously discouraged in XP; it is viewed as a sign of a dysfunctional project, increasingly unhappy people, and decreasing productivity and quality.

4. Developers implement the stories within the agreed timeboxed period, continually collaborating with customers (in a common project room) on tests and requirement details.

5. If not finished for release, return to step 3 for the next iteration.

eXtreme Programming proposes 12 core practices to develop software projects according to the previously defined values. These practices are based on several principles: an entire team working together in a common room, pair programming, constant refactoring, and test-driven development. The practices are:

1. The goal of the Release Planning Game is to define the scope of the next operational release, with maximum value (for the customer) software.

2. The goal of the Iteration Planning Game is to select the stories to implement, and to plan and allocate tasks for the iteration. This is carried out shortly before each iteration.

3. Memorable metaphors aid design communication and capture the overall system or each subsystem to describe the key architectural themes.

4. The design should avoid duplicate code, have a relatively minimal set of classes and methods, and be easily comprehensible.

5. Unit and system tests are written for most code, and the practice of test-driven development (and test-first development) is followed.

6. Frequent refactoring. Refactoring is the effort to simplify the source code and larger design elements, while still ensuring all tests pass.

7. Pair programming. Two engineers working at one computer program the code; they take turns at the keyboard. Pairs may change frequently, for different tasks. The observer is doing a real-time code review and, perhaps thinking more broadly than the typist and considering tests.

8. Team code ownership. This practice means that the entire team is collectively responsible for all the code, so any pair of programmers can improve any code.

9. All checked-in code is continuously re-integrated and tested on a separate build machine in an automated process loop of compiling, running all available tests.

10. Sustainable pace. Frequent overtime is rightly considered a symptom of deeper problems, and does not lead to happy, creative developers, healthy families, or quality maintainable code.

11. The whole team, composed of software engineers and users, work together in a common project room. One or more users work with the team in a part time basis. They are expected to be subject matter experts and empowered to make decisions regarding requirements and their priority.

12. Coding standards. With collective code ownership, frequent refactoring, and regular swapping of pair programming partners, everyone needs to follow the same coding style.

2.2 Scrum

As shown in Figure 1, Scrum is an iterative, incremental framework for application development that structures work in cycles called Sprints (Schwaber & Beedle, 2002). Sprints are "timeboxed," that is, they end on a specific date whether the work has been completed or not, and are never extended. The duration is fixed in advance for each Sprint (normally between one week and one month).

The artifacts produced during the Scrum lifecycle are the Product Backlog, the Sprint Backlog and the Sprint Burndown. The Product Backlog is a list with the requirements of the system containing features, development requirements (nonfunctional), research tasks and bugs. It is a dynamic document that incorporates constantly the needs of the system. The Sprint Backlog is a list of tasks determined by the team to perform a Sprint and achieve, at the end thereof, increased functionality. The Sprint Burndown shows the evolution and the current status of the Sprint and is obtained from the data in the Sprint Backlog.

Scrum focuses mainly on individuals working in teams. The Scrum development team is composed of two types of roles: team members and external stakeholders. Among the team members are the Product Owner, representing, but not necessarily, the client; the Scrum Manager, who manages the problems that may arise; and the software engineers.

Another important aspect in the life cycle of the Scrum methodology is meetings, which can be divided into: Release Planning Meeting, Sprint Planning Meeting, Daily Scrum Meeting, Sprint Review Meeting, and Sprint Retrospective. The Release Planning Meeting consists of the construction of the Product Backlog, discussion about the costs, risks, dates, estimates, etc. and the creation of a high level design. Each Sprint is initiated with a Sprint Planning Meeting, where the Product Owner and Team collaborate on what will be done for the next Sprint, selecting the highest-priority requirements from the Product Backlog. The Daily Scrum Meeting consists of a briefing on what was done the previous day, what is going to be done that day, and what the current obstacles or problems are. The purpose of the Sprint Review Meeting is for the Team to demonstrate to the Product Owner and stakeholders the functionality that is completed. Finally, the Sprint Retrospective consists of inspecting how the process worked during the last Sprint and adjusting it to improve the next one.

Scrum promotes self-directed teams, daily team measurement, and avoidance of prescriptive process. Some key practices include: a self-

Figure 1. Scrum methodology

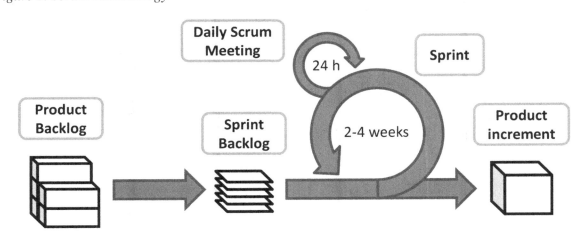

directed and self-organizing team in which tasks are self-assigned by each team member; no external addition of work to a Sprint once started; a daily stand-up meeting to make everyone aware of the project status; a demo to stakeholders at the end of each Sprint to get external feedback. Each Sprint involves client-driven adaptive planning, thus the project can be adapted to the customer's needs.

2.3 Kanban

Kanban is a methodology for developing software products that emphasizes just-in-time delivery, which means making only what is needed, when it is needed, and in the amount needed to avoid the accumulation of work and wasted time. Thus, minimizing the work-in-process allows to maximize the value created by the organization (Anderson, Concas, Lunesu, Marchesi, & Zhang, 2012).

One of the main features of Kanban is that it requires little training to create value. Policies are explicit and understanding them simplifies and reduces the time required for new staff to adapt to the process.

Kanban does not define roles and processes, but rather focuses on improving current processes and roles based on small increments to avoid resistance to change.

A visual task-board is used for managing work in progress. The columns on the board represent the different states or steps in the workflow and the cards/post-it-notes represent a unit of work (feature, user story, task, etc.). Cards are moved along the board through each process stage (i.e. column) to completion. Any team member can easily know what the status of the project is at any time as the dashboard shows which work items are currently within each stage of the process.

Although it does not define processes, Kanban has a set of rules to follow. The first one is to divide the work into blocks, writing each element on a card and placing it on a dashboard. Another rule is to limit the work in progress so as not to overload developers and prevent bottlenecks in the development. The workflow also has to be measured and managed to optimize the process, making it easier to predict and reducing risk of delay. Finally, there must be a collaborative improvement. When teams have a shared understanding of theories

Figure 2. Kanban methodology

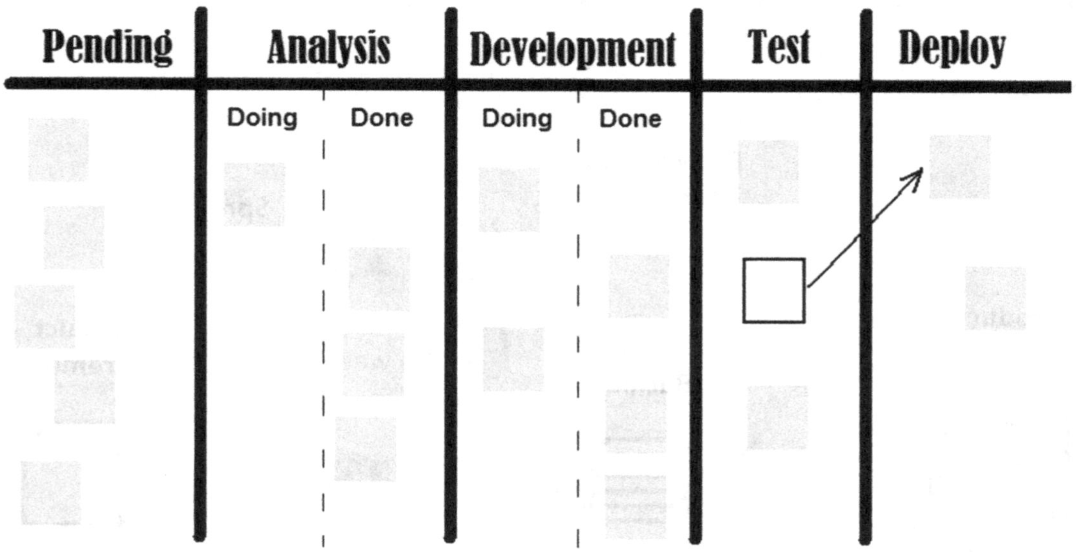

about work, workflow, process, and risk, they are more likely to be able to build a shared comprehension of a problem and suggest improvement actions which can be agreed by consensus. The use of models allows a team to predict the effect of those improvement actions.

2.4 Problems Found in Agile Methodologies Used to Develop Mobile Apps

Although eXtreme Programming, Scrum and Kanban are applied to mobile apps development, these three agile methodologies do not consider several important aspects for the development of mobile apps oriented towards open markets.

First, none of them consider the management of a portfolio of potential apps to develop, but assume there will only be one application to develop. This assumption could be due to the fact that agile methodologies were originally oriented to in-house projects in which an organization requests the development of a specific application to be used by its clients or employees. Mobile apps, however, are not often requested by a clearly stated client, but are developed to fulfill the needs of a group of people within society. In this case, there can be as many potential apps to develop as the number of different needs or opportunities identified. This set of potential apps must, therefore, be managed to select the best one to be developed.

Mobile apps considered in the scope of this chapter are not directly delivered to the client who paid for the development costs, but are usually published in a mobile apps market. The process of releasing the app should then consider some additional activities, such as defining and implementing a marketing strategy. Moreover, the organizations controlling the markets are also stakeholders to be considered because they introduce rules, guides and recommendations that may influence the technical development of the mobile app.

On the other hand, although agile methodologies consider feedback loops, most of the feedback is provided prior to the release of the application. In Scrum, for example, the app is demonstrated to the Product Owner and stakeholders in the Sprint Review Meeting to receive feedback on the completed functionalities. As mentioned above, mobile apps are usually published in a mobile apps market. This new distribution channel opens other feedback loops that should be considered, such as the comments that customers write in the market itself or in the social media.

The most important aspect that agile methodologies lack is marketing, essential to the success of a mobile app (Wooldridge & Schneider, 2010). As mentioned above, mobile apps development brings a change in the philosophy of traditional software development. A mobile app does not usually provide fixed profits from its sale to a particular client, but depends on its price and the number of downloads (i.e. buyers).

Marketing must not be a single process that is completely isolated from development. It should be integrated throughout the project in its different phases, from the conception of the app to its launch in a mobile apps market (Hughes, 2010).

Firstly, when an idea is expressed in the form of a description of the app, several points should be considered, such as the current trends in the market or the differential value that makes the app distinguishable from other apps on the market. It is also important to identify the audience the app is aimed at, since profits will depend on the number of customers who find the app useful. Furthermore, it is necessary to identify the competitors of the app to emphasize those values that make our app different from theirs, and also to learn from them.

Before deciding to develop the app or not, a market analysis is also needed. This process is necessary because the app will be published in a mobile apps market. So, it is necessary to know the market size, assess its profitability, and compare the estimated costs to the expected revenue. The identification of these aspects is important in order to obtain relevant information needed for any decision-making situation in the project.

While the app is being developed, a marketing plan must be created to later publicize the app and make it well-known to the public. The plan must set the goals of the marketing campaign; evaluate the strengths, weaknesses, opportunities and threats involved in the project; establish the channels through which the app will be publicized; and estimate the expected results of the marketing effort and the indicators to measure those results.

Before submitting the app to the market, some marketing-related information must be prepared as this will be needed to publish the app. Elements, such as the screenshots of the app, a keyword list or the description of the app are essential to selling the app because many customers will decide whether to buy the app or not depending on this information.

Finally, when the app is already published in the market, feedback that users provide about the developed app, besides other relevant data, must be gathered to analyze if the app is meeting the goals previously set in the marketing plan or not.

To conclude this section, we have presented some aspects that agile methodologies lack when

applied to mobile app development. To fill this gap, the following section describes a process based on agile methodologies specifically adapted to the development of mobile apps.

3. MISEL SOFTWARE DEVELOPMENT PROCESS (MISEL-SDP)

This section describes a process based on agile methodologies, specifically adapted to the development of mobile apps, named miSEL-sdp. This notation uses SPEM (Software Process Engineering Metamodel and Systems), version 2.0. SPEM is a formal language promoted by the OMG (Object Management Group) that provides concepts to model, document, present, manage, share, and implement methods and development processes (OMG, 2008).

SPEM elements to be used in the diagrams of this section are given in Table 1.

Figure 3 shows the flow through the different processes considered in the proposal:

First, the *Apps Portfolio Management* process identifies all possible apps to develop according

Table 1. SPEM 2.0 elements description

Notation	Description
	Process: element that represents a relationship between instances of activities and roles in the instances.
	Activity: general unit of work assignable to specific performers represented by a role.
	Role: set of skills, competencies and responsibilities of an individual or group performing a process or activity.
	Start: element that represents the beginning of the activities within a process.
	End: element that represents the completion of the activities within a process.
	Decision: choice that allows to split transitions into several alternative outgoing paths.

Figure 3. Processes defined in the proposal

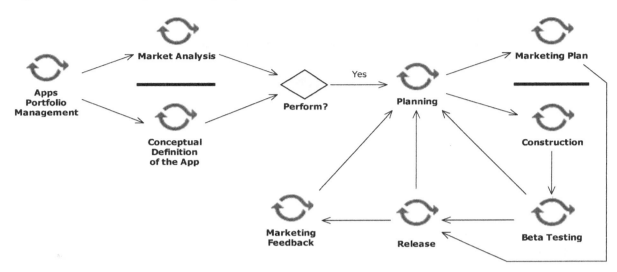

to the customer's needs and market opportunities. These apps are prioritized so that only the highest-priority app is selected to be developed.

Then, the *Conceptual Definition of the App* process and the *Market Analysis* process are conducted in parallel. In these two processes, a conceptual definition of the selected app and a description of the marketing data, necessary for the successful development of the app, are made. The feasibility of the project is determined based on the results of these two processes.

If the development of the app is feasible, the process continues with the *Planning* process, where the tasks needed to develop the app are estimated and assigned to the different team members.

Later, in the *Construction* process the app is designed, coded and tested following an iterative cycle which provides feedback to decide if the new features added to the app fulfill the requirements. In parallel, the *Marketing Plan* aims at analyzing the environment in order to define the marketing strategy and estimate the expected results.

Once the app provides new functionalities, stakeholders validate the entire app in *Beta Testing*. If the app is not approved by the stakeholders, the development process returns to the *Planning* process to fix any problem found.

When the stakeholders approve the app, the *Release* process is carried out. This means that a new version of the app is ready to be submitted to a mobile apps market for distribution. The app is then validated by the market reviewers and made available to customers only if it is approved. Otherwise, the development process returns to the *Planning* process to fix the validation issues.

Finally, in the *Marketing Feedback* process the team receives feedback from users which might raise new issues to fix or provide ideas for new functionalities.

3.1 Apps Portfolio Management

The *Apps Portfolio Management* aims at selecting the app to be developed. To do so, the project team has to identify the customer's needs or the opportunities that arise to develop an app. Then, a list of potential apps can be established and prioritized. The highest-priority app on the list will be the one selected for development.

The activities in this process are performed by the roles shown in Table 2.

Table 2. Roles participating in the apps portfolio management

Roles		Responsibilities
	Team Coordinator	Coordinates the activities required to define and manage the apps portfolio.
	Stakeholder	Identifies needs and opportunities as they arise, and identifies and prioritizes potential apps.
	Software Engineer	Identifies and prioritizes possible apps.

Figure 4. Apps portfolio management activities

Activities to be carried out in this process are shown in Figure 4.

First, the project team must identify the customer's needs or opportunities that arise. A portfolio of apps that may satisfy those needs or take advantage of those opportunities is established, providing an overview of all the potential apps to develop.

Once all the potential apps to be developed are described, the list must be prioritized. The priority of each app must be determined, considering the different points of view from the people involved (i.e. customers, development team, stakeholders). Later, the list could be sorted in descending order to better identify the top-priority apps. The team should select the app with the highest priority for development.

As a result of this process, the app to be developed is selected.

3.2 Conceptual Definition of the App

Prior to the development of the previously selected app, several steps must be taken even before the project planning. These steps include the identi-

fication of the features and restrictions required by the customer and the effort and cost to develop the previously stated functionalities. In addition, several analysis tasks must be carried out, such as identifying the expected characteristics of the mobile app, the differential value, the target audience and competitors.

The conceptual definition of the app has several objectives to achieve. First, it must be clear that this process refers only to the highest-priority app in the apps portfolio established in the previous process. Another objective of this process is to analyze whether the development of this app is feasible or not, besides specifying the features and restrictions that the app will have. A first estimation of the effort and cost for the project should also be made for future planning.

The activities of this process are performed by the roles shown in Table 3.

Activities to carry out in this process are shown in Figure 5.

The first activity consists of identifying the characteristics of the mobile app to develop. The overview of the app specified in the previous process may be a good starting point. The char-

Table 3. Roles participating in the conceptual definition of the app

Roles	Responsibilities
Team Coordinator	Facilitates and coordinates the process to conceptually define an app.
Software Engineer	Identifies functionalities and restrictions, and estimates effort and cost.
Marketing Manager	Identifies characteristics of the app, differential value, target audience, and competitors.

Figure 5. Conceptual definition of the app activities

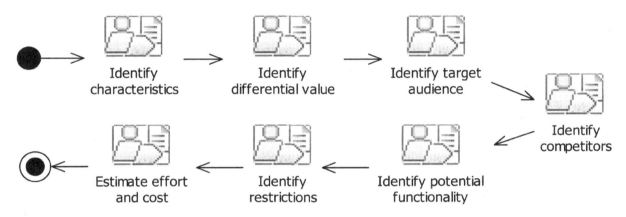

acteristics of the app should represent something unique and provide fresh functionalities. The app should also be aligned with current trends.

Later, to identify the differential value of the app, the strengths of the app must be identified. Finding words that best describe the app is also recommended. These values must distinguish the app developed from those of direct competitors to emphasize them and obtain more income.

Identifying the target audience is also a very important activity in the process. The market should be segmented first to better choose the target audience. The identification of the target audience will help to define the features and restrictions of the app in a better way, orienting them towards the audience.

On the other hand, competitors must also be identified. We should distinguish here between a direct and an indirect competitor. The first offers a similar app for the same target audience, while the other offers a similar app for a different target audience. Once competitors are identified, it is possible to learn from them.

Once the target audience and competitors are identified, the project team should have a much clearer idea about the potential functionalities that the app could provide. The data collected in the previous process and previous activities of this process will also help to identify the restrictions to be taken into account.

Finally, the project team must estimate the effort and cost for the development, and implementing the marketing strategies. This estimation is very important because it will help to decide whether the app is going to be developed or not depending on the results.

From these activities, a conceptual definition of the app is obtained, composed of the features and restrictions of the app, the data needed for the marketing plan, and an estimation to decide whether to develop the app or not.

3.3 Market Analysis

Before deciding if the app is going to be developed, it is important to analyze the market in which the app will be distributed. This process is carried out in parallel with the *Conceptual Definition of the App*. The market analysis is key in the development process to avoid mistakes that could lead to great expense. For instance, without a market analysis the developed app might not obtain the expected profits, resulting in financial losses for the company.

A market analysis determines whether the market is sufficiently attractive to launch the app. This process first requires an understanding the target audience, possible competitors, the characteristics of the app, its differential value and, finally, the time the project will take and the cost.

The activities of this process are performed by the roles shown in Table 4.

Activities to carry out in this process are shown in Figure 6.

First, to identify the market size the team should divide consumers into groups, considering their direct competencies, i.e., skills, market share and weaknesses.

To later assess the profitability of the market, potential buyers must be identified as well as how much they would be willing to pay for the app, how much it would cost to produce, and why they would want to buy our app and not the competitors'.

Finally, performing the cost analysis requires comparing costs and benefits. On the one hand, there must be a list with all the monetary costs that will be incurred during the development of the app, each with an estimated value. On the other hand, there must be a list with the profits that the app will generate. Values must be assigned to each of them.

The outputs to be obtained from these three activities will be the size of the market in which the app will be distributed, the growth rate of this market, as well as the distribution costs analysis.

Table 4. Roles participating in the market analysis

Roles		Responsibilities
	Team Coordinator	Facilitates and coordinates the market analysis process
	Marketing Manager	Calculates market size, considering whether the market in which the app will be introduced is profitable or not, and performs a cost analysis.
	Software Engineer	Provides the information needed for the cost analysis activity

Figure 6. Market analysis activities

3.4 Planning

To conduct the planning process it is necessary to decide first if the development of the app is feasible. The feasibility of the project is based on results of the *Conceptual Definition of the App* and the *Market Analysis* processes. If those results are positive and the development of the app is approved, the planning is performed, including marketing activities, and release.

Planning should be based on the features and restrictions previously identified, which will help to create a list of tasks to be carried out by the different roles involved in the project in order to obtain good results.

The activities of this process are performed by the roles shown in Table 5.

Activities to carry out in this process are shown in Figure 7.

In this process, the first activity consists of creating the different tasks to be carried out to implement the functionalities of the app. A task cannot be too large since it must be finished in a day at most. Otherwise, tasks should be divided into smaller ones.

Once tasks are identified, every task has to be estimated in terms of time and cost. These estimations should be compared to the ones obtained in the *Conceptual Definition of the App* process for the whole project. Some tasks may be re-estimated in consequence.

To conclude this process, the responsibility of each one of the tasks must be assigned to a member of the team. It is recommended that each team member willingly accepts the responsibility of achieving one or several tasks he/she thinks he/she can do better, so that the project manager does not impose tasks on individuals. With this self-assignment of tasks each individual commits to finishing the work.

As a result of this process, some estimated tasks will be assigned to each team member. The cost and effort estimation will also be more accurate because it is made by the development team and is based on smaller tasks. This statement does not mean that the estimations obtained in previous processes are not valid or unnecessary; previous estimations help to decide whether the app is developed or not.

Table 5. Roles participating in the planning

Roles		Responsibilities
	Team Coordinator	Estimates tasks and assigns them.
	Software Engineer	Creates, estimates and assigns tasks.

Figure 7. Planning activities

Create tasks   Estimate time and cost   Assign tasks

3.5 Construction

Once the planning is completed, and having obtained clear and assigned tasks, the construction of the app starts. This process covers not only coding the app, but also includes its design and future tests. Feedback is received through the execution of those tests to validate the requirements. These four activities are performed following an iterative cycle so that the app is first designed, then coded and tested, and finally feedback is produced. If the feedback is positive, this process is finished and a beta version of the app is distributed to the stakeholders. Otherwise, the iterative process starts again with a re-design to fix the issues found in the tests.

Therefore, the aim of this process is to produce a beta version of the app ready to be validated by the stakeholders. Tasks created during the planning are carried out in this iterative process to implement a beta version with desired functionalities based on the features and restrictions of the app.

The activities of this process are performed by the roles shown in Table 6.

Activities to carry out in this process are shown in Figure 8.

In the design activity, tasks are performed to produce different designs needed to code the app, including a data design, an architectural design, a procedural design, and an interface design.

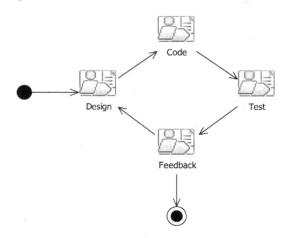

Figure 8. Construction activities

In the coding activity, designs are implemented in code, obtaining different modules that constitute the functionalities of this version of the app.

Once the different modules of the app are coded, tests are executed against those modules. The testing activity includes unit testing, integration testing and system testing. As a result, this activity provides a tested product and the results of the executed tests.

Finally, test results must be analyzed. If results are satisfactory, the construction process is finished. If not, changes are made to the app in order to fix the issues raised during the testing activity, so the cycle starts again.

Table 6. Roles participating in the construction

Roles		Responsibilities
	Team Coordinator	Gets feedback and decides whether to re-design or finish this process.
	Software Engineer	Designs, codes and provides feedback from the tasks within these activities.
	Test Engineer	Validates requirements and provides feedback from the validation.

The results of this process are a tested app ready to be validated by the stakeholders and the feedback from the tests.

3.6 Marketing Plan

One of the great difficulties when producing a mobile app is not the development itself but making the app well-known to public. To achieve this goal it is necessary to implement an appropriate marketing plan for the app.

The aim of this process is to specify a plan to publicize the app, aligned with established goals. The plan will be based on the analysis of the environment where the app will be distributed and the estimation of the results to be obtained according to established metrics. To do so, some previous data are needed such as: market size, growth rate, development costs and distribution channels .

The activities of this process are performed by the role shown in Table 7.

Activities to carry out in this process are shown in Figure 9.

To set the marketing goals, some aspects need to be considered. Not only must the objectives of the product be established, but also objectives related to sales, app pricing and earnings.

On the other hand, the strengths, weaknesses, opportunities and threats (SWOT) analysis must be carried out. The strengths are those characteristics of the business or project that give it an advantage over others. The weaknesses are characteristics that place the team at a disadvantage relative to others. The opportunities are external elements that the project could exploit to its advantage. The threats are external elements in the environment that could cause trouble for the business or project. Comparing the app to similar ones in these terms will provide relevant information needed for any decision-making situation in the project.

The marketing activities include various tasks to be performed. The first one is promotion through different channels, such as traditional media, Web 2.0, and pricing policy. The second task is the communication activities to advertise the app. Another important task should be the deployment of a Website for the app. The latter task considers the diffusion of the app through social networks.

After that, expected results from the marketing effort must be determined. This activity includes determining the objectives to be achieved through the marketing campaign and attracting previous customers so they know about the existence of the app.

Finally, to establish the measurement criteria, metrics must be determined to monitor the marketing campaign. At the end of the development process, data obtained from these metrics could be analyzed to find points of improvement in the app or to help develop future apps.

The expected output of this process is, therefore, to have a marketing plan which includes goals to achieve, advertising channels, the expected results of the marketing campaign, and the metrics to monitor those results.

Table 7. Roles participating in the marketing plan

Roles		Responsibilities
	Marketing Manager	Sets goals, performs a SWOT analysis, performs marketing activities, estimates the results, and establishes metrics.
	Software Engineer	Provides the knowledge required to identify the feasibility of gathering information for the metrics defined in order to follow up marketing strategy

Figure 9. Marketing plan activities

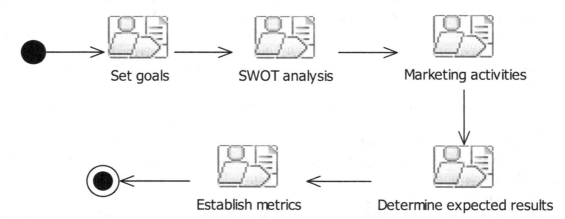

3.7 Beta Testing

The aim of this process is to have the stakeholders validate the beta version of the app in order to find defects that the development team missed in the tests executed in the construction process. When the results from this validation are satisfactory, the app can be released to the mobile apps market. If results are not satisfactory, some new tasks are needed to fix the issues raised and the *Planning* process must be carried out again.

The activities of this process are performed by the roles shown in Table 8.

Activities to carry out in this process are shown in Figure 10.

In the validation activity, the stakeholder must execute every possible test against the app and validate that it has all the features requested and is fully functional.

If a stakeholder does not agree with any of the features, a change may be proposed indicating the new functionality desired. At this point,

Table 8. Roles participating in the beta testing

	Roles	Responsibilities
	Team Coordinator	Facilitates and coordinates the process to prepare, execute and analyze the results of the beta testing process.
	Stakeholders	Perform the beta testing process to validate the app and suggest new features.
	Software Engineer	Analyzes contributions from stakeholders and defines a list of bugs to eliminate or new features to include in future versions of the app.

Figure 10. Beta testing activities

new features or improvements in the app can be proposed too.

If, and only if, the stakeholders provide satisfactory results from their validation, the result of this process will be an app ready to be released in the mobile apps market selected. The result of this process will be an updated list of features to be implemented.

3.8 Release

Publishing an app in a mobile apps market has some advantages, such as giving the app more exposure and directly selling the app to a huge customer base for a small fee without setting up any infrastructure.

All apps to be distributed in the mobile apps market must pass through a validation process before being advertised. This validation is external to the project team as it is conducted by the market reviewers. Depending on the market, different criteria can be applied, so the validation can be more or less rigorous.

The aim of this process is to make the app available in the market for customers to buy and thus obtain the expected profits. If the app fails the market validation, the development process returns to the *Planning* process to fix the validation issues.

The activities of this process are performed by the roles shown in Table 9.

Activities to carry out in this process are shown in Figure 11.

Before advertising the app on the market, it needs to be prepared for release. The different tasks included in the preparation activity are: obtain the screenshots of the app, establish a keyword list, and compose a description of the app. These aspects are very important in order to sell the app because many customers will decide whether to buy or not depending on this information. For instance, keywords will lead customers to our app when they search in the market.

The steps to advertise an app on the market vary depending on the market where the app is submitted. The information prepared before will be required as well as the packaged app. In addition, markets usually perform a validation process to assure that the app meets the criteria established for advertising apps in that market. In that case, it

Table 9. Roles participating in the release

Roles		Responsibilities
	Team Coordinator	Facilitates the process for advertising the mobile app in the market
	Marketing Manager	Prepares the app to be advertised in the market.
	Software Engineer	Performs the technical tasks required to advertise the mobile app

Figure 11. Release activities

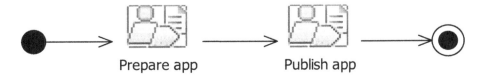

must be taken into account that the app could be rejected, so the process should go back to *Planning* to make the necessary changes for the app to be approved.

The expected output of the release process is the app advertised in the market. If the app does not pass the market validation, the project team will receive feedback from the market reviewers as to why the app was rejected. This feedback must be analyzed to take the appropriate actions to get the app accepted for distribution.

3.9 Marketing Feedback

After buying and using the app, customers can provide personal feedback on their experience with the app. Users' comments can be analyzed to check if users like the app or not. Many users do not provide any feedback, so other indicators should also be taken into account for analysis (e.g., the number of downloads).

The objective of this process is to gather feedback that users provide about the developed app, as well as other relevant data, to be analyzed. This analysis will be useful for identifying issues to fix in the current version of the app or for defining

new functionalities that may be included in future versions. As a consequence, this information should go back to the *Planning* process.

The activities of this process are performed by the roles shown in Table 10.

Activities to carry out in this process are shown in Figure 12.

In this process, the project team must receive and gather all the feedback provided by users on their experience with the app. This feedback could come from comments from users in the market itself, but it could also come from other sources, such as comments in the social media.

The feedback received from users must be used to track marketing activities. The marketing manager has to check if the marketing plan was properly followed, how and when the plan was executed, or if there were any problems.

Finally, all the results must be analyzed according to each one of the objectives. This analysis will help to identify what aspects to improve.

As a result of this process, issues to fix in the current version of the app may arise. Likewise, new functionalities to consider in future versions of the app or in other apps can be identified.

Table 10. Roles participating in the marketing feedback

Roles		Responsibilities
	Team Coordinator	Facilitates the process to analyze feedback obtained from the users of a mobile app
	User	Provides feedback on the app.
	Marketing Manager	Tracks marketing activities and analyzes results.
	Software Engineer	Contributes to the results analysis activity.

Figure 12. Marketing feedback activities

Receive feedback → Track marketing activities → Analyze results

4. CONCLUSION

This chapter describes a process based on agile methodologies specifically adapted to the development of mobile apps called miSEL-sdp. Although agile methodologies adapt quickly to changes, which is very important in the highly dynamic and competitive market of mobile apps, they lack significant aspects that are important for the development of mobile apps oriented to open markets.

The software development process proposed in this chapter includes co-joint management of a portfolio of potential apps to develop, mechanisms to involve end-users in the process of validating and upgrading the apps, and also marketing-related practices to differentiate the app as a product, identify the target customers and possible competitors, publicize the app through different channels to make it known to the public, and follow up marketing efforts, among others.

miSEL-sdp has been followed by the miSEL group at Carlos III University of Madrid for two years. The use of this process has led to the successful development of several mobile apps, including some of the official apps launched by Carlos III University of Madrid, an app to provide information to conference attendees for the VII International Congress on IT Governance and Service Management (ITGSM), and some other apps developed by undergraduate students for their final-year projects. All these apps are available for Android and iOS devices in the Google Play and App Store, respectively.

REFERENCES

Abrahamsson, P. (2007). Agile software development of mobile information systems. In *Proceedings of the 19th International Conference on Advanced Information Systems Engineering (CAiSE) (LNCS)*, (vol. 4495, pp. 1-4). Trondheim, Norway: Springer-Verlag.

Abrahamsson, P., Warsta, J., Siponen, M. T., & Ronkainen, J. (2003). New directions on agile methods: A comparative analysis. In *Proceedings of the 25th International Conference on Software Engineering (ICSE)*, (pp. 244-254). Portland, OR: IEEE Computer Society.

Agile Alliance. (2001). *Manifesto for agile software development*. Retrieved from http://agilemanifesto.org

Anderson, D. (2010). *Kanban: Successful evolutionary change for your technology business*. Sequim, WA: Blue Hole Press.

Anderson, D., Concas, G., Lunesu, M. I., Marchesi, M., & Zhang, H. (2012). A comparative study of scrum and Kanban approaches on a real case study using simulation. In *Proceedings of the 13th International Conference on Agile Software Development* (XP) (LNBIP), (vol. 111, pp. 123-137). Malmö, Sweden: Springer-Verlag.

Beck, K. (1999). *Extreme programming explained: Embrace change*. Boston, MA: Addison-Wesley Professional.

Dybå, T., & Dingsøyr, T. (2008). Empirical studies of agile software development: A systematic review. *Information and Software Technology*, *50*(9-10), 833–859. doi:10.1016/j.infsof.2008.01.006

Gartner Research Group. (2012). *Free apps will account for nearly 90 percent of total mobile app. store downloads in 2012*. Retrieved from http://www.gartner.com/it/page.jsp?id=2153215

Hughes, J. (2010). iPhone and iPad apps marketing. Indianapolis, IN: Que Publishing.

OMG. (2008). *Software & systems process engineering meta-model specification (SPEM) version 2.0*. OMG.

Schwaber, K., & Beedle, M. (2002). *Agile software development with scrum*. Upper Saddle River, NJ: Prentice Hall.

Shen, M., Yang, W., Rong, G., & Shao, D. (2012). Applying agile methods to embedded software development: A systematic review. In *Proceedings of the 2nd International Workshop on Software Engineering for Embedded Systems* (SEES). Zurich, Switzerland: IEEE Computer Society.

Wooldridge, D., & Schneider, M. (2010). *The business of iPhone app development: Making and marketing apps that succeed*. New York, NY: Apress. doi:10.1007/978-1-4302-2734-2

KEY TERMS AND DEFINITIONS

Agile Methodology: An alternative to traditional project management, typically used in software development. It helps teams to respond to unpredictability through incremental, iterative work cadences, known as sprints.

Dashboard: Is a board where one can manage the team of a company.

Marketing: A process that involves the identification of needs and wants of the target market, the development of consumer-oriented objectives, building strategies that create superior value, the implementation of customer relationship and retention of customer value to achieve benefits.

Mobile Applications: Is a software application designed to run on smartphones, tablet computers and other mobile devices.

Product Owner: Representative of all persons interested in the results of the project and single interlocutor with the team, with authority to make decisions.

Stakeholder: Groups together workers, social organizations, shareholders and suppliers, among many other key actors who are affected by the decisions of a company.

Chapter 6
The Influence of Personality Traits on Software Engineering and its Applications

Adrián Casado-Rivas
Universidad Carlos III de Madrid, Spain

Manuel Muñoz Archidona
Universidad Carlos III de Madrid, Spain

ABSTRACT

In Software Engineering, personality traits have helped to better understand the human factor. In this chapter, the authors give an overview of important personality traits theories that have influenced Software Engineering and have been widely adopted. The theories considered are Myers-Briggs Type Indicator, Big Five Personality Traits, and Belbin Roles. The influence of personality traits has provided remarkable benefits to Software Engineering, especially in the making of teams. For software project managers, it is useful to know what set of soft skills correlates to a specific team role so as to analyze how personality traits have contributed to high performance and cohesive software engineering teams. The study of software engineers' personality traits also helps to motivate team members. Creating teams that involve compatible individuals, each working on tasks that suit them, and having a motivated team improves team performance, productivity, and reduces project costs.

DOI: 10.4018/978-1-4666-5182-1.ch006

1. PERSONALITY TRAITS: WHAT THEY ARE AND THEIR RELATION TO SOFTWARE ENGINEERING

It can be said that the development of personality traits is, in part, not linked to peaceful years of recent modern history. Personality traits studies evolved from a branch of psychology known as personality psychology. Psychiatry set the tone for personality psychology until World War II (Udoudoh, 2012). Nowadays, it is possible to categorize studies of personality psychology in order to classify the theories that authors have developed over years of research. The theories can be categorized into biological, behavioral, psychodynamic, humanist and trait theories.

In the literature it is possible to find various definitions of personality. Some authors define personality as a person's moods, attitudes, opinions, motivations, and style of thinking, perceiving, speaking, and acting. It is part of what makes each individual distinct (Jordan, 2011). Other authors say that personality is the combination of all the attributes - behavioral, temperamental, emotional and mental - that characterize a unique individual (Lepri, Mana, Cappelletti, Pianesi, & Zancanaro, 2009). As can be observed, what both definitions have in common is that personality makes a person unique. Nevertheless, it is possible to find people that have some personality attributes in common but most likely, the degree to which they influence the personality of each person is quite different.

Personality psychology is the branch of psychology that studies personality based on the personality differences of individuals. As differences can affect distinct aspects of personality and can be studied from different points of view, personality psychology theories have been classified according to the categories summarized above. The most relevant category for the present research is trait theories.

The best definition that can be used to describe personality traits is the one given by the American Psychiatric Association in 1987. It explains that personality traits are enduring patterns of perceiving, relating to, and thinking about the environment and oneself that are exhibited in a wide range of social and personal contexts. Theories classified as trait theories in the personality psychology domain describe models designed to detect the predominant personality traits of a subject to match his or/her personality to a predefined pattern. Theories that are well-known in the field of personality traits are Myers-Briggs Type Indicator, also known as MBTI, and Big Five Personality Traits or BFPT models. These models are widespread and although they are not recent models, they are still used because they provide good results and are easy to apply in research and real life environments.

In identifying people's personality psychological profile, personality traits theories are not alone. Other contributions that come from psychology converge in what has been denominated soft skills. Researchers have established that people possess hard and soft skills. While hard skills are the technical requirements and knowledge an individual needs to carry out a task (Ahmed, Capretz, & Campbell, 2012), soft skills are non-technical skills referring to a wide range of abilities including flexibility, creativity, problem solving skills and listening skills (Jain & Gupt, 2012). Also, it can be said concisely that soft skills are skills that refer to the personality traits and attitudes that drive a person's behavior (Cloninger, Bayon, & Svrakic, 1998).

Emotional Intelligence is one of the most influential theories when dealing with soft skills. The Emotional Intelligence theory was developed by Daniel Goleman in 1995. Emotional Intelligence refers to the capacity to recognize our own feelings and those of others, to motivate ourselves, and to manage our emotions and its effect on us and our relationships. Goleman groups the skills into five components: self-awareness, self-regulation, motivation, empathy and social skill. One interesting point is that a person, helped by a coach, can improve his or her emotional intelligence skills. The process of designing and developing computer systems is, like any other facet in our lives, driven by emotions (Colomo-Palacios, Casado-Lumbreras, Soto-Acosta, & García-Crespo, 2011).

Personality traits, as mentioned earlier, fall under personality psychology, which is a branch of psychology, and are included together with Emotional Intelligence in the soft skills of a person. Also, important models that deal with personality traits, such as MBTI and BFPT, have been mentioned. So, how are personality traits related to software engineering organizations and why should they be taken into account? As personality makes a person unique, researchers have found that depending on the personality of an individual, some tasks are performed better than others. In an organization no task is personalized for each individual, but it is possible to do the opposite: assign a person to a task to which he or she is suited. Thanks to personality traits theories, it is feasible to relate the personality traits of a person to a pattern of personality. So here is the magic: organizations obtain the personality traits of a software engineer, then match the personality to a pattern and finally assign to the software engineer the task or the role that more correlates with his or her personality pattern. In this way, organizations are sure that a software engineer possesses the necessary soft skills that complement the hard skills required to perform an assigned task. This procedure is also used to assign a role in a team. So in general, it can be said that the procedure is used to entrust an employee with the correct work according to his personality traits.

The benefits of applying personality traits models in software engineering organizations are described later. As human aspects are recognized as one of the main problems associated with software development projects (Colomo-Palacios, Casado-Lumbreras, Soto-Acosta, García-Peñalvo, & Tovar-Caro, 2013), the use of techniques to assign tasks or roles to make teams is translated into improved productivity, reduction in delivery times and project costs and satisfaction of the stakeholders. Additionally, it helps to keep practitioners motivated.

2. TRADITIONAL PERSONALITY TRAITS THEORIES AND THEIR INFLUENCE ON SOFTWARE ENGINEERING

Increasingly software engineers are aware that one key factor to the success of a software development is people. In the field of software engineering, hard skills are highly developed and are continuously improving. Hard skills refer, among others, to programming or designing techniques. It is well known how to teach these skills to trainee software engineers and which is the best for each problem. Nevertheless, soft skills, those that define the personality traits of a software engineer, require more investigation to better understand them in software engineering projects and organizations. Sooner or later, major issues relevant to software engineering boil down to the people involved in software production and their personality traits (Capretz & Ahmed, 2010).

In this section, traditional personality traits theories are introduced and for each one, some research works are briefly analyzed in order to appreciate how these theories influence Software Engineering. Traditional personality traits theories have contributed to understanding soft skills better and to find out which are positive for software engineers both for the different tasks that they can perform, and the colleagues they can work well together with.

2.1 Myers-Briggs Type Indicator (MBTI)

The Myer-Briggs Type Indicator model is the result of a study carried out by Katherine Briggs and Isabel Briggs Myers, mother and daughter, into psychological types theories proposed by Carl Jung. MBTI claims that people always have a preference. Taking this into account, Myers and Briggs refined Jung's theories and established four dimensions where each one is a dichotomy of traits. The dimensions that they proposed are:

Extroversion (E) and Introversion (I): preference between extroversion and introversion is used to identify how a person is energized (Yilmaz & O'Connor, 2012). E's are talkative, outgoing, conversation initiators (Capretz & Ahmed, 2010), while introversion is a preference of individuals who are more interested in themselves (Yilmaz & O'Connor, 2012), which means being discreet and inclined to perform individual activities.

Sensing (S) and Intuition (N): people can perceive in two ways, by living in the present and focusing on what is real and actual (sensing), or looking towards the future and the possibilities (intuition) (Sach, Petre, & Sharp, 2010). S individuals dislike new problems unless prior experience teaches how to solve them. Conversely, N people enjoy solving new problems and dislike performing trivial tasks (Capretz & Ahmed, 2010).

Thinking (T) and Feeling (F): this dimension is about the way people make decisions. People can make decisions using logic and measuring the consequences of the decisions taken, T people, thinking, or being carried along by emotions and intuitions, F people.

Judging (J) and Perceiving (P): people can adopt two different lifestyles. Judging people prefer to know exactly what they are going to do, while perceiving people like to live from day to day. The adherence to deadlines, punctuality, and closure describe J personalities, while the terms open-ended, adaptable and spontaneous apply to P types (Capretz & Ahmed, 2010).

The Myers-Briggs Type Indicator model is categorized as a personality psychology trait theory. It has become a widely used and accessible tool to assess a person's personality type (Sach et al., 2010). To determine the preference of an individual for each dichotomy, the most typical technique is a questionnaire. Predefined questionnaires are available to everybody and additionally, people in charge of evaluating traits can adapt them to a specific domain. Also, researchers work on improving techniques to obtain the predominant preference of a person (Sach et al.,

2010). Instead of questionnaires, it is possible to use cards with a keyword on one side of the card and two different situations that can appear in software engineering jobs on the reverse. The situations that practitioners have to choose from must be related to software engineering to map their traits accordingly.

Research into techniques to obtain personality traits using MBTI can complement other works. One important area where MBTI is also used is in making teams. For the success of software engineering projects it is important to make cohesive teams, obtaining high performance from them. There are researches focused on identifying cohesive personalities (Karn, Syed-Abdullah, Cowling, & Holcombe, 2007), on building tools to make teams (Licorish, Philpott, & MacDonell, 2009), on minimizing effects when no cohesive personalities can be found (Lewis & Smith, 2008) and on identifying soft skills needed to play the software engineer roles to link them with their relative MBTI dimension (Capretz & Ahmed, 2010). Therefore, techniques based on MBTI to obtain the personality traits of software engineers are helpful for team managers to make cohesive teams. On the one hand, they can know practitioners' personalities and on the other, they can know which personalities are cohesive to make a high performance team.

2.2 Big Five Personality Traits (BFPT)

The Big Five Personality Traits, a model proposed by Goldberg in 1990, is categorized, like the Myers-Briggs Type Indicator, as a personality psychology trait theory. It is widely used to classify personality traits (Sodiya, Longe, Onashoga, Awodel, & Omosho, 2007). The model specifies five dimensions of personality, which were empirically established. These are:

Neuroticism: a broad dimension that includes traits like anxiety, moodiness, irritability or frustration (Acuña, Gómez, & Juristo, 2008). Generally defined, it is the tendency to experience unpleasant emotions relatively easily (Sodiya et al., 2007).

Extraversion: the tendency to seek simulation and enjoy the company of other people (Sodiya et al., 2007). It is associated with being sociable, assertive, talkative (Sodiya et al., 2007; Acuña et al., 2008), warm, energetic, adventurous, and enthusiastic (Sodiya et al., 2007).

Openness to experience: especially denotes inquisitiveness about new ideas, values, feelings and interests (Acuña et al., 2008). People who score high in this factor are less suitable for safety critical tasks (Sodiya et al., 2007).

Agreeableness: tendency to be compassionate towards others and not antagonistic (Sodiya et al., 2007). It is a trait that deals with showing altruistic concern and emotional support towards other people (Acuña et al., 2008) and its components include pleasant, tolerant, tactful, helpful, trusting, respectful, sympathetic and modest (Sodiya et al., 2007).

Conscientiousness: a trait of perseverant, scrupulous and responsible behavior (Acuña et al., 2008). Its components include self-disciplined, consultative, competent, orderly, dutiful and thorough (Sodiya et al., 2007).

The Big Five Personality Traits have been used in research into making teams and soft skills identification. Acuña et al. (2008) is an example of using BFPT for making teams. They observed how team personality affects software quality and individual team member satisfaction. The Big Five Personality Traits model is used to obtain the team personality, which is an average of the trait of each team member.

Another study (Rehman, Mahmood, Salleh, & Amin, 2012) focused on reviewing the required personality traits, identified in previous works, for each software engineering role. The references they take match software engineering roles to personality traits using the MBTI model. Nevertheless, as they found that BFPT, rather than MBTI, is highly accepted in software engineering, they used an equivalence table to map dimensions of MBTI to dimensions of BFPT. Next, they linked the personality traits of each kind of software engineering role to BFPT dimensions. The obtained results have been grouped by each analyzed role in Table 1.

Table 1. Soft skills grouped into BFPT dimensions and their relation to software engineering roles

BFPT DIMENSION	Soft Skills	System Analyst	System Designer	System Programmer	System Tester	System Maintenance
Neuroticism						
Extraversion	Ability to work independently			X		
Openness to experience	Communication skills	X				
	Innovative		X			
	Pay careful attention to details			X	X	X
Agreeableness	Interpersonal skills	X				
	Strong analytical and problem-solving skills		X	X		
Conscientiousness	Open and adaptable to changes					X
	Organization skills				X	

Source: Rehman et al., 2012

In Table 1 it can easily be observed to which BFPT dimension each soft skill belongs and roles where is required. The soft skills detected allow managers of software engineering organizations to identify the trait or traits required for each software engineering role. When one or more soft skills are marked for a role, it means that the trait identified with this soft skill is necessary for that role.

2.3 Belbin Roles

R. Meredith Belbin published his theory on roles in 1981 and later a review in 1993. Belbin roles are not to be seen as the functional role of a software engineer in a team, such as the designer or programmer, but rather how an individual fits into a team. The second approach is closer to personality traits and is in line with Belbin's belief that different types of people interact in different ways.

Belbin observed several software engineering teams in different countries in order to discover empirically what roles can be found on a software engineering team. Belbin had knowledge from previous researchers about roles on software engineering and Myers Briggs' Traits Indicator theory. Using the ideas from the theory and the experience gained from observing teams, he defined eight roles that are essential to a software engineering team. The eight roles are shown in Table 2 (Belbin, 1981, 1993).

Similar to the questionnaires used in MBTI to obtain personal traits, Belbin designed a questionnaire that is composed of seven sections, each having one question and eight answers to grade from one to ten. The idea is that each team member has to grade each answer depending on his or

Table 2. Description of Belbin roles

Name	Symbol	Behavioral Description	Typical Features	Positive Qualities	Allowable Weaknesses
Chairman	CH	Guiding and controlling leader, knows the members' abilities well	Calm, self-confident, controlled	A capacity for treating and welcoming all potential contributors on their merits and without prejudice. Strong sense of objectiveness	No more than ordinary in terms of intellect or creative ability
Shaper	SH	Demanding, coercing, confrontational leader, pushes for members to excel	Highly strung	Drive and a readiness to challenge inertia, ineffectiveness, complacency or self-deception	Prone to provocation, irritation and impatience
Plant	PL	Innovator and problem solver, the "idea" member	Individualistic, serious-minded, unorthodox	Genius, imagination, intellect, knowledge	Up in the clouds, inclined to disregard practical details or protocol
Resource Investigator	RI	Contact person for resources external to the team, brings resources into the team	Extroverted, enthusiastic, curious, communicative	A capacity for contacting people and exploring anything new. An ability to respond to challenge	Liable to lose interest once the initial fascination has passed
Monitor-Evaluator	ME	Analyzes, evaluates proposed solutions and choices	Sober, unemotional, prudent	Judgement, discretion, hard-headedness	Lacks inspiration or the ability to motivate others
Company Worker	CW	Implements agreed plans on	Conservative, dutiful, predictable	Organizing ability, practical common sense, hard-working, self-disciplined	Lack of flexibility, un-responsive to unproven ideas
Team Worker	TW	Facilitates team functions, mediates issues within the team	Socially oriented, mild, sensitive	Ability to respond to people and to situations, and to promote team spirit	Indecisive at moments of crisis
Completer-Finisher	CF	Focuses on details and meeting deadlines	Painstaking, orderly, conscientious, anxious	A capacity for follow-through, perfectionism	Tendency to worry about small things, reluctant to "let go"

Source: Belbin, 1981, 1993

her closeness to it. This questionnaire is called Self-Perception Inventory.

An interesting fact that Belbin found is that individuals who possess premium quality in one respect are often lacking in others, and that combining individuals with similar personality traits reduces performance (Licorish et al., 2009). Research carried out in software engineering where Belbin roles are involved are focused on improving team performance. For example, Belbin roles have been used to empirically demonstrate that teams with a lack of leadership roles are less efficient than those with leadership roles (Henry & Stevens, 1999). Also, researchers have conducted studies of how to make teams in which its members effectively work together (Rajendran, 2005).

Belbin roles offer a substantially different vision of personality traits when used in software engineering. While MBTI and BFPT are more focused on determining the personality traits recommended to play a functional role, Belbin roles concentrate on making a good team engine constructed with personality prototypes. Both visions can be considered as complementary to construct a team involving the right software engineers playing the right functional role in a well greased team.

3. APPLYING SOFT SKILLS IN SOFTWARE ENGINEERING PROJECTS: BENEFITS OBTAINED

Team composition is a complex activity because of the differences between individuals' personalities. The composition of teams to undertake software development is subject to the same complexity. Mismatches between personalities may compromise a project's effectiveness, whereas a team made up of compatible individuals can work extremely well as a group (Licorish et al., 2009).

So, to create a group for a software engineering project, it would be highly advantageous to take soft skills into account. Soft skills help to get a work team made up of a mixture of personalities,

which would it to obtain potential benefits in terms of maximizing productivity and improving the likelihood that delivery will occur in a timely and cost-effective manner to the satisfaction of all stakeholders.

Ahmed, Capretz, and Campbell (2012) indicate that soft skills are in demand in the software industry, but only to a limited extent. This is due to the fact that there is a lack of understanding of how to apply social skills to improve the ability and performance of employees. Correct understanding of social skills would also allow the classification of workers in a proper manner, that is, it can assist us to choose what kind of job is more suitable for an individual according to his or her social skills. What is more, if an individual is working in a job related to his soft skills, he or she will be more pleased with his or her work and, therefore, will be more motivated. That is why soft skills are also useful if we want to motivate a team.

In this section we are going to study the application of soft skills in software engineering projects. Not only are we going to talk about how we can apply soft skills when we create a team, but we are also going to describe how soft skills can be used to motivate the team members, and the benefits obtained

3.1 Team Composition

As mentioned before, we are going to describe how soft skills could be applied to get a good team composition. For this reason, some methods and examples are going to be given in this section.

In order to apply soft skills it is necessary to classify individuals according to their personalities. Thanks to the models explained previously, MBTI, BFPT and Belbin roles, we are able to ascertain individuals' personalities properly. However, before classifying the team members' personalities, we need to get information from them. Once the information is obtained, it will be used to design the team composition of a project according to personalities, kind of project, and job.

To start with, we are going to illustrate different ways to get information. As mentioned before, there are different techniques that can be used to get this information: questionnaires, tests, etc. This task may become really complex and tedious in large companies with a big staff. This is why some tools have been developed to make this task easier. Most of these tools are software applications whose aim is to facilitate the management of team composition designs.

For example, in (Feldt, Torkar, Angelis, & Samuelsson, 2008), the author used a Web-based questionnaire as a first step to studying human and personality factors and their effects on software engineering. The questionnaire contained two sections: the first was a personality test, the second a set of questions to probe the attitudes, working style and habits in areas related to software engineering. The alternative answers were mainly categorical, most with Likert scales. So, a complete personality test of an entire organization is carried out in a cheap and simple manner, simply by administrating the tests over the Web.

Although software tools are a good choice to save time and money, they are not mandatory. As an example, in (Sodiya et al., 2007), a well-structured questionnaire was administered to 112 software project team leaders in 19 software development organizations. Later, all the leaders gave personality and performance information on 489 software engineers.

Even though we can gather a lot of information thanks to questionnaires, they are not always the best choice. Questionnaires are good for projects in which we need to obtain personality factors of a great deal of people, but there are some risks which we should be aware of when using them. These risks are related to the fact that sometimes tests do not give us enough information or they are just not reliable. Even if the test is prepared carefully, individuals may try to trick us, or they may answer a question incorrectly if they do not understand it very well. In addition, sometimes test results are not as clear as one could desire. Consequently, if we want to get more accurate results and our resources and budget allow it, it would be a good idea to use a different way of gathering information, such as interviewing people.

Related to interviews, in (Downey & Ali Babar, 2008) the authors propose an instrument to investigate the skills needed by software architects. They believe that such an instrument will enable researchers and practitioners to gather skill-set information by considering the personal traits of the individuals, their behaviors, and the organization they work in together with the artifacts they use. This proposal uses the interview instrument to get information.

The interview proposed in this paper is divided into three sections:

1. **The person:** This section is based on identifying the skill-set needed to perform a given role within the software project. This information is obtained by asking: "what skills do you need in your role?" In addition, a checklist provides a list of skills used in similar surveys carried out in the information systems field. Then, the interviewees' behaviors are examined.

2. **The environment:** To determine the job that a person actually does, a general question is asked: "what do you do?" In this way we can check the duties than the worker is carrying out independently of his job title. Again, a checklist of functional areas is associated with the question so as to ensure that the person's answer can be compared to that of another interviewee.

3. **The behaviors:** This section is focused on determining the person's initial motivation to enter the software world and the way they went about building up the necessary qualifications and experience. To obtain this information, the interviewee is asked: "how did you acquire these skills?" What is more, there is a checklist to fill out about his or her academic history. It also takes into account outside interests.

Other examples of interviews can be found in (Dingsøyr & Røyrvik, 2001). The study in this paper is limited to issues related to skills management, and the authors chose interviews as a data source. They used semi-structured interviews with open-ended questions to allow the respondents to speak more freely on issues they thought were more important, and to let the interviewer develop the interviews. All the interviews were recorded and then transcribed. Then, the transcripts were sent back to the interviewees in case they wanted to make corrections or a comment.

As seen in the interview examples, the information seems to be more accurate and the individual is able to express his thoughts in a better and more understandable way. Besides, misunderstandings and false information is reduced using this method because the interviewee and his answers are more controlled thanks to the presence of an interviewer and the feedback with the interviewee.

Once all the data have been gathered, it is necessary, using models, to classify the individuals according to their personalities. Depending on the model chosen, we will get different personality characteristics of the individuals. Then we will just have to consider what job positions we want in our team and which of the personality characteristics are more suitable for each job position. To make things clear, we are going to use as examples some research papers where soft skills are applied in the design of team composition.

The first example is (Capretz, & Ahmed, 2010). The software life cycle is made of several stages. Each stage needs different kinds of workers or job positions. By mapping soft skills and psychological traits to the main stages of the software life cycle, the authors claim that people assigned according to personality types best suited to a particular stage increases the chances of a project's successful outcome. The MBTP model was used to measure and understand individual personality types. Once all the information has been gathered, and people have been classified according to the MBTP model, the next step is to map job requirements and soft skills to personality types.

For example, system analyst requirements are linked to soft skills such as communication and interpersonal skills. As a result, it is preferable to look for people possessing extrovert and feeling traits. Whereas, a software designer, who should be innovative and with strong analytical and problem-solving skills, requires a combination of intuition and thinking to thrive in design. There are more activities like programming, testing, and maintenance, each one with its own job and soft skills requirements, and personality types.

Last there is the fact that a broad range of personality types is beneficial to the software engineering teams because this diversity of skills and personality traits can solve the big number of problems associated with software development and maintenance (Horwitz, & Horwitz, 2007). In addition, the strongest teams have the most diverse perspectives. The use of personality types can help to achieve these benefits.

BFPT can be utilized instead of MBTI. In (Rehman, Mahmood, Salleh, & Amin, 2012) BFPT is used because, according to the authors, researchers are concerned about MBTI because of its relationships with Jung's theory, whereas BFPT is more acceptable since it broadly encompasses the personality dimension into five main dimensions. So, in this research, BFPT is utilized to categorize software engineers into software management engineers, requirement engineers, program designers, programmers, testers and evaluators. For example, related to the mapping of soft skills, we saw above that a systems analyst needs communication and interpersonal skills. Therefore, if we translate this to BFPT, we need a worker with high levels of openness to experience, and agreeableness. Alternatively, software tester requirements are more suitable for people who have organizational skills and also pay careful attention to details. Therefore, if we map these soft skills requirements to BFPT, a worker with high levels of conscientiousness and openness to experience is more suitable for this kind of job.

The third example is (Licorish et al., 2009). In this paper the authors state that it is necessary to consider the potential impact of personality incompatibilities on software development projects, specifically agile developments in which team cohesion is crucial. Such issues can affect negatively a software project and its goals. They therefore built a prototype software tool which assists software project managers by providing support for personality assessment. The assessment instruments provided to the manager will recommend particular role allocations and team structures according to the team members' personalities and the characteristics of the project. This paper describes the development and evaluation of a tool intended to assist software engineers and project managers in forming agile teams, utilizing information concerning members' personalities as input.

Licorish et al. (2009) used Belbin Roles model to assign roles to the workers, that is, to design the team composition according to the personality of the different individuals. Thanks to their work we can understand why different kinds of projects need different sets of role assignment. But not only there are different ways of composing a team, but also times that the project needs a reassignment may change, as we can see in agile projects where re-assignment may need to take place during the development process.

Another example of how to use personality types in agile software engineering teams can be found in (Karn, Syed-Abdullah, Cowling, & Holcombe, 2007), but, in this case, MBTI is used instead of Belbin Roles to classify the workers according to their personality types.

3.2 Team Motivation

Team motivation is one of the main applications of personal traits in Software Engineering projects. According to (Sharp, Baddoo, Beecham, & Robinson, 2009), motivation in software engineering is recognized as a key success factor for software projects. Software engineers have distinct personality profiles that affect their motivation. Therefore, due to the different characteristics of software engineers, it is a good idea to apply personal traits to team motivation. They state that what motivates software engineers the most to be more productive is identification with the task. That is, the task should have clear goals, be interesting to the individual, be clearly defined and linked to a wider set of activities. Therefore, a good team composition, where people work in their most suitable job position and their tasks are chosen according to their characteristics, will get better results than others.

Motivation is also related to job satisfaction. The more satisfied an individual is with his job; the more motivated he will be while he is working. This job satisfaction is linked to personality, team processes and task characteristics as stated in (Acuña et al., 2009). In order to study how personality can affect the satisfaction of a worker, they measured the personalities of team members based on the BFPT model. Finally, they also considered the characteristics of workers' tasks and team processes such as cohesion and conflict. After getting the results of the experiment, the authors concluded that the teams most satisfied with their job were those with higher scores on the personality factors of agreeableness and conscientiousness. Levels of satisfaction were higher when team members can decide how to develop and organize their work, that is, when the tasks are clear and interesting to the individual.

3.3 Benefits Obtained

According to (Licorish et al., 2009), incompatibilities among the members of a team in terms of their personalities may compromise team effectiveness. Similarly, a team made up of highly compatible individuals may function extremely well as group. Besides, the higher number and greater diversity of individuals involved in software projects may increase the conflicts related to personality incompatibilities, which may affect the project development very negatively. As said at the beginning of the chapter, an optimum mix of personality types in a software development team has the potential to maximize productivity and increase the likelihood of delivery occurring in a timely and cost-effective manner, to the satisfaction of all stakeholders.

Eventually, according to (Sharp et al., 2009), motivation in software engineering projects improves productivity and project delivery time, adherence to budgets, low absenteeism and improved project success. These factors are quite important from an organizational perspective.

4. FUTURE WORKS AND CONCLUSION

Predominant research in software engineering, that use traditional personality trait theories are, in some way, focused on obtaining the traits of software engineers, gathering the soft skills of software engineers and making cohesive software engineer teams. This knowledge can be used in combination with techniques for obtaining personality traits of software engineers to build or improve teams. As traditional techniques and personality traits have been used for a significant amount of years, studies may tend to update knowledge in this area. Nowadays we make software in a different way from how we made it one and two decades ago. Agile methodologies are becoming very popular in software organizations. We have to ask ourselves if the same personality traits obtained as desirable for the software engineering roles are the same needed for software engineers with similar or new roles considered in agile methodologies. Also, it is important to know if the personality traits that allow for a cohesive team, allow for making cohesive teams for agile methodologies projects. Advances in this line have been made. A sample of

related studies are (Licorish & McDonell, 2009), where a tool was developed to make teams for agile developments, and (Karn et al., 2007), where they studied how cohesiveness relates to personality type in XP agile methodology.

Another aspect that researches are focusing on is in the influence of cultural factors on different software engineering research fields. Interesting results may be obtained if we pay attention to how culture influences the soft skills of software engineers. Results may show whether culture interferes or not with the soft skills of software engineers and, consequently, with soft personality, required or recommended for a software engineering role. Results could tell us which cultures influence positively and negatively in the required or recommended soft skills of a functional or a team role.

REFERENCES

Acuña, S. T., Gómez, M., & Juristo, N. (2008). How do personality, team processes and task characteristics relate to job satisfaction and software quality? *Information and Software Technology*, *51*(3), 627–639. doi:10.1016/j.infsof.2008.08.006

Ahmed, F., Capretz, L. Z., & Campbell, P. (2012). Evaluating the demand for soft skills in software development. *IT Professional*, *14*(1), 44–49. doi:10.1109/MITP.2012.7 PMID:23397361

American Psychiatric Association. (1987). *Diagnostic and statistical manual of mental disorders-III-R*. Arlington, VA: American Psychiatric Association.

Belbin, R. M. (1981). *Management teams: Why they succeed of fail*. Oxford, UK: Butterworth Heinemann.

Belbin, R. M. (1993). *Team roles at work*. Oxford, UK: Butterworth Heinemann.

Capretz, L. Z., & Ahmed, F. (2010). Making sense of software development and personality types. *IT Professional*, *12*(1), 6–13. doi:10.1109/MITP.2010.33

Cloninger, C. R., Bayon, C., & Svrakic, D. M. (1998). Measurement of temperament and character in mood disorders: A model of fundamental states as personality types. *Journal of Affective Disorders*, *51*(1), 21–32. doi:10.1016/S0165-0327(98)00153-0 PMID:9879800

Colomo-Palacios, R., Casado-Lumbreras, C., Soto-Acosta, P., & García-Crespo, A. (2011). Using the affect grid to measure emotions in software requirements engineering. *Journal of Universal Computer Science*, *17*(9), 1281–1298.

Colomo-Palacios, R., Casado-Lumbreras, C., Soto-Acosta, P., García-Peñalvo, F. J., & Tovar-Caro, E. (2013). Competence gaps in software personnel: A multi-organizational study. *Computers in Human Behavior*, *29*(2), 456–461. doi:10.1016/j.chb.2012.04.021

Dingsøyr, T., & Røyrvik, E. (2001). Skills management as knowledge technology in a software consultancy company. In Lecture Notes in Computer Science -Advances in Learning Software Organizations, 2176, 96 –103.

Downey, J., & Ali Babar, M. (2008). On identifying the skills needed for software architects. In *Proceedings of the First International Workshop on Leadership and Management in Software Architecture* (pp. 1–6). New York, NY: ACM.

Feldt, R., Torkar, R., Angelis, L., & Samuelsson, M. (2008). Towards individualized software engineering: Empirical studies should collect psychometrics. In *Proceedings of the 2008 International Workshop on Cooperative and Human Aspects of Software Engineering* (pp. 49–52). New York, NY: ACM.

Goleman, D. (1998). *Working with emotional intelligence*. London: Bloomsbury Publishing.

Henry, S. M., & Stevens, K. T. (1999). Using Belbin's leadership role to improve team effectiveness: An empirical investigation. *Journal of Systems and Software*, *44*(3), 241–250. doi:10.1016/S0164-1212(98)10060-2

Horwitz, S. K., & Horwitz, I. B. (2007). The effects of team diversity on team outcomes: A meta-analytic review of team demography. *Journal of Management*, *33*(6), 987–1015. doi:10.1177/0149206307308587

Jain, V., & Gupta, S. (2012). The role of emotional intelligence in improving service quality & work effectiveness in service organizations with special reference to personality traits. *International Journal of Research in IT & Management*, *2*(1), 81–100.

Jordan, M. E. (2011). *Personality traits: Theory, testing and influences*. Nova Science Pub Incorporated.

Karn, J. S., Syed-Abdullah, S., Cowling, A. J., & Holcombe, M. (2007). A study into the effects of personality type and methodology on cohesion in software engineering teams. *Behaviour & Information Technology*, *26*(2), 99–111. doi:10.1080/01449290500102110

Lepri, B., Mana, N., Cappelletti, A., Pianesi, F., & Zancanaro, M. (2009). Modeling the personality of participants during group interactions. Lecture Notes in Computer Science –User Modeling, Adaptation, and Personalization, 5535, 114-125.

Licorish, S., Philpott, A., & MacDonell, S. G. (2009). Supporting agile team composition: A prototype tool for identifying personality (in) compatibilities. In *Proceedings of the 2009 International Conference on Software Engineering* (pp. 66-73). IEEE.

Rajendran, M. (2005). Analysis of team effectiveness in software development teams working on hardware and software environments using Belbin self-perception inventory. *Journal of Management Development*, *24*(8), 738–753. doi:10.1108/02621710510613753

Rehman, M., Mahmood, K. M., Salleh, R., & Amin, A. (2012). Mapping job requirements of software engineers to big five personality traits. In *Proceedings of the International Conference on Computer & [).* Kuala Lumpur, Malaysia: IEEE Computer Society.]. *Information Science*, *2*, 1115–1122.

Sach, R., Petre, M., & Sharp, H. (2010). The use of MBTI in software engineering. In *Proceedings of 22nd Annual Psychology of Programming Interest Group 2010*. Madrid: Universidad Carlos III de Madrid.

Sharp, H., Baddoo, N., Beecham, S., Hall, T., & Robinson, H. (2009). Models of motivation in software engineering. *Information and Software Technology*, *51*(1), 219–233. doi:10.1016/j.infsof.2008.05.009

Sodiya, A. S., Longe, H. O. D., Onashoga, S. A., Awodel, O., & Omosho, L. O. (2007). An improved assessment of personality traits in software engineering. *Interdisciplinary Journal of Information, Knowledge, and Management*, *2*, 163–177.

Udoudoh, S. J. (2012). Impacts of personality traits on career choice of information scientists in Federal University of Technology, Minna, Niger State, Nigeria. *International Journal of Library and Information Science*, *4*(4), 57–70.

Yilmaz, M., & O'Connor, R. V. (2012). Towards the understanding and classification of the personality traits of software development practitioners: Situational context cards approach. In *Proceeding of the Conference Software Engineering and Advanced Applications* (pp. 400–405). Dublin, Ireland: IEEE Computer Society.

KEY TERMS AND DEFINITIONS

Belbin Roles: Model that helps to identify what software engineering team role fits to a person according to his or her personality trait.

Big Five Personality Traits: Personality traits model that identifies the personality of a person by using five dimensions. Each dimension includes a group of soft skills.

Hard Skills: Technical attribute and knowledge required to complete a task.

Myers-Briggs Type Indicator: Personality traits model that identifies the personality of a person by using four dimensions. Each dimension includes a dichotomy of traits.

Personality Trait: Pattern that describes how a person perceives, relates to and thinks about the environment and oneself. The pattern identifies the personality of a person.

Soft Skills: Non-technical skills that drive a person's behavior.

Team Motivation: In Software Engineering, one of the key success factors of a project and where are applicable personality traits models.

Section 2
Software Process Improvement

Chapter 7
Preventing the Increasing Resistance to Change through a Multi-Model Environment as a Reference Model in Software Process Improvement

Mirna Muñoz
Centre of Mathematical Research, Mexico

Jezreel Mejia
Centre of Mathematical Research, Mexico

ABSTRACT

Organizational process improvement offers a key opportunity for organizations to become more efficient. As a consequence, the software industry, among others, is more interested in software process improvement. However, one of the most common issues identified when an organization tries to implement a software process improvement initiative is the difficulty that they face in selecting the reference model and its adaptation to the current organization scenario. Moreover, selecting the wrong reference model according to the way the organization works becomes a trigger to increase resistance to change. This chapter presents a methodology that allows the use of a multi-model environment as a reference model so that the organization can select best practices that best fit the way it works to implement software process improvement. The results of the implementation of an improvement using the methodology proposed are also presented.

DOI: 10.4018/978-1-4666-5182-1.ch007

1. INTRODUCTION

The software industry is becoming an important factor at the core of the economy around the world. Therefore, organizations need to create strategic advantages in order to be competitive (Soto-Acosta et al., 2010). In this context the implementation of software process improvement initiatives is an obvious and logical way to be competitive in the software industry (Gupta et al., 2004; Molina & Marsal, 2002; Turban et al., 2005).

It is well known that the quality of software products is largely dependent on the processes that are used to create them (Williams, 2008). Therefore, the software industry is more and more concerned about software process improvement (SPI) (Mishra & Mishra, 2009).

However, although many organizations are motivated to improve their software processes, very few know how to do so properly. One of the problems of introducing process improvement in organizations is the difficulty that an organization faces when adapting the selected process improvement model to their current scenario (Potter & Sakry, 2006; Morgan, 2007). As a result, most improvement efforts fail, stakeholders feel frustrated, organizations are more convinced than ever that they must continue doing their work as before and the resistance to change in software process improvement increases (Calvo-Manzano et al., 2012).

In this context, a key element that has been identified to achieve a successful software process improvement is the selection of what models or process areas make sense for each organization (Forrester & Wemyss, 2011). This is because even when so many models and standards are available in the market to support organizations in the implementation of process improvements, they are unable to completely address the critical challenges and needs of a software development organization (Conradi & Fuggetta, 2002). As a result two scenarios arise in organizations, resistance to the implementation of software process improvement increases and the process improvement does not obtain the expected results (CMMI working group, 2009).

The goal of this paper is to present a methodology that allows to establish a multi-model environment as a reference when implementing a software process improvement.

The multi-model environment will allow organizations to implement software process improvements with two features: 1) select those best practices that best fit the way the organization works and 2) implement multi-model processes, meaning processes based on the organization's business goals but containing best practices of more than one model or standard in order to get more efficient software processes.

Therefore, the organization is enabled with new processes that reflect the way it works so that users perceive the process as an evolution in working more efficiently.

This chapter is structured as follows: the research context section describes the importance of a multi-model environment in software process improvement; the background section introduces the methodology background; the methodology section includes the description of the methodology phases, the improvement proposed by the methodology, the three main characteristics of the methodology (how it involves stakeholders, the multi-model approach it proposes and the change management activities and knowledge management that it performs to reduce change resistance); the experiment section describes the experiment using the methodology; the results section analyses the results obtained by implementing the methodology, and finally, the conclusions of this research work are presented.

2. RESEARCH CONTEXT

Software Process Improvement (SPI) is a field of research and practice, arising out of the need to solve software development issues (Kautz et al., 2004). Therefore, SPI is the action taken by organizations to change processes, considering the business needs, so that their business goals are achieved in a more effective way (Burke & Howard, 2005). Unfortunately, investments in SPI do not often achieve the expected results (Munk-Madsen & Nielsen, 2011).

In this context, one of the problems that an organization faces when implementing software process improvements is that many organizations are under mandatory or market pressure to use more than one improvement model (Garcia, 2007).

According to Lisa Marino and John Morley (Marino & Morley, 2009), three out of five large organizations are already facing the challenges of using multiple models to meet organizational business goals.

Therefore, organizations worldwide are adopting several international standards and models, such as Capability Maturity Model Integration (CMMI) and ISO 15504 in an effort to improve the processes used to manage their businesses, increase customer satisfaction and maintain a competitive advantage with respect to their competitors (Andelfinger et al., 2009).

However, it is important to take into account that George Box's idea that "all models are wrong, but some are useful" is still valid for Mogilensky and Christian (Mogilensky, 2009), who mention that models are not mutually exclusive even when each one offers unique features and addresses specific problems.

The multi-model environment emerged as a result of a common effort of organizations to integrate international standards and models in order to achieve successful software process improvement (Kirwan et al., 2008; Mogilesnky, 2009).

According to Lawrence and Becker (Lawrence & Becker, 2009), the objectives of a multi-model environment are: reduce redundancy, improve integration, create synergy, leverage best practices and make frameworks transparent.

Besides, authors such as (Andelfinger et al., 2009; Siviy et al., 2008; Siviy et al., 2008b; Srivastava et al., 2009) have identified specific benefits and barriers to using a multi-model in software process improvement. The benefits and barriers are listed below.

On the one hand, according to (Siviy et al., 2008; Siviy et al., 2008b; Srivastava et al., 2009) the benefits of using a multi-model environment are:

- Enables the unification of a single improvement program.
- Focuses on the organization rather than the model.
- Reduces the overall cost in relation to the implementation of a model.
- Builds integrated and cooperative improvement organizations.
- Enables model transparency.
- Implements robust processes without duplication in an ever-evolving regulated world.

On the other hand, according to (Andelfinger et al., 2009; Siviy et al., 2008b; Srivastava et al., 2009) a common set of barriers using a multi-model environment are:

- Proliferation of models that an organization must consider.
- Differences in structure and terminology across standards and models.
- Difficulty in recognizing similarities among standards and models.
- Conflict among different improvement programs within the organization.
- Proliferation of the number and types of audits, assessments, and benchmarking that the organization must undergo while performing the functions needed to manage its business.

3. BACKGROUND

The methodology proposed in this research work is a methodology for a gradual and continuous software process improvement, focusing on minimizing change resistance called MIGME-RRC (its Spanish acronym) (Calvo-Manzano et al., 2012).

MIGME-RRC is a methodology that has been developed taking knowledge from different areas such as knowledge management; change management and multi-model environment. Table 1 shows the knowledge taken as a base for each topic. Besides, the definition of the methodology was supported and supervised by three experts in process improvement from the Polytechnic University of Madrid and one senior manager from everis consulting.

To focus on the methodology, it is important to highlight three key concepts used throughout its phases.

Best Practice: Can be a management or technical practice that has consistently been demonstrated to improve one or more aspects such as productivity, cost, schedule, and quality or user satisfaction (Withers, 2000). Due to its importance,

Table 1. Areas and knowledge base

Areas	Knowledge Taken as Base
Knowledge management activities	is a systematic approach that allows the capture, codification, use and operation of knowledge and experiences to develop better tools, methods and the ability to use them (Williams, 2008)
Change management	is a process of planning, organizing, coordinating and controlling internal and external components in order to ensure that process changes are implemented with the minimum deviation compared to approved plans and overall changes introduction goals (Burke & Howard, 2005)
Multi-model environment	involves all cultural aspects and the knowledge that advises the use of a best practices mix in each process from more than one model or standard to achieve the organization's business goals s (Muñoz et al., 2011)

relevant institutions such as the Software Engineering Institute (SEI), the Project Management Institute (PMI), the Institute of Electrical and Electronics Engineers (IEEE), and the International Organization for Standardization (ISO) have focused on the study of best practices and have developed best practices reference models and standards (Brotbeck et. al, 2002).

Examples of the most widespread models and standards developed are: Capability Maturity Model and Integration for Development (CMMI-DEV) (Chrissis et. al, 2007); Team Software Process (TSP) (Humphrey, 2006); Project Management Body of Knowledge (PMBOK) (IEEE Computer Society, 2004); ISO/IEC15504 Information Technology–Process Assessment (International Organization for Standardization, 2004) ; ISO 9001:2000-Quality Management System (AENOR, 2000) and ISO/IEC 12207-2008 (Standard Committee IEEE 2008, 2008).

Business Goals: is a statement or condition of the organization established by senior management to ensure the continued existence of the organization and enhance its profitability, market and other factors that should be achieved for the organization's success (Object Management Group, 2010). Therefore, when implementing a software process initiative, organizations should focus on their business goals as the main reference in order to achieve the expected success.

Examples of business goals that an organization could establish may include: reducing developed cycle time, reducing the number of change requests during an integration phase, increasing the number of errors found after the second phase; increasing customer satisfaction, reducing the number of projects with any kind of deviation (Chrissis et al., 2007).

Business Indicators: Are words that help organizations to be specific about the measures they need information on business goals (Goethert & Hayes, 2001).

Examples of business indicators are licenses renewal rates, number of customers, quoted lead times, number of common processes, reductions in product development or service cost, management rules, time to accommodate design changes, ration of development time to product life (Goethert & Hayes, 2001).

Therefore, supported by the knowledge taken from knowledge management, change management and multi-model environment and using best practices and business goals with their related business indicators, it is possible to implement a software process improvement focusing on the organization's needs. This allows the organization to know both the need for implementing improvements and where to address the improvement effort so that the business goals could be achieved more efficiently. Then, the resistance to change that increases with the traditional way of implementing improvements is reduced.

4. MIGME-RRC METHODOLOGY

The purpose of the MIGME-RRC methodology is to enable a gradual and continuous process improvement to prevent change resistance in organizations that are interested in implementing a software process improvement initiative.

Therefore, the methodology proposes a different way to implement a software process improvement in an organization as follows:

- First, it analyzes how the organization works by identifying its best practices.
- After, it establishes the performance of its best practices, comparing the business indicators achievement with the identified best practices.
- Then, it analyzes the best practices of different standards and models and selects those practices which best fit the way the organization works, and
- Finally, depending on the internal and external best practices dependences and their impact on achieving the business indicators, new processes and their implementation sequence are defined.

Taking the above into account, four phases of the methodology have been defined as follows:

1. **Identify internal best practices:** Analyzes which practices are really being carried out and produce better results in the organization. Through the identification of its best practices, it is possible to know the organizational current process. In other words, the way the organization works or the organizational work culture.

2. **Assess the organizational performance:** Assesses the organizational processes performance in a different way so that, instead of making a traditional assessment through questionnaires that are adapted from international models and standards, it proposes to make three analyses: coverage, achievement and priority.

3. **Analyze external best practices:** Establishes a multi-model environment that will be used as a reference to implement the improvement processes and allow the organization to choose those external practices that best fit the way it works and make its processes more efficient.

4. **Implement process improvements:** Implements multi-model processes through the integration of internal and external best practices. In this way, the improvement process and its implementation sequence could be established.

It is important to highlight that all the phases are focused on preventing resistance to change. Therefore, to prevent change resistance through the methodology, a set of activities was established. Table 2 shows the set of activities focused on preventing change resistance through the four phases of the methodology.

Due to its nature, the methodology has three main features that allow it to implement a software process improvement in the right way. The following sections describe each feature.

Table 2. Activities focused on preventing change resistance

Phase	Activities Focused on Preventing Change Resistance
Identify internal best practices	1. Present the software process improvement initiative to stakeholders. 2. Involve stakeholders in the extraction and validation of tacit knowledge. 3. Establish a communication plan. 4. Understand the organizational work culture. 5. Perform three activities: observe behaviour, describe and classify behaviour and identify related risk, focusing on senior management.
Assess the organizational performance	1. Show the process performance with the actual internal best practices. 2. Highlight the need to improve the processes to achieve the established business goals. 3. Perform three activities: observe behaviour: describe and classify behaviour and identify related risk, focusing on senior management
Analyze external best practices	1. Select the models and standards, taking into account the business goals and the organizational work culture. 2. Establish a multi-model environment as a reference model.
Implement process improvements	1. Analyze change resistance and risk factors. 2. Select external best practices depending on: impact and adoption difficulty. 3. Select early adopters staff for pilot project. 4. Establish efficient communication (top-down, bottom-up and lateral). 5. Perform continuous support: before, during and after the processes implementation. 6. Prepare the material for processes training taking into account the stakeholders identified, their influence in the change and the proper way to address them.

4.1 Involvement of Stakeholders

In recent years, authors such as O'Connor, Basri, Janh and Nielsen (O'Connor & Basri, 2012; Jahn & Nielsen, 2011) have identified the involvement of stakeholders in the software process improvement as a key aspect in order to achieve a successful software process improvement, so the implication or involvement of stakeholders as a dynamic team in a process improvement project achieves better results.

It is important to highlight that the first feature of the MIGME-RRC methodology is the involvement of stakeholders throughout all the phases. To understand how stakeholders are involved by through the methodology phases, it is important to focus on the main set of stakeholders it identifies.

Next, a list of the main set of stakeholders is presented:

- **Senior management:** Staff that have the power to take strategic decisions regarding business goals. In this set staff such as account managers, senior managers, improvement facilitator and partners are included.

- **Middle management:** Staff that have the power to take operational decisions toward achieving the business goals. This set includes staff such as project managers, quality managers or quality management group; and process improvement managers or process improvement group.

- **Process users:** Staff whose work is directly related to the use of software processes to do their work or staff whose jobs are not directly related to the use of the software process but need information or products produced as output of the performance of software process. In this set staff such as team leaders, team engineers (planning, quality, process, development and support) are included. Besides, depending on the type of process, the methodology allows to involve in an interactive way stakeholders who are interested in participating, providing important information on how the organization works.

Next, a brief description of stakeholders and how the methodology involves them follow:

1. **Identify internal best practices:** Middle management staff and process users have an important role because they are the source of the organization's tacit knowledge. Therefore, they are the only ones who should validate this. It is important to highlight that, in this first phase of the methodology, the validations of best practices are considered a key activity in order to formalize the organization's knowledge because organizational knowledge is formalized in processes using its best practices as a base. Furthermore, at the end of this phase the "documentation findings" are showed to senior management to make them aware of the real organizational software process and the actual gaps in process documentation so that they can appreciate a first methodology work product, which helps to increase their trust and confidence in the methodology.

2. **Assess the organizational performance:** Senior management staff has an important role in this phase of the methodology for three main reasons: first, they establish the business goals and set target values to them; second, they have access to the internal sensitive data such as projects performance audits data; and third, they are able to take a decision about what criteria must be established in order to prioritize the business goals to be achieved. Because this phase ends with communicating the process performance results obtained and where to address the improvement effort, middle management staff and process users are involved in order to increase the need to implement a software process improvement as a strategy toward achieving the business goals identified.

3. **Analyze external best practices:** Middle management staff and process users have an important role in this phase because they are the sources for selecting models and standards to be analyzed. These models and standards are selected depending on the analysis of the practices they perform and the models and standards they mentioned in the interviews. Also, senior management staff provide a list of those models and standards in which they are interested.

4. **Implement process improvements:** Senior management staff have an important role in this phase because they take decisions on the analysis and priority of the change resistance factor and risks associated with the process improvement implementation and the activities to be implemented in order to prevent them. So, middle management staff are involved in selecting those pilot projects which should use the new processes and give feedback that is very important to the success of the launching of the new processes and the success stories using these processes. Finally, at the end of this phase, the process users are involved in launching the improved processes because they have to use these processes and give their opinion of their experience with using them.

4.2 Multi-Model Approach

The second feature of the MIGME-RRC methodology is the use of a multi-model environment as a reference model in the selection of those practices that best fit the way the organization works. This multi-model environment allows to select "external best practices" regardless of the model of standard of precedence. The important thing here is to select the practices, focusing on three aspects: 1) their impact on the achievement of the business goal; 2) how they help to make processes more efficient and 3) how they fit the way the organization works.

The multi-model approach used in this methodology proposed to use the business indicators and the reference model as inputs to select and analyze the external models and standards. Once the business goals and the related business indicators have been prioritized, models and standards that best fit the way the organization works are selected. The selected reference model will enable to know what to do in order to achieve the high priority business goals. And the selected models and standards will provide the best practices, which will indicate "how to do it" in order to achieve the high priority business goals. Figure 1 shows the multi-model approach proposed.

4.3 Change Management Activities and Knowledge Management Implemented to Reduce Change Resistance

The MIGME-RRC methodology is focused on reducing change resistance; in order to achieve this all the methodology phases have been defined taking into account knowledge of change management and knowledge management. Specific

activities related to these have been defined in order to help the organization to reduce change resistance in the implementation of the methodology. Table 3 shows the change and knowledge management activities performed throughout the methodology phases.

5. METHODOLOGY EXPERIMENT

This section describes how the methodology was implemented in a real environment in order to implement a software improvement and analyzes the results. To achieve this, a case study was developed and performed at everis. This section includes the development of the case study carried out according to Runeson and Höst's (Runeson & Höst, 2009) definition of case study.

Figure 1. Multi-model approach proposed by MIGME-RRC

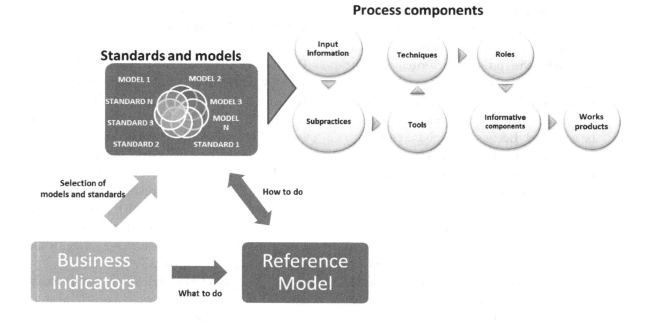

Table 3. Change and knowledge management activities of the MIGME-RRC methodology

Phases	Change Management Activities	Knowledge Management Activities
Identify internal best practices	• Stakeholders' involvement • Observe behavior, describe and classify behavior and identify risk, focusing on middle management and process users • Understand organizational work culture • Establish communication channels	• Extract knowledge • Understand and select knowledge • Characterize and structure knowledge
Assess organizational performance	• Communicate the results of process performance • Highlight the need to implement a process improvement to achieve the established business goals • Observe behavior, describe and classify behavior and identify risk, focusing on senior management	• Analyze, understand and select information related to process performance as historical data • Structure and store information selected as historical data in order to obtain process assets
Analyze external best practices	• Select just those models and standards accorded to the organizational work culture • Select the external practices to be candidates for the new processes accorded to the organizational work culture	• Analyze, select and structure external knowledge through analyzing external best practices • Structure the new knowledge so that it could be easily adopted within the organization
Implement process improvements	• Analyze change resistance factors and risk associated with process implementation and establish actions to prevent them • Analyze the difficulty level of adoption of external best practices • Select pilots projects, focusing on early adopters • Prepare the process presentation material based on the target staff (level of interest in change and influence) • Make the new processes available for all stakeholders • Establish adequate communication channels as follows: top-down (allow to transmit all relevant information to senior manager from middle management and process users); bottom-up (allow to collect feedback and experience using the new processes) and lateral (allows to reinforce commitment to achieve the work) • Allow the organization to adapt the new process at a pace of change they support.	• Analyze the impact of external best practices on the achievement of the business goals • Analyze the internal best practices and external best practices dependences • Define the new processes taking into account external best practices and internal best practices • Structure the new processes based on the organization's needs • Collect feedback of new processes and the experiences of their use and store them as process assets

5.1 Case Study Design and Planning

- **Case study goal:** The goal of the case study is to evaluate and validate the results of implementing an improvement using the MIGME-RRC methodology in an organization.
- **Analysis Unit:** The application scope focused on everis project management because it is an activity with a broad impact on its business goals.
- **Research questions:** To analyze the results of the methodology, three metrics were analyzed and defined as a result of the business goals set by everis' senior management. Figure 2 shows the analysis carried out to define the three metrics.

As Figure 2 shows, an analysis using the Goal-Question-Indicator-Metric methodology (GQ(I)M) was carried out. As a result, three measures were defined to measure the effects of the process improvement: *process use, process performance, and process acceptance.*

- **Data collection methods:** The methods used in this case study were: (1) *analysis of documentation:* analyzing everis' internal audits as source data allowed to evaluate the achievement of business goals; (2) *surveys:* performing surveys allows to get information from staff to analyze the use and usefulness of the processes.

Figure 2. Analysis of business goals

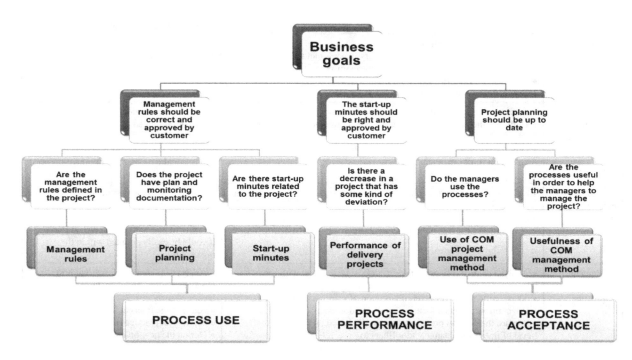

5.2 Collecting Data Approach

The approach for collecting data involved gathering information on change before, during and after the project management improvement. Therefore, data was collected as follows: before (year 2007-2008), during (year 2008-2009) and after (year 2009-2010).

The main sources of data for this case study are: 1) internal audits as source data. These audits allow to identify the noncompliance associated with key indicators, 2) delivery projects with any kind of deviation and 3) surveys carried out by managers involved in project planning at everis' offices around the world; these surveys were carried out through the organization intranet.

As Table 4 shows, the data were collected at three points: before, during and after the improvement.

5.3 The Case Study

This section shows the implementation of the MIGME-RRC methodology at everis in order to improve its project management processes to manage delivery projects.

First of all, it is important to highlight that everis is a multinational consulting firm with factories in Europe and the Latin American region. This company implements best practices to improve the performance of their factories in both Europe and Latin America. Since its creation in 1996, everis has grown steadily in both invoicing and staff in a continuous way. As the case study was carried out in 2009-2010, it is considered important to mention that there were more than 7,000 employees, turnover was over €400m, and over 1,000 projects were open every month within that period.

The scope of the case study was everis' project management because it is an activity with a wide impact on its business goals. Therefore, the project management processes had to be appropriate and

Table 4. Analyzed periods

Fiscal Year (FY)	Date	Period
FY'07	April 2007- March 2008	Before the software process improvement application
FY'08	April 2008- March 2009	During the software process improvement application
FY'09	April 2009- October 2010	After the software process improvement application

timely. The application scope had two aspects: (1) processes related to project management such as project planning and project monitoring and control and (2) staff, which focused on project management carried out by account managers who managed one or more projects; managers, projects managers and team leaders that have a significant role in the validation and feedback during the implementation of the methodology phases.

Finally, the implementation followed the activities proposed by the methodology phases. The activities carried out at everis are briefly described below.

5.3.1 Identify Internal Best Practices

The activities defined in the first phase of the methodology are shown in Figure 3.

The activities (see Figure 3) carried out to identify internal best practices were:

- Interviews with account managers who have managed successful projects (those projects that have a high performance and the best results).
- The information gathered from previous interviews was analyzed, selected and classified in order to establish the *practices diagrams* so that each interview had its own practices diagrams.
- The common practices of all the approved practices diagrams were mapped in order to get a common set of activities called *"generic practices."*
- The organization's process documentation was analyzed in order to identify the activities contained in it and which are carried out in the organization.
- As a final activity, the generic practices diagrams and the practices of the organization's processes documentation were mapped in order to identify its internal best practices.

Figure 3. Identify internal best practices activities

After performing all the activities, the internal best practices identified were approved at three levels: account managers, project managers, and project leaders. In addition feedback was obtained.

5.3.2 Assess the Organizational Performance

The activities defined in the second phase of the methodology are shown in Figure 4.

The activities (see Figure 4) carried out to analyze process performance were:

- The information on internal best practices, business goals, and business indicators were collected. Then, the identification was done using a bottom-up approach and goal diagrams. (Figure 5 shows the analysis carried out.) As Figure 5 shows, the correspondence among best practices, business indicators and business goals is analyzed in order to identify the business goals coverage.
- The information from internal audits carried out at everis every month to monitor their projects was analyzed. Planned target values and actual values of business indicators were identified and collected. Due to confidentiality agreements, only three

of the five indicators and their planned and actual targets values are shown: (1) Percentage of management rules, which are not correct and were not approved by the customer ($\leq 5\%$, 15.30%); (2) Project planning that are not up to date or feasible ($\leq 5\%$, 9.30%) and (3) Start-up minutes that are not correct and were not approved by the customers ($\leq 5\%$, 15.30%)

- A coverage matrix was created and filled in with the actual and planned values. Then it was analyzed to establish the achievement of software process with the actual best practices. Figure 6 shows the matrix with the three business goals included in this analysis.
- A chart to show the achievement of indicators was plotted. The type of chart selected was one often used in the organization to report results.
- A matrix of business indicators prioritization was done to assign weights according to the selected criteria established by senior management: (1) The management rules are a key document at everis because they define the project framework; 2) It is very important that the documentation of project planning be accurate and properly updated, and 3) Management rules are im-

Figure 4. Assess the organizational performance

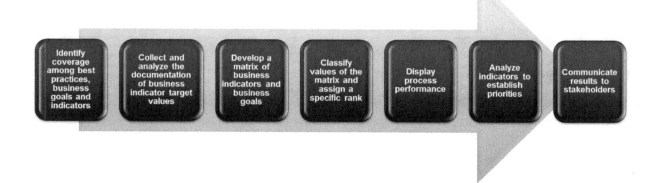

Figure 5. Goal diagram of the correspondence among best practices, business indicators and business goals

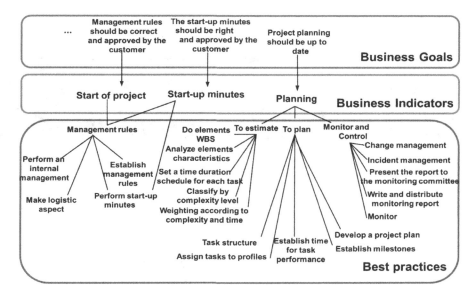

Figure 6. Coverage matrix

Indicator	Business Goals		
	Management should be correct and approved by the costumer	The project planning should be up to date and feasible	Start-up minutes should be correct and approved by the customer
Management rules	10,3%		
Project planning		4.3%	
Start-up minutes			10.3%

portant to establish project operative requirements and customer agreements. The indicators selected were: planning tools, management rules, and start-up minutes.

- As a final activity, minutes were taken to show stakeholders the results of the assessment approach.

5.3.3 Analyze External Best Practices

The activities defined in the third phase of the methodology are shown in Figure 7.

The activities (see Figure 7) carried out to analyze external best practices were:

Figure 7. Analyze external best practices

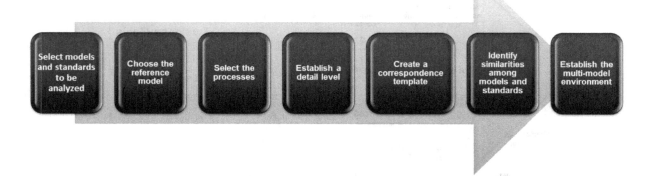

- After analyzing the models and standards mentioned by senior management, middle management and process users, CMMI-DEV v1.2, PMBOOK, PRINCE 2, TSPi, COBIT, ISO9001, and ISO/IEC 15504 were selected.
- CMMI-DEV v1.2 was chosen as the reference model because of its structure and the information it contains best fits the way the organization works.
- Most of the business indicators prioritized in phase 2 are related to project management. Therefore, project planning and project monitoring control processes were chosen because both are considered critical for successful project management.
- The level of mapping selected was "specific practice" level because it is found in all the models and standards analyzed and specific practices help organizations in their process improvement.
- It is important to mention that for this research, "template" is the table in which the process elements such as inputs, subpractices, tools and techniques, work products, and informative components are formalized. The template used in this research is called the "correspondence template." So, the template for each specific practice,

which includes inputs, subpractices, tools and techniques, work products, and informative components, was established.
- The similarities among standards and models were identified and the template for each specific practice was completed.
- As a final activity, each template that contained the best practices was refined to establish the multi-model environment.

5.3.4 Implement Process Improvements

The activities defined in the fourth phase of the MIGME-RRC methodology are shown in Figure 8.

The activities (see Figure 8) carried out to implement the improvements were:

- The main resistance and risk factors associated with the improvement were analyzed. On the one hand, the resistance factors identified were overload perception by staff, lack of line managers' commitment, and any type of reward related to the improvement effort. On the other hand, the risk factors identified were inadequate training material, lack of adequate communication, support, improvement monitoring and staff involvement.

Figure 8. Implement improvements

- The external best practices of a multi-model environment were selected.
- The internal and external best practices were integrated by making two analyses: (1) dependence analysis, and (2) impact analysis and adoption easiness. And because everis needed to develop a project management method as a part of its COrporate Methods methodology (COM), the new improved processes were grouped as the project management method they needed.
- It is important to highlight that the method obtained was validated and approved by everis' quality and methodology group. After the method was validated, pilot projects were performed.

To obtain better results and reduce risk, pilots were chosen, focusing on medium sized projects (no longer than 3 months); a staff of 4-7 people; budget around €100,000-150,000; and a project manager profile of junior project leader.

- As a final activity, the improvement processes were launched through everis' intranet, which allows the improvement process to be available for everis project managers.

5.4 Case Study Results

Control charts were used to analyze the data collected. A control chart is an analytic technique included in the group of techniques adapted from mathematical statistics used for activities such as characterizing process performance, understanding process variation, and predicting outcomes (Calvo-Manzano et al, 2012).

Control charts allow to understand the process variation and to identify whether processes remain "in control" or stable over time because the information provided is useful to obtain visual information of process changes (Chrissis et. al, 2007).

This chart shows simple statistics related to the process such as average and range:

- **Average:** The average of all of the data (iSixSigma, 2010) and
- **Range:** The difference between the Upper Control Limit, (UCL) and the Lower Control Limit, (LCL) (iSixSigma, 2010).

Using control charts as a tool to analyze the noncompliance of processes at everis in order to establish the improvement results has allowed: (1) to understand the process variation; (2) to analyze data for patterns; (3) to monitor the process performance during a specific period of time to detect change signals; and (4) to communicate how a process has been performed within a specific period of time.

To understand the collected data results better, they were classified into two groups: Group I includes data for FY'07 and FY'08; and group II includes data for FY'09.

Next, taking into account the metrics identified in the analysis (carried out and showed in Figure 2), the results obtained focus on process use, process performance and process acceptance at the corporate level.

5.4.1 Process Use

This metric analyzes management rules, project planning, and start-up minutes indicators at the corporate level. The aim is to analyze the degree of best practices performance. Figure 9 shows the results of the three main indicators: management rules; the project planning; and the start-up minutes.

As Figure 9 shows there has been an improvement in the use of those practices contained in the new processes. The improvement has allowed to achieve three key indicators related to the business goals established by senior management at

Figure 9. Three main indicator results

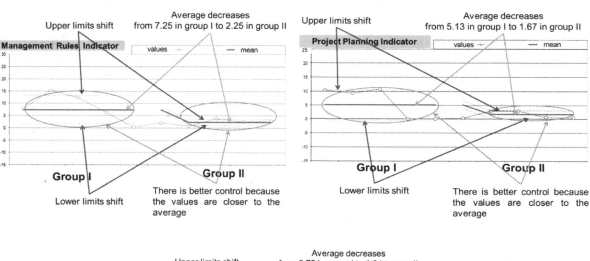

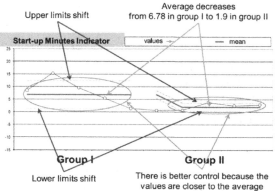

everis. All the control charts show a reduction in the average and in the upper and lower limits. All of them indicate better control because the values are closer to the average.

5.4.2 Process Performance

This metric analyzes the delivery projects at the corporate level so that it is possible to know if there was an improvement in process performance. Projects with any kind of deviation were analyzed. Figure 10 shows the control chart with the results obtained by analyzing those projects that hold any type of internal cost deviation (either in incurred hours, external costs or subcontracting), even when these deviations did not affect the schedules agreed on with the customer.

As Figure 10 shows there has been an improvement in delivery projects because the control chart indicates a reduction in the average and in the upper and lower limits. The reason for better control is because the values are closer to the average.

5.4.3 Process Acceptance

This metric analyzes both process use and process usefulness to know how well or not users accepted the new process. Therefore, it allows to know if there was a reduction in change resistance.

On the one hand, process use analysis was done by analyzing surveys carried out by managers who have used COM to manage their projects. Figure 11 shows the control chart with the results obtained by comparing the percentage of managers that use the COM project management method.

As Figure 11 shows, the control chart on the use of COM showed an improvement because there was a gradual and continuous increase in the average number of managers that use the COM method to manage their projects.

The process usefulness analysis was done by analyzing the percentage of managers who, based on their experience of using the method, described it as useful. It allows to know if the best practices contained in the new process had been appropriated. Figure 12 shows the control chart with the results obtained by comparing the percentage of managers that perceive COM as a useful method.

As Figure 12 shows, the control chart of COM usefulness shows improvement because there is a gradual and continuous increase in the number of managers that perceive the COM method as useful.

6. CONCLUSION

Organizations need to create strategic advantages in order to be competitive and software process improvement is one of the most widely used strategies to achieve this. However, not all software improvement implementations produce the expected result.

The MIGME-RRC methodology has been developed to help organizations to implement software process improvements successfully; it focuses on an organization's needs and uses the minimum process components known as best practices.

The proposed methodology allows to improve an organization's process in two ways. First, through the identification of its organizational best practices in order to capture, codify, operate, communicate and deploy the organizational key knowledge across the organization so that the processes will reflect the way the organization works.

Second, through the adoption of those external practices from the multi-model environment that best fit the way the organization works and make its processes more efficient so that the adoption of

Figure 10. Delivery projects that hold any type of deviation

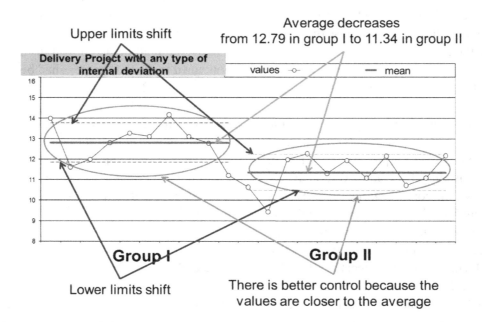

Figure 11. Results of the use of COM

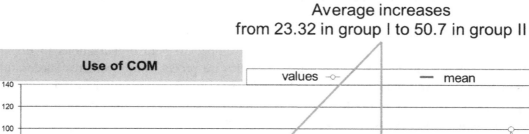

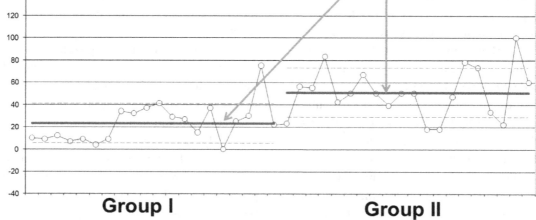

Figure 12. Results of the usefulness of COM

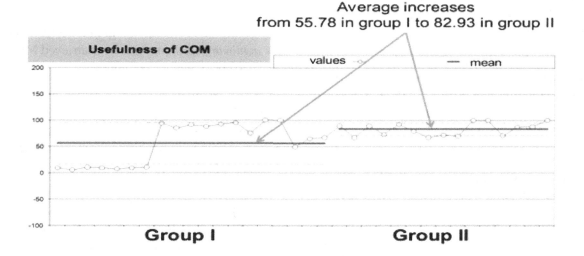

these new practices will be perceived by process users as an evolution in their work.

The above mentioned has been proved with the results obtained from implementing the methodology in a real organization. One important lesson learned was that it is possible to implement a smooth and continuous process improvement that focuses on organizations' business needs because it allows stakeholders to understand and assimilate change and to know the change benefit that is considered a key aspect in order to prevent change resistance. Moreover, in this way, it is possible to steer the perception of process improvement towards an improvement culture instead of focusing on certification as the main target of software process improvement.

REFERENCES

AENOR. (2000). Sistemas de gestión de calidad [Norma Española.]. *ISO, 9001*, 2000.

Andelfinger, U., Heijstek, A., & Kirwan, P. (2009). A unified process improvement approach for multi-model improvement environments. *NEWS AT SEI.* Software Engineering Institute (SEI). Retrieved December 2008 from http://www.sei.cmu.edu/library/abstracts/news-at-sei/feature1200604.cfm

Brotbeck, G., Miller, T., & Statz, J. (1999). A survey of current best practices and utilization of standards in the public and private sectors. *TeraQuest Metrics, Inc, 9*, 15-14. Retrieved November 2, 2012 from https://sw.thecsiac.com/topics/BestPractices/SurveyofBP.pdf

Burke, G. D., & Howard, W. H. (2005). Knowledge management and process improvement: A union of two disciplines. *CrossTalk. The Journal of Defense Software Engineering, 18*(6), 28.

Calvo-Manzano, J. A., Cuevas, G., Gómez, G., Mejia, J., Muñoz, M., & San Feliu, T. (2012). Methodology for process improvement through basic components and focusing on the resistance to change. *Journal of Software Evolution and Process, 24*(5), 511–523. doi:10.1002/smr.505

Chrissis, M. B., Konrad, M., & Shrum, S. (2007). CMMI second Ed. guidelines for process integration and product improvement. Reading, MA: Addison Wesley.

CMMI Working Group. (2009). The economics of CMMI®. *NDIA System Engineering Division, Software Engineering Institute, 1*, 9-21. Retrieved from http://www.sei.cmu.edu/library/assets/Economics%20of%20CMMI.pdf

Conradi, H., & Fuggetta, A. (2002). Improving software process improvement. *IEEE Software, 19*(4), 92–99. doi:10.1109/MS.2002.1020295

Forrester, E., & Wemyss, G. (2011). CMMI and other models and standards. *CMMI Version 1.3 and Beyond*. Retrieved December 2012, from http://www.sei.cmu.edu/

Garcia, S. (2007). Process improvement at the edges. *Software Engineering Institute (SEI) Library*. Carnegie Mellon University. Retrieved June 2009 from http://www.sei.cmu.edu/library/assets/20081218webinar.pdf

Goethert, W., & Hayes, W. (2001). *Experiences in implementing measurement programs* (CMU/SEI-2001-TN-026). Retrieved January 30, 2010, from http://www.sei.cmu.edu/library/abstracts/reports/01tn026.cfm

Gupta, J. N., Sharma, S. K., & Hsu, J. (2008). An overview of knowledge management. In M. Jennex (Ed.), *Knowledge management: Concepts, methodologies, tools, and applications*. Hershey, PA: Information Science Reference.

Humphrey, W. (2006). *Introduction to the team software process*. Reading, MA: Addison-Wesley.

IEEE Computer Society. (2004). IEEE guide adoption of PMI standard A guide to the project management body of knowledge. *IEEE Std 1490-2003 (Revision of IEEE Std 1490-1998)*. IEEE. doi: 10.1109/IEEESTD.2004.94565

International Organization for Standardization. (2004). *ISO/IEC 15504: 2004 information technology – Process assessment, part 1 to part 5*. Author. iSixSigma. (2010). *iSix sigma quality resources for achieving six sigma results*. Retrieved March 11, 2010 from www.isixsigma.com

Jahn, K., & Nielsen, P. A. (2011). A vertical approach to knowledge management: Codification and personalization in software processes. *International Journal of Human Capital and Information Technology Professionals, 2*(2), 26–36. doi:10.4018/jhcitp.2011040103

Kautz, K., Levine, L., Hefley, B., Johansen, J., Kristensen, C., & Nielsen, P. (2004). Networked technologies — The role of networks in the diffusion and adoption of software process improvement (SPI) approaches. *Networked Information Technologies, 138*, 203–211. doi:10.1007/1-4020-7862-5_13

Kirwan, P., Jeannie, S. M., Marino, L., & Morley, J. (2008). Improvement technology classification and composition in multi-model environments. *Software Engineering Institute (SEI)*. Carnegie Mellon University. Retrieved June 2008 from http://www.sei.cmu.edu/library/assets/3.pdf

Lawrence, J., & Becker, N. (2009). *Implementing insights and lesson learned using ISF for excellence*. Paper presented at SEPG 2009 North America Conference. San Jose, CA.

Marino, L., & Morley, J. (2009). Process improvement in a multi-model environment builds resilient organizations. *NEWS AT SEI*. Software Engineering Institute (SEI). Retrieved December 2009 from http://www.sei.cmu.edu/library/abstracts/news-at-sei/02feature200804.cfm

Mishra, D., & Mishra, A. (2009). A software process improvement in SMEs: A comparative view. *Computer Science and Information Systems, 6*(1), 111–140. doi:10.2298/CSIS0901111M

Mogilensky, J. (2009). *Pathological box-checking: The dark side of process improvement*. Paper presented at SEPG 2009 North America Conference. San Jose, CA.

Molina, J. L., & Marsal, M. (2002). Herramientas de gestión del conocimiento, gestión del cambio. In La gestión del conocimiento en las organizaciones (pp. 60-68, 87-94). Colección de Negocios, Empresa y Economía: Libros en red.

Morgan, P. (2007). Process improvement- Is it a lottery? *Methods & Tools, Practical Knowledge for the Software Developer. Tester and Project Manager, 15*(1), 3–12.

Munk-Madsen, A., & Nielsen, P. A. (2011). Success factors and motivators in SPI. *International Journal of Human Capital and Information Technology Professionals, 2*(4), 49–60. doi:10.4018/jhcitp.2011100105

Muñoz, M., Mejia, J., Calvo-Manzano, J. A., San Feliu, T., & Alor, G. (2011). Advantages of using a multi-model environment in software process improvement. In *Proceedings of the Electronics, Robotics and Automotive Mechanics Conference* (CERMA), (pp. 397-402). IEEE. DOI 10.1109/CERMA.2011.85

O'Connor, R., & Basri, S. (2012). The effect of team dynamics on software development process improvement. *International Journal of Human Capital and Information Technology Professionals, 3*(3), 13–26. doi:10.4018/jhcitp.2012070102

Object Management Group. (2010). *Business motivation model, v1.1*. OMG Document Number: formal/2010-05-01. Retrieved November 2012, from http//www.omg.org/spec/BMM/1.1/

Potter, N., & Sakry, M. (2006). Developing a plan. In *Making process improvement work* (pp. 1–49). Reading, MA: Addison-Wesley.

Runeson, P., & Höst, M. (2009). Guidelines for conducting and reporting case study research in software engineering. *Empirical Software Engineering Journal, 14*(2), 131–164. doi:10.1007/s10664-008-9102-8

Siviy, J., Kirwan, P., Marino, L., & Morley, J. (2008). The value of harmonization multiple improvement technologies: A process improvement professional's view. *Software Engineering Institute (SEI) library*. Carnegie Mellon University. Retrieved June 2008 from http://www.sei.cmu.edu/library/assets/whitepapers/multimodelExecutive_wp_harmonizationROI_032008_v1.pdf

Siviy, J., Kirwan, P., Morley, J., & Marino, L. (2008). Maximizing your process improvement ROI through harmonization. *Software Engineering Institute (SEI) Library*. Carnegie Mellon University. Retrieved June 2008 from http://www.sei.cmu.edu/library/assets/whitepapers/multimodelExecutive_wp_harmonization-ROI_032008_v1.pdf

Soto-Acosta, P., Martínez-Conesa, I., & Colomo-Palacios, R. (2010). An empirical analysis of the relationship between IT training sources and IT value. *Information Systems Management, 27*(3), 274–283. doi:10.1080/10580530.2010.493847

Srivastava, N., Singh, S., & Dokken, T. (2009). *Assorted chocolates & cookies in a multi-model box*. Paper presented at SEPG 2009 North America Conference. San Jose, CA.

Standard Comitee, I. E. E. E. (2008). *ISO/IEC/IEEE standard for systems and software engineering - Software life cycle processes (IEEE STD 12207-2008)*. IEEE.

Turban, E., Aronson, J. E., & Liang, T.-P. (2005). Knowledge management. In *Decision support systems and intelligent systems*. Uppers Saddle River, NJ: Prentice Hall.

Williams, T. (2008). How do organizations learn lessons from projects—And do they? *IEEE Transactions on Engineering Management, 55*(2), 248–266. doi:10.1109/TEM.2007.912920

Withers, D. H. (2000). Software engineering best practices applied to the modeling process. In *Proceedings of Simulation Conference* (pp. 432-439). Orlando, FL: Academic Press.

KEY TERMS AND DEFINITIONS

Best Practice: Can be a management or technical practice that has consistently been demonstrated to improve one or more aspects such as productivity, cost, schedule, and quality or user satisfaction.

Business Goals: Is a statement or condition of the organization established by senior management to ensure the continued existence of the organization and enhance its profitability, market and other factors that should be achieved for the organization's success.

Change Management: Is a process of planning, organizing, coordinating and controlling internal and external components in order to ensure that process changes are implemented with the minimum deviation compared to approved plans and overall changes introduction goals.

Knowledge Management: Is a systematic approach that allows the capture, codification, use and operation of knowledge and experiences to develop better tools, methods and the ability to use them.

Multi-Model Environment: Involves all cultural aspects and the knowledge that advises the use of a best practices mix in each process from more than one model or standard to achieve the organization's business goals.

Software Organizations: Organizations which main activity is the development and maintenance of software and related services such as training, documentation, and consulting.

Software Process Improvement: Is the action taken by organizations to change processes, considering the business needs, so that their business goals are achieved in a more effective way.

Resistance to Change: Is the action taken by individuals and groups when they perceive that a change that is occurring as a threat to them especially when they do not have understanding and assimilating the change or they do not know the change benefits.

Chapter 8
Some Key Topics to be Considered in Software Process Improvement

Gonzalo Cuevas
Universidad Politécnica de Madrid, Spain

Jose A. Calvo-Manzano
Universidad Politécnica de Madrid, Spain

Iván García
Universidad Tecnológica de la Mixteca, Mexico

ABSTRACT

This chapter summarizes a set of relevant aspects that may have a strong influence on the effectiveness of software process improvement and, as a consequence, on the competitiveness of software companies. Also included are the results obtained from a survey carried out in large companies on their processing needs in order to be more competitive. The organizational structures seen in different projects highlight the relevance of suitable processes as well as a culture of individual and organizational commitment. With this focus in mind, this chapter provides detailed information about teams, their construction and performance so that they can be effective in developing and implementing the processes. Finally, the chapter provides information about successful change management as well as advice on qualification of the workforce and technological tendencies, which is of key importance to achieve the objectives of competitiveness and process improvement.

1. INTRODUCTION

The capacity of organizations and their products, systems and services to compete, adapt and survive will depend more and more on software. With current products like those in the automobile, aviation or services sectors, software provides the competitive differentiation and the fast adaptability to competitive change. Software facilitates the fast adaptation of products and services to different market sectors to support multicultural global coordination of companies. In the following sections of this chapter, different key topics to be considered in the software process improvement are presented.

DOI: 10.4018/978-1-4666-5182-1.ch008

2. INDUSTRY NECESSITIES

Taking into account the answers provided by representatives of large software companies to the question "Identify necessities of process technologies from an industrial viewpoint as opposed to a researcher's viewpoint," we summarized a list of necessities as follows:

- Guidance on how to apply process improvement, with equal effectiveness, for a multi-faceted, highly integrated, heterogeneous environment (commercial systems, internally developed systems, hybrids). We need to ensure interoperability, quality, and scalability.
- Guidance on how to motivate key stakeholders to "do it right the first time."
- Quantification of quality, privacy, and security.
- Fusion of multiple models (CMMI, Sarbanes-Oxley, COBIT), all with the same people. How a simple checklist can provide guidance to people who ask "are you doing this, and that?"
- Guidance on how to incrementally enable the education/adoption of process improvement "on the fly." Heavyweight solutions are simply impractical.
- Guidance on processes management for multi-vendor projects based on commercial products as components. Expect that at least some of these will have "low maturity."
- How the established science of behavioral modification can be humanely applied to process improvement transformation.
- We have a well-established process improvement tradition in clinical care – How do we link the software process improvement disciplines to clinical care process improvement disciplines?
- How does a high maturity vendor work with a low maturity customer? Process models are needed not only for multi-site development, but also for working with customers at various levels of maturity. So, they need guidance to work together through coaching, counseling, or education.
- Can I, as a software provider, commit myself to a certain quantifiable level of improvement in productivity (e.g., 3-5% towards level 3)?
- When an organization grows rapidly, there is a great deal of churn from the people perspective. A good process works well with competent and good people. What are the links between competent people and process capability? Some companies have integrated People-CMM with CMMI to tie the competency management with process, but would like more guidance on this.
- Relationship management outsourcing, for example. The ends of the spectrum are at one extreme, where bodies are replaced with low-cost bodies, and at the other where the entire application is handled by an outside vendor.
- Looking at things that will be needed in the next 3, 5, and 10 years, we will need process technologies that cross through companies and cultures (including processes with different maturity). Where does process interface between the two?
- Relationships of partners.
- Statistical process control using process simulation. Simulating a social-economical system gives good indicators of what to change to reach certain goals.
- We would like to establish an overall design process. Some companies generally develop their products in product-line; moreover, they want to have an architect that handles product and process at same time.
- Reusable process components, interfaces, etc.

- Estimation. COCOMO is the decent estimation approach mostly used by companies, but this is only used for software. We need the same for systems. A kind of expert system. People are developing their own models.

- Why isn't there more automation? Some companies developed their own tools for peer reviews.

- Lack of definition for measures in systems engineering/integration is where the differentiation will occur in the future.

- Biggest problem in large projects - managing our partners.

- Different estimation procedures across different engineering disciplines.

- "Heavyweight" education and methods do not work; smaller increments are necessary.

- Have processes to provide increased emphasis on the relationship with partners and primes, similar to the current emphasis on subcontractors.

- Extend best practices for software estimation and productivity measures to the rest of engineering fields (systems, hardware, mechanical, etc.).

- Extend statistical process control techniques to engineering development.

- Develop processes for commercial Information Technologies (IT) organizations (e.g. insurance or financial IT groups) based on sound system engineering principles.

- Develop process architectural guidelines to support the "ilities" (e.g. extensibility, flexibility, adaptability, maintainability).

3. COMMITMENT PROCESS

This is a topic implicit in Requirements Management, Software Project Planning, and Project Monitoring and Control as described by Watts Humphrey. Commitment is the basis of CMMI Level 2, just as Level 2 is the foundation for continuously improving any process (Dymond, 1988).

A commitment is simply *"an agreement by one person to do something for another"* (Humphrey, 1989). In an organization, commitments are made and achieved by individuals, but these must also be supported by the organization and by a culture for making and achieving commitments. The support and culture is what the commitment process really means. This process relies on two principles:

1. An attitude for high commitment, and
2. An organizational practice for achieving both big and small commitments.

3.1 High Commitment Attitude

The software commitment process, as Watts Humphrey outlined in his 1989 book, can be illustrated by the pictogram shown in Figure 1 (Dymond, 1998).

The role of the senior manager is explicitly defined in the upper part of the figure. Concretely, the commitment for delivering to external customers is made by the senior manager based on:

- The successful completion of a process for formal review and concurrence, and

- The existence of a mechanism to ensure that reviews have been completed and the concurrence has been obtained. The lower half of the pictogram shows the activities that the senior manager has to perform in order to make an external commitment.

At the center of the software commitment process is a documented project plan than contains estimates of resources, effort, and cost and a reasonable schedule based on these estimates. The plan is the result of a determination that resources are or will be available, and that adequate technical and business inputs show that the com-

Figure 1. Commitment process. Based on Humphrey's "Managing the Software Process" (p. 71).

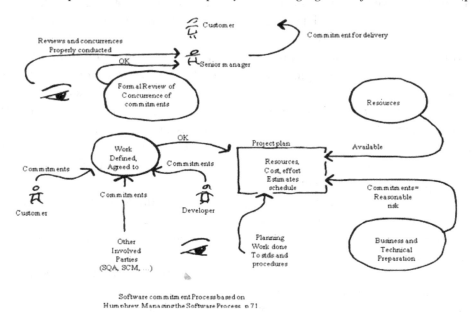

Software commitment Process based on
Humphrey, Managing the Software Process, p 71.

mitments agreed on for the project represent a reasonable risk.

In addition, the work tasks must be defined and agreed on by all parties. These are the developers, other groups (like SQA, SCM, and marketing) and the customer to whom the development group will deliver the product. All these commitments are agreed on before the project plan is issued. There is a review to make sure these planning activities have been carried out fairly and with appropriate negotiation; that is, according to standards and procedures.

3.2 An Organizational Practice for Achieving Both Big and Small Commitments

In addition, there must be a management system in place to make it happen. This system, shown in Figure 2, reconciles the two levels on schedules conflicts in a typical software organization: the project schedule, that responds to customer's project and timing, and the business schedule, which may be quarterly, semi-annual, or annual (Dymond, 1988). The management system must allow for reviews of project plans and progress at project milestones and also for review of operating plans, which most likely are out-of-phase with project milestones. The contentions for resources and delivery dates will naturally arise from the different phasing, so there would be a process to bring the conflicting issues to the surface and then resolve them. This implies another radical behavior change, because surfacing contentions must be the norm, whereas in many organizations the more typical behavior is to bury issues. So, the management system has to foster an environment where people are expected to raise issues and where there is a process—one that is free of blame—to resolve them.

4. MANAGING THE SOFTWARE PROCESSES

Developing software across borders is becoming an important competitive advantage in today's software industry. However, the increased globalization of software development creates software engineering challenges due to the impact of time zones, diversity of culture and communication, or distance. Thus, novel and effective techniques

Figure 2. Pictogram commitment process 2. Based on Humphrey's "Managing the Software Process" (sec. 5.2, pp. 72-80).

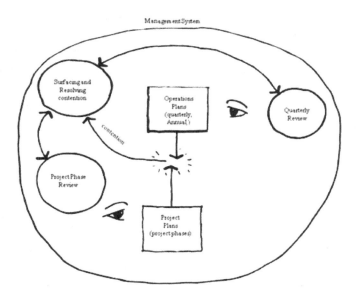

and behaviors to achieve intended productivity and quality targets are required (SEI, 2006).

4.1 Characterizing the Current State of the Practice

Today we have many small companies operating on only one site. Some of these companies operate collaboratively with others, possibly to enhance their capacity or to avail themselves of their specialist skill sets. These collaborations may involve several companies in one country or companies distributed across international borders, where the cost base or political considerations may be important drivers. Such collaborations tend to be managed through subcontractor relationships.

Many large companies may also be split across multiple sites, again either in one country or across several countries. In such circumstances, there may often be a greater tendency to have collaborative working arrangements without the notion of a subcontractor management structure. These projects may be considered more highly

"integrated" than is often achieved through a contractual relationship.

Where higher levels of integration have been successful, integration is, nevertheless, normally organized around development lifecycle stages.

4.2 Characterizing the Desired State of the Practice

In this state, small and large organizations live together in harmony and have culturally infused process awareness. There is a tendency for federations of SMEs (Small and Medium Enterprises) to grow in response to project needs. Even large organizations tend to manage themselves around a federated system. As the projects are completed, the federations are reduced in size. The need for process in this environment is unquestioned. In fact, process compliance is a mandatory requirement for entry into the 'register of suppliers'.

Continuous process improvement is a regular practice in organizations. Education, training and professional awareness support the above concepts. Integrated process standards, including other disciplines and business processes for different domains, are common. Emerging processes for systems engineering of global-scale complex adaptive systems are aligned with stakeholder values. The use of process simulations based on various parameters to reduce risks is common. Process is viewed as an enabler for cooperative working.

Not only do organizations evolve rapidly in this environment to meet business needs, but so too do their individual staff complements. Next, we present the description of the organizational structures considered. They are described in order of complexity and normally one must be controlled before moving on to the next.

4.3 Description of Organizational Structures

The organizations listed below represent progression from an organizational complexity perspective. Most development organizations would move through the three levels as a progression. The issues become more complicated as they progress through the levels.

It is reasonable to believe that good solutions are needed for one level before moving on to the following levels.

4.3.1 Level 1: Operating under Autonomous Control

The process objective of this level is to focus on projects with autonomous control to achieve predictable outcomes in terms of functionality, cost, schedule and quality attributes when developing, evolving and maintaining software. Autonomous control refers to situations where there is one decision authority; everybody works according to the same project process and joint organizational goals. However, it does not exclude distributed development, working across cultural boundaries or having different companies involved. The key issue is that one prime has the decision authority

and that anyone involved in the project uses the same project process instantiation. Some examples of this situation include:

- One company at one or several sites,
- Body shopping with requirement to use the same project process instantiation, and
- Several companies with one prime and they all use the same project process instantiation.

The motivation for operating projects with one decision authority and using the same project process instantiation comes from several sources.

1. Reduction of overhead for communication and interaction.
2. Ease of communications and enhanced ability to share process understanding, though in this environment there may be a lower motivation for process adoption.
3. Other motivations for this organizational structure include the ability to react more quickly to market demands and the ability to be close to particular clients.

4.3.2 Level Two: Managing through Centralized Cooperation

The process objective of this level is to focus on projects with one main decision authority, but using different project process instantiations. These projects are most likely decentralized, made up of a possible mix of mature and/or immature organizations, but having joint organizational goals.

Scenarios within this node could be large projects in one company with multiple development locations or multiple companies. The reasons for development in multiple locations are many, for example access to labor, cost-reduction, presence in a specific country or region, tax incentives to establish work based in economically disadvantaged parts of a country, or where there are pockets of expertise, for example in regions surrounding a university with a good reputation in certain fields. Even just finding enough people can cause companies to establish themselves at multiple locations or to resort to subcontracting other companies. Other reasons include having locations near major clients or near important suppliers.

The objective is to support companies by dividing projects into suitable parts that can be developed at different locations and then, as easily as possible, integrate them into a system. This is a challenge, and it will make more demands on a process than perhaps a single location operation. However, it has a better chance of succeeding where the processes and culture support mutual understanding.

4.3.3 Level Three: Agreeing under Federated Collaboration

The process objective of this level is to focus on projects with shared decision authority and project goals, but with different organizational goals and processes. To truly harness the possibilities for global development, the best companies around the globe must be involved. The objective must be to create strategic alliances with the best players to be competitive.

One scenario at this level is to make use of different expertise at different companies. For example, there may be a split between domain knowledge/expertise (provided by one partner) and systems and software engineering skills (provided by another). The objective could be to create virtual value-added networks by combining the expertise of different companies. In other words, several companies jointly develop a product, where there is an agreement about how to divide income from the sales.

These projects would most likely be decentralized and made up of a possible mix of mature and/or immature organizations. Furthermore, the objective is to create effective and efficient systems, developed independent of times zones, cultures and differences in other aspects, for example development processes.

5. TEAM BUILDING

5.1 Team Definition

A team is a collection of people who work closely together on tasks that are highly interdependent in order to achieve shared objectives. A team reports to a manager who manages the day-to-day activities.

A team is given considerable autonomy to manage and perform its work that a selected workforce within the team may perform (Scholtes, 1991).

Groups that call themselves teams usually have:

- A reason or purpose for working together.
- A need for each other's experience, ability, and a commitment to obtain a mutually held goal.
- A belief that working cooperatively will lead to more effective output than working alone.

The team's performance does not spontaneously improve. The team need to take periodic "time-outs" to assess how they are performing and to develop or improve team process skills. The team must be established by:

- Determining team tasks, knowledge needed, and skills.
- Assigning appropriate team members.
- Establishing governing processes and structure by
  - Developing a shared vision.
  - Establishing a team charter.
  - Defining roles and responsibilities.

- ○ Documenting operating processes and procedures.
- ○ Paying attention to multiple team collaboration, as necessary.

5.2 Introduction to the Drexler-Sibbet Team Performance Model

Figure 3 presents the Drexler-Sibbet model to build efficient teams. The following sections of the chapter provide a brief explanation of each stage (SEI, 2000).

5.2.1 Orientation Concerns

- **Purpose:**
  - ○ Does each of the team members know what the group is formed to do?
  - ○ Can members state the team's purpose clearly and with conviction?

- ○ Can members describe what first sparked the idea to create the team? Do they feel part of a larger process?
- **Personal Fit:**
  - ○ Can each member imagine and describe how their skills will contribute to the team's goals?
  - ○ Can each member see how his or her personal development will be furthered?
- **Membership:**
  - ○ Some individuals may wonder whether the other members of the team will accept them and whether they are qualified to contribute to the work.
  - ○ Feeling a sense of membership frees individuals to move on to the other stages of a team's life and their related concerns.

Figure 3. The Drexler-Sibbet Team Performance Model

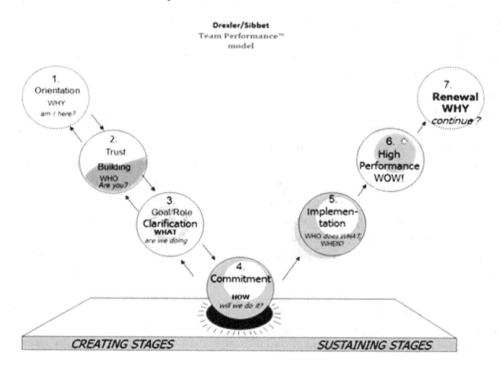

When the team is blocked, uncertainty and fear arise.

5.2.2 Building Trust

- **Mutual Regard:**
  - ○ Teams with mutual regard recognize that each member is important to the team and understand how diverse contributions make up the whole.
  - ○ If the team is highly interdependent and requires a high level of trust, then they need to build respect for individual talents and different points of view.
- **Forthrightness:**
  - ○ Trusting teams are willing to be open and explicit in dealing with each other. Are the team members sharing difficulties?
  - ○ All teams have underlying "second-level" concerns. Does the team work to bring them out into the open or avoid them?
  - ○ The team will require forthrightness in direct proportion to the level of interdependence and high performance they want to attain.
- **Spontaneous Interaction:**
  - ○ A sure sign that members have begun to trust each other is the bubbling conversation associated with free flowing information.
  - ○ Discussion topics allow everyone a chance to participate, build confidence, and help people overcome their fear of being judged.

When the team is blocked, the result is mistrust and caution.

5.2.3 Goal/Role Clarification Concerns

- **Explicit Assumptions:**
  - ○ Assumptions are explicit when they are explored openly in discussions and, better yet, recorded in writing.
- **Clear and Integrated Goals:**
  - ○ Focused teams are able to describe the specific goals and work products necessary for success.
- **Identified Roles:**
  - ○ Before moving to full commitment, the roles probably want to feel that the responsibilities they are being asked to assume are clear and match their skills.

When the team is blocked, the result is apathy, skepticism and irrelevant competition.

5.2.4 Commitment Concerns

- **Shared Vision:**
  - ○ Can members of the team easily and succinctly communicate their vision to the others?
- **Allocated Resources:**
  - ○ Resources usually seem limited in comparison to visions. Resource allocation will be seen as hard, constraining work, but fundamental to success.
  - ○ Resources are allocated when there is a budget, assignments, space and timetables to develop a project.
  - ○ Resources are not allocated when individuals have not been identified to back-fill the responsibilities that were given up to participate as a member of the improvement team.

When the team is blocked, the result is dependence.

5.2.5 Implementation Concerns

- **Clear Processes:**
  - Well-implemented teams have spent the time required to ensure that everyone understands the work processes in use.
  - The training needed to master new technologies and methodologies is scheduled.
- **Alignment:**
  - When a team is aligned, everyone is heading in the same direction. At deeper levels, it means personal values support the work goals.
- **Disciplined Execution:**
  - Well-implemented teams are willing and able to be accountable for deadlines and standards. People will fix problems as they occur instead of passing them on to others.

When the team is blocked, the result is conflict, nonalignment, and missed deadlines.

5.2.6 High Performance Concerns

- **Flexibility:**
  - High performance is marked by an ability to not only achieve goals but to change them if necessary.
  - Changing signals from the senior managers, middle managers, and others are challenges that serve as opportunities to fine-tune procedures and improve results.
- **Intuitive Communication:**
  - It is almost as though thinking and communicating function at a group level, rather than at the individual level. Obstacles and challenges become opportunities for higher performance.

- **Synergy:**
  - Synergy is experiencing a larger result than any single part suggests. In high performance teams, talents will mesh and leap beyond expected results.

When the team is blocked, the result is overload and disharmony.

5.2.7 Renewal Concerns

- **Recognition:**
  - Renewing teams take the time to recognize the achievements of its members.
- **Change Mastery:**
  - Excellent teams take the time to develop new-member orientation practices. If members change frequently, it is essential to learn how to bring them up to speed as quickly and painlessly as possible.
- **Staying Power:**
  - Taking time to learn lessons from whatever is done is a key to staying power. Team performance involves continual reflection and adjustment. As people move to new teams, learning inevitably carries over.
  - Staying power also involves knowing when to rest and take time off. (Workaholics are usually not high performers for long.)

When the team is blocked, the result is boredom and burnout.

5.3 The Team Charter

The team charter is a tool to help ensure a common understanding of issues on which the team have reached consensus. Some important components of a team charter are:

5.3.1 Clear Goals

The Process Group cannot reach its goals systematically if the goals are ambiguous or missing.

- The goals should be clear enough that the group can measure its progress towards them.
- The goals should also be consistent with the mission and vision of the organization.

5.3.2 Appropriate Membership

An effective group has a membership that is carefully selected according to defined criteria, which may include the following:

- Members must bring an appropriate mix of knowledge and skills to successfully complete the task.
- The group should be large enough to handle the task. But every additional member requires that the group spend additional time coordinating activities.
- The composition of the group must be stable enough so that the group can maintain its continuity of effort. Groups that are continually losing and replacing members spend much time orienting the new members and learning how to work together.

5.3.3 Clearly Defined Roles

- Without clear, agreed-upon roles, members can experience conflict and stress.
- Because groups are made up of individuals who fill interdependent roles, members must understand clearly what role each member plays and what behaviors people expect of each role.
- When roles are understood clearly and agreed upon, members can coordinate their actions more easily to complete their tasks.

5.3.4 Sufficient Time

A group needs enough time to complete its work. Specifically, a group needs two kinds of time:

- Performance time, and
- Process time.
    - During performance time, the group prepares and produces its products and services.
    - During process time, the group reflects on how it can improve its performance.
    - Process time enables the group to systematically learn from its experience in order to improve its overall effectiveness.

Typically, groups spend too little time on process, underestimating how process time can enhance the time spent on performance.

5.3.5 Shared Values and Beliefs

In a group with a strong culture, members take actions and make decisions that are consistent with the shared values and beliefs.

Group culture is the set of values and beliefs that members of a group share and that guide their behavior.

- Beliefs are assumptions about what is true (e.g., people are naturally motivated to do a good job).
- Values are assumptions about what is worthwhile or desirable (e.g., practicing what one preaches).

5.3.6 Group Norms

Norms are expectations about how people should or should not behave that all group members share.

5.4 Benefits of Teams

Some benefits provided by teams are:

- Identify and manage interdependencies and objectives.
- Contribute to efficiency of work.
- Facilitate structuring of workforce related processes and practices around workgroups and their objectives.
- Encourage workgroups to tailor processes and roles to achieve their objectives.
- Optimize interdependencies to contribute to efficiency in the organization.
- Lay the foundation for empowering workgroups and achieving higher levels of performance.

6. CHANGE MANAGEMENT: ROLES IN CHANGE AND PERSONALITY

Most teamwork involves change, and change is seldom easy. It is unlikely that anyone will successfully change an organization without first asking its people to change as well (Kasse, 2009).

People do not resist change – they resist being changed. Arbitrary mandates to change normally result in people digging in their heels regardless of whether they recognize the change is good for them or not. First of all, before attempting to change something, time should be taken to understand the background to the problem.

For improvement to take place, people will need to change the way they work. Management would be easy if it were not for the employees. Change is a physical event so it should not be surprising that many people have strong reactions to it. Change does not happen overnight. People must be given sufficient time to change, and supported along the way. Change is a pervasive aspect of our lives and a necessity for economic survival.

6.1 Concepts

Some considerations to bear in mind with respect to change are:

- Change is a process.
- Unexpected results sometimes unfold during change.
- In its raw and most destructive form, change is chaos, decay, and loss of control.
- Change may be a planned or unplanned response.
- It results in new functions and relationships among employees.
- Change creates opportunities and vulnerabilities.
- Change is an attitude - a state of mind.
- Change is a dynamic set of evolving events that must be managed as if it were a major part of one's business, because it is!

6.2 Principles of Process Change

Some principles to consider with respect to change are:

- Senior management must promote major changes.
- The focus is on fixing the process, not assigning blame.
- Current process must be understood first.
- Change is continuous.
- Improvement requires investment.
- Maintaining improvement requires periodic reinforcement.

6.3 Building Support for Change

As Figure 4 shows, changes are supported bottom-up in the organization and legitimacy is given top-down.

Figure 4. Support and legitimacy for change

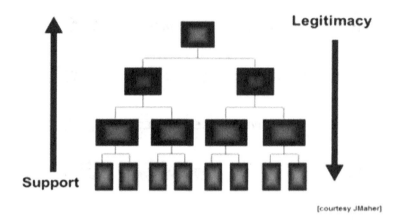

[courtesy JMaher]

6.4 Managing Complex Change Requirements

Five elements are considered for the success of change. Figure 5 shows what happens when all the elements are satisfied and when one of the elements fails.

6.5 A Simple Change Model

As Figure 6 shows, in this model the status quo is broken (unfreezing) and there is a transition state, where the situation goes through different transition states until it finally arrives to the new desired state (refreezing).

During transition, people need: Information, Freedom, Inclusion, Support, Safety, Skills, and Rewards.

6.6 The Response to Change

Commitment to change is a phased process. The sequence of steps before arriving to change is as follows:

- **Status Quo:** First answer in response to the change.

- **Stunned/Paralysis:** Do nothing.
- **Denial:** Through incapacity within the framework to integrate the new information of present reference.
- **Anger, Rage:** Expression of frustration and aggressive defensive behavior may be manifested.
- **Bargaining:** Attempt to delay or to limit the effects of the change.
- **Depression:** Resignation, feeling a victim through lack of energy to confront the situation.
- **Testing:** Partial acceptance or first attempts of execution that allow to regain control of the situation and self-confidence.
- **Acceptance:** Realistic implication to confront the change, while not totally conforming to the new situation. Agreed performance with the new demands.

Figure 7 shows these steps.

6.7 Roles in a Change

In general the roles in a change are:

Figure 5. Elements for successful change

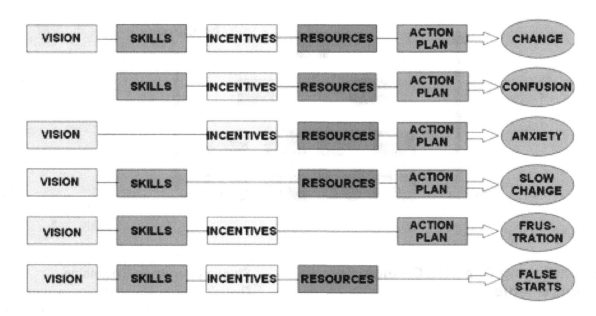

Figure 6. A sample change model

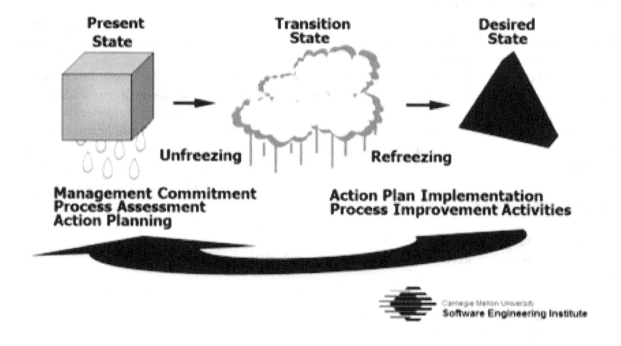

Figure 7. Response to change. Based on Humphrey's "Managing Technological Change," Carnegie Mellon University, Software Engineering Institute.

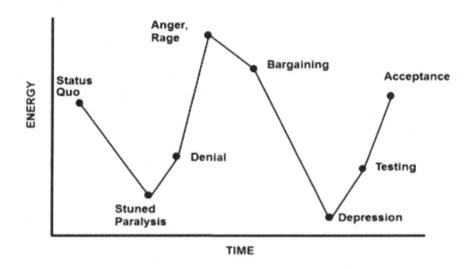

- **Sponsor:** Authorizes and advocates change effort.
- **Champion:** Influences the adoption of new technology.
- **Agent:** Authorized to implement the change.
- **Users:** Individuals who must use new processes.

6.8 Attributes of Successful Changes

Some attributes that contribute to the success of the change are:

- **Management sponsorship.**
- **The change is consistent with the organization's values, mission, and strategy.**
- **Buy-in:** Those affected by the change are involved in designing it.
- **Education and training:** Are provided in the new technology or process, and in managing change concepts.
- **Communication is stressed:** Formal meetings, briefings, reviews, informal discussions, memos, newsletters, handbooks, mentoring, training.
- **Reward systems are modified:** Desired behavior should be rewarded, undesired behavior should not be rewarded, and heroes should be process performers, not best firefighters.
- **The change is planned and budgeted**: Goals and plan should be realistic.
- **Long-term commitment:** Worthwhile changes usually take a long time to implement; maintaining the change requires investment, and maintenance is cheaper than a series of "crash" programs.
- **Champions:** Advocates for the change are necessary, and they should be cultivated and encouraged.
- **Walk your talk:** A process change is weakened every time it is waived for "business" or "organizational" or "personal" reasons, and those sponsoring change should be prepared to use the same processes, if applicable.

6.9 Personality Profile Model Based on Myers-Briggs

The strength of a team depends on the value the team places on the differences of the individual team members. The Myers Briggs personality types based on Carl Jung's preferences are: Where do I focus my attention? (**E**xtraversion-**I**ntroversion), How do I gather data? (**S**ensing-i**N**tuition), How do I make decisions? (**T**hinking-**F**eeling) and, How do I prefer to deal with the world? (**J**udging-**P**erceiving).

Personality is determined by the code of four letters. For example ENFJ (**E**xtroversion, i**N**tuition, **F**eeling and **J**udging).

6.10 The Importance of Getting the Right Mix

The change effort roles are: Inventors, Entrepreneurs, Integrators, Experts, Managers, and Sponsors. Planned change relies on getting the right people with the right attributes into the right roles at the right time.

6.11 Summary

Some conclusions with respect to change are:

- Change is harder than one thinks
  - It takes longer and costs more.
  - People resist.
  - Most organizations are very complex systems.
- Successful process changes are possible with appropriate planning and management, and assigning the right people.

7. SOME IDEAS ON THE QUALIFICATION OF THE WORKFORCE

Forty years ago people thought that technology would reduce the necessity of highly qualified workers, leaving great segments of the population without employment. The opposite has happened. In fact, the demand for highly qualified workers exceeds the offer (Humphrey, 1997).

Organizations are now competing in two markets: a market for their products and services, and another for the necessary talent to produce or execute these products. The success of the organization in the market is determined by its success in the talent market.

The increased demand for skilled personnel is still unabated, but what does appear to have hampered it is having a workforce with the right skills and abilities.

The capacity to compete is related directly to the capacity to attract, develop, motivate, organize and hold on to people with the talent required to achieve strategic business targets.

7.1 Some Terms

Some terms to be considered for the qualification of the workforce are:

- **Competence:** Is "demonstrated ability to apply knowledge, skills and attitudes to achieve observable results."
- **Skill**: Is the "ability to carry out managerial or technical tasks." Managerial and technical skills are components of competences and specify some core abilities that form a competence.
- **Knowledge:** Represents the "set of know-what" (e.g. programming languages, design tools...) and can be described by operational descriptions.
- **Attitude**: Means in this context the "cognitive and relational capacity" (e.g. analysis capacity, synthesis capacity, flexibility, pragmatism, etc.). If skills and knowledge are the components, attitudes are the glue which keeps them together.
- **Process abilities**: Are the capacity to perform individual skills in the sequencing or method used in the organization.

- **Knowledge + Skills + Process abilities = Workforce Competency.**
- **Culture**: Culture represents the way of life of a group of people. It is a complex system of socially transmitted behavioral patterns, ideas, norms, symbols, and values that human beings acquire to become members of a society. Culture is learned, shared, and is essential to human life and is found universally throughout the world.

7.2 Building Process Capability Requires Developing Capable People

In order to build a capable workforce, organizations must develop managers that take responsibility and authority for managing, developing, and motivating the individuals who are under their direction.

Today, organizations are largely dependent on high technology to develop, build, and maintain their products and services. This has created a dependence on a workforce with specialized knowledge and skills.

As mentioned earlier, organizations are now competing in two markets, one for their products and services and the other for the talent required to produce or perform them. Success in the former is determined by success in the latter. The ability to compete is directly related to the ability to attract, develop, motivate, organize, and retain the talented people needed to accomplish strategic business objectives.

Attracting and retaining talented people is the key for any organization's success. Every organization needs to continually improve its ability to attract, develop, motivate, organize, and retain the workforce needed to accomplish its strategic business objectives. The People Capability Maturity Model is a framework that successfully addresses strategic workforce issues. This framework is a guide to help organizations achieve the following:

- Attract, develop, organize, motivate, and retain the workforce required to build their products and deliver their services.
- Align workforce development with strategic business or mission goals.
- Establish an integrated system of workforce practices that is aligned with current and future business objectives.
- Characterize the maturity of workforce practices.
- Guide a program of continuous workforce development.
- Set priorities for improvement actions.
- Integrate workforce development with process improvement.
- Become an employer of choice after describing the rationale and evolution.

CMM Software has been used by software organizations around the world to guide significant improvements in its ability to improve productivity and quality, reduce costs and time to market, and increase customer satisfaction. Based on the best current practices in fields such as human resources, knowledge management, and organizational development, People CMM guides organizations in improving their processes for managing and developing their workforce. People CMM helps organizations to characterize the maturity of their workforce practices, establish a program of continuous workforce development, set priorities for improvement actions, integrate workforce development with process improvement, and establish a culture of excellence (Curtis, Hefley, & Miller, 2009).

The primary objective of People CMM is to improve the capability of an organization's workforce that develop and maintain products and services.

The human side of the equation, essential to sustaining high maturity, is better dealt with and institutionalized using People CMM.

It is only when competent personnel use an able process that performance of predictable process can be guaranteed.

People CMM is designed for application to practices that contribute directly to the workforce's capability and performance of an organization.

People CMM, describes practices for the following:

- Improving individual capability.
- Developing effective work groups and organizational culture.
- Motivating, managing, and quantifying performance.
- Shaping the workforce to meet current and future organizational needs.

Capability is defined as the level of knowledge, skills, and process abilities available within each workforce competency of the organization to build its products or deliver its services. People CMM presents a competence framework. People competencies must constantly evolve.

7.3 Eight Properties of High Maturity Work Cultures

The eight properties of high maturity work cultures that have been identified are based on a ten-year organizational infrastructure project built using a multimodel deployment approach (Curtis, 2011).

These eight properties are:

1. Reinforced sponsorship, commitment with investors to build competencies, and to keep the state of the practice current and fresh.
2. Leadership focus on nurturing an integrated process and competency development framework.
3. Improvement focus at multiple levels: individual, team, competencies and organizational level.

4. Strong performance management focus that is sensitive to problem recognition and problem solving.
5. Competency-based career opportunities that foster retention of competencies.
6. Creating an empowered work culture that constantly works to improve process capability and performance.
7. Positive role models that facilitate and guide in the inculcation of the right behaviors and values.
8. A high trust work environment that promotes loyalty, fair play and a sense of belonging.

7.4 Nine Process Areas from People CMM to Sustain High Process Maturity

While all of the 22 process areas of the People CMM are useful, the nine 'essential' process areas, if one is looking for factors required to sustain High Process Maturity, are:

1. Competency Analysis.
2. Competency Development.
3. Competency Based Assets.
4. Competency Integration.
5. Quantitative Performance Management.
6. Organizational Capability Management.
7. Mentoring.
8. Continuous Capability Improvement.
9. Continuous Workforce Innovation.

7.5 Why Process, Technology, People, and Culture?

To implement enduring process improvement activities in organizations, the elements in Table 1 are necessary:

7.6 Conclusion

- One of the requirements for sustaining a predictable process is for execution out-

Table 1. Essential elements in process improvement activities

Process	The ability to manage and control the complex development, delivery, and maintenance process and the process used to manage and develop the workforce.
Technology	The ability to monitor changes in technology and deploy it to make the work efficient.
People	A workforce (people) that have the appropriate knowledge, skills, and process abilities (competencies) to adapt to rapid changes in a technological environment.
Culture	An organizational culture that supports a rapidly changing and potentially volatile market and is in alignment with policies, business or mission objectives, and strategies.

comes to be repeatable and permanent within acceptable limits of variation.

- It is known today that such possibilities occur if, and only if, competencies are internalized, maybe within competency communities.
- Performance improvement must be the real focus if process predictability is to be established – process + competency improvement.
- While the organization may provide conditions and opportunities for improvement, performance improvement is impossible if individuals do not exploit opportunities.
- Organizations that are able to sustain high process maturity ensure
  - Annual appraisals of both the development process and the competency framework.
  - Exploitation and alignment benefits from both opportunistic and proactive improvements within a multi-model improvement program.
  - Nine process areas of the People CMM are particularly helpful in ensuring that the high process maturity is sustained.
  - It is known where unexplored opportunities lie. Unless thought is given to improving those factors explored in People CMM, sustaining a high process maturity is difficult.

- Process predictability is possible if, and only if, both process capability and workforce capability are improved.

8. THE IT PROFESSION

From 2013, IT professionals will assume roles oriented to business. Medium and large companies will reduce IT staff by 30%. Technical aptitude alone will not be sufficient for IT professionals.

With a versatile staff, the suppliers of services and businesses can increase their budgets more that they could with specialists. Professionals with ample vision, deep knowledge of the process and competences oriented to the sector will help companies to incorporate multiple innovations and perspectives in IT processes, products and services. New castes of IT professionals are foreseen. They have:

- Technical aptitude.
- Local knowledge.
- Knowledge of the processes of the sector.
- Leadership capacity.

Successful professionals will identify themselves not by their occupation but by:

- Sector.
- Process and,

- Programs of change in which they participate. (For example: I helped to design an Internet sales process that increased revenue by 20%).

8.1 Rise of the Versatile

Independently of the current works, the areas of expertise, knowledge and abilities will change. Some of these will be reinforced, others divided, others redistributed and others eliminated.

8.2 Forces That Lead Change in the IT Profession

- **Global source:** Enabled by the global high-speed networks and led by companies that look for great IT capabilities, knowledge and service bases, the global source will become a standard of the company's portfolio and will make many professionals compete against their peers in other geographic markets.
- **Automation of IT:** Most of the outstanding development of software, tests, remote control of systems, operations centers, technical support, storage and work in network will be transformed.
- **The consumption of IT:** Through technologies, such as personal equipment, online services, or mobile telephones, IT will be demystified and tolerance will be reduced not only for complicated systems and applications, but also for the departments and personnel required to work with them.
- **Restructuring of business:** Mergers, acquisitions, disinvestments, consolidations, dismissals, outsourcing, financial engineering, bankruptcies, will challenge the professional positioning of IT and the weakness of employee commitment.

Before this happens, employees will analyze the situation to identify opportunities or the imminent end. This will be the moment to consider whether they want to remain in pure technology or to redirect their efforts to new expert dominions and develop practical experience in industry, market segments and fundamental business processes that will be useful for them in those dominions. The last decade has represented the era of the specialists; this one will mark that of versatility.

8.3 Futures Dominions of Experts in IT

The current field of IT will be subdivided into four dominions:

- **Infrastructure of technology and services:**
  - Opportunities in this dominion, the base of the profession, will grow in services, hardware and software sales (high growth in developing economies and low in client companies).
  - Design of networks will remain strong at all sites.
- **Design and management of the information:**
  - Business intelligence, online services, work improvement initiatives, search and recovery of information (practices), and collaboration, will grow for clients, integrating systems and consultant companies.
  - Linguistic skills, knowledge of business and culture, and knowledge management will be fertile fields.
- **Design and management of the process:**
  - Professionals will observe the process opportunities from three angles:
    - Competitive business processes.

- Processes automation design.
- Operative processes.

The first will be applied to companies, the second to software salesmen, and the third to outsourcing salesmen.

- **Management of sources and relations:**
  - Far from the traditional expertise that IT professionals pursue, the relations and management of sources will gain new ground, demanding competence in the management of intangibles and in the management of peers distributed geographically with different results and cultures.

9. SOME FUTURE TRENDS AND IMPLICATIONS FOR SYSTEMS AND SOFTWARE ENGINEERING PROCESSES

The eight relatively surprise-free trends for Systems and Software Engineering Processes are (Boehm, 2005):

- **The increasing integration of software and systems engineering:**
  - Recent process guidelines and standards, such as the Integrated Capability Maturity Model (CMMI) (CMMI Product Team, 2010), ISO/IEC 12207 for software engineering (ISO/IEC, 2008), and ISO/IEC 15288 for systems engineering (ISO/IEC, 2002) emphasize the need to integrate systems and software engineering processes, along with hardware engineering processes and human engineering processes.
- **An increased emphasis on users and end value:**
  - The "Future of IT" indicates that usability and total ownership cost-benefits, including user inefficiency and ineffectiveness costs, are becoming IT user organizations' top priorities.
  - A recurring user-organization's desire is to have technology that adapts to people rather than the other way round.
- **Increasing SIS criticality and need for dependability:**
  - The IT industry spends the bulk of its resources, both financial and human, on rapidly bringing products to market.
  - Several of the Computerworld "Future of IT" panelists in (Albert & Brownsword, 2009) indicated increasing customer pressure for higher quality and vendor warranties.
- **Increasingly rapid change:**
  - Rapid change also increases the priority of development speed vs. cost in capitalizing on market windows.
  - Hewlett Packard is a good example of successful software process improvement toward rapid change. Some companies are taking initiatives to reduce product line software development times from 48 to 12 months.
  - When added to the trend toward emergent systems requirements, the pace of change places a high priority on systems and software engineering process agility and investments in continuous learning for both people and organizations.
- **Increasing SIS globalization and need for interoperability:**
  - The global connectivity provided by the Internet allows major economies of scale and network economies that drive both an organization's product and process strategies.

- On balance, "Future of IT" panelists felt that global collaboration would be commonplace in the future.
- A standards-based infrastructure is essential for effective global collaboration.

- **Increasingly complex systems of systems:**
  - New frameworks and support packages are making it possible for organizations to reinvent themselves around transformational, network-centric systems of systems. These are necessarily Software-Intensive Systems of Systems (SISOS), and have tremendous opportunities for success and equally tremendous risks of failure.

- **Increasing needs for COTS, reuse, and legacy SIS integration:**
  - Although infrastructure software developers will continue to spend most of their time programming, most application software developers are spending more and more of their time assessing, tailoring, and integrating commercial-off-the-shelf (COTS) products. COTS hardware products are also becoming more pervasive, although they are generally easier to assess and integrate

- **Computational plenty:**
  - Assuming that Moore's Law holds, another 20 years of doubling computing element performance every 18 months will lead to a performance improvement factor of $2^{20}/1.5 = 2^{13.33} = 10,000$ by 2025. Similar factors will apply to the size and power consumption of the competing elements.
  - This computational plenty will spawn new types of platforms (smart dust, smart paint, smart materials, nanotechnology, micro electrical-mechanical systems: MEMS), and new types

of applications (sensor networks, conformable or adaptive materials, human prosthetics).

The two "wild card" trends are:

- **Increasing software autonomy:** "Autonomy" covers technology advancements that use computational plenty to enable computers and software to autonomously evaluate situations and determine best-possible courses of action. Examples include:
  - Cooperative intelligent agents that assess situations, analyze trends, and cooperatively negotiate to determine best available courses of action.
  - Autonomic software, that uses adaptive control techniques to reconfigure itself to cope with changing situations.
  - Machine learning techniques that construct and test alternative situation models and converge on versions of models that will best guide system behavior.
  - Extensions of robots at conventional-to-nanotechnology scales empowered with autonomy capabilities such as the above.

- **Combinations of biology and computing:** Combinations of biology and computing include:
  - Biology-based computing that uses biological or molecular phenomena to solve computational problems beyond the reach of silicon-based technology.

Computing-based enhancement of human physical or mental capabilities, perhaps embedded in or attached to human bodies or serving as alternate robotic hosts for human bodies.

ACKNOWLEDGMENT

This work is sponsored by everis Foundation and Universidad Politécnica de Madrid through the Software Process Improvement Research Chair for Spain and Latin American Region.

REFERENCES

Albert, C., & Brownsword, L. (2009). *Evolutionary process for integrating COTS-based systems (EPIC): An overview (CMU/SEI-20030TR-009)*. Pittsburgh, PA: Software Engineering Institute, Carnegie Mellon University.

Boehm, B. (2005). *The future of software and systems engineering processes* (Technical Report USC-CSE-TR-507). Los Angeles, CA: University of Southern California.

CMMI Product Team. (2010). *CMMI for development (CMMI-DEV, v1.3) (CMU/SEI-2010-TR-033)*. Pittsburgh, PA: Software Engineering Institute, Carnegie Mellon University.

Curtis, B. (2011). Disputation of misinterpreted principles underlying the process maturity framework. Paper presented as keynote at the SEPG 2011 Europe. Dublin, Ireland.

Curtis, B., Hefley, B., & Miller, S. (2009). People capability maturity model (P-CMM), version 2.0 (2nd ed.) (CMU/SEI-2009-TR-003). Pittsburgh, PA: Software Engineering Institute, Carnegie Mellon University.

Dymond, K. M. (1988). *A guide to the CMMI: Understanding the capability maturity model for software*. Annapolis, MD: Process Transition International, Inc.

Humphrey, W. S. (1989). *Managing the software process*. Reading, MA: Addison-Wesley Publishing Company.

Humphrey, W. S. (1997). *Managing technical people*. Boston, MA: Addison-Wesley.

International Standardization Organization / International Electrotechnical Commission. (2002). *ISO/IEC 15288: 2002, information technology – Life cycle management – System life cycle processes*. Geneva, Switzerland: ISO/IEC.

International Standardization Organization / International Electrotechnical Commission. (2008). *ISO/IEC 12207: 2008, systems and software engineering – Software life cycle processes*. Geneva, Switzerland: ISO/IEC.

Kasse, T. (2009). Change management toolkit. Paper presented as Conference Session at the SEPG 2009 North America. Los Angeles, CA.

Scholtes, P. R. (1991). *El manual del equipo*. Madison, WI: Joiner Associates, Inc.

Software Engineering Institute. (2000). *Mastering process improvement course: Introduction to the Drexler-Sibbet team performance model*. Pittsburgh, PA: Software Engineering Institute, Carnegie Mellon University.

Software Engineering Institute. (2006). *A process research framework – The international process research consortium*. Pittsburgh, PA: Software Engineering Institute, Carnegie Mellon University.

KEY TERMS AND DEFINITIONS

Change Management: Judicious use of means to effect a change, or a proposed change, on a product of service.

Commitment: A pact that is freely assumed, visible, and expected to be kept by all parties involved.

Competency: An underlying characteristic of an individual that is causally related to effective and/or superior performance, as determined by measurable, objective criteria, in a job or situation.

Knowledge: The information and understanding that someone must have to perform a task successfully. Knowledge provides the basis for performing a skill.

Mentoring: The process of transferring the lessons of greater experience in a workforce competency to improve the capability of other individuals or workgroups.

Reward: Special recognition outside of the compensation system for accomplishments of significant value to the organization. Usually consists of variable amounts of money, stock, or other considerations provided to individuals or groups at appropriate times without any prior agreement as to conditions of receipt. Rewards are distinguished from recognition in that rewards typically involve financial considerations.

Role: A defined set of work tasks, dependencies, and responsibilities that can be assigned to an individual as a work package. A role describes a collection of tasks that constitute one component of a process, and would normally be performed by an individual.

Skills: The behaviors that an individual must be able to perform in order to accomplish committed work. Skills may involve behaviors that directly accomplish the task or that provide the support of, or coordination with, others involved in accomplishing tasks.

Workgroup Team: A collection of people who work closely together on tasks that are highly interdependent to achieve shared objectives and who exercise a level of autonomy in managing their activities in pursuit of those objectives.

Chapter 9
Managing Tacit Knowledge to Improve Software Processes

Alberto Heredia
Carlos III University of Madrid, Spain

Javier García-Guzmán
Carlos III University of Madrid, Spain

Fuensanta Medina-Domínguez
Carlos III University of Madrid, Spain

Arturo Mora-Soto
Carlos III University of Madrid, Spain

ABSTRACT

In general, software process improvement entails significant benefits such as increased software product quality, decreased time and development cost, and decreased risks. To obtain these, organizations must apply knowledge management because the identification of new knowledge is considered key to success when improving software processes. Existing knowledge is, however, difficult to find, and when found, it is often difficult to reuse in practice. This is due to the fact that a considerable part of the knowledge that is useful for executing software processes is tacit and not all of it can be captured and made explicit. The purpose of this chapter is to present a framework for software process improvement based on the enrichment of organizational knowledge by means of the acquisition of tacit knowledge from individuals working in different teams and environments. The framework includes the specification of roles, processes, and tools, and is based on a process asset library and the introduction of configuration and change management mechanisms.

DOI: 10.4018/978-1-4666-5182-1.ch009

1. INTRODUCTION

In recent years, software has become indispensable to society. However, Software Engineering is a discipline that still does not seem to have reached maturity. Seeing software development as a process has significantly helped to identify the different dimensions of software development and the problems to be addressed to establish effective practices. Researchers and practitioners focus on the study and improvement of the process by which software is developed because of the direct correlation between the process quality and software quality development (Humphrey, 1989).

Since the early 90s, Software Process Improvement (SPI) has tried to meet the challenges of improving quality and efficiency in software engineering practices, facilitating the identification and implementation of changes in management activities and software development (Allison & Merali, 2007).

SPI projects usually begin with an assessment of the practices currently implemented in the organization, identifying bottlenecks, problems or opportunities to prioritize potential improvements in the existing software development process. The long-term goal in SPI is to implement and institutionalize in the organization the improved practices of software development, i.e., create new knowledge at the organizational level. This knowledge will be acquired individually by the participants of the process and subsequently extended to the organizational level to be applied in new projects.

In general, the SPI provides significant benefits including:

- Improved quality of software products (Allison & Merali, 2007).
- Reduced costs (Niazi, Wilson, & Zowghi, 2006).
- Reduced risks (Dybå, Kitchenham, & Jørgensen, 2005).
- A positive ROI (Capell, 2004).

- Increase in customer satisfaction (Mathiassen, Ngwenyama, & Aaen, 2005).
- Improvement in morale, responsibility and communication in teamwork (Capell, 2004).
- A higher rate of project success (Capell, 2004).

2. KNOWLEDGE MANAGEMENT IN SPI

In the mid-90s, organizations began to consider seriously the possibility of managing their knowledge since this can be registered not only in documents or repositories, but also in organizational processes, practices, routines and rules. This movement was called Knowledge Management.

Knowledge Management (KM) can be defined as the discipline that studies the creation, preservation, application and reuse of knowledge available in an organization, its goal being the creation of shared knowledge among all users (Alavi & Leidner, 2001). KM simplifies the process of sharing, distributing, creating, capturing and understanding knowledge of an organization.

To improve the software development process and get the benefits mentioned above, organizations must apply the principles of KM to manage their knowledge (Dingsøyr et al., 2009). Thus, KM becomes an essential part of the efforts in SPI as the identification of new knowledge is considered a key to success in improving processes.

2.1 Knowledge Lifecycle

Knowledge assets are not static resources; they change their form according to a life cycle. The philosopher Michael Polanyi was the first to propose a distinction between two types of knowledge, tacit and explicit, although this distinction was applied in the field of business and knowledge management by Ikujiro Nonaka.

Tacit knowledge is highly personal, hard to formalize and communicate, intuitive and derived from experience and beliefs. Explicit knowledge, however, is formal and systematic, and can be expressed unambiguously through texts, drawings, databases, etc. (Assimakopoulos & Yan, 2006).

The theory of knowledge creation proposed by Nonaka suggests that knowledge alternates between tacit and explicit forms, so tacit knowledge can lead to the creation of explicit knowledge and vice versa. This knowledge conversion occurs in four processes –socialization, externalization, combination and internalization–, known as the "SECI model" (Nonaka, von Krogh, & Voelpel, 2006).

2.2 Knowledge Repositories

Knowledge repositories are usually one of the basic structures in any knowledge management system. These repositories store artifacts so that knowledge can be easily recovered and reused in order to generate higher quality products (Gupta, Jingyue, Conradi, Rønneberg, & Landre, 2009) and to improve organizational performance (Maier, 2007).

Focusing on software engineering organizations, this type of repository that can manage organizational knowledge is known as a Process Asset Library (PAL). A PAL is an organized, well-indexed, searchable repository of process assets that is easily accessible by anyone who needs process guidance information, examples, data, templates or other process support materials (Garcia, 2004).

In software organizations, a PAL can be used as a key element of the infrastructure that is necessary to support the learning and dissemination of effective practices among software engineers within the organization, increasing their skills and abilities. A PAL not only contains knowledge about how to perform the processes, but also lessons learned from previous projects in order to improve the processes. The software development projects can improve their performance –in terms of cost, quality and planning– by reusing lessons learned in previous projects (Basili & Seaman, 2002) stored in a PAL.

2.3 Enriching Organizational Knowledge

Although existing knowledge within the environment of an organization can be beneficial, it is usually difficult to find knowledge that is useful and relevant, and when found, it is often difficult to reuse in practice (Komi-Sirviö, Mäntyniemi, & Seppänen, 2002). The problem is that, within organizations, much of the knowledge that is useful for the execution of software processes is tacit (Assimakopoulos & Yan, 2006), and only a part of all the knowledge on software processes can be captured and made explicit (Rus & Lindvall, 2002). In addition, this tacit knowledge can only be revealed through practice and, to capture it, it is often necessary for people to be part of a work team (Goffin & Koners, 2011).

Despite the poor economic conditions of recent years, organizations continue to invest substantial amounts of their resources to manage their own knowledge and to provide opportunities for employees to learn the processes of the organization, according to the American Association for Training and Development (ASTD). However, few organizations obtain the expected benefits in relation to the investment in management and organizational knowledge transfer (Strong, Davenport, & Prusak, 2008).

Therefore, it would be interesting to find mechanisms to enrich organizational knowledge about software process, adding personal knowledge (tacit) to the pre-existing one to improve the organizational software processes, and also to facilitate its reuse for learning purposes.

To evolve and enrich the organizational knowledge a transformation of tacit knowledge into explicit, and vice versa, is needed, since it is this alternation which can lead to the creation of new knowledge (Nonaka & von Krogh, 2009). To promote this alternation of knowledge it is necessary for all the members of the organization to be able to create, modify and/or reuse knowledge in a collaborative manner.

Wikis are one of the technologies enabling collaborative generation of knowledge, thereby supporting the management of knowledge about the processes of an organization. According to Majchrzak, Wagner, and Yates (2006), participation in organizational wikis allows three main types of benefits: enhanced reputation, easier learning, and helping the organization to improve its processes through the effective use of knowledge elicited during the collaborative learning processes.

3. ITAKA FRAMEWORK

ITAKA (Interactive TAcit Knowledge Administration) is a solution based on the principles of KM that provides a framework consisting of a model of knowledge, processes to manage it and a technology platform for the interactive and collaborative management of the tacit knowledge needed to facilitate the improvement of software processes (Heredia, Garcia-Guzman, Amescua, & Sanchez-Segura, 2013).

The ITAKA framework provides mechanisms to (1) acquire tacit knowledge that individuals obtain while working in different teams to col-laboratively enrich organizational knowledge, and (2) disseminate the evolved organizational knowledge among different project teams. This proposal is initially oriented –but not limited– to environments that require learning and adoption of new processes (e.g., continuous process improvement initiatives and the integration of new people into the organization).

Knowledge flows through ITAKA following the same phases the SECI model proposes (Nonaka et al., 2006) (see Figure 1). First, the pre-existing knowledge is acquired and stored in the organizational repository, allowing an initial distribution of different views of knowledge for different teams in the organization. Then, tacit knowledge that resides in a project team is exchanged (*socialization*) to achieve a better understanding of the software processes of the organization, resulting in the creation of new knowledge. This new tacit knowledge has to be preserved, so it is formalized and transformed into explicit knowledge (*externalization*). Once made explicit, the new knowledge is combined with the explicit one that was already stored in the organizational repository (*combination*) and is again distributed through the different views. This enriched knowledge can be later applied to other projects by engineers who assimilate new knowledge (*internalization*). The cycle continues again to socialization when individuals share this newly acquired tacit knowledge.

Figure 1. SECI model

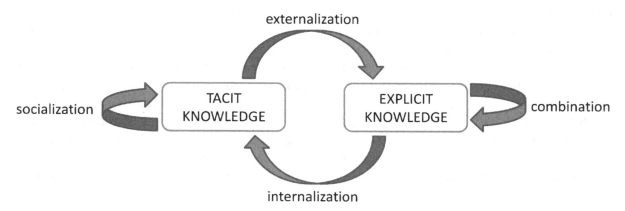

The results of using ITAKA have shown that this framework is effective in the capture, formalization and distribution of tacit knowledge that arises from the different interactions among members of a software engineering organization. ITAKA thus provides a suitable environment for the improvement of processes and practices to develop quality software. In spite of the little effort required to use the system's functionalities, it takes some time to get used to the framework and to get users involved in the improvement of the organizational processes. Thus, the improvement in the quality of the products developed is not immediate but becomes evident with time.

4. KNOWLEDGE STRUCTURE IN ITAKA

The knowledge stored in the repository must be organized according to some structure so that any particular asset (knowledge element) can be located within that structure.

The PAL in ITAKA consists of a set of assets, which are those entities that the organization considers useful. All assets have associated information about its version and its change history. In addition, an asset can be composed in turn of other assets. The same asset can be instantiated several times for reuse in other projects; that is, the contents of the asset can be adapted in each instance for each specific project. Assets contain explicit knowledge (i.e., formal) and may also contain tacit knowledge (i.e., personal). On the one hand, explicit knowledge can be textual or enriched by using multimedia elements (mainly documents and videos). On the other hand, tacit knowledge is in the form of examples (obtained from the application of active projects and offering a possible solution to a particular problem), and in the form of lessons learned during the implementation of each project (obtained from the discussions created to exchange ideas and opinions among members of the same team).

To store these assets, ITAKA has a single knowledge repository that acts as a version control platform aimed at arranging and preserving all the knowledge on software processes of the organization. These assets usually contain a textual description and rich contents, and some of them (mainly activities and processes) may also contain tacit knowledge that was formalized and stored in the form of examples and lessons learned. All the organizational knowledge is stored in this repository as text files and other multimedia files such as images, documents or videos.

The structure of the knowledge repository proposed in ITAKA emphasizes procedural knowledge, i.e., tasks that people know how to do based on gradually acquired skills through practice. The content of this structure allows to store knowledge about which actions to take, who should perform them, when to perform them, and how they can be performed.

5. PROCESS MODEL OF ITAKA

The process model of ITAKA includes a description of the various elements that define each of these processes. This notation uses SPEM (Software Process Engineering Metamodel and Systems), version 2.0. SPEM is a formal language promoted by the OMG (Object Management Group) that provides concepts to model, document, present, manage, share, and implement methods and development processes (OMG, 2008).

SPEM elements to be used in the diagrams of this section are given in Table 1.

In order to manage knowledge, which is useful and relevant to an organization, ITAKA defines the set of processes shown in Figure 2. First, knowledge is acquired through the processes of *identification* and *formalization*, resulting in pre-existing knowledge that is registered in the organizational repository. This initial knowledge is then passed on to the *distribution* process through which different views of this knowledge are tai-

Table 1. SPEM 2.0 elements description

Notation	Description
	Process: element that represents a relationship between instances of activities and roles in the instances.
	Activity: general unit of work assignable to specific performers represented by a role.
	Role: set of skills, competencies and responsibilities of an individual or group performing a process or activity.
●	**Start**: element that represents the beginning of the activities within a process.
◉	**End**: element that represents the completion of the activities within a process.
◇	**Decision**: choice that allows to split transitions into several alternative outgoing paths.

Figure 2. Processes defined in ITAKA

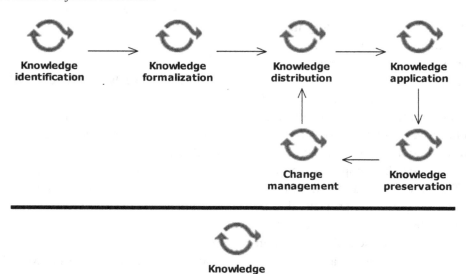

lored to suit the specific needs of the different project teams within the organization. The *application* of this knowledge in each of the projects of the organization can lead to the creation of new tacit knowledge, which is elicited by a *preservation* process. Later, the feedback loop is closed by a *change management* process that merges all new knowledge each of the teams preserved with the pre-existing knowledge stored in the organizational repository. Parallel to these processes, a *measurement* process assesses whether the knowledge of the organization is managed properly and efficiently. The following sections describe in more detail each of these processes.

To carry out all these processes it is necessary to involve certain roles in the various activities of these processes. Specifically, defined roles and responsibilities within ITAKA are listed in Table 2.

5.1 Knowledge Identification

One of the key problems that appear repeatedly in the literature related to knowledge management is the difficulty in encouraging people to use the knowledge repositories and participate in enriching them through new contributions. First, there is no reason why anyone would want to use a knowledge repository if it does not provide relevant contents. On the other hand, it is difficult to obtain relevant contents if users do not participate in the knowledge repository. Thus, the importance of feeding the knowledge repository with initial contents is evident. To do this, an organization can use different methods, one of which is based on storing in the repository pre-existing knowledge.

The *Knowledge Identification* process therefore aims to obtain and characterize this pre-existing knowledge, which is necessary to carry out the

processes of the organization. The knowledge identified will be later stored in the organizational repository so that it is available for continuous use in projects.

The pre-existing knowledge is obtained from the software development processes of the organization, from the most effective practices taken from the existing literature on software engineering, and from the experience of the most relevant experts within the organization.

Activities to carry out in this process are shown in Figure 3.

First, the information to define the processes that take place in the organization has to be gathered. It is necessary to identify which processes, techniques and tools are available, which are useful and where all the information is located.

References to books, articles, guides and other bibliographic elements related to the processes carried out in the organization that will increase knowledge about these processes are also compiled.

Table 2. Roles and responsibilities within ITAKA

Roles	Responsibilities
Expert	- Compile processes to identify knowledge - Compile bibliography to identify knowledge - Compile experiences to identify knowledge - Create knowledge assets to formalize knowledge - Connect knowledge assets to formalize knowledge - Review changes in assets during change management knowledge
Librarian	- Register knowledge assets to formalize knowledge - Select knowledge assets to distribute knowledge - Integrate knowledge assets to distribute knowledge - Generate a view to distribute knowledge - Identify changes in assets to manage changes in knowledge - Assimilate changes in assets to manage changes in knowledge - Measure the knowledge to determine the effectiveness of the framework - Measure the knowledge to determine the quality of knowledge - Measure the knowledge to determine user satisfaction
Software Engineer	- Consult knowledge assets to apply in a project - Instantiate knowledge assets to apply in a project - Register examples to preserve knowledge - Participate in discussions to preserve knowledge - Edit knowledge assets to preserve knowledge

Figure 3. Activities of the knowledge identification process

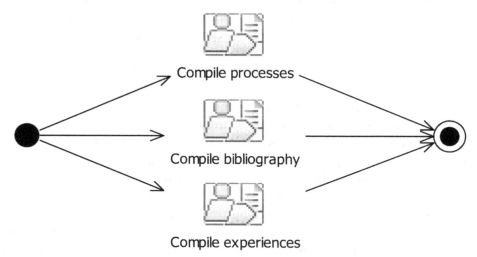

Compile processes

Compile bibliography

Compile experiences

Finally, it is important to collect experiences from previously developed projects to complement the explicit knowledge compiled previously in relation to the processes of the organization. These experiences can be collected through individual interviews with experienced personnel or through focus groups where participants discuss the implementation of the various projects they were involved in.

As a result, the *Knowledge Identification* process provides the set of assets that define the pre-existing knowledge of the organization.

5.2. Knowledge Formalization

The knowledge of a specific domain can be represented using different levels of formality, from natural language text to rules or logic models. Each of these levels of formalization has its advantages and disadvantages. Thus, knowledge in textual form is very common and can be easily elicited as it requires no prior experience for representation, but recovery of textual knowledge is only possible by comparing character strings. In addition, it is not possible to automate the reasoning using textual knowledge with the existing methods. Conversely, the logic rules that are well suited for automated reasoning also allow semantic query process.

However, obtaining rules or models is generally complex and time consuming.

It is very important, therefore, to select an appropriate level of formality. Since the knowledge of an organization is usually in text form (explicit knowledge) or resides in individuals (tacit knowledge), ITAKA uses text to represent organizational knowledge, structured using semantic annotations and supplemented with some multimedia (images and videos). To structure the data we propose the use of templates and forms so that knowledge can be introduced at a basic level using as much natural language as possible.

In this second process, once the pre-existing knowledge is identified, it must be converted into explicit knowledge and then stored in the organizational repository. This process of formalization is accomplished by using a pre-existing knowledge editor for structuring and standardizing knowledge, thus defining a process guide that will be registered in the organizational repository ready to be distributed later.

Activities to carry out in this process are shown in Figure 4.

In this process, knowledge assets are first created. Using the pre-existing knowledge editor, the definition of the different elements of the process guide must be inserted as part of the initial knowl-

Figure 4. Activities of the knowledge formalization process

edge of the organization as well as other general descriptions such as the principles and organizational culture, organizational governance, or the process model to be followed in the projects. After that, the description, states, transitions between states, and different fields of each work item are introduced. The next step will be to insert the description and the entry and exit criteria of each organizational process. Afterwards, the description and the entry and exit criteria of each of the activities performed within the organizational processes are introduced. Then, the description of the various roles involved in the activities and processes of the organization are also inserted. This is followed by the work products required to develop the tasks during the execution of the processes of the organization. Finally, the technical instructions that explain how to extract a particular activity are introduced.

Once knowledge assets have been created it is necessary to establish links between them by using the pre-existing knowledge editor. These links provide access from the knowledge asset that is being displayed to other related knowledge assets. So each activity should connect with the corresponding process in which it is carried out, every role should connect with the processes and activities in which it participates, and each work product should connect with the activities and processes in which it is used, and so on.

Finally, knowledge assets that were previously created and interrelated should be stored in the organizational knowledge repository. These assets are formalized and thus become part of the organizational knowledge, and made available for distribution to project teams within the organization from that moment on.

The result of this formalization of the pre-existing knowledge leads to the definition of a process guide, whose elements are stored in the repository of organizational knowledge.

5.3 Knowledge Distribution

During the execution of a project, for learning purposes or simply in order to keep up to date, the work teams may need access to some kind of knowledge about the different processes of the organization. To meet this need to access the organizational knowledge, that knowledge must first be distributed to those who require it.

The purpose of the distribution of the organizational knowledge is to facilitate the knowledge that was previously registered and formalized in the repository of organizational knowledge for potential users. This process enables the deployment of a view that provides access to a version of the organizational knowledge.

Since not all the teams have the same needs, they should be offered the possibility of deploying different types of views tailored to each specific need. Therefore, we propose three types of views:

- **Static offline view:** Provides access to a version of the organizational knowledge without the need for Internet connection; it does not include the functionality to collect new tacit knowledge to enrich the organizational knowledge.
- **Static online view:** Provides access to a version of the organizational knowledge through the Internet; it does not include the functionality to collect new tacit knowledge to enrich the organizational knowledge.

- **Dynamic online view:** Provides access to a version of the organizational knowledge through the Internet; it includes the functionality to collect new tacit knowledge to enrich the organizational knowledge.

Activities to carry out in this process are shown in Figure 5.

First, the knowledge assets to be distributed are selected among all the assets available in the repository of organizational knowledge. These assets are selected according to the software development methodology used in the project and the tasks to be undertaken by the members of the project team. Any knowledge asset that may be useful in the scope of the project is likely to be selected.

Once the assets have been selected, they should be integrated into a single knowledge package. This activity starts from a basic skeleton that defines the hierarchical structure in which the elements of the view will be assembled. All the selected knowledge assets will be assembled in the skeleton in turns. Additionally, the unidirectional links manually created in the previous process during the activity named "Connect knowledge assets" are automatically transformed into bidirectional links. This mechanism simplifies the activity of connecting knowledge assets so that when an asset is connected to another, the backwards connection is automatically added in the other asset.

The last step is to create and publish a view that allows access to a version of the organizational knowledge generated from previously selected assets and their subsequent integration. Different generation mechanisms will allow to obtain each one of the three types of views mentioned above.

As a result, each work team will get a view according to its needs. So, any team can get a view with a static format available offline, a static format available online, or an editable format available online.

5.4 Knowledge Application

The work teams should really know about the processes of the organization and this knowledge should be effectively applied during the project execution.

Once the organizational knowledge has been distributed through the views, this can be accessed and used by people involved in the processes of future projects. An asset can be accessed by navigating through the view, or adapted to another project, creating an instance of that asset (these instances are text documents, spreadsheets, tables, figures, etc. generated with external tools).

With the distribution of knowledge and its subsequent application, the internalization phase that Nonaka defined in the SECI model (Nonaka et al., 2006) is completed, so the teams can acquire new tacit knowledge from the explicit one stored in the organizational repository.

Activities to carry out in this process are shown in Figure 6.

Users of a view can navigate through hyperlinks to locate the asset they want to consult. In the views there are two forms of navigation: in the first one the user selects a process or activity from which to access a work item or a work product; for instance, while in the second the user selects a role to access a process or activity in which that role participates. The first type of navigation is recommended when specific information about

Figure 5. Activities of the knowledge distribution process

Select knowledge assets   Integrate knowledge assets   Generate views

Figure 6. Activities of the knowledge application process

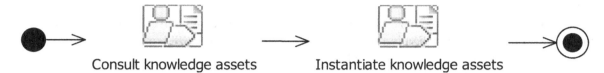

Consult knowledge assets　　　　　Instantiate knowledge assets

an asset is needed, while the other is recommended when the user wants to know the next process or activity to carry out. Furthermore, the views provide a search box in which the user can enter keywords so that the view will present a list of assets in which those keywords appear.

In addition, users of a view can adapt a knowledge asset according to the characteristics and needs of a project, creating an instance of that asset.

As a result of this process, distributed knowledge assets are applied in the execution of the different projects of the organization.

5.5 Knowledge Preservation

The application of existing organizational knowledge (explicit) can result in the generation of new knowledge (tacit) from everyday experience gained when carrying out the processes of the organization in different types of projects. This new knowledge can be relevant to the organization, so it must be captured for preservation.

The interaction between projects and organizational knowledge establishes two loops that can lead to this generation of new tacit knowledge. The first is at the project level, where new knowledge is obtained during process execution, which is represented by the *Knowledge Preservation* process. The second is at the organizational level, represented by the *Change Management* process.

With the preservation of knowledge, the socialization and externalization stages are complete as defined by Nonaka in the SECI model (Nonaka et al., 2006), so software engineers share their experiences gained during the implementation of projects, converting tacit knowledge into explicit.

Activities to carry out in this process are shown in Figure 7.

The new tacit knowledge generated during the execution of the projects can be captured in the form of examples from the artifacts produced by carrying out the processes in the organization. These examples can be useful to the project team or other teams within the organization and offer possible solutions to problems identified. Therefore, during the execution of the organizational processes it is desirable to register examples that can be useful in the future. To register an example, the appropriate information has to be introduced through the tacit knowledge collector. The information needed to register an example is the context, the problem addressed and the solution proposed. For a more effective reuse of the examples, this type of contribution requires first to be de-contextualized and then re-contextualized. To de-contextualize the example, the software engineer must remove those details that are not relevant to understanding, thus isolating it from the project and obtaining clean material. To re-

Figure 7. Activities of the knowledge preservation process

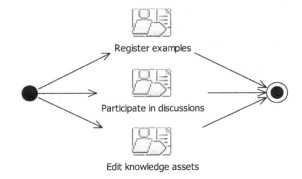

contextualize, the software engineer must compose a new context so that the example has sufficient significance for reuse. The processes of de-contextualization and re-contextualization of an example help to identify the conditions under which the example is applicable independent of the project.

Likewise, the new tacit knowledge generated during the execution of the projects can be captured in the form of discussions created to exchange ideas and opinions among members of a team. These discussions can be useful to the project team or other teams within the organization as they offer different views on the processes or provide new ideas for implementation. Therefore, during the execution of the processes of the organization it is appropriate to participate in the discussions that may be useful in the future. Discussions can be obtained in different ways depending on the platform used by the organization: email discussions, comments on a wiki, forum posts, etc. A software engineer can start a new discussion related to an asset or may make contributions to the discussions already started by himself or by any other software engineer.

Finally, the new tacit knowledge generated during the projects execution can be captured by editing the formalized knowledge assets. Editing assets can be useful to maintain updated and error-free organizational knowledge. Therefore, during the execution of the processes of the organization it is convenient to edit those assets that contain incorrect information. The content of any asset can be easily modified through the tacit knowledge collector.

As a result of this process all the contributions made by software engineers are publicly available to the team to which they belong (dynamic online view, mainly). These contributions can be in the form of examples, discussions or changes in knowledge assets.

5.6 Change Management

As mentioned previously, the interaction between projects and organizational knowledge establishes two loops that can lead to the generation of new tacit knowledge. The first is at the project level, represented by the *Knowledge Preservation* process. The second is at the organizational level, where the new knowledge obtained from projects is gathered in the repository of organizational knowledge and made available to all the members within the organization for reuse in other projects, which is represented by the *Change Management* process.

The aim of this process is therefore to improve the knowledge stored in the repository of organizational knowledge by including contributions by software engineers –in the form of examples, discussions or changes in knowledge assets– preserved during the execution of the projects. We propose a feedback mechanism that allows change management of the organizational knowledge using two alternatives: review changes (contributions are supervised by an expert) or do not review changes (contributions are not supervised).

With the management of changes in the knowledge stored in the organizational repository, the combination phase is completed as defined by Nonaka's SECI model (Nonaka et al., 2006), so the new knowledge made explicit during the externalization phase is now part of the repository of organizational knowledge. Thus, a new version of the different views can be distributed and the enriched organizational knowledge is made available to all teams regardless of whom contributed new knowledge.

Activities to carry out in this process are shown in Figure 8.

The first activity consists in the identification of the changes made in the knowledge assets and the new contributions made to the knowledge

Figure 8. Activities of the change management process

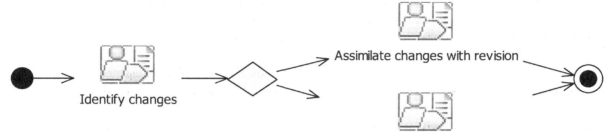

assets in the form of examples or discussion. The tacit knowledge collector can be configured to facilitate the execution of this activity. For instance, it can automatically notify the librarian by email every time an asset is edited, whenever someone starts or contributes a discussion, or every time someone registers a new example, that is when one of the activities of the *Knowledge Preservation* process is carried out. Once the assets that were modified have been identified, all the new knowledge preserved in these assets must be collected and prepared for inclusion in the repository of organizational knowledge.

When an organization chooses not to perform the review of changes in this process, the repository of organizational knowledge directly assimilates all the new contributions. On the other hand, when the review of changes is included each contribution is supervised by an expert who decides to discard, edit or accept it. Only if the contribution is not rejected, will it be incorporated into the repository of organizational knowledge. The tasks involved in this supervised activity depend on the type of contribution:

- For new examples, these are reviewed by the expert to decide whether they are useful and relevant to the organization or not. The expert also checks that they were correctly de-contextualized and re-contextualized so that they are applicable to other projects.

Finally, each example must be checked to ensure it is associated with an appropriate asset, otherwise the expert has to relocate it. Once an example has been reviewed and accepted, it is registered in the repository of organizational knowledge and appended to the list of examples related to the corresponding asset.

- For discussions, the expert reviews the contributions and, when needed, they can be modified to facilitate understanding. Discussions on the same topic can be unified to be more easily located. Finally, each discussion must be checked to ensure it is associated with an appropriate asset, otherwise the expert has to relocate it. Once a discussion has been reviewed and accepted, it turns into a lesson learned and is merged with the existing list of lessons learned associated with the corresponding asset in the repository of organizational knowledge.

- Finally, changes in existing knowledge assets are reviewed by the expert who verifies whether these modifications really enrich the organizational knowledge or not. Once changes in an asset have been reviewed and accepted, the knowledge asset is updated in the repository of organizational knowledge.

As a result of this process, organizational knowledge is enriched by adding new tacit knowledge to the organizational repository from the various contributions made during the execution of different projects throughout the organization.

5.7. Knowledge Measurement

García, Amescua, Sanchez-Segura, and Bermón (2011) suggest that the use of stored assets must be monitored to assess whether organizational knowledge is managed properly and efficiently. Furthermore, the success of process improvement using ITAKA depends heavily on user satisfaction and other factors that may increase users' intentions regarding the continued use of ITAKA, such as the quality of knowledge stored.

To measure and evaluate all of these factors prior measurement targets must be established, a set of issues related to the objectives raised, and a set of metrics (indicators) specified to try to respond in a measurable way to the issues raised.

The aim of this process is therefore to analyze the use of ITAKA from the measures taken in order to identify opportunities for improvement by introducing corrective changes in the future.

The data collected will be analyzed to establish which aspects of ITAKA require adjustments.

Specifically, it must obtain statistics about user behavior, measures related to new contributions to the repository of organizational knowledge, and data on the subjective assessment of the usefulness and quality of new knowledge and products obtained in the projects.

Activities to carry out in this process are shown in Figure 9.

On the one hand, it is necessary to collect and analyze the data collected to determine if the mechanisms are effective for acquiring tacit knowledge.

On the other hand, the data must be collected and analyzed to determine the quality of the new knowledge elicited.

Also, the data must be collected and analyzed to determine if the functionality offered by the system meets the needs of users.

As a result, the statistics obtained allow to analyze the level of effectiveness of the system in capturing new tacit knowledge, the level of quality of the organizational knowledge, and the level of user satisfaction.

Figure 9. Activities of the knowledge measurement process

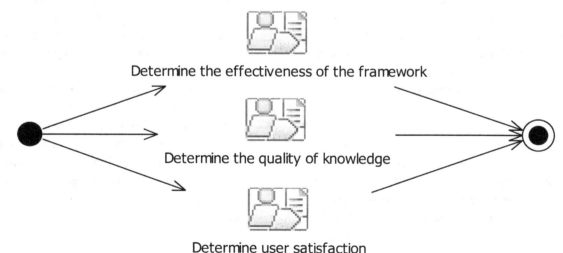

Determine the effectiveness of the framework

Determine the quality of knowledge

Determine user satisfaction

6. ITAKA TECHNOLOGY PLATFORM

The three-layered scheme in Figure 10 shows the architecture of the framework described in this chapter, and knowledge sharing that occurs between the various modules involved. Knowledge flows through ITAKA alternating between tacit and explicit forms, and vice versa, following the continuous cycle of processes presented in the previous section. As can be seen, the *Knowledge Identification* process is not covered in this architecture since its implementation does not require the use of any software tool.

First, the pre-existing knowledge editor enables the *Knowledge Formalization* process, structuring and standardizing knowledge through the definition of different knowledge assets of the organization and the relationships between them. These assets are registered in the repository of organizational knowledge assets thanks to the pre-existing knowledge codifier. Assets stored can be selected as inputs of the *Knowledge Distribution*

process through the knowledge publisher, resulting in the creation of different views of knowledge (static offline, static online and dynamic online). Each knowledge browser allows the team to consult the organizational knowledge to carry out the *Knowledge Application* process within the project in which the team are involved. During the execution of the various projects of the organization new tacit knowledge can be generated. This tacit knowledge can be registered via the tacit knowledge collector in the *Knowledge Preservation* process since new knowledge is temporarily stored in the database associated with the project in which it was generated. This new tacit knowledge is later exported from the databases of the different projects, so part of the organizational knowledge changes during the *Change Management* process. Finally, a Web analytics engine allows the *Knowledge Measurement* process to monitor and analyze the use of the framework and the evolution of organizational knowledge through a report generator.

Figure 10. Architecture of ITAKA

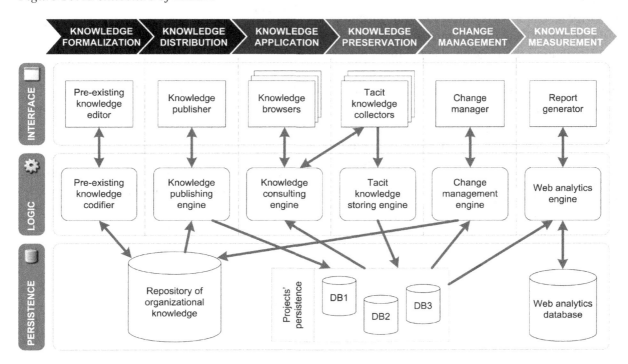

7. CONCLUSION

This chapter presents a framework to support the improvement of software processes called ITAKA (Interactive TAcit Knowledge Administration). The objective of ITAKA is the enrichment of the organizational knowledge through the elicitation of high-quality tacit knowledge assets in the form of examples, discussions, lessons learned and changes in the pre-existing knowledge, as these assets are generated during the execution of the organizational software processes. Thus, ITAKA supports the interaction and exchange of experiences among software engineers working in different project teams and/or different sites and using different means to access the same organizational knowledge assets.

This framework proposes two alternative mechanisms to feed the tacit knowledge from projects back into the organizational repository: supervised change management in which an expert evaluates the quality of the new knowledge and decides whether to add it to the repository or not, and unsupervised change management in which the new knowledge is directly accepted to become part of the repository of organizational knowledge.

ITAKA is effective in capturing, formalizing and distributing the tacit knowledge that arises from different interactions among the members of a software engineering organization. This new knowledge enriches the organizational knowledge and empowers the improvement of processes, obtaining, in consequence, high levels of quality in the products developed. Not only does ITAKA provide an effective environment in order to improve the software processes, but also to learn and adopt new processes and practices to develop quality software.

REFERENCES

Alavi, M., & Leidner, D. (2001). Knowledge management and knowledge management systems: Conceptual foundations and research issues. *MIS Quaterly*, *25*(1), 107–136. doi:10.2307/3250961

Allison, I., & Merali, Y. (2007). Software process improvement as emergent change: A structurational analysis. *Information and Software Technology*, *49*(6), 668–681. doi:10.1016/j.infsof.2007.02.003

Assimakopoulos, D., & Yan, J. (2006). Sources of knowledge acquisition for Chinese software engineers. *R & D Management*, *36*(1), 97–106. doi:10.1111/j.1467-9310.2005.00418.x

Basili, V. R., & Seaman, C. (2002). The experience factory organization. *IEEE Software*, *19*(3), 30–31.

Capell, P. (2004). *Benefits of improvement efforts* (Special Report CMU/SEI-2004-SR-010). Pittsburgh, PA: Software Engineering Institute (SEI), Carnegie Mellon University.

Dingsøyr, T., Bjørnson, F. O., & Shull, F. (2009). What do we know about knowledge management? Practical implications for software engineering. *IEEE Software*, *26*(3), 100–103. doi:10.1109/MS.2009.82

Dybå, T., Kitchenham, B. A., & Jørgensen, M. (2005). Evidence-based software engineering for practitioners. *IEEE Software*, *22*(1), 58–65. doi:10.1109/MS.2005.6

García, J., Amescua, A., Sanchez-Segura, M. I., & Bermón, L. (2011). Design guidelines for software processes knowledge repository development. *Information and Software Technology*, *53*(8), 834–850. doi:10.1016/j.infsof.2011.03.002

Garcia, S. (2004). *What is a process asset library? Why should you care?* Boston, MA: Aimware Professional Services Inc.

Goffin, K., & Koners, U. (2011). Tacit knowledge, lessons learnt, and new product development. *Journal of Product Innovation Management, 28*(2), 300–318. doi:10.1111/j.1540-5885.2010.00798.x

Gupta, A., Jingyue, L., Conradi, R., Rønneberg, H., & Landre, E. (2009). A case study comparing defect profiles of a reused framework and of applications reusing it. *Empirical Software Engineering, 14*(2), 227–255. doi:10.1007/s10664-008-9081-9

Heredia, A., Garcia-Guzman, J., Amescua, A., & Sanchez-Segura, M. I. (2013). Interactive knowledge asset management: Acquiring and disseminating tacit knowledge. *Journal of Information Science and Engineering, 29*(1), 133–147.

Humphrey, W. S. (1989). *Managing the software process*. Reading, MA: Addison-Wesley Professional.

Komi-Sirviö, S., Mäntyniemi, A., & Seppänen, V. (2002). Toward a practical solution for capturing knowledge for software projects. *IEEE Software, 19*(3), 60–62. doi:10.1109/MS.2002.1003457

Maier, R. (2007). *Knowledge management systems: Information and communication technologies for knowledge management* (3rd ed.). Heidelberg, Germany: Springer. doi:10.4018/978-1-59904-933-5.ch046

Majchrzak, A., Wagner, C., & Yates, N. (2006). Corporate wiki users: Results of a survey. In *Proceedings of the 2006 International Symposium on Wikis (WikiSym)*, (pp. 99-104). Odense, Denmark: ACM Press.

Mathiassen, L., Ngwenyama, O. K., & Aaen, I. (2005). Managing change in software process improvement. *IEEE Software, 22*(6), 84–91. doi:10.1109/MS.2005.159

Niazi, M., Wilson, D., & Zowghi, D. (2006). Critical success factors for software process improvement implementation: An empirical study. *Software Process Improvement and Practice, 11*(2), 193–211. doi:10.1002/spip.261

Nonaka, I., & von Krogh, G. (2009). Tacit knowledge and knowledge conversion: Controversy and advancement in organizational knowledge creation theory. *Organization Science, 20*(3), 635–652. doi:10.1287/orsc.1080.0412

Nonaka, I., von Krogh, G., & Voelpel, S. (2006). Organizational knowledge creation theory: Evolutionary paths and future advances. *Organization Studies, 27*(8), 1179–1208. doi:10.1177/0170840606066312

OMG. (2008). *Software & systems process engineering meta-model specification (SPEM) version 2.0*. OMG.

Rus, I., & Lindvall, M. (2002). Knowledge management in software engineering. *IEEE Software, 19*(3), 26–38. doi:10.1109/MS.2002.1003450

Strong, B., Davenport, T. H., & Prusak, L. (2008). Organizational governance of knowledge and learning. *Knowledge and Process Management, 15*(2), 150–157. doi:10.1002/kpm.306

KEY TERMS AND DEFINITIONS

Collaborative Learning: Situation in which several people actively interact by sharing experiences in order to acquire new knowledge together.

Knowledge Distribution: Dissemination of previous experiences among individuals within the organization.

Knowledge Elicitation: Acquisition of understanding through experience gained when carrying out the organizational processes.

Organizational Knowledge Enrichment: Enhancement of company's knowledge assets through the addition of new tacit knowledge acquired by individuals in their daily work.

Process Adoption: Assimilation of effective practices by an organization to improve its competitiveness.

Process Asset Library: Organized, well-indexed, searchable repository of process assets that is easily accessible by anyone who needs process guidance information, examples, data, templates or other process support materials.

Software Process Improvement: Approach to the systematic and continuous enhancement of the organization's ability to produce and deliver quality software within time and budget constraints.

Tacit Knowledge Management: Process of capturing, developing, sharing, and effectively using knowledge which is highly personal, hard to formalize and communicate, intuitive and derived from experience and beliefs.

Chapter 10
Towards Knowledge Management to Support Decision Making for Software Process Development

Edrisi Muñoz
Centro de Investigación en Matemáticas A.C., Mexico

Elisabeth Capón-García
Safety and Environmental Technology Group, Switzerland

ABSTRACT

The complexity of decision making in software process development and the need for highly competitive organizations require new supporting tools to coordinate and optimize the information flow among decision levels. Decision levels are related to strategic planning, tactical process management, and operational activities development and control. This chapter presents the theory for developing a framework that integrates the different decision levels in software development companies in order to reach their business objectives. Furthermore, the proposed framework coordinates the information exchange among the different modeling paradigms/conventions currently used.

INTRODUCTION

Nowadays, software represents a main building block in developing the activities of many companies and organizations since it creates added value to products and services, thus improving the competitiveness and differentiation of enterprises.

For example, many automotive, avionic, telecommunication applications and financial services rely on complex software-intensive systems. As a result of the increasing importance of software, new challenges and demands on software development, operation and maintenance have emerged (Münch et al., 2012).

A software process can be defined as a goal-oriented activity in the context of engineering-style software development. However, software

DOI: 10.4018/978-1-4666-5182-1.ch010

engineering is a relatively young discipline whose terminology has not been standardized yet. In addition, an imprecise usage of terms can be found in practice, along with misuse of modeling approaches and concepts stemming from other disciplines.

In software development, an ever-changing environment must be faced in order to deal with actual customer needs. The management of a software process involves collecting and processing huge amounts of data, which are further used and can be considered a valuable source of information for decision-making.

For many years, companies have developed management information systems to help process users to exploit data and models which can be used in discussions and decision-making. Decision-support systems (DSS) are computer technology solutions which can support complex decision making and problem solving (Shim et al., 2002). DSS are defined as computer-aided systems at the company management level which combine data and sophisticated analytic models (Simon & Murray, 2007). Classic DSS design comprises components for sophisticated database management capabilities with access to internal and external data, information, and knowledge; modeling functions accessed by a model management system; simple user interface designs that enable interactive queries, reporting, and graphing functions; and optimization by mathematic algorithms and/or intuition/knowledge.

Figure 1 describes what probably is became the most commonly used model of the decision-making process in a DSS environment. Typically, the phases overlap and blend together, with frequent looping back to earlier stages as more is learned about the problem, as solutions fail, and so forth. A first step is the recognition of the problem. Once the problem has been recognized, it is defined as a term that facilitates the creation of the model. Some authors consider that the emphasis is on the next two steps: model development and alternatives analysis. Then, the choice is made and implemented. As a final step, and if necessary, a new recognition is performed. Obviously, no decision process is this clear-cut in an ill-structured situation (Shim et al., 2002).

There has also been a huge effort in the DSS field to build a group support system (GSS) or

Figure 1. Scheme of the decision making process in a DSS environment

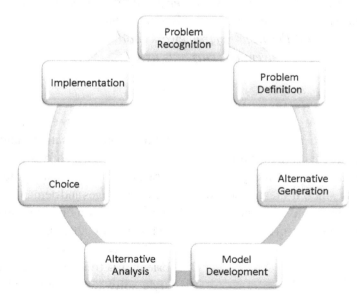

collaboration support system to enhance the communication-related activities of team members who are engaged in computer-supported cooperative work. The communication and coordination activities of team members are facilitated by technologies that can be characterized along the three continua of time, space, and level of group support (Alavi & Keen, 1989; Shim et al., 2002). Teams can communicate synchronously or asynchronously; they may be located together or remotely; and the technology can provide task support primarily for the individual team member or for the group's activities. These technologies are utilized to overcome the space and time constraints that burden face-to-face meetings, to increase the range and depth of information access, and to improve group task performance effectiveness, especially by overcoming "process losses."

From the previous discussion, it is clear that the need for infrastructures that continuously and coherently support fast and reliable decision-making activities related to the software process is of utmost importance (Münch et al., 2012). This need is more evident when we consider recent activity in the fields of data warehousing, online analytical processing (OLAP), data mining and Web-based DSS, followed by the treatment of collaborative support systems and optimization-based decision support (Shim et al., 2002). It is quite common for software process activities to have large databases. Hence, an enormous amount of information is created, stored and shared and it may be hard to find the right information when it is required. Furthermore, because of the possible use of different computer languages and differences in conceptualization, the interoperability between information in different systems is one of the most critical aspects in the daily operation of many organizations.

One key aspect is information extraction, which should result in the extraction of information quality. Information quality can be defined as precise information in terms of time, content, and clarity (Eppler, 2006). A common problem is that this data extraction process may be performed using blind methods in many cases. However, the performance of such methods can be drastically improved by combining them with knowledge or expertise of the process.

More specifically, information is data that is processed to be useful. Knowledge is the application of data and information through the development of a system which models, in a structured way, the experience gained in some domain. Knowledge exists as soon as human interaction is or has been made available in any step of the product/process development (Gebus & Leiviskä, 2009). In recent years, effort has been made to create knowledge with minimum human interface, either in a straight and formal way (e.g. expert systems) or in a conceptual manner.

The use of multiple models to represent detailed and abstract knowledge of software processes has been taken into account recently for many activities related to systematic coordination, synchronization, monitoring, and improvement of software development, maintenance and operational activities, and so forth (Münch et al., 2012). However, there is no unique set of ideal process models that can be used for process software development. The suitability of a process model depends on the characteristics and goals of a project. In fact, the choice of the model requires a deep understanding of the process.

In order to address the aforementioned lack of consensus, the conceptual and terminological confusion should be reduced and a shared understanding of the software process should be reached. Such an understanding can function as a unifying framework for the different viewpoints of the knowledge management that can be adopted to develop an integrated framework through the definition and semantic description of data and information. This is the basis for modeling the different forms of knowledge that are to be organized or the contextualized information that can be used to produce new meanings and generate new information.

Precisely, the use of ontologies in this work constitutes a means of specifying the structure of a domain of knowledge in a generic way that can be read by a computer (formal specification) and presented in a human readable form (informal specification). Ontologies are emerging as a key solution to knowledge sharing in a cooperative business environment (Missikoff & Taglino, 2002). Since they can express knowledge (and its relationships) with clear semantics, they are expected to play an important role in forthcoming information-management solutions to improve the information search process (Gruber, 1993; Obrst, 2003).

In this work, we propose the application of the semantic technologies to the field of software process development in order to obtain a common model for aiding decision support systems. The proposed ontology should be general enough to be applied to any software process system. Additionally, it may be used as a straightforward guideline for standardizing software process management and improvement. The ontology stands for an opportunity to improve data, information and knowledge sharing. In particular, this knowledge representation must enable to identify process sections together with their functionalities, objectives and relations within the process. This allows the improvement of the generation of different alternatives to the software process development problem, organized in integrated hierarchical levels of abstraction.

BACKGROUND

The creation and application of ontology-enabled tools for software engineering purposes have received increased attention in the literature. Indeed, some recent attempts to demonstrate their benefits

towards flexible and transparent infrastructures in organizations already exist.

One initial attempt to model software engineering concepts with ontologies is the representation formalism for software engineering ontologies (REFSENO) proposed by Tautz and von Wangenheim (1998). Such an approach has been used for the development of ontologies to model and reuse experience from industry, and to manage the software maintenance process (Rodriguez et al., 2010). The range of the application of ontologies in software engineering activities was extended by García et al. (2009). The authors proposed a framework for the integrated management of modeling and measurement of software processes, and incorporated the elements necessary to ease the integrated management of the definition and evaluation of software processes.

A general software engineering ontology model was developed by Wongthongtham et al. (2006), and later improved by Wongthongtham et al. (2009), based on the Guide to the Software Engineering Body of Knowledge (SWEBOK) and a software engineering book by the same authors. The model comprises five different ontologies related to the business domain, software engineering principles, project management, ontological, technical and managerial issues domain, as well as solution and knowledge issues. These ontologies were developed to serve software agents who support multi-site software development by accessing data from the project-ontology repository.

Rodriguez et al. (2010) present how software processes modeled using the Software & Systems Process Engineering meta-model (SPEM) can be translated into ontologies. SPEM was developed by the OMG (Object Management Group) using standards such as MOF (Meta-Object Facility) and UML (Unified Modelling Language). The authors generated an OWL (Web ontology language) ontology model based on SPEM and represented the data derived from actual projects. This is a first step towards providing reasoning capabilities for consistency checking, model validation, project and resource analysis, and so forth.

More recently, Vizcaíno et al. (2012) created an ontology for global software development in order to facilitate communication and avoid misunderstanding between researchers and practitioners. Their work was aimed at the development of methodologies and the necessary technological support for the global development of software and quality improvement. However, the proposed ontology used is limited to the establishment of a common terminology.

Valiente et al. (2012) present an ontological approach that integrates business and IT, thus building a bridge between IT service management processes and software engineering processes for service quality improvement. Their work provides a standard-based solution for effective support for the development of software components that underpin the services delivered to customers.

Previous works represent a very important step forward to define software engineering terms and processes for common understanding and knowledge sharing, but most of them do not incorporate the relationships and formalisms necessary for reasoning and exploiting knowledge. In addition, the different software processes are usually considered separately and not within the whole managerial structure of the enterprise.

In the field of the enterprise structure, Muñoz et al. (2011) designed and deployed an ontological framework which contains an integrated representation of the whole enterprise, ranging from the supply chain management to the scheduling function and comprising activities related to the operational, tactical and strategic functions. The model is based on the understanding and management of operational concepts stemming from process standards, and complemented with other handbooks and reviews. As a result of the knowledge derived from such modeling experience, this work further applies it to software process development.

ANALYSIS REQUIREMENTS

In order to increase the knowledge about the domain to be modeled, an analysis of the particular elements of the software process involved in current ontology development must be described. Nowadays, many companies and organizations mainly base their business on software. Software adds significant value to many products and services and allows for competitive differentiation in the market. The problem with software process management has been studied in many works (Conradi, 2002; Fitzgerald, 1999). These works derived from the so-called software crisis, which is a consequence of unmet due dates, high costs and of not covering the main goals previously planned at the strategic level of the enterprise. The problems with software process management found in enterprises lie with two principal aspects: i) the lack of analysis of the software process management; and ii) the chaotic, undisciplined and inflexible processes adopted for years (Gainer, 2006).

When an organization is developing a project, a multitude of activities are performed in parallel. This requires good coordination so that the results of these tasks fit together in a planned way. Even more, there are many relationships between those activities which have temporal dependencies. Also, many activities need to be synchronized so that they contribute to overall project goals. The above-mentioned tasks demand optimal process management, which can be structured according to the enterprise decision levels and the enterprise functional elements.

On the one hand, the software process management system can be divided into three levels, namely strategic, tactical and operational (Figure 2). The strategic level is concerned with the long-term view of the organization and deals with tasks related to the planning of software projects in order to fulfill the business objectives. The planning level tackles the software process management from the project development perspective. Finally, the operational level considers the control, evaluation and maintenance tasks of the software process.

On the other hand, software process development relates to different elements of the enterprise structure which have been identified as key elements that affect the success of software processes, specifically: i) procedural functionality, related to software tasks and activities, ii) physical elements, which include the enterprise infrastructure and human resources, and iii) process, related to software process models and functions (Figure 2).

Next, the elements of the enterprise structure are described, and the final problem statement is defined.

Infrastructure and Human Resources

Due to the nature of the software process business, the day-to-day activities depend on hundreds or thousands of people. The activities performed are called processes in the software domain environment. Additionally, the existing infrastructure necessary to adequately support processes must be supplied to the right people in order to develop the processes. This includes providing sufficient number of tools, workplaces, hardware resources such as engine test beds or test vehicles, as well as educational resources such as classrooms, personnel for helpdesk services.

Systematic coordination and cooperation mechanisms are needed in order to successfully create customer value and fulfill project goals under given project constraints such as budget limitations or deadlines. In addition, software fulfills more critical functions in its use, thereby increasing the complexity even more. All the above-mentioned factors make it difficult to manage software process management.

As business and technological environments change so fast, innovation in infrastructure for software needs to be developed in a rapid and flexible way at acceptable quality levels. To cope with this, new techniques, methods, and

Figure 2. Scheme of the software process management structure

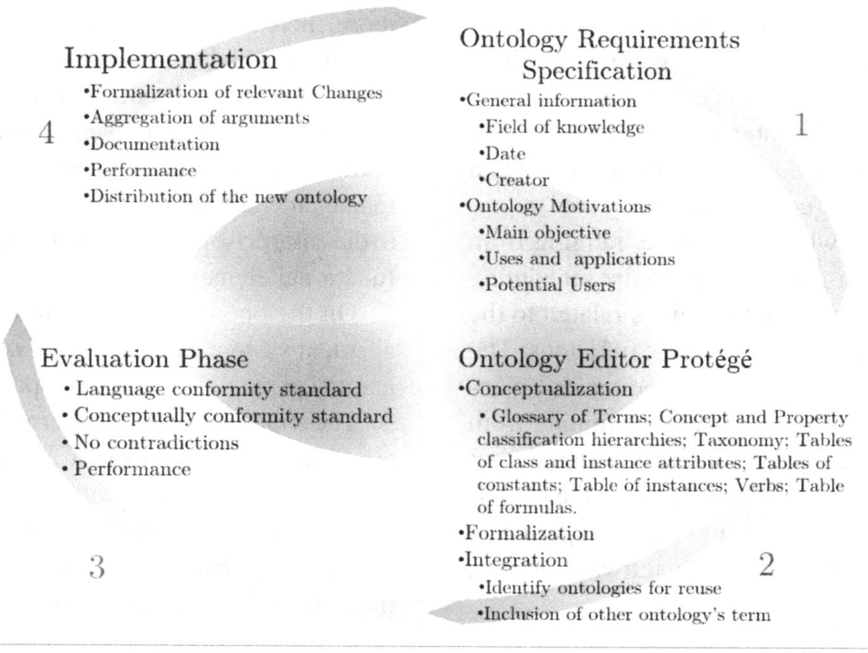

Implementation
4
- Formalization of relevant Changes
- Aggregation of arguments
- Documentation
- Performance
- Distribution of the new ontology

Ontology Requirements Specification
1
- General information
  - Field of knowledge
  - Date
  - Creator
- Ontology Motivations
  - Main objective
  - Uses and applications
  - Potential Users

Evaluation Phase
3
- Language conformity standard
- Conceptually conformity standard
- No contradictions
- Performance

Ontology Editor Protégé
2
- Conceptualization
  - Glossary of Terms; Concept and Property classification hierarchies; Taxonomy; Tables of class and instance attributes; Tables of constants; Table of instances; Verbs; Table of formulas.
- Formalization
- Integration
  - Identify ontologies for reuse
  - Inclusion of other ontology's term

tools are being developed constantly. Even more, new programming paradigms and languages are being introduced to improve the quality of software development and the resulting products. Each tool or programming paradigm has its own benefits and disadvantages. The hugely popular object-oriented programming, for example, makes construction of large systems possible in the first place and improves product quality in most cases. Nevertheless, engine control software is still being developed mostly in a functional manner because using object-oriented technology would make the system more complex and slower.

The software process infrastructure and human resources are closely related to the different decision levels of the organization. Indeed, the design and retrofit of existing resources are performed at the strategic level. At the tactical level, the existing infrastructure is allocated to ongoing projects and activities, and at the operational level, the infrastructure is actually being used in the process.

Models and Functions

The solution to problems and the development of certain goals are based most of the time on models. Process models aim to capture specifications about how to perform the different tasks and activities that make up a process depending on its functions. Process models can be used for different purposes, such as coordinating, synchronizing, monitoring, and improving software development, maintenance, and operation activities. The software process functions consist of the goal specification, design, modeling, execution, monitoring and optimization, and are related to the activities presented in the next subsection.

It is widely accepted that there is not a unique set of ideal process models that can be used for software systems and services. Regularly, the success of a process model depends on the characteristics of the project's development environment and the appropriate definition of the project's goals. The

choice of adequate process models and the establishment of the correct development environment are important and require sufficient understanding of the effects of the processes. Therefore, software development organizations should invest effort in determining the effects of processes in the nature of their businesses.

The increasing development of models and new trends aim to solve those problems in order to improve the probability of the success of the software process. Different organizations such as the Software Engineering Institute (SEI), the Project Management Institute (PMI), the Institute of Electric, Electronic Engineers (IEEE), the Information Technologies Government Institute (ITGI) and the International Standard Organization (ISO) are continuously developing successful process performance of models and standards. Besides, these models and standards are encompassed by different tools in order to verify, control and evaluate their results.

Tasks and Activities

Software process management activities aim to develop the software process functions, namely goal specification, design, modeling, execution, monitoring and optimization. First of all, the main business functions refer to the strategic vision and goals of an organization. Each function is attached to a list of processes. Multiple processes are aggregated to functional accomplishments and multiple functions are aggregated to achieve organizational goals. Therefore, the process design encompasses the assignment and adaptation of existing processes and/or the design of new processes to fulfill the goals identified in the previous function. Thus, a good design can reduce problems over the lifetime of the process. The objective of the activities related to the design function consists of ensuring the development of a correct and efficient design. The following set of activities are related to modeling, and consists of taking the previously specified design and trying different combinations of features in order to analyze how the system would behave under different probable scenarios.

After the implementation, the execution activities take place. They consist of running a software program which automatically performs the tasks specified previously. In order to facilitate this execution, the system uses services in connection with applications to perform business operations. However, automating a process definition requires flexible and comprehensive infrastructure, which typically rules out implementing these systems in a legacy IT environment. After that, monitoring encompasses activities related to tracking individual processes features, which are of interest for the performance evaluation aimed at fulfilling an enterprise's goals. In addition, the information resulting from monitoring can be used to work with customers and suppliers to improve their connected processes. Finally, the optimization activities are based on the information received from the monitoring function aimed at identifying improved conditions for process development.

Final Problem Statement

This work argues that the lack of structuring and order in the software process management system results in unsuccessful software process improvement efforts. Hence, a robust definition of the strategic, tactical and operational hierarchical structures must be done. Within those hierarchical structures, key aspects such as activities, methods, and practices that guide people in the production of software must be taken into account. In addition, the need to integrate the different modeling approaches in a hierarchical decision-support system means that consistent terminology and concepts must be used to improve the communication and collaboration tasks over the entire system.

METHODOLOGY: ONTOLOGICAL FRAMEWORK

The most widely cited definition of ontology in computing and artificial intelligence consists of "an explicit specification of a conceptualization" (Gruber, 1993). In this concise explanation, "specification" stands for a formal and declarative representation; and "conceptualization" means an abstract, simplified view of the world. According to Neches et al. (1991), an ontology defines the basic terms and relations that comprise the vocabulary of a topic area as well as the rules for combining terms and relations to define extensions to the vocabulary. Such definition stresses the use of vocabulary and rules, which are necessary for sharing and standardization purposes. Thus, an ontology has been described as a hierarchically structured set of terms for describing a domain that can be used as a skeletal foundation for a knowledge base (Swartout, Neches, & Patil, 1993). Therefore, the hierarchical organization of concepts is highlighted as a means for knowledge organization. In this sense, Hendler (2001) suggests the application of ontologies for reasoning and creating knowledge, defining an ontology as "a set of knowledge terms, including the vocabulary, the semantic interconnections, and some simple rules of inference and logic for some particular topic."

As a whole, ontologies can be defined as formal structures enabling acquiring, maintaining, accessing, sharing and reusing information (Gruber, 1993; Fensel, 2001). They are hierarchical domain structures that provide a domain theory, have a syntactically and semantically rich language, and a shared and consensual terminology (Klein, Fensel, Kiryakov, & Ognyanov, 2002). Ontologies provide shared and common domain structures required for the semantic integration of information sources. They were created to help in knowledge reuse and sharing: reuse means building new applications by assembling components that have already been built, while sharing occurs when different applications use the same resources. Reuse and sharing properties are advantageous, since they are cost, time and resource effective (Fensel, 2001).

Ontologies have been applied to a wide range of disciplines, and although it is still difficult to find consensus among ontology developers and users, there is some agreement on protocols, languages and frameworks. In this work, the basis for constructing an ontology for software process development is presented. The resulting ontology should be able to support the management of different concepts involved in the software process as well as their categorization and the relationships among them. As a result, all activities concerning software processes should be properly represented.

Language

Different ontology languages provide diverse features for the ontology developer. Any language used to codify ontology-underpinned knowledge should be expressive, declarative, portable, domain independent and semantically well defined. The language used in an ontology is essential for its future implementation and sharing.

In this work, we adopt Web ontology language (OWL), as it has good characteristics for ontologies (Bechhofer et al., 2004). OWL has been designed for use by applications that need to process the content of information, instead of just presenting the information to humans. OWL facilitates greater machine interpretability of Web content than that supported by extensible markup language (XML), resource description framework (RDF), and resource description framework schema (RDF-S), as it provides additional vocabulary along with formal semantics.

The ontology formally describes the meaning of the terminology used in documents. If machines are expected to perform useful reasoning tasks on these documents, the language must go beyond the basic semantics of RDF schema.

OWL has been designed to meet this need for a Web ontology language, and is part of the growing stack of W3C recommendations that are related to the semantic Web.

- XML provides a surface syntax for structured documents, but imposes no semantic constraints on the meaning of these documents (XML-Core-Working-Group, 2009).
- XML Schema is a language that restricts the structure of XML documents and extends XML with data types (McQueen & Thompson, 2000).
- RDF is a data model for objects ("resources") and relations between them. It provides simple semantics for data models, which can be represented in XML syntax (Klyne & Carroll, 2002).
- Schema is a vocabulary for describing properties and classes of RDF resources. It includes semantics for generalization hierarchies of these properties and classes (Brickley & Guha, 2002).

OWL adds more vocabulary for describing properties and classes, including the relations between classes (e.g. disjointedness), cardinality (e.g. "exactly one"), equality, richer typing of properties, characteristics of properties (e.g. symmetry), and enumerated classes. The semantics in the ontology build on XML's ability to define customized tagging schemes and RDF's flexible approach to representing data. This unifying aspect makes it easier to establish, through collaboration and consensus, the utilitarian vocabularies (between ontologies) needed for far-flung cooperative and integrative applications using the Word Wide Web and internal servers.

The uses of these languages are helpful for the first task of the ontology, which is to become a standard tool for vocabulary, format, and definitions. Restrictions and reasoning make communication possible between the different system elements.

Ontology Development Methodology

Numerous ontologies have been developed and used in various research areas. Each development project usually follows its own set of principles in order to design criteria and phases in the ontology development process. An ontology development methodology comprises a set of established principles, processes, practices, methods, and activities used to design, construct, evaluate, and deploy ontologies (Gasevic et al., 2009).

Various methodologies have been reported to guide the theoretical approach, and numerous ontology building tools are available; however, there is a lack of consensus on a uniform approach to designing and maintaining these ontologies (Gasevic et al., 2009). There is no single best methodology to develop ontologies, because there is no "correct" way to model a domain.

The absence of standard guidelines and methods hinders the following: the development of shared and concentrated ontologies within and between projects; the extension of a given ontology by others; and its reuse in other ontologies and final applications. It is widely recognized that constructing ontologies, or domain models, is an important step in the development of knowledge-based systems (KBSs). Many points are common to the various methodologies, although they are named differently. The problem is that these procedures have not coalesced into popular development styles or protocols, and the tools have not yet matured to the degree one would expect in other software instances.

The methodology applied in this work is based on two ontology development methodologies "Methontology" (López et al., 1999) and "On-To-Knowledge" (Sure & Studer, 2002). Methontology provides support for the entire life cycle of ontology development. It enables experts and ontology makers who are unfamiliar with implementation environments to build ontologies from scratch. Methontology identifies the following activities in the development of an ontology: specifica-tion, knowledge acquisition, conceptualization, integration, implementation, evaluation, and documentation. The life cycle of the ontology is based on the refinement of a prototype and ends with a maintenance state. The most distinctive aspect of Methontology is the focus on this maintenance stage.

In contrast, On-To-Knowledge methodology includes the identification of goals that should be achieved by knowledge management tools and is based on an analysis of usage scenarios. The steps proposed by On-To-Knowledge are: (i) kick-off, in which some competency questions are identified, potentially reusable ontologies are studied and a first draft of the ontology is built; (ii) refinement, in which a mature and application-oriented ontology is produced; (iii) evaluation, in which requirements and competency questions are checked and the ontology is tested in the application environment; and finally (iv) ontology maintenance. On-To-Knowledge stresses that the ontology modeling process should start with a definition of the abstraction level, which is strongly dependent on the usage of the ontology.

The aforementioned methodologies have been inserted into a Plan, Do, Check/Study and Act Cycle (PDCA or PDSA), which results in an ordered sequence of steps that are easy to understand and track (Figure 3).

The PDSA Cycle is a four-step cycle for problem solving, which includes: planning (definition of a problem and a hypothesis about possible causes and solutions), doing (implementing), checking (evaluating the results), and action (back to plan if the results are unsatisfactory or standardization if the results are satisfactory). The PDSA cycle emphasizes the prevention of error recurrence by establishing standards and the ongoing modification of those standards. Even before the PDCA cycle is employed, it is essential that the current standards be stabilized. The process of stabilization is often called SDCA (standardize-do-check-action) cycle.

Figure 3. Methodology applied for developing software process development ontology based on the PDSA cycle

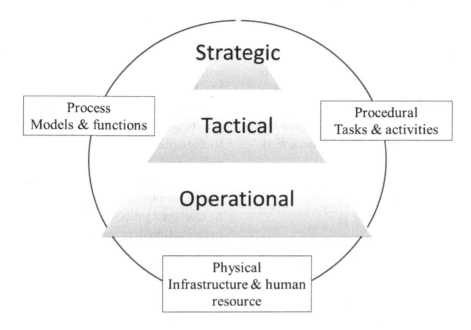

The PDSA cycle is applicable to all types of organizations and to all groups and levels in an organization. The following well-known issues are attained:

- It provides a framework for the application of improvement methods and tools guided by theory of knowledge:
  - It encourages planning to be based on theory.
  - Its theory leads to appropriate questions, which provide the basis for learning.
  - Its questions lead to predictions, which guide the user in identifying the necessary data, methods and tools to answer the questions relative to the theory in use.
  - It emphasizes and encourages the iterative learning process of deductive and inductive learning.

- It allows project plans to adapt as learning occurs.
- It provides a simple way for people to empower themselves to take action that leads to useful results in the pragmatic tradition of learning.
- It facilitates the use of teamwork to make improvements.

Regarding the PDSA cycle, it is worth mentioning that spending the right time in each phase or activity of the PDSA cycle is imperative to having a smooth and meaningful quality improvement process. Cycle elements involve a reflective process based on scientific method, and ensure improvement efforts are carried out by the success to be achieved.

Domain Sources of Knowledge

The underlying idea in software process improvement is that product quality is heavily influenced by the quality of the software processes associated with development and maintenance. However, even though the methods are quite comprehensible, they differ in a wide variety of features, which increases the complexity of selecting the most appropriate model for the organization. In this section, a brief analysis of the capability maturity model integration (CMMI) and ISO12207 standard is shown. These models are the bases of the domain for constructing an ontological framework for software process improvement.

Capability Maturity Model Integration (CMMI)

According to the software engineering institute (SEI), CMMI is a model that provides organizations with the essential elements for obtaining effective processes. It improves the performance of the processes found within an organization. The activities related to process improvement, included in CMMI, provide guidance for applying best practices. The basis of this guidance lies in identifying the process's strengths and weaknesses by adopting the adequate practices for developing quality products and services to meet the needs of customer and end users in order to turn weaknesses into strengths (CMMI Product Team, 2010).

According to SEI, the quality of the process used to develop and maintain a specific system or product derives from the quality of the product itself. Therefore, the CMMI model aims to guide the software development process in order to achieve product quality. Even more, CMMI intends to help process areas to achieve tasks with high quality, using standards and best practices so that they can deliver products and services better, faster and cheaper. It tries to avoid stovepipes and barriers caused by the lack of planning, poor requirements analysis and the wrong design (CMMI Product Team, 2010).

Finally, CMMI supports two improvement paths called "representations." The first one in-crementally improves processes corresponding to individual process areas or group of process areas; this representation is related to "capability levels" and is called "continuous." It uses four capability levels, namely: (0) Incomplete, which refers to processes that are not performed; (1) Performed, which refers to processes that accomplish the work needed to produce work products; (2) Managed, which refers to processes that are planned and executed in accordance with policy and resources, are monitored, controlled and reviewed, produce controlled outputs and can be evaluated; and (3) Defined, which refers to managed processes that are tailored from the organizational processes according to tailoring guidelines (CMMI Product Team, 2010). The second representation incrementally improves a set of related processes corresponding to a set of process areas. This representation is related to "maturity levels" and is called "staged." It uses five levels of maturity, namely: (1) Initial level, which refers to unpredictable processes and is poorly controlled and reactive; (2) Managed level, in which processes are characterized for projects and is often reactive; (3) Defined level, processes are characterized for the organization and is proactive; (4) Quantitatively managed level, where processes are measured and controlled; and (5) Optimizing level, which focuses on process improvement (CMMI Product Team, 2010).

ISO 12207 Standard

This standard covers the software life cycle from the conceptualization of an idea to the final stages. The ISO 12207 standard groups the activities that may be performed during the life cycle of a software system into seven process groups (Singh, 1996). Each life cycle process within those groups is described in terms of its purpose, desired outcomes and list of activities needed to achieve organization goals. The seven processes groups are defined as follows:

- **Agreement Processes:** They define the activities necessary to establish an agreement between two organizations. Even more, they provide a means for conducting a project to produce goods or a service.
- **Organizational Project-Enabling Processes:** They enable the organization's capability to manage the supply chain of products or services in a project.
- **Project Processes:** They establish and develop the planning of a project to assess actual achievement and progress against the plans and provide control execution.
- **Technical Processes:** These are activities that enable functions to optimize the benefits. Thus, they reduce the risks that arise from technical decisions and actions.
- **Software Implementation Processes:** They produce a specified software item implemented in software, resulting in elements that satisfy the system requirements.
- **Software Support Processes:** They are a specifically focused set of activities for performing a specialized software process, contributing to the success and quality of the software project.
- **Software Reuse Processes:** They support the ability to reuse software elements across projects.

Ontology Layering and Architecture

The architecture of the proposed ontological framework could be considered as nominal ontology and high ontology, taking into account the factors that influence its complexity, such as concepts, taxonomy, patterns, constraints and instances.

The basis for the construction of this particular ontology includes concepts and relations taken from software process models, standards and expert knowledge. The coherence between the concepts ensures that there is compatibility between the software elements at different hierarchical levels. This provides more opportunities for applications in which information can be updated at the same rate as data are received.

Logics are added to concepts, which express the relationships with relations. The proposed ontology is logic-based, and includes the logics considering six main layers. Figure 4 introduces the six layers that are seen as the main axis of the ontology architecture. The layers represent the following:

- **Concepts:** A concept defines a basic and abstract idea that is commonly used in an ontology domain. It is represented as a word or phrase.

Figure 4. Scheme of the ontology construction layering

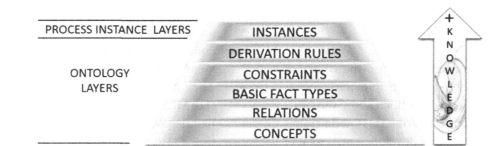

- **Relations:** A relation describes the way in which two or more concepts are inter-related. It is usually described by a verb or verb phrase (basic properties).
- **Basic fact types:** A basic fact type is a kind of primitive sentence or fact. It is composed of concepts and relations. If the basic fact type is always true in the ontology that contains it, it can play a role as an axiom in the logic-based ontology (detailed properties).
- **Constraints:** A constraint is the restriction that is applied to a fact type (binary or numerical restrictions for properties).
- **Derivation rules:** These are rules, functions or operators (including mathematical calculations or logical inference) that are used to derive new facts from existing ones.
- **Instances:** Instances have the distinctiveness of the reality and are specifications in the applications of the upper layers.

Concepts

The concepts that must be taken into account are found in the CMMI model and ISO12207 standard. They contain models and terminology which define the main concepts that describe the software process domain. The two sources of knowledge have been studied separately. At the moment, a total of 333 concepts have been identified in CMMI, whereas from ISO 12207, a total of 64 concepts have been obtained.

Relations

The basic relations were taken from the assertions of the models established in the previous sources of knowledge. These assertions show the basic relations, which can be described in flow diagrams.

In the current state of development, a total of 81 relations have been derived from the CMMI model, and 112 relations from ISO 12207.

Constraints and Derivation Rules

Some information about basic fact types is required. This assertion leads to the use of constraints. In addition, rules are used to link parts within the classes and properties.

Development Environment

Apart from the ontology representation language selection, the ontology developer must address the organization of the overall conceptual structure issues of the ontology related concepts, relations, properties, constraints and logics. In the literature, there is a wide range of ontology editors available who eventually help to develop the ontology.

In this work, Protégé has been selected as a tool for ontology editing and knowledge acquisition (Horridge et al., 2007). This system additionally acts as an inference engine to check data consistency and validity. Protégé is the most widely used open-source ontology and knowledge base editor with a friendly user interface (Gasevic et al., 2009).

Thus, Protégé allows the exportation of ontologies to other knowledge-representation systems, such as:

- Resource description framework (RDF), mainly intended for use in the semantic Web, but it has also been described as a content management technology, a knowledge management technology, a portal technology, and as one of the pillars of e-commerce (Klyne & Carroll, 2002).
- Ontology inference layer (OIL), intended to solve the findability problem, support e-commerce, and enable knowledge management (Horrocks et al., 2000).
- The DARPA agent markup language (DAML), focused on supporting the semantic Web, though one would assume that it also has other uses (Pagels, 2006).

Given its wide range of functionalities, Protégé is a very suitable environment to build the software process development ontology.

Ontology Use

The proposed ontology is intended to promote transversal process-oriented management, to enable crossover among the different functionalities related to the software process development process. In order to obtain and manage a comprehensive view of the overall software process, new modeling structures have to be developed.

It is envisaged that this transversal ontology can be extended to incorporate higher decision-making hierarchies and to include the entire life cycle of the organization, from the design stages of the software process to the delivery of the projects.

CONCLUSION

The fields of ontology, knowledge management and decision-support systems have matured significantly in recent years. Currently, the integration of various fields and technological solutions facilitate knowledge creation, storage and sharing in a specific domain, and improve the effectiveness of decision-support systems. In this work, the fundamentals for structuring and understanding the domain of software processes in the strategic, tactical and operational levels have been established. In addition, this ontology opens the way for successful information flow among the processes, which results in better monitoring and control of the activities. Since software engineering is still a young discipline, this research work establishes the basis to help in the standardization of the terminology by means of the semantic approach. Thus, this work presents the basis for creating a general model which can be very reusable depending on the organization, and with much usability to be able to develop all the activities of the organization. Finally, this work represents a step forward to support the integration (not just "communication") of different software tools applicable to the management and exploitation of process information, resulting in an enhancement of the entire software engineering management.

REFERENCES

Alavi, M., & Keen, P. G. W. (1989). Business teams in an information age. *The Information Society*, *6*(4), 179–195. doi:10.1080/01972243.1989.9960081

Bechhofer, S., van Harmelen, F., Hendler, J., Horrocks, I., McGuinness, D. L., Patel-Schneider, P. F., & Stein, L. A. (2004). *OWL web ontology language reference-website*. Retrieved from http://www.w3.org/TR/2004/REC-owl-ref-20040210/

Brickley, D., & Guha, R. (2002). *RDF vocabulary description language 1.0: RDF schema*. Retrieved from http://www.w3.org/TR/2002/WD-rdf-schema-20021112/

CMMI Product Team. (2010). *CMMI for development, version 1.3*. Retrieved from http://resources.sei.cmu.edu/asset_files/TechnicalReport/2010_005_001_15287.pdf

Conradi, H., & Fuggetta, A. (2002). Improving software process improvement. *IEEE Software*, *19*(4), 92–99. doi:10.1109/MS.2002.1020295

Eppler, M. J. (2006). *Introducing the notion of information quality* (2nd ed.). Berlin, Germany: Springer.

Fensel, D. (2001). *Ontologies: A silver bullet for knowledge management and electronic commerce*. Berlin, Germany: Springer. doi:10.1007/978-3-662-04396-7

Fitzgerald, B., & O'kane, T. (1999). A longitudinal study of software process improvement. *IEEE Software*, *16*(3), 37–45. doi:10.1109/52.765785

Gainer, J. (1998). *Best practices: Informal, effective process improvement*. Retrieved from http://www.jeffgainer.com/bestprac.html

García, F., Ruiz, F., Calero, C., Bertoa, M. F., Vallecillo, A., Mora, B., & Piattini, M. (2009). Effective use of ontologies in software measurement. *The Knowledge Engineering Review*, *24*(1), 23–40. doi:10.1017/S0269888909000125

Gasevic, D., Djuric, D., & Devedzic, V. (2009). *Model driven engineering and ontology development* (2nd ed.). Berlin, Germany: Springer.

Gebus, S., & Leiviskä, K. (2009). Knowledge acquisition for decision support systems on an electronic assembly line. *Expert Systems with Applications*, *36*(1), 93–101. doi:10.1016/j.eswa.2007.09.058

Gruber, T. R. (1993). A translation approach to portable ontology specifications. *Knowledge Acquisition*, *5*(2), 199–220. doi:10.1006/knac.1993.1008

Hendler, J. (2001). Agents and the semantic web. *IEEE Intelligent Systems*, *16*(2), 30–37. doi:10.1109/5254.920597

Horridge, M., Jupp, S., Knublauch, H., Moulton, G., Rector, A., Stevens, R., & Wroe, C. (2007). *A practical guide to building OWL ontologies using Protégé 4 and CO-ODE tools*. Manchester, UK: The University of Manchester.

Horrocks, F. D., Broekstra, J., Decker, S., Erdmann, M., Goble, C., van Harmelen, F., & Motta, E. (2000). *Ontology inference layer oil*. Retrieved from http://www.researchgate.net/publication/2384931_The_Ontology_Inference_Layer_OIL

Klein, M. C. A., Fensel, D., Kiryakov, A., & Ognyanov, D. (2002). Ontology versioning and change detection on the web. In A. Gómez-Pérez & V.R. Benjamins (Eds.), *Proceedings of the 13th International Conference on Knowledge Engineering and Knowledge Management* (pp. 197–212). London, UK: Springer-Verlag.

Klyne, G., & Carroll, J. J. (2002). *Resource description framework (RFD), concepts and abstract syntax reference-website*. Retrieved from http://www.w3.org/TR/2002/WDrdf-concepts-20021108/

López, M. F., Gómez-Pérez, A., Sierra, J. P., & Sierra, A. P. (1999). Building a chemical ontology using methontology and the ontology design environment. *IEEE Intelligent Systems*, *14*(1), 37–46. doi:10.1109/5254.747904

McQueen, S., & Thompson, H. (2000). *XML schema reference-website*. Retrieved from http://www.w3.org/XML/Schema

Missikoff, M., & Taglino, F. (2002). Business and enterprise ontology management with SymOntoX. In I. Horrocks, & J. Hendler (Eds.), *The semantic web—ISWC 2002* (pp. 442–447). Berlin, Germany: Springer.

Münch, J., Armbrust, O., Kowalczyk, M., & Soto, M. (2012). *Software process definition and management*. Berlin, Germany: Springer. doi:10.1007/978-3-642-24291-5

Muñoz, E., Capon-Garcia, E., Lainez, J., Espuña, A., & Puigjaner, L. (2011). Ontological framework for the enterprise from a process perspective. In J. Filipe & J.L.G. Dietz (Eds.), *Proceedings of the International Conference on Knowledge Engineering and Ontology Development* (pp. 538–546). SciTePress.

Neches, R., Fikes, R., Finin, T., Gruber, T., Patil, R., Senator, T., & Swartout, W. R. (1991). Enabling technology for knowledge sharing. *AI Magazine, 12*(3), 36–56.

Obrst, L. (2003). Ontologies for semantically interoperable systems. In D. Kraft (Ed.), *Proceedings of the Twelfth International Conference on Information and Knowledge Management* (pp. 366–369). New York: ACM. DOI: 10.1145/956863.956932

Pagels, M. (2006). *The DARPA agent markup language (DAML) reference website.* Retrieved from http://www.daml.org/

Rodríguez, D., García, E., Sánchez, S., & Rodríguez-Solano, C. (2010). Defining software process model constraints with rules using OWL and SWRL. *International Journal of Software Engineering and Knowledge Engineering, 20*(4), 533–548. doi:10.1142/S0218194010004876

Shim, J. P., Warkentin, M., Courtney, J. F., Power, D. J., Sharda, R., & Carlsson, C. (2002). Past, present, and future of decision support technology. *Decision Support Systems, 33*(2), 111–126. doi:10.1016/S0167-9236(01)00139-7

Simon, F., & Murray, T. (2007). Decision support systems. *Communications of the ACM, 50*(3), 39–40. doi:10.1145/1226736.1226762

Singh, R. (1996). International standard ISO/IEC 12207 software life cycle processes. *Software Process Improvement and Practice, 2*(1), 35–50. doi:10.1002/(SICI)1099-1670(199603)2:1<35::AID-SPIP29>3.0.CO;2-3

Sure, Y., & Studer, R. (2002). A methodology for ontology-based knowledge management. In J. Davies, D. Fensel, & F. van Harmelen (Eds.), *Towards the semantic web: Ontology-driven knowledge management* (pp. 33–46). Chichester, UK: Wiley. doi:10.1002/0470858060.ch3

Swartout, W., Neches, R., & Patil, R. (1993). Knowledge sharing: Prospects and challenges. In K. Fuchi & T. Yokoi (Eds.), *Proceedings of the International Conference on Building and Sharing of Very Large-Scale Knowledge Bases.* Tokyo, Japan: Academic Press.

Tautz, C., & von Wangenheim, C. G. (1998). *REFSENO: A representation formalism for software engineering ontologies* (IESE-015.98/E). Kaiserslautern: Fraunhofer IESE.

Valiente, M. C., García-Barriocanal, E., & Sicilia, M. A. (2012). Applying ontology-based models for supporting integrated software development and IT service management processes. *IEEE Transactions on Systems, Man, and Cybernetics. Part C, 42*(1), 61–74.

Vizcaíno, A., García, F., Caballero, I., Villar, J. C., & Piattini, M. (2012). Towards an ontology for global software development. *IET Software, 6*(3), 214–225. doi:10.1049/iet-sen.2011.0087

Wongthongtham, P., Chang, E., Dillon, T., & Sommerville, I. (2006). Ontology based multi-site software development methodology and tools. *Journal of Systems Architecture, 52*(11), 640–653. doi:10.1016/j.sysarc.2006.06.008

Wongthongtham, P., Chang, E., Dillon, T., & Sommerville, I. (2009). Development of a software engineering ontology for multisite software development. *IEEE Transactions on Knowledge and Data Engineering, 21*(8), 1205–1217. doi:10.1109/TKDE.2008.209

XML-Core-Working-Group. (2009). *Extensible markup language (XML) reference website.* Retrieved from http://www.w3.org/XML/

ADDITIONAL READING

Allison, I., & Merali, Y. (2007). Software process improvement as emergent change: A structurational analysis. *Information and Software Technology*, *49*(6), 668–681. doi:10.1016/j.infsof.2007.02.003

Apostolou, D., Mentzas, G., & Abecker, A. (2008). Ontology-enabled knowledge management at multiple organizational levels. In A.S.C. Fernandes (Ed.), *Engineering Management Conference, 2008.* Paper presented at Engineering Management Conference IEEE 2008 International, *Estoril, Portugal 28-30 June* (pp. 1–6). *N.p.: IEEE International.*

Benestad, H. C., Anda, B., & Arisholm, E. (2009). Understanding software maintenance and evolution by analyzing individual changes: a literature review. *Journal Of Software Maintenance And Evolution-Research And Practice*, *21*(6), 349–378. doi:10.1002/smr.412

Chrissis, M. B., Konrad, M., & Shrum, S. (2007). CMMI Second Ed. Guidelines for Process Integration and Product Improvement. United States: Addison Wesley.

Cuevas Agustín, G. (2002). *Gestión del Proceso Software*. Madrid, España: Editorial Centro de Estudios Ramón Areces.

Fernandez-Lopez, M., Gomez-Perez, A., & Juristo, N. (1997). METHONTOLOGY: from Ontological Art towards Ontological Engineering. *Proceedings of the AAAI97 Spring Symposium* (pp. 33–40), March, Stanford, USA.

French, S., & Turoff, M. (2007). Decision support systems. *Communications of the ACM*, *50*(3), 39–40. doi:10.1145/1226736.1226762

Grüninger, M., & Fox, M. S. (1995). Methodology for the Design and Evaluation of Ontologies. *International Joint Conference on Artificial Inteligence (IJCAI95), n.p. Workshop on Basic Ontological Issues in Knowledge Sharing.*

ISOIEC 15504. (2004). *Information technology – Process assessment.* N.p.: International Organization for Standardization Liao, S.H. (2003). Knowledge management technologies and applications–literature review from 1995 to 2002. *Expert Systems with Applications*, *25*(2), 155–164.

Mathiassen, L., & Ngwenyama, O. K., & AAEN, I. (2005). Managing change in software process improvement. *IEEE Software*, *22*(6), 84–91. doi:10.1109/MS.2005.159

Mcfeeley, B. (1996). IDEALSM: A User's Guide for Software Process Improvement (CMU/SEI-96-HB-001). Pittsburgh, USA: Software Engineering Institute (SEI), Carnegie Mellon University.

Muñoz, E., Espuña, A., & Puigjaner, L. (2012). *Knowledge Management Tool for Integrated Decision-making in Industry: Technology for ontology development aimed at integrated decision support systems in process industries. N.p.* LAP LAMBERT Academic Publishing.

Muñoz, M. A., Cuevas Agustin, G., & San Feliu Gilabert, T. (2012). *Metodología Multimodelo para Implementar Mejoras de Procesos Software. N.p.* Editorial Académica Española.

Power, D. J., & Sharda, R. (2007). Model-driven decision support systems: Concepts and research directions. *Decision Support Systems*, *43*(3), 1044–1061. doi:10.1016/j.dss.2005.05.030

Shim, J. P., Warkentin, M., Courtney, F. J., Power, J. D., Sharda, R., & Carlsson, C. (2002). Past, present, and future of decision support technology. *Decision Support Systems*, *33*(2), 111–126. doi:10.1016/S0167-9236(01)00139-7

Sicilia, M. A., Garcia-Barriocanal, E., Sanchez-Alonso, S., & Rodriguez-Garcia, D. (2009). Ontologies of engineering knowledge: general structure and the case of Software Engineering. *The Knowledge Engineering Review*, *24*(3), 309–326. doi:10.1017/S0269888909990087

Sure, Y., Erdmann, M., Angele, J., Staab, S., Studer, R., & Wenke, D. (2002). Ontoedit: Collaborative ontology development for the semantic web. In I. Horrocks, & J. Hendler (Eds.), *The semantic web—ISWC 2002*. Paper presented at First International Semantic Web Conference, Sardinia, Italy, 9–12 June (pp. 221–235). Berlin/Heidelberg, Germany: Springer.

Uschold, M., & Gruninger, M. (1996). Ontologies: principles, methods, and applications. *The Knowledge Engineering Review*, *11*(2), 93–155. doi:10.1017/S0269888900007797

van Heijst, G., Schreiber, A. T., & Wielinga, B. J. (1997). Using explicit ontologies in KBS development. *International Journal of Human-Computer Studies*, *46*(2–3), 183–292. doi:10.1006/ijhc.1996.0090

Varma, V. A., Reklaitis, G. V., Blau, G. E., & Pekny, J. F. (2007). Enterprise-wide modeling & optimization - an overview of emerging research challenges and opportunities. *Computers & Chemical Engineering*, *31*(5–6), 692–711. doi:10.1016/j.compchemeng.2006.11.007

Williams, T. J. (1989). *A reference model for computer integrated manufacturing (CIM)*. North Carolina, USA: Instrument Society of America.

KEY TERMS AND DEFINITIONS

Decision-Support System: Set of information technology elements, which aim to support decision-making in organizations.

Knowledge Management: A collection of processes, strategies and practices, which aim to identify, create, distribute and use knowledge within the organization.

Information Quality: The precise information in terms of time, content, and clarity.

Ontology: Formal structures enabling acquiring, maintaining, accessing, sharing and reusing information.

Process Improvement: Set of organized actions taken to identify, analyze and improve the process to meet the organizational goals.

Software Engineering: A systematic and disciplined approach to create, operate and maintain software based on computer science and engineering principles and practices.

Software Process: A goal-oriented activity in the context of engineering-style software development.

Chapter 11
Software Process Improvement in Small Organizations:
A Knowledge–Management Perspective

Ismael Edrein Espinosa-Curiel
Centro de Investigación Científica y de Educación Superior de Ensenada, Mexico

Josefina Rodríguez-Jacobo
Centro de Investigación Científica y de Educación Superior de Ensenada, Mexico

José Alberto Fernández-Zepeda
Centro de Investigación Científica y de Educación Superior de Ensenada, Mexico

Ulises Gutiérrez-Osorio
Centro de Investigación Científica y de Educación Superior de Ensenada, Mexico

ABSTRACT

Recently, many micro and small-sized enterprises (MSEs) have implemented a model-based Software Process Improvement (SPI) initiative. An initiative like this is a knowledge-intensive activity that uses and creates knowledge related to multiple areas (SPI knowledge) that should be managed. However, MSEs do not usually manage their SPI knowledge, which results in its erosion and eventual loss. This chapter discusses the importance of Knowledge Management (KM) for those MSEs that are implementing an SPI initiative. It also presents the knowledge created or required to accomplish the implementation of this type of initiative. Finally, it discusses the characteristics that a software tool should have to effectively support this KM process.

INTRODUCTION

The micro and small-sized enterprises (MSEs) play an important role in the development of software products and services. MSEs are organizations with fewer than 50 employees and, in some countries, represent 94% of the software development organizations (Fayad, Laitinen, & Ward, 2000). Competition in the software market encourages many MSEs to start a model-based Software Process Improvement (SPI) initiative. The goal of these initiatives is to increase the productivity and quality of these organizations'

DOI: 10.4018/978-1-4666-5182-1.ch011

software processes and products, reduce their associated time and costs, and increase customer satisfaction (Paulk, Curtis, Chrissis, & Weber, 1993). MSEs have limitations, particularities, and special conditions that SPI managers need to consider to design effective SPI initiatives (e.g., MSEs have a reduced number of employees; they have limited funds and they are very vulnerable to market conditions) (Demirors & Demirors, 1998; Horvat, Rozman, & Gyorkos, 2000). Because of these limitations and characteristics, MSEs use special SPI strategies and methodologies. For instance, MSEs usually implement tailored versions of some well-known Process Reference Models (PRMs) (e.g., CMMI, ISO/IEC 15504, or ISO/IEC 12207), or implement PRMs designed especially for their characteristics (e.g., MoProSoft (Oktaba & Vázquez, 2008), Competisoft (Oktaba et al., 2008), or MR-MPS.BR (Montoni et al., 2006)). In spite of these innovations, there is a high failure rate of SPI initiatives, estimated at 70% (Niazi, 2006).

The model-based SPI in MSEs is complex, resource-demanding, and a long-term activity (Mishra & Mishra, 2008; Niazi, Wilson, & Zowghi, 2006). During this activity, to meet the specifications of the PRM, MSEs make several major changes in their current processes (e.g., reallocation of activities flow), structure (e.g., change of roles and responsibilities), policies (e.g., changes in work performance expectations), culture (e.g., introduction of habits, beliefs, or values), employees (e.g., changes in status, benefits or influence), tools (e.g., introduction of new support tools), and software development methodologies (e.g., introduction of new methodologies) (Mathiassen, Ngwenyama, & Aaen, 2005; Moitra, 2005). Because of the magnitude and diversity of these changes, an SPI initiative is a knowledge-intensive activity that uses and creates knowledge related to multiple areas (e.g., software engineering, project management, organizational change, human motivation, etc.). To make these changes, the employees involved (directly or indirectly) in the SPI

initiative (called *SPI stakeholders*) acquire new knowledge, work collaboratively, make decisions, learn from others, share their knowledge, and learn from the results and experiences obtained during the performance of their SPI activities. However, very often MSEs do not manage (identify, create, maintain, update, evaluate, access, transfer, apply and preserve) the knowledge created or acquired in all of the above activities (called *SPI knowledge*). This situation may cause MSEs many difficulties (e.g., repeating the same mistakes, making ineffective decisions, overdependence on the very experienced people, increasing the time and cost of the initiative, and eroding the SPI knowledge or its eventual loss (Wickert & Herschel, 2001)). Sometimes the SPI initiatives may fail (Komi-Sirviö, Mäntyniemi, & Seppänen, 2002). In this sense, SPI knowledge management, tailored to the characteristics of MSEs, may help to solve some of the above problems and increase the success of their SPI initiatives.

The purpose of this chapter is threefold: first, to raise awareness of the importance of SPI KM in MSEs and discuss the general problems that MSEs face when they want to manage their SPI knowledge; second, to present an SPI knowledge taxonomy to help MSEs to determine the type of knowledge they require to manage their SPI initiatives; and third, to provide an overview of the features that a technological tool should have to support the management of SPI knowledge and the limitations to its adoption.

BACKGROUND

Nowadays, knowledge is a very important factor for organizations' competitiveness. Davenport and Prusak (1998) consider knowledge as "a fluid mix of framed experience, contextual information, values and expert insight that provides a framework for evaluating and incorporating new experiences and information." Polanyi (1966) classified knowledge into two dimensions: tacit and explicit. Tacit knowledge (TK) is more personal, difficult to formalize, and difficult to communicate and share with others. Explicit knowledge (EK) is codified and can be expressed in words or numbers and shared in the form of data, documents, manuals, etc. In addition, Nonaka (1994) classified knowledge as individual and collective. He also defines knowledge creation as a "knowledge spiral" in which there is continuous interaction among individuals and continuous conversion from EK to TK and vice versa. This process has the following four basic conversion patterns: socialization (TK to TK), externalization (TK to EK), combination (EK to EK), and internalization (EK to TK).

Knowledge Management

Organizations need to effectively capitalize their knowledge and use it as a source of growth and profit. However, this action depends on the organizational efforts to explicitly manage their knowledge. Alavi and Leidner (2001) define *Knowledge Management* (KM) as "an organizational systematic framework to capture, acquire, organize and communicate tacit and explicit knowledge to employees, so that employees can use it and thus be more effective and productive in their work, maximizing the knowledge of the organization." KM can provide several benefits to organizations (e.g., better decision making, faster time to response to key issues, improvement of productivity, cost reduction, quality improvement, process improvement, learning, innovation, and increased staff satisfaction) (Alavi & Leidner, 1999).

The KM process consists of the following eight activities (Beijerse, 2000; Dayan & Evans, 2006; Natali & Falbo, 2002; Ribiere, 2001; Rus & Lindvall, 2002).

1. **Identify gaps/needs of knowledge:** The organization identifies the knowledge that is necessary to reach its objectives. The organi-

zation also identifies its present knowledge and knowledge gaps.

2. **Acquire/create/capture knowledge:** The organization's employees create knowledge through learning, problem solving, innovating, or they obtain it from external sources. The organization's employees capture knowledge in explicit forms (e.g., written material or knowledge base systems).

3. **Organize knowledge:** Organizations classify and group knowledge to facilitate searching for and accessing specific knowledge.

4. **Access/retrieve information:** The organization's employees have a fast, accurate and friendly access to specific knowledge.

5. **Transfer/share knowledge:** Organizations distribute knowledge through education, training programs, knowledge-based systems, or expert networks.

6. **Apply/use knowledge:** The organization's ultimate goal is to apply knowledge (this is the most important part of the KM life cycle). In this situation, knowledge helps to create organizational capability (e.g., directives, organizational routines, and self-contained tasks).

7. **Maintain/update/evaluate knowledge:** This activity involves updating or evaluating existing knowledge. The organization's employees update or evaluate knowledge through learning, problem solving, or innovating.

8. **Preserve knowledge:** Organizations must consider mechanisms to preserve their knowledge since it is part of their assets and, if properly managed, may produce income.

Organizations perform some level of knowledge management; however, this management is not systematic. For this reason, the objective of KM is to expand, improve and systematize these practices. In general, it is convenient to use consultants who can assist in designing the knowledge map, assessing the status of current knowledge, and educating managers and employees in fundamental aspects of KM.

To support the KM process, some researchers have developed several models and implementation guides. Abecker, Bernardi, Hinkelmann, Kuhn and Sintek (1998) proposed a KM model that requires a hybrid solution that involves people and technology. For this model, it is necessary to identify and structure the elements of KM and their interactions. Wong and Aspinwall (2004) proposed a KM implementation framework that synthesizes the existing KM implementation frameworks and related KM literature. They argue that the lack of support and guidelines can make organizations struggle with KM and unable to reach their full potential. Lindvall, Rus and Sinha (2003) present a literature review of KM technologies. They argue that KM relies heavily on technology, but it is important to appreciate that technology alone will never be the solution to KM. They specify that a KM system implementation needs to address the socio-cultural and organizational components to assure its acceptance and success.

Knowledge Management in SPI Initiatives

KM is an expanding and promising discipline in the software industry. Software organizations need to perform KM process activities to increase the probability of successfully implementing an SPI initiative (e.g., documenting their software processes). If they can do so in a fast and effective way, they can cope with some pressing business issues (e.g., decrease time and cost, increase quality, make better decisions, and adapt to market changes). Meehan and Richardson (2002) claim that KM is a core component of SPI initiatives, where employees continuously create, capture, and transfer SPI knowledge. Espinosa-Curiel, Rodríguez-Jacobo and Fernández-Zepeda (2013) argue that KM is a key factor that influences the success of SPI initiatives and impact the processes,

the people, the organization, the improvement project, and the development process.

Several researchers developed methodologies to support KM in SPI. Santos, Montoni, Figueiredo and Rocha (2007) used KM to support their proposed process-centered approach strategy, called SPI-KM. They based their strategy on well-known PRMs and standards. Montoni, Cerdeiral, Zanetti and Rocha (2008) presented a KM approach to support SPI initiatives. This approach captures knowledge related to critical success factors, issues, and best practices of SPI implementations. In addition, some researchers proposed KM tools. Montoni et al. (2006) developed an SPI system that provides support to the KM of software development processes, preserves organizational knowledge, and fosters the initialization of a learning software organization. In another study, Montoni et al. (2008) proposed a tool that integrates SPI and KM technologies.

SPI Knowledge Management in MSEs

Wong and Aspinwall (2004) argue that most of the literature on KM focus on large organizations and usually neglect KM in small settings; however, they specify that KM has the same importance in large and small organizations. Since MSEs have special characteristics and needs, their KM strategies have particularities in scope, scale, and how they will be carried out. Although some researchers have conducted several studies on KM in software organizations, few of these studies focus on SPI in the context of MSEs. Figure 1 shows the elements of an MSE and the elements of the model-based SPI initiative. Usually, MSEs do not consider the SPI KM process (black box on the right side of the figure), but it is important to perform an SPI initiative.

In general, MSEs are not aware of the importance and the benefits of SPI KM because they mainly focus on core business processes and are busy with their day-to-day operations. Even more,

Figure 1. KM in a model-based SPI initiative in MSEs

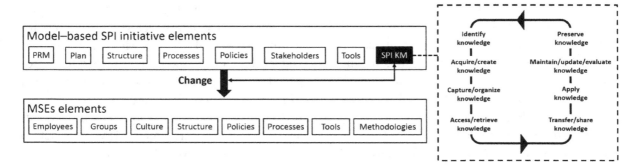

there is a lack of knowledge and experience related to the implementation of SPI initiatives in MSEs. Usually, these organizations only provide stakeholders with hardcopies of the PRM manuals and some templates (technical knowledge). However, this information does not support all the changes at the personal, social and organizational levels required by an SPI initiative. For MSEs, it is hard to assign dedicated staff to implement an SPI initiative. Therefore, they depend heavily on external SPI initiative consultants. In general, the SPI activities in MSEs are informal with low standardization and their division is unclear.

MSE managers (frequently the owners) strongly impact and shape the organizational culture. They influence the direction of SPI initiatives and determine how important KM is in the SPI initiative; however, they usually have little formal training for effective business management.

SPI stakeholders normally know each other well, have face-to-face contact, their collaboration is often good, and they recognize the importance of KM (especially because of the high turnover rate). On the other hand, stakeholders are poorly specialized in SPI and they usually do not know how to fulfill their responsibilities without increasing time and cost of the initiative. They are overloaded with work and do not have time to think about KM strategies. Communication among them is brief and direct and their interactions are informal and poorly documented. Even more, the informal ways in which stakeholders conduct their SPI activities may inhibit the implementation of a formal and comprehensive KM system.

In general, MSEs lack formal and integrated SPI KM activities. Next, we present some examples of the SPI KM activities performed by MSEs (Rodríguez-Jacobo, Espinosa-Curiel, Gutiérrez-Osorio, Ocegueda-Miramontes, & Fernández-Zepeda, 2012).

- **Identify knowledge:** MSEs focus their attention on defining a general SPI plan, and frequently they do not make a plan of the knowledge needed to adopt a PRM. Usually, the consultants define the SPI knowledge needed by the SPI initiatives and provide some support material and templates. Existing SPI knowledge is difficult to find and, when found, is not reusable. As a result, it is hard for MSEs to determine the knowledge gap within their SPI initiative.

- **Acquire/create/capture knowledge:** SPI stakeholders focus mainly on the SPI activities rather than on the SPI documentation process. In general, to acquire knowledge, SPI stakeholders depend mainly on self-learning, the support of coworkers, and on the guidance of SPI consultants and experts. SPI stakeholders use external sources of information such as books, Web pages, templates, documents, and formal training courses. However, these courses focus mainly on understanding the process of a specific PRM and lack of action knowledge. Moreover, the creation of knowledge occurs when SPI stakeholders perform their SPI activities and responsibilities. The documentation of the knowledge used and created during SPI activities is usually insufficient, informal and individual. Stakeholders document most of the information in digital format. The SPI leaders and some SPI team members perform most of the documentation process, but they usually focus only on describing their activities. In general, the SPI stakeholders feel that a great deal of the SPI knowledge is being wasted.

- **Access/transfer knowledge:** In general, MSEs do not have a tool to manage their SPI knowledge. Stakeholders transfer the SPI knowledge in informal ways (e.g., through open and direct discussions with other stakeholders and by providing informal guidance, printed or digital material, etc.). Sometimes, the SPI stakeholders that attended the training courses replicate the information they learned within the company.

- **Apply knowledge:** Usually, the application of the SPI knowledge is individual. It does not become an organizational capability as self-contained tasks or routines.

- **Maintain/update/evaluate knowledge:** In general, MSEs lack a systematic approach to maintain, update and evaluate their knowledge. Stakeholders update SPI knowledge in informal ways (e.g., through open and direct discussions with other stakeholders and by receiving informal guidance, printed or digital material, etc.).

CLASSIFICATION OF SPI KNOWLEDGE

This section provides a brief description of the knowledge generated or required in an SPI initiative. This knowledge is the result of the integration of two different sources of information. First, from the knowledge that we identified in some case studies (Rodríguez-Jacobo et al., 2012); and second, the knowledge that Espinosa-Curiel (2013) identified from the analysis of the implementation guides for MSEs and from a set of case studies conducted by other researchers in software development MSEs. We classified knowledge into three hierarchical levels. The first level divides knowledge into three categories: personal, social and technical. The second level divides each of the categories into subcategories. The third level makes a further division of the subcategories (see Table 1). Finally, each subcategory contains knowledge items. According to Zack (1999), the knowledge items can be any of the following six types: declarative (know-about), procedural (know-how), causal (know-why), conditional (know-when), relational (know-with) and pragmatic (experiences and lessons learned). Next, we describe our categories and subcategories.

Table 1. SPI knowledge classification

First Classification	Second Classification	Third Classification Examples
Personal	Self-awareness	Emotional-awareness
	Self-management	Emotional self-control
Social	Social awareness	Organizational awareness
	Relation management	Team work and collaboration
Technical	SPI project management	Resources and time estimation
	Processes	Process modeling

- **Knowledge for personal development**: It is the knowledge that employees are required to know how to be and how to behave. We divided this category into the following subcategories:
  - ○ **Self-awareness:** It is the knowledge related to the development of emotional awareness, self-assessment, self-confidence, and self-development.
  - ○ **Self-management:** It is the knowledge related to the development of responsibility, analytical thinking, creativity and innovation, decision making, emotional self-control, ethics and integrity, flexibility, initiative, and results and achievements orientation.
- **Knowledge for social development**: It is the knowledge that employees need to know how to relate and how to collaborate with others. We divided this category into the following subcategories:
  - ○ **Social sensitivity:** It is the knowledge related to the development of communication, social awareness, and organizational awareness.
  - ○ **Relationship management:** It is the knowledge related to the development of conflict management, development and empowerment of others, the adoption of and support for change, negotiation and influence, work networking, teamwork and collaboration.
- **Technical knowledge**: It is the knowledge that employees need to know what to do and how to do it. We divided this category into the following subcategories:
  - ○ **Software Engineering:** It is the knowledge related to the processes of requirement management; design, construction, testing and software maintenance; configuration management, process engineering, software quality management, project management and support tools and systems for software development.
  - ○ **PRMs:** It is the knowledge related to the characteristics, advantages, disadvantages, and restrictions of PRMs. It includes concepts, terms, basic definitions, and supporting material. It also includes specific knowledge related to the PRM to be adopted (e.g., the structure, stages, roles, processes, activities, outputs, outcomes and benefits in the short, medium and long term, the initial requirements, etc.).
  - ○ **Implementation guides (IGs):** It is the knowledge related to the characteristics, advantages, and disadvantages of the IGs. It includes concepts, terms, definitions, and support material for the IGs. It also includes specific knowledge related to the IGs that the organization uses (e.g., phases, roles, activities, products, initial requirements, etc.).
  - ○ **Organizational analysis:** It is the knowledge related to the identification of the situation and needs of the organization.
  - ○ **Processes modeling:** It is the knowledge related to the techniques and methodologies for analyzing and modeling the processes of the organization.
  - ○ **Processes assessment:** It is the knowledge related to the evaluation of the maturity of the processes (both formal and informal), the analysis of the results, and the identification of areas for SPI.
  - ○ **SPI initiative definition:** It is the knowledge related to the definition of the goals and principles of the SPI initiative, the alignment of these with respect to the goals and needs of the

organization, and the high-level planning of the SPI initiative.

○ **SPI project management:** It is the knowledge required to plan, organize, direct and control the SPI project. This subcategory includes the knowledge related to prioritizing areas for improvement, estimating the resources (human, material, financial) and the time required for the improvements (in stages and levels, processes), including the development of an SPI initiative plan and the definition of improvement actions. In addition, this subcategory includes the knowledge related to knowledge, quality, and risk management methodologies; and communication, feedback, training, and rewards mechanisms.

○ **Support structure for SPI initiative:** It is the knowledge related to the definition of roles and responsibilities, training and integration of work groups that will support the SPI initiative, the metrics, methods, tools, and systems to evaluate the performance of the support team, and the knowledge to design training plans.

○ **Competencies:** It is the knowledge and methodologies related to the identification, evaluation and development of the skills, knowledge and behavior required by the managers, the SPI leader, the improvement team, consultants, and employees.

○ **Change management:** It is the knowledge related to the identification, evaluation and implementation of personal, social, and organizational changes required by the SPI initiative. This subcategory includes knowledge related to methodologies and strategies to mitigate and control the resis-

tance to change, motivate and engage employees and managers, increase the integration and collaboration of employees, manage and resolve personal and work conflicts, and respond appropriately to staff turnover.

○ **Process improvement:** It is the knowledge required to design the transition process from the current state to the desired state. This subcategory includes the knowledge to maintain the configuration of the processes, improve existing processes, or develop new processes.

○ **Implementation process:** It is the knowledge required to establish new or improved processes in the organization. This subcategory includes the knowledge required to design and implement pilot tests for processes, analyze the tests results, and for the institutionalization of new or improved processes.

○ **Processes Metrics:** It is the knowledge related to the definition and evaluation of metrics (e.g., time, cost, satisfaction, errors and rework) to help assess the processes improvements.

○ **Postmortem analysis and knowledge management:** It is the knowledge required to analyze the results of the improvements and lessons learned, and to store them in a manageable way.

○ **Tools and support systems for SPI:** It is the knowledge required to use and adapt the tools and support systems of the SPI initiative (e.g., electronic guides for processes, processes evaluation systems, project management systems, knowledge management systems, etc.).

KM SYSTEMS

A *knowledge management system* (KM system) is a technological support tool for all the activities of the KM process. KM systems are classified into two types: commercial and research systems. The KM research systems were created to support research in the KM area and are not available to the general public. Among these systems, we can mention the following:

Acknowledge (Montoni, Miranda, Rocha, & Travassos, 2004) is a KM system related to software development. The purpose of this tool is to acquire, filter and package the tacit and explicit knowledge of the members of the organization to become organizational knowledge. This system temporarily stores the acquired knowledge in a knowledge base until a moderator filters it to identify the knowledge relevant to the organization. In addition, the system allows employees to make comments on knowledge to facilitate evaluation and maintenance.

TechSolution (Figueiredo et al., 2006) is a system to manage the knowledge of the architectural design of a software system. The system takes the design criteria from the input project and displays information from architectural patterns consistent with those characteristics. It also displays information on how to perform tasks related to the architectural pattern selected.

AdaptPro (Montoni et al., 2005) is a system that helps to institutionalize standardized processes in software development projects. This system provides information (both knowledge and experience) related to the processes activities to facilitate their adaptation to the particular characteristics of a project (e.g., adapt the life cycle, estimates, etc.). It also provides information about the activities of similar projects.

Jasmine (Shin, Choi, & Baik, 2007) is a personal knowledge management tool. It consists of two subsystems: a management tool for personal processes, and a model guide for Personal Software Process (PSP) that has a repository of experiences.

While users perform their processes based on PSP, they can store their experiences, artifacts, related knowledge, etc. in the data base of the system. Jasmine also allows software developers to share their experiences among members of their development team.

Sharebox (Rodríguez-Jacobo et al., 2012) is a KM system designed specifically to support an SPI initiative in MSEs. (Table 3 shows the features of ShareBox.) They determined the features and functions that KM systems should have, based on the information provided by a literature review, and the results from some case studies in Mexican MSEs that develop software (Rodríguez-Jacobo et al., 2012). Unlike Sharebox, none of the above four tools were designed to specifically manage knowledge to foster an SPI initiative. The following section evaluates ShareBox.

Likewise, there are many commercial KM systems. Gutiérrez-Osorio (2011) presented a list of ten commercial systems and their costs. We present this list in Table 2. Since our research group designed and implemented ShareBox, and to facilitate its comparison with the commercial systems, we included ShareBox in this Table.

We present a classification of the main features of these systems and divide them into two categories: those features required by the KM process and those that support KM systems. We divided the first categories into eight subcategories which match the eight activities of the KM process, so it is easy to determine which feature supports each activity. Table 3 shows our classification and provides examples of the most common features in each subcategory. We also divided the second category into four subcategories.

Gutiérrez-Osorio (2011) also compared the features of the eleven KM systems of Table 2. The features he evaluated are an extension of those shown in Table 3.

In his comparison, Gutiérrez-Osorio (2011) only indicates whether there is evidence, based on the information available, that the feature is present in the KM system or not. He never had

Table 2. Some commercial KM systems and Sharebox (Gutiérrez-Osorio, 2011)

#	Knowledge Management Systems	Home Pages	Annual Costs (US Dollars)
1	Knowledge Base Manager Pro	www.web-site-scripts.com	500 - 20,000
2	Alfresco	www.alfresco.com	Not available
3	KB Publisher	www.kbpublisher.com	1000 - 12,000
4	KMS	www.en.enage.com	Not available
5	Interspire Knowledge Manager	www.static.interspire.com	495 - 9,095
6	Knowledge Base	www.moxiesoft.com	Not available
7	Lumoflow	www.lumoflow.com	480 – unlimited
8	Omnistar Kbase	www.omnistarkbase.com	324 - 3,564
9	Parature Knowledge base	www.parature.com	Not available
10	Traction Team Page	www.traction.tractionsoftware.com	3,750 - 60,000
11	ShareBox	www.sharebox.gisep.com.mx	Not for sale

access to the systems, so it is possible that some systems have more features than those specified in his comparison. He did not evaluate the quality of the features implementation. In Table 4, we present a reduced version of his comparison. A check symbol indicates that the KM system has such a feature.

EVALUATION OF THE ADOPTION OF SHAREBOX

Rodríguez-Jacobo et al. (2012) evaluated Share-Box. The purpose of this evaluation was to determine whether Sharebox works as a support tool for organizations and stakeholders, and to identify the factors that influence its adoption. This evaluation proceeded in two stages. In the first stage, SPI professionals provided their thoughts about the system. In the second stage, two MSEs started the adoption of Sharebox with the aim of reducing the time for learning, facilitating the capture, formalizing and increasing knowledge for their stakeholders, and increasing collaboration and communication among them.

The interviewees mentioned that Sharebox seems to be easy to use and is intuitive, easily supports the capture of knowledge (because it provides templates), facilitates the managing, sharing, searching and updating of knowledge, and classifies the knowledge according to different criteria (e.g., categories and sub-categories, SPI stages, roles, focus). The interviewees agreed that Sharebox can help to make better decisions, reduce dependence on certain employees, learn from past experiences, avoid repeating the same mistakes, ease the training of new stakeholders, and help to support their professional development in a holistic way (personal, social, and technical). Additionally, KM in their organizations is more effective, because Sharebox can provide the right information at the right time; however, they were concerned about the seriousness and reliability of the information stored in the knowledge base, the anonymity of the information, and the time needed to capture knowledge. On the other hand, the interviewees indicated that the technical knowledge was easier to identify than the personal and social knowledge; nevertheless, they considered that all types of knowledge is fundamental for a successful SPI initiative.

The results of this evaluation showed that the features of ShareBox satisfy the requirements of a tool intended to support knowledge management in an SPI initiative. Our knowledge classification covers most of the knowledge required by

Table 3. Classification of the features provided by knowledge management systems

Features Required by the KM Process	
1. Identify Knowledge	**Description of the Feature**
Contents	It shows a list of the information for a specific category, subcategory, topic, etc.
Pending knowledge acquisition	It records a list of knowledge required by the organization.
2. Acquire/Create/Capture Knowledge	**Description of the Feature**
Import information	It allows to acquire unstructured information from different digital sources (e.g., web pages, data bases, e-mails, pdf documents, etc.).
Related knowledge	It provides related knowledge on a specific topic to help users to create knowledge.
Auto save	It allows automatic periodical saves during knowledge capture.
Attachments	It allows to attach files (e.g., pdf documents, images, videos, etc.) on specific knowledge topics.
Glossary	It allows to capture the meaning of certain terminology for future consultation.
Draft manager	Il allows to capture incomplete or preliminary versions of a knowledge topic.
Spell checker	It checks spelling and grammar.
3. Organize Knowledge	**Description of the Feature**
Knowledge structure	It provides the capability to create and edit templates to store knowledge.
Taxonomy	It allows the construction of categories and subcategories to classify knowledge.
Ontology	It allows the definition of vocabulary in the system to facilitate communication, searches, storage and representation of knowledge.
Similar knowledge	It allows users to identify similar knowledge topics to integrate them into a single topic to avoid redundancy.
Document manager	It allows the management of different types of documents.
Knowledge approval	It allows the publication of knowledge.
Contents moderator	It allows to the system manager to publish and remove stored knowledge.
4. Access/Retrieve Information	**Description of the Feature**
Search	It allows to search and filter (most voted, most recent, etc.) specific knowledge topics or files in the system.
Subscription	It allows users to subscribe to specific types of knowledge and periodically receive a bulletin or newsletter.
Navigation	It allows users to access references on specific topics.
5. Apply Knowledge	**Description of the Feature**
Lessons learned	It allows to record the results of applying specific knowledge.
6. Transfer/Share Knowledge	**Description of the Feature**
Share	It provides modules that allow knowledge exchange among users or organizations (exchange of knowledge links, e-mail, documents, etc.).
Social network	It supports the collaboration and communication of users with common interests and needs (some common tools are boards and real time communication).
Forum	It provides a place to share opinions about specific topics, facilitating collaboration among peers and team members.
Export information	It allows information transfer in digital form to external systems.
7. Update/Evaluate Knowledge	**Description of the Feature**
Feedback	It allows users to indicate if the information is useful, correct, incomplete, etc., providing feedback for proper maintenance.
Knowledge rating	It provides a mechanism to evaluate the quality of knowledge.
Version control	It records historical changes and updates of knowledge.
8. Maintain/Preserve Knowledge	**Description of the Feature**
Backups	It generates security information backups to assure the integrity of the information.
Knowledge access	It manages the access of users or groups to knowledge.

continued on following page

Table 3. Continued

Features that Support the KM system	
1. User Management/Accessibility	**Description of the Feature**
Registration	It allows to define the profile of each user (e.g., interests, experience and image).
Accessibility	Users can access the system from different locations (intranet, Internet, etc.) and devices (i.e, smart phones).
Authentication	It allows to manage users' access to the system.
Users directory	It provides a list of the users of the system.
2. Metrics	**Description of the Feature**
Measurability	It provides tools to report statistics (most relevant topics, users' activities, system error, etc.).
Reputation	It indicates the importance of the contributions of a specific user (to motivate and encourage users).
3. Proactivity	**Description of the Feature**
Proactivity	It provides new knowledge, the most rated knowledge, and the most accessed knowledge, among others according to users' profile.
4. Adaptability	**Description of the Feature**
Legacy systems integration	It allows the migration of knowledge stored in previous systems to the new system.
Flexibility	It allows the system to incorporate new modules and functions or to edit HTML files.

an SPI initiative. Even more, the results of the evaluation allowed to identify some barriers that organizations should consider when implementing Sharebox. Table 5 lists these barriers.

Rodríguez-Jacobo et al. (2012) proposed the following recommendations that may help organizations to mitigate some of the barriers listed in Table 5.

- **Integration:** Organizations should define a strategy to integrate the SPI KM activities within SPI activities and define formal time periods to use Sharebox.
- **Support:** Managers should take an active role and exemplify the desired behavior for KM. They should also create an environment that encourages the preservation, use and transfer of knowledge. Organizations should provide training, support material (documents, manuals, videos, etc.) and templates.
- **Policies:** Organizations should define a clear policy manual to regulate the use, capture, update and sharing of knowledge. The use of this manual may increase the quality and reliability of information. Also, organizations should provide mechanisms

to manage access to knowledge and, when required, the anonymity of the information.
- **Awareness, commitment, and incentives:** It is important that the whole organization be committed to including Sharebox in all the SPI activities, conducting activities to increase the awareness of the importance of KM, and implementing incentives to recognize and to potentiate the use of Sharebox and knowledge creators.
- **Visibility:** It would be useful to identify the early adopters of Sharebox and include them in a strategy to strengthen the "visibility of the use" of Sharebox.
- **Culture:** Organizations should create a culture that encourages the exchange of knowledge and motivates staff to share the SPI initiative.

CONCLUDING REMARKS

During an SPI initiative, organizations use and create SPI knowledge from several areas. Organizations need to manage this knowledge to improve decision making and to facilitate learning for SPI stakeholders. Some MSEs erroneously consider

Table 4. Features of the KM systems analyzed

No.	Features of KM Systems	KM systems										
		1	2	3	4	5	6	7	8	9	10	11
1	Multi-platform	√	√	√	√	√	√	√	√	√	√	√
2	Multi-language	√	√	√	√	√	√	√	√	√	√	
3	Open source		√									√
4	KM mobile						√				√	
5	Internet	√	√	√		√		√	√		√	√
6	Intranet	√	√	√	√	√	√	√	√	√	√	√
7	Help	√	√	√		√	√					√
8	Flexibility (code availability)											√
9	Legacy systems integration											
10	Metadata management		√	√		√	√	√	√	√	√	
11	Information export	√	√	√	√	√	√	√	√	√	√	√
12	Information import	√		√	√		√				√	
13	System errors report					√		√				√
14	System usage report					√		√	√	√		√
15	Search engine	√	√	√	√	√	√	√	√	√	√	√
16	Search filtering		√			√	√		√		√	
17	Similar knowledge	√	√	√	√		√	√		√		√
18	Role-oriented search results		√					√			√	
19	Contents based on category		√								√	√
20	Document management	√	√	√	√		√	√				√
21	File finder		√									
22	Version management	√	√		√	√	√			√	√	
23	Draft manager	√		√	√						√	√
24	Lessons learned											√
25	Knowledge approval			√	√	√	√					√
26	Auto save	√									√	
27	Spell checker	√	√	√	√	√	√	√	√	√	√	√
28	HTML editor		√	√	√	√	√	√	√	√	√	√
29	Forum	√	√	√	√	√	√	√	√	√	√	√
30	E-mail	√	√		√	√	√	√	√	√	√	√
31	Social board							√		√		√
32	Subscriptions	√	√	√	√	√	√	√	√	√	√	
33	Private message			√	√	√		√	√	√	√	√
34	Comments	√	√	√	√	√	√	√	√	√	√	√
35	Information sharing	√	√	√	√	√	√	√	√	√	√	√
36	Selective broadcasts	√	√	√	√	√	√	√	√	√	√	√
37	Real time communication					√				√	√	√
38	Inter-organizational interaction											√
39	SPI knowledge taxonomy											√
40	Knowledge structure											√

continued on following page

Table 4. Continued

41	Multi-category	√	√	√	√	√			√	√		√
42	Knowledge integration	√		√	√	√				√		
43	Glossary	√		√			√		√			
44	Ontology											
45	Users and groups management	√	√	√	√	√	√	√	√	√	√	√
46	Users directory		√					√	√			√
47	Contents moderator			√	√	√	√					√
48	Authentication	√	√	√	√	√	√	√	√	√	√	√
49	Information privacy management	√	√	√	√	√	√	√	√	√	√	√
50	Information safeguarding	√	√									√
51	Popularity lists	√	√	√	√	√	√	√	√	√	√	√
52	Reputation				√	√				√	√	√
53	Proactivity (information)					√						
54	Virtual incentives				√	√				√	√	√
	Total	28	28	32	30	32	28	27	26	28	31	39

Table 5. Barriers that organization may encounter when implementing ShareBox

#	Description
1	Lack of capable users due to insufficient training.
2	Failure to integrate KM into daily working practices.
3	The employees are overloaded with work, so they have little time to perform KM activities.
4	Lack of time to learn how to use the system because of its unfriendly design.
5	Users are sceptical about the benefits of the system.
6	Users are not committed to the implementation of the system.
7	Difficulties in transforming tacit knowledge into explicit knowledge.
8	There are no incentives for capturing, sharing, using and evaluating knowledge.
9	Information overload (too much knowledge is created and it is difficult to capture and organize).
10	The policies on the use of the system are unclear.

that only technical knowledge is relevant for an SPI initiative. However, we coincide with other authors that argue that personal and social knowledge is also important for this activity. For this reason, the classification that we have presented in this chapter clearly specifies that stakeholders need knowledge at the personal, social and technical levels. Personal knowledge helps stakeholders to know how to be and how to behave. Social knowledge helps stakeholders to know how to be with others. Technical knowledge helps stakeholders to know what to do and how to do it.

Several KM systems can support KM in SPI initiatives. However, to select the appropriate system, it is necessary to consider two factors: first, the special characteristic of the MSEs and second, the characteristics of the SPI knowledge. Additionally, the KM system should include a set of basic features. Organizations that are planning to acquire a KM system may want to use our comparison analysis to help them to decide the most appropriate tool.

We compared a KM system, called Sharebox, with some commercial KM systems. Unlike the other KM systems, Sharebox is designed to support the management of the SPI knowledge. We also discussed the results of the use of ShareBox in two MSEs. To successfully adopt Sharebox, we established that MSEs need to implement awareness and motivation strategies, gain the commitment of the whole organization, provide support and training resources, develop KM policies, monitor the use of the system, and recognize the employees that create knowledge. Finally, it is important to highlight that the impact of Sharebox depends on the amount and quality of knowledge managed by the organization. It is also important to note that the competitive advantages of KM should not be measured only by the amount of knowledge that the organization gathers and stores, but rather by the use the organization makes of it. Therefore, it is necessary to adopt an organizational culture that fosters exchange and collaboration.

REFERENCES

Abecker, A., Bernardi, A., Hinkelmann, K., Kuhn, O., & Sintek, M. (1998). Toward a technology for organizational memories. *IEEE Intelligent Systems and their Applications, 13*(3), 40–48.

Alavi, M., & Leidner, D. E. (1999). Knowledge management systems: Issues, challenges, and benefits. *Commun. AIS, 1*(2).

Alavi, M., & Leidner, D. E. (2001). Review: Knowledge management and knowledge management systems: Conceptual foundations and research issues. *Management Information Systems Quarterly, 25*(1), 107–136. doi:10.2307/3250961

Beijerse, R. U. (2000). Knowledge management in small and medium-sized companies: Knowledge management for entrepreneurs. *Journal of Knowledge Management, 4*(2), 162–179. doi:10.1108/13673270010372297

Davenport, T. H., & Prusak, L. (1998). *Working knowledge: How organizations manage what they know*. Boston, MA: Harvard Business School Press.

Dayan, R., & Evans, S. (2006). KM your way to CMMI. *Journal of Knowledge Management, 10*(1), 69–80. doi:10.1108/13673270610650111

Demirors, O., & Demirors, E. (1998). Software process improvement in a small organization: difficulties and suggestions. In V. Gruhn (Ed.), *Software Process Technology* (pp. 1–12). Springer Berlin Heidelberg. doi:10.1007/3-540-64956-5_1

Espinosa-Curiel, I. (2013). *Mecanismos de soporte al proceso de adopción de un modelo de referencia de procesos en las micro, pequeñas y medianas empresas*. (Doctoral dissertation). Department of Computer Science, CICESE, Ensenada, Mexico.

Espinosa-Curiel, I. E., Rodríguez-Jacobo, J., & Fernández-Zepeda, J. A. (2013). A framework for evaluation and control of the factors that influence the software process improvement in small organizations. *Journal of Software: Evolution and Process, 25*(4), 393–406.

Fayad, M. E., Laitinen, M., & Ward, R. P. (2000). Thinking objectively: Software engineering in the small. *Communications of the ACM, 43*(3), 115–118. doi:10.1145/330534.330555

Figueiredo, S., Santos, G., Montoni, M., Rocha, A. R., Barreto, A., Barreto, A., & Ferreira, A. (2006). Taba workstation: supporting technical solution through knowledge management of design rationale. In U. Reimer, & D. Karagiannis (Eds.), *Practical Aspects of Knowledge Management* (pp. 61–72). Springer Berlin Heidelberg. doi:10.1007/11944935_6

Gutiérrez-Osorio, U. (2011). *Una estrategia para la implementación de un sistema de administración del conocimiento en la mejora de procesos de software*. (Master Thesis). Department of Computer Science, CICESE, Ensenada, Mexico.

Horvat, R. V., Rozman, I., & Gyorkos, J. (2000). Managing the complexity of SPI in small companies. *Software Process Improvement and Practice, 5*(1), 45–54. doi:10.1002/(SICI)1099-1670(200003)5:1<45::AID-SPIP110>3.0.CO;2-2

Komi-Sirviö, S., Mäntyniemi, A., & Seppänen, V. (2002). Toward a practical solution for capturing knowledge for software projects. *IEEE Software, 19*(3), 60–62. doi:10.1109/MS.2002.1003457

Lindvall, M., Rus, I., & Sinha, S. S. (2003). Technology support for knowledge Mmanagement. In S. Henninger, & F. Maurer (Eds.), *Advances in Learning Software Organizations* (pp. 94–103). Springer Berlin Heidelberg. doi:10.1007/978-3-540-40052-3_9

Mathiassen, L., Ngwenyama, O. K., & Aaen, I. (2005). Managing change in software process improvement. *IEEE Software, 22*(6), 84–91. doi:10.1109/MS.2005.159

Meehan, B., & Richardson, I. (2002). Identification of software process knowledge management. *Software Process Improvement and Practice, 7*(2), 47–55. doi:10.1002/spip.154

Mishra, D., & Mishra, A. (2008). Software process improvement methodologies for small and medium enterprises. In A. Jedlitschka, & O. Salo (Eds.), *Product-Focused Software Process Improvement* (pp. 273–288). Springer Berlin Heidelberg. doi:10.1007/978-3-540-69566-0_23

Moitra, D. (2005). Managing organizational change for software process improvement. In S. T. Acuña, & N. Juristo (Eds.), *Software Process Modeling* (pp. 163–185). Springer, US. doi:10.1007/0-387-24262-7_7

Montoni, M., Miranda, R., Rocha, A. R., & Travassos, G. H. (2004). Knowledge acquisition and communities of practice: an approach to convert individual knowledge into multi-organizational knowledge. In G. Melnik, & H. Holz (Eds.), *Advances in Learning Software Organizations* (pp. 110–121). Springer Berlin Heidelberg. doi:10.1007/978-3-540-25983-1_11

Montoni, M., Santos, G., Rocha, A., Figueiredo, S., Cabral, R., Barcellos, R., et al. (2006). Taba workstation: Supporting software process deployment based on CMMI and MR-MPS.BR. In J. Münch, & M. Vierimaa (Eds.), Product-Focused Software Process Improvement, (pp. 249–262). Springer Berlin Heidelberg.

Montoni, M., Santos, G., Villela, K., Rocha, A., Travassos, G., Figueiredo, S., & Mian, P. (2005). Enterprise-oriented software development environments to support software products and processes quality improvement. In F. Bomarius, & S. Komi-Sirviö (Eds.), *Product Focused Software Process Improvement* (pp. 370–384). Springer Berlin Heidelberg. doi:10.1007/11497455_30

Montoni, M. A., Cerdeiral, C., Zanetti, D., & Cavalcanti da Rocha, A. R. (2008). A Knowledge management approach to support software process improvement implementation initiatives. In R. V. O'Connor, N. Baddoo, K. Smolander, & R. Messnarz (Eds.), *Software Process Improvement* (pp. 164–175). Springer Berlin Heidelberg. doi:10.1007/978-3-540-85936-9_15

Natali, A. C. C., & Falbo, R. (2002). Knowledge management in software engineering environments. In *Proceedings of the XVI Brazilian Symposium on Software Engineering*, (pp. 238–253). Gramado, Brazil.

Niazi, M. (2006). Software process improvement: A road to success. In J. Münch, & M. Vierimaa (Eds.), Product-Focused Software Process Improvement (pp. 395–401). Springer Berlin Heidelberg.

Niazi, M., Wilson, D., & Zowghi, D. (2006). Critical success factors for software process improvement implementation: An empirical study. *Software Process Improvement and Practice, 11*(2), 193–211. doi:10.1002/spip.261

Nonaka, I. (1994). A dynamic theory of organizational knowledge creation. *Organization Science*, *5*(1), 14–37. doi:10.1287/orsc.5.1.14

Oktaba, H., Alquicira, C., Pino, F. J., Ruíz, F., Piattini, M., Martínez, T., & García, F. (2008). COMPETISOFT: An improvement strategy for small latin-american software organizations. In H. Oktaba, & M. Piattini (Eds.), *Software Process Improvement for Small and Medium Enterprises: Techniques and Case Studies* (pp. 212–222). Hershey, PA: IGI Global. doi:10.4018/978-1-59904-906-9.ch011

Oktaba, H., & Vázquez, A. (2008). MoProSoft®: A software process model for small enterprises. In H. Oktaba, & M. Piattini (Eds.), *Software Process Improvement for Small and Medium Enterprises: Techniques and Case Studies* (pp. 170–176). Hershey, PA: IGI Global. doi:10.4018/978-1-59904-906-9.ch008

Paulk, M. C., Curtis, B., Chrissis, M. B., & Weber, C. V. (1993). Capability Maturity Model, version 1.1. *IEEE Software*, *10*(4), 18–27. doi:10.1109/52.219617

Polanyi, M. (1966). *The tacit dimension*. New York, NY: Doubleday.

Ribiere, V. M. (2001). *Assessing knowledge management initiative successes as a function of organizational culture*. (Doctoral dissertation). The George Washington University, Washington, DC.

Rodríguez-Jacobo, J., Espinosa-Curiel, I. E., Gutiérrez-Osorio, U., Ocegueda-Miramontes, V., & Fernández-Zepeda, J. A. (2012). Knowledge management in software process improvement initiatives in small organizations. *Proceedings of the 19th European Systems & Software Process Improvement and Innovation*, (pp. 10.1–10.10.) Vienna, Austria.

Rus, I., & Lindvall, M. (2002). Knowledge management in software engineering. *IEEE Software*, *19*(3), 26–38. doi:10.1109/MS.2002.1003450

Santos, G., Montoni, M., Figueiredo, S., & Rocha, A. (2007). SPI-KM - Lessons learned from applying a software process improvement strategy supported by knowledge management. In J. Münch, & P. Abrahamsson (Eds.), Product-Focused Software Process Improvement, (pp. 81–95). Springer Berlin Heidelberg.

Shin, H., Choi, H.-J., & Baik, J. (2007). Jasmine: a PSP supporting tool. In Q. Wang, D. Pfahl, & D. M. Raffo (Eds.), *Software Process Dynamics and Agility* (pp. 73–83). Springer Berlin Heidelberg. doi:10.1007/978-3-540-72426-1_7

Wickert, A., & Herschel, R. (2001). Knowledge-management issues for smaller businesses. *Journal of Knowledge Management*, *5*(4), 329–337. doi:10.1108/13673270110411751

Wong, K. Y., & Aspinwall, E. (2004). Knowledge management implementation frameworks: A review. *Knowledge and Process Management*, *11*(2), 93–104. doi:10.1002/kpm.193

Zack, M. H. (1999). Developing a knowledge strategy. *California Management Review*, *41*(3), 125–145. doi:10.2307/41166000

KEY TERMS AND DEFINITIONS

IGs (Implementation Guides): They are models that define a set of steps that software development organizations need to follow to improve their software development processes.

KM (Knowledge Management): It is a systematic framework that helps to identify, create, maintain, update, evaluate, access, transfer, apply and preserve the tacit and explicit knowledge.

KM System: Technological tools (software system) that support the KM activities.

MSEs (Micro-Sized and Small-Sized Enterprises): MSEs are organizations with fewer than 50 employees.

PRMs (Process Reference Models): They are models that define standardized software development processes.

SPI Initiative: It is a temporal effort that software organizations make to improve their software development processes.

SPI KM: The knowledge management process of SPI knowledge.

SPI Knowledge: Knowledge created or acquired during the activities of an SPI initiative.

SPI Stakeholders: The employees of the organization who are involved directly or indirectly in the SPI initiative.

SPI: Software process improvement.

Chapter 12
On Software Architecture Processes and their Use in Practice

Perla Velasco-Elizondo
Autonomous University of Zacatecas, Mexico

Humberto Cervantes
Autonomous Metropolitan University, Mexico

ABSTRACT

Software architecture is a very important software artifact, as it describes a system's high-level structure and provides the basis for its development. Software architecture development is not a trivial task; to this end, a number of methods have been proposed to try to systematize their related processes to ensure predictability, repeatability, and high quality. In this chapter, the authors review some of these methods, discuss some specific problems that they believe complicate their adoption, and present one practical experience where the problems are addressed successfully.

1. INTRODUCTION

In recent years, software architecture has begun to permeate mainstream software development and, according to Shaw and Clements (Shaw & Clements, 2006), since the year 2000, architecture has entered a "popularization" period characterized by aspects such as increased attention to the role of the software architect and the introduction of software architecture processes into organizations. As part of this trend, a number of methods have

appeared to try to systematize these processes to ensure predictability, repeatability, and high quality outcomes.

The software architecture of a software system is the structure (or structures) of this system, which comprises software elements, the externally visible properties of those elements, and the relationships among them (Clements et al., 2010). In this chapter, by software architecture development we refer to the activities that are typically performed early in a software development project, which contribute to creating the different structures that shape the architecture. Despite the

DOI: 10.4018/978-1-4666-5182-1.ch012

availability of methods to support the processes related to software architecture development, we consider that there is a set of specific problems that complicate the adoption of such methods in practice. A summary of these problems can be stated as follows:

1. **Selection of methods for the software architecture lifecycle:** Ideally, software architecture development should be carried out within the context of a software architecture lifecycle, which imposes a structure on the activities for developing it. Existing software architecture development methods typically focus only on a particular phase of the lifecycle and do not cover it completely. Thus, an appropriate combination of methods to cover the complete lifecycle must be chosen.

2. **Heterogeneity of the existing methods**: Many existing software architecture development methods have been defined by different authors "in isolation," i.e. independently of methods used in other lifecycle phases. This results in having them defined in terms of different activities, work products and terminology. This heterogeneity requires that, once a particular combination of methods is chosen, they must often be analyzed and modified to avoid mismatches, omissions or repetitions.

3. **No consideration of the software development process:** Software architecture development methods are typically defined independent of a particular software development process. Therefore, the introduction of architectural development methods into an organization often demands adapting both the organization development process and the architectural development methods to fit properly (Kazman, Nord, & Klein, 2003).

4. **Architectural design methods are decoupled from everyday practice:** To support the design of an architecture many methods use abstract concepts such as tactics and patterns. These concepts are frequently not the ones that software architects use the most in their day-to-day activities, as many architects tend to favor the selection of technologies such as software frameworks during design. Thus, it is necessary to find ways to include commonly used concepts into architectural design methods (Cervantes, Velasco-Elizondo, & Kazman, 2013).

5. **Difficulty of organizational deployment:** The introduction of architectural methods into an organization often involves costs related to process change, human resources training and technology investment. To promote the successful adoption of software architecture development methods in an organization it is necessary to follow a systematic deployment process.

Based on the problems listed above, in this chapter we propose some actions to address them and describe the observed benefits when implementing them in an industrial setting, specifically, in a large software development company in Mexico City, currently rated at CMMI-DEV level 5, which develops custom software for government and private customers.

This chapter is organized as follows. In Section 2, we introduce the notion of software architecture lifecycle and, within this context, review some well-known processes and methods to support it. Next, we discuss in more detail in section 3 the set of problems that we consider have complicated the adoption of these methods in practice. In Section 4, we describe a specific instance where these problems were addressed in practice. Section 5 presents a discussion. Finally, in the last section, we draw some conclusions and describe paths of future work.

2. REVIEW OF SOFTWARE ARCHITECTURE PROCESSES AND METHODS

Before starting the review of software architecture processes and methods, it is important to introduce the notion of an architecture development lifecycle. Ideally, software architecture development should be carried out within the context of a software architecture lifecycle, which imposes a structure on the activities for developing it. The architecture development lifecycle can be seen as a general model that comprises all the activities and work products required to develop a software architecture. The software architecture development lifecycle is composed of a set of phases depicted in Figure 1: architectural requirements analysis, architectural design, architectural documentation, and architectural evaluation. It should also be noted that, although these phases are not necessarily performed sequentially, there is a sequential information dependency between them, i.e. the design phase depends on the availability

Figure 1. Phases of the software architecture development lifecycle

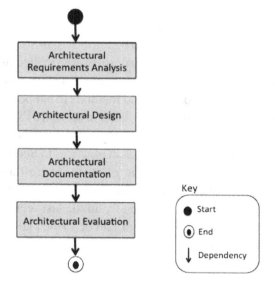

of the information generated during the requirements analysis phase (Hofmeister et al., 2007).

Each one of the phases of the software architecture development lifecycle is supported by a general process; to this end a number of methods have appeared to try to systematize these processes to ensure predictability, repeatability, and high quality outcomes. In the following sections, we describe the focus of each one of these processes and review some well-known methods to support them.

2.1 Architectural Requirement Analysis Process and Methods

The architectural requirements analysis process involves the activities of eliciting, analyzing, specifying and prioritizing architectural requirements so that they can later be used to drive the design of the architecture. A representative output of this process is the architectural drivers, which represent the main functional and non-functional requirements, where the latter include quality attributes requirements and constraints.

The Quality Attribute Workshop (QAW) (Barbacci et al., 2003) is a method to elicit, analyze, specify and prioritize quality attributes requirements, e.g. performance, availability, security or testability. In the QAW quality attributes requirements are specified as scenarios, which are textual descriptions of how the system responds, in a measurable way, to some particular stimulus. For example, "…when a door sensor detects an object in the door's path, the door motion is stopped in less than one millisecond" is an excerpt of a performance scenario. Scenarios are described according to a suggested 6-part template with the active participation of the main system stakeholders, who propose and prioritize them. The results of the QAW include a list of quality attributes requirements as well as a prioritized and refined set of scenarios.

Another relevant method in this context is the Architecture Centric Design Method (ACDM) (Lattanze, 2009). ACDM considers a set of eight sequential stages; most of them focus on architectural design and evaluation. Stages 1 and 2 of ACDM discover architectural drivers and establish project scope, focus on eliciting, analyzing and specifying architectural requirements. As in the QAW, these stages require the active participation of the main system stakeholders and scenarios are utilized to specify the quality attribute requirements of the system. Other types of architectural drivers are also addressed in stages 1 and 2 of ACDM, i.e. functional requirements and constraints.

Within the context of the Rational Unified Process (RUP) (Kroll, Kruchten, & Booch, 2003) (Jacobson, Booch, & Rumbaugh, 1999), FURPS+ (Eeles, 2012) is a model defined to support the elaboration of a supplementary (requirements) specification. The supplementary specification contains the requirements that are not captured in the use case model and is generated as part of the Requirements discipline in the Elaboration Phase of the RUP. FURPS+ stands for Functionality, Usability, Reliability, Performance and Supportability. The "+" in the acronym denotes other important development concerns, such as constraints, that must be taken into account. In contrast to the methods described earlier, FURPS+ does not prescribe a particular way of analyzing, specifying and prioritizing quality attributes requirements.

2.2 Architectural Design Process and Methods

Within the context of the architectural development lifecycle, the process supporting the architectural design phase focuses on identifying and selecting the different structures that compose the architecture and that will allow the drivers identified in the architectural requirements analysis to

be satisfied. Next, we describe some methods to support the activities of this process.

The Attribute Driven Design (ADD) (Bachmann et al., 2000) is a method to design a software architecture based on the selection of patterns and tactics. In software engineering, patterns are understood as conceptual solutions to recurring problems in specific design contexts. Patterns have names associated with them that facilitate their identification e.g. the layers pattern. Although it is difficult to classify patterns, it is generally accepted that architectural patterns (Buschmann, Henney, & Schmidt, 2007) and design patterns (Gamma et al., 1995) exist. On the other hand, architectural tactics are understood as design decisions that influence the control of a quality attribute response (Bass, Clements, & Kazman, 2012), e.g. the use of a redundancy tactic promotes the degree of availability and the use of an authentication tactic promotes the degree of security. ADD assumes the existence of a set of quality attribute scenarios and follows a top-down recursive decomposition-based approach where, at each iteration, tactics and patterns are selected and applied to satisfy a subset of the system's quality attribute scenarios. In the first iteration the element to decompose is generally the entire system. Subsequent interactions focus on the application of tactics and patterns to the resulting design structures from previous iterations. The architectural design is considered complete when all the scenarios have been satisfied.

As introduced before, ACDM is an eight-stage method that mostly concerns architectural design and evaluation. Once the architectural drivers have been identified in stages 1 and 2 of ACDM, stage 3 focuses on the creation of a design for the system architecture as well its documentation. Thus, architectural design and architectural documentation are not separate stages in ACDM. Although this method does not promote a particular design approach, compared to ADD, it suggests a set of techniques to create the architectural design.

RUP also supports the architectural design activity via specific workflows in the Analysis and Design discipline of the Elaboration Phase. In these workflows, the focus is on creating an initial architecture for the system and completing it by analyzing the system behavior. A similar approach is adopted in OpenUP (OpenUP, 2012), which is a lightweight open-source instance of RUP.

2.3 Architectural Documentation Process and Methods

The architectural documentation process involves creating the documents that describe the different structures that compose the architecture for the purpose of communicating it efficiently to the different system stakeholders. An important output of this process is a set of architectural views, which represent the system's structures, their composing elements and the relationships among them. Because all the details of a software architecture are hard to represent in a single view, documenting the architecture involves creating a set of relevant views which can be classified into different types: module views, which show structures where the elements are implementation units; component-and-connector views, which show how the elements in the structures behave at run time; and allocation views, which show how the elements in the structures are allocated to physical resources like the hardware, file systems, and people (Clements et al., 2010) .

The 4+1 view model (Kruchten, 1995) is an architectural documentation method adopted by RUP. This method considers the generation of five interrelated views: the Logical View, the Process View, the Physical and the Development View. The fifth view corresponds to the Use Case view around which the other views revolve. The views are meant to be documented iteratively based on existing information in previously developed artifacts such as use cases and the supplementary specifications. In the 4+1 view model, the syntax suggested for documenting the architecture is UML.

Views and Beyond (V&B) (Clements et al., 2010) is another method to document architectural views. The V&B approach defines two main stages for architectural documentation: (1) selecting the views that are worth documenting and (2) documenting them using a specific template. The template includes elements such as a primary representation, an architectural elements catalog, a context diagram, a variability guide and an architecture background. Multiple related views can be grouped in a view package that includes the views and information to relate these views to each other.

Another method to support the architectural documentation process is Viewpoints and Perspectives (Rozanski & Woods, 2005). A viewpoint defines a view in which content and conventions for constructing it are standardized. A perspective is a collection of guidelines to achieve a particular quality property relevant to a number of architectural views. The method provides a framework for choosing the relevant views based on the structures that are inherent in the software architecture. Six viewpoints (i.e. functional, information, concurrency, development, deployment and operational) and seven perspectives (e.g. security, performance, availability, usability, accessibility, location and regulation) are defined. Both viewpoints and perspectives are described in detail in a set of documents, which include information such as definition, concerns addressed, applicability, related stakeholders, activities, common problems and pitfalls, and a set of checklists to guide the architecture definition.

In previous sections we introduced the ACDM method and mentioned that architectural documentation is part of stage 2 that focuses on architectural design. Thus, the output of stage 2 comprises the initial, or the refined, architectural design and the associated documentation artifacts. ACDM considers static, dynamic and physical views, which are analogous to the module, component-and-connector and allocation views mentioned before, and suggests organizing them according to a specific template. The ACDM does not emphasize the use of a specific notation.

2.4 Architectural Evaluation Process and Methods

Software architecture evaluation focuses on assessing a software architecture design to determine whether it satisfies the required architectural requirements. Next, we describe some relevant methods that support this process.

The Software Architecture Analysis Method (SAAM) (Kazman et al., 1996) is a scenario-based evaluation method. Although SAAM works for scenarios related to different quality attributes requirements, it is considered that the main one SAAM analyzes is modifiability. SAAM can be used either for a single architecture or for comparison of multiple ones. For a single architecture, SAAM's activities are scenario development, which requires the presence of all stakeholders, SA description, individual scenario evaluation and scenario interaction. In this case, the cost of scenario modification is estimated by listing the components and the connectors that are affected and then counting the number of changes. In the case of using SAAM to compare multiple architectures, scenarios and the scenario interactions are weighted according to their importance. This metric is used to determine an overall evaluation of the candidate architectures.

The Architecture Tradeoff Analysis Method (ATAM) (Clements, Kazman, & Klein, 2002) is an evaluation method based on SAAM. However, and in contrast to the former, ATAM explores quality attribute scenarios of any type to discover sensitivity points, trade-off points and risks within a set of candidate architectural structures. In ATAM a sensitivity point is a property resulting from a design decision which directly impacts the achievement of a particular quality attribute. A trade-off point is a property that affects multiple quality attributes. A risk is a design decision that was incorrectly taken or not taken at all. Finally, it is important to mention that ATAM is designed to support the evaluation of systems whose quality attribute requirements may not have been documented when the evaluation took place. Thus, ATAM considers, as part of its initial steps, the identification of the quality attributes requirements.

In ACDM, the eight-stage method introduced in the previous sections, stages 4-6 focus on evaluation. In stage 4, the architectural design is reviewed to discover issues that may compromise the satisfaction of the architectural drivers. In order to do so, the architecture design team evaluate the initial architectural design (or reevaluate the refined design after architectural evaluation and experimentation, see stages 5-6 below). Based on this review, it is determined in stage 5 whether the architectural design is ready for production or not. If it is not, some experimentation is carried out in stage 6 to address the issues that were discovered during the review. Based on the results of the experiments, the team refine the architecture design (ACDM stage 3 described in the architectural design section). This sequence of activities is repeated until all the issues have been addressed.

In RUP, within the architecture refinement activity there is a task named Review the Architecture whose focus is to perform an architectural evaluation. The review is conducted as a meeting and there are recommendations with respect to the approaches that can be used to do the review. These include reviewing the architectural model (representation-driven review), reviewing data and measurements (information-driven review) and reviewing scenarios (scenario-driven review). RUP does not provide more specific guidelines on how to conduct these particular reviews, and the Review the Architecture task script only emphasizes the fact that issues must be identified during the review and assigned to the person responsible for their resolution.

Some other methods that support software architecture are Architecture-Level Modifiability Analysis (ALMA) (Bengtsson et al., 2000) (Lassing et al., 2002), Performance Assessment of Software Architecture (PASA) (Ali Babar & Gorton, 2004) and Active Reviews for Intermediate Designs (ARID) (Clements, 2000).

3. PROBLEMS WITH ADOPTING SOFTWARE ARCHITECTURE PROCESSES AND METHODS

Unfortunately, despite a growing body of methods to support software architecture processes during the past years, at present we consider that not many organizations have adopted these methods in practice, at least, not as they are currently defined. The following list includes what we consider the main problems that have contributed to this:

1. Selection of methods for the software architecture lifecycle.
2. Heterogeneity of the existing methods.
3. No consideration for the software development process.
4. Architectural design methods are decoupled from everyday practice.
5. Difficulty of organizational deployment.

It is important to highlight that we have heard about these problems from practitioners in the field as well as from our own experience with clients and industry contacts. In the following sections, we describe these problems in more detail.

3.1 Problem #1: Selection of Methods for the Software Architecture Lifecycle

Table 1 shows (in grey) the phases of the software architecture lifecycle covered by the methods reviewed in this chapter. As this table shows, only ACDM and RUP cover the complete lifecycle. RUP, however, is a general software development process and the guidance that it provides with

Table 1. Phases of the software architecture development lifecycle covered by the methods reviewed

Method	Architecture Lifecycle Phase			
	Requirements	Design	Documentation	Evaluation
QAW	▓			
FURPS+	▓			
ADD		▓		
4+1 view model			▓	
Views and Beyond			▓	
Viewpoints and Perspectives			▓	
SAAM	▓			▓
ATAM	▓			▓
ALMA				▓
RUP	▓	▓	▓	▓
ACDM	▓	▓	▓	▓

respect to each of the phases in the architecture lifecycle is limited. The rest of the methods only cover specific phases of the architecture lifecycle.

The fact that architecture methods generally focus on particular phases of the lifecycle requires selecting an appropriate combination of methods. Table 1 also shows that there is more than one method to choose from for a particular phase of the lifecycle. As can be implied, not only can the number of available methods complicate the selection, but also the lack of knowledge of software architecture and experience in using these methods.

3.2 Problem #2: Heterogeneity of the Existing Methods

In the previous section we discussed the problem of selecting an adequate combination of methods to cover the architecture lifecycle. However, choosing the methods is not all that is needed. In order to progress beyond the selection of individual methods, it is necessary to stand back and identify how the selected methods should properly be used together. This is not a trivial task because these methods have usually been defined by different authors "in isolation," and therefore they are defined in terms of different activities, work products and terminology.

We have noticed that even methods that share a common heritage do not provide explicit support to combine them. To give an example, consider ATAM, the method to support the architecture evaluation process; and QAW, the method to support the architectural requirements analysis process, both developed by the Software Engineering Institute (SEI) (Software Engineering Institute, 2012). At the beginning, ATAM requires quality attributes for the system to be identified. This is because ATAM can be performed on a system whose quality attributes are not documented. However, if a requirements method such as QAW has been used previously, the initial steps of ATAM may be unnecessary.

Thus, once a particular combination of methods is chosen, the architect must often analyze and modify them to avoid mismatches, omissions or repetitions.

3.3 Problem #3: No Consideration of the Software Development Process

Another important problem is that architectural development methods are typically defined independently of a particular software development process. As far as we know, only the author of ACDM provides a detailed description of how to integrate it with different software development processes such as Extreme Programming, Scrum, Team Software Process (TSP), Rational Unified Process (RUP) and Agile Unified Process (AUP) (Lattanze, 2009). For the rest of the methods very little or no guidance is given to help architects to use them within the context of specific software development processes. Thus, the introduction of architectural development methods into an organization often requires adapting both the organization's development process and the architectural development methods to fit properly (Kazman, Nord, & Klein, 2003).

It is important to highlight that, when provided, the guidance is typically generic and therefore difficult to apply to specific situations. Success often depends on the context and characteristics of the organization interested in using the methods. The adaptation of the architectural development methods and the development are part of the activities of organizational deployment discussed in section 3.6.

3.4 Problem #4: Architectural Design Methods Are Decoupled from Everyday Practice

Architectural design is performed by applying design decisions to satisfy a set of architectural requirements. Examples of design decisions, within the context of the categories discussed in (Bass, Clements, & Kazman, 2012), are shown in Table 2. All the design decisions listed in this table are very important for the success of the system and for its evolution. However, the final category of design decisions and choice of technology are very critical to the success of the system.

Unfortunately, most software architecture design methods say very little on the choice of technology (Hofmeister et al., 2007) and often deal in abstract concepts such as tactics and patterns. These concepts are different from the ones that software architects use in their day-to-day work, which mostly come from development frameworks such as JSF (Java Server Faces), Spring, Hibernate or Axis (Cervantes, Velasco-Elizondo, & Kazman, 2013). Frameworks are related to patterns and tactics because they instantiate these concepts. However, as the mapping among all these concepts is not very evident in architectural design methods, software architects are often unwilling to use them.

3.5 Problem #5: Difficulty of Organizational Deployment

The introduction of architectural methods into an organization, whose processes are documented and used, often has a high initial cost due to the need to change several existing process elements. This cost is not only limited to the cost of making changes in the processes elements, it also often comprises the cost of training and technology investment.

Table 2. Examples of design decisions within the context of the categories discussed in (Bass, Clements, & Kazman, 2012)

Category	Examples
Allocation of responsibilities	• Determination of basic system functions. • Definition of the architectural infrastructure. • Determination of how responsibilities are allocated to architectural elements.
Coordination model	• Determination of the elements of the system that must be coordinated. • Definition of coordination properties, e.g. timeliness, currency, completeness, correctness, and consistency. • Selection of communication mechanisms to support coordination properties.
Data model	• Determination of main data abstractions. • Definition of operations and properties of data abstractions. • Definition of any metadata needed for consistent interpretation of data abstractions.
Management of resources	• Determination of the resources that must be managed. • Determination of the system elements that manage each resource. • Selection of the strategies employed when there is contention for or saturation of resources.
Mapping among architectural elements	• Specification of the mapping of runtime elements that are created from each module. • Specification of the modules that contain the code for each runtime element. • Specification of the assignment of runtime elements to processors and data items in the data model to data stores
Binding time decisions	• Establishment of the point in the life cycle and the mechanism for achieving a variation.
Choice of technology	• Determination of the available technologies to realize the decisions made in the other categories. • Determination of the available tools to support technology choices, e.g. IDEs, testing tools. • Determination of the side effects of technology choices.

Training is a fundamental aspect when introducing architecture development methods. Software architects are generally proficient developers with considerable experience. However, this does not guarantee that they are knowledgeable about software architecture concepts. Thus, training courses and coaching activities are often required not only for the software architect, but also for the people that the architect deals with within the organization. Technological support is also an important issue as the selection of appropriate tools is crucial to allow the architects to develop the architecture and communicate it in an easy and, ideally, in an automated or semi-automated manner.

It should also be noted that when an organization decides to use a new method to perform a specific activity, it is creating a change in the way people work. This can generally have a negative impact on (people's) productivity in the early stages. It should also be noted that an organization might need to invest a significant amount of effort to get people to adapt to the new processes.

4. USING ARCHITECTURE PROCESSES IN PRACTICE

This section discusses how the five issues listed previously were addressed in a large software development company in Mexico City through the introduction of software architecture development processes and methods. This company, which is currently rated at CMMI-DEV level 5, develops software for government and private customers using the Team Software Process (TSP) (Humphrey, 2000). In 2010 the architecture method introduction project was conducted on some aspects of the company as follows:

- The company had, at that time, a CMMI level 3 rating which means, among other things, that all of its processes associated with requirements and design were documented.
- There was a lack of experience in capturing quality attribute requirements. Furthermore, typical customers encountered difficulties while trying to express these types of requirements.
- The role of the software architect existed and the organization tried to assign a software architect to every team, although sometimes this was not possible due to the insufficient number of architects in the organization. People who took on the architect role were typically highly experienced developers with high technical proficiency, but usually little theoretical foundation in software architecture.
- The architect, along with the team leader and core developers, were selected at the beginning of the project and they usually worked together throughout the project where they participated in several activities such as requirements, high-level design, component development and testing.
- Development contracts typically required all of the requirements to be elicited initially.
- The project's cost and schedule were determined very early on before the actual requirements phase was performed. During this initial estimate, quality attributes were not frequently considered but an initial architecture proposal had to be established nonetheless.

The particular context of this company introduces specific constraints that affect the way the five problems discussed in section 3 were addressed.

4.1 Addressing Problem #1: Selection of Methods

As previously discussed, the first problem to be addressed involves the selection of methods for the software architecture lifecycle. Next, we discuss how methods for every phase of the architecture lifecycle were selected (see summary in Table 3).

4.1.1 Requirements Phase

For the requirements phase, the methods listed in section 2.1 were considered. While QAW is the most complete method with respect to quality attribute requirements, it was decided not to adopt it initially because of the lack of maturity in the company on elicitation of quality attributes as well as the difficulties associated in conducting meetings with relevant stakeholders. The decision, instead, was to define a custom method for requirements engineering of quality attributes, which would complement the existing requirements process of the company and which would help provide some initial level of maturity with respect to quality attribute elicitation. The scenario technique was

retained along with an impact analysis technique associated with FURPS+. Prioritization was performed with the customer using a technique taken from ATAM where every scenario is given two ratings, which can take a Low, Medium or High value. The two ratings correspond to the importance of a quality attribute scenario for the customer and the difficulty of implementation from the architect's perspective.

4.1.2 Design Phase

For the design phase, only ADD was considered because this method provides the most detailed process for designing in a systematic way. Selecting ADD posed no significant problems since the company did not have any architectural design process in place.

4.1.3 Documentation Phase

For the documentation phase, the fact that the company already had several artifacts in place for documenting the software architecture had to be considered. These artifacts included a design document based on the 4+1 Views method. It was not necessary to make a complete change to the document so it was decided that only the concept of view packages and the associated templates from the V&B would be adopted.

Table 3. Summary of information on method selection

Architectural Lifecycle Phase	Constraints	Selected Method
Requirement analysis	- Lack of experience in quality attributes - Existing requirement process - Difficulty in involving customers	Custom quality attribute elicitation method
Design	- Existing architectural sketch from early estimation	ADD
Documentation	- Existing standard based on the 4+1 Views method	V&B (only view packages and templates)
Evaluation	- Availability of other architects for the evaluation team - Architects' limited time	ACDM stage 4 ("Evaluate the architectural design")

4.1.4 Evaluation Phase

For the evaluation phase, there was no equivalent activity in the existing organizational process. One benefit associated with the size of the company is that there was a reasonable number of architects that could participate as members of an architecture evaluation team so that performing scenario-based evaluations could be achieved. The constraint, however, was that their availability was limited, so the evaluation meeting had to be performed in a short time. Among the scenario-based evaluation methods, both ATAM and ACDM Stage 4 (Evaluate the Architectural Design) were considered. ATAM was discarded because it typically requires two days to carry out an evaluation and, furthermore, some steps of ATAM are rendered unnecessary because quality attributes are captured using the requirements method. The final decision was to select the process defined by ACDM's Stage 4.

4.2 Addressing Problem #2: Adapting and Connecting the Methods

The second problem involved adapting the methods to overcome heterogeneity, resulting from the fact that methods are defined in isolation. Next, we discuss how methods for every phase of the architecture lifecycle were adapted to overcome this heterogeneity.

4.2.1 Requirements Phase

Since the process for the requirements phase was a custom method, it required no particular adaptation of an existing method. However, one aspect that was considered, in addition to elicitation of quality attributes requirements, was the identification of other architectural drivers, including functional requirements and constraints. These architectural drivers were identified by adding a primary use case selection activity and listing constraints (which had not been formally identified

previously). Complementing the quality attribute elicitation custom method with the selection of primary use cases and constraint identification provided all the necessary inputs for the design phase.

4.2.2 Design Phase

The ADD method was adopted with minor modifications. One important aspect that was considered was that the initial design iteration does not start "from scratch," but rather with a preliminary architecture sketch that is established as part of the early estimation process. This preliminary architecture constrains the decisions that the architect can make during the design process. Furthermore, the design process based on ADD emphasizes the use of technology, besides patterns and tactics, and the creation of an executable architecture as one of the outputs of the design process. Other aspects that were considered were guidelines to model the architecture in a case tool so that the documentation packages could be produced in a very straightforward way.

4.2.3 Documentation Phase

Regarding the documentation method, the view template from V&B was adopted without modifications. Since the company already had an architecture document based on 4+1 Views which mandated the inclusion of module, allocation and component-and-connector views, the view selection activity from V&B was not adopted. The original views were replaced with view packages and at least one view package associated with the module, component-and-connector and allocation was included.

4.2.4 Evaluation Phase

The process defined in ACDM Stage 4 was used without modifications. This process, however, was complemented by adding a preparation phase where an "evaluation package" was assembled. This package includes information concerning the business goals, the architectural drivers and the views produced in the documentation phase. Furthermore, once the evaluation method is performed, a follow-up activity is performed to support the architect in dealing with the observations raised during the evaluation meeting.

4.3 Addressing Problem #3: Integrating the Methods with the Team Software Process

The Team Software Process, as its name suggests, is a development process oriented towards teams, which is built on top of the Personal Software Process (PSP) (Humphrey, 2005). Data collected from the TSP projects reveal that projects developed using TSP do indeed achieve substantially better results than typical projects (0.06 defects/KLOC versus 7.5 defects/KLOC after delivery) (Davis & Mullaney, 2003).

A TSP software project is performed as a series of development cycles, where each cycle begins with a planning process called a launch and ends with a closing process called a postmortem. Within each development cycle, activities belonging to different phases can be performed. These phases include: requirements (REQ), high-level design (HLD), implementation (IMPL) and testing (TEST). The REQ phase of TSP focuses on producing a complete System Requirements Specification document (SRS). The main goal of the HLD phase is to produce a high-level design that will guide product implementation. This high-level design must define the components that compose the system and that have to be designed and developed independently using PSP in the IMPL phase. Finally, the TEST phase focuses on performing integration and system testing and on preparing the delivery of the system. It must be noted that the lifecycle model of a particular

project (waterfall, incremental) is defined by the phases that are performed in each cycle.

TSP does not give full consideration to software architecture development. None of the roles defined in TSP are that of software architect, which (generally speaking) denotes the person responsible for performing the process of software architecture development discussed previously. Furthermore, the script for the REQ phase does not provide specific guidelines to support the identification of architectural drivers, which are necessary to design the architecture. The HLD script focuses on designing a general structure to guide development, but no explicit consideration is given to satisfying quality attributes in this process. A further problem involves the fact that TSP does not mandate an architectural evaluation to be performed. The closest activities include a design walkthrough and the inspection of the design document. These activities, however, are performed by other team members, who may have less experience than the architect with respect to designing and, as a consequence, may not detect complex design problems.

The UML activity diagram in Figure 2 shows a general overview of the introduction strategy of software architecture development into the TSP (Cervantes, Martinez, Castillo, Montes de Oca, 2010). Vertical swimlanes represent the roles that participate in architecture development activities and horizontal swimlanes represent TSP phases (REQ and HLD). Within the HLD phase, two regions represent distinct stages. Composite activities, such as Perform Architectural Design, represent architectural development methods and objects represent artifacts produced by these methods.

As the diagram shows, the requirements method is included as part of the REQ phase of TSP and its execution produces a list of scenarios. The remaining methods are all part of the HLD phase and they are performed as the initial activities of this phase. The HLD phase is thus di-

Figure 2. Overview of architecture lifecycle phases introduced into TSP

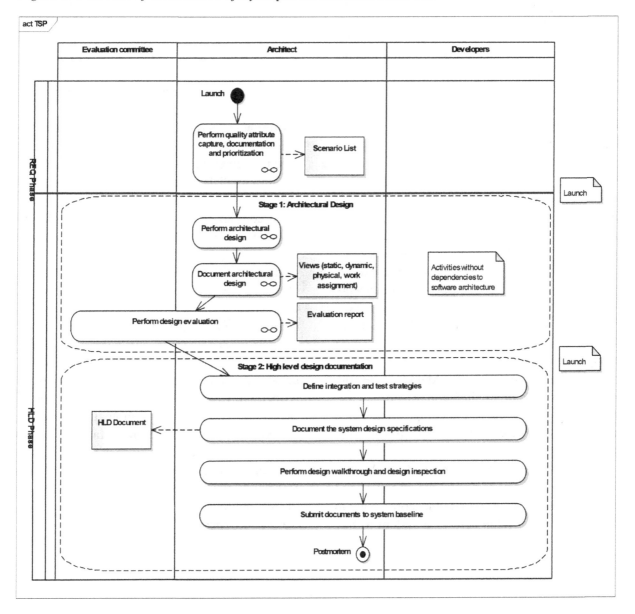

vided into two stages: architectural design stage and high-level design and documentation stage. During the architectural design stage, the activities previously discussed that culminate in an evaluated architectural design are performed. This initial stage is performed mainly by the architect, but other architects from outside the project also participate during the evaluation of the architecture. In the high-level design and documentation stage, the team design and document the rest of

the system based on the architectural design. This design typically involves creating sequence diagrams for all of the use cases, which allow the interfaces of all of the components to be specified. This specification is later used in the development phase (IMPL) for performing detailed design and development of the components.

The benefits of this approach is that the high-level design and documentation stage is performed using an architecture that has been evaluated.

211

Furthermore, the evaluation team participate in the architectural evaluation while other team members with less experience participate in the inspection of the architecture document at the end of the HLD phase.

4.4 Addressing Problem #4: Considering Frameworks during Architectural Design

We have discussed the problem that many software architecture design methods often deal with abstract concepts such as tactics and patterns, while software architects mostly use those that come from development frameworks. To address this problem we proposed an approach where frameworks are used as design concepts on par with tactics and patterns. The approach was realized as an extension to the ADD method. However, it can be applied to other architecture design methods as well.

Recalling section 2.2, the ADD assumes the existence of a set of architectural drivers and follows a top-down recursive decomposition-based approach where, at each iteration, tactics and patterns are applied to satisfy a subset of drivers. Table 4, shows an excerpt of what results from the first design iterations when frameworks are considered as design concepts. The iterations correspond to the greenfield development of a system to buy

bus tickets: a typical enterprise application where large numbers of users interact with the system through a browser or mobile apps and perform processes such as checking bus schedules that act on data in a database. Functional architectural requirements include searching for bus schedules. The most important quality attribute scenario is performance: performing searches for timetables in less than 10 seconds, and constraints include time to market for the initial system release and having a small development team with experience in JSF, Spring and Hibernate.

In contrast to the traditional manner of performing the ADD, several frameworks are selected in early iterations. Although many frameworks exist, the ones selected were favored because of one of the architectural drivers in iteration 2. Once frameworks are chosen, further design iterations are impacted by this decision. To satisfy the performance scenario, in iteration 3, at the data layer, performance was addressed by configuring the parameters provided by the framework (Hibernate Community Documentation, 2004). In this case, Hibernate incorporates the Lazy Load Pattern, but it also incorporates tactics such as support for a cache (an instance of the "Maintain Multiple Copies" tactic) that allow performance to be improved. A detailed description of this design approach can be found in (Cervantes, Velasco-Elizondo, & Kazman, 2013).

Table 4. Excerpt of the initial ADD design iterations when using frameworks as design concepts

Iteration	Architectural Drivers	Element to Decompose and Designs Decisions
1	• Web access and support for mobile apps • Time to market for the initial release • Small development team	• Element: The whole system • Design Decisions: Apply the 3-Layers Pattern (presentation, business and data)
2	o Searching for bus schedules • Team experience with frameworks	• Element: The 3-Layers • Design Decisions: Apply the Application Service Pattern, Use of JSF, Spring and Hibernate for the presentation, business and data layers respectively.
3	• Performance scenario	• Element: The data layer • Design Decisions: Apply the Lazy Loading Pattern and the Maintain Multiple Copies tactic, both by configuring Hibernate support for lazy associations and caches.

4.5 Addressing Problem #5: Method Deployment

The deployment of architecture development methods in an organization is an endeavor that may be complicated depending on the scope of the changes and the size of the organization. The methods that were previously discussed were introduced into the company by following a systematic approach based on the Organizational Performance Management process area (OPM) of CMMi (Chrissis, Konrad & Shrum, 2010). Figure 3 shows the general steps that were followed. Next, we describe them.

- **Diagnose:** During this step, several activities were performed. These include analyzing the existing processes of the organization, observing development teams, interviewing architects, and studying work products. This step revealed many issues, an example is poor documentation of quality attribute requirements.

Figure 3. Steps followed in the introduction of architecture development methods

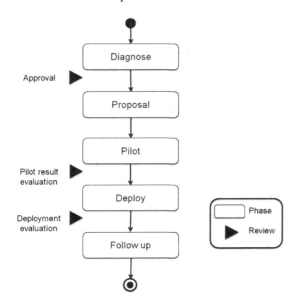

- **Proposal:** During this step, the activities discussed in sections 4.1, 4.2 and 4.3 were performed in order to address the problems identified during the diagnosis.
- **Pilot:** Piloting the proposal is necessary in order to 1) understand whether the proposal can really be applied in the context of a real project and 2) make adjustments to the proposal based on the results of its use. During the pilots, adjustments to the methods were made. An example of this is the modification of ADD to consider frameworks as design concepts, as discussed in section 4.4.
- **Deploy:** This is one of the most complex steps as it requires many activities to be performed. These activities include creating training materials and then training the architects, modifying the existing organizational processes and also championing the use of architecture methods.
- **Follow-up:** Follow-up involved coaching the architects and also collecting data about the results of the use of the methods.

Although the deployment of the methods is treated here very briefly, the aspects associated with organizational change management are complex and need to be given serious consideration in order to successfully introduce architectural development methods into an organization.

5. DISCUSSION

In the following sections we provide a discussion on (1) general observations and lessons learnt from the implementation of the actions described in this paper and (2) specific observations derived from coaching architects.

5.1 General Observations and Lessons Learnt

The material presented in the above sections provides an example of how the five problems listed were addressed in the software company. While it would be unwise to draw definitive conclusions from it, it is possible to make some general observations and discuss some valuable lessons learnt for most of the problems addressed.

With respect to problems 1 and 2, method selection is a complex task as it depends on the context of the organization. As there are many methods, both commercial and academic, each one of them defining heterogeneous activities and work products, it is necessary to properly use all this information not only to select the "best combination of methods" but also to adapt them. Method selection and, in particular, method adaptation also requires process engineers to work closely with software architects in order to make useful adaptations.

Regarding problem 3, it is important to consider the impact of the introduction of architectural methods into existing organizational processes. Although in the context of the company studied these changes seem significant, in the end the number of affected process elements was relatively small compared to the overall process repository. We believe, however, that to minimize the risk of process change, a process engineer should systematically perform analyses not only to identify the affected process elements but also to estimate the quantitative impact of the change on people performance.

Regarding problem 4, reducing the de-coupling between methods and everyday practice is often the result of performing pilot projects with the proposed methods. It is important to bridge this gap between theory and practice to facilitate the adoption of the methods.

Finally, with respect to problem 5, the aspects associated with organizational change management are complex and need to be given serious consideration in order to successfully introduce architectural development methods into an organization. If these aspects are not taken into consideration, no matter how well architectural methods are selected, connected and adapted to the development process, the possibility of them being deployed in the organization in a successful way is limited. The introduction of architecture development methods can be simplified by having somebody knowledgeable about the methods coaching the architects. In the organization studied, one of the authors performed this task, which allowed the observation of some specific aspects that are discussed in the next section.

5.2 Specific Observations from Coaching Architects

Regarding architectural drivers, specifying quality attribute requirements as scenarios was a difficult task. The identification of quality attribute types is not straightforward and deriving them from business goals requires certain experience. The most difficult part, however, is the definition of a measure to express the scenario's response in a quantitative manner. The SEI suggests the use of quality attribute scenario generation tables, which are templates that provide many choices for creating scenarios for a particular quality attribute category. To be effective these tables need, however, to be suited to the organization's type of products and this requires the study of many quality attribute scenarios produced by the organization, something that would not be possible during the initial introduction.

On the other hand, it was observed that the architects often needed to have clear criteria to establish how much architectural design is appropriate. Before the proposal was presented to the organization in question, there was great variation among architects with respect to the criteria used for end design. Currently, architects are asked to make a list of architectural drivers and to perform design activities until decisions have been taken for all of the architectural drivers. Although this may not always be possible depending on the time allocated to HLD in the project, this has proven to be a good criterion because even if an architect does not finish his design, he is aware of the drivers that he has not considered.

Some other aspects that are worthy of mention are the participation of customers in software architecture development activities and how software architecture supports software estimation and allocation of work. Regarding the first aspect, involving customers in activities related to software architecture development was not feasible in the early stages of the introduction of the methods into the organization. This is mainly due to the lack of maturity with respect to the use of these methods. For example, in the organization studied the identification and correct specification of quality attributes took some time. If QAW is used for architectural requirements analysis, this could build false expectations from customers. Regarding the second aspect, the availability of a software architecture helps not only to reduce the risks associated with software estimates but also to develop better work assignment. In the organization studied, many projects were planned and estimated based only on information pertaining to functional aspects of the system. Currently, there is also information about quality attributes, which is prioritized according to its importance for the customer and the difficulty of implementation. It should also be noted that in the context of the organization studied, the creation of a work assignment structure is essential in TSP to guide development in the IMPL phase. Furthermore, this structure also provides a clear guide to identify which interfaces must be documented thoroughly.

6. CONCLUSION

Over the past years, attention to the introduction of software architecture development has increased as software architecture has been recognized as an important artifact for high quality system development. Although software architecture development is supported by a variety of methods, their adoption is complicated because many of the methods have been defined without considering all the software architecture development activities, a specific organization environment or a particular software development life-cycle.

In this chapter we have described some actions to address the problems mentioned above and described the benefits observed when implementing them in an software development company in Mexico City, currently rated at CMMI-DEV level 5, which develops custom software for government and private customers. Although there is not enough data to evaluate quantitatively the real benefits of these actions, there are some preliminary positive results that have led to some valuable lessons learnt.

In order to improve the evaluation of the benefits of the actions described in this paper, we plan to carry out a systematic analysis of defects related to software architecture found during evaluations, system tests or after the system has been transitioned to customers. This type of analysis, however, may not be possible in the short term as it requires a long testing period and a significant number of projects to be performed so that sufficient data can be gathered.

ACKNOWLEDGMENT

The authors wish to thank CIMAT and the editors of this book for their kind invitation to be part of this project. We would also like to thank Quarksoft S.A. de C.V., the company where the software architecture methods were introduced.

REFERENCES

Ali Babar, M., & Gorton, I. (2004). Comparison of scenario-based software architecture evaluation methods. In *Proceedings of the Asia-Pacific Software Engineering Conference* (pp. 600-607). IEEE Computer Society.

Bachmann, F., Bass, L., Chastek, G., Donohoe, P., & Peruzzi, F. (2000). *The architecture based design method* (Technical Report CMU/SEI-2000-TR-001). Pittsburgh, PA: Software Engineering Institute, Carnegie Mellon University.

Barbacci, M., Ellison, R. J., Lattanze, A. J., Stafford, J. A., Weinstock, C. B., & Wood, W. G. (2003). *Quality attribute workshops (QAWs)* (Technical Report CMU/SEI-2003-TR-016). Pittsburgh, PA: Software Engineering Institute, Carnegie Mellon University.

Bass, L., Clements, P., & Kazman, R. (2012). *Software architecture in practice* (3rd ed.). Reading, MA: Addison-Wesley Professional.

Bengtsson, P., Lassing, N., Bosch, J., & Vliet, H. (2000). *Analyzing software architectures for modifiability* (Technical Report HK-R-RES–00/11-SE). Högskolan Karlskrona/Ronneby.

Buschmann, F., Henney, K., & Schmidt, D. (2007). Pattern-oriented software architecture: Vol. 4. *A pattern language for distributed computing*. Chichester, UK: Wiley.

Cervantes, H., Martinez, I., Castillo, J., & Montes de Oca, C. (2010). Introducing software architecture development methods into a TSP-based development company. In *Proceedings of SEI Architecture Technology User Network (SATURN 2010) Conference*. Pittsburgh, PA: Software Engineering Institute, Carnegie Mellon University.

Cervantes, H., Velasco-Elizondo, P., & Kazman, R. (2013). A principled way of using frameworks in architectural design. *IEEE Software*, *30*(2), 46–53. doi:10.1109/MS.2012.175

Chrissis, M. B., Konrad, M., & Shrum, S. (2010). *CMMi for development: Guidelines for process integration and product improvement* (3rd ed.). Reading, MA: Addison-Wesley Professional.

Clements, P. (2000). *Active reviews for intermediate designs* (Technical Report CMU/SEI-2000-TN-009). Pittsburgh, PA: Software Engineering Institute, Carnegie Mellon University.

Clements, P., Bachmann, F., Bass, L., Garlan, D., Ivers, J., Reed, L., & Nord, R. (2011). *Documenting software architectures: Views and beyond* (2nd ed.). Reading, MA: Addison-Wesley Professional.

Clements, P., Kazman, R., & Klein, M. (2002). *Evaluating software architectures: Methods and case studies*. Reading, MA: Addison-Wesley Professional.

Davis, N., & Mullaney, J. (2003). *The team the team software ProcessSM (TSPSM) in practice: A summary of recent results (Technical Report, CMU/SEI-2003-TR-014)*. Pittsburgh, PA: Software Engineering Institute, Carnegie Mellon University.

Eeles, P. (2012). *Capturing architectural requirements*. Retrieved from http://www.ibm.com/developerworks/rational/library/4710.html

Gamma, E., Helm, R., Johnson, R., & Vlissides, J. (1995). *Design patterns: elements of reusable object-oriented software*. Reading, MA: Addison-Wesley Professional Computing Series.

Hibernate Community Documentation. (2004). *Improving performance*. Retrieved from http://docs.jboss.org/hibernate/orm/3.3/reference/en/html/performance.html

Hofmeister, C., Kruchten, P. B., Nord, R., Obbink, H., Ran, A., & America, P. (2007). A general model of software architecture design derived from five industrial approaches. *Journal of Systems and Software*, *80*(1), 106–126. doi:10.1016/j.jss.2006.05.024

Humphrey, W. (2000). *The team software process (TSP)* (Technical Report CMU/SEI-2000-TR-023). Pittsburgh, PA: Software Engineering Institute, Carnegie Mellon University.

Humphrey, W. (2005). *PSP, a self-improvement process for software engineers*. Reading, MA: Addison-Wesley Professional.

Jacobson, I., Booch, G., & Rumbaugh, J. (1999). *The unified software development process.* Boston, MA: Addison-Wesley.

Kazman, R., Abowd, G., Bass, L., & Clements, P. (1996). Scenario-based analysis of software architecture. *IEEE Software, 13*(6), 47–55. doi:10.1109/52.542294

Kazman, R., Nord, R., & Klein, M. (2003). *A life-cycle view of architectural analysis and design methods (Technical Note CMU/SEI-2003-TN-026)*. Pittsburgh, PA: Software Engineering Institute, Carnegie Mellon University.

Kroll, P., Kruchten, P. B., & Booch, G. (2003). *The rational unified process made easy*. Reading, MA: Addison-Wesley Professional.

Kruchten, P. B. (1995). The 4+1 view model of architecture. *IEEE Software, 6*(12), 42–50. doi:10.1109/52.469759

Lassing, N., Bengtsson, P., Vliet, H., & Bosh, J. (2002). Experience with ALMA: Architecture-level modifiability analysis. *Journal of Systems and Software, 61*, 47–57. doi:10.1016/S0164-1212(01)00113-3

Lattanze, A. J. (2009). *Architecting software intensive systems: A practitioners guide*. Boca Raton, FL: CRC Press.

OpenUP. (2012). Retrieved from http://epf.eclipse.org/wikis/openup

Rozanski, N., & Woods, E. (2012). *Software systems architecture: Working with stakeholders using viewpoints and perspectives*. Reading, MA: Addison-Wesley.

Shaw, M., & Clements, P. (2006). The golden age of software architecture. *IEEE Software, 2*(23), 31–39. doi:10.1109/MS.2006.58

Software Engineering Institute. (2012). Retrieved from http://www.sei.cmu.edu/

KEY TERMS AND DEFINITIONS

Architectural Design: The phase of the software architecture development lifecycle that focuses on identifying and selecting the different structures that compose the architecture and that will allow architectural requirements to be satisfied.

Architectural Documentation: The phase of the software architecture development lifecycle that focuses on creating the documents that describe the different structures that compose the architecture for the purpose of communicating it efficiently to the different system stakeholders.

Architectural Evaluation: The phase of the software architecture development lifecycle that focuses on assessing a software architecture design to determine whether it satisfies the required architectural requirements.

Architectural Requirements Analysis: The phase of the software architecture development lifecycle that focuses on eliciting, analyzing, specifying and prioritizing architectural requirements so that they can later be used to drive the design of the architecture.

Software Architecture Development Lifecycle: It imposes a structure on the activities for software architecture development. The software architecture development lifecycle is composed of the following phases: architectural requirements analysis, architectural design, architectural documentation, and architectural evaluation. Each one of the phases involves principles, practices and methods used to develop software architecture.

Software Architecture Development: It is the set of activities that are typically performed early in a software development project, which contribute to creating the software architecture of a system.

Software Architecture: It is the structure (or structures) of this system, which comprises software elements, the externally visible properties of those elements, and the relationships among them (Clements et al, 2010).

Chapter 13
A Method to Design a Software Process Architecture in a Multimodel Environment:
An Overview

Mery Pesantes
Research Centre in Mathematics (CIMAT, A.C.), Mexico

Jorge Luis Risco Becerra
University of São Paulo – Escola Politécnica, Brazil

Cuauhtémoc Lemus
Research Centre in Mathematics (CIMAT, A.C.), Mexico

ABSTRACT

In the multimodel improvement context, Software Organizations need to incorporate into their processes different practices from several improvement technologies simultaneously (i.e. CMMI, PSP, ISO 15504, and others). Over the last few years, software process architectures have been considered a means to harmonize these technologies. However, it is unclear how to design a software process architecture supporting a multimodel environment. In this chapter, an overview of the method to design a software process architecture is presented, identifying basic concepts, views, phases, activities, and artifacts. In addition, important aspects in the creation of this method are explained. This method will assist process stakeholders in the design, documentation, and maintenance of their software process architecture.

1. INTRODUCTION

Multimodel Software Process Improvement (MSPI) aims to achieve business goals, develop quality products through a mature process applying multiple improvement technologies best prac-

tices simultaneously, and reduce time-to-market and production costs (Siviy, Penn, & Stoddard, 2008; Unterkalmsteiner, Gorschek, Islam, Cheng, Permadi, & Feldt, 2012). Therefore, software organizations are analyzing their processes, selecting appropriate improvement technologies and adopting best practices from each technology.

Problems have arisen within organizations working under this multimodel environment

DOI: 10.4018/978-1-4666-5182-1.ch013

(Kelemen, Kusters, & Trienekens, 2011), where multiple technologies, which may be used in different ways, address the same need with significant overlap. Therefore, the decision to simultaneously adopt multiple technologies can be complex and can depend as much on how they will be implemented as on their specific features and benefits.

The need to harmonize technologies emerges as a solution toward working simultaneously with multiple improvement technologies (Kirwan, Marino, Morley, & Siviy, 2008a; Lawrence, 2009; Pardo, 2010). Currently, there are many harmonization approaches (Calvache, Pino, García, & Piattini, 2009; Kirwan et al., 2008a), methods and techniques (Halvorsen & Conradi, 2001; Mutafelija & Stromberg, 2003; Wang & King, 2000). Some techniques, such as mapping and comparison, are widely used but many other techniques have not yet been clearly defined, making harmonization of multiple technologies a difficult endeavor for organizations.

Software Process Architectures have been recognized as a means to harmonize multiple technologies within an organization that develops software products (Kirwan et al., 2008a; Kirwan, Marino, Morley, & Siviy, 2008b). Software process architecture in a multimodel environment is defined as "a set of process elements and its relationships that support adding, removing or modifying any improvement technology and allowing it to be derived from standard processes" (Pesantes, Lemus, Mitre, & Mejia, 2012a).

Several methods have been published to address the problem of how to design a process architecture (Borsoi & Becerra, 2008; Dai, Li, Zhao, Yu, & Huang, 2008; Green & Ould, 1996; Maldonado & Velázquez, 2006). However, it is unclear how to design a software process architecture that supports a multimodel software process improvement environment.

This research presents a method to design a software process architecture that supports a multimodel environment. This method considers creating a software process architecture that will receive as input a set of harmonized heterogeneous technologies and obtain as output a set of standard processes. It is based on a statistical thinking approach, analysis method and internal structured analysis technique.

Accordingly, the contents herein are structured as follows: section 2 presents a background of available efforts regarding methods to design a process architecture. Section 3 presents important aspects considered to create the method. Section 4 describes the basic concepts of the method. Section 5 shows the basic constructors of a software process architecture. Section 6 gives a general description of the method. Section 7 describes the method's phases, with their respective activities and artifacts. The last section summarizes conclusions and future works of this research.

1.1 Background

Today, researchers are concerned with understanding and improving the quality of software, which is being used in a variety of areas and applications and becoming more complex as the functionality required to provide services is evolving. As software increases in usage, complexity and size, the cost of building and maintaining it has increased as well. Software exhibits unexpected and undesirable behaviors that may even cause severe problems and damage that affect its quality. Hence, the software process approach has emerged to address these concerns and, recently, the research area of process architecture is emerging with it.

The software process approach is centered on the process through which software is developed. A software process is defined as "the set of partially ordered steps used to develop or enhance a software product" (Feiler & Humphrey, 1993). This approach is based on the assumption that there is a direct correlation between the quality of the process and the quality of the developed software. Evidence indicates that a well-defined software process appears to be one way to decrease the cost and increase the productivity of developing software (Herbsleb, Carleton, Rozum, Siegel, & Zubrow, 1994).

Therefore, since the 1990s, organizations are moving toward a process oriented approach to develop software. A strategy to achieve some level of control in product quality is to use appropriate processes, methods, models and standards in product development. But, problems have arisen with the adoption of several of these elements in a software organization to achieve process improvement. In this section, we discuss this issue and show how the idea of using a process architecture emerges to generate software processes from the proper combination of models, methods or standards. Thus, three areas were identified and will be explained: software process improvement, multimodel environment and process architecture.

1.1.1 Software Process Improvement

As stated earlier, methods, models and standards are being used as tools to improve product quality. One way to improve quality is by improving the process constantly. Software Process Improvement (SPI) examines how to improve an organization's software development practices, once the software process evaluation has clarified what the current state of the process is. SPI is not planned as a single step to excellence but is performed gradually by transitions from one maturity level to the next.

There are many approaches and frameworks to support SPI. These implement the selected standards and then measure the effectiveness of the new processes. The most popular approaches and frameworks are (Plan-Do-Check-Act) PDCA cycle (Moen & Norman, 2006), IDEAL model (McFeely, 1996), ISO TR 15504 (ISO/IEC, 1998), CMMI (Capability Maturity Model Integrated) (CMMI Product Team, 2010), ISO 9001:2000 (ISO, 2000), and others.

However, SPI initiatives are not easy to implement; they carry a significant risk of failure (Aaen, 2003). The complexity of implementing SPI requires commitment, proper skills and re-

sources. These all need to be assured to obtain a successful SPI. Tailoring multiple approaches and frameworks to the company's needs is a time-consuming process and needs special expertise. This could be especially difficult in the global environment.

Software organizations do not sequentially implement the necessary approaches or frameworks in their improvement project, but rather several approaches or frameworks simultaneously. They find that models and standards often overlap in the requirements when they decide to implement the best practices for the situation.

1.1.2 Multimodel Environment

Numerous models, standards, methods, approaches and frameworks are available to software and systems engineering organizations. The long list of reference models, standards, best practices, regulatory policies and other types of practices that help organizations in their improvement effort is called improvement technologies (Kirwan, Marino, Morley, & Siviy, 2008c). A multimodel environment within an organization is denoted by the simultaneous use of improvement technologies to implement their improvement approach.

Many problems in this multimodel environment are identified (Kelemen et al., 2011). Selection of the most appropriate improvement technologies becomes an issue. Strategies and selection of technologies and solution implementation are closely connected to multimodel SPI, and these are considered new research topics (Kirwan, Marino, Morley, & Siviy, 2008d). The decision to adopt simultaneous multiple technologies is not always easy. Technologies that address the same needs and those that address different needs may significantly overlap. Also, the way these are implemented influence the decision-making process.

Organizations often struggle with the interpretation of technologies because of their different structure, terminology, level of detail and point of view on quality. Additionally, their integration is not always clear as the granularity of their descriptions and scope of applicability vary considerably.

Another problem with multimodel environments is the competition between technologies when several initiatives are concurrently implemented at difference hierarchical levels. This leads to competition for resources by the different approaches to satisfy their specific needs. The overlapping efforts are costly and the benefits of each technological approach are undermined by the conflicting approaches. This results in lack of effectiveness of the multiple technological approaches.

In the last decade several attempts have been made to define solutions for the harmonization of multimodels such as mappings (Mutafelija & Stromberg, 2003), taxonomies (Halvorsen & Conradi, 2001; Paulk, 2008; Kirwan et al., 2008d), combined models, combined appraisals (Griffith University, 2007), standardization (Kelemen, 2009), formal solutions (Ferreira, Machado, & Paulk, 2010), a multimodel framework (Balla, 2001)(Kirwan et al., 2008a), and other research on multimodel process improvement (Software Engineering Institute, 2010).

In the context of the harmonization framework, we will conduct research to design an improvement solution using a process architecture. We are going to discuss this issue in the section which follows.

1.1.3 Process Architecture

The simultaneous use of existing and new improvement technologies is causing many problems. Software organizations usually have "ad-hoc processes" describing spur of the moment processes and "processes of different technologies" implementing improvement technologies. These processes are grouped into "process repositories," where it is unclear whether relations between them are well defined to ensure that they will work well together and support any change. This happens because there are no methodologies or techniques

that guide the generation of a flexible and robust structure of processes.

Thus, software organizations need tools to convert selected improvement technologies to execute processes and to design an improvement solution. One tool could be process architecture (Kirwan et al., 2008b). It provides process components and characteristics to design the processes. It is an aid for visualizing the relationships of a process with other existing and future processes, identifying relationships between process elements and external processes, describing interfaces, interdependencies and supporting the dynamic business context.

Process architecture (PA) is an emergent area of research, with little understanding and experience and with confusing terminology that makes it difficult to express technical issues and concerns, along with its progress. The value of process architectures has to rise to the challenge to aggregate value within a company that develops software products. Consequently, this is leading organizations to invest resources in the development of their process architecture (Wolf & Harmon, 2012).

This work considers that a Software Process Architecture (SPA) is derived from the general structure of a PA (Pesantes, Lemus, Mitre, & Mejia, 2012b). Thus, many SPA methods and efforts generating awareness, ideas and approaches have been found in the literature as follows:

- (Ould, 1997) creates a process architecture from the essential business entities (EBEs). After, EBEs are converted to essential units of work diagrams (EUOW) and relations between them are identified, and tools like RADmodeller and visio stencils (plug-in) are built.
- (Jeston & Nelis, 2006) propose a framework to implement BPM (Business Process Management) programs and projects. The framework considers a process architecture phase. It specifies that a process architec-

ture must be composed of overall objectives, general principles, process guidelines and process models. Also, (Harmon, 2003) mentions that a useful way to embed a process architecture in the organization is the establishment of a "business process architecture committee."

- (Maldonado & Velázquez, 2006) present a method for defining the process architecture using concepts such as Zachman's framework and value configuration (chain, workshop and network). This method develops a process architecture as the artifact using a Planner and Function in Zachman's framework.

- (Borsoi & Becerra, 2008) propose a process architecture as a set of views (structural, behavioral, organizational and automation) represented by models and relationships between them. In this work, the fundamentals of object-oriented methodology are applied to represent processes (processes and their components are handled as objects).

- (Dai et al., 2008) define a process architecture made of evolution process components (EPC) and connectors. They argue that a process architecture may realize process component-based software process reuse as well as software architecture does in a component-based software reuse.

- (Fu, Li, & Hu, 2009) present a process architecture using Aspect Oriented Programming (AOP) methodology. Software evolution process components, software evolution process connectors, aspect connectors and constraint relations among them are put together in the aspect oriented software evolution process architecture (AOSEPA).

- (Boehm & Wolf, 1996) introduce an open process architecture and examine some architectural element interfaces.

- (Mutafelija & Stromberg, 2003) make reference to three views of a process architecture. First, a functional view shows task descriptions. Second, a behavioral view shows when and how tasks are performed. And third, an organizational view identifies who performs the tasks.

- (Carr, Dandekar, & Perry, 1995) provide a process interface description language, called Mini-interact, which is a simple approach to describe process interfaces accessible to both programmers and non-programmers.

- (Kasser, 2005) identifies a new role named process architect. This role will cover the gap in the functions performed by the three organizational roles (systems architecting, systems engineering and project management) when viewed from the perspective of planning and implementing the development of a system.

On the basis of a literature review (Kitchenham, Pearlbrereton, Budgen, Turner, Bailey, & Linkman., 2009), the methods found to design process architecture do not address multimodel environment issues, thus it is the purpose of this research.

2. IMPORTANT ASPECTS TO BUILD THE METHOD

This section shows the most relevant aspects considered to build the proposed method. These aspects are organized as follows: first, criteria used to design software process architecture in a multimodel environment; second, an organizational model which may contribute supporting a multimodel environment within a software organization and third, the multimodel framework on which the method was developed.

2.1 Criteria to Design a Software Process Architecture in a Multimodel Environment

The criteria used to design a Software Process Architecture (SPA) that supports a multimodel environment were identified from problems in the multimodel environment, important issues, principles and attributes for a good process architecture (Pesantes et al., 2012a).

Figure 1 shows the problems, issues, and attributes considered to derive these criteria. The multimodel environment problems considered were (Kelemen et al., 2011):

- Correlation among improvement technologies: different terminology; requirements overlap; different internal structures, granularity, size and complexity; and chaotic relationships.
- Changeability of these technologies because organizations need to modify their business.

Figure 1. Design criteria of software process architecture

Multimodel Environment Problems	PA Critical Issues				Good PA Attributes
	Definition	Design	Properties	Evaluation	
Correlation	✔		✔		Set of rules, principles and models.
Changeability			✔	✔	Dynamic
Traceability		✔			Aligned with organization strategy and objectives, and business, information and technical architecture.
Solution Documentation	✔				Basis for design and realization of processes and easy to understand.
Multiple Appraisal	✔				Easy to stakeholders.

Quality

Handling different inputs - General - Quality

Traceability - General

Documentation

Documentation

Design Criteria

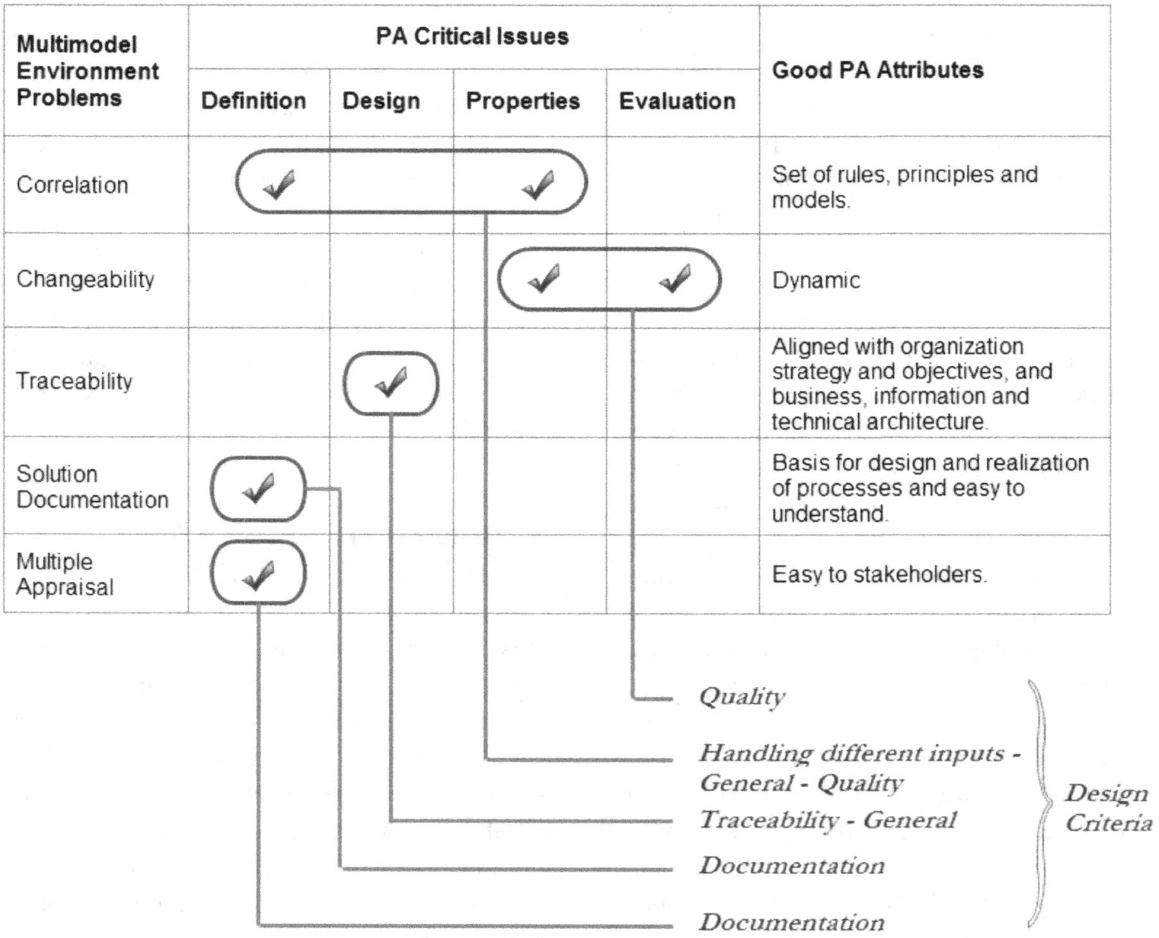

- Traceability of elements from improvement technologies to standard process description is not well established.
- Documentation of multimodel solution because several multimodel initiatives describe only the final multimodel result.
- Multiple appraisals such as assessments, audits, reviews, benchmarks or measurements, which are aimed at the discovery of the conformity of organizational processes to a quality approach.

The SPA issues that would resolve the multimodel environment problems are:

- Process Architecture adopts different definitions from the point of view of Process Management (PM), Business Process Management (BPM), Enterprise Architecture (EA) and Software Process Engineering (SPE). From the PM perspective, it is important for the general management system of organizations. From the BPM perspective, it is necessary to achieve the business goals, to model the business and manage change within the business. From the EA perspective, it is an important part of enterprise structure. In addition, the SPE perspective makes its interest clear from the internal structure of PA.
- Design identifies how an SPA is created and that a method consists of process elements, relations, views, stakeholders, tools and architectural level properties.
- Properties at the level of process and architectural.
- Evaluations, forms to classify and evaluate methods, would be useful for organization process researchers and for those engaged in developing process centric organizations if they could access a critical comparative analysis of different approaches for identifying and modeling process architectures.

The good process attributes considered were (Jeston & Nelis, 2006):

- There must be a set of rules, principles and models for the processes.
- The process architecture must be dynamic, that is, easily adaptable to the evolving process, business and enterprise changes.
- Processes must be related to organization strategy and objectives.
- Processes must be aligned with the business architecture, and information and technical architecture, which equates to an organization driven enterprise architecture.
- There must be a basis for design and realization of processes of the organization.
- Processes must be easy for all relevant stakeholders to understand and apply.

These criteria are summarized as follows:

1. **General criteria:**
   - Identify organizational and process objectives: processes must be related to organization strategy and objectives.
   - PA supports the process life cycle (i.e. elicitation, analysis, design, implementation, enactment, assessment).
   - PA supports multimodel process improvement.
   - PA supports the maintenance of processes: it supports changes and dynamic environment, and keeps in balance the return of investment for improvement projects.
2. **Criteria for handling different inputs:**
   - Identify correlation among technologies (terminology, requirements, granularity, size and complexity).
   - Identify static and dynamic elements of technologies (internal structure).

○ Identify internal and external relationships between process elements of PA (compatibility).

3. **Criteria of traceability:**
   ○ Business objectives and improvement technologies.
   ○ Technologies elements and PA elements.
   ○ PA elements and elements of process descriptions.

4. **Criteria of quality:**
   ○ Process level: easy for all stakeholders to understand and apply, support modularity, and granularity.
   ○ Architectural level: reuse, decomposition of processes hierarchically, flexibility, comprehensibility, facilitate communication, ease of maintenance and utility.

5. **Criteria of documentation:**
   ○ Views to describe a software process architecture.
   ○ Tools to support the design, implementation and maintenance of a software process architecture in a software organization.

Finally, these criteria will be used as a checklist to verify that the proposed method may be used to design a software process architecture, which supports a well-defined set of quality attributes in a multimodel environment.

2.2 Organizational Model

A software organization will be defined under the organizational model of an Integrated Software Factory. An organizational model is defined as a sub-model of a software process model which describes the organizational component types, their structure, and properties (Lonchamp, 1993). An Integrated Software Factory identifies a set of views such as application, infrastructure, process, quality and business. These views are based on the Reference Model of the Open Distributed Processing (RM-ODP) methodology. Based on (Dominguez Dias, 2010) an Integrated Software Factory is defined as "an enterprise that contains all the necessary organizational departments to carry out their main activity and whose main business process is to develop software; hence, its primary department is denoted as Software Factory" (see Figure 2). It is important to mention that from

Figure 2. Composition of an integrated software factory

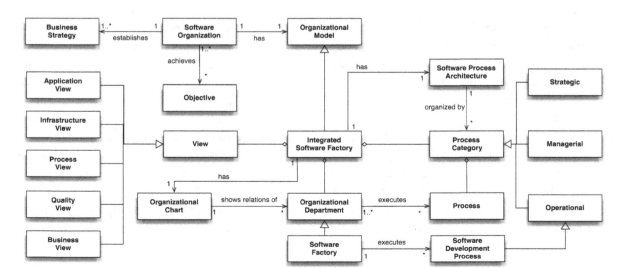

the combination of quality and process views a software process architecture in a multimodel environment is created. Also, these views may be detailed even further.

A hierarchical model of roles in an integrated software factory is shown in Figure 3. Based on the literature (Borsoi, 2008; Harmon, 2003; Humphrey, 2000; Kasser, 2005; McFeely, 1996), three basic levels to organize an integrated software factory are identified: strategic, managerial and operational.

- The general management group carries out activities that are strategic to the integrated software factories.
- The project management group is at the managerial level and has the following responsibilities: define project planning, identify risks, develop measures to mitigate risks, solve problems, manage the project, budget and schedule and perform quality control.
- The process group is also at the managerial level and is responsible for maintaining the entire organization's processes and

the Software Process Architecture. They also establish and maintain the alignment between the organization's strategic objectives and the process goals. This group has its own internal structure and can be subdivided. Due to the scope of their responsibilities, they can directly influence the project group.

- At the operational level is the development team, which is composed of: Team Leader, Development Manager, Planning Manager, Quality/Process Manager and Support Manager. This is a proposal of how a team can be organized to develop software. This proposal was chosen because it supports small organizational structures and their measurement framework.

2.3 Multimodel Framework

The reasoning framework generated in (Kirwan et al., 2008a, 2008d; Siviy et al., 2008) was tailored and detailed to build the basis of our method. This framework for harmonization is according to relevant principles and practices, which result

Figure 3. Model of the hierarchical structure of roles

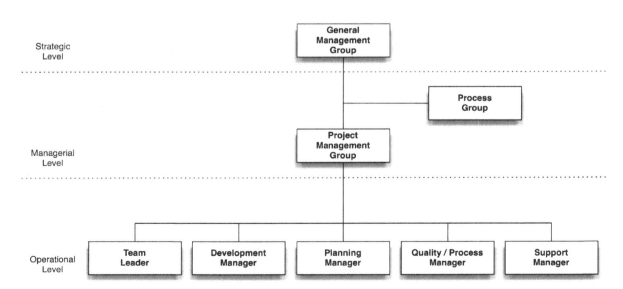

in a vertically aligned set of layers addressing multimodel design and implementation from mission to strategy and from tactics to execution. This framework adheres to the paradigm of statistical thinking (Janis & Shade, 2000) that considers:

- Everything is a process.
- All processes have inherent variability.
- Data is used to understand variation and to drive decisions to improve the processes.

Based on currently available knowledge and research, the key components of this multimodel framework are explained below:

1. **Choose improvement technologies:**
   a. Alignment of organizational and improvement objectives. The mission and highest-level strategic objectives must be decomposed into operational objectives.
   b. Improvement technologies should be selected on the basis of their ability to enable process features and capabilities that are needed to achieve mission and operational objectives (each is independently selected).
2. **Analysis of technologies synergy:**
   a. Each selected improvement technology is examined for its high-level relationship among each other; these relationships aid selection decisions and alignment with objectives. This strategic categorization can be used to refine the list of technologies selected by identifying gaps and enabling high-level validation and verification.
   b. It is an iterative process that needs to be performed each time new improvement technologies are considered for inclusion in the organization's process landscape.

   c. Taxonomies for improvement frameworks can be used to support categorization. Some examples are (Halvorsen & Conradi, 2001; Kirwan et al., 2008d; Kirwan, Marino, Morley, & Siviy, 2008e; Paulk, 2008).
3. **Construction of an integrated model:** Technologies need to be customized for rollout within a software organization. For multimodel process improvement, this framework complements strategic categorization with composition of selected improvement technologies and process architecture. These are not necessarily sequential, but may be quite iterative and the starting point may vary.
   a. Technology composition using element classification and other tactical technology connections:
      i. It is critical to understand the details about how technologies connect with each other. This is a specialized task to examine overlapping, distinctive, and enabling functionality among technologies.
      ii. The practical integration of the selected technologies is through the understanding of the relationships of the selected technologies to each other, the types of elements the selected technologies contain, and technology mapping and process implementation.
      iii. When considering pairs or small groups of technologies, their relationships often emerge or detailed mappings may be created. But when you add more technologies into the mix, it is more complex. In this task it is necessary to use taxonomies or other tools to

classify technology elements. For example, (Kirwan et al., 2008e).

b. Process architecture

  i. It is a big leap from technology composition to process architecture and process descriptions.

  ii. In practice, a PA is derived from multiple improvement technologies and it may lead to defining descriptions of standard software processes. This gap will be covered by our proposed method.

4. **Adaptation of the integrated model to the organization context:**

  a. Clear traceability between project objectives and business drivers will be necessary. Project teams are called upon to integrate in their projects the process improvements selected. Such projects are probably most effective at integrating new process solutions when they address project performance goals or points.

  b. In the context of multimodel process improvement, the process group face several implementation challenges, distinct from linear model improvement: shared/coordinated roles and responsibilities; integrated and/or coordinated training; coordinated (possibly shared) audit and appraisal processes and data; and coordinated improvement project portfolio management.

  c. Other factors that affect the integration of improvement solutions in a software organization are the organizational culture and change resistance (Muñoz, Mejia, Calvo-Manzano, Cuevas, & San Feliu, 2012).

5. **Measuring results:**

  a. Considering that these improvement technologies will solve a problem or enable a higher level of performance, measurement of impact is an important step.

b. Baseline data are necessary but not always available in the early stages of software process improvement. The impact measurement is a long-term proposition. Depending on the size and quantity of projects, it may take multiple years to determine the effectiveness of an improvement.

c. Therefore the meta-measures of performance become the main part of the model: performance snapshots based on single projects or even sub-projects, engineering measures, and measures of model standard institutionalization (such as maturity levels).

Finally, this work is focused on the creation of a method to design a software process architecture that supports a multimodel environment. This method considers the design of a software process architecture derived from heterogeneous improvement technologies as input and it allows the creation of standard process descriptions as output.

3. THE DESIGN METHOD

This section describes the method to design a software process architecture in a multimodel environment. First, basic concepts used in the method are defined. Second, the general design of the method is substantiated. Third, basic constructors of software process architecture are given. Fourth, a hierarchy of software process architecture is shown. Finally, method phases are explained.

3.1 Basic Concepts

The definition of the proposed method and its ingredients were influenced by (Kronlöf, 1993) who identified four main parts: 1) an underlying model, 2) a language, 3) defined steps and ordering of these steps and 4) guidance for applying the method:

- An underlying model which provides a conceptual representation of the product of a method. Most system engineering methods in fact incorporate more basic methods (each with their own model) in a "uses" or "inherits" hierarchy. As a method increases its repertoire and scope it will have a collection of inherited underlying models. Kronlöf keeps it simple by identifying a single underlying model, even though that "model" may actually be a set of models.
- A language, which is the concrete means of describing the product of the method and the user interface of the underlying model of the method. It is used to describe the process models represented by the method, and is the concrete counterpart of the underlying model. As with the model, Kronlöf denotes it as a unique method's single language, even though that language may in fact be a set of languages.
- Defined steps and the order of those steps. It is the process model of the method.
- Guidance for applying the method, which typically takes the form of informal text in manuals, handbooks, guides etc.
- Tools to support different activities of the method. The tools support the documentation of process architecture design. The tools assist the method user in his or her work, thereby not only making the design process faster, but also preventing human mistakes in the process.

Based on (IEEE, 2000), a description of software process architecture is composed of a set of views represented by models and their relationships. These models have different degrees of abstraction and are represented by diagrams. The basic constructors compose the diagrams. Both elements and relationships display a certain type of behavior and are subject to restrictions. The relationships can be static or represent sequence and data flows.

The proposed method, according to Figure 4, is composed of phases, and the notation of process elements is depicted using basic constructors (modeling syntax and semantics). These elements are obtained from the internal structure analysis of the improvement technologies. For this work, Business Process Management Notation (BPMN) was selected to complement our notation.

The phases represent the sequence of steps to elicit and model the information used to compose process models. The basic concepts provide "what" will be modeled and the notation defines "how" it will be modeled. "What" refers to the process elements and the concepts that represent these elements. "How" refers to the syntax used to represent the types of elements that compose the process models.

The method to design a software process architecture in a multimodel environment basically describes the activities that must be performed to obtain process views of the model. Thus, phases are the main parts of the method. The phases are sequential and aimed at defining the process architecture model. Each method phase produces models that comprise the process architecture with different degrees of abstraction. To represent these models, basic concepts and notations for elements were defined.

Software process architecture can be built for software organizations, organizational departments or software projects. These can be restricted to a specific domain (for example, organization size, technology used or kind of projects). In this work, guidance and tools of the method are not shown.

3.2 General Design

Meta-Object Facility (MOF) (OMG, 2006), reference architecture theory (Bass, Clements, & Kazman, 2003) and the main elements to model a software process system (Wang & King, 2000) were used to organize the proposed method.

Figure 4. Basic concepts of the method

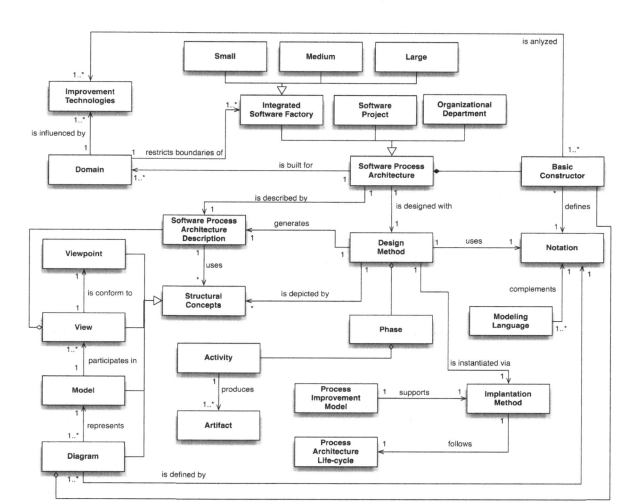

Figure 5 shows the method as a four-layered architecture based on MOF (OMG, 2006). Each layer represents distinct abstraction levels. From the perspective of this method, each layer is a phase and each phase generates elements that form the basis for the next phase. The phases represented as rectangles are interrelated. That is, each rectangle represents distinct abstraction levels of the same model, and all models use the basic concepts and notational elements defined in the conceptual architecture phase. Theses phases are executed sequentially. Considering the process improvement context, Figure 5 highlights

the main elements in a software process system: process reference model, process assessment model and process improvement model (Wang & King, 2000). These elements are represented as circles. A process reference model is a model of a process system that describes process organization, hierarchy, interrelationship and tailoring. A process assessment model consists of a process capability model (measurement framework) and a process capability determination method. A process improvement model is an operational model that provides guidance for improving a process system capability by changing, updating,

Figure 5. General design of the method

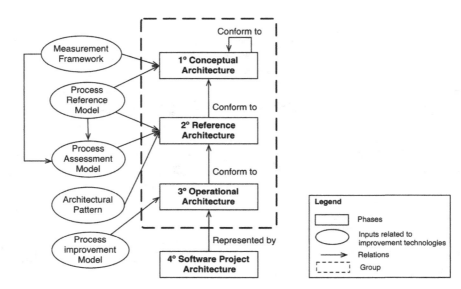

enhancing existing processes based on the findings provided in a process assessment. In general, conceptual architecture, reference architecture and operational architecture phases are grouped together since they generate conceptual process models and the software project architecture phase generates enacted process models.

The conceptual architecture phase defines the basic concepts, basic constructors of a process element and the notational elements. Constructors are identified from an internal structural analysis of multiples process reference model and process assessment model. The maturity requirements of a process element are extracted from measurement frameworks. Viewpoints, views, models and diagrams are defined.

The reference architecture phase includes process meta-models customized to a domain. The reference architecture is defined as a process reference model and/or process assessment model mapped onto process elements and the data flows between them. The meta-models are built from the concepts defined in the previous phase. A meta-model defines a set of practices and relationships between them. Also, an architectural pattern is a description of element and relation types together with a set of constraints on how they may be used. In the proposed method, an architectural pattern is considered a set of constraints of a process architecture, the element types and their patterns of interaction. These constraints define a set or family of architectures that satisfy them. These definitions are adapted from (Bass et al., 2003).

The operational architecture phase comprises process models that are customized by business requirements (for example, maturity level). These process models are defined as standard processes. These processes may be customized and thus allow the instantiation of distinct projects. Also, a process improvement model is selected to define improvement mechanisms for a process system.

The software project architecture phase defines process instances for implementation and enactment. This layer is referred to as instantiated architecture because the process models are instantiated through a software project considering its requirements. In this phase the software project processes are executed.

In addition, traceability among elements of these phases must be clearly defined. That is, basic elements of improvement technologies are transformed into constructors. These basic constructors are transformed into process meta-models, which are in turn transformed into process models. And process models are transformed into project process instances.

3.3 Basic Constructors of Software Process Architecture

Based on the internal structure analysis of some improvement technologies (CMMI, TSP, PSP, Bootstrap, ISO 15505 and ISO 9001) and process elements proposed in (Bhuta, Boehm, & Meyers, 2005), a software process architecture is composed of process elements and its relationships. A process element is a set of activities and/or sub-process elements (granularity level). Both activities and sub-process elements are classified as variants or invariants. Pre-conditions are dependencies (artifacts and information needed for execution) and project effort, schedule and resources estimates. Post-conditions define results from its execution (these may be abstract models, information and analysis or simple risk reduction). The process

element is related to a knowledge base to take into consideration the implications of past projects both inside and outside the organization. Process element needs to incorporate past project efforts, schedules and relationships of information within the process elements and project plans. Additionally, process element may also include organizational and industry best practices (see Figure 6).

3.4 Hierarchy of Software Process Architecture

A hierarchy of software process architecture designs supporting a multimodel environment is shown in Figure 7. The phases of the proposed method are considered artifacts. This hierarchy shows a way to order the creation of software process architectures. First, a conceptual architecture; second, a reference architecture composed of multimodel-reference architecture and domain references architecture by organization size (small, medium, large); third, an operational architecture by maturity level; and fourth, a software project architecture (evidences of organizational maturity and process capability).

Figure 6. Basic constructors of software process architecture

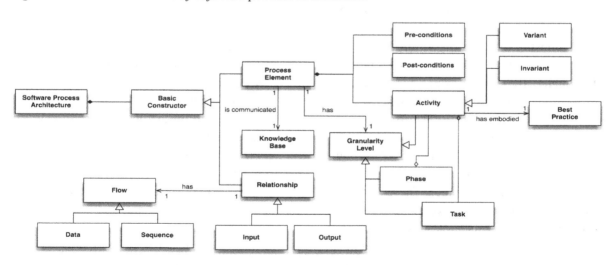

Figure 7. Hierarchy of software process architecture in a multimodel environment

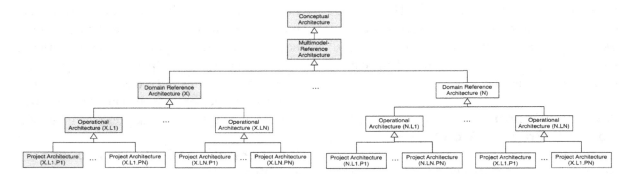

3.5 Phases of the Method

This section shows phases, activities and artifacts of the proposed method. It is based on basic concepts of process element and their relationships. The Business Process Management Notation (BPMN) was used to exemplify the process model generation. The method is not linked to specific languages; any language that allows the representations from the models obtained in the method phases and the notational elements may be used.

In Figure 8 the relationships between the SPA and the knowledge base is highlighted. At project and organizational levels, process elements must take into consideration the implications of past projects both inside and outside the organization. Consideration of previous project efforts, schedule and relationship information within the process elements will empirically prove project plans. Additionally, these plans should also include organizational and industry best practices.

Based on (Ahlgren, 2007), the goal of knowledge base management is a practical one: to improve organizational capabilities through better use of the organization's individual and collective knowledge resources. These resources include skills, capabilities, experience, routines, and norms, as well as technologies. This work is concerned with products that enable communication between process architecture and knowledge base rather than how to perform knowledge base management activities. In a general manner, knowledge base management (Ahlgren, 2007) should perform the following activities:

- Knowledge identification, companies should know what knowledge and expertise exist both inside and outside their own walls.
- Knowledge acquisitions, four "import channels" were identified to acquire knowledge: knowledge held by other organizations, stakeholder knowledge, experts and knowledge products (i.e. software, patents and others).
- Knowledge development consists of all the management activities intended to produce new internal or external knowledge at both the individual and collective levels.
- Knowledge distribution consists of making knowledge available and usable across the whole organization. Technical knowledge distribution infrastructures can support efficient knowledge exchange within organizations and connect formerly separated experts through an electronic network.
- Knowledge use means the productive deployment of organizational knowledge in the production process. The successful identification and distribution of critical knowledge does not ensure its daily use. And without consistent use, there is a high

Figure 8. Design method phases and external relationships

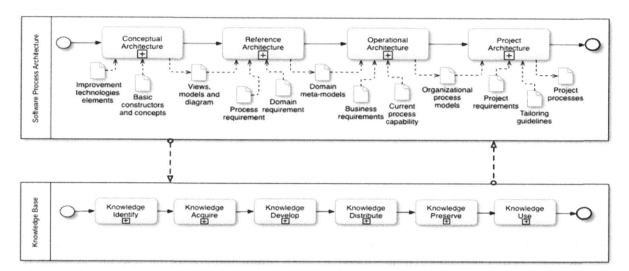

probability that new knowledge systems will decline in quality, and the investment will be wasted. The potential user of knowledge has to see a real advantage in order to change his or her behavior and "adopt" the knowledge.

- Knowledge preservation, after knowledge has been acquired or developed, it must be carefully preserved. Many companies complain that in the process of reorganization they have lost part of their corporate memory. To avoid the loss of valuable expertise, companies must shape the processes of selecting valuable knowledge for preservation, ensuring its suitable storage, and regularly incorporating it into the knowledge base.

- Knowledge measurement, the evaluation and measurement of organizational knowledge present the biggest challenge in the field of knowledge management. Knowledge Managers have no tested toolbox of accepted indicators and measurement processes. They are pioneers. And the subject they need to measure is particularly elusive. Knowledge and capabilities

can rarely be tracked to a single influencing variable. Furthermore, the cost of measuring knowledge is often seen as too high or socially unacceptable. Nevertheless, knowledge measurement holds considerable potential value, as has been demonstrated in a related field by human resources managers, who have had to prove the impact of training investments.

3.5.1 Phase 1: Conceptual Architecture

The conceptual architecture phase (Figure 9) includes the following activities:

- Identify goals, elicit requirements, and define stakeholders and their interests. They all form the basis to group together these meta-models in the defined views.
- Identify basic concepts and constructors; selection of different methodologies to define software process architecture and its elements (i.e. aspect-oriented, object-oriented, software component, services). Concerns are important to define quality attributes that must support the process

Figure 9. Conceptual architecture phase

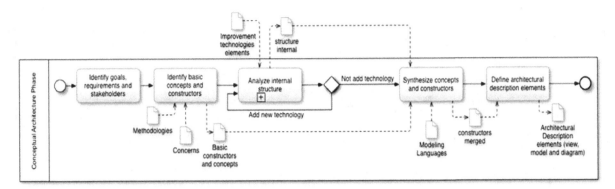

architecture and its elements. Thus, basic constructors and concepts are identified and will be used in each phase of the method.

- Analyze internal structure; the technologies selected are analyzed to identify concepts or elements of a software process architecture, generating diagrams of internal structure of each technology, process elements and operational elements. This activity will be repeated every time that a new technology is added or any changes are made to it.

- Synthesize concepts and constructors; this complements the basic constructors with other elements detected in the technologies. Modeling languages can support the identification of an appropriate notation.

- Define architectural description elements; with the previous concepts, constructors and stakeholders' interests are identified viewpoints, views, models and diagrams that describe a software process architecture.

3.5.2 Phase 2: Reference Architecture

The reference architecture phase (Figure 10) includes the following activities:

- Design the multimodel reference architecture; this consists of selecting practices (or process requirements) from technologies, analyzing the impact level of practices, integrating practices and identifying variant and invariant practices. The mapping matrix of practices of all technologies selected is obtained.

- Using a domain, customize the reference architecture; a domain is considered along with the size of the organization (small, medium and large). But each organization has some considerations as domain requirement (these may be technology or specific improvement technology), an organizational chart and role set. The main outcome is a meta-model expressed as a set of practices.

3.5.3 Phase 3: Operational Architecture

The operational architecture phase (Figure 11) includes the following activities:

- Obtain and categorize business requirement; the business requirements are elicited. These categories may be: process, roles, policies, stakeholders, and others. This categorization is important to evaluate its impact on reference architecture elements.

Figure 10. Reference architecture phase

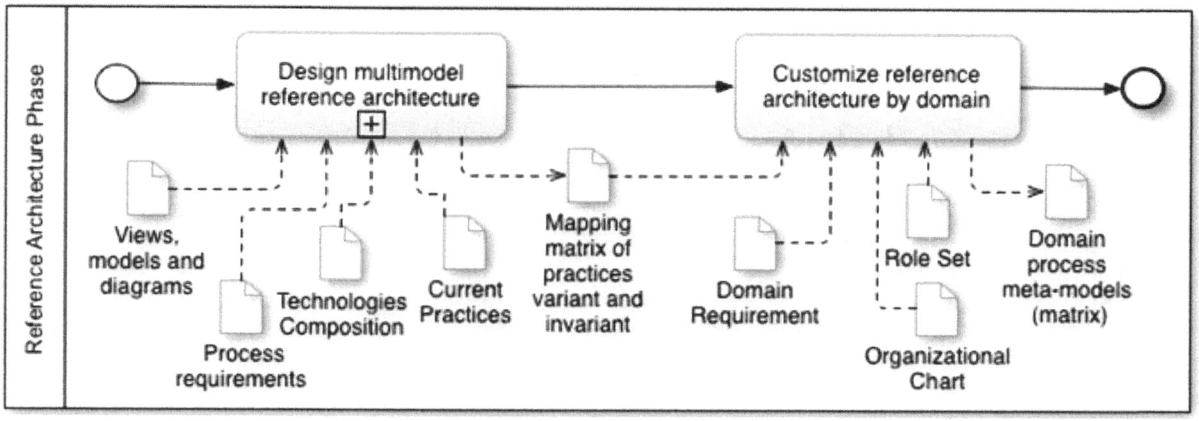

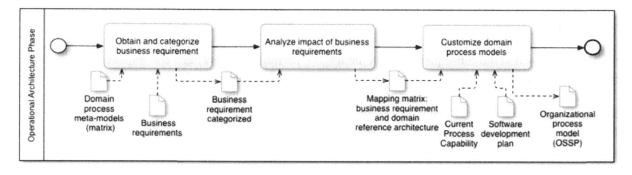

Figure 11. Operational architecture phase

- Analyze impact of business requirements such as mapping between business requirement and domain reference architecture.
- Customize domain process models; using the previous mapping and the current process capability or maturity level, the organizational process models or organizational standard software processes (OSSP) are created. Software development plans are created using OSSP.

3.5.4 Phase 4: Software Project Architecture

The software project architecture (Figure 12) includes the following activities:

- Customize organizational process model; the organizational process models are customized by project requirements, software cycle and tailoring guidelines. The software development plan contains standard processes, which may be modified.
- Instantiate project processes; the defined project process of a specific project are executed.

4. CONCLUSION

In this work, we have presented an overview of the method to design a software process architecture supporting a multimodel environment: general design, basic concepts, phases, activities and ar-

Figure 12. Software project architecture phase

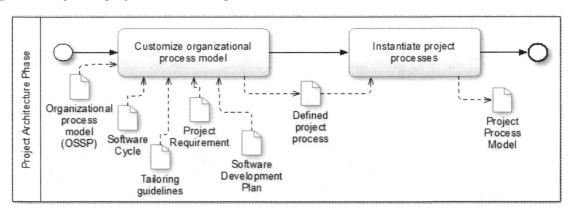

tifacts. The challenge of multimodel improvement is to select, compose and sequence the desired set of improvement technologies. In addition, the organization must develop processes to deliver the capability of each technology in a way that enables work to get done and the subsequent achievement of business objectives.

Thus, Software Process Architecture would be a means to derive standard process description from improvement technologies. It was defined as a set of process elements and its relationships; and its basic constructors were also defined. The proposed method is composed of phases, activities and artifacts. And the description of a software process architecture makes use of views, models and diagrams.

Also, a method to implement the design of a software process architecture in a Software Organization will be built, considering a process architecture lifecycle and process improvement model. We are currently working on a software tool to support the design and implementation methods.

Some topics extracted from the review for future research are: mechanisms to validate quality attributes and generic mechanisms in the design of a software process architecture to collect quantita-

tive information. Thus, it is necessary to develop a methodology for creating software process architecture that supports a multimodel environment. It must be flexible to support changes in the business. We are currently working on a methodology that permits us to evaluate the impact of aggregating a technology and designing a flexible software process architecture.

REFERENCES

Aaen, I. (2003). Software process improvement: Blueprints versus recipes. *IEEE Software*, *20*(5), 86–93. doi:10.1109/MS.2003.1231159

Ahlgren, R. (2007). Facilitating design knowledge management by tailoring software patterns to organizational roles. [AMCIS.]. *Proceedings of AMCIS*, *07*, 463–463.

Balla, K. (2001). *The complex quality world, developing quality management systems for software companies*. Eindhoven, The Netherlands: University of Technology Eindhoven.

Bass, L., Clements, P., & Kazman, R. (2003). *Software architecture in practice* (2nd ed.). Reading, MA: Addison-Wesley Professional.

Bhuta, J., Boehm, B., & Meyers, S. (2005). Process elements: Components of software process architectures. In *Proceedings of the 2005 International Conference on Unifying the Software Process Spectrum* (pp. 332–346). Berlin: Springer-Verlag. doi:10.1007/11608035_28

Boehm, B., & Wolf, S. (1996). An open architecture for software process asset reuse. In *Proceedings of Software Process Workshop,* (pp. 2-4). IEEE.

Borsoi, B. T. (2008). *Arquitetura de processo aplicada na integraçaõ de fábricas de software.* (Doctoral dissertation, Ph. D Thesis). Escola Politécnica da Universidade de Sao Paulo, Sao Paulo, Brazil.

Borsoi, B. T., & Becerra, J. L. R. (2008). A method to define an object oriented software process architecture. In *Proceedings of Software Engineering* (pp. 650–655). IEEE.

Calvache, C. J. P., Pino, F. J., García, F., & Piattini, M. (2009). Homogenization of models to support multi-model processes in improvement environments. In *Proceedings of ICSOFT* (pp. 151–156). ICSOFT.

Carr, D. C., Dandekar, A., & Perry, D. E. (1995). Experiments in process interface descriptions, visualizations and analyses. In *Software process technology* (pp. 119–137). Berlin: Springer. doi:10.1007/3-540-59205-9_48

CMMI Product Team. (2010). *CMMI for development (CMMI-DEV, v1.3) (CMU/SEI-2010-TR33).* Pittsburgh, PA: Software Engineering Institute, Carnegie Mellon University.

Dai, F., Li, T., Zhao, N., Yu, Y., & Huang, B. (2008). Evolution process component composition based on process architecture. In *Proceedings of Intelligent Information Technology Application Workshops* (pp. 1097–1100). IEEE.

Dias, L. D. (2010). *Método de instanciação de uma arquitetura de processos aplicado em fábrica de software.* (Master dissertation). Escola Politécnica de Universidade de Sao Paulo, Sao Paulo, Brazil.

Feiler, P., & Humphrey, W. S. (1993). Software process development and enactment: Concepts and definitions. In *Proceedings of Software Process* (pp. 28–40). Berlin, Germany: IEEE Computer Society Press.

Ferreira, A. L., Machado, R. J., & Paulk, M. C. (2010). Size and complexity attributes for multi-model improvement framework taxonomy. In Proceedings of Software Engineering and Advanced Applications (SEAA), (pp. 306-309). IEEE.

Fu, Z., Li, T., & Hu, Y. (2009). An approach to aspect-oriented software evolution process architecture. In *Proceedings of Intelligent Computation Technology and Automation* (pp. 144–147). IEEE.

Green, S., & Ould, M. A. (1996). The primacy of process architecture. In *Proceedings of CAiSE Workshops* (pp. 154-159). CAiSE.

Griffith University. S. Q. I. (SQI). (2007). *Tool: Appraisal assistant beta.* Retrieved from http://www.sqi.gu.edu.au/AppraisalAssistant/about.html

Halvorsen, C., & Conradi, R. (2001). A taxonomy to compare SPI frameworks. In *Proceedings of Software Process Technology* (pp. 217–235). Berlin: Springer. doi:10.1007/3-540-45752-6_17

Harmon, P. (2003). Business process change: A manager's guide to improving, redesigning, and automating processes. *Business Process Trends, 1*(3), 529.

Herbsleb, J., Carleton, A., Rozum, J., Siegel, J., & Zubrow, D. (1994). *Benefits of CMM-based software process improvement: Initial results (CMU/SEI-94-TR-013).* Pittsburgh, PA: Carnegie-Mellon University, Software Engineering Institute.

Humphrey, W. S. (2000). *Introduction to the team software process (sm)*. Addison-Wesley Professional. Retrieved from http://books.google.com/books?id=0-Gzw8v-S0YC&pgis=1

IEEE. (2000). *IEEE recommended practice for architectural description of software-intensive systems (Technical Report IEEE Std 1471-2000)*. IEEE Computer Society.

ISO. (2000). *ISO 9001 : 2000 quality management systems — Requirements*. Geneva, Switzerland: ISO.

ISO/IEC. (1998). *ISO/IEC TR 15504:1998 information technology — Software process assessment part 2: A reference model for processes and process capability*. Geneva, Switzerland: ISO/IEC.

Janis, S. J., & Shade, J. E. (2000). *Improving performance through statistical thinking*. Milwaukee, WI: ASQ Quality Press.

Jeston, J., & Nelis, J. (2006). *Business process management: Practical guidelines to successful implementations*. Oxford, UK: Butterworth-Heinemann.

Kasser, J. E. (2005). Introducing the role of process architecting. In *Proceedings of 15th International Symposium of the International Council on Systems Engineering (INCOSE)*. Rochester, NY: INCOSE.

Kelemen, Z. D. (2009). A process based unification of process-oriented software quality approaches. In *Proceedings of Global Software Engineering* (pp. 285–288). IEEE.

Kelemen, Z. D., Kusters, R., & Trienekens, J. (2011). Identifying criteria for multimodel software process improvement solutions – Based on a review of current problems and initiatives. *Journal of Software Maintenance and Evolution Research and Practice*, 24(8), 895–909.

Kirwan, P., Marino, L., Morley, J., & Siviy, J. (2008a). *The value of harmonizing multiple improvement technologies: A process improvement professional's view* (White paper). Retrieved from http://www.sei.cmu.edu/library/abstracts/whitepapers/multimodelSeries_wp1_harmonizationValue_052008_v1.cfm

Kirwan, P., Marino, L., Morley, J., & Siviy, J. (2008b). *Process architecture in a multimodel environment* (White paper). Retrieved from http://www.sei.cmu.edu/library/abstracts/whitepapers/multimodelSeries_wp4_processArch_052008_v1.cfm

Kirwan, P., Marino, L., Morley, J., & Siviy, J. (2008c). *Maximizing your process improvement ROI through harmonization* (White paper). Retrieved from http://www.sei.cmu.edu/library/abstracts/whitepapers/multimodelExecutive_wp_harmonizationROI_032008_v1.cfm

Kirwan, P., Marino, L., Morley, J., & Siviy, J. (2008d). *Strategic technology selection and classification in multimodel environments* (White paper). Retrieved from http://www.sei.cmu.edu/library/abstracts/whitepapers/multimodelSeries_wp2_techSelection_052008_v1.cfm

Kirwan, P., Marino, L., Morley, J., & Siviy, J. (2008e). *Improvement technology classification and composition in multimodel environments* (White paper). Retrieved from http://www.sei.cmu.edu/library/abstracts/whitepapers/multimodelSeries_wp2_techSelection_052008_v1.cfm

Kitchenham, B., Pearlbrereton, O., Budgen, D., Turner, M., Bailey, J., & Linkman, S. (2009). Systematic literature reviews in software engineering – A systematic literature review. *Information and Software Technology*, 51(1), 7–15. doi:10.1016/j.infsof.2008.09.009

Kronlöf, K. (1993). *Method integration: Concepts and case studies*. New York, NY: John Wiley & Sons, Inc.

Lawrence, J. (2009). Implementing insights and lesson learned using ISF for excellence. In *Proceedings of SEPG 2009 North America Conference*. SEPG.

Lonchamp, J. (1993). A structured conceptual and terminological framework for software process engineering. In *Proceedings of Software Process* (pp. 41–53). IEEE.

Maldonado, A., & Velázquez, A. (2006). A method to define the process architecture. In *Proceedings of AMCIS 2006*. AMCIS.

McFeely, B. (1996). *IDEAL: A users guide for software process improvement* (Tech. Rep. CMU/SEI-96-HB-001). Retrieved from www.sei.cmu.edu

Moen, R., & Norman, C. (2006). *Evolution of the PDCA cycle*. Retrieved August 12, 2012, from http://kaizensite.com/learninglean/wp-content/uploads/2012/09/Evolution-of-PDCA.pdf

Muñoz, M., Mejia, J., Calvo-Manzano, J. A., Cuevas, G., & San Feliu, T. (2012). Method to evaluate process performance focused on minimizing resistance to change. *International Journal of Human Capital and Information Technology Professionals*, 4(2), 1–15. doi:10.4018/jhcitp.2013040101

Mutafelija, B., & Stromberg, H. (2003). *Systematic process improvement using ISO 9001:2000 and CMMI*. Artech House.

OMG. (2006). *Meta object facility (MOF) core specification version 2.0*. OMG.

Ould, M. A. (1997). Designing a re-engineering proof process architecture. *Business Process Management Journal*, 3(3), 232–247. doi:10.1108/14637159710192284

Pardo, C. (2010). A systematic review on the harmonization of reference models. In *Proceeding of ENASE 2010* (pp. 40–47). ENASE.

Paulk, M. C. (2008). A taxonomy for improvement frameworks. In *Proceedings of Fourth World Congress for Software Quality*. Bethesda, MD: Academic Press.

Pesantes, M., Lemus, C., Mitre, H. A., & Mejia, J. (2012a). Identifying criteria for designing a process architecture in a multimodel environment. In Proceedings of Software and System Process (ICSPP), (pp. 83–87). IEEE.

Pesantes, M., Lemus, C., Mitre, H. A., & Mejia, J. (2012b). Software process architecture: Roadmap. In *Proceedings of the 2012 IEEE Ninth Electronics, Robotics and Automotive Mechanics Conference* (pp. 83–87). Cuernavaca, Mexico: IEEE Computer Society.

Siviy, J., Penn, M. L., & Stoddard, R. W. (2008). *CMMI and six sigma: Partners in process improvement*. Upper Saddle River, NJ: Pearson Education

Software Engineering Institute. (2010). *SEI prime project*. Retrieved from http://www.sei.cmu.edu/process/research/prime.cfm

Unterkalmsteiner, M., Gorschek, T., Islam, A. K. M. M., Cheng, C. K., Permadi, R. B., & Feldt, R. (2012). Evaluation and measurement of software process improvement - A systematic literature review. *IEEE Transactions on Software Engineering*, 38(2), 398–424. doi:10.1109/TSE.2011.26

Wang, Y., & King, G. (2000). *Software engineering processes: Principles and applications*. Boca Raton, FL: CRC Press.

Wolf, C., & Harmon, P. (2012). The state of business process management - 2012. *BPTrends Market Surveys*. Retrieved from http://www.bptrends.com/surveys_landing.cfm

KEY TERMS AND DEFINITIONS

Design Method: In this context, a design method is a systematic process to build or develop a software process architecture. It is composed of an underlying model, language, a set of steps, guidance and tools to apply the method.

Harmonization: Approach used in the multimodel improvement to define and configure the most suitable way to do and to put two or more models in tune with each other. It is about developing an appropriate solution to meet individual organizational objectives. To accomplish this harmonization requires understanding and leveraging the properties of the technologies of interest as well as composing these properties and the process architecture into a harmonized solution.

Improvement Technologies: In general, this is a long list of reference models, standards, best practices, regulatory policies and other types of practices that an organization may use simultaneously.

Multimodel Environment: The organizations' environment based on several improvement technologies that are required to be used simultaneously to implement an improvement.

Multimodel Improvement: Multimodel Improvement aims to achieve business goals, develop quality products through a mature process applying multiple improvement technologies best practices simultaneously, and reduce time-to-market and production costs.

Software Process Architecture (SPA): As a result of this multidisciplinary approach, SPA is considered a conceptual framework for designing and maintaining processes and their relationships, which must be aligned with business objectives and strategies, and enterprise architecture. Moreover, considering that a software process is composed of process elements, a process element is composed of activities, input and output interfaces, defined by pre-conditions and post-conditions and a knowledge base.

Chapter 14
A Successful Case of Software Process Improvement Programme Implementation

Antonia Mas
Universitat de les Illes Balears, Spain

Antoni Lluís Mesquida
Universitat de les Illes Balears, Spain

ABSTRACT

This chapter describes the experience of a Spanish software company founded in 2000, which bet strongly on quality as the way to progress towards maturity. The authors discuss the continuous evolution the company experienced through the implementation of quality standards. The actions related to the deployment and improvement of both the management and production processes are detailed. The most significant results and lessons learned during the improvement path are presented. The experience gained from continuous improvement has facilitated the deployment of a knowledge reuse strategy that enables an effort and cost reduction when implementing a new quality standard.

1. INTRODUCTION

"Many are those who want good luck, but few are willing to pursue it. Creating good luck consists in preparing conditions for opportunity. But opportunity has nothing to do with luck or chance: it is always there. Good luck depends on the creation of the necessary conditions, and the creation of these circumstances depends only on oneself."

We have used this excerpt from the book "Good Luck" (Rovira & Trías De Bes, 2004) as a reference to illustrate the behaviour of the company whose case is presented in this chapter. The company began its journey in 2000 and today, in spite of the current economic situation, it is an established and recognized company in

DOI: 10.4018/978-1-4666-5182-1.ch014

its sector located in the Balearic Islands, Spain. However, it has not reached this stage by chance because it has been lucky, but rather because the company has been able to create the appropriate circumstances. Many factors have influenced the success of the company.

The organization is an innovative company that has committed to quality and excellence from its inception. Along the way, it has had to adapt to the constant technological changes in the ICT sector. These changes have greatly influenced people's habits, forcing companies to develop applications for environments and devices that did not exist a few years ago. Therefore, continuous adaptation to cover both new user needs and development issues and also to offer new services to stay in the market has been required throughout the history of the company. The changes resulting from this situation have taken place throughout the entire structure of the organization, both at top management level, by developing new strategies and in the culture of employees. Making the adjustments to new needs, considering the expectations of all employees, is never easy because of resistance to change.

The chapter is structured as follows: section 2 presents the company background. Section 3 describes the company's evolution, from the beginnings to the current situation. Section 4 details the software process improvement programme the company followed. Section 5 shows the evolution of the processes implemented. Section 6 describes how the knowledge gained through the implementation of best practices recommended by quality standards has been managed and reused. The final section concludes this chapter.

2. COMPANY BACKGROUND

The company began its activity in 2000 with a staff of six. Today, it has 120 employees dedicated to the development of Internet-based marketing and management applications and the implementation of the infrastructure which supports them. The company provides tailored, unique and global solutions that include consultancy, training and the technology necessary for the evolution of customers' businesses and needs. It has four main business lines:

- **Software Factory and Applications:** Its mission is to provide customers with software development projects based on the latest technologies.
- **Systems, Communications and Security:** Its mission is to provide customers with systems, communications and security projects based on technologies from leading manufacturers.
- **Incoming & Select4U:** Its mission is to provide qualified personnel in key development, systems, communications and security technologies to work directly in the clients' office and under their direction.
- **IT Infrastructure Management:** Its mission is to provide customers with IT infrastructure maintenance services to ensure maximum availability and performance of their systems.

Since the creation of the company, innovation and continuous improvement are the bases of a culture assumed by all those working in the organization, not only to grow as a company, but with the clear objective to share the improvements with customers to help them to innovate in their business through knowledge and technology. Quality applied to all the areas will allow a company to achieve its business objectives, meeting the needs and expectations of its customers.

3. COMPANY EVOLUTION: THE ROAD TOWARDS MATURITY

This section summarizes the evolution that has taken place in the company after incorporating the good practices of recognized models and standards. The commitment to implement several international standards has had an impact on different areas of the company, such as integrated management, software development processes, information security management and environmental management. This has allowed the growth and improvement of the company in all aspects, its consolidation in the software and services development sector in the Balearic Islands, and a competitive position, thanks to the recognition obtained.

3.1 The Beginnings: 2000-2004

The company started its journey in the year 2000 with the development of management applications as one of the highlights of its strategic plan. From its inception, the company opted for quality and took part in the first edition of the QuaSAR project (Amengual & Mas, 2007). This project was a successful initiative that allowed the analysis of the software development sector in the Balearic Islands and provided guidance for the participant companies to improve their software processes and to be ISO 9001 (ISO, 2008a) certified. At that time, ISO/IEC 15504 (SPICE) (ISO, 2006) had still not been released as an international standard and companies were interested not only in a software process improvement path, but also in an ISO 9001 certification.

Thanks to the participation in the QuaSAR project, the company established its first Quality Management System (QMS) and obtained the ISO 9001 certification in 2003. Moreover, the organization laid the foundations for its software development processes and was motivated by continuous process improvement.

3.2 The Evolution: 2005-2012

The implementation of a quality management system and the ISO 9000 certification obtained by the company initiated what has become one of the main insignias of the company: quality as a management strategy. In 2005, the company introduced the EFQM Excellence Model (EFQM, 2013) into its QMS. Figure 1 shows the nine criteria of the EFQM Excellence Model.

Figure 1. EFQM excellence model

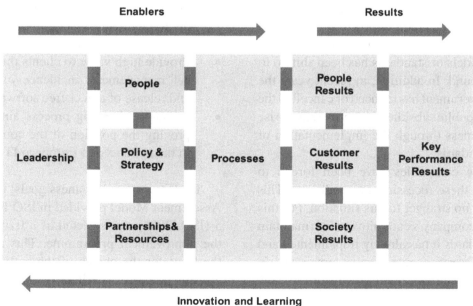

In 2006, the company reorganized its product and offered new solutions and services. During that year the company made an important commitment to environmental management and obtained the ISO/IEC 14001 (ISO, 2009) certification in 2007.

As recognition for its effort, the company obtained the Balearic Silver Award for Excellence in Management in 2006 and the Golden Award in 2008.

In 2007, it initiated a software process improvement programme, thanks to public subsidies from the Spanish government, making an enormous effort to adapt some of its software development processes to the best practices proposed by the ISO/IEC 15504 international standard for process assessment and improvement. After a formal assessment and an improvement phase, the company achieved capability level 2 in some of its processes.

In 2009, as set out in its new strategic plan, the company incorporated information security management in its existing management model and obtained the ISO/IEC 27001 (ISO, 2005a) certification.

3.3 The Future

The adverse economic situation has forced organizations to redirect their efforts to survive in the market. As a consequence, the interest in applying new models or standards has been shifted to the background. In addition, in recent years the Spanish government has reduced or cancelled the majority of public subsidies to improve enterprise competitiveness through the implementation of process standards.

Software companies have been forced to compete in these recessionary conditions. This company is no stranger to this situation. For this reason, the company's commitment is to maintain all the standards it has already implemented and improve IT service management processes. In order to facilitate sustained growth of this new business line, the organization plans to implement ISO/IEC 20000-1 (ISO, 2011) and obtain certification of this standard during 2013.

4. SOFTWARE PROCESS IMPROVEMENT PROGRAMME

As mentioned before, the company initiated an SPI programme in 2007 to adjust its production processes to the ISO/IEC 15504 international standard. This programme followed the steps of a conformant process assessment according to the requirements described in ISO/IEC 155045-2 (ISO, 2003) and in ISO/IEC 15504-3 (ISO, 2004b). In this section, the application of these steps, as detailed in ISO/IEC 15504-4 (ISO, 2007), is described.

4.1 Initiating Process Improvement

From an analysis of the company's business goals and the existing stimulus to improve, the following objectives were set:

- Achieve quality and productivity standards for the company's technological innovation to gain visibility and recognition in order to facilitate collaboration with partners as well as to participate in large projects.
- Provide high value to clients through project management, incidence management and release of defect-free software.
- Initiate a changing process aimed at improving the position of the company both in the national and European IT sectors.

To address these business goals, the Process Assessment Model provided in ISO/IEC 15504-5 (ISO, 2006) was selected as a framework for the improvement programme. This model was the basis for the choice of the software development processes, defined by ISO/IEC 12207

(ISO, 2004a), to be assessed and the setting of the improvement targets. The first task consisted of identifying which of the efforts could be useful when deploying specific technical software development processes in order to implement ISO 9001 and EFQM.

As the intention of the company was to reach maturity level 2 according to ISO/IEC 15504-7 (Assessment of Organizational Maturity) (ISO, 2008b), the 22 processes of these two maturity levels were selected (Table 1).

As recommended by the standard, the process improvement programme was implemented as a project in its own right with defined project management, budget, milestones and accountability. Thus, a Process Improvement Plan was produced.

The following sections describe each one of the tasks performed through the improvement programme.

Table 1. Work groups and improvement areas

Work Group	Processes
Management	MAN.3 Project management MAN.5 Risk management SUP.4 Joint review SUP.9 Problem resolution management ENG.12 Software and system maintenance
Analysis	ENG.1 Requirements elicitation ENG.4 Software requirements analysis ENG.8. Software testing
System	ENG.2 System requirements analysis ENG.3 System architectural design ENG.9 System integration ENG.10 System testing
Design Construction Integration Installation Release	ENG.5 Software design ENG.6 Software construction ENG.7 Software integration ENG.11 Software installation SPL.2 Product release
Quality Assurance	SUP.1 Quality assurance SUP.2 Verification SUP.7 Documentation SUP.8 Configuration management SUP.10 Change request management

4.2 Assessing Current Capability

In any improvement programme an initial process assessment is undertaken to understand the capability of the processes which have been previously selected for the improvement. This assessment was conducted by an independent assessment team of two competent assessors. A result of this assessment was the identification of a set of strengths and weaknesses that were used to develop an action plan. The strengths identified were the following:

- The availability of a quality report which considers different organizational and management aspects as well as some product development aspects.
- The performance of project management, problem resolution and non-conformity management activities with the support of a CASE tool.
- The identification and assignment of human resources for the different project processes based on established profiles.
- The professionalism of the employees, the individual experience of the people in previous projects, the positive work atmosphere and the fluent communication among team members.

The list of improvement actions compiled from the weaknesses identified was the following:

- Tailoring the company's standard processes to each particular project.
- Individual management of project processes.
- Explicit adjustment of plans when deviations occur.
- Management of process work products.

- Management of data on the implementation of the standard processes to demonstrate their suitability and effectiveness as well as to identify continuous improvement of these standard processes.

4.3 Planning Improvements

4.3.1 Participants

For the implementation of the improvement project, the following roles were defined:

- **Sponsor:** The sponsor had the responsibility and the authority to make sure that adequate resources and competencies were made available. This role was performed by the Service and Project Manager of the company.
- **Project Manager:** The project manager should manage the project, validate achieved improvements, coordinate and control current projects. This role was performed by the Quality Manager.
- **Organizer:** The role of the organizer was to simplify the work of the teams and identify common objectives. The tasks of the organizer were the organization of work sessions, supporting process improvement and controlling projects. This role was performed by an assessor with experience in teamwork.
- **Quality specialist:** The quality specialist gave support to the definition of the processes and participated in the inspection and control of the currents projects.

4.3.2 Work Groups

For the improvement of the different areas identified, five work groups were formed. Each work group was responsible for a set of processes. The leader of each group had to develop the plan and assign tasks to reach the objectives identified. Each group was formed by people with different skills and abilities to assure that they would have distinct points of view of the processes to improve. All of the members of the development area were part of one of the five groups. Table 1 shows these work groups.

4.3.3 Action Plan

The quality manager and the assessor analysed the strengths and weaknesses identified in the previous assessment to identify: strong processes, improvement areas, and evidence of corrective actions. It was decided that the actions to be performed should provide the planned results in nine months.

Each work group had full autonomy to undertake the process improvement. Different communication channels were established in order to facilitate information interchange among groups. Firstly, the company's intranet would be used to spread the implemented improvements and to inform about their achievement level. Secondly, the corporate blog would be used to inform about technical improvements. Finally, workshops would be held every fifteen days.

The organizer had to give support to the different work groups by focusing the work on achieving results through the definition of the processes and their documentation, the management of the tasks and the adaptation of the processes to the standard.

The quality manager had to review the results of each work group to validate if the standard requirements were satisfied. If so, the process could be published and made accessible to the organization. Otherwise, the deficiency in the process could be identified and the process would be adjusted to adapt to the standard.

4.4 Implementing Improvement Actions

The implementation of the improvement actions in every project in the company was performed with the support of joint reviews, quality controls and training actions.

The quality team coordinated and participated in periodical joint reviews with the project managers and the different specialists assigned to the projects. The main goal of these meetings was to communicate and support the improvement actions performed. During these reviews, the work products of the different processes were adjusted. It is important to note that some of the improvements resulted in a significant change in the organization's processes and also in the way the employees approached their tasks.

In parallel with the joint reviews, the quality team performed quality controls by randomly inspecting current projects, examining in each control a previously established set of processes. As a result of these controls, preventive and corrective actions were defined both at a project level and at a process level.

Throughout the project, training sessions were prepared and executed.

4.4.1 Internal Workshops

During the first months of the project, workshops were held every fifteen days. The attendees to these workshops were the project sponsor, the leader of each work group, and the quality team: the manager, the assessor, and the specialist.

The objectives of the workshops were:

- The revision of global achievements and team progression.
- The alignment of the effort of the different work groups.
- The identification of transversal improvement areas and the decision of the optimal solution.
- The information about decisions that could affect the project advancement.

The agenda was opened one week before the workshop, allowing the inclusion of the different

items to be considered by any one of the attendees. During the workshop the items were addressed in the same order as set out in the agenda.

As the project progressed, the workshops were no longer held periodically. Instead, they were convened by any one of the interested parties.

4.4.2 External Checkpoints

The improvement plan included two assessments, an initial diagnosis assessment and a final certification assessment. Moreover, three external monitoring checkpoints were planned. These checkpoints allowed to evaluate the level of achievement of the implemented improvements and to check whether the improved processes were aligned with the standard best practices.

From the results of these checkpoints the changes were validated and adjusted, and new corrective actions were proposed.

4.4.3 Working Day with the Client

With the aim of aligning the improvement actions, it was decided in the middle of the project to organize a working day with the client. A set of clients was selected, using criteria such as representative and experience, and they were invited to participate in a working day.

This working day was carried out as team dynamics in which the clients could present their problems, experiences, and the improvement areas that they had identified in their projects. The leaders of each team attended this session as the person responsible for the progress of the projects.

The analysis of the results of this session confirmed that the effort made and the approach of the improvement project were appropriate since the improvement areas identified by the clients were aligned with the improvement actions that were being performed internally in the company. Moreover, from the ideas provided by the clients, it was possible to refine and adjust some of the resulting work products.

4.5 Final Assessment

At the time of planning the final assessment, it was decided to reduce to eight the number of processes to be evaluated and plan a checkpoint for four other processes included in the improvement project. The main reason for this decision was that some of the improvement actions to perform were still in the implementation phase in some of the projects. Moreover, they depended on new software tools that had been acquired recently. Therefore, since these improvement actions had not been performed in all of the projects, there was no sense in assessing these processes.

The result of the final assessment was satisfactory because, although the established goal was not reached, four of the eight processes assessed achieved capability level 2. The other four processes reached capability level 1, achieving 95 per cent of level 2 attributes. With some more adjustments in the capability level 1 base practices for these processes, it would be possible to reach capability level 2.

Regarding the checkpoint results, it is important to highlight that the improvement actions performed in three of the four processes achieved the necessary quality level. Therefore, it was confirmed that the improvement actions considered were appropriate.

4.6 Lessons Learned

Throughout the performance of the improvement actions a set of weaknesses has directly influenced the project schedule and resources. These weak points are the following:

- **Lack of knowledge of the standard:** At the end of the improvement project it was confirmed that the importance of understanding the standard and interpreting its best practices for each one of the software life cycle processes was underestimated.

- **Greater effort than expected:** The effort to adapt the project tasks to the best practices defined by the standard was not appropriately estimated.

- **Implementation of changes in the processes and information about them:** Information about new established tasks, concept assimilation and the deployment of new ways of working were hindered by an aggressive planned schedule.

- **Project support tools:** The implementation of a set of the best practices recommended in the standard has shown that it is essential to have case tools to support the work.

On the other hand, the strengths that have been the key to the success of the improvement project are the following:

- **Active participation:** Awareness and motivation of all the participants in the project.

- **The role of the organizer:** This was a key role since it gave continuous support to each team, helping them to reach their objectives and acting as an intermediary to achieve coherence among common improvement areas.

- **Periodical monitoring of the improvements in the current projects:** The improvement programme had a very ambitious schedule and the number of improvement actions was important. Without the joint reviews and the understanding of the improvement actions by the team, the cost of implementing the improvement would have been higher.

- **Support tools:** The availability of a case tool for project management and change control made it easier to achieve some process base practices. The acquisition of a case tool, such as Enterprise Architect, also facilitated traceability, configuration management and verifications.

5. EVOLUTION OF THE PRODUCTION PROCESSES

The evolution of the production processes of the company is shown in Table 2. The first column shows the processes deployed in the company. Columns two and three detail the actions and changes that these processes have undergone during the evolution to maturity.

Having implemented a QMS according to ISO 9001 enabled the company to reach values "L" or "P" for ISO/IEC 15504 capability level 3 process attributes in some processes because these processes were defined, standardized and measured within the organization. The implementation of the ISO/IEC 15504 standard helped the company to consolidate the processes already deployed, focusing on the best practices and aspects that were not previously detailed.

5.1 Adaptation of the Production Processes to Support ISO/IEC 27001 Implementation

After consolidating the process improvement programme according to ISO/IEC 15504, the company realized that it had already performed some important steps in order to implement some of the ISO/IEC 27002 (ISO, 2005b) security controls, which are necessary for the implementation of an information security management system since these controls were considered by ISO/IEC 15504-5 base practices.

From the analysis of all the existing relations between ISO/IEC 15504-5 base practices and ISO/IEC 27002 security controls presented in (Mas, Mesquida, Amengual, & Fluxà, 2010; Mesquida, Mas, & Amengual, 2011), the work of the company consisted of modifying or amplifying the deployed ISO/IEC 15504-5 processes in order to make them compliant with the security requirements of the related ISO/IEC 27002 controls. Each change could affect different process components: process purpose, base practices and/or work products. In

order to cover a specific security control, four different types of actions could be performed on the processes:

- Use the process purpose or its base practices to manage the security requirements of the related control without any process modification.
- Modify or extend one or more base practices.
- Add a new base practice from the related control objective, closely related to the existent base practices.
- Modify or extend the process purpose.

It should be noted that although some ISO/IEC 15504-5 processes were easily adapted to cover some requirements of the ISO/IEC 27002 security controls, other security controls that did not have any relation to the deployed ISO/IEC 15504-5 processes had to be implemented as indicated in the ISO/IEC 27002 standard.

6. KNOWLEDGE MANAGEMENT STRATEGY

One of the most important strengths of the evolution of the company has been its knowledge management strategy. In 2002, with the main goal of supporting and improving the management system of the company, the quality department was established. Without this department, which served to define, centralize and support the implementation of the processes that were needed in the rest of the departments, the company might not have reached the current process maturity level.

Given the process management approach that drives the organization, different macro processes were identified, defined and deployed: business management, project management, software engineering, systems engineering, infrastructure management, human resource management and quality management and assurance. Each of these

Table 2. Evolution of the company's production processes

ISO/IEC 12207 Software life cycle processes	ISO 9001 and EFQM implementation (before 2007)	ISO/IEC 15504-5 implementation (2007 onwards)
ACQ.1 Acquisition preparation ACQ.2 Supplier selection ACQ.3 Contract agreement ACQ.4 Supplier monitoring ACQ.5 Customer acceptance	Deployed during ISO 9001 implementation. Focused on material procurement.	The scope of these processes was expanded to cover subcontracting. Supplier monitoring related to the project management process.
SPL.2 Product release	-	Deployed.
ENG.1 Requirements elicitation ENG.4 Software requirements analysis	Deployed during ISO 9001 implementation.	Existing requirements elicitation and analysis assets were improved by taking into account ISO/IEC 15504 base practices.
ENG.3 System architectural design ENG.5 Software design	Deployed in a single process during ISO 9001 implementation.	Improved.
ENG.6 Software construction	Deployed during ISO 9001 implementation.	Improved.
ENG.7 Software integration	-	Improved.
ENG.8 Software testing	Deployed during ISO 9001 implementation.	No significant changes.
ENG.11 Software installation	Deployed during ISO 9001 implementation.	Installation was improved by completing the installation registration procedure. Delivery was fully standardized and consolidated.
ENG.12 Software and system maintenance	Deployed during ISO 9001 implementation.	Improved.
MAN.1 Organizational alignment	Deployed during ISO 9001 implementation and considerably improved with EFQM implementation.	No significant changes.
MAN.2 Organizational management	Deployed during ISO 9001 implementation and considerably improved with EFQM implementation.	No significant changes.
MAN.3 Project management	Deployed during ISO 9001 implementation.	Improved and consolidated through the implementation of project management best practices. Existing project management assets were expanded by including new activities.
MAN.4 Quality management	Deployed during ISO 9001 implementation and considerably improved with EFQM implementation.	No significant changes.
MAN.5 Risk management	-	Deployed. Focused on projects. Security risk analysis was included in project risk management. Having defined a risk management strategy facilitated ISO/IEC 27001 implementation.
MAN.6 Measurement	Deployed during ISO 9001 implementation. Focused on organizational measurement.	No significant changes.
RIN.1 Human resource management	Partially deployed during ISO 9001 implementation and improved with EFQM implementation.	No significant changes.
RIN.2 Training	Deployed during ISO 9001 implementation.	No significant changes.
RIN.4 Infrastructure	Deployed internal maintenance, user management and backup processes during ISO 9001 implementation.	No significant changes.
SUP.1 Quality assurance	-	Partially deployed.

continued on following page

Table 2. Continued

ISO/IEC 12207 Software life cycle processes	ISO 9001 and EFQM implementation (before 2007)	ISO/IEC 15504-5 implementation (2007 onwards)
SUP.2 Verification	-	Partially deployed in several processes by defining verification checklists.
SUP.4 Joint review	-	Deployed.
SUP.5 Audit	Deployed during ISO 9001 implementation. Focused on organizational audit.	No significant changes.
SUP.7 Documentation	-	Deployed.
SUP.8 Configuration management	Partially deployed during ISO 9001 implementation.	Improved. Introduction of new tools to manage code.
SUP.9 Problem resolution management	Partially deployed during ISO 9001 implementation.	Improved.
SUP.10 Change request management	Partially deployed during ISO 9001 implementation.	Improved.

macro processes includes a set of processes of the same field with a greater level of detail. For example, the infrastructure management macro process includes a set of processes, such as user management, internal maintenance, access control and logical security.

The centralization of knowledge, together with the skills and competencies of the quality department, has enabled knowledge reuse and therefore the reduction of effort in implementing standards in the company.

6.1 Establishment of an Integrated Management System

From the ISO 9001 (ISO, 2008a) QMS and, after consolidating the implemented EFQM Excellence Model (EFQM, 2013), the company realized that many requirements of the environmental management system defined by ISO 14001 (ISO, 2009) and the information security management system defined by ISO/IEC 27001 (ISO, 2005a) had many similarities with the requirements of the QMS implemented and therefore could be integrated into a global Integrated Management System (IMS). The IMS of the company is shown in Table 3.

The relationships between the requirements of the three management systems that were inte-grated are structured into five categories, which correspond to the five 'Enabler' criteria of the EFQM Excellence Model. Next, the most important changes and decisions taken and the lessons learned during the integration process are detailed.

The decisions related to the 'Leadership' criteria were as follows:

- Management commitments regarding environmental aspects and information security were integrated into the existent quality policy of the company, resulting in the new 'Integrated Management System policy.'
- The existence of an IMS allowed the integration of all top management review activities.
- The vast majority of information security responsibilities were integrated into the profile of the quality manager. The other responsibilities were assigned to the information systems manager.
- A committee, combining the functions of the three management systems, was set up as the governing body of the IMS. Some information security responsibilities were assigned to a security sub-committee.

Table 3. Integrated Management System of the company

EFQM	ISO 9001:2008	ISO 14001:2004	ISO/IEC 27001:2005
1. Leadership	5.1. Management commitment 5.3. Quality policy	4.2. Environmental policy	5.1. Management commitment
	5.6. Management review	4.6. Management review	7. Management review of the ISMS
	5.5.1. Responsibility and authority 5.5.2. Management representative	4.4.1. Resources, roles, responsibility and authority	6. Organization of information security
	4. Quality management system	-	4.2.1. Establish the ISMS
2. Strategy	5.4.1. Quality objectives 5.6. Management review 8.4. Analysis of data	4.3.3. Objectives, targets and programme(s) 4.6. Management review	4.2.3. Monitor and review the ISMS 5.1. Management commitment 7. Management review of the ISMS
3. People	6.1. Provision of resources	-	5.2.1. Provision of resources
	6.2. Human resources	4.4.2. Competence, training and awareness	5.2.2. Training, awareness and competence
	5.5.3. Internal communication	4.4.3. Communication	-
	6.1. Provision of resources	-	5.2.1. Provision of resources
4. Partnerships & Resources	-	4.4.6. Operational control	-
	6.3. Infrastructure 6.4. Work environment 7.4. Purchasing 7.6. Control of monitoring and measurement equipment	4.3.1. Environmental aspects	4.2.1. Establish the ISMS 4.2.2. Implement and operate the ISMS
	-	4.4.7. Emergency preparedness and response	14. Business continuity management
5. Processes, Products and Services	4. Quality management system 5.2. Customer focus 5.4.2. Quality management system planning 7.1. Planning of product realization 7.2. Customer-related processes 7.3. Design and development 7.4. Purchasing 7.5. Production and service provision 8.2.1. Customer satisfaction	4.3.1. Environmental aspects 4.4.6. Operational control	4.2.2. Implement and operate the ISMS
	5.6. Management review	4.6. Management review	7. Management review of the ISMS
	8.2.3. Monitoring and measurement of processes 8.2.4. Monitoring and measurement of product 8.4. Analysis of data	4.5.1. Monitoring and measurement	4.2.3. Monitor and review the ISMS
	7.2.1. Determination of requirement related to the product	4.3.2. Legal and other requirements 4.5.2. Evaluation of compliance	15.1. Compliance with legal requirements
	8.3. Control of nonconforming product 8.5. Improvement	4.5.3. Nonconformity, corrective action and preventive action	4.2.4. Maintain and improve the ISMS 8. ISMS improvement 13. Information security incident management
	8.2.2. Internal audit	4.5.5. Internal audit	6. Internal ISMS audits
	4.2. Documentation requirements 4.2.3. Control of documents 4.2.4. Control of records	4.4.4. Documentation 4.4.5. Control of documents	4.3. Documentation requirements 4.3.2. Control of documents 4.3.3. Control of records

Regarding the 'Strategy' criteria, the decisions were:

- In order to satisfy existing and future customers demand for higher levels of quality and management, the company decided to continue investing in the implementation of internationally recognized quality standards such as ISO/IEC 15504, ISO/IEC 27001 and ISO/IEC 20000-1. This strategic decision is related to EFQM sub-criterion 2a (Strategy is based on understanding the needs and expectations of both stakeholders and the external environment).
- New strategy and supporting policies were developed, reviewed and updated according to EFQM Sub-criterion 2c (Strategy and supporting policies are developed, reviewed and updated to ensure economic, societal and ecological sustainability).
- A management model including objective allocation of both leadership and middle management was established. A systematic policy to define and formalize personal action plans from the company's objectives was implemented. The definition of the objectives, goals and action plans follows EFQM Sub-criterion 2b (Strategy is based on understanding internal performance and capabilities).

Regarding the 'People' criteria, the decisions were:

- An annual training plan with annual training activities for all staff and specific actions for technical profiles related to security management were established.
- The existing stakeholders' communication record was also used for recording information security and environmental issues related to customers and suppliers.

The results related to the 'Partnerships & Resources' criteria were:

- The integration of the ISO/IEC 27001 information security management system facilitated compliance with EFQM Sub-criterion 4d (Technology is managed to support the delivery of strategy) and 4e (Information and knowledge are managed to support effective decision making and to build the organizational capability) by considering information systems management and maintenance activities, risk analysis, asset identification, backup and user access and responsibility management.
- The integration of the ISO 14000 environmental management system facilitated compliance with EFQM Sub-criterion 4c (Buildings, equipment, materials and natural resources are managed in a sustainable way).
- The business continuity plan was complemented with the existing emergency plan.

Regarding the 'Processes, Products and Services' criteria, the decisions were:

- All the clauses related to security and environmental aspects were included in the subcontractor management process. In addition, the procurement process, initially intended for material purchasing during ISO 9001 implementation, was expanded to systematize part of the subcontractor management process.
- The scope of the evaluation of the legal compliance process was expanded with all the applicable security legislation.
- The same channel and the same software tool used to support the registration of non-conformities of the existent QMS were used to record and manage security incidents.

- IMS internal and external audits were added to the existing audit program. Qualification criteria for security auditors were incorporated into the internal audit process.
- The existing document control and record control processes were improved by including information classification, confidential or public, and adding review and approval responsibilities.

7. CONCLUSION

The case study presented in this paper is an example of a company which firmly bet on quality standards to improve its production processes at a time when few companies in its sector and environment were doing so. One of the keys to success of the company's evolution towards maturity has been the active participation, commitment and motivation of top management. Top management provided and trained the necessary human resources to achieve the stated objectives and support the business strategy. Moreover, important financial investment to facilitate the implementation and standardization of new procedures, establishing new departments or areas and incorporating new support tools, was required. These changes gave the feeling of continuous improvement in all the departments and at all levels of the company. At the moment, it is not only top management that is promoting improvement; changes are also requested by the different departments and people in the company.

All these efforts have borne fruit. The company has evolved from a company of 6 people in 2000 to a company of 120 employees to date. The higher the maturity level, the easier it has been for the company to tackle new projects and gain an advantage over its competitors.

Because the road to maturity is long, this organization will follow the path to quality by continually improving its internal processes. There is no single way to reach the goal. This chapter has presented the steps to maturity this company took

ACKNOWLEDGMENT

This research has been supported by CICYT-TIN2010-20057-C03-03 *Simulación aplicada a la gestión de equipos, procesos y servicios*, Sim4Gest.

REFERENCES

Amengual, E., & Mas, A. (2007). Software process improvement in small companies: An experience. In *Proceedings of 14th European Software Process Improvement Conference*. Springer.

EFQM. (2013). *The EFQM excellence model*. Retreived from http://www.efqm.org

ISO. (2003). *ISO/IEC 15504-2:2003 information technology - Process assessment - Part 2: Performing an assessment*. International Organization for Standardization.

ISO. (2004a). *ISO 12207:1995/Amd 1:2002/Amd 2:2004 systems and software engineering - Software life cycle processes*. International Organization for Standardization.

ISO. (2004b). *ISO/IEC 15504-3:2004 information technology - Process assessment - Part 3: Guidance on performing an assessment*. International Organization for Standardization.

ISO. (2005a). *ISO/IEC 27001:2005 information technology - Security techniques - Information security management systems - Requirements*. International Organization for Standardization.

ISO. (2005b). *ISO/IEC 27002:2005 information technology - Security techniques - Code of practice for information security management*. International Organization for Standardization.

ISO. (2006). *ISO/IEC 15504-5:2006 information technology - Process assessment - Part 5: An exemplar process assessment model.* International Organization for Standardization.

ISO. (2007). *ISO/IEC 15504-4:2007 information technology - Process assessment - Part 4: Guidance on use for process improvement and process capability determination.* International Organization for Standardization.

ISO. (2008a). *ISO 9001:2008 quality management systems - Requirements.* International Organization for Standardization.

ISO. (2008b). *ISO/IEC TR 15504-7:2008 information technology - Process assessment - Part 7: Assessment of organizational maturity.* International Organization for Standardization.

ISO. (2009). *ISO 14001:2004/Cor 1:2009 environmental management systems - Requirements with guidance for use.* International Organization for Standardization.

ISO. (2011). *ISO/IEC 20000-1:2011 information technology - Service management - Part 1: Service management system requirements.* International Organization for Standardization.

Mas, A., Mesquida, A., Amengual, E., & Fluxà, B. (2010). ISO/IEC 15504 best practices to facilitate ISO/IEC 27000 implementation. In *Proceedings of 5th International Conference on Evaluation of Novel Approaches to Software Engineering* (ENASE) (pp. 192-198). Athens, Greece: SciTePress.

Mesquida, A., Mas, A., & Amengual, E. (2011). An ISO/IEC 15504 security extension. *Communications in Computer and Information Science, 155*(2), 64–72. doi:10.1007/978-3-642-21233-8_6

Rovira, A., & Trías De Bes, F. (2004). *Good luck: Creating the conditions for success in life and business.* New York: John Wiley & Sons.

Chapter 15
A Brief Overview of Software Process Models:
Benefits, Limitations, and Application in Practice

Sanjay Misra
Covenant University, Nigeria

Martha Omorodion
Federal University of Technology, Nigeria

Luis Fernández-Sanz
Universidad de Alcalá, Spain

Carmen Pages
Universidad de Alcalá, Spain

ABSTRACT

Software process development in software engineering does not seem to offer a solid view of what they have in reality. Although many models have already been developed, recommended, or even used in the industry, these proposals have still not been able to come to terms with what is available. This chapter evaluates the benefits and limitations of some of the software development models while offering a comparative analysis and data on their real usage. In particular, an attempt has been made to evaluate the problems and strengths of a good variety of software process models and methodologies. Some conclusions and lines of future research are presented.

DOI: 10.4018/978-1-4666-5182-1.ch015

1. INTRODUCTION

In our fast-paced society, judging from the recent technological advances within the past two decades and the rate at which they become obsolete, one is tempted to ask, "How do they come up with such ideas? What does it take to move from one stage to the next? How does the developer suddenly feel that the next best thing since sliced bread that customers want is a car with GPS (global positioning system) and not just that, it talks to you as well?"

The basis of all these developments fits into a single word, "software." Within the past two decades this abstract concept has consumed a vital part of our society and on a regular basis. We all demand improvements, systems that are more sophisticated than what we already have, features and services that are almost insurmountable to the layman. Yet at the end of the day, we get them through systems we often refer to as "computerized."

Computerized systems range from laptops, air traffic control systems to even architecture and building operations and trading. Achieving all these involve a lot of complex activities. Occasionally, problems arise within our components that are software-based. These problems did not appear out of the blue. In some cases, they were embedded in the systems during the development stages. This is due, in part, to the fact that these systems and their applications are products of complex activities that are really very difficult to develop, integrate and test.

The aim of this paper is to give insight into the various activities technically known as software processes and how they are organized into different models to achieve the sophisticated software-based products that we have today. Also, focus will be placed on highlighting the benefits and limitations of each model and recommendations made for improvements on what is available to ease the problems involved in the production of these software-based systems, while creating better outputs in the process.

Section two of this paper deals with the definition of terms and a list of other software development processes that are not evaluated in this paper; section three shows the comparative analysis of the processes that are evaluated. Section four outlines their benefits and limitations in tables. The recommendations made are quite elementary but are useful for consideration when designing a process model.

1.1 Motivation for This Chapter

While teaching software engineering courses to undergraduates and masters students for the past six years, one of the authors has observed that students are often confused about the different software process models. Each book on software engineering explains these models in its own way. For example, in the well-known book "Software Engineering" by (Sommerville, 2010), the author describes the models under three categories: waterfall, iterative and CBSE. However, we do not feel comfortable considering CBSE as a model because it is essentially based on the development of components and very close to object-oriented development. Furthermore, most of the available models are similar in many ways, which make them difficult to discriminate from one another. For example, spiral, iterative/evolutionary models (waterfall, incremental, spiral models, prototyping, Cleanroom, and object-oriented techniques) show similarities in their processes. Additionally, several new software process models/methodologies based on the basic models have been developed and applied in the industries in the last decade. There is lack of clear-cut explanation and discrimination between these models in the literature except for the basic ones. This contributes to insufficient knowledge in the learning community regarding these models. To the best of our knowledge, no existing research paper available has provided the explanation and discrimination of these models in a clear way. In this paper we evaluate and explain each available model and present them to the learning community in a more comprehensible way to help discriminate between them easily.

2. DEFINITION OF TERMS

The concept of software process development cannot be discussed without prior knowledge of software processes. The selection of a suitable model is based on these generic process activities commonly used in all software process models.

2.1 Software Processes

Simply stated, a software process is the path taken in order to produce software. The processes include:

- **Software Requirements Specification:** At this stage, the end users are consulted and the stage for the services and stated functions and abilities of the product is set.
- **Software Design and Implementation:** At this stage, the hardware and software requirements of the system are partitioned.
- **Software Validation (Integration and Testing):** Simply, a software check. It is generally referred to as verification and validation (V & V).
- **Software Evolution:** This deals with the installation and maintenance of the software product and it depends on the flexibility of the system.

2.2 Software Process Models

A software development process is a structure imposed on the development of a software product and a process model is the structure imposed on the process of development of a software product (Gull, Azam, Haider, & Iqbal, 2009). There are

several models for such processes, each describing approaches to a variety of tasks or activities that take place during the process.

Authors sometimes refer to them as "Software Life Cycle Models" (Aggarwal & Singh, 2008) (Royce, 1987). The Software Life Cycle Model is considered a more general term than software process model - a more specific term. These processes involve systematic procedures, organization and methods that are useful for the development of a software project. In practice, developers do not necessarily follow strictly the systematic procedures involved in a particular model. What they do is to select aspects of different models that they believe will give them the best results.

While a model is an excellent example that deserves to be imitated, a methodology, which is synonymous to technique, is a systematic way of doing something; it is an orderly thought. As such, the two schools of thought should be separated in this paper as the three terminologies are used often.

Prior to the development of the generic software process models, the Build and Fix Model (Aggarwal & Singh, 2008) was in use. This model was comprised of just two stages: writing the code and fixing problems in the code. Basically, there are two broad models which all other processes take after: the sequential models, which emphasize movement from one phase to another after completing the previous phase, and the evolutionary process models, which do not depend on the conclusion of one phase before moving to the next. These ones involve iteration (Crnkovic, Larsson, & Chaudron, 2006).

There are three generic software process models on which most models are based:

- **The Waterfall Model:** The first formal description of the waterfall model is often cited from an article published in 1970 by Winston W. Royce, although Royce did not use the term "waterfall" in his article. Royce was presenting this model as an example of a flawed, non-working model

(Royce, 1987; Scacchi, 2001). It obtained its name from the way it cascades like waterfalls from one phase to another in its diagrammatic representation. Sometimes it is referred to as the 'Classic Software Life Cycle Model' (Pressman, 2001). The fundamental process activities of Requirement Specification, Design and Implementation, Integration and Testing and Installation and Maintenance are represented as separate process phases.

- **The Iterative** (Aggarwal & Singh, 2008) **(Evolutionary)** (Sommerville, 2007) **Process Model:** This model focuses on development in small increments. The conclusions reached are subjected to user comments and then refined through many stages until a final validated system is developed.
- **Rapid Application Development Model (RAD)** (Pressman, 2001): This model is considered to be an incremental development and its emphasis is on a short development cycle. In this case, there is software reuse in new systems with minor or no modification. It is sometimes referred to as "Component Based Software Engineering" (Stapleton, 2003) because rapid development is accomplished by using component-based construction.

Software developers sometimes integrate these models so that they can enjoy the benefits of each process and discard those attributes that may not be useful to them. Thus, there are several alternative models and methods used for software development. These models include:

- **The Rapid Prototyping Model (RPM)** (Jawadekar, 2004): It falls under the evolutionary process. This model is useful when users are not sure about their requirements. A prototype model is then developed to verify the specification.

- **The Spiral Model** (Boehm, 1988): It falls under the evolutionary model. This system avoids backtracking and it places more emphasis on risk analysis.
- **V-Model:** It improves on the waterfall model and does not move in a linear way; its process steps are bent upwards to form a V-shape (Gull, Azam, Haider, & Iqbal, 2009).
- **V-Model XT Process Framework:** The VM XT, (XT - eXtreme Tailoring) is an improvement on the V-Model (20). It is a recent model announced as the standard for public-sector projects in Germany and its framework has a flexible customizing ability focused on meeting the requirements specifications (Biffl, Winkler, Höhn, & Wetzel, 2006).
- **The Divide and Conquer Model (DCM):** It has three phases and one can move from any one phase to the other (Gull, Azam, Haider, & Iqbal, 2009).
- **The WinWin Spiral Model (WSM):** This model deals mainly with how to handle negotiations between customer and developer so that, at the end of the day, the customer wins by getting a product that satisfies most of his needs while the developer wins by being able to work out achievable budgets and time limits (Boehm, Egyed, Kwan, Port, Shah, & Madachy, 1998).
- **The Concurrent Process Model (CPM):** It involves a series of activities that take place during development, existing simultaneously but still remaining in different developmental stages (Cockburn, 2001).
- **The Formal Systems Development Model (FSDM):** Its development process is based on formal mathematical transformation of system models to executable programs. Though it is similar to the waterfall model, it has clearly defined phase boundaries. Sometimes it is called the Formal Methods Model (FMM) (Pressman, 2001).

- **Component-Based Development Model (CBDM):** This model seems similar to the CBSE but they differ in the sense that while CBSE places more emphasis on re-use of components, CBDM focuses on development of systems using components (Crnkovic, Larsson, & Chaudron, 2006).

The following are development methodologies named as methodologies, techniques, processes or approaches:

- **Adaptive Project Framework (APF)** (Highsmith, 1999): This method allows for constant adjustment of the project so as to ensure the delivery of maximum business value.

- **Family-Oriented Software Development Process (FSDP):** This process focuses on clarifying the properties of family-related systems and not the individual systems. It is useful mainly for aero-engine software. It follows the traditional lifecycle process (Allenby et al., 2001).

- **Incremental Delivery (IDR)** (Sommerville, 2007): It falls under the evolutionary process. Also called the Incremental Development and Release. It combines the advantages of the iterative and waterfall approach.

- **Joint Application Development:** This is a technique that involves the use of a group of software developers, testers, and possible end-users to interact to generate requirements and prototypes of the software being produced (Scacchi, 2001).

- **Agile Software Development** (Ambler, 2002): This approach is a broad concept that represents an iterative approach and not a methodology. It was developed as a result of the numerous weaknesses of the waterfall concept and uses an iterative approach with shorter development cycles. Thus, it has various forms that have individual ideas. They are Extreme Programming, Scrum, Lean Development, Unified Process and a host of others. The agile approach started in 1994 with trials of *semi*-formal agile methodologies, such as RAD, DSDM, XP, Crystal, Scrum. These methodologies are based on *agile methods*. Agile methods are adaptive rather than predictive (Bodea, 2005).

- **The Rational Unified Process (RUP)** (Sommerville, 2007): It is sometimes simply referred to as the unified process (Highsmith, 1999). It emphasizes the development and maintenance of models and is normally described from three perspectives: dynamic, static and practice.

- **Extreme Programming (XP)** (Beck, 2003): It is actually a deliberate and disciplined approach to Agile software development. One of the first approaches to gain main-stream success, Extreme was found to be most successful in smaller companies especially during the dot-com boom. It involves team work (Bodea, 2005).

- **Scrum:** This method involves an agile approach to software development. It is a framework and not a full process or methodology. Thus, it does not provide a complete detail of descriptions of how the project is done. It has a team called the Scrum team, which make many of the decisions during the project. Team work is emphasized (Schwaber & Beedle, 2002).

- **Lean Software Development (LSD)** (Poppendieck & Poppendieck, 2003): Lean Network describes lean as "A systematic approach to identifying and eliminating waste through continuous improvement, flowing the product at the pull of the customer in pursuit of perfection."

- **Crystal Methodologies (CM):** It employs an evolutionary process and involves the use of team work; it is also an agile process that consists of three different methods viz: crystal clear, crystal orange, crystal orange/web. The method was created with different requirements or problems posed by the customer. It is useful for customized products (Cockburn, 2001).

- **The Dynamic Systems Development Method (DSDM)**: It is an agile software system technique. Here, time is a fixed and functionality variable as opposed to traditional development methodologies where functionality is fixed, and time and resources are variables. It is useful when the time required for delivery is short, thus it uses incremental prototyping in a controlled environment with each increment delivering enough functionality to move to the next increment (Stapleton, 2003).

- **Feature Driven Development (FDD)** (Coad, LeFebvre, & DeLuca, 1999): It is very iterative and collaborative and it is an agile development method. It is composed of five processes: Develop an Overall Model, Build a Features List, Plan By Feature, Design By Feature, Build By Feature. FDD has eight practices: domain object modeling, developing by feature, individual class ownership, feature teams, inspections, regular builds, configuration management, reporting/visibility of results.

- **Adaptive Software Development (ASD)** (Crnkovic, Larsson, & Chaudron, 2006): It is an agile method which involves teamwork and the use of JAD approach for requirements gathering. It is mission driven, component-based, iterative, risk driven and change tolerant. It evolved from RAD.

- **Test Driven Development:** It is an agile method. It produces tests that specify and validate what the code does before the final the production code is designed (Beck, 2003).

- **The Fourth Generation Techniques (4GT)** (Pressman, 2001): It is a modern-day technique that involves the use of automated code generation. This technique deals with the ability to use specialized language forms to identify software that explains the problems that need to be solved in ways customers will understand.

2.3 Other Development Methods Not Described

Many other models have been developed over the years, such as Structured programming developed in 1969, Structured Systems Analysis and Design Methodology (SSADM) in 1980, Object-oriented Programming (OOP) developed since the early 1960s and was the dominant programming methodology during the mid-1990s. Different methodologies were proposed as mandatory (de jure standards) for development projects in certain countries, such as Metrica v2 (MAP, 1995) and v3 (MAP, 2000), Merise (Matheron, 1994) in France or the above mentioned SSADM in the UK. Settlement of compulsory processes models, life cycles or methodologies was also a practice adopted by powerful/state-run/large organizations like DoD, NATO, NASA or ESA through specific standards which were creating direct or inverse relationships with general standards for the whole world. For example, some specific standards were finally adapted and published for general purpose as standards in IEEE, ISO, while others were the inverse, i.e. adaptation of certain IEEE standards for specific organizations (e.g. ESA). Of course, at the very beginning, during the seventies, some very specific and limited approaches were established as the first real guiding methods for developing software, at least at the level of programming and low-level design: Warnier (Warnier, 1981), Jackson (JSP) (Jackson, 1975) and JSD (Jackson, 1983), Bertini (Bertini & Tallineau, 1974), etc.

Another approach worth mentioning is Team software process developed by Watts Humphrey at the Software Engineering Institute (SEI). Personal Software Process (Humphrey, 1996) was also developed by Watts Humphrey in an attempt to apply the underlying principles of the Software Engineering Institute's (SEI) Capability Maturity Model (CMM) (Humphrey, 1996) to a developer's software development practices. Integrated Methodology (QAIassist-IM) since 2007, Systems Development Life Cycle (SDLC) (Alexandrou, n.d.). Clean Your Room (CYR) (Haase, 2008) is a response to the Cleanroom Software Engineering process; its focus is on implementing cool, new features and not on tests, documentation, or bug-fixes. Cliff, developed as a response to the Waterfall model, leaps suddenly from the starting point (known as the Hairbrained Idea) to the end (known as the Product, but informally Cliff teams refer to it as the Corpse) (Haase, 2008). Testosterone-Driven Development, (Haase, 2008), like Test-driven Development, focuses on testing first but is extremely aggressive, requiring that entire test suites be produced. Fragile Programming (Haase, 2008) is an important element of the Delicate software pattern related to Agile

programming, Conference Drive Development (CDD) and Cleanroom Software Engineering (Haase, 2008) but they are not explained in any detail in this report.

3. COMPARATIVE ANALYSES OF THE GENERIC MODELS

A comparative analysis of the three generic models is shown in Table 1. Only these three models have been analyzed because, as stated earlier, all the other models and methodologies are variations of these three. Table 2 shows the benefits and limitations of all the models mentioned in this paper, about 27, but some other models and methodologies may have either been overlooked or simply not found.

4. RESULTS, DISCUSSION, AND RECOMMENDATIONS

Table 2 shows the benefits and limitations of the generic and some recent software development models. While some of the models support rapid

Table 1. Comparison of the three generic models

Waterfall Model	Evolutionary Process Model	CBSE
It lacks flexibility.	It is very flexible.	It is relatively flexible.
It is useful when long life complex systems are being built.	Useful mainly when small systems are being developed.	Useful mainly for commercial systems.
Delivery is relatively fast.	Delivery is slow.	It is characterized by fast delivery.
Very low risks.	High risks.	Low risks.
Greater chance that user needs will not be met.	Needs are definitely met, otherwise the product will not be released.	May not meet needs because of requirement compromise and time limit.
Badly structured systems.	Poorly structured systems.	Relatively well structured systems.
It is simple and stable. It is static.	Fairly clear but needs confirmation. It is dynamic.	Fairly clear, stable and large. It is fairly dynamic.
It is not cost effective.	It is not cost effective.	It is relatively cost effective.

Table 2. The benefits and limitations of various models

Models	Benefits	Limitations
Waterfall Model	Lots of useful documentation. Fits in with other engineering process models.	Static. Lacks flexibility. Restricts looping. Excessive documentation. Amendment incorporation is difficult. Deadlines are not met easily. Tedious.
Evolutionary Process Model	Needs are met. Incremental development possible. New developments reflected in products.	Poor structure. Not cost effective. It is a slow process. High risk. Excessive user involvement. Develops problems in large, complex, long-life systems. Late delivery.
RAD	System reuse. Low risk. Stable. Active user involvement. Requirements are met. Rapid delivery. Reduced costs. Supports future development and maintenance. Adapts to system analysis and design techniques.	Control over system evolution is lost. Requirements not always met. Reduction in features occurs to meet time limit. Not suitable for all types of application development. Technological needs may not be met. Timeline is fixed.
FSDM	Phases are fewer. Possibility of errors is reduced. Useful for systems in which safety, reliability and security needs are high.	Not cost effective. Cannot be used for small systems because of cost and system development effort.
DCM	Good for large software projects. Emphasizes looping to any phase. Cost effective.	
V-Model	The model was designed in such a way that checks are made automatically to ensure that needs are met.	Not too different from waterfall model. Does not consider every detail.
RPM	User requirements are met. Useful when requirements change rapidly. Minimizes risks. Active user involvement.	Too many iterations. Not cost effective. Idea is vague. Time consuming. May contain features users cannot utilize. The problem must be understood.
Spiral Model	The system tries to eliminate risks. Cost effective. Useful for large projects. Process modules can be reshaped.	Risk analysis could be poor. Time consuming. Cannot be used for large, complex projects. Need for improvement on technical focus.
WSM	Majority of customer's needs are met. Time limit is met. Cost effective.	The customer and developer may not reach an agreement. Involves compromise during negotiations.
CPM	Applicable to most software development. Shows the current state of a project accurately. Defines a network of activities and is not sequential. Activities are carried out simultaneously. Creates room for improvement during production.	May result in too many iterations. Events in an activity trigger transitions in other activities.

continued on following page

Table 2. Continued

Models	Benefits	Limitations
CBDM	Less time consuming. Cost effective. Higher productivity. Component reuse.	Requirements may not be met. Development of systems depends on available components. No user involvement.
FSDP	Several process models can be represented using this model. Has reuse capability. Categorizes the system boundary unequivocally. Defines which types of systems are going to be analyzed.	Value creation poses a threat to it and it is required to realign requirements and engineering solutions. Cannot be used for all software applications. Little system reuse. Family oriented rather than individual.
The V-Model XT	Understanding user requirements is emphasized, converting them to IT requirements and engineering solutions and integrates user contributions. Tender and bidding situations for contractors and customers. Involved in guidelines for hardware development, logistics, project management and process improvement.	
IDR	Early product delivery. Most requirements are met. Room for improvement before delivery.	Excessive user involvement. Excess time is consumed on user involvement. Poorly defined scope because of variations at each increment.
DSDM	User involvement is active. Decision making is rapid. Changes are reversible Needs are met.	Too many iterations. Product may not be perfect.
FDD	Analysis and design practices are thorough, less time consuming, well stated development practices. Five sub-processes, with defined entry and exit criteria. Useful for both large and small systems.	Time constraints could lead to poorly developed processes. May not be cost effective because of technical drive.
APF	Needs are met. Not speculative. Cost effective.	Too many iterations. Not cost effective. Excessive user involvement.
Agile	Software reliability. Lesser risks. Rapid delivery.	
RUP	Flexible. Has user-visible features.	
ASD	Responds to change. Involves team work. Very flexible. Useful in complex environments.	Time consuming. Its ability to adapt to change may mean reviewing the whole process.
XP	Consumer needs are met. Time conscious. Changes can be made even late in the development process. User involvement. Simplicity.	

continued on following page

Table 2. Continued

Models	Benefits	Limitations
Scrum	Rapid delivery. Risks are minimized. Progress is monitored.	Involves too many iterations. Wasteful. Too many meetings.
LSD	Cost effective. Rapid delivery. Eliminates waste.	Decision making is slow. Involves many iterations.
TDD	Automated.	Tests may not be thorough because of time constraints. ime consuming as the tests may fail when run. Too many iterations. The test code may be useless at the end of the day.
4GT	Automated. Less time consuming for small and intermediate applications. Viable approach for many applications. Offers solutions for many software problems. Reduced amount of design and analysis. Can be combined with component-based development approach.	The 4GT tool may not be able to interpret user requirements. May not be too applicable for large applications.
CM	Flexible. The method used depends on the software or system to be developed. Involves team work. User involvement. Incremental delivery (2-3 months). Two user viewings per release.	A new method is formulated each time a system is to be developed. Too many meetings.

delivery and flexibility as their strong points (including user involvement and looping), others focus more on cost effectiveness and matching user requirements. In some cases, excessive focus on these points leads to a limitation of the model and vice versa.

The reality of software development has not been properly analyzed in the literature in terms of real application of models in surveys of wide samples of organizations or companies. However, some available results can give us some idea of the reality of industrial practice. An anonymous Web-based inquiry conducted during early spring 2009 that intended to survey current processes, practices, and methods in the software industry shows that the most used software development processes are waterfall, agile and adaptive. The response rates to the current software development process question are: agile (23.8%), adaptive (21.4%), waterfall (21.4%), spiral (2.3%) or ad hoc with different configurations (RUP-based,

V-model, etc.) (7.2%) while CMMI levels were of almost all types: 1 (16.6%), 2 (9.5%), 3 (11.9%), 4 (0%) and 5 (2.3%); the rest are not known because they were never assessed (Causevic, Krasteva, Land, Sajeev, & Sundmark, 2009). The result of an empirical study of software processes in practice in 15 Irish software companies shows that most of the companies used the Rational Unified Process (RUP) or an approximation of it (46%); others used XP (20%) though not applying all 12 elements of XP. The remainder used either versions of the waterfall model or some form of iterative development approach (Coleman, 2005).

Observing the practical use of software process models in industry, interestingly, few or no companies follow a process model exactly, choosing instead either to drop elements from their chosen model or develop something proprietary instead (Coleman, 2005). Customization adapts a generic process model to make it more effective in the given software project (Pérez, El Emam, & Madhavji,

1995). Of course, the idea behind all this is that companies tend to adopt the specific approach which best fits their specific circumstances. In fact, increase in productivity, reduced time for development, client and development team satisfaction, operational excellence and feedback from discussion are considered the most important measures of success by small and medium Web development organizations using software process improvement models/techniques (Sulayman & Mendes, 2009). These goals certainly influence their decisions on the specific models for their development projects. Thus, some contributions have focused on the analysis of which factors and characteristics are most impacted by some of the models like ISO 9000 or CMMi (Kuilboer & Ashrafi, 2000), giving some guidelines on expected results to organizations which are implementing them .

It is true that general models for Software Process Improvement like CMMi or ISO are not contradictory (as general guidelines) and have flexibility in the explicit model for software development but the extreme variety of models and methods tend to create confusion in members of the software community. Each generic model has its area of usefulness and shortcomings. Consequently, to make recommendations for the design of a new model adapted to each situation and with its roots in the already existing models, the following factors must be taken into consideration:

- First and most important, one needs to consider the main goal of software engineering, which is to produce cost effective software products and have them delivered within the shortest time possible.
- Second, user requirements and involvement are also very important at every step.
- Last, homogeneity, maintainability, flexibility and risk are factors that also have to be considered.

One cannot design a perfect method which will meet the needs of all these factors and be suitable for all areas of application. However, whatever area a model fits into, it should be able to meet at least 75-95% of these conditions. In fact, sometimes software products are used in areas where life is a paramount issue, such as in air traffic systems and railway systems. A developer should always bear in mind that no matter how hard s/he tries, the needs and wants of consumers cannot fully be met as observed with most of the models.

Out of curiosity, a software developer, Douglas Stein, in response to "The Difference between Waterfall, Iterative Waterfall, Scrum and Lean Software Development (In Pictures!)" posted online, proposed a configuration of a team which is right-sized to the skills and scale of the project. He also proposed a fixed sprint size of about 2-3 weeks if you prefer scrum or 6-8 weeks for XP composed of 3-4 iterations of 2 weeks. Then, the client should have the opportunity to change anything they want for the next sprint or iteration. As a give and take situation, the client has to be sure there is a single voice and not a committee available to the team. He also suggested that the client should be assured that he could cancel at the end of any release with no penalty and that needs will be met eventually. He further declared assertively that he has applied this method in some of his strategic engagements as well, stating that clients stop development at around 85-90% of the original budget because the product is good enough to ship and make money and thereby save costs.

As a consequence, when designing a model or in the process of designing software, a developer can decide on a specific period of time for requirements and specification, say one-fourth of the time designated for the development of the system. During the collecting requirements process, the design and development stage can be initiated with whatever requirements are available and then, during the period assigned for design and development, the necessary finishing touches can then be included wherever they are needed in the design. This way a little time can be bought indirectly and then backtracking will not necessarily be seen as a burden or as a time-consuming task. Similarly, while design and development are going on, validation can be carried out so that errors can be corrected along the line. Then, whatever requirements come in during these two latter stages, they can be managed if they can still be added; if not, they should then be left for evolutionary processes. Some emphasis should also be placed on the risk involved in whatever activity or action is to be taken next at each stage of development. The suggested guidelines above allow some degree of flexibility even though they appear rigid in daily practice.

5. CONCLUSION

From observation, software development seems to be in a dilemma over how the needs of consumers can be met and, as shown, about 27 models are mentioned in this paper, though many have not; all in the bid to develop that one perfect model. This goal seems to be evasive as more problems are sometimes created.

Software process models diversity requires continuous adaptation of software development to changing and complex user requirements. Establishing the necessary criteria to choose the most suitable process model in each case is worth noting in software process modeling literature. Fundamentally, the choice depends on the development team's experience and problem type as well as organizational circumstances. To meet user requirements needs, the models can be used in flexible and adaptive combinations.

As the goal of this chapter is to evaluate the problems and strengths of some software process models as well as conduct analyses on the results and make recommendations, we think our work has been clear enough to contribute to a better understanding of the panorama of software process models. We hope that the information it contains will be useful to any interested reader and to the software community as a whole.

REFERENCES

Aggarwal, K. K., & Singh, Y. (2008). *Software engineering* (3rd ed.). New Delhi: New Age International Publishers.

Alexandrou, M. (n.d.). *Systems development life cycle (SDLC)*. Retrieved December 10, 2013, from http://www.mariosalexandrou.com/methodologies/systems-development-life-cycle.asp

Allenby, K., Bardill, M., Burton, S., Buttle, D., Hutchesson, S., & McDermid, J. .... Stephenson, A. (2001). A family-oriented software development process for engine controllers. In *Proceedings of the Third International Conference on Product Focused Software Process Improvement* (pp. 210-226). Berlin: Springer.

Ambler, S. W. (2002). *Agile modeling*. New York, NY: John Wiley and Sons.

Beck, K. (2003). *Test driven development: By example*. Boston: Addison Wesley Professional.

Bertini, M. T., & Tallineau, Y. (1974). Le Cobol structuré, un modèle de programmation. Paris: Ed.s d'informatique (in French).

Biffl, S., Winkler, D., Höhn, R., & Wetzel, H. (2006). Software process improvement in Europe: Potential of the new V-modell XT and research issues practice section. *Software Process Improvement and Practice*, *11*(3), 229–238. doi:10.1002/spip.266

Bodea, C. (2005). Agile software project management methodologies: The agile approach. *Ecological Informatics*, *5*(4), 27–31.

Boehm, B. (1988). A spiral model of software development and enhancement. *Computer*, *21*(5), 61–72. doi:10.1109/2.59

Boehm, B., Egyed, A., Kwan, J., Port, D., Shah, A., & Madachy, R. (1998). Using the WinWin spiral model: A case study. *Computer*, *31*(7), 33–44. doi:10.1109/2.689675

Causevic, A., Krasteva, I., Land, R., Sajeev, A. S. M., & Sundmark, D. (2009). *An industrial survey on software process practices, preferences and methods*. Malardalen University.

Coad, P., LeFebvre, E., & DeLuca, J. (1999). Feature-driven development. *Java Modeling in Color with UML*, 182-203.

Cockburn, A. (2001). *Agile software development*. Reading, MA: Addison Wesley Longman.

Coleman, G. (2005). An empirical study of software process in practice. In *Proceedings of the 38th Hawaii International Conference on System Sciences*. IEEE Computer Society.

Crnkovic, I., Larsson, S., & Chaudron, M. (2006). Component-based development process and component lifecycle. In *Proceedings of the International Conference on Software Engineering Advances* (pp. 44-44). IEEE.

Gull, H., Azam, F., Haider, W. B., & Iqbal, S. Z. (2009). A new divide & conquer software process model. *World Academy of Science. Engineering and Technology*, *60*, 255–260.

Haase, C. (2008). *Crystal methodology*. Retrieved December 10, 2006, from http://weblogs.java.net/blog/chet/archive/2008/01/crystal_methodo.html

Highsmith, J. (1999). *Adaptive software development*. New York, NY: Dorset House.

Humphrey, W. S. (1996). Using a defined and measured personal software process. *IEEE Software*, *13*(3), 77–88. doi:10.1109/52.493023

Jackson, M. A. (1975). *Principles of program design*. London: Academic Press.

Jackson, M. A. (1983). *System development*. London: Prentice Hall.

Jawadekar, W. S. (2004). *Software engineering: Principles and practices*. New Delhi: Tata McGraw-Hill Publishing Company Limited.

Kuilboer, J. P., & Ashrafi, N. (2000). Software process and product improvement: An empirical assessment. *Information and Software Technology*, *42*(1), 27–34. doi:10.1016/S0950-5849(99)00054-3

MAP. (1995). *Métrica version 2.1*. Madrid: Tecnos.

MAP. (2000). *Metodología MÉTRICA versión 3*. Madrid: MAP.

Matheron, J. P. (1994). *Comprendre merise: Outils conceptuels et organisationnels*. Paris: Eyrolles.

Pérez, G., El Emam, K., & Madhavji, N. H. (1995). Customising software process models. In *Software process technology* (pp. 70–78). Berlin: Springer. doi:10.1007/3-540-59205-9_43

Poppendieck, M., & Poppendieck, T. (2003). *Lean software development: An agile toolkit*. Upper Saddle River, NJ: Addison-Wesley Professional.

Pressman, R. S. (2001). *Software engineering: A practitioner's approach*. New York: McGraw-Hill.

Royce, W. W. (1987). Managing the development of large software systems. In *Proceedings of IEEE 9th International Conference on Software Engineering* (pp. 328-338). IEEE.

Scacchi, W. (2001). *Process models in software engineering*. New York: John Wiley and Sons, Inc.

Schwaber, K., & Beedle, M. (2002). *Agile software development with SCRUM*. Upper Saddle River, NJ: Prentice-Hall.

Sommerville, I. (2007). *Software engineering*. Harlow, UK: Addison Wesley.

Sommerville, I. (2010). *Software engineering*. Boston: Addison-Wesley.

Stapleton, J. (2003). *DSDM: The method in practice*. Reading, MA: Addison Wesley Longman.

Sulayman, M., & Mendes, E. (2009). A systematic literature review of software process improvement for small and medium web companies. In *Proceedings of Advances in Software Engineering* (pp. 1–8). Berlin: Springer. doi:10.1007/978-3-642-10619-4_1

Warnier, J. D. (1981). *Logical construction of systems*. New York: Van Nostrand Reinhold Company.

KEY TERMS AND DEFINITIONS

Iterative Model: A software development technique in which requirements definition, design, implementation, and testing occur in an overlapping, iterative (rather than sequential) manner, resulting in incremental completion of the overall software product.

Rapid Application Development Model: Software development methodology that uses minimal planning in favor of rapid prototyping in which emphasis is placed on developing prototypes early in the development process to permit early feedback and analysis in support of the development process.

Software Development Methodologies: A framework that is used to structure, plan, and control the process of developing an information system.

Software Development: Development of a software product.

Software Life Cycle Model: The framework selected by each using organization on which to map the activities to produce the software project life cycle.

Software Process Improvement: A set of software engineering activities which pretend to improve the state of software engineering practices within an organization.

Software Process Model: A model for the process by which user needs are translated into a software product.

Waterfall Model: A model of the software development process in which the constituent activities (normally phases like concept, requirements analysis, design, implementation, test and installation) are performed in that order, possibly with overlap but with little or no iteration.

Chapter 16
Learning to Innovate:
Methodologies, Tools, and Skills for Software Process Improvement in Spain

Félix A. Barrio
National Institute for Information and Communication Technologies, Spain

Raquel Poy
Universidad de León, Spain

ABSTRACT

Using a large sample of Spanish organizations, in this chapter, the authors empirically reveal the state of health of the Spanish software industry in terms of software process improvement, both in the monitoring of working methodologies and the usage of tools, and they provide the necessary information in order to understand the real skills and efforts to improve the quality of products and end-user services. Having found that a significant number of organizations do not have specific training programs or their own software quality department, it is an essential point of departure for professionals to increase awareness of the need to implement quality processes to improve the competitiveness of the company. The state of knowledge of the methodologies aimed at quality and existing national and international standards shows that these are barely known by professionals in Spanish companies, especially among SMEs and micro-enterprises. However, most Spanish small businesses and large enterprises think the CMMI model best suits their needs, both business and technical. This growing interest is the main reason behind the fact that Spain has almost 38% of the European CMMI certifications, including 22 new certifications since 2010, and is the fourth country in the world in terms of number of CMMI appraisals.

DOI: 10.4018/978-1-4666-5182-1.ch016

1. INTRODUCTION

There are many wide-ranging methodologies and tools, which may be involved in a software project, that are viewed as the entire project life cycle from its creation as a business necessity to its operation and maintenance.

The developing interest of organizations in cementing their relationship with customers and improving competitiveness and productivity is leading an increasing number of companies, both those with a demand for software products and services and those supplying this area, to make efforts to ascertain and monitor the quality of products and end-user services.

With the arrival of new working models and the heterogeneity of services, we are also seeing an increase in activities and complex processes, making it more difficult to monitor the quality of an organization.

In this regard, organizations maintain as their main initiatives the underpinning of basic tasks, intended to control costs, increase quality and reduce the time to market of software products.

In Spain, where the fabric of small and medium-sized enterprises (SMEs) amounts to 99% of all companies (94% of these being organizations with fewer than 10 employees), the situation is decidedly different from that of other industrialized countries, and particular attention and effort should therefore be focused on SMEs.

Within this context, the aim of our study has been to reveal the state of health of Spanish companies in terms of software process improvement, both in the monitoring of working methodologies and the usage of tools, and to provide the necessary information in order to understand their real skills and efforts to improve the quality of products and end-user services.

2. METHODOLOGY

For this study an online survey was conducted within Spain by the Spanish National Laboratory for Quality Software and the Observatory of the National Institute for Communications Technology[1] between July 2008 and December 2012. 2,925 company managers and professionals from across the country were selected on the basis of their position within the software products and services market (supply and demand) and by their sector of activity in accordance with the CNAE[2]. In addition to the national sample, an oversample of 75 general managers, who are representatives of software factories located in Spain, were interviewed. Parallel documentary research and analysis were undertaken. These included previous works and studies, both national and international articles on software quality with particular reference to the knowledge and use of methodologies and tools in software projects.

The main reason behind this distinction is that business needs and objectives are believed to be different for organizations belonging to the supply side as opposed to the demand side and vice versa. In order to guarantee the representation of the study at a national level, *the following research focus strata are defined:*

- The geographical scope of the study extended to the entire national territory, divided into seventeen autonomous regions and the two autonomous cities of Ceuta and Melilla.

- The sectorial scope was defined by supply and demand with each of the following types of company included in accordance with the National Economic Activity Classification (CNAE):

○ **Supply:** Software service and development companies, including IT Activities (CNAE 72) and Research and Development (CNAE 73).

○ **Demand:** Companies, public authorities, development centers and major integrators with the capacity to sub-contract in the following sectors of activity: Industry (CNAE 15-41), Construction (CNAE 45), Services (CNAE 50-52, 551, 552, 60-64, 70-74 and 921, 922), Public Authorities, Defense and mandatory Social Security (CNAE 75) and Other Professional Activities (CNAE 74).

• The professional scope was also defined from a perspective of supply and demand in accordance with the types of occupation defined by the Spanish National Statistics Institute in its National Occupation Classification (CNO) codes:

○ **Supply:** Advanced level information technology professionals (CNO 203), senior engineers (CNO 205), medium-level information technology professionals (CNO 263) and technical IT staff (CNO 303).

○ **Demand:** Heads of technology purchasing at organizations and businesses identified as demand-side within the sectorial scope.

• The questionnaire was divided into two major blocks, one covering the level of knowledge and usage of methodologies, and the other focusing on tools for software projects. The data obtained were aggregated and cross-checked against several variables defined in order to establish a more precise vision of the situation of the methodologies and tools employed in Spain on software projects[3]. This division has the following aims:

○ To identify the profile of the company surveyed through an analysis of the responses given to different quota control variables and different classification variables.

○ To cover all relevant aspects regarding the current situation of the methodologies and tools employed in software projects at any phase, in particular with regard to SMEs.

○ To uncover the skills performance and the level of penetration of the quality culture at organizations.

The associated sample error for a level of confidence of 95.5% was ±1.69%, thus providing adequate representativeness for all the strata defined on the basis of the market position variables (supply-demand), type of organization, size of enterprise and sector of activity. This avoided any concentration of the sample selection in certain strata or groups as a result of random selection. The stratification criteria applied to the present study was the following:

1. Market position (supply-demand), proposing a balanced distribution across the two as illustrated in Table 1.

2. Sector of activity. According to National Economic Activity Classification. Table 2 sets out the distribution of companies positioned within the supply side by sector of economic activity, *with practically all of these falling within the* information technology field.

Table 1. Distribution of organizations according to market position

Market Position	Universe	Sample
SUPPLY	88,749	1,277
DEMAND	3,334,521	1,648
STUDY TOTAL	**3,423,270**	**2,925**

Table 2. Distribution of supply-side organizations by sector of activity

Sector of Activity	Supply
IT Activities (CNAE 72)	1,096
R&D in natural and technical sciences (CNAE 731)	181
Total	1,277

2.1 Profile of Respondents

Table 3 sets out the distribution of companies positioned on the demand side by sector of economic activity. The majority fall within the service sector, followed by industry, then construction and public authorities.

One key fact worthy of note is that the organizations' position on the demand and supply sides were mainly set up between 1997 and 2003 both inclusive, and 1987 and 1993.

Confirmation was provided of the feature which clearly marks out the fabric of Spanish enterprise: most Spanish companies are organizations with fewer than 10 employees, also known as micro-enterprises. Together with organizations made up of between 10 and 49 employees, they represent 70% of Spain's business fabric.

Most professionals in supply-side organizations fall within the management, development and technical areas. Meanwhile, the professionals on the demand side are mainly in the management and technical areas.

The main levels of qualifications and training currently in existence were applied, with only post-graduate studies being excluded from the questionnaire (Master's and PhDs). The majority of survey respondents had advanced or medium-level university qualifications, making up slightly more than 60% of the entire population covered by the study. Meanwhile, within this group those professionals with advanced level university qualifications predominated.

The next group, although considerably behind, was made up of professionals with advanced or medium-level vocational training. As in the previous case, more advanced levels again predominate.

The smallest group was made up of school-leavers with basic or lower-level education, with a particularly low percentage of those with basic and lower levels of education compared with all other levels of qualifications.

Professionals with more than ten years' experience in the software project area make up the bulk. They are followed by professionals with between five and ten years of experience, and lastly by those with no more than five years' experience or less.

In accordance with the profile of professional experience, most of the **respondents** are aged between 30 and 44 (almost 62%). They are followed by professionals aged under 30 and those aged between 45 and 59. The proportion of professionals aged above 60 makes up only 1% of the total.

Table 3. Distribution of demand-side organizations by sector of activity

Sector of Activity	Supply
Industry (CNAE 15-41)	264
Construction (CNAE 45)	152
Services (CNAE 50-52, 551, 552, 60-64, 70-74, 921, 922)	1,109
Public Authorities (CNAE 751)	123
Total	**1,648**

3. KNOWLEDGE OF METHODOLOGIES AND LEVEL OF USAGE

A methodology is a set of working methods. These methods, which are defined, ordered and integrated, help to guarantee quality for those employing them throughout the process in question. There is a large and ever-increasing number of methodological approaches to software projects.

The demand for this type of system is dictated by the requirements of the sector and the commercial approach to supply, making them similar to other types of business.

Nonetheless, the results of the survey reveal limited awareness of the methodological approaches in existence, with two out of every three respondents on the demand side (64.8%), and one in three on the supply side (37.6%) having no knowledge whatsoever of the benchmarks, official standards and methodologies focusing on software process improvement. In accordance with international trends, almost half (47.7%) of the companies demanding software projects consider the establishment of service level agreements with their suppliers.

The key causes presumed to be behind this situation would be, on the one hand, the limited visibility of the benefits which methodologies can provide within already complicated business processes (Mas & Amengual, 2005), and on the other, the low level of interest shown in any of the options: 14.5% for CMMI (*Capability Maturity Model Integration*), 11% for Métrica 3, 8.4% for ISO 9001, 2.8% for ITIL, and just 1% for ISO/IEC 15504 (SPICE).

The final factor is the lack of knowledge of public grants, as only one in ten respondents (11%) claims to be aware of the specific training programs and governmental subsidies in the field of software quality provided by the public authorities (Figure 1).

3.1 Demand Side

Companies with a demand for software projects, given their focus on the business sector (within which they operate), have a lower level of interest in aspects connected with methodologies to improve products and end-user services in spite of their role as consumers.

Nonetheless, this level of interest increases notably with the size of the company with a considerable difference being evident in terms of software quality in accordance with the company's capacity.

Figure 1. Knowledge of public programs and grants for software quality (%)

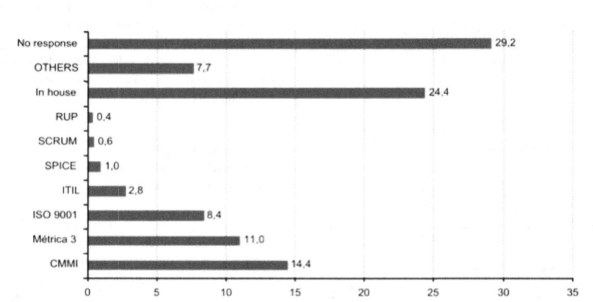

Table 4 illustrates under the context of the lack of information on the demand side, greater awareness among professionals in larger companies, who see methodologies as valid and effective instruments in improving their internal processes, in terms of both business and support for other areas of the organization.

Particular mention should be made of the fact that those professionals with the greatest shortcomings are those in managerial positions (70.1%) while contrary to expectations, the individuals most familiar with project methodologies are from the development area: software architects (52.8%) and functional analysts (49.0%) rather than from the quality area.

The presence within the central zone of the country of the various national and international bodies connected to the world of quality (SEI Partners, the Spanish Association for Standardization-AENOR, Excellence in Management Club, the Spanish Association for Quality, etc., headquartered at Madrid) makes companies in this area more familiar with international standards and methodologies (30.4%). By region, the greatest lack of awareness is found in several peripheral regions.

In line with the high level of general unawareness within the field of quality, a considerable percentage of companies (65.7%) have not considered introducing software quality methodologies or standards in the short term.

Those organizations which have plan to implement a methodology show a clear preference for the CMMI model (21.0%), focused essentially on software engineering. This trend is also corroborated by the fact that it likewise receives the greatest demand for training among the professionals surveyed.

The other benchmark models (ISO 9001, ISO/IEC 15504 (SPICE), Métrica 3, ITIL, etc.) are positioned behind the development of a company-specific methodology (4.2%), with more than half of those surveyed (57.1%) stating that they had no knowledge or interest in the model to be implemented. This figure highlights the high degree of confusion which abounds as a result mainly of misinformation and the large number of methodologies which exist.

In terms of distribution by sectors of activity, the highest levels of awareness are seen in finance (56.2%) and public authorities (55.6%) as opposed to companies of sectoral activity (27.9%) and others (21.3%), where awareness is lower.

In terms of the nature of the organization, Métrica 3 is widely familiar among professionals in the public sector (27.4%) and is the methodology defined by the Government of Spain. ISO 9001 is the most well-known standard (22.3%) within the private sector.

Awareness of public training programs and subsidies for specific training in the field of software quality is inadequate (23.8%) and only 13.7% of those organizations positioned on the demand side stated that they are or have been involved in programs, seminars or other events connected with software quality. This same trend is revealed among professionals at micro-enterprises and SMEs, as depicted in Table 5.

Organizations and their professional staff essentially maintain contact with universities (26.8%), and to a lesser extent (6.0%) with associations, laboratories and software process methodology flagship centers –including the European Software Institute Tecnalia, located in Bilbao, the Spanish Association of Information Technology System Metrics-AEMES, the Information Technology Institute of Valencia-ITI,

Table 4. Knowledge of standards and methodologies on the demand side, by size of organization (%)

Number of Workers	Yes	No	Do not Know (DNK)	No Response (NR)
Under 10	17.5	75.9	5.0	1.6
From 10 to 49	23.6	71.2	3.1	2.1
From 50 to 250	42.0	49.7	3.8	4.5
Over 250	64.8	24.7	6.2	4.4

Table 5. Involvement in training programs, by size of company (%)

Company Business	Yes	No	DNK	NR
Under 10	7.1	88.9	4.0	0.0
From 10 to 49	13.3	82.4	2.9	1.5
From 50 to 250	16.9	78.5	1.6	3.0
Over 250	34.7	54.1	6.5	4.7

AENOR, ISO, the Excellence for Management Club.

The CMMI (5.9%) and Métrica 3 (6.9%) models are the most commonly employed of the existing standards, although 49.9% of organizations choose to employ their own methodologies, or to combine formal and/or existing methodologies with in-house models (Figure 2).

According to the nature of the organization, and following the use of company-specific methodologies, enterprises in the public sector mainly use Métrica 3 (25.4%) while those within the private sector use an existing, unspecified methodology (13.3%).

The Standard ISO/IEC 9126[4] gives a wide-ranging definition of the characteristics of software product quality, and is supplemented by Standard ISO/IEC 14598[5], which identifies the different phases and tasks involved in implementing a quality evaluation process. Taking as a benchmark the international standards IEEE/EIA 12207.2008, the Standard for Systems and Software Engineering - Software Life Cycle Processes, which include a *Software Life Cycle Process Management Good Practice Guide*, it would be fair to state that less than half of Spanish companies (41.2%) manage their software projects properly (Table 6).

The methodologies of demand-side organizations focus mainly on the administration of costs. Risks, human resources and providers, meanwhile, are lower priority areas. In addition, a quarter of Spanish enterprises (25.4%) are unaware of the usage of indicators to monitor projects while one-third (34.6%) do not employ them (Figure 3).

Figure 2. Methodologies most employed in the demand sector (%)

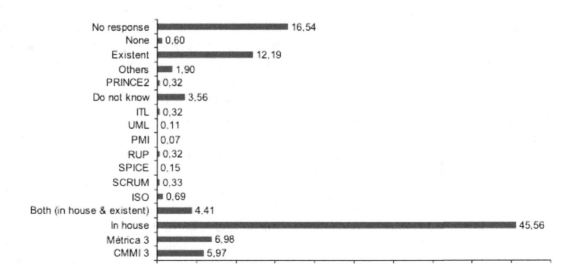

Figure 3. Usage of project management indicators (%)

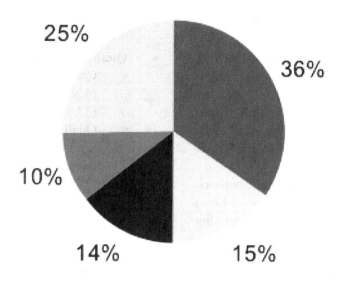

25% 36%

10%

14% 15%

■None   Process indicators ■Execution indicators ■Product indicators   DNK/NR

Table 6. Scope of project management methodology (%)

Project Management Area	Yes	No	DNK	NR
Product scope	43.0	41.8	9.5	5.8
Time	45.5	41.5	7.1	6.0
Costs	48.8	38.8	6.8	5.6
Quality	42.3	44.4	6.7	6.6
Integration	39.4	43.4	9.1	8.1
Human Resources	37.7	46.7	8.0	7.5
Communications	40.9	42.5	8.4	8.2
Risks	35.0	48.4	8.3	8.3
Providers	38.1	43.7	9.3	8.9

An indicator represents a "target to be met," meaning that the information which they provide must be classified in order to guarantee that processing and analysis correspond to the information needs at each level of the company addressed (management, architecture, quality, systems, etc.). This classification allows decisions to be taken as far as possible in real time. An analysis of the most important areas leads us to the following conclusions:

- **Time management:**
  - Organizations whose economic activity lies within software product validation and verification services (72.4%), technological consultancy (69.8%), strategic consultancy (68.9%), applications integration (68,9%) and the development of bespoke applications (61.7%) give the greatest importance to time management within their methodologies.
  - By sectors of activity, public authorities (48.3%) and industry (54.6%) place the least emphasis on defining and planning the project schedule.
- **Cost management:**
  - Organizations within the public sector pay the least attention to cost management within their methodologies, compared with the private sector.
  - Professional staff in the quality (66.9%) and technical areas (59.6%) give the greatest consideration in their methodology to the management of software project costs.
  - Irrespective of the services, size and sector of economic activity of companies, most of them (48.8%) implement cost management.
- **Quality management:**
  - Companies in the public sector employ this least in their methodologies (37.5%).
  - Quality management is at its lowest levels of implementation within the management areas of organizations (39.6%). This figure illustrates the fact that, although quality has become increasingly institutionalized over recent years, the desired levels have still not been attained.
  - Public authorities give the lowest importance to quality (47.6% of those surveyed said that it was not included in their methodology), as opposed to service and health companies.

It should be pointed out that, without their own in-house software quality department and specific training programs in this area, one in

Figure 4. Activities to verify the quality of products and services contracted (%)

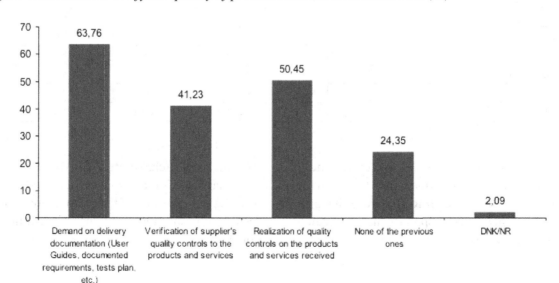

two Spanish enterprises (50.5%) undertakes its own controls in order to verify the quality of their products and services.

Figure 4 presents the data for the requirements of those companies which do perform such checks, and which generally require their suppliers to deliver formal project documentation before prior quality controls are performed.

Professionals in the quality area (66.3%), the technical office (57.3%) and development (57.0%) areas are the most concerned with their methodology to ensure that the end product or software complies with the technical and non-technical requirements agreed with the client. It should be pointed out that, in terms of the professional category of the respondents, the above trend is not seen among heads of purchasing.

Those organizations whose activity lies within the fields of software product verification and validation (79.3%), technological consultancy (75.9%) and strategic consultancy and applications integration (75.3%), dedicate the greatest efforts to product verification management. On the one hand, public authorities, micro-enterprises and SMEs perform the least verification to test the product complies with the characteristics agreed with the supplier. Industry and services are at the other end of the scale.

In general, only 16% of Spanish companies require suppliers to apply some methodology to monitor software projects. 18.1% require them to hold CMMI certification, the level falling to 9.1% in the case of ITIL.

Figure 5 is even more striking if we take into consideration the fact that only 19.7% of companies require any specific training and/or qualification on the part of their suppliers' staff, whether technical or methodological.

It is of interest that, in line with the current best practice of the government in Information

Figure 5. Technical and methodological certifications required from suppliers (%) – Yes, technical certifications

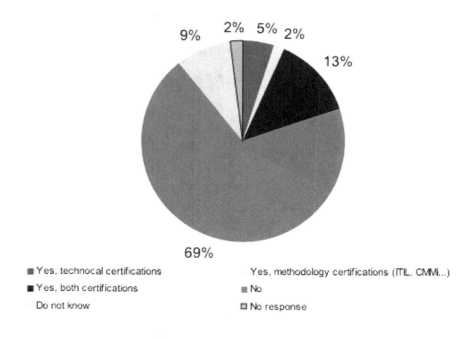

Technologies (Cobit, ITIL), almost half the companies surveyed (47.7%) have plans to establish Service Level Agreements (SLAs) with their suppliers, in particular within the public sector and among professionals with more than ten years' experience. Professional staff within the technical and quality areas have the greatest interest in establishing Service Level Agreements with suppliers in order to use these as control and monitor instruments for projects.

As opposed to the benchmark figures for other countries, such as the United States where two out of every three projects end unsuccessfully or without meeting expectations (Standish Group International, 2006), the outcome would seem to be quite the opposite in Spain. Two out of three respondents (67.8%) said they were satisfied with the results of their software projects in terms of both quality and the price of the services they receive from their suppliers (Figure 6).

3.2 Supply Side

Given the nature of the supply side, slightly more than one half of organizations (50.8%) are familiar with the benchmarks, official standards and methodologies focusing on software quality while 37.6% say they are unaware of them.

The staff of micro-enterprises and SMEs are less familiar with software quality methodologies, benchmarks and standards, compared with those at large organizations (Table 7).

In the short term, only a quarter of organizations (26.0%) are considering the possibility of introducing a software quality methodology. The greatest demand is for CMMI: 35.8% of those surveyed hope to introduce it.

In line with the level of awareness of each methodology and standard, mention should be made of the limited interest shown by organizations in certification programs (56.0% state they

Figure 6. Technical and methodological certifications required of suppliers (%) – NOT appropriate/ UNappropriate

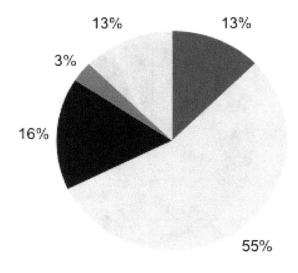

■ Very appropriate   Appropriate ■ Less appropriate ■ No appropriate   DNK/NR

Table 7. Awareness of benchmarks, official standards and methodologies (%)

Number of Workers	Yes	No	DNK	NR
Under 10	35.1	52.7	6.5	5.7
From 10 to 49	49.0	41.0	5.3	4.7
From 50 to 250	61.6	29.8	3.0	5.6
Over 250	68.3	17.2	7.1	7.4

are not certified). The greatest interest is focused on Level 3 CMMI certification (6.8%).

It should be highlighted that 16.4% of the organizations surveyed do not know of the existence of the responsive methods (XP, Scrum, Crystal, etc.) applicable to development cycles while 40.5% have no plans to implement them. These figures confirm the limited penetration so far of these methods as an alternative to more complete or formal methodologies.

In geographical terms, those organizations located in the northern areas (Asturias, Cantabria, Galicia, Leon, Navarre, the Basque Country and La Rioja) have a higher percentage of awareness of levels for methodologies and official standards, as seen in Table 8.

Those sectors of the economy which see the greatest penetration on the part of methodologies are the public authorities (69.2%), companies involved in software quality consultancy (64.5%) and companies in the financial sector (60.8%). At many such organizations, while also being a line of business in itself, there is a high technological component, which demands the standardization of internal processes and requires that the organization improve its image over its competitors.

The greater levels of awareness seen among professionals with a moderate level of experience (54.3%) is a trend that is consistent with an increase in the quality culture at organizations over recent years.

Only 26.2% of organizations state that they are or have been involved in training programs, seminars or other events connected with software quality, mainly connected with the CMMI model. Familiarity with public programs and governmental subsidies for specific training in software quality is inadequate, with only 10% stating that they are aware of them.

Slightly more than half of the organizations are familiar with the national and international standards and methodologies focused on software quality currently in existence, with a predominance of applications developed in-house (38.2%) to define and standardize deliverables at each stage of the development cycle. Figure 7 illustrates this situation, further highlighting the fact that the CMMI model is the most commonly employed, followed by Métrica 3.

The private sector tends to choose its own in-house project management methodologies (39.0%) and the CMMI model (17.0%).

Table 8. Awareness of methodologies and standards by geographical zone (%)

Geographical Zone	Yes	No	DNK	NR
Northern Areas	58.6	32.2	4.6	4.5
Central Areas	57.6	30.2	5.9	6.3
Southern Areas	50.9	34.8	7.2	7.1
Eastern Areas	41.8	47.1	5.7	5.4

Figure 7. Usage of formal and company-specific methodologies (%) – based on

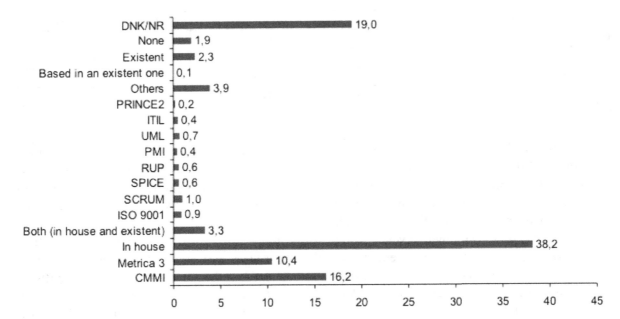

Project management methodologies focus mainly on product verification, time management and cost management, while risks and providers would seem to be the least important aspects (Table 9).

The monitoring and management of project risks do not take place systematically, but rather on an informal and ad hoc basis, with the consequent negative impact on costs and delivery deadlines for the end product.

The use of indicators is more widespread among supply-side companies, with two out of three of the companies surveyed employing indicators (66.0%), either for the product (14.0%), process (26.0%) or implementation (26.0%) (Figure 8).

Although those organizations on the demand side do not require their suppliers to undertake quality controls to verify the quality of deliverables and the end product, most suppliers do perform such checks, 57% in the case of deliverables and 65% for the end product. The percentage (5.8%) of companies which state that they do not know

what quality control is or what it is for is thus not representative.

Quality checks are not always undertaken by individuals independent of development work as recommended in the standard IEEE-STD 1012-2012 (*Standard for System and Software Verification and Validation*).

At those organizations which make provision for a specific quality area, fewer individuals are assigned (13.3%) while the development area has a higher percentage of resources allotted (38.4%).

As depicted in Figure 9, the use of responsive methods at the various stages of the development life cycle takes place mainly in the business of information analysis and software design, user and system requirements specification, and finally in the coding of the software product.

The specification of requirements is undertaken mainly by means of informal methods such as interviews or questionnaires (7.9%), followed by more formal methods, such as test cases (5.6%).

For analysis and design, meanwhile, there is a major preference for the usage of more formal

Table 9. Scope of project management methodology (%)

Project Management Area	Yes	No	DNK	NR
Product scope	73.2	15.0	5.3	6.5
Time	74.9	17.9	2.9	4.3
Costs	70.3	20.2	4.5	5.0
Quality	60.6	28.9	4.8	5.7
Integration	65.0	21.7	6.9	6.5
Human Resources	54.9	30.1	7.2	7.8
Communications	55.6	27.6	9.5	7.3
Risks	45.9	37.9	8.3	7.9
Providers	44.2	34.7	12.5	8.6

Figure 8. Usage of indicators (%)

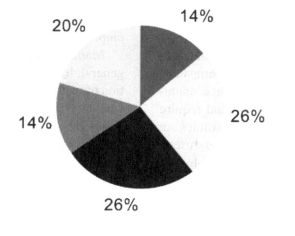

■None   Process indicators ■Execution indicators ■Product indicators   DNK/NR

methods, mainly Unified Modeling Language or UML (10.1%).

Building or coding is the least controlled phase. Mention should be made of the inadequate usage of responsive development methods, such as eXtreme Programming (4.3%).

4. KNOWLEDGE OF TOOLS AND LEVEL OF USAGE

Technological advances have led to the progressive appearance on the market of a diverse range of software project support tools. The characteristics and functionalities of such tools have

Figure 9. Use of responsive methods (%) – specification

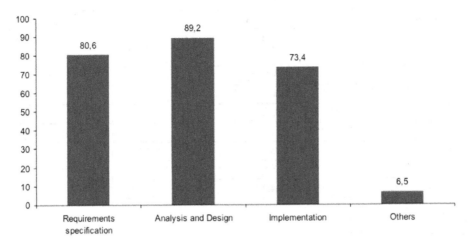

also expanded, providing complete coverage for services and the software life cycle.

In the opinion of the experts consulted, commercial tools (in use at 21.3% of the companies surveyed) are, despite the efforts of their manufacturers, increasingly complicated and require technological know-how, which constitutes an additional effort and added challenge for end users.

Company-specific tools, developed in-house, are the option most often employed by organizations (26.8%), although they are generally short on functionality, and their evolution becomes an almost impossible challenge without embarking on a costly project offering limited guarantees of success.

Alternatives in the field of open source projects fail to win over consumers, with only 13.1% of respondents stating that they had made use of such programs.

Within this context, 22.5% of organizations do not use software project support tools, or use them partially in support of specific processes and tasks.

No analysis is performed from the point of view of demand side, based on a position that the professional profile and type of company selected correspond mainly to activities involving the management of requirements and management of suppliers, processes which do not generally employ such tools.

Management of requirements is performed, in general, by word of mouth, with no documentation of interlocutors or changes (Calvo-Manzano, Cuevas, García, San Feliú, Serrano, Arcilla, Arboledas, & Ruiz de Ojeda, 2005). There is no traceability of requirements over the course of the project, and no review is conducted of the project plans, activities or products in order to guarantee that these are consistent with the system requirements. As for the management of suppliers, the most common system is to identify, select and establish agreements through specifications and calls for tender. However, processes intended to control and monitor projects properly are inadequate or non-existent.

For the sake of comprehensiveness, the analysis of the level of knowledge and usage of tools is applied separately to each of the phases making up the software development cycle.

One initial conclusion which could be drawn from an observation of the data is the predominance of organizations employing some form of tool as a support for software life-cycle phases (61.4%), as opposed to those which employ no type of tool, although the latter make up one out of every five organizations within the sample (22.5%).

Although the tools with the lowest levels of penetration are those based on an open source approach, if we analyze the data in line with the different stratification variables defined for this study, there is no uniformity in terms of the penetration of company-specific or commercial tools.

It should finally be stressed that organizations do not apply tools covering the entire software project life cycle, but rather specific tools for each phase.

4.1 Project Management Tools

As seen in Figure 10, there is a slight percentage difference in favor of the use of tools developed by the organizations themselves, rather than commercial off-the-shelf products. Open source tools make up 11% of the overall sample.

In terms of the nature of the organization, commercial tools enjoy greater penetration in the public sector than in-house systems, with the opposite trend being seen in the private sector.

4.2 Requirements Management Tools

It is a fairly widespread position that requirements may be modified over the course of the software project, with a minimal impact on the cost and time required to implement the project, meaning that management is not considered a priority here.

This trend is corroborated in those organizations involved in the study, with 33.8% employing no type of tool for requirements management whatsoever. With regard to commercial tools versus those developed in-house, the latter predominate, with levels of 24.8% compared with 15.8% for the former (Figure 11).

Mention should also be made of the high levels of unawareness which likewise exist regarding this type of tool, with 17.2% of those surveyed stating that they had no knowledge, a figure corroborated by the fact that no requirement management tool was included in the list of those named.

Figure 10. Usage of project management tools (%)

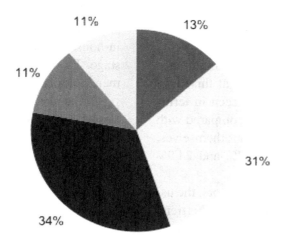

■ No   Commercial ■ In house ■ Open source   DNK/NR

Figure 11. Usage of requirements management tools (%)

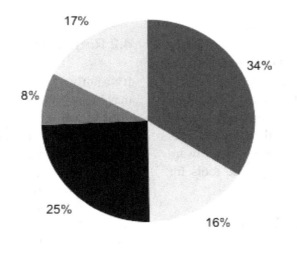

17%

34%

8%

25%

16%

■ No   Commercial ■ In house ■ Open source   DNK/NR

An analysis of the data based on the nature of the organization reveals lower levels of usage of these tools in the public sector (48.7%) and the private sector (32.5%), with a higher level of penetration of in-house tools in the private sector (25.7%) compared with commercial tools (15.8%).

4.3 Analysis and Design Tools

Most of the organizations do give importance to the usage of some type of tool at this stage (65.8%), with a slight difference seen in terms of the usage of commercial tools compared with those developed at the organizations themselves, the respective figures being 28.7% and 24.9% (Figure 12).

In both the private and public sectors, the usage of commercial tools predominates. This trend is also reflected across the different professional categories at enterprises (Table 10).

4.4 Coding Tools

Given the complexity that is always involved in the business of writing code, the usage of support tools with a large proportion pre-written code is increasingly necessary, thereby reducing the influence of the human factor. This is the opinion held at organizations, with 72.7% using some form of in-house, commercial or open source tool at this stage. The highest percentage figure is for commercial tools (33.8%).

Of the many tools available, Figure 13 identifies Microsoft Visual Studio (4.7%) and Eclipse (5.7%) as the most commonly employed, followed by company-specific software. These are also practically the only ones known to the organizations surveyed.

Figure 12. Usage of analysis and design tools (%)

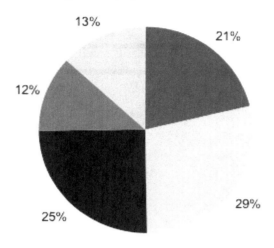

■ No   Commercial ■ In house ■ Open source   DNK/NR

Table 10. Usage of design and analysis tools, by professional category (%)

Professional Category	No	Commercial	In-House Development	Open Source	DNK/NR
Management Area	22.2	21.7	29.1	13.0	14.0
Technical Office Area	19.2	32.1	23.9	15.5	9.3
Quality Area	19.5	34.8	23.8	14.1	7.9
Development Area	22.4	32.9	20.0	14.6	10.1
Operations and Maintenance Area	22.5	24.1	25.5	16.9	11.0

4.5 Testing Tools

In recent years, the management of testing has taken on greater importance within the software development cycle, with organizations dedicating increasing financial and technical resources here.

This growth has been accompanied by greater penetration and consolidation of the concept of Software Quality Assurance (SQA), understood as a set of activities to be implemented throughout the entire lifecycle of the project, and not at one-off points, such as prior to the release of the software (Figure 14)

In accordance with this trend, the statistical data obtained in the survey revealed:

- The consolidation of organizations using testing management tools (61.1%).
- A greater presence at micro-enterprises and SMEs of tools based on company-specific development (35.2% and 32.7%, respectively), while at larger companies the usage of commercial tools predominates (27.9%).

Figure 13. Most commonly employed coding tools (%) (identified by respondents) – do not know – Visual Studio

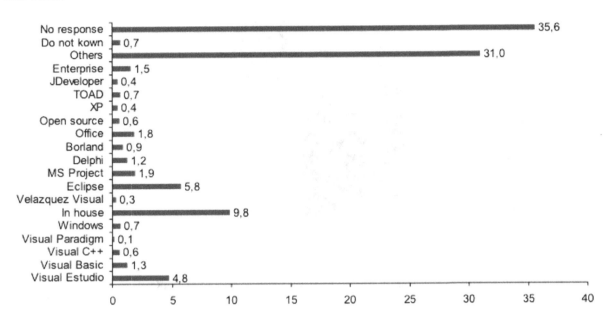

Figure 14. Usage of testing tools (%)

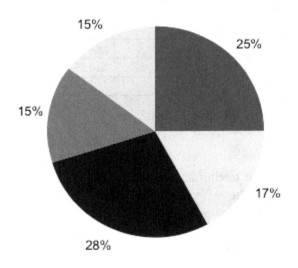

■ No Commercial ■ In house ■ Open source DNK/NR

4.6 Configuration Management Tools

Within the life cycle of the project, configuration management is a relatively recent activity, and consequently has enjoyed limited implementation within software projects.

Although more than one half of organizations (53.9%) have implemented some type of tool, 46.0% are unaware that they exist or use none (Figure 15)

4.7 Roll-Out Management Tools

Alongside requirements management, this is the software project activity with the lowest level of penetration of commercial tools (13.6%). This fact, together with the high percentage of unawareness of their existence (22.6%) constitutes the most significant data (Figure 16).

4.8 Incident Management Tools

As with project and requirements management, organizations use their own platforms –based on Excel, Word and others– to manage incidents, rather than more specialized tools (Figure 17).

Management takes place on an informal basis, with no methodology applied, allowing for the systematic and ongoing monitoring of incidents to record their status, the individual in charge and the solutions adopted. The most significant consequence of this is the impossibility of reusing them in other projects to reduce costs and shorten the end product delivery time.

5. COMPARATIVE ANALYSIS OF SMES AND LARGE COMPANIES

The difference in values in a large company means it is better equipped to undertake projects to improve software quality. On the one hand, they have bigger budgets than micro-enterprises and SMEs with which to achieve their objectives, and on the other hand, they have more human resources for the efficient completion of the tasks required.

For a micro-enterprise or SME, these actions represent an additional effort in all senses. Therefore, greater reliance is placed on partial allocation of resources, prioritization of work and budget readjustments. In SMEs, because of the small size of the workforce, there is little specialization or

Figure 15. Usage of configuration management tools (%)

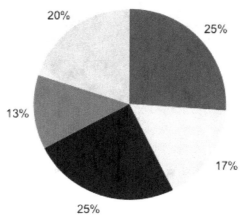

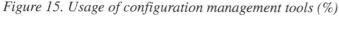

Figure 16. Usage of roll-out tools (%)

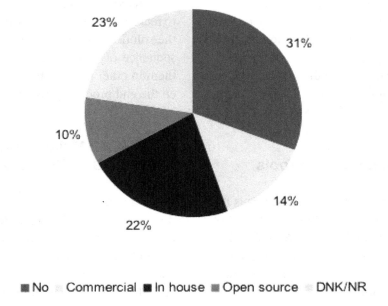

Figure 17. Usage of incident management tools (%)

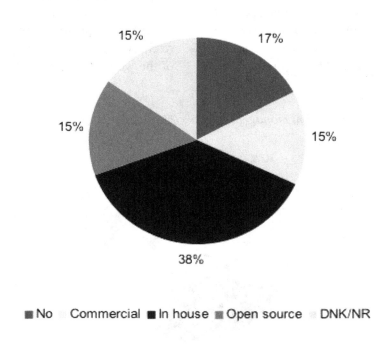

clearly defined responsibilities, and they depend heavily on individual effort.

The lack of training and poor visibility of the benefits and assistance has a direct impact on the motivation of SMEs when compared with larger companies. Access to information and training also poses an added problem for micro and SMEs, which have lower investment opportunities, albeit with greater individual motivation.

Nevertheless, their small size also gives them a number of advantages over large companies, such as flexibility in their organization, their willingness to change and the involvement of personnel.

Regarding the relationship between SMEs and quality related institutions, the following observations need to be made:

- Demand-side organizations maintain the least contact with institutions (those with fewer than 10 employees, 86% say they consult, whereas in those with fewer than 250 workers, the percentage drops to 74%).
- The percentage among supply-side companies is lower, though still important (72% in firms with fewer than 10 employees, 57% in those with fewer than 250).
- In large companies, an average of 63.5% (including supply-side and demand-side) say they maintain no contact with universities, associations, laboratories or centers of learning.

The data regarding the level of knowledge of methodologies and standards indicate that SMEs have more knowledge about ISO 9001 Standard (19.7%) than CMMI (18.8%), equivalent to the levels in a big company, but the use of CMMI (22.5%) is higher than for ISO 9001:2000 (22.4%). According to the results, it is observed globally that the methodology and standards with a higher degree of penetration in small and medium enterprises is the CMMI model (7.9%), as with large companies where it reaches 23.9%. Other methodologies and standards (IEEE, ITIL, RUP[6],

etc.) do not have a significant percentage, in some cases below 1% of the total results.

This increased penetration of the CMMI Model is because both small and medium enterprises as well as large enterprises consider that the methodology is best suited to their business needs and techniques. Consequently, it is the model that the majority of organizations have considered implementing in the short-term (45% in large enterprises, compared with 38.2% in medium-sized enterprises, 35.1% in small businesses and 6.1% in micro-enterprises).

The sharp contrast detected within SMEs can be explained by the different vision of the benefits that the implementation of methodologies provides. Developer supply-side companies consider that its implementation can improve their internal processes, image and therefore their competitiveness in the market. These reasons are not applicable to demand-side (client) companies as their business needs are totally different.

This high degree of interest is the main reason behind the fact that Spain has almost 38% of the European CMMI certifications including 22 new certifications since 2010 (Table 11).

Only the level of knowledge and use of tools from the supply side have been compared. It is considered that the profile of SMEs and large demand-side enterprises respond primarily to activities related to the management of needs and suppliers, and there is no relevant data on this aspect.

For SMEs and large firms, Table 12 compares the data on their use of a number of tools: e.g. company-specific, commercial, open source. It can be seen that, regardless of the size of the organization, there is ignorance of the tools existing on the market today. This is probably due to the excessive number of existing tools as well as their rapid evolution.

Regarding the level of deployment in enterprises of different types of tools, it can be seen that the number of workers is not a decisive factor either. Both large enterprises and small and me-

Table 11. Top 10 countries with certifications: most reported CMMI appraisals[7] per year by country

Country	2006	2008	2010	2012	Total
China	1	273	499	560	2,425
United States	3	238	307	317	1,519
India	5	80	110	136	662
Spain	0	30	43	54	273
Korea, Republic of	0	29	34	46	198
Japan	0	46	33	24	191
Brazil	0	27	40	25	174
Mexico	0	18	35	46	165
United Kingdom	0	16	13	10	86
Germany	0	16	14	9	77

Source: Carleton, 2009; CMMI Institute, 2013

Table 12. Comparison of the use of tools by SMEs and large enterprises (%) (identified by the respondents)

Tool	Less than 10	From 10 to 49	From 50 to 250	More than 250
Visual Studio	4.3	6.8	3.2	4.1
Visual Basic	2.0	0.5	0.7	1.4
Visual C++	0.6	0.3	1.3	0.3
Visual Paradigm	0.0	0.5	0.0	0.0
Windows	1.2	0.2	0.8	0.3
Company specific	12.7	11.7	5.2	7.1
Velazquez Visual	0.9	0.0	0.0	0.0
Eclipse	3.5	4.8	9.1	7.6
MS Project	1.0	1.4	3.3	2.7
Delphi	3.2	1.1	0.8	0.0
Borland	1.3	1.1	0.0	0.7
Office	2.4	1.4	1.6	1.8
Open source	1.0	0.8	0.0	0.2
XP	0.9	0.4	0.3	0.0
TOAD	1.2	0.0	1.0	0.5
JDeveloper	0.5	0.5	1.2	0.0
Enterprise	1.0	0.7	2.8	2.2
Others	25.6	33.2	38.4	30.9
Unknown	0.2	1.0	1.1	0.8
No response	36.3	34.4	29.1	39.5

dium sized ones use tools developed by the organizations themselves.

Finally, the large number of tools specified by the companies surveyed, grouped in the "Others" column in Table 12, is worth mentioning. This fact shows that, except for the tools already indicated (Eclipse and MS Visual Studio), there is a great variety of tool types deployed in organizations where there is no significant concentration of one or more specific manufacturers. The representativeness of other tools is not significant, some of them … between 1% and 2% at most).

6. CONCLUSION

As indicated in the initial section, the purpose of this study is to determine the level of implementation and use of methodologies and tools in software projects in Spain and their impact on the quality of products and end-user services.

Having found that organizations do not have specific training programs or their own software quality department, it is an essential point of departure for professionals to raise awareness of the need to implement quality processes to improve the competitiveness of the company.

The state of knowledge of the methodologies aimed at quality and existing national and international standards shows that these are barely known by professionals in Spanish companies, especially among SMEs and micro-enterprises.

As a result, organizations tend to apply their own methodologies when managing their projects, or combine them with formal or existing methodologies, the best known being the CMMI model, Metric 3 or the ISO 9001 standard.

In addition, very few organizations are aware of the specific training and support programs regarding quality software available to them. To try to remedy this lack of information, organizations within the sector are calling on all parties for a concerted effort in the same direction, with the ultimate goal of achieving greater dissemination of best practices related to national and international quality software.

Software project management is based on experience and not upon a systematic approach, to the detriment of quality, human resources, communication, risks and acquisitions. In this regard, improvements have been identified for possible application in organizations:

- Increased application of process, implementation or product indicators as effective management control tools for software projects.
- Implementation of quality controls by people who are not connected with development, as recommended by the IEEE-SDT 1012-2012 *Standard for System and Software Verification and Validation*. These activities must be supported by a group outside the development context.
- Increased deployment of service level agreements (SLAs) between development companies and customers, thereby complying with international best practices for information technology governance (COBIT, ITIL, etc.).
- Demands on suppliers to monitor specific methodologies in the software industry, and demands on their staff to possess the certification to prove this.

The study makes it clear that the use of tools throughout the entire software life cycle is essential for organizations. They place their trust in commercial tools or their own developments to support the software life cycle, with open source options having very little penetration.

The study also reveals that one in four Spanish companies do not use any kind of tool for management of needs, testing and deployment of applications. This has a knock-on, negative effect on the objectives of cost, quality and application time and delivery of the products and end user services.

As regards the use of tools to support methodologies applicable to the software life cycle, a united effort from all parties is also essential. Everyone needs to be pulling in the same direction so that they can improve their knowledge and application in projects developed by Spanish organizations.

Finally, both demand-side and supply-side companies must improve their internal circuits, allowing for the processing and analysis of information as to the progress made on the project, and the implementation of quality controls, with individuals who are independent of the development work being allocated to such roles wherever the structure of the organization permits.

Spain is suffering from a very serious economic crisis that began in 2007 and the continuous efforts made nationally and at the European Union level to overcome this crisis are beginning to show results. As a result of the global economic crisis, the software industry experienced a serious downturn in sales and profitability, especially between 2008 and 2012. The software industry in particular is expected to show a sustained recovery in 2013 and a return to pre-financial crisis levels in terms of growth rates. The software industry can be the driving force behind Spain's economic recovery bringing in revenues and creating more jobs.

Within this context, innovation in the software production process can be considered a strategic factor. However, experts and institutions are agreed on the fact that quality, in the short term, will continue to constitute unfinished business in Spanish companies, although two out of every three demand-side companies are satisfied with the value for money offered by the services received from their suppliers.

One essential aspect of a common agreement is that, throughout this process of adaptation of methodologies and tools, the public authorities should be playing a lead role in increasing the awareness of professionals in Spanish companies. Some possible actions would include publicity campaigns, tax breaks for companies obtaining certification, definition of requirements for bidding in public tenders and greater cooperation with cutting-edge companies in each sector of the economy.

REFERENCES

Calvo-Manzano, J. A., Cuevas, G., García, I., San Feliú, T., Serrano, A., & Arcilla, M. … Ruiz de Ojeda, F. (2005). Experiences of Spanish public administration in requirements management and acquisition management processes. In *Proceedings of the Fourth International Conference on Information Research and Applications*. Sofia, Bulgaria: FOI Commerce.

Carleton, A. (2009). *CMMI impact*. Pittsburgh, PA: Software Engineering Institute. Retrieved from http://www.sei.cmu.edu/library/assets/cmmiimpact-jac-eg.pdf

CMMI Institute. (2013). *Maturity profile reports*. Pittsburgh, PA: CMMI Institute. Retrieved from http://cmmiinstitute.com/assets/presentations/2013MarCMMI.pdf

Mas, A., & Amengual, E. (2012). La mejora de los procesos de software en las pequeñas y medianas empresas (pyme): Un nuevo modelo y su aplicación a un caso real. *REICIS: Revista Española de Innovación. Calidad e Ingeniería del Software*, *1*(2), 7–29.

Standish Group International. (2006). *The chaos report*. Retrieved from www.standishgroup.com/sample_research/PDFpages/Chaos2006.pdf

KEY TERMS AND DEFINITIONS

CNAE: National Economic Activity Classification used by the Spanish National Statistics Institute (INE).

Innovation Management: The discipline of managing processes related to the invention and implementation of a practice, process, structure, or technique that is new to the state of the art and is intended to further organizational goals.

Software Process Improvement: The improvement of the set of activities, methods, and practices that guide people in the production of software.

ENDNOTES

[1] The Spanish National Institute for Communication Technologies was founded in 2006. The Institute is a governmental agency attached to the Ministry of Industry, Tourism and Trade through the State Secretariat for Telecommunications and the Information Society, whose business aim is to manage, provide advice on, promote and disseminate technology projects within the framework of the information society. The National Software Quality Laboratory acts as a technological observatory for the quality sector, defining benchmarks and standards, forms of certification, awareness-raising services, working methodologies and the desirability of adopting applications. It offers advice and skills development to companies within the sector, assistance with standards of application and services intended to underpin the proper promotion of excellence within the software industry in Spain.

[2] National Economic Activity Classification used by the Spanish National Statistics Institute (INE).

[3] The data analysis was carried out at the University of León using the programme suite Statistical Package for the Social Sciences IBM SPSS Statistics 21.0.

[4] ISO/IEC 9126 "Software Engineering – Product Quality"

[5] ISO/IEC 14598 "Information Technology – Software Product Evaluation"

[6] Rational Unified Process, IBM.

[7] Over 5,000 businesses use CMMI models from over 70 countries in 2012.

Chapter 17
Social Network Analysis for Processes Improvement in Teams

Alejandra García-Hernández
Centre of Mathematical Research (CIMAT), Mexico

ABSTRACT

There is a vast amount of literature showing the effects of social networks in different organizational settings, such as innovation, knowledge transfer, leadership, and organizational culture. Recently, business process literature has recognized the impact of Social Network Analysis (SNA) in process improvement by observing the real collaborative relationships between employees, or the SNA impact in detecting communication structures in a large software team. However, little is known about how the teams' network structures may impact on the teams' productivity. This chapter analyzes different network properties that may have an impact on the teams' productivity and generates knowledge that may help to improve processes in the organizations.

1. INTRODUCTION

Knowledge creation is an important task for organizations (Tsai & Wu, 2010). An important research stream for the knowledge management area is the study of social network structures because they may have important implications for organizational performance (Argote & McEv-

DOI: 10.4018/978-1-4666-5182-1.ch017

ily et al., 2003). Knowledge creation requires abilities and capacities from different actors; the interaction and communication between different actors becomes a key determinant for knowledge production (Gulati & Gargiulo, 1999; Moenaert, Caeldries, Lievens, & Wauters, 2000).

From the social network perspective it is possible to explain variance in such traditional organizational outcomes as innovation, productivity, quality and different performance indicators

(Brass, Galaskiewicz, Greve, & Tsai, 2004). Network research perspective is distinctive from other research streams because it focuses on relations among actors. According to the social network literature, actors are embedded within networks of interconnected relationships that provide opportunities and constraints on behaviors (Brass & Galaskiewicz et al., 2004). Social Network research focuses on how the structural properties of social networks may explain organizational outcomes (Sparrowe, Liden, Wayne, & Kraimer, 2001).

There is a general consensus among social networks research academics that networks are important; however, the effect of network properties over performance is still unclear (Ahuja, 2000). Recent research proposes to focus on team level research, because teams are the nearest organizational structure for knowledge creation (Cummings & Cross, 2003; Cross, Ehrlich, Dawson, & Helferich, 2008). According to Kratzen (2001), current research "fails to offer a set of criteria for deciding whether the existing networks need to improve, what kinds of relational structure are desirable or undesirable, and what an improved network would look like." Some research supports the proposition that a high level of team communication benefits performance; however the relationship between communication frequency and team performance is not clear (Kratzen, 2001).

In the business process literature some researchers are recognizing the impact of Social Network Analysis in processes improvement. For example, the research of Bush and Fettke (2011) examine with the social network methodology the true working relationships between different employees of an organization. Their study case is exploratory and they conclude that the intersection between social network analysis research and business process literature may be important for business process improvements. The work of Wolf, Schroter, Damian, Panjer and Nguyen (2009) is another example of the importance of detecting the real working relationships between employees because this may impact the flow of communication and, as a consequence, the business processes. Wolf et al. focused on detecting communication structures between a large distributed software team and found that the quality of software projects depends on the quality of team members' communication and relationships. However, in the literature review an important gap that is addressed in the present paper was observed: prior research recognized the importance of network relationships between teams or organizational employees; there is a consensus that social networks may have a positive impact on team performance, but little is known about how teams' network structures may affect its performance. Our main objective is to review the social network research literature and identify key network properties that can affect organizational processes and performance.

In this paper, it is assumed that some organizations develop collaboration strategies between their employees, and these strategies build the team collaboration network structure. The principal hypothesis of this paper is that different strategies may impact differently on the organizational processes, and organizational performance. Recent research stresses the importance of analyzing internal and external team networks (Ancona, 1990; Reagans & Zuckerman, 2001; Oh, Labianca, & Chung, 2006) because both may have implications for flow communication impact (Moenaert & Caeldries et al., 2000). In Oh et al., (see Figure 1), the researchers take into account both the team internal network to examine how teams handle relationships and internal resources as well as the team external network in order to have a broader view of the availability of team resources through their external contacts. Oh et al. propose three different team network structure configurations and consider density, centrality, network efficiency and size among other variables (Oh & Labianca et al., 2006).

In Figure 1 Oh et al. consider that the optimal team network structure is the second diagram, because within the team there is a moderate relationship between team members, but outside the

Figure 1. Optimal model for group social capital

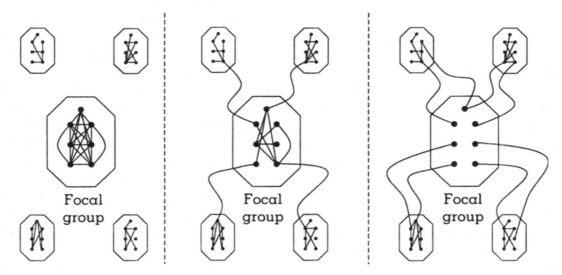

team, the members also have a communication flow with other teams within the organization.

Thus, for the literature review several network properties were considered: centrality, density, network size and network efficiency. The different network structures within the internal/external team's network perspective are similar to those depicted in Oh et al.'s (2006) study on corporate teams (see Figure 1).

Finally, the research review of this paper may have important implications for the design of collaboration strategies between organizational employees.

2. BACKGROUND

2.1 Social Network Perspective

The principal research focus from the social network perspective is to identify the kinds of structures that inhibit or enhance organizational performance. The principal network properties analyzed for performance are density, centrality, size, and network structural holes or network efficiency. There is a large body of literature

that relates network structure properties to performance at different organizational levels. According to Burt (2001), the principal metaphor is that "actors who do better are somehow better connected." However, what is better connected still remains unclear. The relationship between network structure and performance is marked by an intense debate between two different views: the optimistic and pessimistic point of view in each network property (Reagans & Zuckerman, 2001).

Burt argues that the different social capital points of view have one thing in common: all agree that network structure is a form of social capital for teams and gives them a competitive advantage because of their position in the social structure (Burt, 2007). Better connected people enjoy higher returns (Burt, 2001). The disagreement between the different points of view begins with what being better connected means.

For example, network density measures the proportion of relations among team members on the maximum number of relationships that may exist. The density takes values in a range from zero to one and the maximum value is determined by the number of actors in the network (Wasserman & Faust, 1994). Network density has often been proposed as an indicator of team cohesiveness (Kratzen, 2001), and the debate about the benefits of network density on team performance is highlighted by two different theoretical points of view: the positive point of view about network density or team cohesiveness is postulated by Coleman (1988). The principal thesis is that cohesive networks facilitate the creation of trust and norms between actors, making it possible to monitor and guide behavior, and to support social exchange and collective action. This form of social capital facilitates productive activities, because a team with trust is able to accomplish much more than a comparable team without trust and trustworthiness (Coleman, 1988). The creation of trust and norms enhance organizational efficiency because they facilitate task coordination, diminishing the probability of opportunism (Oh, Chung, & Labianca, 2004), limiting competition between teams inside an organization (Reagans & McEvily, 2003), permitting the joining of individual interest to the pursuit of common initiatives (Reagans & Zuckerman, 2001; Reagans, Zuckerman, & McEvily, 2004) and also providing security in transferring knowledge and valuable resources (Granovetter, 1983; Coleman, 1988). According to Reagans & Zuckerman (2001), teams with low levels of relation between members face many barriers to success.

But network cohesion or density can also be costly because people need time and effort to communicate the knowledge to all the team members. Excessively closed teams can lead to strong norms against associating with members of out-teams and restrict access to more diverse resources and innovative information available beyond the closed team. Also, in a closed team the information that is available is often homogeneous and redundant (Oh & Chung et al., 2004). Figure 2 shows the differences observed in a team with high density level or high cohesion and a team with low density network where there is no relationship between team members.

Figure 2. Network density levels

Parallel to Coleman, Burt observes other points of view about the benefits of social capital. In this second line of thinking, Burt postulated that in an open network the actors can build relationships between disconnected clusters and use these connections to take both advantage and control of information over the clusters (Burt, 1992). The principal premise in the thesis of structural holes is the benefits of information access and control when an actor builds a network with many structural holes (Burt, 1992). A structural hole exists when an actor's contacts have no relationship between them, and as a consequence, the information that flows to each contact is different, and the actor's knowledge sources are not redundant. With access to different knowledge pools the actor may act as intermediary and control the knowledge flow between different teams (Burt, 2001). The actors that build networks that are rich in structural holes, expand their access to more opportunities and get faster and more diverse information (Burt, 2001). They therefore have a competitive advantage over those that are restricted to a single team (Burt, 1992; Gabbay & Zuckerman, 1998). Burt's arguments describe social capital as a function of the brokerage opportunities. For Burt, a redundancy indicator is measured through social cohesion: when all the actors are strongly connected in the network, this leads to access to redundant information and resources (Burt, 2001).

According to Coleman (1988), an optimal social structure is generated by a dense and interconnected network because an open structure does not facilitate trust, an important aspect for the creation of social capital. According to Burt (1992), building a network structure with disconnected contacts is the optimal strategy. Thus, analyzing different network properties may be relevant from the perspective of effective and efficient network design (Ahuja, 2000).

An emerging research line emphasizes that an optimal network structure combines elements of network cohesion and structural holes (Walker, Kogut, & Shan, 1997; Burt, 2001; Reagans & Zuckerman, 2001; Reagans & McEvily, 2003; Burt & Ronchi, 2007).The principal thesis in this emergent research line highlights that the two mechanisms are far from opposing and are complementary. The greatest organizational benefits are found when two social capital forms are present: when within the team there is network cohesion and there are structural holes beyond the team (Reagans & Zuckerman, 2001; Reagans & McEvily,2003; Oh & Labianca et al., 2006; Burt & Ronchi, 2007). The results of Walker et al., (1997) suggest that the two forms of social capital may be applied to different contexts; social cohesion is a better predictor of cooperation and collaboration. At the same time the structural holes theory has greater interest for the strategic action of entrepreneurs and can be more applied in networks of market transactions than in networks of cooperative relationships (Walker et al., 1997).

Network centrality reflects the extent to which the team's network relations are concentrated on a small number of individuals rather than distributed equally among all the team members. The network centrality identifies the most important actors in the network or the actor with the greatest number of relationships (Wasserman & Faust, 1994). At the individual level the principal premise is that the central actors may have a competitive advantage because they have more alternatives to satisfy their needs, more access to resources and are less dependent (Hanneman & Riddle, 2005). The central actors also are considered stars actors, and frequently this property is associated with power and dependence (Hanneman & Riddle, 2005). A high level of centrality could be an indicator of the actor's experience and ability to give advice. This is the reason why many other actors have a relationship with the central actor. The central actors also have an advantageous position because they may act as intermediaries and take advantage of the information flowing through them because they can distort or restrict this flow of information (Krackhardt, 1992).

At the individual level the positive advantages generated for the central actors seem clearer, but at the team level the relationship between network centrality and team performance is not as clear. Early studies have found that centrality had an influence in the rapid evolution of organizations because organizations were more stable and had fewer errors in performance (Bavelas, 1950). However, it affected the satisfaction levels of the periphery actors. Also, it was found that task complexity was a predictor of the relationship between centrality and team performance. Teams with simple tasks worked better in centralized networks (Bavelas, 1950), and teams with complex tasks performed more effectively in decentralized networks (Shaw, 1964). The results of Sparrowe et al. (2001) coincide with Shaw's (1964) research: the central position benefits the central actor, but at the team level, network decentralization is a better predictor of team performance for complex tasks. Figure 3 shows a team with a centralized network structure and a team with a decentralized network structure.

The relationship between centrality and team performance has sometimes been tied to leadership aspects. According to Luo (2005), a strong leadership is represented by a centralized network; at the same time a null level of leadership represents a decentralized network. On the one hand, strong leadership means a high level of control and better coordination, but reduces freedom for creative actions. On the other hand, a null level of leadership may affect the organization's tasks but enhance creative actions.

Figure 3. Network centrality levels

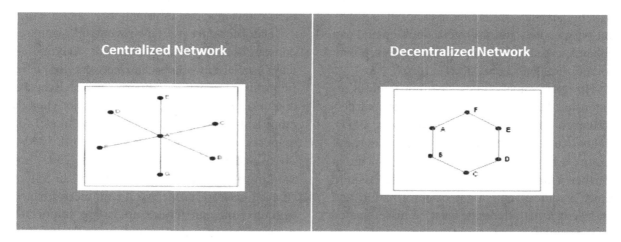

In a more recent study, Yousefi-Nooraie, Akbari-Kamrani, Hanneman, and Etemadi, (2008) found that research centers show a high level of centrality, and the central researchers were also the formal leaders of their organization. Yousefi-Nooraie et al., found that central leaders are characterized by a high level of connections inside and outside their organization, and played an important role in promoting research projects and connecting the center to their scientific community. Therefore, the central actors have experience, know-how and greater influence in their research area (Allen, 1977; Lowrie & McKnight, 2004; van der Leij & Goyal, 2006; Yousefi-Nooraie et al., 2008), making the presence of star researchers important for the network (van der Leij & Goyal, 2006). However, a high level of centrality also could be a sign of scarce researchers with the ability to manage projects and be independent, which can threaten the sustainability of the research center and also decrease the knowledge flow between members due to the high level of leadership and control (Yousefi-Nooraie et al., 2008).

Degree centrality measures the number of an actor's direct contacts; in some cases degree is also denominated an actor's network size (Tichy, Tushman, & Fombrun, 1979; Burt, 1983). The actor network size in this case refers to the number of the actor's direct contacts; the principal arguments of the benefits of network size are related to the benefits gained through degree centrality. A high level of network size means greater and faster access to resources, opportunities and information sources. The network size is the actor's capacity to connect to other actors or teams (Burt, 1983).

According to the network perspective, the higher the number of contacts or direct actors, the greater the opportunities to get the resources needed (Borgatti, Jones, & Everett, 1998). The study of the team's external network size is important, the direct contacts of the team may generate resources benefits, information and greater external knowledge (Ahuja, 2000). Some studies have found that knowledge transfer with external contacts has a positive influence on team performance (Ancona, 1990), and on product quality (Wong, 2008). According to Wong, the team's effectiveness depends on its capacity to synthesize different ideas and create innovative solutions. This capacity is possible through team relations with external contacts; the teams are exposed to different ideas, experiences, and activities and have more interaction with different actors. Therefore, teams may import more diverse knowledge and enhance synthesis capacity and creative solutions (Allen, 1977; Burt, 1992;

Levine & Moreland, 2004; Wong, 2008). Teams with bigger networks are more exposed to different perspectives and divergent thinking and can enhance creative learning and creative problem solving (Reagans et al., 2004).

However some studies have not found a relationship between team network size and performance (Baldwin, Bedell, & Johnson, 1997). Baldwin et al.'s research suggests teams may not require a high level of external communication. Further, a large number of direct contacts require time, resources and a lot of information and knowledge that afterward must be disseminated by the team.

Another important network property for team performance is the efficiency of its external network. According to Burt, the efficiency of an external network refers to the level of redundancy between the team's direct contacts (Burt, 1983). A higher density between external contacts results in a higher level of redundancy of contacts (Burt, 1983; Borgatti, 1997). An efficient team's external network is characterized by the presence of structural holes. There is a debate concerning the benefits of an external network, rich in structural holes proposed by Burt, and the benefits of an external density network are supported by Coleman's arguments (Reagans & Zuckerman, 2001). From a strategic point of view, teams benefit from an efficient external network, rich in structural holes because structural holes enhance team creativity (Burt, 2004). When a team has relationships with different disconnected teams, it has access to different points of view, information and perspectives (Heinze & Bauer, 2007) and can act as an intermediary to control the resources flow and use information for its own benefit (Burt, 1992). An efficient external network also promotes competition and decreases collaboration between external contacts. As mentioned earlier, a high level of density is important to building trust

between contacts, collaborating and transferring tacit knowledge and information.

The literature review revealed a general consensus about the importance of studying the team's social networks because networks may have important implications for performance (Reagans & Zuckerman, 2001). Still, there is not enough empirical evidence about an optimal model for team social network structure. Oh et al. (2004, 2006) and Reagans and Zuckerman (2001) are working in this research line. Also, the effect of each network property on team performance remains unclear. There are some important mechanisms that may influence the relationship between network structure and team performance. The first is the type of task done by the team. Some properties could be influential in complex tasks but not in simple tasks; perhaps some tasks require a high level of collaboration and others require a strategic network of competition (Burt, 2001); in general, different types of structures are better suited for different tasks (Ahuja & Carley, 1999). Another important mechanism is team level of analysis; some properties are more effective at the internal level of analysis and other properties can have a positive influence only at the external level. Therefore, it is important to analyze different levels of analysis and to consider different network properties (Reagans & Zuckerman, 2001). The final important mechanism is the kind of team performance or result being considered. Castilla, Hwang, Granovetter and Granovetter (2000) argue that "the interesting problem is not whether networks are important in a region, but what kinds of networks are associated with what kinds of outcomes.

In the next two sections, the above arguments about each team network property were taken into account, and the possible effects of each network property on two performance indicators, team productivity and product quality were reviewed separately.

3. PRODUCTIVITY AND NETWORK STRUCTURE

Organizational performance is an area of research interest because of the increase in the demand for efficient organizations and efficient teams, and because of the actual organizational competitive environment between firms in different sectors. However, evaluating performance is a complex and multidimensional process which includes, among the most used indicators, organizational productivity and product quality.

In this paper productivity is defined as the total organizational outputs completed over a period of time (Print & Hattie, 1997). An important determinant of productivity is collaboration among employees. Team productivity depends largely on its members' abilities to exploit the flow of information and knowledge networks (seen in Leenders et al., 2003); the team communication network is the most important explanatory variable (Leenders et al., 2003).

Some studies provide evidence of a positive relationship between team density and productivity (Reagans & Zuckerman, 2001; Reagans & McEvily, 2003; Reagans et al., 2004). Network density enhances productivity because the creation of trust and norms support coordination tasks and the teams are able to accomplish much more with an effective assignment of resources. Density also enhances the organizational efficiency because the creation of trust and norms decreases the probability of opportunism and competition between team members (Coleman, 1988).

However, teams with low levels of relation between members may face many barriers to success. In this kind of network with low density, it is very difficult to create trust because team members work separately and resources may not be managed effectively and, as a consequence, may not provide a good level of productivity.

Team productivity is mainly affected by institutional characteristics and leadership (Bland, Center, Finstad, Risbey, & Staples, 2005). Network centrality is related to aspects of leadership like coordination and control. Centralized communication or direct supervision is seen as an important means to coordinate work-teams (Kratzen, 2001). Teams require a kind of control structure to provide appropriate organizational support for both internal and external exchanges that are essential to the team's survival and success (Liebeskind, Oliver, Zucker, & Brewer, 1996). The central actors have knowledge about team resources, information and capabilities, meaning they can communicate with disconnected members and act as a resource integrator (Balkundi & Harrison, 2006). From this point of view, team productivity is enhanced through the organization and coordination of tasks in a centralized network and strong leadership. According to some researchers, the role of a central actor or leader is essential for international projects. The leader acts as the driving force, maintaining the continuity of projects, selecting the necessary skills, monitoring and controlling the information flows, executing the projects, and managing internal and external team relations (Allen, 1977; Moenaert & Caeldries et al., 2000; Lowrie & McKnight, 2004; Leij & Goyal, 2006; Yousefi-Nooraie & Akbari-Kamrani et al., 2008). From this perspective, the central actor is associated with team leadership (Luo, 2005). Effective leadership can clarify the goals of the team and shorten the time to completion of research activities. Therefore, the team can have effective planning in resource allocation. A decentralized network with null level of leadership may affect the organization and coordination of tasks and, as a consequence, the team may encounter many obstacles to success (Reagans & Zuckerman et al., 2004).

As mentioned earlier, network size refers to the number of a team's external contacts. This property may also influence the team's productivity when team tasks are complex and require a wide range of experience, resources, techniques and skills (Katz & Martin, 1997) usually found outside the team or organization. Teams that are more open to outside connections with a wide range of resources have more chances of division of work compared to teams with only a few contacts (Ahuja, 2000; Bozeman & Lee, 2005; Yousefi-Nooraie et al., 2008). According to the network perspective, a higher number of contacts or direct actors increases the opportunities to obtain the resources needed at the precise time (Borgatti & Jones et al., 1998). The ability to obtain resources is an important aspect for productivity: the shorter the time required to obtain the desired results, the more productive the system is. Aral and Alstyne (2007) found that the number of network contacts is related to the number of projects executed (productivity).

Some empirical works also show that network efficiency is related to productivity. At the individual level, for example, researchers with efficient networks produce more publications than scientists with redundant networks (Rumsey-Wairepo, 2006). At the team level some researchers also found a relationship between efficiency and productivity (Reagans & Zuckerman, 2001). Teams with efficient networks can mediate between other teams and contacts, and they benefit from controlling the flow of information between teams separated by "structural holes" (Burt, 1992). In these kinds of networks teams are more able to identify opportunities (Burt, 2007). In an efficient network teams get the benefits of control and coordination of the disconnected teams and have the advantage of acting faster than external contacts, thereby increasing their productivity. Teams with an efficient network act as intermediaries, and thus have power and control over the disconnected teams.

4. PRODUCT QUALITY AND NETWORK STRUCTURE

Quality is another important organizational output. The productivity indicator (quantity) may not reflect the quality of the organizational products (Ahuja & Carley, 1999). According to Ahuja and Carley (1999), studies should also try to include product quality as well as quantity produced in objective measures of organizational performance.

For product quality, it is important to have a social network structure that encourages creativity. From this point of view, creativity is the result of complex interrelationships between team members. A critical role for creativity in teams is communication between members; when there are interactions between members, the results can be more creative, innovative and useful because the members can contribute different ideas (Leenders et al., 2003), and in this way knowledge flows between employees, and thus increasing creativity (Laudel, 2001; Yousefi-Nooraie et al., 2008).

Creativity and originality can emerge as a result of interactions and team work (Laudel, 2001). Creativity requires the combination and integration of ideas and resources of different members (Leenders et al., 2003), thus network density is generally associated with scientific creativity and product quality (Rigby & Edler, 2005). However, some recent research has highlighted the importance of moderate levels of network density within a team (Oh et al., 2006). High density levels lead to the transmission of redundant information among team members, which could limit the capacity for creativity (Burt, 1992). Also, high density levels can affect creativity because they are conducive to the creation of mutual beliefs between team members, which reduces the quantity and quality of the solutions to problems (Leenders et al., 2003). Low density level is neither good for creativity nor product quality because this means poor interaction between team members. Following this line of thought it is possible that a moderate density level is more appropriate for quality results.

A high centrality network implies greater information control by the central actors. Greater information control may reduce members' independence (Luo, 2005), or limit members' interactions and flows of knowledge among them, all of which may influence creative abilities (Yousefi-Nooraie et al., 2008). In a highly centralized network there is no relationship between actors and the ideas are not shared between them; the central actor receives all the information, and for this reason is likely to experience information overload (Leenders et al., 2003). Perhaps a network of high centrality promotes effective resources management (Kratzen, 2001), but it seems that when it comes to innovation, creativity or quality, centralized communication can result in information failing to reach the intended recipient or becoming distorted (Leenders et al., 2003). Besides, team members need a level of freedom for a creative environment and high centrality makes that difficult (Leenders et al., 2003).

According to network size, effective communication between an organization and its external contacts reduces the life cycle of product development and enhances product quality (Moenaert et al., 2000). Information acquisition is related to contact quantity; large networks provide access to diverse and novel information (Aral & Alstyne, 2007).

Employees exposed to larger networks are able to improve their communication skills and their capacity to synthesize knowledge and external information. Creativity and quality increases with the number of collaborators because of the increased opportunities for interaction and discussion of ideas, methods and results (Melin, 2000).

Network efficiency is also related to creativity and the generation of ideas. According to Heinze and Bauer, scientists with efficient networks publish papers that are seen as creative and of high quality by their peers (Heinze & Bauer, 2007). The mediators of efficient networks have access to various knowledge pools and novel information, and the actors are exposed to alternative ways of thinking and behaving (Burt, 2004; Reagans et al., 2004). They can develop different ways to understand and solve problems and generate creative and innovative solutions (Balkundi & Kilduff et al., 2007).

The above arguments suggest that each network property has different effects if are considered different organizational outputs. In this case, it was observed that the effect of some team network properties may be different for productivity and creativity or quality because all the properties are related to different aspects of organizational outcomes, and therefore, require different strategies.

In Table 1 the principal arguments about the effect of each team network variable in team productivity and the quality of team products are summarized, based on the literature reviewed in this paper.

Table 1 shows that most of the arguments for the effect of the team network variables on productivity and product quality are positive, with

Table 1. Effect of team network properties on productivity and product quality

	Productivity	**Product Quality**
Centrality	Positive Relationship (+) Greater leadership clarifies goals and reduces time for completion of tasks.	Negative Relationship (-) Less freedom and independence, and therefore, less creativity.
Density	Positive Relationship (+) Increased coordination and cooperation.	Moderate Relationship (U-inverted) Too much density: redundant information between team members reduces creativity. Moderate density: enhances the team work component necessary for creativity.
Network Size	Positive Relationship (+) Better division of labor.	Positive Relationship (+) Improves communication skills; research can be discussed among collaborators.
Network Efficiency	Positive Relationship (+) Competitive advantage of acting as mediator: greater control of information and fast identification of opportunities.	Positive Relationship (+) Access to different knowledge pools and novel information. Mediators develop different ways to understand and solve problems, and generate creative solutions.

the exception of centrality and product quality, where the proposed relationship is negative. Another exception is the relation between network density and product quality, where the level of density that enhances product quality may be moderate.

5. CONCLUSION

The objective of this paper was to extend the research line about the effect of teams' social networks on performance. The literature review presented above gives rise to some conclusions. First, there is a general consensus in the research literature that there is an effect between some team social network variables and team performance, specifically with productivity and product quality. Second, the literature reviewed showed that the effect on the network structure variables differs if productivity or quality is considered as a performance indicator: some network properties may have a positive effect on a team's productivity but a negative effect on product quality. Third, the research about teams' social networks showed how each one of the network variables studied may affect different team performance indicators.

From this literature review it is possible to conclude that following a social network perspective to analyze teams' performance is a research alternative, especially for the business processes and teams' processes because researchers are recognizing the impact of social network analysis in processes improvement. Through the teams' networks it is possible to identify the employees who participate internally and externally in team knowledge production processes, and the study of both levels of analysis has important implications on the teams' results.

Finally, it is expected that these results will set the stage for future research into collaboration networks of teams and business processes.

In particular, our future research will extend this literature review and evaluate each one of our hypotheses about the effects of each network variable on team productivity and product quality. The findings presented here are limited to teams. Therefore it may be interesting to extrapolate our literature review to other organizational levels.

REFERENCES

Ahuja, G. (2000). Collaboration networks, structural holes, and innovation: A longitudinal study. *Administrative Science Quarterly, 23*(2), 425–455. doi:10.2307/2667105

Ahuja, M. K., & Carley, K. M. (1999). Network structure in virtual organizations. *Organization Science, 10*(6), 741–757. doi:10.1287/orsc.10.6.741

Allen, T. J. (1977). *Managing the flow of technology*. Boston: Halliday Lithograph.

Ancona, D. G. (1990). Outward bound: Strategies for team survival in an organization. *Academy of Management Journal, 33*(2), 334–365. doi:10.2307/256328

Aral, S., & Alstyne, M. V. (2007). Network structure & information advantage. In *Proceedings of the Academy of Management Conference*. Philadelphia, PA: Academy of Management.

Argote, L., & McEvily, B. et al. (2003). Managing knowledge in organizations: An integrative framework and review of emerging themes. *Management Science, 49*(4), 571–582. doi:10.1287/mnsc.49.4.571.14424

Baldwin, T. T., Bedell, M. D., & Johnson, J. L. (1997). The social fabric of a team-based MBA program: Network effects on student satisfaction and performance. *Academy of Management Journal, 40*(6), 1369–1397. doi:10.2307/257037

Balkundi, P., & Harrison, D. A. (2006). Ties, leaders, and time in teams: Strong inference about network structure's effects on team viability and performance. *Academy of Management Journal, 49*(1), 49–68. doi:10.5465/AMJ.2006.20785500

Balkundi, P., Kilduff, M., Barsness, Z. I., & Michael, J. H. (2007). Demographic antecedents and performance consequences of structural holes in work teams. *Journal of Organizational Behavior, 28*(2), 241–260. doi:10.1002/job.428

Bavelas, A. (1950). Communication patterns in task-oriented groups. *The Journal of the Acoustical Society of America, 22*(6). doi:10.1121/1.1906679

Bland, C. J., Center, B. A., Finstad, D. A., Risbey, K. R., & Staples, J. G. (2005). A theoretical, practical, predictive model of faculty and department research productivity. *Academic Medicine, 80*(3), 225–237. doi:10.1097/00001888-200503000-00006 PMID:15734804

Borgatti, S. P. (1997). Structural holes: Unpacking Burt's redundancy measures. *Connections, 20*(1), 35–38.

Borgatti, S. P., & Foster, P. C. (2003). The network paradigm in organizational research: A review and topology. *Journal of Management, 29*(6), 991–1013.

Borgatti, S. P., Jones, C., & Everett, M. G. (1998). Network measures of social capital. *Connections, 21*(2), 27–36.

Bozeman, B., & Lee, S. (2005). The impact of research collaboration on scientific productivity. *Social Studies of Science, 35*(5), 673–702. doi:10.1177/0306312705052359

Brass, D. J., Galaskiewicz, J., Greve, H. R., & Tsai, W. (2004). Taking stock of networks and organizations: A multilevel perspective. *Academy of Management Journal, 47*(6), 795–817. doi:10.2307/20159624

Burt, R., & Ronchi, D. (2007). Teaching executives to see social capital: Results from a Weld experiment. *Social Science Research, 36*, 1156–1183. doi:10.1016/j.ssresearch.2006.09.005

Burt, R. S. (1992). *Structural holes: The social structure of competition.* Cambridge, MA: Harvard University Press.

Burt, R. S. (2001). Structural holes versus network closure as social capital. In N. Lin, K. Cook, & R. S. Burt (Eds.), *Social capital: Theory and research.* New York: Aldine de Gruyter.

Burt, R. S. (2004). Structural holes and good ideas. *American Journal of Sociology, 110*(2), 349–399. doi:10.1086/421787

Burt, R. S. (2007). Seconhand brokerage: Evidence on the importance of local structure for managers, bankers, and analysts. *Academy of Management Journal, 50*(1), 119–148. doi:10.5465/AMJ.2007.24162082

Burt, R. S., Minor, M. J., & Alba, R. D. (1983). *Applied network analysis: A methodological introduction.* Beverly Hills, CA: Sage Publications.

Busch, P., & Fettke, P. (2011). Business process management under the microscope: The potential of social network analysis. In *Proceedings of System Sciences (HICSS).* IEEE.

Castilla, E. J., Hwang, H., Granovetter, E., & Granovetter, M. (2000). Social networks in Silicon Valley. In *The Silicon Valley edge: A habitat for innovation and entrepreneurship* (pp. 218–247). Academic Press.

Coleman, J. S. (1988). Social capital in the creation of human capital. *American Journal of Sociology, 94*, S95–S120. doi:10.1086/228943

Cross, R., Ehrlich, K., Dawson, R., & Helferich, J. (2008). Managing collaboration at the point of execution: Improving team effectiveness with a network perspective. *California Management Review, 50*(4), 74–98. doi:10.2307/41166457

Cummings, J. N., & Cross, R. (2003). Structural properties of work groups and their consequences for performance. *Social Networks, 25*, 197–210. doi:10.1016/S0378-8733(02)00049-7

Gabbay, S. M., & Zuckerman, E. W. (1998). Social capital and opportunity in corporate R&D: The contingent effect of contact density on mobility expectations. *Social Science Research, 27*, 189–217. doi:10.1006/ssre.1998.0620

Granovetter, M. S. (1983). The strength of weak ties: A network theory revisited. *Sociological Theory, 1*, 201–233. doi:10.2307/202051

Gulati, R., & Gargiulo, M. (1999). Where do interorganizational networks come from? *American Journal of Sociology, 104*(5), 1439–1493. doi:10.1086/210179

Hanneman, R. A., & Riddle, M. (2005). *Introduction to social network methods. Riverside, CA.* Riverside: University of California.

Heinze, T., & Bauer, G. (2007). Characterizing creative scientists in nano-S&T: Productivity, multidisciplinarity, and network brokerage in a longitudinal perspective. *Scientometrics, 3*, 811–830. doi:10.1007/s11192-007-0313-3

Katz, J. S., & Martin, B. R. (1997). What is research collaboration? *Research Policy, 26*, 1–18. doi:10.1016/S0048-7333(96)00917-1

Krackhardt, D. (1992). The strength of strong ties: The importance of philos in organizations. In N. Nohria, & R. Eccles (Eds.), *Networks and organizations: Structure, form, and action.* Boston, MA: Harvard Business School Press.

Kratzen, J. (2001). *Communication and performance: An empirical study in innovation teams.* Amsterdam: Tesla Thesis Publishers.

Laudel, G. (2001). Collaboration, creativity and rewards: Why and how scientists collaborate. *Int. J. Technology Management, 22*(7/8), 762–781.

Leenders, R. T. A., Van Engelen, J. M., & Kratzer, J. (2003). Virtuality, communication, and new product team creativity: A social network perspective. *Journal of Engineering and Technology Management, 20*(1), 69–92. doi:10.1016/S0923-4748(03)00005-5

Levine, J. M., & Moreland, R. L. (2004). Collaboration: The social context of theory development. *Personality and Social Psychology Review, 8*(2), 164–172. doi:10.1207/s15327957pspr0802_10 PMID:15223516

Liebeskind, J. P., Oliver, A. L., Zucker, L., & Brewer, M. (1996). Social networks, learning, and flexibility: Sourcing scientific knowledge in new biotechnology firms. *Organization Science, 7*(4), 428–443. doi:10.1287/orsc.7.4.428

Lowrie, A., & McKnight, P. J. (2004). Academic research networks: A key to enhancing scholarly standing. *European Management Journal, 22*(4), 345–360. doi:10.1016/j.emj.2004.06.011

Luo, J.-D. (2005). Social network structure and performance of improvement teams. *Int. J. Business Performance Management, 7*(2), 208–223. doi:10.1504/IJBPM.2005.006491

Melin, G. (2000). Pragmatism and self-organization: Research collaboration on the individual level. *Research Policy, 29*, 31–40. doi:10.1016/S0048-7333(99)00031-1

Moenaert, R. K., Caeldries, F., Lievens, A., & Wauters, E. (2000). Communication flows in international product innovation teams. *Journal of Product Innovation Management, 17*(5), 360–377. doi:10.1016/S0737-6782(00)00048-5

Oh, H., Chung, M. H., & Labianca, G. (2004). Group social capital and group effectiveness: The role of informal socializing ties. *Academy of Management Journal, 47*(6), 860–875. doi:10.2307/20159627

Oh, H., Labianca, G., & Chung, M. H. (2006). A multilevel model of group social capital. *Academy of Management Review*, *31*(3), 569–582. doi:10.5465/AMR.2006.21318918

Print, M., & Hattie, J. (1997). Measuring quality in universities: An approach to weighting research productivity. *Higher Education*, *33*, 453–469. doi:10.1023/A:1002956407943

Reagans, R., & McEvily, B. (2003). Network structure and knowledge transfer: The effects of cohesión and range. *Administrative Science Quarterly*, *48*, 240–267. doi:10.2307/3556658

Reagans, R., Zuckerman, E., & McEvily, B. (2004). How to make the team: Social networks vs. demography as criteria for designing effective teams. *Administrative Science Quarterly*, *49*(1), 101–133.

Reagans, R., & Zuckerman, E. W. (2001). Networks, diversity, and productivity: The social capital of corporate R&D teams. *Organization Science*, *12*(4), 502. doi:10.1287/orsc.12.4.502.10637

Rigby, J., & Edler, J. (2005). Peering inside research networks: Some observations on the effect of the intensity of collaboration on the variability of research quality. *Research Policy*, *34*, 784–794. doi:10.1016/j.respol.2005.02.004

Rumsey-Wairepo, A. (2006). *The association between co-authorship network structures and successful academic publishing among higher education scholars*. (Doctoral Dissertation). Department of Educational Leadership and Foundations, Brigham Young University, Salt Lake City, UT.

Shaw, M. (1964). *Comunication networks*. Advances in experimental social psychology New York: Academic Press.

Sparrowe, R. T., Liden, R. C., Wayne, S. J., & Kraimer, M. L. (2001). Social networks and the performance of individuals and groups. *Academy of Management Journal*, *44*(2), 316–325. doi:10.2307/3069458

Tichy, N. M., Tushman, M. L., & Fombrun, C. (1979). Social network analysis for organizations. *Academy of Management Review*, *4*(4), 507–519.

Tsai, W., & Wu, C. H. (2010). From The editors: Knowledge combination: A cocitation analysis. Academy of Management Journal, 53(3), 441–450.

van der Leij, M. J., & Goyal, S. (2006). Strong ties in a small world (No. 06-008/1). Tinbergen Institute.

Walker, G., Kogut, B., & Shan, W. (1997). Social capital, structural holes and the formation of an industry network. *Organization Science*, *8*(2), 109–125. doi:10.1287/orsc.8.2.109

Wasserman, S. (1994). *Social network analysis: Methods and applications* (Vol. 8). Cambridge, UK: Cambridge University Press. doi:10.1017/CBO9780511815478

Wolf, T., Schroter, A., Damian, D., Panjer, L. D., & Nguyen, T. H. (2009). Mining task-based social networks to explore collaboration in software teams. *IEEE Software*, *26*(1), 58–66. doi:10.1109/MS.2009.16

Wong, S. S. (2008). Task knowledge overlap and knowledge variety: The role of advice network structures and impact on group effectiveness. *Journal of Organizational Behavior*, *29*, 591–614. doi:10.1002/job.490

Yousefi-Nooraie, R., Akbari-Kamrani, M., Hanneman, R. A., & Etemadi, A. (2008). Association between co-authorship network and scientific productivity and impact indicators in academic medical research centers: A case study in Iran. *Health Research Policy and Systems, 6*(1), 9. doi:10.1186/1478-4505-6-9 PMID:18796149

KEY TERMS AND DEFINITIONS

Centrality: Centrality reflects the extent to which the team's network relations are concentrated on a small number of individuals rather than distributed equally among all the team members.

Density: Measures the proportion of relations among team members on the maximum number of relationships that may exist. The density takes values in a range from zero to one and the maximum value is determined by the number of actors in the network.

Network Efficiency: Refers to the level of redundancy between the team's direct contacts. A higher density between external contacts results in a higher level of redundancy of contacts. An efficient team's external network is characterized by the presence of structural holes.

Network Size: Number of nodes in the network.

Social Network Analysis: Is focused on discovery and analysis the patterning of people's interaction.

Social Network: A specific set of linkages among a defined set of persons, with the additional property that the characteristics of these linkages as a whole may be used to interpret the social behavior of the persons involved.

Chapter 18
Cloud Computing Decisions in Real Enterprises

Manuel Pérez-Cota
Universidade de Vigo, Spain

Ramiro Gonçalves
Universidade de Trás-os-Montes e Alto Douro, Portugal

Fernando Moreira
Universidade Portucalense Infante D. Henrique, Portugal

ABSTRACT

Money is one of the most important things for enterprises today. Computer Centers represent a large part of the total costs of enterprises, irrespective of their size. This chapter describes some (real) ways to convince enterprises to use Cloud computing in order to save money and obtain better returns from their computer (hard and soft) resources.

1. INTRODUCTION

Enterprises have grown over the years and have increased their computer resources in line with their needs accordingly. The current economic crisis is deeply affecting people and enterprises, and consequently some of them have chosen to optimize their resources while others have opted to share resources with others.

The word "Cloud," a collective term for a large number of developments and possibilities, is now in fashion after words such as "Grid" and "Virtualization." Petri (2010) states that this is not an invention but more of a "practical innovation." However, the term was first defined by Prof. Kenneth K. Chellapa in 1997 as "a computing paradigm where the boundaries of computing would be determined by economic rationale rather than technical limits." Wikipedia provides more details on how the name and use was defined: "Cloud computing is the use of computing resources (hardware and software) that are delivered as a service over a network (typically the Internet). The name comes from the use of a cloud-shaped symbol as an abstraction for the complex infrastructure it contains in system diagrams. Cloud computing

DOI: 10.4018/978-1-4666-5182-1.ch018

entrusts remote servers with a user's data, software and computation" (Wikipedia, 12/2012).

On the other hand, the NIST (National Institute of Standards and Technology www.nist.gov) provides a clearer definition: "Cloud computing is a model for enabling ubiquitous, convenient, on-demand network access to a shared pool of configurable computing resources (e.g., networks, servers, storage, applications, and services) that can be rapidly provisioned and released with minimal management effort or service provider interaction. This cloud model is composed of five essential characteristics, three service models, and four deployment models" (NIST, 2011).

When computer experts in enterprises were asked what they thought about Cloud Computing, the answers varied from "this is a new paradigm" to "this is a mix between Grid and Virtualization." Other answers were even more complex such as "this is when you are using infrastructures, platforms and applications that are not yours but they seem to be yours," that is like the scenario of your new vision. Reality is in this case about professionals. What about ordinary people, where the idea of computing is "any complex device that contains a microprocessor," and when you ask them about Cloud the answer normally is "everything is a Cloud nowadays, you never know where things are." It clarifies what is happening with this new paradigm. Things may be clear, but they are not clear enough, so it is necessary to explain what is happening from within. Documents such as "The top 5 truths behind what the Cloud is not " (CITRIX, 2012), can show, clearly, that our idea of computer people, for users and ordinary people, the term Cloud is far from clear.

This moves us to try to find out how people are using the Cloud nowadays, and as we can see in many documents (Infoworld (www.infoworld.com, 2008), Gartner Group (www.gartner.com, 2012), Microsoft (www.microsoft.com/nube, 2012), Oracle (www.oracle.com/Cloud-Compting, 2012) IBM (www.ibm.com/Computacion/Nube, 1012), Hewlett-Packard (www.hp.com/go/

Cloud, 2012), Spanish Cloud distributor (http://nube.es, 2012), Amazon (www.amazon.com, 2012) and others (the list today is probably longer)) the problem is, as we said in the previous paragraph, that definitions of Cloud are very different, and consequently how people use it is also very different. We define cloud as, "the use of services, platforms and applications using the net, taking all or some of them from the net." Therefore, almost everybody who is using a smartphone, a tablet, a PC or any other device plugged into the net and using services or applications offered or provided (and of course their platforms) in using the net.

In a conference held in Chapman University (Schmid College of Science and Technology), available in video from iTunes U (www.apple.com since 2011) and entitled "Cloud Computing: The Power of the Cloud" Dr. Jim Doti, Dr. Renee Bergeron, Dr. Menas Kafatos and Dr. Narinder Singh (among others), made a very interesting analysis about what people, academics, and enterprises think use, assume or opine about Cloud Computing. Even within academia, opinions that are varied, and some of them are very simple while others are complex. Nevertheless, they give a clear vision about the enterprise-academic view of the Cloud. It should probably be academic-enterprise because it was the academic world that invited the enterprise to show them the advantages of using the Cloud.

Kenneth and Jane Laudon, in their famous book "Management Information Systems" (Laudon, 2012), made a study on how to apply Cloud Computing in the new digital enterprises. They analyze, from almost all points of view, the application of computer technologies to make enterprises use digital systems. And, in their 12th edition, they also apply the use of the Cloud (explained in previous editions, but in greater detail in this one) as one of the most interesting parts of computers to be used in actual enterprises, that is, they analyze problems with using Cloud.

In this chapter, we present solutions for enterprises, beginning with an analysis of the computing models in order to clarify the idea of actual systems management. Then we reflect on the characteristics of the actual Cloud. The Cloud is alive, so we know that some things will change. Consequently we present ideas on how to be prepared for those changes. Next, we explain the different types of clouds trying to make clear what can be interesting for what kind of enterprise, showing the characteristics that any enterprise (or including a private user) should analyze carefully in order to benefit from the Cloud. Some questions that users should answer carefully are listed. We also talk about the types of Cloud users in order to show that the Cloud can offer a variety of solutions for different types of users.

2. COMPUTING MODELS

When talking about how enterprises use computers, it is important to specify the most important characteristics that need to be considered. Here the user can discover their model type, or the one that adapts best to his/her enterprise's computer model.

We agree with Renee Bergeron (Chapman University, www.apple.com, 2011) who divides computer models into 3 types:

- On Premise
- Managed Services
- Cloud Service Model

Basically, if you examine these, you will understand that they probably cover all the types needed to show how an enterprise can use computers. After studying these three types you can discover easily why one or another model is being applied for a concrete type of business.

We are going to analyze each of these models, focusing only on the five main ones and the different features of each one.

The OnPremise model can be called the classic one, because its use can range from individuals to very large enterprises (although large enterprises do not use this model nowadays), but it is usually the initial model for SMEs (Small and Medium-sized Enterprises).

If we analyze the characteristics of this model; to summarize, we can establish the following five key points:

- Clients own both the hardware and software
- Dedicated infrastructure designed for peak volume
- Fixed cost
- CAPEX intensive
- Client owns the risks

As we can see, everything is there to be controlled by the owner of systems in this model. From the beginning we say "Clients own hardware and software." This can be very interesting if you are a company that wants to have no risks with your infrastructure, but to be the owner of hardware and software means that you will need to control both of them. This is not an easy choice because the costs of computer hardware and software are very difficult to determine. Let's begin with "el economista" (www.eleconomista.es, 2013) which said that "spending on Data Center Systems will increase by 4.5% to 147,000 million dollars (±111,803 million euros), while corporate spending on software will grow by 6.4% to 296,000 million (±225,130 million euros)." If we analyze this information, it translates to ±15.97€ per global citizen in hardware and ±32.16€ per global citizen in software. Somebody might say that this is not that much money, but in fact it is. This means that enterprises are struggling to maintain their hardware and software infrastructures in a global recession. We should bear in mind that more than a half of the human population do not use computers (so we need to double these numbers) and if we analyzed these numbers they would increase much more.

Other important data taken from the Annual Report on European SMEs (Ecorys, 2012), said that the number of SMEs dedicated to information and communications decreased in 2012, but will increase in 2013. (This is a market problem in Europe because of crisis.)

Enterprises want to maintain their computer services. The principal idea for the On-Premise model is that every client maintains his/her own infrastructure. The reasons can be highlighted using the acronym SACC:

- Security
- Availability
- Confidence
- Control

Security, because the users own their equipment, they know the positive and the negative aspects of each, and when someone is isolated, in some way, your security levels are greater. Outsiders doing harm to one's systems would be much more difficult. This will be dealt with in more detail below because this also involves risks.

The system is always going to be available when needed; the software is going to be customized and, normally, by one's own IT team. Therefore, what is going to happen and when is known. Only very external events can interrupt service, such as electrical damage or natural disasters, but other events are almost impossible. Availability is almost always guaranteed.

Confidence normally depends on the IT team in very small computer centers. Everything usually works properly when there is confidence in the teams. The limits are known, but solutions are provided when needed and at a reasonable cost, because everybody knows the requirements and work in the same direction.

And finally, control in SMEs, this is normally carried out by the owners or by those responsible for every department (especially in the computer center). Nobody likes to take unnecessary risks. Everybody depends on the quality and availability

of their systems, so there is no room for errors. Everybody knows his/her position and everybody does his/her job the best way he/she knows.

The second key point is "dedicated infrastructure designed for peak volume," where the IT team (in the case of SMEs) are very aware of the limits of their hardware and software. They cannot take unnecessary risks. Normally, an IT team know that the proper functioning of the company depends largely on them. If the IT fails, the company fails.

The problem is how to maintain hardware and software in optimal conditions, because, when a company buys a computer or its accessories, they know that they are going to be obsolete very quickly. So it is necessary to get the best at the cheapest price. This is the same with software; what is more valuable, buying or designing? A thorough market study must be carried out "with the real necessities of enterprise" to know what kind of software is appropriate for the business. Buying means that what the market has to offer may have to be adapted. Creating and designing means that it needs to be done as quickly as possible. Sometimes the costs are unpredictable.

In general, we can say that, there are no problems with normal everyday work, but what happens when there are unexpected peak loads? The enterprise needs to be prepared. All the hardware and software will have to be adapted accordingly. There is no other choice if the company does not want to share. Many private projects have been presented to control the balance load in computer centers (the number of papers written about this is really extensive) (Pérez Cota, 2012), and there are formulas that help IT to maintain control, but it normally depends on good planning of your information systems (Laudon, 2011).

The Managed Services model basically is an evolution when enterprises discover that it is sometimes much better to share the risks of computer installations and the use of software, instead of going it alone. But this evolution it is not a free decision of the enterprises. It is usually the result of the increase in costs for services, software and hardware, and the difficulties of knowing what is "really" going to happen to one's own enterprise in the future.

At other times, the decision to manage services comes directly from analyzing what is best for the enterprise under specific market conditions. Some may say "it is a question of money." Therefore not only costs, but when there is an essential product change, a crisis or fluctuations in sales forecasts can force companies to take decisions to keep some computer infrastructures and share part of others.

As in the previous model, we can analyze the five key points of this one:

- Client and provider own hardware and software
- Dedicated infrastructure designed for peak volume
- Predictable monthly recurring fee
- Move from CAPEX to OPEX
- Client and provider share risks

Starting from the bottom both the client and the provider share risks because they both have their infrastructures in hardware and software (these include net resources). Let's look at a real enterprise in Vigo, a shipyard, we will call "Buques." "Buques" shipyard usually build medium sized boats, medium tankers and fishing boats. Their production is normally stable; they have a large number of permanent employees and about 15% temporary ones. Years before the crisis, three ships would be built simultaneously.

This company had their own computer center with very good net systems where they shared the resources they needed among all the departments of the company; twin frame servers that supported all the requirements of the company, with many small servers giving particular service to the special needs of specific departments.

The software they used for designing, calculating, producing the payroll, storing and other tasks were designed by their very good IT teams. But only some applications, such as MS Office and, in this case, specifically Excel and Word, were external, so outsourcing was not uncommon for them.

Surprisingly, and contrary to market logic, they received a very big order for ships that had to be built within a specific deadline. They decided that they needed to buy new servers and software because the capacity of the ones they had at that moment was not enough for such an important order. Another problem arose: although their CAD/CAM/CIM software was very good, it was outdated for these new challenges. Another secondary but very important problem was discovered: they did not want to share their unique shipping building technology for assembling, soldering and other specific processes.

"Buques" had to decide as soon as possible so as not to lose the order, and increase the future earnings. The future of shipyards was not very clear for companies in the south of Europe. They needed to take a quick and clear present decision so as to remain competitive in the future.

The company's IT team directors began contacting a few companies that could provide the infrastructure (hardware and software), while maintaining control of their own technologies. They succeeded and discovered that they could continue with their own proprietary technology but when necessary they could rely on the hardware and software rented from their providers.

That was one advantage; they had access to their critical and proprietary local resources and for more open software, they outsourced. The infrastructure (the service) was designed for peak situations. They had access to the hardware and software exactly when needed. When the contract finished they were sure that all their "things" were protected, but the work had been done.

A program of work and load were designed between the IT directors and the providers, and they knew almost exactly how much every minute of the external resources was going to cost. Training of the personnel was very easy because they used standard software for that part of the business, and the cost increase for net use was almost negligible compared to any other option.

The only thing that was more complex was the move from CAPEX to OPEX, but because the company needed to do so in other areas, it was not so difficult in the computer department. As defined in Wikipedia (www.wikipedia.org, 2012) "An operating expense, operating expenditure, operational expense, operational expenditure or OPEX is an ongoing cost for running a product, business, or system. Its counterpart, a capital expenditure (CAPEX), is the cost of developing or providing non-consumable parts for the product or system. For example, the purchase of a photocopier involves CAPEX, and the annual paper, toner, power and maintenance costs represent OPEX. For larger systems like businesses, OPEX may also include the cost of workers and facility expenses such as rent and utilities."

Some of their staff was temporary. They adapted the same philosophy for their IT services.

One of the most important things, as we said at the beginning, was risk sharing. If you get a good service provider, risks are really low. Nowadays, a wide variety of computer infrastructure hardware and software providers exist with very adjustable cost control. The difficulties are that users must define very clearly and with the highest level of accuracy. The client must define the schedule of hardware and software needs and how, where and when they are going to be available. The provider should define the possible changes that the client will need for his/her strategy in order to obtain the best results. Planning then, as in every computer activity, it is very important.

The rest of this document deals with the Cloud Service Model. To summarize, we can present this model using the same premises that we used for the other two models.

First some definitions of Cloud will be given in order to understand this complex but interesting model. This is not the future of computing, but rather the present.

Eric Knorr and Galen Gruman in Infoworld (www.infoworld.com, 2008), collected some definitions of Cloud, but the two paragraphs at the beginning of their paper give us a clear idea of what it is happening with the Cloud. They quote Ben Pring of Garter Group, "It's become the phrase du jour".... "The problem is that (as with Web 2.0) everyone seems to have a different definition. As a metaphor for the Internet, "the cloud" is a familiar cliché, but when combined with "computing," the meaning gets bigger and fuzzier. Some analysts and vendors define cloud computing narrowly as an audited version of utility computing: basically virtual servers available over the Internet. Others go very broad, arguing anything you consume outside the firewall is "in the cloud," including conventional outsourcing." As we can see, in those days the definitions were not very precise.

Nowadays, we prefer to use the NIST (National Institute of Standards and Technology) definition, which is closer and better identifies the current idea of the cloud, with some minimal adaptations over the years. We will summarize the document, pointing out the most important ideas, then we will analyze the five critical items as in the other two models.

According to NIST, U.S. Department of Commerce's definition (summarized from Peter Mell and Timothy Grance's (NIST, 2011) draft document) there are five fundamental characteristics, three fundamental service models and four deployment models:

- **Characteristics:**
  - On-demand self-service
  - Broad network access
  - Resource pooling
  - Rapid elasticity
  - Measured Service
- **Service Models:**
  - Cloud Software as a Service (Saas)
  - Cloud Platform as a Service (Paas)

- ○ Cloud Infrastructure as a Service (Iaas)
- **Deployment Models:**
  - ○ Private cloud
  - ○ Community cloud
  - ○ Public cloud
  - ○ Hybrid Cloud

As will be seen later on, nowadays only three deployment models are being considered: private, hybrid and Public.

We can analyze the cloud model even further based on these premises, in the same way as the other two models were analyzed. The five premises are:

- Provider owns hardware and software (Not recommended)
- Shared infrastructure (multi-tenant) provisioned based on usage
- Utility based pricing
- OPEX intensive
- Provider owns risks (Not recommended)

When we say that the provider owns hardware and software we are talking about the hardware and software that provide us the principal support in an enterprise (small, medium, big, private use). The problem is that (normally because of incorrect information) some people think that they do not need hardware and software of their own. Nothing further from reality. In fact, the basic communication is needed, that is a computer (smartphone, tablet, desk pc, etc.) with access to Internet, and a compatible browser (compatible with the software provider). This element or device is going to be the link between the user and the cloud; the interface will be the browser.

This link is very important and, as in our last model, we will explain the problems with a real example.

Tourism is one of the most important economic activities in Spain and Portugal (as in Mexico).

Some places are outside the best economic and touristic routes because of "communications."

Some investors in the north of Europe were very interested in creating a tourist route in the southwest of Galicia (Spain) where communications by road are good but complex (roads are not very wide and the amount of bends are indescribable, making people feel sick if they need to cover a great distance of many kilometers). But the very small towns connected by these roads are incredibly beautiful, with very friendly people, wonderful landscapes, good food, really comfortable lodgings. These investors were convinced enough to create that tourist route. They stipulated one condition: "their customers must have a very good Internet connection and perfect access to mobile telephony." The reason was that their customers would be business people who needed to "control their business independently of where they were."

The telephone and Internet companies wanted a usage guarantee in order to make the huge investment needed to maintain the infrastructures required for communication availability at the levels the investors wanted. In the end, there was no way of solving this problem (until 2013). Sometimes the question arises: Do people in isolated places have the same right to be connected as people in the big cities? The answer is yes, but there is no money to do so, and unfortunately this is the reality.

Can you imagine trying to use unplugged cloud services? Of course not. And this is not only a problem of connecting speed, it is also a problem of availability as well as the use of compatible devices. You need to use devices (browsers in your computer) that are fully compatible with the software and communication devices that you use from your provider in the cloud.

The providers own the principal IaaS, PaaS and Saas, but you as a user need to have the compatible devices and software to connect to them.

Another reason is the infrastructure that you share with them. The principal providers (IBM,

Microsoft, Amazon, Google, to name a few) can provide a wide range of capacities to share their resources, but cloud integrators in companies should study the comparative strengths and weaknesses of every distributor and their own very carefully.

This is not only a question of money but of the real use of devices contracted when you sign on. The balance, as we will explain later, depends on very well planned and scheduled service necessity. Peaks on loads should be clear for hardware and software services, because every minute you use the equipment (hardware and software) is invoiced; connections that are not used can still cost money.

Probably the best thing is to know one's own enterprise very well, prepare a plan and the needs, "talk" with a number of providers, read the small print in the contracts carefully (the most dangerous of all), talk with other users that have the same needs or that have been working with the providers.

This brings us to the third point, the utility based pricing. When we are using the SOA model (Software Oriented Architecture), we are talking about interoperable services. We are going to use many different services from many different providers (sometimes we do not have this sensation, because transparency is one of the great characteristics of the cloud).

How can we obtain utility? It can be obtained through the correct use of the services. If we calculate that we will need 10-minutes machine-time to carry out an activity, the final machine-time used should be that and no other. We will waste money if we do not control this. Sometimes a question arises: What if I can do the same with my systems? Sometimes you can, but that is why having a good plan and schedule is important. If you do so with real costs (not the ones you imagined but the ones that you obtain with real work) your probabilities of earning money using the cloud are very high.

When the provider was the owner of the risks, we thought that we would have no problems. The providers own the risks of "their things." You, as a user, must take care of "your things," and the

rule was initially called an extended version of SACC, but is now:

- Security
- Reliability
- Fastness
- Scalability
- Economy
- Independence

Security can be the most complex item to cover; we will expand on this, but state only a few essential comments here. Sometimes when we talk with our students or friends or family and we ask them why they put personal information on some social networks, they assure us that the information is secure on Internet. Only "their friends" are going to see the information. When you demonstrate how easy that information can be accessed by undesirable people, they seem incredulous and do not give credit to this problem.

The second question is hard for computer people to admit, but unfortunately true. Is the net and Internet 100% secure? Fortunately, almost everybody agrees here. No network is fully secure; you never know if your information is 100% safe. You can put all your effort towards keeping information secure, but it is impossible to reach 100%. The only way for your information to be 100% secure is to keep it locked in your brain (and some psychologists are not sure about that either).

It is very important to read the fine print in contracts regarding this aspect and the others (reliability, scalability, economy, independence) as well as some other facts that we will comment these in the next sections.

To summarize, the advance in computer organization and models have given us a variety of ways to use computers (stand alone, shared, multi-tenant, etc.), but the most important thing is to know our own business, our own work, our own enterprise.

In order to prepare plans to switch from one model to another, to combine them or to stay with the most comfortable and economical one for your business, remember that it is only a matter proper planning.

Open your mind and recognize your own weaknesses without fear of always making changes in order to progress.

3. VALUE OF CLOUD COMPUTING

We will now expand on every point about cloud computing, beginning with the values within this technology.

Supposing that your enterprise and your providers (observe that we are talking in the plural, only to say that we can have more than one) are following all the rules for your cloud to work well, we can say that the principal values that cloud computing provides are:

- Agility
- Utility
- Ubiquity

Agility is the ability to give instant access to the computing power and scale in accordance with your necessities.

Here we need to return to the previous section where we talked about planning. What do we need exactly to get all the computer power that is inside the cloud? We talked about browsers, we talked about the net, we talked about the resources in our company. All of them are necessary. We can demonstrate this with an example: is it possible to take advantage of all the power in a 275hp car if you use very thin wheels? Of course not! Likewise, how can you access all the power in the cloud if you have a bad Internet connection? It's not possible. The first thing we need is good bandwidth which will allow us to access all the services, software and infrastructures hidden in the cloud, a software compatible browser necessary to access them, and the characteristics of the client device .

The advantage for some companies is that old devices may only need a good Internet connection and a specific browser to access the important services that we may contract with all the available suppliers.

Utility means that you pay for the goods that you consume.

For new users this is becoming one of the most important reasons for entering the cloud. Why pay for licenses that you are not going to use? Why buy complete packages if you only need a small part of the software package? Why pay for terabytes that you do not need? Why pay for processors that you only use one or two days a year? We can ask hundreds of questions like these only to come to a final one: Why do I need to use cloud computing?

Let's look at an example of one of the ways that small enterprises are entering cloud computing here in the south of Europe. The problem principally comes from the use of integrated office packages: Microsoft Office from Microsoft Corporation, Open Office from Apache Software Foundation and Libre Office from the Document Foundation. The first one has a cost, and the other two are free. When a company uses them, the first problem is that you buy or download the full package to use only a small part of it. The second problem is that any update means that you need to update all the devices that are using that package, not only the small part of it that you are using. Third problem is the compatibility among them in any case, difficult when using a wide variety of devices. If you use the cloud and, for example, you are using Microsoft Office 365 or any other version of your software provider, you are going to use only the part that you need, and you are going to pay for that part and not the whole. The problem of updating is for the provider and not for the user. The contract should stipulate all the available characteristics and compatibilities very clearly as well as in those devices that you have within the contract terms. Many enterprises are shifting to this type of license and the cost is only a fraction of the normal fee.

Another important thing is the use of space. When you have your own space to save your information, you need backup disks. Control over them and over the information is your responsibility. In any case, you are paying for space that you will probably never use, but you need to buy it because the scales for today's disks are hundreds of gigabytes. If you rent space, the problem of a backup is for your provider's as well as the cost. This is another reason to move to the cloud.

Ubiquity means that something is accessible from anywhere, for anyone at any time. This says it all.

As we mentioned earlier, why pay for three licenses for an office package (one for home, one for the office, and another one for the tablet)? If I can use only one for all three, always the latest version, paying for only the part I need, accessing my information from anywhere, that's enough! Nevertheless, this contains the major risk of cloud computing. Let's carefully analyze the facts of this ubiquity.

Accessible from anywhere: as mentioned earlier, it is not easy to access Internet from some places. Some people may say this is not a problem in some countries. We can assure you that good Internet access is not as good as it should be in developed countries (look at the coverage maps of Internet providers in the main developed countries). We will give examples later on.

For some people this is a joke. In a test that we gave to our students at the University, we observed that more than 25% of them forgot their initial password to some applications (fortunately for them there were ways to recover it). In cloud, maintaining a good password policy is very important. Forgetting this rule can prevent access and isolate you from your cloud services.

At any time: it will clash with the same problem of the previous two. When you use the cloud,

having good discipline, a good connection, and a good browser (at least a compatible one with your cloud provider) are the three most important things.

It is also important to remember that when there are problems, it is necessary to evaluate the impact that those problems can have on our business. Stephen S. G. Lee and Veerappa Rajan published a document in IEEE Spectrum (ieeespectrum, 12/2012) called Understanding Cloud Failures. They proposed an increase in the types of failures that CSA indicates normally. The report by CSA (Cloud Security Alliance, cloudsecurityalliance. org, 2010) says that there are 7 causes of problems:

- Abuse and Nefarious Use of Cloud Computing
- Insecure Interfaces and APIs
- Malicious Insiders
- Shared Technology Issues
- Data Loss or Leakage
- Account of Service Hijacking
- Unknown risk Profile

In addition to Lee's and Rajan's proposal, they recommended five more categories:

- Hardware failure
- Natural disaster
- Service closure
- Cloud-related malware
- Inadequate infrastructure planning

They provide a very interesting graph that shows the increase in these problems. Responsible people should think when they are planning the use of cloud computing services. Their last proposal is "Inadequate infrastructure planning," and the first one is "hardware failure." We can see that these are more and less problems that we have been detecting in the use of computers not connected to the cloud. However, if they are, things can become worse.

Planning is basic to achieve success, as we have said repeatedly. Good planning is very important to make your cloud and your business work properly.

4. CLOUD TYPES AND USE

One of the most curious things about cloud computing is the types of clouds. We say "curious" because, except for very specific cases, in reality people and many enterprises are using different types of cloud for their own convenience.

Let's begin with the types and the changes for people to see that this is something alive, that it is moving and changing.

There are three cloud computing types:

- Public cloud
- Hybrid cloud
- Private cloud

You may recall that NIST (2011) proposed another type called community cloud which we need to delete.

Community cloud: The cloud infrastructure is shared by several organizations and supports a specific community that has shared concerns (e.g., mission, security requirements, policy, and compliance considerations). It may be managed by the organizations or a third party and may exist on premise or off premise.

In fact, this is considered within a private cloud nowadays and this is why we only refer to three types. Instead of the NIST definitions we are going to use the one modified by Howard Cohen in his article "Managing a Reliable Cloud Environment" (QuinStreet, Inc., 2012).

- **Public cloud:** The cloud infrastructure is owned by a cloud services provider who makes it available to the general public or a large industry group. SaaS is usually delivered from a public cloud.
- **Private cloud:** The cloud infrastructure is designed, developed, and deployed for use by one organization and it is usually located on premises owned by that organization. If the infrastructure is instead located at provider's data center, it is referred to as a Virtual Private Cloud or Remote Private Cloud.
- **Hybrid cloud:** Especially in the early period of transition and continuing in many environments where some specific types of data must remain on premises by regulatory or fiduciary requirements, some customers will construct systems that combine their on-premises resources with cloud services. NIST specifies that hybrid clouds are composed of two or more private or public clouds bound together by technology that enables data and application portability.

In order to explain all of these in depth, it is important to explain which services the cloud offers in order to analyze the questions that an enterprise or an individual should ask when planning whether or not to use the cloud (Figure 1).

We are going to look at the service models as they appear in Howard Cohen's paper, 'Managing a Reliable Cloud Environment' (QuinStreet, Inc., 2012):

Software-as-a-Service (Saas) in where the customer uses the provider's software that is running on a cloud infrastructure and is typically accessed using a Web browser.

Platform-as-a-Service (PaaS) allows the customer to develop his/her own applications using programming tools and utilities supported by the provider.

Infrastructure-as-a-Service (IaaS) provides processing, storage, networking and other fundamental computing resources. While customers

Figure 1. View of the whole structure

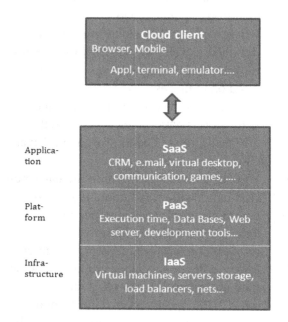

do not manage or control the underlying infrastructure, they do not manage operating systems, applications and data. We would like to add that the Integrator, the people responsible for doing this work, is very important.

Let's take a deeper look at what is really happening in cloud computing that makes all these things work.

In private clouds, what we have is a complex development of a network (intranet) within an enterprise or a group of enterprises that decide, because of costs, to share infrastructures, use of software; in short, they make better use of their computing resources, by sharing everything on their private cloud. This makes them adapt to the philosophy of the cloud to plan all the things that they want to do together. In fact, it is becoming a very successful way of using computers for large enterprises because they have transferred their on-premise computer systems to a group of private resource sharers.

Any of them will be able to share their plans and decisions with the rest. This means that all are going to have their own systems but shared with the rest of partners. Every system or software is going to be available everywhere in their private cloud. Trust is therefore of most importance.

Imagine automobile manufacturers, their associated companies and distributors. They are all interested in having the highest level of secrecy in the models they distribute. This means that they are going to do everything possible to maintain their patents, requirements, offers and distribution channels, in the strictest confidence. These automobile companies began sharing resources from "a central" computer center at the main factory to share characteristics, prices, models, distribution. They discovered that this allowed better distribution of their products and big cost savings (see Planning Systems in Laudon, 2011). More than that, they began to avoid manufacturing large series of cars without knowing the real response from the market. Why? Because they could obtain their distributors' opinion in real time and decide on production well in advance and therefore require less stock, as well as advice their partners to do the same. The next step was to share more information on what their customers liked, the defects they discovered, that is, real user information. All this information shared properly saves the industry a great deal of money. In the end, they decided to create their own closed private clouds, which were a complete success.

Is it possible for SMEs to do the same? Yes, it is possible. The problem is having the size to make the cloud economically viable. In general, SMEs in the south of Europe, do not have real computer centers as many of their services are outsourced, thus making it more difficult to create private clouds.

The option is to go directly to a public cloud. As we saw above, the public cloud is where the greater public (anyone from private users to big companies) can obtain services by renting the items they need. Of course, control comes from a different source. You are not the owner of your resources, your infrastructure or your services. You are going to share everything. In fact the public cloud is like a hotel; you can use the room, but you never know if you are going to use the same room or another the following evening (in a hotel you can sleep one day in one room, the next day in another and so on if desired). A private cloud is like having your own house, everything is yours, except the taxes you need to pay.

Returning to the public cloud, the biggest advantage is that the supply is very large. The bibliography below lists the major distributors of public clouds. If you look around, we are sure you can find many small or medium sized public cloud distributors that earn good money sharing resources and software (they get some of their cloud from bigger distributors). Many local customers are interested in saving money, but they also want to know who their distributor is (this is unlikely as behind the local distributor there is probably a big company).

What are the main features of this public cloud? As we deduced from the previous paragraph, this is a multi-tenant system, where, as in a hotel, you pay for the things you use. It is important to take great care in only planning your needs. Otherwise, you will pay for services that you are not going to use. As we have emphasized throughout this paper, it is very important to forecast, and make a plan, to have a deep understanding of your real situation, your real needs. This means asking what software you need from the cloud (this or that package or application, with these or those characteristics). What are the real services you require? Is it necessary to contract a 10 Mbits/sec line if we need only 5 Mbits/sec? (Imagine the real amount of information moving at those speeds, and you are doing business not playing games!). How much space do we need for our database, our Website, our applications? All this should be studied very carefully. Costs are not linear and the fine print in contracts is usually very difficult to understand for a novice, and often for experts as well. You are going to pay-per-use, but remember, plan your use.

The most complex part is probably access over the Web, using browsers. All of us know the classic browsers (Internet Explorer from Microsoft (www.microsoft.com), Mozilla Firefox from Mozilla (www.mozilla.org), Google Chrome from Google Inc. (www.google.com), Safari from Apple Inc. (www.apple.com), Opera from Opera Software ASA (www.opera.com) or Maxthon, the self-acclaimed cloud browser from Maxthon Ltd. (www.maxthon.com), etc.), and many others that are "not" as standard as these are. What we do not know are the problems that can arise when we are using browsers. A small example can illustrate this.

If you open the Web page of one of the authors (http://cuautla.uvigo.es/mpcota/) what you are going to discover is that Website has a W3C, xhtml 1.0 approval. In theory, the Website should appear the same way in all the browsers, but for an expert eye, the visualization is not exactly the same. In this example it is not a problem because any user can search for and find the information desired without any problem.

But if you are in the cloud, trying to use software and services that you rented, and you have only one browser in your computer, things can become more complex. Wrong visualization of graphical items, improper interface view, wrong colors, etc., can create a real problem for you because you cannot use the resources you need or those that you are paying for. You must consider browsers with 100% availability in your contracts.

And this point leads us to the next, security. Here security is at its lowest, and this must be studied carefully with your distributors to know the compatibilities or the possible problems that can arise when you use the cloud. Keep in mind that this is not a minor problem.

Time is another point to consider but we will look at this in "Questions time." We are not referring here only to the usage time. We are talking about the average time between failures or disruptions of connections and related issues. It is a complex problem.

The hybrid cloud is growing faster and faster because you can combine the characteristics of the two previously defined types. If you are an SME and you have some of your services well covered with your own systems or with the public cloud or public outsourcing, you have problems at peak times, but you do not want to increase your internal resources. The solution is clear: use the services that the cloud offers you without putting out your own cloud. The combination is always a good choice, but always remember to prepare a previous plan.

5. QUESTIONS TIME

Throughout this paper we have been talking about planning and preparing for changes in IT resources. There are some simple questions that must be asked in order to make a plan.

Before asking these questions, we are going to present some data that will give you an idea of how cloud computing is growing. We are not talking about the biggest countries; we are talking about our countries.

According to the Bankinter Foundation, in 2009 (the most recent reliable data on the crisis and provider misinformation should not be used) there were 3,350,000 companies in Spain (11,000 in Galicia in the northwest of Spain), 5,375 of which had more than 200 employees (only 10 in Galicia, and this was before the crisis). The important data is that 99.84% of these companies were SMEs. This may explain why we insist on some things in this paper.

We have a very high rate of access to Internet (96.2%) and mobile telephony (90.9%). This is very interesting for us, but speed is a problem. Even the telephone companies admit it is very slow.

If we analyze the Websites and their quality (a study is being done by the authors of this paper in the north of Portugal and the south of Galicia) we can see that only 60% of companies have their own Websites and the majority is only a simple page.

Another study from TNS WorldPanel from April 2008 to March 2009 states that two million Spanish people buy goods via Internet (mainly food and OTC drugs). This amounts to 13.4% of all homes, twice a year for an average of 65€ (sixty five euros). In Galicia this drops to 58€ (fifty-eight euros) and 1.4 times a year.

How can we convince people to adopt the use of Internet and the use of the cloud? We are going to provide pros and cons to be discussed, as we are going to see, in contradictory ways.

Initially, the main reason to move to the cloud is cost, but if the cost is not considered carefully it can backfire. All costs must be carefully studied to avoid surprises. The small print of any contract must be analyzed and a good spreadsheet can help to compute and evaluate everything. If you obtain more or less the same average between your actual systems and the one you can obtain using cloud, your option is your system. Cloud must be positively balanced. If it is not, better to remain with your own system.

Security importance. If the security of your information is a very important part of your business, and it can be very critical or dangerous or private, do not put them in cloud, at least not in the current cloud, this can change (with difficulties) in future.

The time to go to the market, cloud can really help, but the question is, what are the markets that you are interested in? When you publish a Website, anybody from anywhere can visit it. You should evaluate the consequences of this depending on the way you want to grow. Some people may think that this is not a problem but it is a big one if you do not properly analyze the inherent facts. Imagine that somebody from abroad wants to be a competitor in your own city, and you are a small furniture store, they know your information and from the Web they can prepare a way to destroy you. It depends on you to be prepared, not to be destroyed and win. As before, prepare a good plan.

The conclusion is that it is not only very important to build your business strategy but also your cloud strategy.

What are the six principal aspects that you must analyze in order to create your cloud strategy? Those that we presented above (security, reliability, fastness, scalability, economy and independence).

- Security means that information is saved and it is moved under the right conditions knowing that it will not be changed without authorization (violated).
- Reliability and availability mean that the system is available when it is needed.
- Fastness means that the systems respond within the acceptable time conditions (up and down loading).
- Scalability is enabling the use of the system that should grow or shrink based on the needs of the user.
- Economy means the use of the system should cost less than maintaining a proprietary system (on premise).
- Independence exists when the system in the cloud permits access to the users through any browser-based system.

To build this type of cloud we should ask some very specific questions. If it is done properly, success is not guaranteed but it will be easier. Here is a list of the main questions to be asked:

1. What kind of enterprise is it? An SME, a large company, or an individual?
2. What kind of software tools do I want to own?
   a. Are they critical ones?
   b. Were they created by my team and do they work well?
   c. Are they specific and can I access them in the cloud?
   d. Can I use some tools that exist in the cloud?
3. How can security affect my connections?
4. How are the providers offering me the use, storage, growth, peak loads, failures conditions?
5. What kind of guarantee do they offer me?
6. What is the average response time of these providers?
7. What is the average time between failures (that they offer)?

This is a very simple way to take the first decision, if we answer these questions properly, the rest, the full plan is going to be easier because it will depend on us and the proposition that we can make to providers, and in the end, the kind of relationship.

If we analyze each of these questions, we can see that it is important to analyze from an owner status and the status of owned computers to the status that can be offered by cloud providers, but these same questions can allow for a decision if it can be proposed for other users to create a private cloud among them.

The first question is crucial, and it forces me to decide the type of enterprise that I am because in this way I can discover whether my idea of my business is correct or whether I need revisit my plan and look at other ways of working.

The second one forces me to discover what the strengths and weaknesses of my business are. When a business does an internal audit, they discover that they have got a lot of underutilized resources and that, if they use them properly, they do not need to outsource. On the other hand, they may discover that the tools in the cloud are better and cheaper.

Connection security is a very important area. Remember the availability of service in some zones, not only due to natural communication problems but also to natural disasters, weather, overloads, and so on. This must be taken into account in zones where services or availability may be poor.

Providers are another headache for the user. There is no choice if there is only one provider.

However, nowadays there are several and their offers are interesting. Therefore, it is very important to have a complete proposal, and offers must be studied carefully without being afraid to ask questions. Every question may mean a possible problem avoided.

Providers can offer very good information without excess of data. We must ask for the warranty code. Oblige them to offer customer quality.

The two last questions seem to be the same but they are very different in meaning. The first one refers to the time they offer to provide a solution to some need that may arise suddenly in a concrete situation. This may be the result, for example, of one my customers sending me a file in a specific format that is not contemplated in my contract. My provider should be able to offer a solution within a short space of time, without my having to search another provider or do it by myself.

The second one refers to the period of time that they guarantee without failures. This is important in critical conditions. Assume that you have sufficient time to do the payroll, but a failure in your cloud connection delays this process. You may tell your team to work harder but you cannot tell them that they are not going to be paid because there is a problem with the system.

6. CONCLUSION

Cloud computing is the most modern way to make systems, software, platforms available for a wide range of the population and enterprises. Good planning of your cloud strategy can make an enterprise succeed or fail.

We have offered a brief account of the actual cloud world, with the advantages and disadvantages, the rules and caution that enterprises (SME, big, particular) should heed in order to be satisfied with the cloud.

The future is the present, it is moving all the time, and we must be prepared to move forward and make computers our tools for success.

REFERENCES

Amazon. (2013). *Anything digital, securely stored, available anywhere*. Retrieved from http://www.amazon.com/gp/feature.html?ie=UTF8&docId=1000796931&ref_=cd_lm_rd_fp

Apple. (2013). *Cloud computing: The power of cloud*. Retrieved from http://store.apple.com/es-edu

Bankinter. (2010). *The outlook for cloud computing in Spain (Cap. 6)*. Retrieved from http://www.fundacionbankinter.org/system/documents/7697/original/The_outlook_for_cloud_computing_in_Spain.pdf

Chen, J., Wang, Y., & Wang, X. (2012). On-demand security architecture for cloud computing. *Computer*, *45*(7), 73–78. doi:10.1109/MC.2012.120

CITRIX. (2012). *The top 5 truths behind what the cloud is not*. Retrieved from http://www.citrix.com/wsdm/restServe/skb/attachments/RDY7415/The%20top%205%20truths%20behind%20what%20the%20cloud%20is%20not.pdf

Erbes, J., Motahari Nezhad, H. R., & Graupner, S. (2012). The future of enterprise it in the cloud. *Computer*, *45*(5), 66–72. doi:10.1109/MC.2012.73

Google. (2013). *Tools for modern applications*. Retrieved from http://cloud.google.com

Gruman, G., & Knorr, E. (2008). *What cloud computing really means*. San Francisco, CA: InfoWorld.

HP. (2013). *Meet the cloud that enterprises rely on*. Retrieved from http://www.hp.com/go/Cloud

IBM. (2013). *Server and cloud platform*. Retrieved from http://www.microsoft.com/es-es/server-cloud/default.aspx#fbid=yFhqG_9NKmPe

IEEE. (2013). *IEEE cloud computing*. Retrieved from http://cloudcomputing.ieee.org

Infoworld. (2013). *Cloud computing*. Retrieved from http://www.infoworld.com/d/cloud-computing

Laudon, K., & Traver, C. G. (2012). *E-commerce 2013*. Upper Saddle River, NJ: Pearson Higher Ed.

Laudon, K. C., & Laudon, J. P. (2012). *Management information systems: Managing the digital firm*. London, UK: Pearson.

Mell, P., & Grance, T. (2011). The NIST definition of cloud computing (draft). *NIST Special Publication*, *800*(145), 7.

Microsoft. (2013). *Cloud computing*. Retrieved from http://www.microsoft.com/spain/enterprise/soluciones-microsoft/soluciones-de.aspx?tema=cloud-computing

Mozilla. (2013). *De todos para todos*. Retrieved from http://www.mozilla.org

Newman, A., & Cohen, H. (2012). *Cloud computing: Discover the skills that power the cloud*. Foster City, CA: QuinStreet Inc. doi:10.1109/PST.2012.6297945

nube.es. (2013). *Nube: Cloud computing*. Retrieved from http://nube.es

Oracle. (2013). *Oracle cloud solutions*. Retrieved from http://www.oracle.com/webapps/dialogue/ns/dlgwelcome.jsp?p_ext=Y&p_dlg_id=13613910&src=7665776&Act=78&sckw=WWMK12062962MPP019

Pérez Cota, M. (2012). *Cloud computing and planning of information systems*. Mikkeli-Polytechnic. Retrieved from http://www2.mamk.fi/singlenews-info.asp?id=505&menu_id=64&selected=64&companyId=1&show=2

Petri, G. (2010). *Shedding light on cloud computing*. New York, NY: The Cloud Academy.

Pezzini, M., & Lheureux, B. J. (2011). *Integration platform as a service: moving integration to the cloud*. Stanford, CT: Gartner.

Tyndall, I. (2010). *The end of corporate IT? Cloud computing literature review*. New York, NY: Ian Tyndall.

VMWare. (2013). *Cloud computing*. Retrieved from http://www.vmware.com/es/cloud-computing/

Wikipedia. (2013). *Cloud computing*. Retrieved from http://en.wikipedia.org/wiki/Cloud_computing

Worldpanel. (2009). *Informe TNS*. Retrieved from http://www.kantarworldpanel.com/es

KEY TERMS AND DEFINITIONS

Cloud Computing: Cloud computing is a model for enabling ubiquitous, convenient, on-demand network access to a shared pool of configurable computing resources (e.g., networks, servers, storage, applications, and services) that can be rapidly provisioned and released with minimal management effort or service provider interaction. (NIST, 2011).

Evaluation: To think carefully about something before making a judgment about its value, importance, or quality (MacMillan, 2013).

Grid Computing: Grid computing is the collection of computer resources from multiple locations to reach a common goal (Wikipedia, 2013).

IT: Information Technology (IT) is the application of computers and telecommunications equipment to store, retrieve, transmit and manipulate data, often in the context of a business or other enterprise. The term is commonly used as a synonym for computers and computer networks (Wikipedia, 2013).

Services: To do work or to perform duties for a person, an organization, or a community (MacMillan, 2013).

Virtualization: Virtualization adds a low-level software layer that allows multiple, even different operating systems and applications to run simultaneously on a host (NIST, 2010).

Compilation of References

Aaen, I. (2003). Software process improvement: Blueprints versus recipes. *IEEE Software, 20*(5), 86–93. doi:10.1109/MS.2003.1231159

Abecker, A., Bernardi, A., Hinkelmann, K., Kuhn, O., & Sintek, M. (1998). Toward a technology for organizational memories. *IEEE Intelligent Systems and their Applications, 13*(3), 40–48.

Abrahamsson, P. (2007). Agile software development of mobile information systems. In *Proceedings of the 19th International Conference on Advanced Information Systems Engineering* (CAiSE) (LNCS), (vol. 4495, pp. 1-4). Trondheim, Norway: Springer-Verlag.

Abrahamsson, P., Warsta, J., Siponen, M. T., & Ronkainen, J. (2003). New directions on agile methods: A comparative analysis. In *Proceedings of the 25th International Conference on Software Engineering* (ICSE), (pp. 244-254). Portland, OR: IEEE Computer Society.

Acuña, S. T., Gómez, M., & Juristo, N. (2008). How do personality, team processes and task characteristics relate to job satisfaction and software quality? *Information and Software Technology, 51*(3), 627–639. doi:10.1016/j.infsof.2008.08.006

AENOR. (2000). Sistemas de gestión de calidad[). Norma Española.]. *ISO, 9001*, 2000.

Agile Alliance. (2001). *Manifesto for agile software development*. Retrieved from http://agilemanifesto.org

Ahlgren, R. (2007). Facilitating design knowledge management by tailoring software patterns to organizational roles.[AMCIS.]. *Proceedings of AMCIS, 07*, 463–463.

Ahmed, F., Capretz, L. Z., & Campbell, P. (2012). Evaluating the demand for soft skills in software development. *IT Professional, 14*(1), 44–49. doi:10.1109/MITP.2012.7 PMID:23397361

Ahuja, G. (2000). Collaboration networks, structural holes, and innovation: A longitudinal study. *Administrative Science Quarterly, 23*(2), 425–455. doi:10.2307/2667105

Ahuja, M. K., & Carley, K. M. (1999). Network structure in virtual organizations. *Organization Science, 10*(6), 741–757. doi:10.1287/orsc.10.6.741

Akbar, R., Hassan, M. F., & Abdullah, A. (2011). A review of prominent work on agile processes software process improvement and process tailoring practices. In J. M. Zain, W. M. bt Wan Mohd, & E. El-Qawasmeh (Eds.), Software engineering and computer systems (Vol. 181, pp. 571–585). Berlin: Springer.

Alavi, M., & Leidner, D. E. (1999). Knowledge management systems: Issues, challenges, and benefits. *Commun. AIS, 1*(2).

Alavi, M., & Keen, P. G. W. (1989). Business teams in an information age. *The Information Society, 6*(4), 179–195. doi:10.1080/01972243.1989.9960081

Alavi, M., & Leidner, D. (2001). Knowledge management and knowledge management systems: Conceptual foundations and research issues. *MIS Quaterly, 25*(1), 107–136. doi:10.2307/3250961

Albert, C., & Brownsword, L. (2009). *Evolutionary process for integrating COTS-based systems (EPIC): An overview (CMU/SEI-20030TR-009)*. Pittsburgh, PA: Software Engineering Institute, Carnegie Mellon University.

Alexandrou, M. (n.d.). *Systems development life cycle (SDLC)*. Retrieved December 10, 2013, from http://www.mariosalexandrou.com/methodologies/systems-development-life-cycle.asp

Ali Babar, M., & Gorton, I. (2004). Comparison of scenario-based software architecture evaluation methods. In *Proceedings of the Asia-Pacific Software Engineering Conference* (pp. 600-607). IEEE Computer Society.

Allenby, K., Bardill, M., Burton, S., Buttle, D., Hutchesson, S., & McDermid, J. ... Stephenson, A. (2001). A family-oriented software development process for engine controllers. In *Proceedings of the Third International Conference on Product Focused Software Process Improvement* (pp. 210-226). Berlin: Springer.

Allen, T. J. (1977). *Managing the flow of technology*. Boston: Halliday Lithograph.

Allison, I., & Merali, Y. (2007). Software process improvement as emergent change: A structurational analysis. *Information and Software Technology*, *49*(6), 668–681. doi:10.1016/j.infsof.2007.02.003

Amazon. (2013). *Anything digital, securely stored, available anywhere*. Retrieved from http://www.amazon.com/gp/feature.html?ie=UTF8&docId=1000796931&ref_=cd_lm_rd_fp

Ambler, S. W. (2002). *Agile modeling*. New York, NY: John Wiley and Sons.

Amengual, E., & Mas, A. (2007). Software process improvement in small companies: An experience. In *Proceedings of 14th European Software Process Improvement Conference*. Springer.

American Psychiatric Association. (1987). *Diagnostic and statistical manual of mental disorders-III-R*. Arlington, VA: American Psychiatric Association.

Ancona, D. G. (1990). Outward bound: Strategies for team survival in an organization. *Academy of Management Journal*, *33*(2), 334–365. doi:10.2307/256328

Andelfinger, U., Heijstek, A., & Kirwan, P. (2009). A unified process improvement approach for multi-model improvement environments. *NEWS AT SEI*. Software Engineering Institute (SEI). Retrieved December 2008 from http://www.sei.cmu.edu/library/abstracts/news-at-sei/feature1200604.cfm

Anderson, D., Concas, G., Lunesu, M. I., Marchesi, M., & Zhang, H. (2012). A comparative study of scrum and Kanban approaches on a real case study using simulation. In *Proceedings of the 13th International Conference on Agile Software Development* (XP) (LNBIP), (vol. 111, pp. 123-137). Malmö, Sweden: Springer-Verlag.

Anderson, D. (2010). *Kanban: Successful evolutionary change for your technology business*. Sequim, WA: Blue Hole Press.

Andersson, C., & Runeson, P. (2007). A spiral process model for case studies on software quality monitoring—Method and metrics. *Software Process Improvement and Practice*, *12*(2), 125–140. doi:10.1002/spip.311

Apple. (2013). *Cloud computing: The power of cloud*. Retrieved from http://store.apple.com/es-edu

Aral, S., & Alstyne, M. V. (2007). Network structure & information advantage. In *Proceedings of the Academy of Management Conference*. Philadelphia, PA: Academy of Management.

Argote, L., & McEvily, B. et al. (2003). Managing knowledge in organizations: An integrative framework and review of emerging themes. *Management Science*, *49*(4), 571–582. doi:10.1287/mnsc.49.4.571.14424

Asociación Española de Normalización y Certificación AENOR. (1996). *ISO 9000*. Asociación Española de Normalización y Certificación.

Assimakopoulos, D., & Yan, J. (2006). Sources of knowledge acquisition for Chinese software engineers. *R & D Management*, *36*(1), 97–106. doi:10.1111/j.1467-9310.2005.00418.x

Bachmann, F., Bass, L., Chastek, G., Donohoe, P., & Peruzzi, F. (2000). *The architecture based design method* (Technical Report CMU/SEI-2000-TR-001). Pittsburgh, PA: Software Engineering Institute, Carnegie Mellon University.

Baker, E., & Fisher, M. (2007). *Basic principles and concepts for achieving quality*. Software Engineering Institute.

Baldwin, T. T., Bedell, M. D., & Johnson, J. L. (1997). The social fabric of a team-based MBA program: Network effects on student satisfaction and performance. *Academy of Management Journal*, *40*(6), 1369–1397. doi:10.2307/257037

Balkundi, P., & Harrison, D. A. (2006). Ties, leaders, and time in teams: Strong inference about network structure's effects on team viability and performance. *Academy of Management Journal*, *49*(1), 49–68. doi:10.5465/AMJ.2006.20785500

Balkundi, P., Kilduff, M., Barsness, Z. I., & Michael, J. H. (2007). Demographic antecedents and performance consequences of structural holes in work teams. *Journal of Organizational Behavior*, *28*(2), 241–260. doi:10.1002/job.428

Balla, K. (2001). *The complex quality world, developing quality management systems for software companies.* Eindhoven, The Netherlands: University of Technology Eindhoven.

Bankinter. (2010). *The outlook for cloud computing in Spain (Cap. 6)*. Retrieved from http://www.fundacion-bankinter.org/system/documents/7697/original/The_outlook_for_cloud_computing_in_Spain.pdf

Barbacci, M., Ellison, R. J., Lattanze, A. J., Stafford, J. A., Weinstock, C. B., & Wood, W. G. (2003). *Quality attribute workshops (QAWs)* (Technical Report CMU/SEI-2003-TR-016). Pittsburgh, PA: Software Engineering Institute, Carnegie Mellon University.

Basha, S., & Ponnurangam, D. (2010). Analysis of empirical software effort estimation models. *International Journal of Computer Science and Information Security*, *7*(3), 68–77.

Basili, V. R., & Seaman, C. (2002). The experience factory organization. *IEEE Software*, *19*(3), 30–31.

Bass, L., Clements, P., & Kazman, R. (2012). *Software architecture in practice* (3rd ed.). Reading, MA: Addison-Wesley Professional.

Bavelas, A. (1950). Communication patterns in task-oriented groups. *The Journal of the Acoustical Society of America*, *22*(6). doi:10.1121/1.1906679

Bechhofer, S., van Harmelen, F., Hendler, J., Horrocks, I., McGuinness, D. L., Patel-Schneider, P. F., & Stein, L. A. (2004). *OWL web ontology language reference-website*. Retrieved from http://www.w3.org/TR/2004/REC-owl-ref-20040210/

Beck, K. (1999). *Extreme programming explained: Embrace change*. Boston, MA: Addison-Wesley Professional.

Beck, K. (2003). *Test driven development: By example.* Boston: Addison Wesley Professional.

Beck, K., & Fowler, M. (2001). *Planning extreme programming*. Reading, MA: Addison-Wesley Professional.

Beijerse, R. U. (2000). Knowledge management in small and medium-sized companies: Knowledge management for entrepreneurs. *Journal of Knowledge Management*, *4*(2), 162–179. doi:10.1108/13673270010372297

Belbin, R. M. (1981). *Management teams: Why they succeed of fail.* Oxford, UK: Butterworth Heinemann.

Belbin, R. M. (1993). *Team roles at work.* Oxford, UK: Butterworth Heinemann.

Bengtsson, P., Lassing, N., Bosch, J., & Vliet, H. (2000). *Analyzing software architectures for modifiability* (Technical Report HK-R-RES–00/11-SE). Högskolan Karlskrona/Ronneby.

Bernard, T., Gallagher, B., Bate, R. A., & Wilson, H. (2005). *CMMI acquisition module, version 1.1 software engineering institute* (Technical Report CMU/SEI-2005-TR-011). Pittsburgh, PA: Carnegie Mellon.

Bertini, M. T., & Tallineau, Y. (1974). Le Cobol structuré, un modèle de programmation. Paris: Ed.s d'informatique (in French).

Bhuta, J., Boehm, B., & Meyers, S. (2005). Process elements: Components of software process architectures. In *Proceedings of the 2005 International Conference on Unifying the Software Process Spectrum* (pp. 332–346). Berlin: Springer-Verlag. doi:10.1007/11608035_28

Biffl, S., Winkler, D., Höhn, R., & Wetzel, H. (2006). Software process improvement in Europe: Potential of the new V-modell XT and research issues practice section. *Software Process Improvement and Practice*, *11*(3), 229–238. doi:10.1002/spip.266

Bland, C. J., Center, B. A., Finstad, D. A., Risbey, K. R., & Staples, J. G. (2005). A theoretical, practical, predictive model of faculty and department research productivity. *Academic Medicine*, *80*(3), 225–237. doi:10.1097/00001888-200503000-00006 PMID:15734804

Bodea, C. (2005). Agile software project management methodologies: The agile approach. *Ecological Informatics*, *5*(4), 27–31.

Boehm, B. (2005). *The future of software and systems engineering processes* (Technical Report USC-CSE-TR-507). Los Angeles, CA: University of Southern California.

Boehm, B., & Wolf, S. (1996). An open architecture for software process asset reuse. In *Proceedings of Software Process Workshop,* (pp. 2-4). IEEE.

Boehm, B. (1988). A spiral model of software development and enhancement. *Computer, 21*(5), 61–72. doi:10.1109/2.59

Boehm, B. W., Madachy, R., & Steece, B. (2000). *Software cost estimation with Cocomo II with Cdrom.* Upper Saddle River, NJ: Prentice Hall PTR.

Boehm, B., Egyed, A., Kwan, J., Port, D., Shah, A., & Madachy, R. (1998). Using the WinWin spiral model: A case study. *Computer, 31*(7), 33–44. doi:10.1109/2.689675

Borgatti, S. P. (1997). Structural holes: Unpacking Burt's redundancy measures. *Connections, 20*(1), 35–38.

Borgatti, S. P., & Foster, P. C. (2003). The network paradigm in organizational research: A review and topology. *Journal of Management, 29*(6), 991–1013.

Borgatti, S. P., Jones, C., & Everett, M. G. (1998). Network measures of social capital. *Connections, 21*(2), 27–36.

Borsoi, B. T. (2008). *Arquitetura de processo aplicada na integraçaõ de fábricas de software.* (Doctoral dissertation, Ph. D Thesis). Escola Politécnica da Universidade de Sao Paulo, Sao Paulo, Brazil.

Borsoi, B. T., & Becerra, J. L. R. (2008). A method to define an object oriented software process architecture. In *Proceedings of Software Engineering* (pp. 650–655). IEEE.

Bozeman, B., & Lee, S. (2005). The impact of research collaboration on scientific productivity. *Social Studies of Science, 35*(5), 673–702. doi:10.1177/0306312705052359

Brass, D. J., Galaskiewicz, J., Greve, H. R., & Tsai, W. (2004). Taking stock of networks and organizations: A multilevel perspective. *Academy of Management Journal, 47*(6), 795–817. doi:10.2307/20159624

Brickley, D., & Guha, R. (2002). *RDF vocabulary description language 1.0: RDF schema.* Retrieved from http://www.w3.org/TR/2002/WD-rdf-schema-20021112/

Brotbeck, G., Miller, T., & Statz, J. (1999). A survey of current best practices and utilization of standards in the public and private sectors. *TeraQuest Metrics, Inc, 9*, 15-14. Retrieved November 2, 2012 from https://sw.thecsiac.com/topics/BestPractices/SurveyofBP.pdf

Burke, G. D., & Howard, W. H. (2005). Knowledge management and process improvement: A union of two disciplines. *CrossTalk. The Journal of Defense Software Engineering, 18*(6), 28.

Burt, R. S. (1992). *Structural holes: The social structure of competition.* Cambridge, MA: Harvard University Press.

Burt, R. S. (2001). Structural holes versus network closure as social capital. In N. Lin, K. Cook, & R. S. Burt (Eds.), *Social capital: Theory and research.* New York: Aldine de Gruyter.

Burt, R. S. (2004). Structural holes and good ideas. *American Journal of Sociology, 110*(2), 349–399. doi:10.1086/421787

Burt, R. S. (2007). Seconhand brokerage: Evidence on the importance of local structure for managers, bankers, and analysts. *Academy of Management Journal, 50*(1), 119–148. doi:10.5465/AMJ.2007.24162082

Burt, R. S., Minor, M. J., & Alba, R. D. (1983). *Applied network analysis: A methodological introduction.* Beverly Hills, CA: Sage Publications.

Burt, R., & Ronchi, D. (2007). Teaching executives to see social capital: Results from a Weld experiment. *Social Science Research, 36*, 1156–1183. doi:10.1016/j.ssresearch.2006.09.005

Buschmann, F., Henney, K., & Schmidt, D. (2007). Pattern-oriented software architecture: Vol. 4. *A pattern language for distributed computing.* Chichester, UK: Wiley.

Busch, P., & Fettke, P. (2011). Business process management under the microscope: The potential of social network analysis. In *Proceedings of System Sciences (HICSS).* IEEE.

Calvache, C. J. P., Pino, F. J., García, F., & Piattini, M. (2009). Homogenization of models to support multi-model processes in improvement environments. In *Proceedings of ICSOFT* (pp. 151–156). ICSOFT.

Calvo-Manzano Villalón, J. A., Agustín, G. C., Hurtado, G. G., & San Feliu Gilabert, T. (2009). State of the art for risk management in software acquisition. *ACM SIGSOFT Software Engineering Notes*, *34*(4), 1–10. doi:10.1145/1543405.1543426

Calvo-Manzano, J. A., Cuevas, G., García, I., San Feliú, T., Serrano, A., & Arcilla, M. … Ruiz de Ojeda, F. (2005). Experiences of Spanish public administration in requirements management and acquisition management processes. In *Proceedings of the Fourth International Conference on Information Research and Applications.* Sofia, Bulgaria: FOI Commerce.

Calvo-Manzano, J. A., Cuevas, G., Gómez, G., Mejia, J., Muñoz, M., & San Feliu, T. (2012). Methodology for process improvement through basic components and focusing on the resistance to change. *Journal of Software Evolution and Process*, *24*(5), 511–523. doi:10.1002/smr.505

Calvo-Manzano, J. A., Cuevas, G., & San Feliu, T. (2008). A process asset library to support software process improvement in small settings. In *Proceedings of EuroSPI 2008, CCIS 16* (pp. 25–35). Berlin: Springer-Verlag.

Capell, P. (2004). *Benefits of improvement efforts* (Special Report CMU/SEI-2004-SR-010). Pittsburgh, PA: Software Engineering Institute (SEI), Carnegie Mellon University.

Capretz, L. Z., & Ahmed, F. (2010). Making sense of software development and personality types. *IT Professional*, *12*(1), 6–13. doi:10.1109/MITP.2010.33

Carleton, A. (2009). *CMMI impact.* Pittsburgh, PA: Software Engineering Institute. Retrieved from http://www.sei.cmu.edu/library/assets/cmmiimpact-jac-eg.pdf

Carr, D. C., Dandekar, A., & Perry, D. E. (1995). Experiments in process interface descriptions, visualizations and analyses. In *Software process technology* (pp. 119–137). Berlin: Springer. doi:10.1007/3-540-59205-9_48

Carr, M. J., Konda, S. L., Monarch, I., Ulrich, F. C. A., & Walker, C. F. (1993). *Taxonomy-based risk identification.* Software Engineering Institute.

Castilla, E. J., Hwang, H., Granovetter, E., & Granovetter, M. (2000). Social networks in Silicon Valley. In *The Silicon Valley edge: A habitat for innovation and entrepreneurship* (pp. 218–247). Academic Press.

Causevic, A., Krasteva, I., Land, R., Sajeev, A. S. M., & Sundmark, D. (2009). *An industrial survey on software process practices, preferences and methods.* Malardalen University.

Cervantes, H., Martinez, I., Castillo, J., & Montes de Oca, C. (2010). Introducing software architecture development methods into a TSP-based development company. In *Proceedings of SEI Architecture Technology User Network (SATURN 2010) Conference.* Pittsburgh, PA: Software Engineering Institute, Carnegie Mellon University.

Cervantes, H., Velasco-Elizondo, P., & Kazman, R. (2013). A principled way of using frameworks in architectural design. *IEEE Software*, *30*(2), 46–53. doi:10.1109/MS.2012.175

Chen, J., Wang, Y., & Wang, X. (2012). On-demand security architecture for cloud computing. *Computer*, *45*(7), 73–78. doi:10.1109/MC.2012.120

Chidamber, S. R., & Kemerer, C. F. (1994). A metrics suite for object oriented design. *IEEE Transactions on Software Engineering*, *20*(6), 476–493. doi:10.1109/32.295895

Chrissis, M. B., Konrad, M., & Shrum, S. (2010). *CMMi for development: Guidelines for process integration and product improvement* (3rd ed.). Reading, MA: Addison-Wesley Professional.

CITRIX. (2012). *The top 5 truths behind what the cloud is not.* Retrieved from http://www.citrix.com/wsdm/restServe/skb/attachments/RDY7415/The%20top%205%20truths%20behind%20what%20the%20cloud%20is%20not.pdf

Clarke, P., & O'Connor, R. V. (2012). The influence of SPI on business success in software SMEs: An empirical study. *Journal of Systems and Software*, *85*(10), 2356–2367. doi:10.1016/j.jss.2012.05.024

Clements, P. (2000). *Active reviews for intermediate designs* (Technical Report CMU/SEI-2000-TN-009). Pittsburgh, PA: Software Engineering Institute, Carnegie Mellon University.

Clements, P., Bachmann, F., Bass, L., Garlan, D., Ivers, J., Reed, L., & Nord, R. (2011). *Documenting software architectures: Views and beyond* (2nd ed.). Reading, MA: Addison-Wesley Professional.

Clements, P., Kazman, R., & Klein, M. (2002). *Evaluating software architectures: Methods and case studies.* Reading, MA: Addison-Wesley Professional.

Cloninger, C. R., Bayon, C., & Svrakic, D. M. (1998). Measurement of temperament and character in mood disorders: A model of fundamental states as personality types. *Journal of Affective Disorders, 51*(1), 21–32. doi:10.1016/S0165-0327(98)00153-0 PMID:9879800

CMMI Institute. (2013). *Maturity profile reports.* Pittsburgh, PA: CMMI Institute. Retrieved from http://cmmi-institute.com/assets/presentations/2013MarCMMI.pdf

CMMI Product Team. (2010). *CMMI for development, version 1.3.* Retrieved from http://resources.sei.cmu.edu/asset_files/TechnicalReport/2010_005_001_15287.pdf

CMMI Working Group. (2009). The economics of CMMI®. *NDIA System Engineering Division, Software Engineering Institute, 1,* 9-21. Retrieved from http://www.sei.cmu.edu/library/assets/Economics%20of%20CMMI.pdf

Coad, P., LeFebvre, E., & DeLuca, J. (1999). Feature-driven development. *Java Modeling in Color with UML,* 182-203.

Cockburn, A. (2001). *Agile software development.* Reading, MA: Addison Wesley Longman.

Cohn, M. (2004). *User stories applied: For agile software development.* Reading, MA: Addison-Wesley Professional.

Cohn, M. (2005). *Agile estimating and planning.* Englewood Cliffs, NJ: Prentice Hall.

Coleman, G. (2005). An empirical study of software process in practice. In *Proceedings of the 38th Hawaii International Conference on System Sciences.* IEEE Computer Society.

Coleman, J. S. (1988). Social capital in the creation of human capital. *American Journal of Sociology, 94,* S95–S120. doi:10.1086/228943

Colomo-Palacios, R., Casado-Lumbreras, C., Soto-Acosta, P., & García-Crespo, A. (2011). Using the affect grid to measure emotions in software requirements engineering. *Journal of Universal Computer Science, 17*(9), 1281–1298.

Colomo-Palacios, R., Casado-Lumbreras, C., Soto-Acosta, P., García-Peñalvo, F. J., & Tovar-Caro, E. (2013). Competence gaps in software personnel: A multi-organizational study. *Computers in Human Behavior, 29*(2), 456–461. doi:10.1016/j.chb.2012.04.021

Conradi, H., & Fuggetta, A. (2002). Improving software process improvement. *IEEE Software, 19*(4), 92–99. doi:10.1109/MS.2002.1020295

Cooper, J. A., & Fisher, M. (2002). *Software acquisition capability maturity model version 1.03 (CMU/SEI-2002-TR-010).* Pittsburgh, PA: Software Engineering Institute Carnegie Mellon.

Cottmeyer, M. (2011). *The real reason we estimate.* Retrieved December 2013 from http://www.leadingagile.com/2011/09/the-real-reason-we-estimate/

Crnkovic, I., Larsson, S., & Chaudron, M. (2006). Component-based development process and component lifecycle. In *Proceedings of the International Conference on Software Engineering Advances* (pp. 44-44). IEEE.

Cross, R., Ehrlich, K., Dawson, R., & Helferich, J. (2008). Managing collaboration at the point of execution: Improving team effectiveness with a network perspective. *California Management Review, 50*(4), 74–98. doi:10.2307/41166457

Cummings, J. N., & Cross, R. (2003). Structural properties of work groups and their consequences for performance. *Social Networks, 25,* 197–210. doi:10.1016/S0378-8733(02)00049-7

Curtis, B. (2011). Disputation of misinterpreted principles underlying the process maturity framework. Paper presented as keynote at the SEPG 2011 Europe. Dublin, Ireland.

Curtis, B., Hefley, B., & Miller, S. (2009). People capability maturity model (P-CMM), version 2.0 (2nd ed.) (CMU/SEI-2009-TR-003). Pittsburgh, PA: Software Engineering Institute, Carnegie Mellon University.

Dai, F., Li, T., Zhao, N., Yu, Y., & Huang, B. (2008). Evolution process component composition based on process architecture. In *Proceedings of Intelligent Information Technology Application Workshops* (pp. 1097–1100). IEEE.

Davenport, T. H., & Prusak, L. (1998). *Working knowledge: How organizations manage what they know*. Cambridge, MA: Harvard Business Press.

Davis, N., & Mullaney, J. (2003). *The team the team software ProcessSM (TSPSM) in practice: A summary of recent results (Technical Report, CMU/SEI-2003-TR-014)*. Pittsburgh, PA: Software Engineering Institute, Carnegie Mellon University.

Dayan, R., & Evans, S. (2006). KM your way to CMMI. *Journal of Knowledge Management, 10*(1), 69–80. doi:10.1108/13673270610650111

Demirors, O., & Demirors, E. (1998). Software process improvement in a small organization: Difficulties and suggestions. In *Software Process Technology (LNCS)* (Vol. 1487, pp. 1–12). Berlin: Springer. doi:10.1007/3-540-64956-5_1

Dias, L. D. (2010). *Método de instanciação de uma arquitetura de processos aplicado em fábrica de software*. (Master dissertation). Escola Politécnica de Universidade de Sao Paulo, Sao Paulo, Brazil.

Dingsøyr, T., & Røyrvik, E. (2001). Skills management as knowledge technology in a software consultancy company. In Lecture Notes in Computer Science -Advances in Learning Software Organizations, 2176, 96 –103.

Dingsøyr, T., Bjørnson, F. O., & Shull, F. (2009). What do we know about knowledge management? Practical implications for software engineering. *IEEE Software, 26*(3), 100–103. doi:10.1109/MS.2009.82

Downey, J., & Ali Babar, M. (2008). On identifying the skills needed for software architects. In *Proceedings of the First International Workshop on Leadership and Management in Software Architecture* (pp. 1–6). New York, NY: ACM.

Dyba, T. (2000). An instrument for measuring the key factors of success in software process improvement. *Empirical Software Engineering, 5*(4), 357–390. doi:10.1023/A:1009800404137

Dybå, T., & Dingsøyr, T. (2008). Empirical studies of agile software development: A systematic review. *Information and Software Technology, 50*(9-10), 833–859. doi:10.1016/j.infsof.2008.01.006

Dybå, T., Dingsøyr, T., & Moe, N. B. (2004). *Process improvement in practice: A handbook for IT companies*. Boston: Kluwer Academic.

Dybå, T., Kitchenham, B. A., & Jørgensen, M. (2005). Evidence-based software engineering for practitioners. *IEEE Software, 22*(1), 58–65. doi:10.1109/MS.2005.6

Dymond, K. M. (1988). *A guide to the CMMI: Understanding the capability maturity model for software*. Annapolis, MD: Process Transition International, Inc.

Eeles, P. (2012). *Capturing architectural requirements*. Retrieved from http://www.ibm.com/developerworks/rational/library/4710.html

EFQM. (2013). *The EFQM excellence model*. Retreived from http://www.efqm.org

Elliott, M., Dawson, R., & Edwards, J. (2009). An evolutionary cultural-change approach to successful software process improvement. *Software Quality Journal, 17*(2), 189–202. doi:10.1007/s11219-008-9070-7

Eppler, M. J. (2006). *Introducing the notion of information quality* (2nd ed.). Berlin, Germany: Springer.

Erbes, J., Motahari Nezhad, H. R., & Graupner, S. (2012). The future of enterprise it in the cloud. *Computer, 45*(5), 66–72. doi:10.1109/MC.2012.73

Espinosa-Curiel, I. (2013). *Mecanismos de soporte al proceso de adopción de un modelo de referencia de procesos en las micro, pequeñas y medianas empresas*. (Doctoral dissertation). Department of Computer Science, CICESE, Ensenada, Mexico.

Espinosa-Curiel, I. E., Rodríguez-Jacobo, J., & Fernández-Zepeda, J. A. (2011). A framework for evaluation and control of the factors that influence the software process improvement in small organizations. *Journal of Software Maintenance and Evolution: Research and Practice*. doi:10.1002/smr.569

Espinosa-Curiel, I. E., Rodríguez-Jacobo, J., & Fernández-Zepeda, J. A. (2013). A framework for evaluation and control of the factors that influence the software process improvement in small organizations. *Journal of Software Maintenance and Evolution: Research and Practice*.

Extreme Chaos. (2001). The Standish Group.

Fayad, M. E., Laitinen, M., & Ward, R. P. (2000). Thinking objectively: software engineering in the small. *Communications of the ACM, 43*(3), 115–118. doi:10.1145/330534.330555

Feiler, P., & Humphrey, W. S. (1993). Software process development and enactment: Concepts and definitions. In *Proceedings of Software Process* (pp. 28–40). Berlin, Germany: IEEE Computer Society Press.

Feldt, R., Torkar, R., Angelis, L., & Samuelsson, M. (2008). Towards individualized software engineering: Empirical studies should collect psychometrics. In *Proceedings of the 2008 International Workshop on Co-operative and Human Aspects of Software Engineering* (pp. 49–52). New York, NY: ACM.

Fensel, D. (2001). *Ontologies: A silver bullet for knowledge management and electronic commerce*. Berlin, Germany: Springer. doi:10.1007/978-3-662-04396-7

Ferreira, A. L., Machado, R. J., & Paulk, M. C. (2010). Size and complexity attributes for multimodel improvement framework taxonomy. In Proceedings of Software Engineering and Advanced Applications (SEAA), (pp. 306-309). IEEE.

Figueiredo, S., Santos, G., Montoni, M., Rocha, A. R., Barreto, A., Barreto, A., & Ferreira, A. (2006). Taba workstation: Supporting technical solution through knowledge management of design rationale. In *Practical Aspects of Knowledge Management (LNCS)* (Vol. 4333, pp. 61–72). Berlin: Springer. doi:10.1007/11944935_6

Firesmith, D. (2005). *A taxonomy of security-related requirements*. Software Engineering Institute.

Fitzgerald, B., & O'kane, T. (1999). A longitudinal study of software process improvement. *IEEE Software, 16*(3), 37–45. doi:10.1109/52.765785

Forrester, E., & Wemyss, G. (2011). CMMI and other models and standards. *CMMI Version 1.3 and Beyond*. Retrieved December 2012, from http://www.sei.cmu.edu/

Fu, Z., Li, T., & Hu, Y. (2009). An approach to aspect-oriented software evolution process architecture. In *Proceedings of Intelligent Computation Technology and Automation* (pp. 144–147). IEEE.

Gabbay, S. M., & Zuckerman, E. W. (1998). Social capital and opportunity in corporate R&D: The contingent effect of contact density on mobility expectations. *Social Science Research, 27*, 189–217. doi:10.1006/ssre.1998.0620

Gainer, J. (1998). *Best practices: Informal, effective process improvement*. Retrieved from http://www.jeffgainer.com/bestprac.html

Gamma, E., Helm, R., Johnson, R., & Vlissides, J. (1995). *Design patterns: elements of reusable object-oriented software*. Reading, MA: Addison-Wesley Professional Computing Series.

Garcia, S. (2007). Process improvement at the edges. *Software Engineering Institute (SEI) Library*. Carnegie Mellon University. Retrieved June 2009 from http://www.sei.cmu.edu/library/assets/20081218webinar.pdf

García, F., Ruiz, F., Calero, C., Bertoa, M. F., Vallecillo, A., Mora, B., & Piattini, M. (2009). Effective use of ontologies in software measurement. *The Knowledge Engineering Review, 24*(1), 23–40. doi:10.1017/S0269888909000125

Garcia, I., Pacheco, C., & Calvo-Manzano, J. (2010). Using a web-based tool to define and implement software process improvement initiatives in a small industrial setting. *IET Software, 4*(4), 237–251. doi:10.1049/iet-sen.2009.0045

García, J., Amescua, A., Sánchez, M.-I., & Bermón, L. (2011). Design guidelines for software processes knowledge repository development. *Information and Software Technology, 53*(8), 834–850. doi:10.1016/j.infsof.2011.03.002

Garcia, S. (2004). *What is a process asset library? Why should you care?* Boston, MA: Aimware Professional Services Inc.

Gartner Research Group. (2012). *Free apps will account for nearly 90 percent of total mobile app. store downloads in 2012*. Retrieved from http://www.gartner.com/it/page.jsp?id=2153215

Gasca-Hurtado, G. P. (2010). *Metodología para la gestión de riesgos de adquisición de software en pequeños entornos MEGRIAD. (Tesis para optar al grado de Doctor)*. Madrid, Spain: Universidad Politécnica de Madrid.

Gasevic, D., Djuric, D., & Devedzic, V. (2009). *Model driven engineering and ontology development* (2nd ed.). Berlin, Germany: Springer.

Gebus, S., & Leiviskä, K. (2009). Knowledge acquisition for decision support systems on an electronic assembly line. *Expert Systems with Applications*, *36*(1), 93–101. doi:10.1016/j.eswa.2007.09.058

Gibbs, W. W. (1994). Software's chronic crisis. *Scientific American*, *271*(3), 86–95. doi:10.1038/scientificamerican0994-86

Goethert, W., & Hayes, W. (2001). *Experiences in implementing measurement programs* (CMU/SEI-2001-TN-026). Retrieved January 30, 2010, from http://www.sei.cmu.edu/library/abstracts/reports/01tn026.cfm

Goffin, K., & Koners, U. (2011). Tacit knowledge, lessons learnt, and new product development. *Journal of Product Innovation Management*, *28*(2), 300–318. doi:10.1111/j.1540-5885.2010.00798.x

Goleman, D. (1998). *Working with emotional intelligence*. London: Bloomsbury Publishing.

Google. (2013). *Tools for modern applications*. Retrieved from http://cloud.google.com

Granovetter, M. S. (1983). The strength of weak ties: A network theory revisited. *Sociological Theory*, *1*, 201–233. doi:10.2307/202051

Green, S., & Ould, M. A. (1996). The primacy of process architecture. In *Proceedings of CAiSE Workshops* (pp. 154-159). CAiSE.

Griffith University. S. Q. I. (SQI). (2007). *Tool: Appraisal assistant beta*. Retrieved from http://www.sqi.gu.edu.au/AppraisalAssistant/about. html

Gruber, T. R. (1993). A translation approach to portable ontology specifications. *Knowledge Acquisition*, *5*(2), 199–220. doi:10.1006/knac.1993.1008

Gruman, G., & Knorr, E. (2008). *What cloud computing really means*. San Francisco, CA: InfoWorld.

Grütter, G., & Ferber, S. (2006). The personal software process in practice: Experience in two cases over five years. In Proceedings of Software Quality—ECSQ 2002, (pp. 165-174). ECSQ.

Gulati, R., & Gargiulo, M. (1999). Where do interorganizational networks come from? *American Journal of Sociology*, *104*(5), 1439–1493. doi:10.1086/210179

Gull, H., Azam, F., Haider, W. B., & Iqbal, S. Z. (2009). A new divide & conquer software process model. *World Academy of Science. Engineering and Technology*, *60*, 255–260.

Gupta, A., Jingyue, L., Conradi, R., Rønneberg, H., & Landre, E. (2009). A case study comparing defect profiles of a reused framework and of applications reusing it. *Empirical Software Engineering*, *14*(2), 227–255. doi:10.1007/s10664-008-9081-9

Gupta, J. N., Sharma, S. K., & Hsu, J. (2008). An overview of knowledge management. In M. Jennex (Ed.), *Knowledge management: Concepts, methodologies, tools, and applications*. Hershey, PA: Information Science Reference.

Gutiérrez-Osorio, U. (2011). *Una estrategia para la implementación de un sistema de administración del conocimiento en la mejora de procesos de software*. (Master Thesis). Department of Computer Science, CICESE, Ensenada, Mexico.

Haase, C. (2008). *Crystal methodology*. Retrieved December 10, 2006, from http://weblogs.java.net/blog/chet/archive/2008/01/crystal_methodo.html

Habra, N., Alexandre, S., Desharnais, J.-M., Laporte, C. Y., & Renault, A. (2008). Initiating software process improvement in very small enterprises: Experience with a light assessment tool. *Information and Software Technology*, *50*(7–8), 763–771. doi:10.1016/j.infsof.2007.08.004

Halvorsen, C., & Conradi, R. (2001). A taxonomy to compare SPI frameworks. In *Proceedings of Software Process Technology* (pp. 217–235). Berlin: Springer. doi:10.1007/3-540-45752-6_17

Hanneman, R. A., & Riddle, M. (2005). *Introduction to social network methods. Riverside, CA*. Riverside: University of California.

Harmon, P. (2003). Business process change: A manager's guide to improving, redesigning, and automating processes. *Business Process Trends*, *1*(3), 529.

Heinze, T., & Bauer, G. (2007). Characterizing creative scientists in nano-S&T: Productivity, multidisciplinarity, and network brokerage in a longitudinal perspective. *Scientometrics*, *3*, 811–830. doi:10.1007/s11192-007-0313-3

Hendler, J. (2001). Agents and the semantic web. *IEEE Intelligent Systems*, *16*(2), 30–37. doi:10.1109/5254.920597

Henry, S. M., & Stevens, K. T. (1999). Using Belbin's leadership role to improve team effectiveness: An empirical investigation. *Journal of Systems and Software*, *44*(3), 241–250. doi:10.1016/S0164-1212(98)10060-2

Herbsleb, J., Carleton, A., Rozum, J., Siegel, J., & Zubrow, D. (1994). *Benefits of CMM-based software process improvement: Initial results (CMU/SEI-94-TR-013)*. Pittsburgh, PA: Carnegie-Mellon University, Software Engineering Institute.

Heredia, A., Garcia-Guzman, J., Amescua, A., & Sanchez-Segura, M. I. (2013). Interactive knowledge asset management: Acquiring and disseminating tacit knowledge. *Journal of Information Science and Engineering*, *29*(1), 133–147.

Hibernate Community Documentation. (2004). *Improving performance*. Retrieved from http://docs.jboss.org/hibernate/orm/3.3/reference/en/html/performance.html

Highsmith, J. (1999). *Adaptive software development*. New York, NY: Dorset House.

Hitz, M., & Montazeri, B. (1995). Measuring coupling and cohesion in object-oriented systems. In *Proceedings of the International Symposium on Applied Corporate Computing* (Vol. 50, pp. 75-76). Academic Press.

Hofmeister, C., Kruchten, P. B., Nord, R., Obbink, H., Ran, A., & America, P. (2007). A general model of software architecture design derived from five industrial approaches. *Journal of Systems and Software*, *80*(1), 106–126. doi:10.1016/j.jss.2006.05.024

Hollenbach, C., & Frakes, W. (1996). Software process reuse in an industrial setting. In *Proceedings of the 4th International Conference on Software Reuse* (ICSR '96) (pp. 22–30). IEEE.

Horridge, M., Jupp, S., Knublauch, H., Moulton, G., Rector, A., Stevens, R., & Wroe, C. (2007). *A practical guide to building OWL ontologies using Protégé 4 and CO-ODE tools*. Manchester, UK: The University of Manchester.

Horrocks, F. D., Broekstra, J., Decker, S., Erdmann, M., Goble, C., van Harmelen, F., & Motta, E. (2000). *Ontology inference layer oil*. Retrieved from http://www.researchgate.net/publication/2384931_The_Ontology_Inference_Layer_OIL

Horvat, R. V., Rozman, I., & Gyorkos, J. (2000). Managing the complexity of SPI in small companies. *Software Process Improvement and Practice*, *5*(1), 45–54. doi:10.1002/(SICI)1099-1670(200003)5:1<45::AID-SPIP110>3.0.CO;2-2

Horwitz, S. K., & Horwitz, I. B. (2007). The effects of team diversity on team outcomes: A meta-analytic review of team demography. *Journal of Management*, *33*(6), 987–1015. doi:10.1177/0149206307308587

HP. (2013). *Meet the cloud that enterprises rely on*. Retrieved from http://www.hp.com/go/Cloud

Hughes, J. (2010). iPhone and iPad apps marketing. Indianapolis, IN: Que Publishing.

Humphrey, W. (2000). *The team software process (TSP)* (Technical Report CMU/SEI-2000-TR-023). Pittsburgh, PA: Software Engineering Institute, Carnegie Mellon University.

Humphrey, W. S. (2000). *Introduction to the team software process (sm)*. Addison-Wesley Professional. Retrieved from http://books.google.com/books?id=0-Gzw8v-S0YC&pgis=1

Humphrey, W. (2006). *Introduction to the team software process*. Reading, MA: Addison-Wesley.

Humphrey, W. S. (1989). *Managing the software process*. Reading, MA: Addison-Wesley Publishing Company.

Humphrey, W. S. (1996). Using a defined and measured personal software process. *IEEE Software*, *13*(3), 77–88. doi:10.1109/52.493023

Humphrey, W. S. (1997). *Managing technical people*. Boston, MA: Addison-Wesley.

Humphrey, W. S. (2005). *Psp (sm), a self-improvement process for software engineers*. Reading, MA: Addison-Wesley Professional.

IBM. (2013). *Server and cloud platform*. Retrieved from http://www.microsoft.com/es-es/server-cloud/default.aspx#fbid=yFhqG_9NKmPe

IEEE Computer Society. (2004). IEEE guide adoption of PMI standard A guide to the project management body of knowledge. *IEEE Std 1490-2003 (Revision of IEEE Std 1490-1998)*. IEEE. doi: 10.1109/IEEESTD.2004.94565

IEEE. (1998). *IEEE recommended practice for software acquisition*. Institute of Electrical and Electronics Engineers.

IEEE. (2000). *IEEE recommended practice for architectural description of software-intensive systems (Technical Report IEEE Std 1471-2000)*. IEEE Computer Society.

IEEE. (2013). *IEEE cloud computing*. Retrieved from http://cloudcomputing.ieee.org

Infoworld. (2013). *Cloud computing*. Retrieved from http://www.infoworld.com/d/cloud-computing

Institute of Electrical and Electronics Engineers. (1998). *IEEE Std 1062: 1998 recommended practice for software acquisition software engineering standards committee of the IEEE computer society*. IEEE.

International Organization for Standardization. (2004). *ISO/IEC 15504: 2004 information technology – Process assessment, part 1 to part 5*. Author. iSixSigma. (2010). *iSix sigma quality resources for achieving six sigma results*. Retrieved March 11, 2010 from www.isixsigma.com

International Organization for Standardization. (2008). *Systems and software engineering —Software life cycle processes (ISO/IEC 12207)*. Author.

International Standardization Organization / International Electrotechnical Commission. (2002). *ISO/IEC 15288: 2002, information technology – Life cycle management – System life cycle processes*. Geneva, Switzerland: ISO/IEC.

International Standardization Organization / International Electrotechnical Commission. (2008). *ISO/IEC 12207: 2008, systems and software engineering – Software life cycle processes*. Geneva, Switzerland: ISO/IEC.

ISO. (2000). *ISO 9001 : 2000 quality management systems — Requirements*. Geneva, Switzerland: ISO.

ISO. (2003). *ISO/IEC 15504-2:2003 information technology - Process assessment - Part 2: Performing an assessment*. International Organization for Standardization.

ISO. (2004a). *ISO 12207:1995/Amd 1:2002/Amd 2:2004 systems and software engineering - Software life cycle processes*. International Organization for Standardization.

ISO. (2004b). *ISO/IEC 15504-3:2004 information technology - Process assessment - Part 3: Guidance on performing an assessment*. International Organization for Standardization.

ISO. (2005a). *ISO/IEC 27001:2005 information technology - Security techniques - Information security management systems - Requirements*. International Organization for Standardization.

ISO. (2005b). *ISO/IEC 27002:2005 information technology - Security techniques - Code of practice for information security management*. International Organization for Standardization.

ISO. (2006). *ISO/IEC 15504-5:2006 information technology - Process assessment - Part 5: An exemplar process assessment model*. International Organization for Standardization.

ISO. (2007). *ISO/IEC 15504-4:2007 information technology - Process assessment - Part 4: Guidance on use for process improvement and process capability determination*. International Organization for Standardization.

ISO. (2008a). *ISO 9001:2008 quality management systems - Requirements*. International Organization for Standardization.

ISO. (2008b). *ISO/IEC TR 15504-7:2008 information technology - Process assessment - Part 7: Assessment of organizational maturity*. International Organization for Standardization.

ISO. (2009). *ISO 14001:2004/Cor 1:2009 environmental management systems - Requirements with guidance for use*. International Organization for Standardization.

ISO. (2011). *ISO/IEC 20000-1:2011 information technology - Service management - Part 1: Service management system requirements*. International Organization for Standardization.

ISO/IEC. (1998). *ISO/IEC TR 15504:1998 information technology — Software process assessment part 2: A reference model for processes and process capability*. Geneva, Switzerland: ISO/IEC.

ITSqc Carnegie Mellon. (2006). eSCM-CL v1.1, part 1. Pittsburgh, PA: Carnegie Mellon.

Iversen, J., & Ngwenyama, O. (2006). Problems in measuring effectiveness in software process improvement: A longitudinal study of organizational change at Danske data. *International Journal of Information Management*, *26*(1), 30–43. doi:10.1016/j.ijinfomgt.2005.10.006

Jackson, M. A. (1975). *Principles of program design.* London: Academic Press.

Jackson, M. A. (1983). *System development.* London: Prentice Hall.

Jacobson, I., Booch, G., & Rumbaugh, J. (1999). *The unified software development process.* Boston, MA: Addison-Wesley.

Jahn, K., & Nielsen, P. A. (2011). A vertical approach to knowledge management: Codification and personalization in software processes. *International Journal of Human Capital and Information Technology Professionals*, *2*(2), 26–36. doi:10.4018/jhcitp.2011040103

Jain, V., & Gupta, S. (2012). The role of emotional intelligence in improving service quality & work effectiveness in service organizations with special reference to personality traits. *International Journal of Research in IT & Management*, *2*(1), 81–100.

Jalote, P. (2002). *Software project management in practice.* Reading, MA: Addison-Wesley Professional.

Janis, S. J., & Shade, J. E. (2000). *Improving performance through statistical thinking.* Milwaukee, WI: ASQ Quality Press.

JArchitect. (2012). *Java metrics.* Retrieved December 2013 from http://www.javadepend.com/Metrics.aspx

Jawadekar, W. S. (2004). *Software engineering: Principles and practices.* New Delhi: Tata McGraw-Hill Publishing Company Limited.

Jean-Claude, D., & Oquendo, F. (2004). Key issues and new challenges in software process technology. *Novatica. European Journal for the Informatics Professional*, *5*(5), 15–20.

Jeffries, R., Anderson, A., & Hendrickson, C. (2000). *Extreme programming installed.* Reading, MA: Addison-Wesley Professional.

Jeston, J., & Nelis, J. (2006). *Business process management: Practical guidelines to successful implementations.* Oxford, UK: Butterworth-Heinemann.

Johnson, J. (2006). *My life is failure: 100 Things you should know to be a successful project leader.* West Yarmouth, MA: Standish Group International.

Jones, C. (1995). Risks of software system failure or disaster. *American Programmer*, *8*(3), 2–9.

Jordan, M. E. (2011). *Personality traits: Theory, testing and influences.* Nova Science Pub Incorporated.

Jørgensen, M. (2004). A review of studies on expert estimation of software development effort. *Journal of Systems and Software*, *70*(1), 37–60. doi:10.1016/S0164-1212(02)00156-5

Jorgensen, M., Boehm, B., & Rifkin, S. (2009). Software development effort estimation: Formal models or expert judgment? *IEEE Software*, *26*(2), 14–19. doi:10.1109/MS.2009.47

Jorgensen, M., & Grimstad, S. (2012). Software development estimation biases: The role of interdependence. *IEEE Transactions on Software Engineering*, *38*(3), 677–693. doi:10.1109/TSE.2011.40

Jorgensen, M., & Shepperd, M. (2007). A systematic review of software development cost estimation studies. *IEEE Transactions on Software Engineering*, *33*(1), 33–53. doi:10.1109/TSE.2007.256943

Karn, J. S., Syed-Abdullah, S., Cowling, A. J., & Holcombe, M. (2007). A study into the effects of personality type and methodology on cohesion in software engineering teams. *Behaviour & Information Technology*, *26*(2), 99–111. doi:10.1080/01449290500102110

Kasse, T. (2009). Change management toolkit. Paper presented as Conference Session at the SEPG 2009 North America. Los Angeles, CA.

Kasser, J. E. (2005). Introducing the role of process architecting. In *Proceedings of 15th International Symposium of the International Council on Systems Engineering (INCOSE).* Rochester, NY: INCOSE.

Katz, J. S., & Martin, B. R. (1997). What is research collaboration? *Research Policy*, *26*, 1–18. doi:10.1016/S0048-7333(96)00917-1

Kautz, K., Levine, L., Hefley, B., Johansen, J., Kristensen, C., & Nielsen, P. (2004). Networked technologies — The role of networks in the diffusion and adoption of software process improvement (SPI) approaches. *Networked Information Technologies, 138*, 203–211. doi:10.1007/1-4020-7862-5_13

Kazman, R., Abowd, G., Bass, L., & Clements, P. (1996). Scenario-based analysis of software architecture. *IEEE Software, 13*(6), 47–55. doi:10.1109/52.542294

Kazman, R., Nord, R., & Klein, M. (2003). *A life-cycle view of architectural analysis and design methods (Technical Note CMU/SEI-2003-TN-026)*. Pittsburgh, PA: Software Engineering Institute, Carnegie Mellon University.

Kelemen, Z. D. (2009). A process based unification of process-oriented software quality approaches. In *Proceedings of Global Software Engineering* (pp. 285–288). IEEE.

Kelemen, Z. D., Kusters, R., & Trienekens, J. (2011). Identifying criteria for multimodel software process improvement solutions – Based on a review of current problems and initiatives. *Journal of Software Maintenance and Evolution Research and Practice, 24*(8), 895–909.

Kirwan, P., Jeannie, S. M., Marino, L., & Morley, J. (2008). Improvement technology classification and composition in multi-model environments. *Software Engineering Institute (SEI)*. Carnegie Mellon University. Retrieved June 2008 from http://www.sei.cmu.edu/library/assets/3.pdf

Kirwan, P., Marino, L., Morley, J., & Siviy, J. (2008a). *The value of harmonizing multiple improvement technologies: A process improvement professional's view* (White paper). Retrieved from http://www.sei.cmu.edu/library/abstracts/whitepapers/multimodelSeries_wp1_harmonizationValue_052008_v1.cfm

Kirwan, P., Marino, L., Morley, J., & Siviy, J. (2008b). *Process architecture in a multimodel environment* (White paper). Retrieved from http://www.sei.cmu.edu/library/abstracts/whitepapers/multimodelSeries_wp4_processArch_052008_v1.cfm

Kirwan, P., Marino, L., Morley, J., & Siviy, J. (2008c). *Maximizing your process improvement ROI through harmonization* (White paper). Retrieved from http://www.sei.cmu.edu/library/abstracts/whitepapers/multimodelExecutive_wp_harmonizationROI_032008_v1.cfm

Kirwan, P., Marino, L., Morley, J., & Siviy, J. (2008d). *Strategic technology selection and classification in multimodel environments* (White paper). Retrieved from http://www.sei.cmu.edu/library/abstracts/whitepapers/multimodelSeries_wp2_techSelection_052008_v1.cfm

Kirwan, P., Marino, L., Morley, J., & Siviy, J. (2008e). *Improvement technology classification and composition in multimodel environments* (White paper). Retrieved from http://www.sei.cmu.edu/library/abstracts/whitepapers/multimodelSeries_wp2_techSelection_052008_v1.cfm

Kitchenham, B., Pearlbrereton, O., Budgen, D., Turner, M., Bailey, J., & Linkman, S. (2009). Systematic literature reviews in software engineering – A systematic literature review. *Information and Software Technology, 51*(1), 7–15. doi:10.1016/j.infsof.2008.09.009

Klein, M. C. A., Fensel, D., Kiryakov, A., & Ognyanov, D. (2002). Ontology versioning and change detection on the web. In A. Gómez-Pérez & V.R. Benjamins (Eds.), *Proceedings of the 13th International Conference on Knowledge Engineering and Knowledge Management* (pp. 197–212). London, UK: Springer-Verlag.

Klyne, G., & Carroll, J. J. (2002). *Resource description framework (RFD), concepts and abstract syntax reference-website*. Retrieved from http://www.w3.org/TR/2002/WDrdf-concepts-20021108/

Komi-Sirviö, S., Mäntyniemi, A., & Seppänen, V. (2002). Toward a practical solution for capturing knowledge for software projects. *IEEE Software, 19*(3), 60–62. doi:10.1109/MS.2002.1003457

Korsaa, M., Johansen, J., Schweigert, T., Vohwinkel, D., Messnarz, R., Nevalainen, R., & Biro, M. (2012). The people aspects in modern process improvement management approaches. *Journal of Software: Evolution and Process*. doi:10.1002/smr.570

Krackhardt, D. (1992). The strength of strong ties: The importance of philos in organizations. In N. Nohria, & R. Eccles (Eds.), *Networks and organizations: Structure, form, and action*. Boston, MA: Harvard Business School Press.

Kratzen, J. (2001). *Communication and performance: An empirical study in innovation teams*. Amsterdam: Tesla Thesis Publishers.

Kroll, P., Kruchten, P. B., & Booch, G. (2003). *The rational unified process made easy.* Reading, MA: Addison-Wesley Professional.

Kronlöf, K. (1993). *Method integration: Concepts and case studies.* New York, NY: John Wiley & Sons, Inc.

Kruchten, P. B. (1995). The 4+1 view model of architecture. *IEEE Software, 6*(12), 42–50. doi:10.1109/52.469759

Kuilboer, J. P., & Ashrafi, N. (2000). Software process and product improvement: An empirical assessment. *Information and Software Technology, 42*(1), 27–34. doi:10.1016/S0950-5849(99)00054-3

Laanti, M., Salo, O., & Abrahamsson, P. (2011). Agile methods rapidly replacing traditional methods at Nokia: A survey of opinions on agile transformation. *Information and Software Technology, 53*(3), 276–290. doi:10.1016/j.infsof.2010.11.010

Lassing, N., Bengtsson, P., Vliet, H., & Bosh, J. (2002). Experience with ALMA: Architecture-level modifiability analysis. *Journal of Systems and Software, 61*, 47–57. doi:10.1016/S0164-1212(01)00113-3

Lattanze, A. J. (2009). *Architecting software intensive systems: A practitioners guide.* Boca Raton, FL: CRC Press.

Laudel, G. (2001). Collaboration, creativity and rewards: Why and how scientists collaborate. *Int. J. Technology Management, 22*(7/8), 762–781.

Laudon, K. C., & Laudon, J. P. (2012). *Management information systems: Managing the digital firm.* London, UK: Pearson.

Laudon, K., & Traver, C. G. (2012). *E-commerce 2013.* Upper Saddle River, NJ: Pearson Higher Ed.

Lawrence, J., & Becker, N. (2009). *Implementing insights and lesson learned using ISF for excellence.* Paper presented at SEPG 2009 North America Conference. San Jose, CA.

Leenders, R. T. A., Van Engelen, J. M., & Kratzer, J. (2003). Virtuality, communication, and new product team creativity: A social network perspective. *Journal of Engineering and Technology Management, 20*(1), 69–92. doi:10.1016/S0923-4748(03)00005-5

Lepri, B., Mana, N., Cappelletti, A., Pianesi, F., & Zancanaro, M. (2009). Modeling the personality of participants during group interactions. Lecture Notes in Computer Science –User Modeling, Adaptation, and Personalization, 5535, 114-125.

Levine, J. M., & Moreland, R. L. (2004). Collaboration: The social context of theory development. *Personality and Social Psychology Review, 8*(2), 164–172. doi:10.1207/s15327957pspr0802_10 PMID:15223516

Levy, M., & Hazzan, O. (2009). Knowledge management in practice: The case of agile software development. In *Proceedings of Cooperative and Human Aspects on Software Engineering* (pp. 60–65). IEEE.

Licorish, S., Philpott, A., & MacDonell, S. G. (2009). Supporting agile team composition: A prototype tool for identifying personality (in)compatibilities. In *Proceedings of the 2009 International Conference on Software Engineering* (pp. 66-73). IEEE.

Liebeskind, J. P., Oliver, A. L., Zucker, L., & Brewer, M. (1996). Social networks, learning, and flexibility: Sourcing scientific knowledge in new biotechnology firms. *Organization Science, 7*(4), 428–443. doi:10.1287/orsc.7.4.428

Lindvall, M., Rus, I., & Sinha, S. S. (2003). Technology support for knowledge management. In *Advances in Learning Software Organizations (LNCS)* (Vol. 2640, pp. 94–103). Berlin: Springer. doi:10.1007/978-3-540-40052-3_9

Lonchamp, J. (1993). A structured conceptual and terminological framework for software process engineering. In *Proceedings of Software Process* (pp. 41–53). IEEE.

López, P. (2005). *Taxonomía unificada de referencia de fallos accidentales de software crítico.* (PhD Dissertation). Universiad Politécncia de Madrid, Madrid, Spain.

López, M. F., Gómez-Pérez, A., Sierra, J. P., & Sierra, A. P. (1999). Building a chemical ontology using methontology and the ontology design environment. *IEEE Intelligent Systems, 14*(1), 37–46. doi:10.1109/5254.747904

Lowrie, A., & McKnight, P. J. (2004). Academic research networks: A key to enhancing scholarly standing. *European Management Journal, 22*(4), 345–360. doi:10.1016/j.emj.2004.06.011

Luo, J.-D. (2005). Social network structure and performance of improvement teams. *Int. J. Business Performance Management*, *7*(2), 208–223. doi:10.1504/IJBPM.2005.006491

Mahnič, V., & Hovelja, T. (2012). On using planning poker for estimating user stories. *Journal of Systems and Software*, *85*(9), 2086–2095. doi:10.1016/j.jss.2012.04.005

Maier, R. (2007). *Knowledge management systems: Information and communication technologies for knowledge management* (3rd ed.). Heidelberg, Germany: Springer. doi:10.4018/978-1-59904-933-5.ch046

Majchrzak, A., Wagner, C., & Yates, N. (2006). Corporate wiki users: Results of a survey. In *Proceedings of the 2006 International Symposium on Wikis (WikiSym)*, (pp. 99-104). Odense, Denmark: ACM Press.

Maldonado, A., & Velázquez, A. (2006). A method to define the process architecture. In *Proceedings of AMCIS 2006*. AMCIS.

MAP. (1995). *Métrica version 2.1*. Madrid: Tecnos.

MAP. (2000). *Metodología MÉTRICA versión 3*. Madrid: MAP.

Marino, L., & Morley, J. (2009). Process improvement in a multi-model environment builds resilient organizations. *NEWS AT SEI*. Software Engineering Institute (SEI). Retrieved December 2009 from http://www.sei.cmu.edu/library/abstracts/news-at-sei/02feature200804.cfm

Martin, R. C. (2000). *Design principles and design patterns*. Object Mentor.

Martin, R. C. (2002). The single responsibility principle. In *The principles, patterns, and practices of agile software development* (pp. 149–154). Upper Saddle River, NJ: Prentice Hall.

Martin, R. C., & Martin, M. (2007). *Agile principles, patterns, and practices in C*. Upper Saddle River, NJ: Prentice-Hall PTR.

Mas, A., Mesquida, A., Amengual, E., & Fluxà, B. (2010). ISO/IEC 15504 best practices to facilitate ISO/IEC 27000 implementation. In *Proceedings of 5th International Conference on Evaluation of Novel Approaches to Software Engineering* (ENASE) (pp. 192-198). Athens, Greece: SciTePress.

Mas, A., & Amengual, E. (2012). La mejora de los procesos de software en las pequeñas y medianas empresas (pyme): Un nuevo modelo y su aplicación a un caso real. *REICIS: Revista Española de Innovación. Calidad e Ingeniería del Software*, *1*(2), 7–29.

Matheron, J. P. (1994). *Comprendre merise: Outils conceptuels et organisationnels*. Paris: Eyrolles.

Mathiassen, L., Ngwenyama, O. K., & Aaen, I. (2005). Managing change in software process improvement. *IEEE Software*, *22*(6), 84–91. doi:10.1109/MS.2005.159

Matturro, G., & Saavedra, J. (2012). Considering people CMM for managing factors that affect software process improvement. *IEEE Latin America Transactions*, *10*(2), 1603–1615. doi:10.1109/TLA.2012.6187605

McConnell, S. (2006). *Software estimation: Demystifying the black art*. Microsoft Press.

McFeely, B. (1996). *IDEAL: A users guide for software process improvement* (Tech. Rep. CMU/SEI-96-HB-001). Retrieved from www.sei.cmu.edu

McQueen, S., & Thompson, H. (2000). *XML schema reference-website*. Retrieved from http://www.w3.org/XML/Schema

Meehan, B., & Richardson, I. (2002). Identification of software process knowledge management. *Software Process Improvement and Practice*, *7*(2), 47–55. doi:10.1002/spip.154

Melin, G. (2000). Pragmatism and self-organization: Research collaboration on the individual level. *Research Policy*, *29*, 31–40. doi:10.1016/S0048-7333(99)00031-1

Mell, P., & Grance, T. (2011). The NIST definition of cloud computing (draft). *NIST Special Publication*, *800*(145), 7.

Mesquida, A., Mas, A., & Amengual, E. (2011). An ISO/IEC 15504 security extension. *Communications in Computer and Information Science*, *155*(2), 64–72. doi:10.1007/978-3-642-21233-8_6

Messnarz, R., Bachmann, O., Ekert, D., & Riel, A. (2010). SPICE level 3 - Experience with using e-learning to coach the use of standard system design best practices in projects. In A. Riel, R. O'Connor, S. Tichkiewitch, & R. Messnarz (Eds.), *Systems, software and services process improvement* (Vol. 99, pp. 213–221). Berlin: Springer. doi:10.1007/978-3-642-15666-3_19

Microsoft. (2013). *Cloud computing*. Retrieved from http://www.microsoft.com/spain/enterprise/soluciones-microsoft/soluciones-de.aspx?tema=cloud-computing

Mishra, D., & Mishra, A. (2008). Software process improvement methodologies for small and medium enterprises. In *Product-Focused Software Process Improvement (LNCS)* (Vol. 5089, pp. 273–288). Berlin: Springer. doi:10.1007/978-3-540-69566-0_23

Mishra, D., & Mishra, A. (2009). A software process improvement in SMEs: A comparative view. *Computer Science and Information Systems*, 6(1), 111–140. doi:10.2298/CSIS0901111M

Missikoff, M., & Taglino, F. (2002). Business and enterprise ontology management with SymOntoX. In I. Horrocks, & J. Hendler (Eds.), *The semantic web—ISWC 2002* (pp. 442–447). Berlin, Germany: Springer.

Moen, R., & Norman, C. (2006). *Evolution of the PDCA cycle*. Retrieved August 12, 2012, from http://kaizensite.com/learninglean/wp-content/uploads/2012/09/Evolution-of-PDCA.pdf

Moenaert, R. K., Caeldries, F., Lievens, A., & Wauters, E. (2000). Communication flows in international product innovation teams. *Journal of Product Innovation Management*, 17(5), 360–377. doi:10.1016/S0737-6782(00)00048-5

Mogilensky, J. (2009). *Pathological box-checking: The dark side of process improvement*. Paper presented at SEPG 2009 North America Conference. San Jose, CA.

Moitra, D. (2005). Managing organizational change for software process improvement. In *Software process modeling* (pp. 163–185). New York: Springer US. doi:10.1007/0-387-24262-7_7

Molina, J. L., & Marsal, M. (2002). Herramientas de gestión del conocimiento, gestión del cambio. In La gestión del conocimiento en las organizaciones (pp. 60-68, 87-94). Colección de Negocios, Empresa y Economía: Libros en red.

Moløkken-Østvold, K., & Jørgensen, M. (2004). Group processes in software effort estimation. *Empirical Software Engineering*, 9(4), 315–334. doi:10.1023/B:EMSE.0000039882.39206.5a

Montoni, M., Santos, G., Rocha, A., Figueiredo, S., Cabral, R., & Barcellos, R. ... Lupo, P. (2006). Taba workstation: Supporting software process deployment based on CMMI and MR-MPS.BR. In Product-Focused Software Process Improvement (LNCS), (vol. 4034, pp. 249–262). Berlin: Springer.

Montoni, M., Santos, G., Villela, K., Rocha, A., Travassos, G., & Figueiredo, S. ... Mian, P. (2005). Enterprise-oriented software development environments to support software products and processes quality improvement. In Product Focused Software Process Improvement (LNCS), (vol. 3547, pp. 370–384). Berlin: Springer.

Montoni, M. A., & Cavalcanti da Rocha, A. R. (2011). Using grounded theory to acquire knowledge about critical success factors for conducting software process improvement implementation initiatives. *International Journal of Knowledge Management*, 7(3), 43–60. doi:10.4018/jkm.2011070104

Montoni, M. A., Cerdeiral, C., Zanetti, D., & Cavalcanti da Rocha, A. R. (2008). A knowledge management approach to support software process improvement implementation initiatives. In *Software process improvement* (pp. 164–175). Berlin: Springer. doi:10.1007/978-3-540-85936-9_15

Montoni, M., Miranda, R., Rocha, A. R., & Travassos, G. H. (2004). Knowledge acquisition and communities of practice: An approach to convert individual knowledge into multi-organizational knowledge. In *Advances in Learning Software Organizations (LNCS)* (Vol. 3096, pp. 110–121). Berlin: Springer. doi:10.1007/978-3-540-25983-1_11

Morgan, P. (2007). Process improvement- Is it a lottery? *Methods & Tools, Practical Knowledge for the Software Developer. Tester and Project Manager*, 15(1), 3–12.

Mozilla. (2013). *De todos para todos*. Retrieved from http://www.mozilla.org

Muller, S. D., Kraemmergaard, P., & Mathiassen, L. (2009). Managing cultural variation in software process improvement: A comparison of methods for subculture assessment. *IEEE Transactions on Engineering Management*, 56(4), 584–599. doi:10.1109/TEM.2009.2013829

Müller, S. D., Mathiassen, L., & Balshøj, H. H. (2010). Software process improvement as organizational change: A metaphorical analysis of the literature. *Journal of Systems and Software*, *83*(11), 2128–2146. doi:10.1016/j.jss.2010.06.017

Münch, J., Armbrust, O., Kowalczyk, M., & Soto, M. (2012). *Software process definition and management*. Berlin, Germany: Springer. doi:10.1007/978-3-642-24291-5

Munk-Madsen, A., & Nielsen, P. A. (2011). Success factors and motivators in SPI. *International Journal of Human Capital and Information Technology Professionals*, *2*(4), 49–60. doi:10.4018/jhcitp.2011100105

Muñoz, E., Capon-Garcia, E., Lainez, J., Espuña, A., & Puigjaner, L. (2011). Ontological framework for the enterprise from a process perspective. In J. Filipe & J.L.G. Dietz (Eds.), *Proceedings of the International Conference on Knowledge Engineering and Ontology Development* (pp. 538–546). SciTePress.

Muñoz, M., Mejia, J., Calvo-Manzano, J. A., San Feliu, T., & Alor, G. (2011). Advantages of using a multi-model environment in software process improvement. In *Proceedings of the Electronics, Robotics and Automotive Mechanics Conference* (CERMA), (pp. 397-402). IEEE. DOI 10.1109/CERMA.2011.85

Muñoz, M., Mejia, J., Calvo-Manzano, J. A., Cuevas, G., & San Feliu, T. (2012). Method to evaluate process performance focused on minimizing resistance to change. *International Journal of Human Capital and Information Technology Professionals*, *4*(2), 1–15. doi:10.4018/jhcitp.2013040101

Mutafelija, B., & Stromberg, H. (2003). *Systematic process improvement using ISO 9001:2000 and CMMI*. Artech House.

Natali, A. C. C., & Falbo, R. (2002). Knowledge management in software engineering environments. In *Proceedings of the XVI Brazilian Symposium on Software Engineering*, (pp. 238–253). Gramado, Brazil: Academic Press.

Neches, R., Fikes, R., Finin, T., Gruber, T., Patil, R., Senator, T., & Swartout, W. R. (1991). Enabling technology for knowledge sharing. *AI Magazine*, *12*(3), 36–56.

Nelson, P., Richmond, W., & Sidmann, A. (1996). Two dimensions of software acquisition. *Communications of the ACM*, *39*(7), 29–35. doi:10.1145/233977.233986

Nevalainen, R., & Schweigert, T. (2010). A European scheme for software process improvement manager training and certification. *Journal of Software Maintenance and Evolution: Research and Practice*, *22*(4), 269–277. doi: doi:10.1002/spip.438

Newman, A., & Cohen, H. (2012). *Cloud computing: Discover the skills that power the cloud*. Foster City, CA: QuinStreet Inc. doi:10.1109/PST.2012.6297945

Niazi, M. (2011). An exploratory study of software process improvement implementation risks. *Journal of Software Maintenance and Evolution: Research and Practice*. doi:10.1002/smr.543

Niazi, M. (2006). Software process improvement: A road to success. In *Product-Focused Software Process Improvement (LNCS)* (Vol. 4034, pp. 395–401). Berlin: Springer. doi:10.1007/11767718_34

Niazi, M. (2009). Software process improvement implementation: Avoiding critical barriers. *CROSSTALK: The Journal of Defense Software Engineering*, *22*(1), 24–27.

Niazi, M., Babar, M. A., & Verner, J. M. (2010). Software process improvement barriers: A cross-cultural comparison. *Information and Software Technology*, *52*(11), 1204–1216. doi:10.1016/j.infsof.2010.06.005

Niazi, M., Wilson, D., & Zowghi, D. (2005). A framework for assisting the design of effective software process improvement implementation strategies. *Journal of Systems and Software*, *78*(2), 204–222. doi:10.1016/j.jss.2004.09.001

Niazi, M., Wilson, D., & Zowghi, D. (2006). Critical success factors for software process improvement implementation: An empirical study. *Software Process Improvement and Practice*, *11*(2), 193–211. doi:10.1002/spip.261

Nonaka, I. (1994). A dynamic theory of organizational knowledge creation. *Organization Science*, *5*(1), 14–37. doi:10.1287/orsc.5.1.14

Nonaka, I., & von Krogh, G. (2009). Tacit knowledge and knowledge conversion: Controversy and advancement in organizational knowledge creation theory. *Organization Science*, *20*(3), 635–652. doi:10.1287/orsc.1080.0412

Nonaka, I., von Krogh, G., & Voelpel, S. (2006). Organizational knowledge creation theory: Evolutionary paths and future advances. *Organization Studies*, *27*(8), 1179–1208. doi:10.1177/0170840606066312

Nube.es. (2013). *Nube: Cloud computing*. Retrieved from http://nube.es

O'Connor, R. V. (2012). Evaluating management sentiment towards ISO/IEC 29110 in very small software development companies. In A. Mas, A. Mesquida, T. Rout, R. V. O'Connor, & A. Dorling (Eds.), *Software process improvement and capability determination* (Vol. 290, pp. 277–281). Berlin: Springer. doi:10.1007/978-3-642-30439-2_31

O'Connor, R., & Basri, S. (2012). The effect of team dynamics on software development process improvement. *International Journal of Human Capital and Information Technology Professionals*, *3*(3), 13–26. doi:10.4018/jhcitp.2012070102

Object Management Group. (2010). *Business motivation model, v1.1*. OMG Document Number: formal/2010-05-01. Retrieved November 2012, from http//www.omg.org/spec/BMM/1.1/

Obrst, L. (2003). Ontologies for semantically interoperable systems. In D. Kraft (Ed.), *Proceedings of the Twelfth International Conference on Information and Knowledge Management* (pp. 366–369). New York: ACM. DOI: 10.1145/956863.956932

Oh, H., Chung, M. H., & Labianca, G. (2004). Group social capital and group effectiveness: The role of informal socializing ties. *Academy of Management Journal*, *47*(6), 860–875. doi:10.2307/20159627

Oh, H., Labianca, G., & Chung, M. H. (2006). A multilevel model of group social capital. *Academy of Management Review*, *31*(3), 569–582. doi:10.5465/AMR.2006.21318918

Oktaba, H., Alquicira, C., Pino, F. J., Ruíz, F., Piattini, M., Martínez, T., & García, F. (2008). COMPETISOFT: An improvement strategy for small Latin-American software organizations. In *Software process improvement for small and medium enterprises: Techniques and case studies* (pp. 212–222). Hershey, PA: IGI Global. doi:10.4018/978-1-59904-906-9.ch011

Oktaba, H., & Vázquez, A. (2008). MoProSoft®: A software process model for small enterprises. In *Software process improvement for small and medium enterprises: Techniques and case studies* (pp. 170–176). Hershey, PA: IGI Global. doi:10.4018/978-1-59904-906-9.ch008

OMG. (2006). *Meta object facility (MOF) core specification version 2.0*. OMG.

OMG. (2008). *Software & systems process engineering meta-model specification (SPEM) version 2.0*. OMG.

OpenUP. (2012). Retrieved from http://epf.eclipse.org/wikis/openup

Oracle. (2013). *Oracle cloud solutions*. Retrieved from http://www.oracle.com/webapps/dialogue/ns/dlgwelcome.jsp?p_ext=Y&p_dlg_id=13613910&src=7665776&Act=78&sckw=WWMK12062962MPP019

Organization for Standardization/International Electrotechnical Commission. (2004). *International standard ISO/IEC 15504 software process improvement and capability determination*. Author.

Ould, M. A. (1997). Designing a re-engineering proof process architecture. *Business Process Management Journal*, *3*(3), 232–247. doi:10.1108/14637159710192284

Pagels, M. (2006). *The DARPA agent markup language (DAML) reference website*. Retrieved from http://www.daml.org/

Pardo, C. (2010). A systematic review on the harmonization of reference models. In *Proceeding of ENASE 2010* (pp. 40–47). ENASE.

Parnas, D. L. (1972). On the criteria to be used in decomposing systems into modules. *Communications of the ACM*, *15*(12), 1053–1058. doi:10.1145/361598.361623

Passos, O. M., Dias-Neto, A. C., & da Silva Barreto, R. (2012). Organizational culture and success in SPI initiatives. *IEEE Software*, *29*(3), 97–99. doi:10.1109/MS.2012.52

Paulk, M. C. (2008). A taxonomy for improvement frameworks. In *Proceedings of Fourth World Congress for Software Quality*. Bethesda, MD: Academic Press.

Paulk, M. C., Curtis, B., Chrissis, M. B., & Weber, C. V. (1993). Capability maturity model, version 1.1. *IEEE Software*, *10*(4), 18–27. doi:10.1109/52.219617

Pérez Cota, M. (2012). *Cloud computing and planning of information systems*. Mikkeli-Polytechnic. Retrieved from http://www2.mamk.fi/singlenewsinfo.asp?id=505&menu_id=64&selected=64&companyId=1&show=2

Pérez, G., El Emam, K., & Madhavji, N. H. (1995). Customising software process models. In *Software process technology* (pp. 70–78). Berlin: Springer. doi:10.1007/3-540-59205-9_43

Pesantes, M., Lemus, C., Mitre, H. A., & Mejia, J. (2012a). Identifying criteria for designing a process architecture in a multimodel environment. In Proceedings of Software and System Process (ICSPP), (pp. 83–87). IEEE.

Pesantes, M., Lemus, C., Mitre, H. A., & Mejia, J. (2012b). Software process architecture: Roadmap. In *Proceedings of the 2012 IEEE Ninth Electronics, Robotics and Automotive Mechanics Conference* (pp. 83–87). Cuernavaca, Mexico: IEEE Computer Society.

Petersen, K., & Wohlin, C. (2010). Software process improvement through the lean measurement (SPI-LEAM) method. *Journal of Systems and Software*, *83*(7), 1275–1287. doi:10.1016/j.jss.2010.02.005

Petri, G. (2010). *Shedding light on cloud computing*. New York, NY: The Cloud Academy.

Pezzini, M., & Lheureux, B. J. (2011). *Integration platform as a service: moving integration to the cloud*. Stanford, CT: Gartner.

Ply, J. K., Moore, J., Williams, C. K., & Thatcher, J. (2012). IS employee attitudes and perceptions at varying levels of software process maturity. *MIS Quarterly-Management Information Systems*, *36*(2), 601.

Polanyi, M. (1966). *The tacit dimension*. New York: Doubleday.

Poppendieck, M., & Poppendieck, T. (2003). *Lean software development: An agile toolkit*. Upper Saddle River, NJ: Addison-Wesley Professional.

Potter, N., & Sakry, M. (2006). Developing a plan. In *Making process improvement work* (pp. 1–49). Reading, MA: Addison-Wesley.

Pressman, R. S. (2001). *Software engineering: A practitioner's approach*. New York: McGraw-Hill.

Print, M., & Hattie, J. (1997). Measuring quality in universities: An approach to weighting research productivity. *Higher Education*, *33*, 453–469. doi:10.1023/A:1002956407943

Rajendran, M. (2005). Analysis of team effectiveness in software development teams working on hardware and software environments using Belbin self-perception inventory. *Journal of Management Development*, *24*(8), 738–753. doi:10.1108/02621710510613753

Reagans, R., & McEvily, B. (2003). Network structure and knowledge transfer: The effects of cohesión and range. *Administrative Science Quarterly*, *48*, 240–267. doi:10.2307/3556658

Reagans, R., & Zuckerman, E. W. (2001). Networks, diversity, and productivity: The social capital of corporate R&D teams. *Organization Science*, *12*(4), 502. doi:10.1287/orsc.12.4.502.10637

Reagans, R., Zuckerman, E., & McEvily, B. (2004). How to make the team: Social networks vs. demography as criteria for designing effective teams. *Administrative Science Quarterly*, *49*(1), 101–133.

Rehman, M., Mahmood, K. M., Salleh, R., & Amin, A. (2012). Mapping job requirements of software engineers to big five personality traits. In *Proceedings of the International Conference on Computer &[)*. Kuala Lumpur, Malaysia: IEEE Computer Society.]. *Information Science*, *2*, 1115–1122.

Reißing, R. (2001). Towards a model for object-oriented design measurement. In *Proceedings of 5th International ECOOP Workshop on Quantitative Approaches in Object-Oriented Software Engineering* (pp. 71-84). ECOOP.

Ribiere, V. M. (2001). *Assessing knowledge management initiative successes as a function of organizational culture*. (Doctoral dissertation). The George Washington University, Washington, DC.

Rigby, J., & Edler, J. (2005). Peering inside research networks: Some observations on the effect of the intensity of collaboration on the variability of research quality. *Research Policy, 34*, 784–794. doi:10.1016/j.respol.2005.02.004

Ringstad, M. A., Dingsøyr, T., & Moe, N. B. (2011). Agile process improvement: Diagnosis and planning to improve teamwork. In R. V. O'Connor, J. Pries-Heje, & R. Messnarz (Eds.), *Systems, software and service process improvement, communications in computer and information science* (pp. 167–178). Berlin: Springer. doi:10.1007/978-3-642-22206-1_15

Rodríguez, D., García, E., Sánchez, S., & Rodríguez-Solano, C. (2010). Defining software process model constraints with rules using OWL and SWRL. *International Journal of Software Engineering and Knowledge Engineering, 20*(4), 533–548. doi:10.1142/S0218194010004876

Rodríguez-Jacobo, J., Espinosa-Curiel, I. E., Gutiérrez-Osorio, U., Ocegueda-Miramontes, V., & Fernández-Zepeda, J. A. (2012). Knowledge management in software process improvement initiatives in small organizations. In *Proceedings of the 19th European Systems & Software Process Improvement and Innovation*. Vienna, Austria: Academic Press.

Ropponen, J., & Lyytinen, K. (1997). Can software risk management improve system development: An exploratory study. *European Journal of Information Systems, 6*(1), 41–50. doi:10.1057/palgrave.ejis.3000253

Rovira, A., & Trías De Bes, F. (2004). *Good luck: Creating the conditions for success in life and business*. New York: John Wiley & Sons.

Royce, W. W. (1987). Managing the development of large software systems. In *Proceedings of IEEE 9th International Conference on Software Engineering* (pp. 328–338). IEEE.

Rozanski, N., & Woods, E. (2012). *Software systems architecture: Working with stakeholders using viewpoints and perspectives*. Reading, MA: Addison-Wesley.

Rumsey-Wairepo, A. (2006). *The association between co-authorship network structures and successful academic publishing among higher education scholars*. (Doctoral Dissertation). Department of Educational Leadership and Foundations, Brigham Young University, Salt Lake City, UT.

Runeson, P., & Höst, M. (2008). Guidelines for conducting and reporting case study research in software engineering. *Empirical Software Engineering, 14*(2), 131–164. doi:10.1007/s10664-008-9102-8

Rus, I., & Lindvall, M. (2002). Knowledge management in software engineering. *IEEE Software, 19*(3), 26–38. doi:10.1109/MS.2002.1003450

Sach, R., Petre, M., & Sharp, H. (2010). The use of MBTI in software engineering. In *Proceedings of 22nd Annual Psychology of Programming Interest Group 2010*. Madrid: Universidad Carlos III de Madrid.

Santos, G., Montoni, M., Figueiredo, S., & Rocha, A. (2007). SPI-KM - Lessons learned from applying a software process improvement strategy supported by knowledge management. In *Product-Focused Software Process Improvement (LNCS)* (Vol. 4589, pp. 81–95). Berlin: Springer. doi:10.1007/978-3-540-73460-4_10

Scacchi, W. (2001). *Process models in software engineering*. New York: John Wiley and Sons, Inc.

Schneider, G., & Winters, J. P. (2001). *Applying use cases: A practical guide*. Que Publishing.

Scholtes, P. R. (1991). *El manual del equipo*. Madison, WI: Joiner Associates, Inc.

Schwaber, K. (2004). *Agile project management with Scrum*. Microsoft Press.

Schwaber, K., & Beedle, M. (2002). *Agile software development with SCRUM*. Upper Saddle River, NJ: Prentice-Hall.

SEI Blog. (2012). Retrieved from http://www.blog.sei.cmu.edu/

Sellers, B. H. (1996). *Object-oriented metrics: Measures of complexity*. Upper Saddle River, NJ: Prentice-Hall, Inc.

Sharp, H., Baddoo, N., Beecham, S., Hall, T., & Robinson, H. (2009). Models of motivation in software engineering. *Information and Software Technology*, *51*(1), 219–233. doi:10.1016/j.infsof.2008.05.009

Shaw, M. (1964). *Comunication networks*. Advances in experimental social psychologyNew York: Academic Press.

Shaw, M., & Clements, P. (2006). The golden age of software architecture. *IEEE Software*, *2*(23), 31–39. doi:10.1109/MS.2006.58

Shen, M., Yang, W., Rong, G., & Shao, D. (2012). Applying agile methods to embedded software development: A systematic review. In *Proceedings of the 2nd International Workshop on Software Engineering for Embedded Systems (SEES)*. Zurich, Switzerland: IEEE Computer Society.

Shepperd, M., & MacDonell, S. (2012). Evaluating prediction systems in software project estimation. *Information and Software Technology*, *54*(8), 820–827. doi:10.1016/j.infsof.2011.12.008

Shih, C.-C., & Huang, S.-J. (2010). Exploring the relationship between organizational culture and software process improvement deployment. *Information & Management*, *47*(5–6), 271–281. doi:10.1016/j.im.2010.06.001

Shim, J. P., Warkentin, M., Courtney, J. F., Power, D. J., Sharda, R., & Carlsson, C. (2002). Past, present, and future of decision support technology. *Decision Support Systems*, *33*(2), 111–126. doi:10.1016/S0167-9236(01)00139-7

Shin, H., Choi, H.-J., & Baik, J. (2007). Jasmine: A PSP supporting tool. In *Software Process Dynamics and Agility (LNCS)* (Vol. 4470, pp. 73–83). Berlin: Springer. doi:10.1007/978-3-540-72426-1_7

Simon, F., & Murray, T. (2007). Decision support systems. *Communications of the ACM*, *50*(3), 39–40. doi:10.1145/1226736.1226762

Singh, R. (1995). *International standard ISO/IEC 12207 software life cycle processes*. Federa Aviation Administration.

Singh, R. (1996). International standard ISO/IEC 12207 software life cycle processes. *Software Process Improvement and Practice*, *2*(1), 35–50. doi:10.1002/(SICI)1099-1670(199603)2:1<35::AID-SPIP29>3.0.CO;2-3

Siviy, J., Kirwan, P., Marino, L., & Morley, J. (2008). The value of harmonization multiple improvement technologies: A process improvement professional's view. *Software Engineering Institute (SEI) library*. Carnegie Mellon University. Retrieved June 2008 from http://www.sei.cmu.edu/library/assets/whitepapers/multimodelExecutive_wp_harmonizationROI_032008_v1.pdf

Siviy, J., Kirwan, P., Morley, J., & Marino, L. (2008). Maximizing your process improvement ROI through harmonization. *Software Engineering Institute (SEI) Library*. Carnegie Mellon University. Retrieved June 2008 from http://www.sei.cmu.edu/library/assets/whitepapers/multimodelExecutive_wp_harmonizationROI_032008_v1.pdf

Siviy, J., Penn, M. L., & Stoddard, R. W. (2008). *CMMI and six sigma: Partners in process improvement*. Upper Saddle River, NJ: Pearson Education Software Engineering Institute. (2010). *SEI prime project*. Retrieved from http://www.sei.cmu.edu/process/research/prime.cfm

Sodiya, A. S., Longe, H. O. D., Onashoga, S. A., Awodel, O., & Omosho, L. O. (2007). An improved assessment of personality traits in software engineering. *Interdisciplinary Journal of Information, Knowledge, and Management*, *2*, 163–177.

Software Engineering Institute. (2000). *Mastering process improvement course: Introduction to the Drexler-Sibbet team performance model*. Pittsburgh, PA: Software Engineering Institute, Carnegie Mellon University.

Software Engineering Institute. (2002). *Capabitlity maturity model integration - CMMI-SE/SW, V1.1*. Author.

Software Engineering Institute. (2006). *A process research framework – The international process research consortium*. Pittsburgh, PA: Software Engineering Institute, Carnegie Mellon University.

Software Engineering Institute. (2010). *CMMI for acquisition, version 1.3*. Author.

Software Engineering Institute. (2012). Retrieved from http://www.sei.cmu.edu/

Sommerville, I. (2004). *Software engineering*. International Computer Science Series.

Soto-Acosta, P., Martínez-Conesa, I., & Colomo-Palacios, R. (2010). An empirical analysis of the relationship between IT training sources and IT value. *Information Systems Management, 27*(3), 274–283. doi:10.1080/10580530.2010.493847

Sparrowe, R. T., Liden, R. C., Wayne, S. J., & Kraimer, M. L. (2001). Social networks and the performance of individuals and groups. *Academy of Management Journal, 44*(2), 316–325. doi:10.2307/3069458

Srivastava, N., Singh, S., & Dokken, T. (2009). *Assorted chocolates & cookies in a multi-model box*. Paper presented at SEPG 2009 North America Conference. San Jose, CA.

SSQC. (2011). Software estimation bootcamp. In *Proceedings of the SEPG Conference 2011*. Portland, OR: SEPG.

Standard Comitee, I. E. E. E. (2008). *ISO/IEC/IEEE standard for systems and software engineering - Software life cycle processes (IEEE STD 12207-2008)*. IEEE.

Standish Group International. (2006). *The chaos report*. Retrieved from www.standishgroup.com/sample_research/PDFpages/Chaos2006.pdf

Stapleton, J. (2003). *DSDM: The method in practice*. Reading, MA: Addison Wesley Longman.

Strong, B., Davenport, T. H., & Prusak, L. (2008). Organizational governance of knowledge and learning. *Knowledge and Process Management, 15*(2), 150–157. doi:10.1002/kpm.306

Sulayman, M., & Mendes, E. (2009). A systematic literature review of software process improvement for small and medium web companies. In *Proceedings of Advances in Software Engineering* (pp. 1–8). Berlin: Springer. doi:10.1007/978-3-642-10619-4_1

Sulayman, M., Urquhart, C., Mendes, E., & Seidel, S. (2012). Software process improvement success factors for small and medium web companies: A qualitative study. *Information and Software Technology, 54*(5), 479–500. doi:10.1016/j.infsof.2011.12.007

Sun, Y., & Liu, X. (2010). Business-oriented software process improvement based on CMMI using QFD. *Information and Software Technology, 52*(1), 79–91. doi:10.1016/j.infsof.2009.08.003

Sure, Y., & Studer, R. (2002). A methodology for ontology-based knowledge management. In J. Davies, D. Fensel, & F. van Harmelen (Eds.), *Towards the semantic web: Ontology-driven knowledge management* (pp. 33–46). Chichester, UK: Wiley. doi:10.1002/0470858060.ch3

Swartout, W., Neches, R., & Patil, R. (1993). Knowledge sharing: Prospects and challenges. In K. Fuchi & T. Yokoi (Eds.), *Proceedings of the International Conference on Building and Sharing of Very Large-Scale Knowledge Bases*. Tokyo, Japan: Academic Press.

Tarr, P., Ossher, H., Harrison, W., & Sutton, S. M., Jr. (1999). N degrees of separation: Multi-dimensional separation of concerns. In *Proceedings of the 21st International Conference on Software Engineering* (pp. 107-119). ACM.

Tautz, C., & von Wangenheim, C. G. (1998). *REFSENO: A representation formalism for software engineering ontologies* (IESE-015.98/E). Kaiserslautern: Fraunhofer IESE.

The CMMi Easy Button. (2012). *CMMI level 2 - MA*. Retrieved 10th December 2013, from http://www.software-quality-assurance.org/cmmi-measurement-and-analysis.html

Tichy, N. M., Tushman, M. L., & Fombrun, C. (1979). Social network analysis for organizations. *Academy of Management Review, 4*(4), 507–519.

Tsai, W., & Wu, C. H. (2010). From The editors: Knowledge combination: A cocitation analysis. Academy of Management Journal, 53(3), 441–450.

Turban, E., Aronson, J. E., & Liang, T.-P. (2005). Knowledge management. In *Decision support systems and intelligent systems*. Uppers Saddle River, NJ: Prentice Hall.

Tyndall, I. (2010). *The end of corporate IT? Cloud computing literature review*. New York, NY: Ian Tyndall.

Udoudoh, S. J. (2012). Impacts of personality traits on career choice of information scientists in Federal University of Technology, Minna, Niger State, Nigeria. *International Journal of Library and Information Science, 4*(4), 57–70.

United States Government Accountability Office. (2009a). *Challenges in aligning space system components (Vol. GAO 10-55)*. Washington, DC: Author.

United States Government Accountability Office. (2009b). *DOD faces substantial challenges in developing new space systems*. Washington, DC: Author.

United States Government Accountability Office. (2009c). *Issues to be considered for army's modernization of combat systems*. Washington, DC: Author.

United States Government Accountability Office. (2009d). *Many analyses of alternatives have not provided a robust assessment of weapon system options (Vol. GAO 09-665)*. Washington, DC: Author.

United States Government Accountability Office. (2009e). *Opportunities exist to achieve greater commonality and efficiencies among unmanned aircraft systems*. Washington, DC: Author.

Unterkalmsteiner, M., Gorschek, T., Islam, A. K. M. M., Cheng, C. K., Permadi, R. B., & Feldt, R. (2012). Evaluation and measurement of software process improvement - A systematic literature review. *IEEE Transactions on Software Engineering*, 38(2), 398–424. doi:10.1109/TSE.2011.26

Valiente, M. C., García-Barriocanal, E., & Sicilia, M. A. (2012). Applying ontology-based models for supporting integrated software development and IT service management processes. *IEEE Transactions on Systems, Man, and Cybernetics. Part C*, 42(1), 61–74.

van der Leij, M. J., & Goyal, S. (2006). Strong ties in a small world (No. 06-008/1). Tinbergen Institute.

van Solingen, R. (2004). Measuring the ROI of software process improvement. *IEEE Software*, 21(3), 32–38. doi:10.1109/MS.2004.1293070

van Solingen, R. (2009). A follow-up reflection on software process improvement ROI. *IEEE Software*, 26(5), 77–79. doi:10.1109/MS.2009.120

Vega Zepeda, V., Gasca-Hurtado, G. P., & Calvo-Manzano, J. A. (2012). *Identifying patterns of software acquisition projects through the application of the MECT method*. Paper presented at the Information Systems and Technologies (CISTI). Madrid, Spain.

Vizcaíno, A., García, F., Caballero, I., Villar, J. C., & Piattini, M. (2012). Towards an ontology for global software development. *IET Software*, 6(3), 214–225. doi:10.1049/iet-sen.2011.0087

Vlaanderen, K., Brinkkemper, S., & van de Weerd, I. (2012). On the design of a knowledge management system for incremental process improvement for software product management. *International Journal of Information System Modeling and Design*, 3(4), 46–66. doi:10.4018/jismd.2012100103

VMWare. (2013). *Cloud computing*. Retrieved from http://www.vmware.com/es/cloud-computing/

Walker, G., Kogut, B., & Shan, W. (1997). Social capital, structural holes and the formation of an industry network. *Organization Science*, 8(2), 109–125. doi:10.1287/orsc.8.2.109

Wang, Y., & King, G. (2000). *Software engineering processes: Principles and applications*. Boca Raton, FL: CRC Press.

Warnier, J. D. (1981). *Logical construction of systems*. New York: Van Nostrand Reinhold Company.

Wasserman, S. (1994). *Social network analysis: Methods and applications* (Vol. 8). Cambridge, UK: Cambridge University Press. doi:10.1017/CBO9780511815478

Wickert, A., & Herschel, R. (2001). Knowledge-management issues for smaller businesses. *Journal of Knowledge Management*, 5(4), 329–337. doi:10.1108/13673270110411751

Wikipedia. (2013). *Cloud computing*. Retrieved from http://en.wikipedia.org/wiki/Cloud_computing

Williams, T. (2008). How do organizations learn lessons from projects—And do they? *IEEE Transactions on Engineering Management*, 55(2), 248–266. doi:10.1109/TEM.2007.912920

Withers, D. H. (2000). Software engineering best practices applied to the modeling process. In *Proceedings of Simulation Conference* (pp. 432-439). Orlando, FL: Academic Press.

Wolf, C., & Harmon, P. (2012). The state of business process management- 2012. *BPTrends Market Surveys*. Retrieved from http://www.bptrends.com/surveys_landing.cfm

Wolf, T., Schroter, A., Damian, D., Panjer, L. D., & Nguyen, T. H. (2009). Mining task-based social networks to explore collaboration in software teams. *IEEE Software*, *26*(1), 58–66. doi:10.1109/MS.2009.16

Wong, K. Y., & Aspinwall, E. (2004). Knowledge management implementation frameworks: A review. *Knowledge and Process Management*, *11*(2), 93–104. doi:10.1002/kpm.193

Wong, S. S. (2008). Task knowledge overlap and knowledge variety: The role of advice network structures and impact on group effectiveness. *Journal of Organizational Behavior*, *29*, 591–614. doi:10.1002/job.490

Wongthongtham, P., Chang, E., Dillon, T., & Sommerville, I. (2006). Ontology based multi-site software development methodology and tools. *Journal of Systems Architecture*, *52*(11), 640–653. doi:10.1016/j.sysarc.2006.06.008

Wongthongtham, P., Chang, E., Dillon, T., & Sommerville, I. (2009). Development of a software engineering ontology for multisite software development. *IEEE Transactions on Knowledge and Data Engineering*, *21*(8), 1205–1217. doi:10.1109/TKDE.2008.209

Wooldridge, D., & Schneider, M. (2010). *The business of iPhone app development: Making and marketing apps that succeed*. New York, NY: Apress. doi:10.1007/978-1-4302-2734-2

Worldpanel. (2009). *Informe TNS*. Retrieved from http://www.kantarworldpanel.com/es

XML-Core-Working-Group. (2009). *Extensible markup language (XML) reference website*. Retrieved from http://www.w3.org/XML/

Yilmaz, M., & O'Connor, R. V. (2011). A software process engineering approach to improving software team productivity using socioeconomic mechanism design. *SIGSOFT Softw. Eng. Notes*, *36*(5), 1–5. doi:10.1145/2020976.2020998

Yilmaz, M., & O'Connor, R. V. (2012). Towards the understanding and classification of the personality traits of software development practitioners: Situational context cards approach. In *Proceeding of the Conference Software Engineering and Advanced Applications* (pp. 400–405). Dublin, Ireland: IEEE Computer Society.

Yousefi-Nooraie, R., Akbari-Kamrani, M., Hanneman, R. A., & Etemadi, A. (2008). Association between co-authorship network and scientific productivity and impact indicators in academic medical research centers: A case study in Iran. *Health Research Policy and Systems*, *6*(1), 9. doi:10.1186/1478-4505-6-9 PMID:18796149

Zack, M. H. (1999). Developing a knowledge strategy. *California Management Review*, *41*(3), 125–145. doi:10.2307/41166000

About the Contributors

Ricardo Colomo-Palacios is an Associate Professor at the Computer Science Department of the Universidad Carlos III de Madrid. His research interests include applied research in Information Systems, software project management, and people in software projects. He received his PhD in Computer Science from the Universidad Politécnica of Madrid (2005). He also holds a MBA from the Instituto de Empresa (2002). He has been working as Software Engineer, Project Manager, and Software Engineering Consultant in several companies including Spanish IT leader INDRA. He is also an Editorial Board Member and Associate Editor for several international journals and conferences and Editor-in-Chief of *International Journal of Human Capital and Information Technology Professionals*.

Jose A. Calvo-Manzano Villalon holds a PhD in Computer Science. He is an assistant professor in the Facultad de Informática at the Universidad Politécnica de Madrid, where he teaches Software Engineering, specifically Software Process Management and Improvement. He has participated in more than 20 research projects (European, Spanish Public Administration, as well as with private enterprises). He is the author of more than 50 international papers. He is the author of several books on software process improvement and software engineering topics as well. He is the Director of the Research Chair for Software Process Improvement for Spain and the Latin American Region, where he was a member of the team that translated CMMI-DEV v1.2 and v1.3 into Spanish. He also holds the ITIL® v2 and v3 Foundation and CMDB Certifications.

Antonio de Amescua Seco is a full professor in the Computer Science Department at Carlos III University of Madrid. He has been working as a software engineer in a public company (Iberia Airlines) and a private company (Novotec Consultores) as a software engineering consultant. He also founded Progresión, a spin-off company, in order to offer advanced Software Process Improvement services. His research interests include software process improvement, software reuse, and software project management.

Tomás San Feliu Gilabert holds a PhD in Computer Science. He is an assistant professor in the Facultad de Informática at the Universidad Politécnica de Madrid. He teaches Software Engineering, specifically software process management and improvement. He has participated in more than 20 research projects (European, Spanish public administration, as well as with private enterprises). He is author of more than 50 international papers. He is also the author of books related to software process improvement and software engineering. He is a member of the Research Chairs for Software Process Improvement for Spain and the Latin American Region and has been a member of the team that translated CMMI-DEV v1.2 and v1.3 to Spanish.

* * *

María Clara Gómez Álvarez is a professor in the Facultad de Ingeniería at the Universidad de Medellín, Colombia. She teaches Software Engineering, specifically requirements engineering. She is the head of the Research Group ARKADIUS.

Magdalena Arcilla holds a PhD in Computer Science. She is assistant professor in the Languages and Computer Science Department of UNED (Spanish Open University). She teaches Software Engineering. She has also worked in the Computer Science Department of the Carlos III University of Madrid and has 8 years' experience as a software developer at CustomWare Company. She is the author of several international papers on software engineering and of a book on the software engineering. She holds the ITIL® v2 and v3 Foundation certificates.

Jaime Alberto Echeverri Arias is an associate professor in the Facultad de Ingeniería at the Universidad de Medellín, Colombia. He teaches Software Engineering. He is the author of international papers related to software. He is member of the Research Group ARKADIUS.

Félix A. Barrio holds a PhD in Science and Technology Management from the University of Salamanca. He is the Head Manager of the Innovation and Quality Department at the National Institute for Information and Communication of Technologies, an agency of the Spanish Government. He was the head of the National Laboratory for Quality of Software between 2007 and 2012, where he has promoted actively the translation of CMMI-DEV v1.2 and v1.3 to Spanish. He has been teaching in the Master's of Information Security programme of the Open University of Catalonia (UOC) and in the Master's of IT Security programme at the Universidad of Leon since 2007, both in the area of Information Security Management and IT governance. He has participated in more than 20 research projects (European, Spanish public administration, as well as private enterprises). He also holds the CISM Certification.

Jorge Becerra is a professor and researcher of computer engineering and head of the Software Factory Group at Escola Politécnica da Universidade de São Paulo (Brazil). His research interests are software architecture, process architecture, software factory, business process management, and enterprise architecture. He has a PhD in Computer Engineering from Escola Politécnica da Universidade de São Paulo.

Adrián Casado-Rivas obtained his B.Sc. in Computer Science Engineering in October 2012 from Universidad Carlos III de Madrid. Currently, he is pursuing an Information Science and Technology Master's Degree at the same university. Adrián has been working for a year and a half with the Software Engineering Lab research group at UC3M (SEL-UC3M) as a junior researcher. His areas of interest are people, projects and process management, and the improvement of daily life supported by mobile applications.

Victor Navarro Belmonte obtained a Master's degree in Software Engineering at the Research Center in Mathematics (CIMAT) in Zacatecas, México.

Leonardo Bermon-Angarita is a professor at the National University of Colombia in Manizales, Colombia. He holds a PhD in Computer Science from the Carlos III University of Madrid (Spain, 2010). During his research at the Carlos III University of Madrid, he worked on collaborative environments to improve process asset libraries by providing them with new features and capabilities for the reuse of knowledge. His current interests are software process improvement, knowledge management, agile software development, and software product and process quality.

Elisabet Capón-García is a Chemical and Industrial Engineer from Universitat Politècnica de Catalunya (UPC). She obtained her PhD at UPC in the area of Process Systems Engineering. She is currently working at ETH Zürich in the Safety and Environmental Technology Group. Her research interests include decision-making and optimization in the process industry.

Humberto Cervantes is a professor of Software Engineering at the Autonomous Metropolitan University in Mexico City. His primary research interests include software architecture design methods and their adoption in industrial settings. Dr. Cervantes is also a consultant for software development companies in topics related to software architecture. He has helped Quarksoft, a leading Mexican development company, to integrate architecture methods with the Team Software Process (TSP) and Capability Maturity Model Integration (CMMI). Dr. Cervantes holds a PhD from Université Joseph Fourier in France, and he has received the Software Architecture Professional and ATAM Evaluator certificates from the Software Engineering Institute.

Manuel Pérez Cota is Professor and Researcher at the University of Vigo (UVIGO) in Vigo, Spain. He has a degree in Electrical Engineering (Universidad La Salle) and Electronics and Communications Engineering (Universidad Nacional Autónoma de México – UNAM, 1980), a PhD in Industrial Engineering (Universidad de Santiago de Compostela, 1990). He is the director of the international research group SI1-GEAC (http://cuautla.uvigo.es/si1-geac/). He was the first director and developer of the Computer Department (Computer Science School of the University of Vigo). He collaborates in different Master and PhD programs in Spain, Portugal, Germany, Argentina and Bolivia, and has been supervisor of several PhDs. He has been involved in different European and International projects. He has published quite extensively and has many publications (including books, book chapters, Scientific Citation Index journal articles, and international journal articles, as well as publications in refereed conference proceedings). He is a member of different international committees and associations (ACM, IEEE, AISTI, AIPO, ANALCT).

Gonzalo Cuevas was awarded his MSc degree in Computer Science in 1972 at the Computer Science Faculty of the Universidad Politécnica de Madrid and his PhD degree in Telecommunications from the School of Telecommunications in 1974 from the same university. He was a professor in Software Engineering at the Computer Science Faculty of the Universidad Politécnica de Madrid from 1970 to 2010. He joined the faculty as professor in 1970 and became full professor in 1996. He was a systems analyst at the Spanish national railway company (RENFE) from 1965 to 1969. He was the director of software development, data processing, data transmission software development, and Software Process Improvement (SPI) at Iberia Airlines (now AIG). He has been project leader and evaluator in European projects on software best practices. He was also the founder and director of the Master's program in Software Engineering in association with Carnegie Mellon University at the Computer Science Faculty of Universidad Politécnica de Madrid. His current research interests are models and methods for process assessment and process improvement, and process deployment. He has worked as an SPI Consultant in different organizations since 1990. He was a member of the IPRC coordinated by SEI. Also, he was a member of CMMI V1.3 Translation Team, where he coordinated the translation of CMMI-DEV V1.2 and V1.3 into Spanish.

Ismael Edrein Espinosa-Curiel received his BSc in Computational Systems in 2005 and his MSc and PhD in Computer Science at CICESE in 2008 and 2013, respectively. His research interests focus on software process improvement in small companies, software engineering, knowledge management, and the impact of social and personal factors in software engineering.

Roberto Esteban-Santiago holds a BSc in Computer Science and Engineering and is pursuing an MSc in Information Technology and Science at Carlos III University of Madrid. He develops iOS apps in the Software Engineering Lab research group at the university, one of which has already been published on the App Store. His current research interests focus on mobile app development and agile software development.

Luis Fernández-Sanz is an associate professor at the Dept. of Computer Science of Universidad de Alcalá (UAH). He earned a degree in Computing in 1989 at Universidad Politecnica de Madrid (UPM) and his Ph.D. in Computing with a special award at University of the Basque Country in 1997. With more than 20 years of research and teaching experience (at UPM, Universidad Europea de Madrid, and UAH), he is also engaged in the management of the main Spanish Computing Professionals association (ATI: www.ati.es) as vice president and is chairman of ATI Software Quality group. He is now vice president of CEPIS (Council of European Professional Informatics Societies: www.cepis.org). He has made a large number of contributions to refereed impact international journals, conferences, and books. His main research interests include technical fields like software quality and engineering and testing and non-technical fields like computing education, especially in multinational settings, IT profession and professionalism, and requirements and skills for IT jobs.

José Alberto Fernández-Zepeda received his BSc in Electronic Engineering in 1991, MS degree in Electronic Engineering in 1994, and PhD in Computer Engineering in 1999. He is currently an associate professor in the Computer Science Department at CICESE. Some of his research interests include software process improvement in small companies, the impact of social and personal factors in software engineering, and design and analysis of algorithms.

Ivan Garcia has a PhD in Software Engineering at the Universidad Politécnica de Madrid and is a full-time professor at the Postgraduate Division of the Universidad Tecnológica de la Mixteca, Mexico. He is the author of international papers on Software Engineering and, more specifically, Software Process Improvement. Garcia is a member of the Technical Committee of the International Association of

Science and Technology for Development (IASTED) and is also a reviewer of international journals and conferences in Mexico. He has participated in more than 15 software project management and software process improvement projects in the Mexican software industry. In Latin America, Garcia has participated in several institutional research projects in industry (IBM Global Services) and in academia. At present, he is a member of the IMPROWEB project to improve software processes in 32 Spanish enterprises. He was a member of the team that translated CMMI-DEV v1.2 and CMMI-DEV v1.3 into Spanish.

Javier Garcia-Guzman is an associate professor in the Computer Science Department at Carlos III University of Madrid. He holds a BSc in Engineering and a PhD in Computer Science. Javier has participated in numerous knowledge management research projects in software engineering organizations. He has published several books and numerous international scientific papers on software engineering and collaborative working environments.

Alejandra García-Hernández holds a Ph.D. in Engineering and Innovation Projects from the Polytechnic University of Valencia (2010). She is currently a researcher and professor in the Master's program of Software Engineering at CIMAT. She is an Industrial and Systems Engineer from the Instituto Tecnológico y de Estudios Superiores de Monterrey and she is certified in Supply Chain Management (2004). She was a researcher in the Institute of Innovation and Knowledge Management – INGENIO (2007-2010), a joint institute of the Spanish Council for Scientific Research and the Polytechnic University of Valencia. She has participated in R&D projects funded by the Ministerio de Economía y Competitividad de España, CONACyT and private enterprises. She has submitted several papers to International congresses and published papers in international journals. Her research activities mainly concern social network analysis, innovation and knowledge management, teams and organizational performance, networks and software engineering.

Gloria Piedad Gasca-Hurtado holds a Ph.D. in Computer Science. She is an assistant professor in the Facultad de Ingeniería at the Universidad de Medellín, Colombia. She teaches Software Engineering, specifically software process management and improvement. She has participated in research projects. She is author of international papers related to software process improvement and other software engineering topics as well. She is member of the "Research Group ARKADIUS" and was a member of the team that translated CMMI-DEV v1.2 and v1.3 to Spanish.

Ramiro Gonçalves is an Associate Professor at the state-owned University of Trás-os-Montes e Alto Douro (UTAD) in Vila Real, Portugal, and a researcher with INESC TEC. He has a degree in computer management (Universidade Portucalense Infante D. Henrique, 1991), a master of science in computer science (Universidade do Minho, 1998), and a PhD in information systems (Universidade de Trás-os-Montes e Alto Douro, UTAD, 2005). At UTAD, he is currently a member of the Coordination Committee of the Doctoral Program in Computer Science (since 2010). He is widely sought after as a supervisor in the area of computer science and as such has been responsible for the supervision of several PhDs and MScs. He has published quite extensively and has around 120 publications (including book chapters, Scientific Citation Index journal articles, and international journal articles, as well as publications in refereed conference proceedings).

Ulises Gutiérrez-Osorio received a BSc in Computer Science in 2009 and MSc in Computer Science in 2011. His research interests focus on software process improvement in small companies, software engineering, and knowledge management.

Alberto Heredia is an assistant professor in the Computer Science Department at Carlos III University of Madrid. He holds a BSc in Telecommunication Engineering and a PhD in Computer Science and Technology. His current research interests focus on software engineering and knowledge management, especially mobile app development and agile software development.

Antonia Mas is a university lecturer of Software Engineering and Project Management at the University of the Balearic Islands. Her research interests include software process improvement, project management, and service management. She has promoted and coordinated the QuaSAR Project, a software process improvement initiative in small software companies in the Balearic Islands. She received her degree in Computer Science from UAB (Catalonia, Spain) and her PhD in Computer Science from the University of the Balearic Islands. She has been a member of the Software Quality Group of ATI Spain since 1998 and is a member of the editorial board of the REICIS journal. She has also served as program committee chair and program committee member of scientific conferences and workshops related to software quality. She is an ISO/IEC 15504 assessor and focuses on assessing small companies.

Manuel Muñoz Archidona got his B.S. in Computer Science Engineering in June 2012 from Universidad Carlos III de Madrid. He is currently studying the Information Science and Technology Master's Degree at Universidad Carlos III de Madrid, where he has been working for two years with the Computer Architecture, Communications and Systems Group (ARCOS) as a research assistant. At present, Manuel is working on a project related to the simulation of the Spanish railway network electricity consumption in collaboration with the railway infrastructure company ADIF.

Edrisi Muñoz Mata has an MSc. in Industrial Engineering from Instituto Tecnológico de Orizaba in Mexico and a PhD in Chemical Process Engineering from Universitat Politècnica de Catalunya (UPC) in Spain. His research focuses on knowledge management through the development of ontologies and management frameworks for decision-making support in different areas. He is currently a member of Centro de Investigación en Matemáticas A.C (CIMAT) in Mexico and collaborates with the UPC as part of the research team, participating in different Mexican and European research projects.

Fuensanta Medina-Dominguez holds a BSc and a PhD in Computer Science from the Carlos III University of Madrid, Spain. She has been working in the field of software engineering since 2000 and has been a faculty member of the Computer Science Department in the Carlos III University of Madrid since 2004. Her research interests include software engineering, knowledge management, knowledge reuse, and software process improvement focusing on technology transfer in organizations through the use of new trends in computer-supported collaborative work technology.

Jezreel Mejia holds a PhD in Computer Science. He is currently a researcher in software engineering at the Research Center in Mathematics, Zacatecas, México. He is a member of Research Chair in Software Process Improvement for Spain and the Latin American Region. His research field is software engineering, including both technology (methods, techniques, tools, and formalisms) and management. His current research interests are: software process improvement, multi-model environment, project management, acquisition and outsourcing process, agile methodologies, software process improvement models and standards, knowledge management software quality, team software process, and IT security. He has published several technical papers on project management, software teams, software process improvement, acquisition and outsourcing processes. He was a member of the team that translated CMMI-DEV v1.2 and v1.3 into Spanish.

Antoni Lluís Mesquida is an assistant lecturer of Software Engineering and Project Management at the University of the Balearic Islands. His research interests include software process improvement, project management, and service management. He has participated in the QuaSAR project, a software process improvement programme in small software companies in the Balearic Islands. He received his PhD in Computer Science from the University of the Balearic Islands.

Sanjay Misra is a professor of Computer Engineering at Covenant University, OTA, Nigeria. He served as head of department of Computer Engineering from February 2010 to October 2011 and head of the Cyber Security department from October 2011 to September 2012 at Federal University of Technology, Minna, Nigeria. He is a software engineer and has previously held academic positions at Federal University of Technology Minna, Nigeria, Atilim University, Turkey, Subharati University, and UP Technical University, India. He is also Adjunct/Visiting Professor at the University of Alcalá, Spain; UNICEN, Tandil, Argentina, and Atilim University, Turkey. He is the author of more than 100 research papers and has received several awards for outstanding publications. He is chief editor of the International Journal of Physical Sciences and founder chair of several annual international workshops (Software Engineering Process and Applications [Springer], Tools and Techniques in Software Development Process [2009, 2010, 2011, 2012, IEEE], Software Quality [2009, 2011, 2012, IEEE]).

Hugo A. Mitre is a software engineering researcher at CIMAT Zacatecas, Mexico, member of the Mexican national researchers system (SNI), and member of the SEL-UC3M (Software Engineering Lab, sel.inf.uc3m.es) group at Carlos III University of Madrid. He holds a PhD in Computer Science and Technology from the Carlos III University of Madrid (Spain, 2010) and has participated in numerous research projects related to software engineering, IT governance, strategic management, incubation of software companies and legal systems financed by public (Mexican and Spanish) and private funds. His current interests are software process improvement, strategic management in Software Engineering Organizations (SEO), IT governance, agile software development, knowledge measurement, knowledge management, product and process measurement, and ICT clusters management.

Arturo Mora-Soto holds a PhD in Computer Science and Technology from Carlos III University of Madrid. He is an assistant professor at the Computer Science Department of Carlos III University of Madrid. His research involves collaborative learning, Web technologies (especially Web 2.0), knowledge management (use, reuse, assessment, and capitalization), data analysis, and process improvement, especially applying Six Sigma in software engineering. He has been working as a software engineer as well as university lecturer in Mexico since 2002.

Fernando Moreira has a degree in Computer Science (1992), M.Sc. in Electronic Engineering (1997), and Ph.D. in Electronic Engineering (2003), both obtained from the Faculty of Engineering of the University of Porto. He has been a member of the Department of Innovation, Science and Technology at University Portucalense since 1992, currently as Associate Professor. He teaches undergraduate and post-graduate studies and supervises several Ph.D. and M.Sc. students. He is a (co-)author of several peer-reviewed scientific publications with national and international conferences. He has served as a member of the Editorial Advisory Board for several books. He regularly serves as a member of Programme and Organizing Committees of national and international conferences, namely ICEIS, CISTI, InSITE, PATTERNS, INTELLI, Elpub, and CENTRIS. He is the coordinator of the M.Sc. of Computation. He is associated with NSTICC, ACM, and IEEE.

Mirna Muñoz holds a PhD in Computer Science. She is currently a researcher in computer science at the Research Center in Mathematics (CIMAT), Zacatecas, México. She is a member of Research Chair in Software Process Improvement for Spain and the Latin American Region. Her research field is software engineering, including both technology (methods, techniques, tools, and formalisms) and management. Her current research interests are: how to implement software process improvements focused on minimizing change resistance and the use of multi-model environments and software tools in software process improvements, software process improvement models and standards, project management, change management, knowledge management, software quality, and team software process ad IT security. She has published several technical papers on project management, multi-model environment and process improvement. She was a member of the team that translated CMMI-DEV v1.2 and v1.3 into Spanish.

Cuauhtémoc Lemus Olalde received his PhD in Computer Science from the Graduate School at Tulane University (New Orleans, LA, 1996). He was a visiting researcher from 1996 to 1998 as Postdoctoral Fellow in the Aerospace Program at Houston University – Clear Lake in partnership with the National Aeronautics and Space Administration (NASA) and the Johnson Space Center (JSC). Currently, he is the Branch Director of the Research Centre in Mathematics at Zacatecas, México. His research interests include systemic thinking, TRIZ tools applied to software, six sigma tools applied to software.

Martha Fofo Omorodion has obtained her Bachelor of Engineering in electrical and computer engineering from Federal University of Technology, Minna, Nigeria. Her area of interest includes software engineering, software process improvements, software process models, agile software development, and software metrics. She is a talented researcher and has authored several papers on these topics.

Carmen Pagés obtained her University degree in Computer Science at the Technical University of Madrid and PhD from the University of Alcalá. She worked in private telecommunication companies as analyst, project manager, and consultant between 1987 and 2003. She has extensive teaching experience and, at present, holds the position of assistant Ph.D. lecturer at the Department of Computer Science (University of Alcalá, Spain). She has practical experience from software process technology and modeling methodologies to software projects planning and managing, software maintenance and international ERP projects. Her research interests include learning technology and quality issues in education as well as software engineering and management.

Mery Pesantes obtained her Master's Degree in Software Engineering at the Research Centre in Mathematics (CIMAT, Mexico) in 2006. She is an SEI-authorized Personal Software Process Developer. She was involved in several TSP[SM] and PSP[SM] projects in academia. In addition, she participated in process assessments and implementation of quality models, such as CMMI and MOPROSOFT. She is currently a PhD student in Computer Science at CIMAT. Her research interests include multimodel environment, process architecture, software process improvement, and software quality.

Raquel Poy holds a PhD in Psychology and Education from the University of Leon. She is an assistant professor in the Faculty of Education at the same university. She is teaching in the Department of Theory of Education, specifically in the area of Technology in Education. She has participated in more than 10 research projects (European and Spanish Public Administration). She is the director of the research area at the Latin-American Federation for Learning Diseases. She also holds a certificate in Expert in ICT Management from the University of Alcalá. She is the author of more than 20 academic papers related to digital skills development.

Josefina Rodríguez-Jacobo received her BSc in Physics in 1986, MSc in Computer Science in 1993 and PhD in Psychology in 2003. She is currently working in the Computer Science Department at CICESE. Her main research interests include software process improvement in small companies, software engineering, knowledge management, and the social and personal factors related to software engineering.

Jorge Manjarrez Sanchez obtained a PhD in Computer Science in Parallel Databases at the University of Nantes, France. At the writing of this article, he was an Associate Professor in the Master's in Software Engineering at the Research Center in Mathematics (CIMAT) in Mexico. He is now an entrepreneur and independent software consultant in large scale data analytics and parallel software engineering.

Perla Velasco-Elizondo is a professor of Software Engineering at the Autonomous University of Zacatecas. Her main research interests include software composition, architecture-centered software development and software engineering education. From 2008-2012, she was an associate researcher at the Center for Mathematical Research and faculty member of the Master of Software Engineering Program of this institution. From 2010-2011, she was a visiting researcher at The Institute for Software Research of The Carnegie Mellon University. She has received several training courses at The Software Engineering Institute and holds the SOA Architect Professional certificate from this institute. Dr. Velasco-Elizondo received her PhD from the University of Manchester, UK.

Index